OSTHANDEL AND OSTPOLITIK

MONOGRAPHS IN GERMAN HISTORY

Osthandel and Ostpolitik

*German Foreign Trade Policies in Eastern Europe
from Bismarck to Adenauer*

Robert Mark Spaulding

Berghahn Books
Providence • Oxford

First published in 1997 by

Berghahn Books

Editorial offices:
165 Taber Avenue, Providence, RI 02906, USA
3, NewTec Place, Magdalen Road, Oxford, OX4 1RE, UK

© Robert Mark Spaulding 1997

Library of Congress Cataloging-in-Publication Data

Spaulding, Robert Mark, 1957–
    Osthandel and Ostpolitik : German trade policies in Eastern Europe
from Bismarck to Adenauer / Robert Mark Spaulding.
        p.   cm. -- (Monographs in German history ; v. 1)
    Includes bibliographical references and index.
    ISBN 1-57181-039-0 (alk. paper)
    1. Germany--Foreign economic relations--Europe, Eastern.
    2. Europe, Eastern--Foreign economic relations--Germany.
    3. Germany--Commerce--Europe, Eastern--History. 4. Europe, Eastern-
    -Commerce--Germany--History.   I. Title. II. Series.
    HF1546.15.E852S68   1996
    337.43047--dc20   96-20811
                                                                       CIP

British Library Cataloguing in Publication Data

A catalogue record for this book is available from
the British Library.

Printed in the United States on acid-free paper.

CONTENTS

LIST OF GRAPHS AND TABLES

Graphs

Tables

ABREVIATIONS AND USAGE

ADAP	Akten zur deutschen auswärtigen Politik
AVI	Working Group of Iron Finishing Industries
BA	Bundesarchiv
BdI	Bundesverband deutscher Industrie, industrial Bundesverband
CEH	Central European History
DDP	Deutsche Demokratische Partei, Democrats
DBFP	Documents on British Foreign Policy
DGFP	Documents on German Foreign Policy
DNVP	Deutschnationale Volkspartei, German Nationalists
DVP	Deutsche Volkspartei, People's Party
FRUS	Foreign Relations of the United States
GStA PK	Geheimes Staatsarchiv Preussischer Kulturbesitz
HPA	Handelspolitischer Ausschuss, Trade Policy Committee
HZ	Historische Zeitschrift
JCH	Journal of Contemporary History
JEH	Journal of Economic History
JEIA	Joint Export-Import Agency
JMH	Journal of Modern History
MFN	most favored nation
OA	Ostauschuss, Eastern Committee
OMGUS	Office of Military Governor, U.S. Zone
PAAA	Politisches Archiv des Auswärtigen Amtes
RdI	Reichsverband deutscher Industrie, industrial Reichsverband
RWWA	Rheinisch-Westfälisches Wirtschaftsarchiv
SPD	Sozialdemokratische Partei Deutschlands, Socialists
VdESI	Verein deutscher Eisen- und Stahlindutrieller, Union of Iron and Steel Industrialists
VfZ	Vierteljahrshefte für Zeitgeschichte
ZfG	Zeitschrift für Geschichtsunterricht

ACKNOWLEDGEMENTS

In the course of writing this book, I have received first-rate financial, scholarly, and personal support from a number of organizations, institutions, and individuals. I suspect that at times this support taxed each provider's sense of the reasonable. This book cannot even those scores, but it can serve as a downpayment on those debts. Financial support for this topic was generously provided by the German Academic Exchange Service (DAAD) on two occasions for research at the Bundesarchiv in Koblenz, the Political Archive of the Foreign Office in Bonn, the Rheinisch-Westfälisches Wirtschaftsarchiv in Cologne, the Bayer-Archiv in Leverkusen, the Mannesmann Archiv in Dusseldorf, the Haniel Archiv in Duisburg, the Bundesverband deutscher Industrie in Cologne, and the Ludwig Erhard Archiv in Bonn. The Ford Foundation Program in Western Security and European Society also supported research at German archives in Koblenz and in Bonn. The International Research and Exchanges Board (IREX) supported my research at the former Zentrales Staatsarchiv Potsdam of the GDR (now the Bundesarchiv, Abteilungen Potsdam) and at the former Zentrales Staatsarchiv Merseburg of the GDR (now part of the Geheimes Staatsarchiv Preussischer Kulturbesitz, Berlin-Dahlem). Financial and scholarly support were provided by post-doctoral programs at the Center for International Affairs and at the Center for European Studies, both at Harvard University.

A large a number of perceptive colleagues willing to offer conceptual, methodological and editorial improvements has been my great fortune. Portions of the manuscript have benefited immeasurably from readings by Volker Berghahn, Günter Bischof, Gerald

Feldman, Peter Grupp, Christopher Jackson, Charles Maier, Susan McCaffray, and Thomas Schwartz. Irreplaceable scholarly and personal support were provided by Charles Maier, who encouraged my conceptualization of these issues in a long-term framework that many considered impractical. I hope this book can reward his patience. I will always be grateful to Marion Berghahn at Berghahn Books, who accepted an author's large first book on political economy when many other presses had set formalistic limits on length.

The support of my wife, Phyllis, cannot be measured, nor can I imagine how it might be repaid. I can only promise a life-long endeavor to do so.

for my parents:
finis coronat opus

GERMANY AND EASTERN TRADE ISSUES

*E*clipsed by the scope of the Atlantic economy, obscured by Anglo-German rivalry, and nearly destroyed by the post-1945 division of Europe, the flow of goods across East Central Europe has been, nonetheless, an immensely significant pattern of European economic exchange. For Germany, the Osthandel (Eastern trade) was both a blessing and a curse; its bounty provided much of the raw material for the rise of German economic and political power in Europe, while its lure tantalized German ambitions to the point of madness. Despite the enduring importance of this commerce, no monograph has yet made this pattern of trade the centerpiece of its treatment of German-East European relations. This study puts this important pattern of German-East European trade into the center of discussion and views an extended period of German foreign policy toward Eastern Europe through this lens.

Excluding the "working class question" (loosely defined), no other economic issue has been or is now more important than trade policy for the functioning of an industrial economy in Germany. Macroeconomic measures of trade vulnerability before 1914 show that among European countries the Reich had the second-largest stake in foreign trade, behind only the United Kingdom. Even prior to German unification in 1990, the Federal Republic had emerged as one of the world's premier exporting nations. The Germans themselves have acutely perceived their dependence on foreign trade. When West German politicians dubbed trade "the alpha and omega of our economic future," they spoke from long experience with the

German position in the European economy. Even in prosperous times, (e.g., 1900 to 1914) the military security, financial posture, and social peace of the Reich could be severely affected by fluctuations in Germany's Eastern trade. The evolving yet surprisingly stable pattern of trade under consideration here has sent value-added goods from Germany to Eastern Europe in exchange for agricultural products, raw materials, and cheap manufactures for over 100 years. Few other issues of comparable importance in German political economy can be investigated for the same extended period. In view of the worldwide consequences of German involvement in Eastern Europe, no other aspect of German foreign economic policy has been as fateful.

This study examines in detail Germany's most important trade policy actions over a period of seventy years (1890 to 1960) vis-à-vis three key partners in the Eastern trade: Poland, Czechoslovakia, and Imperial Russia/Soviet Union. The critical analysis and interpretation of German foreign trade policy spans the years from the very first trade treaty between the German and Russian empires to the postwar establishment of full commercial relations between the Federal Republic and the Soviet Union. The period embraces four distinct German regimes: the imperial authoritarian monarchy, the Weimar "corporatist" democracy, the Third Reich Nazi dictatorship, and the postwar "neo-corporatist" Federal Republic. I have endeavored to explain German trade policy choices in Eastern Europe over an extended period and to use those choices for an enhanced understanding of German attitudes and actions, both public and private.

If this study suggests some recurring patterns of German foreign economic policies, it has been able to do so by employing a long-term perspective and a multicountry focus. The underlying methodological hypothesis is that a study both "vertically" comparative over time and "horizontally" comparative across space will reveal in new ways the domestic and international origins of German actions. In taking the comparative approach to four different German regimes, the intention is to get beyond a purely economic history of German-Eastern European trade that might be written with relatively little regard for political regime changes. This comparative scope allows a more comprehensive evaluation of the pressures on policymaking than is usually the case. One can begin to sort out enduring versus transient strategies of German foreign economic policy.

An underlying theme of German economic superiority vis-à-vis Eastern Europe runs throughout the period.[1] The persisting differentials of economic development between Germany and Eastern Europe serve as a steady backdrop against which we can evaluate the political choices of German governments as they attempted to shape the flow of trade across East Central Europe. The widely divergent degrees of success exhibited by four German regimes affirm the uniqueness of each political system, despite its participation in enduring patterns of trade and in recurring strategies of trade policy.[2] Traditionally two types of studies touch on the subject at hand. One type concentrates on the connections between German domestic political developments and German foreign economic policy in much shorter periods, e.g., 1900 to 1914 or 1925 to 1929. A second type of study treats Germany's foreign trade policy as a small subplot in histories of Germany or of Germany's foreign relations with Poland, Czechoslovakia, or the Soviet Union during one German regime, e.g., 1933 to 1939. Inasmuch as these shorter-term, one-country approaches have presented only portions of the story, they have obscured the long-term significance of key developments.

A multicountry comparison of German experiences with Poland and Czechoslovakia between the wars allows a differentiation of political and economic impediments to German economic cooperation with its Eastern neighbors. A longer-term of review German-Soviet trade in the 1920s and 1930s suggests both a reperiodization of Nazi-Soviet relations and a reinterpretation of Stalin's policy in the years immediately preceding the 1939 nonaggression pact. In a broader context, Chancellor Konrad Adenauer's 1958 trade treaty with the Soviets appears as the beginning of the Federal Republic's Ostpolitik. Shorter studies also have not fostered a wider appreciation of the longevity of certain political and economic trends in German-Eastern European trade. Only by viewing the "longue durée" we can appreciate the gradually declining economic significance and increasing political role of German trade with Eastern Europe. There is a real need to examine the long record of German-East European trade in a single, coherent study.[3] One hundred years of foreign trade policy provide an historical record rich in insights into the continuity of German policies in the East.[4]

The nature of German foreign trade issues – contested by state and societal forces at the intersection of foreign and domestic economic policies – allows an explication of German trade policy to addresses several critical areas of historical political economy. Most fundamentally, this work is intended to help complete the historical record of German-East European relations, specifically economic relations. This contribution involves extending and, in some cases, revising our understanding of economic interaction in East-Central Europe. Extending the historical record means investigating the political economy of post-1945 trade relations between the Federal

Republic and these important East European economies. Tracing these trade relations through the restoration of normalized commercial relations between the Federal Republic and the USSR extends our study of these issues through the end of 1950s. The passage of thirty years since the events of 1960 just now gives us the ability to write a detailed history of the Federal Republic's early foreign trade policies using government and private-sector records comparable to those long available for earlier German regimes. Understanding the Federal Republic's Eastern trade policies also extends the comparative framework for assessing German policies by broadening the study to four German regimes. We gain a preliminary interpretation of early West German policies as well as a better understanding, through comparison, of the policy constraints faced by earlier German regimes.

In extending and reexamining the historical record, this work probes Germany's ability to apply trade leverage to its Eastern neighbors throughout this period. My study seeks to explain how, when, and why Germany has or has not been able to apply economic diplomacy in East Europe and to evaluate the success of those applications. Understanding Eastern Europe's (in)vulnerability to German economic pressure is an important step in re-creating the historical connections between the East and West European economies. For the post-1945 period, it helps us assess the relationship between these centrally planned economies and the reconstructed liberal-capitalist world economy. Communist responses to West German economic sticks and carrots are important indicators of how extensively these Eastern economies were able to insulate themselves from events in the noncommunist world economy. In exploring this issue, my work endeavors to understand the interaction of Germany and East Europe by illuminating the preconditions for Germany's successful application of trade pressure in its relations with Poland, Czechoslovakia, and Russia/Soviet Union. Accordingly, my view of Central Europe focuses on the changing international environment and German domestic structures in terms of how these obstructed or facilitated German attempts to apply trade pressure in the East.

An investigation into the processes by which successive German regimes and governments formulated and implemented their Eastern trade policies constitutes a second major theme pursued throughout this work.[5] A major portion of this study is devoted to comparing how these four different regimes responded to the various and complex conflicts involved in conducting foreign trade with their Eastern neighbors. I have sought to clarify the changing mixture of international (systemic) and domestic (state and private-sector) forces that combined to produce Germany's Eastern trade policies under four distinctly different regimes.

These two subjects – the process of policy construction and the policies of trade leverage that emerged as products of that process – are best understood together. The participation of leading private-sector groups in the deliberative processes of trade policy formulation decisively influenced the range of policy end products available for application to Germany's Eastern neighbors. Conversely, the state's desire to apply policies of trade leverage strongly influenced the process of policy formation as state agents sought to restrict private-sector participation in policy debates as a way of subordinating the business urge for short-term profits to longer-term political goals. The long-term themes of German trade leverage in Eastern Europe and the process of German trade policy formation are discussed throughout this work in a way that emphasizes their interconnection. Tracing the development of Germany's trade policies in the East along the lines of these two large themes serves as the narrow end of a wedge for opening up a new understanding of the international and German domestic systems of the period.

German trade with Poland, Czechoslovakia, and the USSR produced its own characteristic pattern of exchange across East Central Europe. Nonetheless, German-East European trade must be understood in the larger contexts of the international economy and the domestic framework of German decision-making. Forces originating within these larger contextual frameworks often helped determine the particular courses of German-Polish, German-Czechoslovak, and German-Soviet trade relations. The international and domestic characters of trade polices demand that a detailed examination of these three trade patterns place the unique economic and political aspects of each trade relationship in the larger settings of European international developments and German domestic politics. In placing trade policies in these frameworks of larger forces the intention has not been to diminish the role or responsibility of individuals and their decisions, but to make those roles more understandable. Each of the policies initiated, the agreements achieved, and the opportunities foregone is the result of human action. The historian's task lies in recreating the interplay between environments and individuals.

Within the overall comparative strategy of this study, tactics have varied. Explicating the many international and domestic factors that shaped German trade policies has led me to employ a number of approaches in explaining the course of German trade policy. No single explanatory method can account for both the common features and the unique variations in the Eastern experiences of successive

German regimes during this extended period. I have drawn on a number of interpretive approaches to questions of German foreign policy as well as on the multilevel approaches of foreign economic policy studies to construct conjunctural explanations of trade policy choices.[6] These explanations emphasize the unique combinations of (sometimes recurring) external and internal forces that produced final outcomes. In the course of constructing these explanations, some conceptual approaches may be revealed as more useful and efficacious than others, but my intention has not been to test the utility or effectiveness of any particular methodology. An historical awareness of the subtleties of time and space precludes a primary emphasis on theory-testing or model-building.

In analytic narrative, this study locates German trade policy decisions first in their international contexts and then in the domestic context of state-society relations. The changing international environment decisively affected German willingness and ability to manipulate trade flows for political advantage in Eastern Europe and also determined the way trade issues were understood and contested in Germany. For each phase of German trade policy under discussion here, the analyses of German-East European trade relations begin by indicating how the international environment engendered opportunities, pressures, and constraints on German trade policies.[7] The nature of the prevailing international trade regime (the "rules of the game") receives substantial attention throughout this work as an important component of the international environment.

German trade polices in the East were a response to the economic and political challenges posed by the international order. Germany responded most immediately to the policies pursued by the Polish, Czechoslovak, and Russian/Soviet governments. Drawing on published sources, I have presented summary interpretations of the relevant foreign economic policies of these three countries. In cases where information available from the German side has cast these East European policies in a new light, I have developed the discussion beyond the limits of what is strictly necessary for an understanding of German actions, in the belief that our view of Eastern Europe might be sharpened by illumination from another direction. In concentrating on an in-depth analysis of German policies, I have deliberately and necessarily forgone attempts to explain the varied economic and political structures that underlay Polish, Czechoslovak, and Russian/Soviet foreign policy choices.

Trade policy is foreign policy and domestic policy simultaneously. Successful trade policies locate and reside in areas of congruity between the international political economy and domestic politics.

The constraints of the international framework invariably allow a multiplicity of trade policy responses to any given situation. The findings of this study suggest that the goals of trade policy are framed initially in response to the international framework, but that policy achievements are determined ultimately by the distributions of power within the domestic framework. In other words, while international developments set the parameters for the range of policy choices, only political struggles and outcomes in Germany could determine which options were actually chosen.[8] In Germany, domestic political conflicts over trade policy involved two sets of struggles: those between various private-sector actors and those between the private sector as a whole and portions of the state.

Accounting for the coexistence of powerful private-sector actors with a strong and active state apparatus constitutes one of the major interpretive challenges in modern German history. An investigation into trade policy must meet this challenge head-on since the mutual interest and reciprocal dependence of the state and society in regulating trade dictates an investigation into both the public and private components of the domestic framework for trade policy formulation.

The immediate interest of private-sector groups in regulating trade is a straightforward one – to sculpt the flow of trade in a manner that most benefits or least damages their own particular branch of production, commerce, or labor. Consequently, discussion of the domestic framework begins with an analysis of the effects of the international economy on German civil society as presented in a production profile. This means assessing how changes in the international economy affect the leading German economic actors: agriculture, domestically oriented heavy industry, export-oriented industries, the merchant community, and labor.

International trade does not distribute its benefits and disadvantages evenly across societies.[9] Trade with Eastern Europe initiated changes in domestic incomes, location, and political power that were felt for many years across the various economic sectors in Germany. The pressure of Eastern trade issues produced societal fractures that often ran counter to general class cleavages. Trade issues pitted workers, employees, managers, and owners of export industries against those of domestically oriented producers so that ad hoc cross-class alliances were created and intraclass divisions were generated. The intensity of private-sector struggles over Eastern trade policy destroyed established class alliances in 1894, 1924, and 1930, and helped to make Germany virtually ungovernable in the years immediately thereafter. For these reasons, comparing how different regimes sought to manage the impact of East European trade from

1890 through 1960 provides a new and revealing way of viewing the balance of political and economic power in German society.

The mixed effects of the Eastern trade on various branches of the German economy brought trade policy directly to the attention of the leading private-sector actors. Looking at the commodity structure of Germany's Eastern trade we can see how it generated an enduring cluster of domestic economic conflicts with grave social and political consequences. Developing a sense of the scope and composition of the trade exchanges between Germany and the East is the starting point for understanding the ferocious private-sector struggles to influence trade flows. German economic groups naturally sought to defend their existing positions or to ensure their own expansion as a response to international economic changes. The leading economic sectors and their intermediate associations (interest groups and political parties) sought resolution of these interest conflicts across four successive German political systems.[10] Many German trade policy choices can be explained as the outcomes of alliances and struggles between these commercial, agricultural, and industrial private-sector groups. Liberal pluralism, social corporatism, and Marxism offer variants of this society-centered explanation.[11]

Not only the size of the material stakes, but also other characteristics of trade policy issues contributed to the ferocity of private-sector struggles over German trade relations with the East. Trade issues and the economic consequences of trade policy decisions are highly transparent. Industrial, agricultural, commercial, and consumer groups were readily able to perceive, and therefore to articulate, their interests in trade policy decisions. The flexible, selective nature of trade controls themselves also played a crucial role in the forceful articulation of these interests. Tariffs, treaties, and regulatory administrative action all lent themselves to commodity-specific constructions that selectively included or excluded certain categories of goods. Implementing any trade strategy required decisions on hundreds or thousands of individual tariff positions. The possibility that some items might be excluded from benefit or protection encouraged and preserved a high level of interest-group activity.[12] Germany experienced an increase in interest-group lobbying after passage of the 1925 Tariff Law because of the wide discretionary powers of implementation given to the finance minister. In addition, the immense size and regional concentration of several key German industrial sectors may have facilitated their protectionist campaigns.[13]

Ironically for an industrial country, the agricultural interest groups set the limits on Germany's use of politicized trade in Eastern Europe. Successive chancellors from Bismarck to Adenauer were beholden to agricultural support and, later, to farmers' votes. Any policy designed to increase German influence in Eastern Europe through an expansion of trade was possible only if and when imports from the East did not threaten domestic German agricultural price levels. Radical tariff, quota, and price-control protection for German agriculture from 1930 to 1939 provided one solution to the Eastern European agricultural threat. After 1950, the poor economic performance of Poland and Czechoslovakia (specifically the difficulty of regularly producing exportable agricultural surpluses) provided another solution – one that had appeared in Soviet Russia after 1917. The end of any genuine East European threats to West German agriculture and manufacturing in the 1950s is one reason why the Federal Republic has been more successful in wielding economic diplomacy in East Europe than its Weimar predecessor was, in spite of a greatly reduced volume of German-East European trade.

Although the leading economic interest groups exerted enormous influence during the period under consideration here, the activities of domestic constituencies do not by themselves account entirely for the course of German trade policies in the East. Stresemann's important 1925 economic treaty with Soviet Russia had little or no private-sector support. Adenauer was able to thwart the desires of West German industrial leaders for an early commercial treaty with the Soviets. Explaining these important trade policy decisions requires complementing the explication of international and societal pressures with an understanding of the state both as an institution and an actor.

Throughout the period under consideration here, states played the central role in regulating international trade. All private-sector actors acted through or ultimately relied on the institutions of state in their attempts to shape trade flows for particular private advantage. The traditional mechanisms for molding trade – tariffs, quotas, and administrative barriers – were formal state actions. Even ad hoc private international trade agreements and more durable cartels ultimately depended on the alternative of state actions in the event of private failure. The state's indispensable role in regulating trade flows compels an investigation into the legislative and executive institutions of state that fashioned those regulatory mechanisms. In the domestic context, the organizational structure of successive German states helped determine both the character of the private-sector policy contests going on within it, and the outcomes of those contests.[14] The institutional role of the state emerges most clearly when the process of trade policy formation is examined. The closed-door manner in which chancellors Caprivi and Bülow generated and implemented their trade policies reveals the contours of power in

Wilhelmine Germany more accurately than do the diametrically opposed contents of those two sets of policies. Even in the weak regime of the Weimar Republic, the institutional structure of the state played a central role in shaping the process and product of German trade policy formation.[15]

In Germany, the institutional role of the state was augmented by the active role played by state agents in framing trade policy. The modern German state had powerful motives for regulating trade. The traditional state interest in the tariff derived from the role of customs receipts as a major source of revenue. After 1880 new state interests arose from the growing interdependence of the European national economies and the unprecedented importance that trade assumed in the public life of many industrial economies, and in Germany in particular. One consequence of the Great Depression of 1873 to 1896 was the realization that trade had become too important to be left to the "invisible hand" described by economist Adam Smith. Foreign trade was the area of the economy in which the state first began to intervene in the late nineteenth century. Throughout the seventy-year period under consideration here, trade with the East remained one area of the economy in which the state intervened most extensively.

A third, more purposeful state interest in shaping trade flows emerged from repeated German attempts to use trade as a foreign policy instrument in Eastern Europe. Beginning with Chancellor Caprivi's 1894 Russian treaty, successive German governments became increasingly aware of the utility of trade and trade agreements as foreign policy instruments in pursuit of political goals. Successive German states from the Empire to the Federal Republic have employed trade leverage on an increasing scale in Eastern Europe. Trade has clearly been the Federal Republic's most useful foreign policy tool in dealing with the East.

Manipulating trade flows in accordance with larger foreign policy goals necessitated a far greater degree of state control over trade policy than the ordinary extent of state intervention required for simply managing the German economy.[16] In each of these German political systems, state officials were frequently able to shape trade policy in accordance with their own goals – goals that distinguished themselves from any private-sector objectives. Periods of forceful state control over the direction of Eastern trade policy can be found under the Empire, in the Third Reich, and during the Federal Republic. The strong state character of German regimes from the Imperial Obrigkeitsstaat (authoritarian state) to Adenauer's Kanzlerdemokratie (chancellor democracy) is widely recognized. Weimar provided a notable exception to this pattern and, anticipating our findings, also failed to produce a functioning trade policy in the East. For the other political systems, institutional impermeability combined with state ambitions for the political use of trade policy to produce remarkably strong, highly autonomous regimes in Eastern trade policy issues.[17] As public and private forces contended for the dominant voice in German trade policy, the state's agents were brought into collision and collusion with representatives from the most important economic sectors. The conflicting claims of the state and the private-sector were embodied in the struggle between the ministerial bureaucracy and the interest groups for control over Eastern trade policy. There were few one-sided victories in this struggle; Chancellor Bülow's spurning of private-sector demands for a voice in the 1904 Russian trade treaty negotiations came closest to complete government victory. Rather, various forms of accommodation were arranged in which both state and at least some private-sector voices were heard when planning trade strategy.

Investigating the pattern of state/private-sector accommodation and investigating further the specific manner of forging or imposing accommodation brings us directly into the heart of the power relationships in each of these regimes. Explicating the process of setting trade policy lays bare the focal points of decisionmaking in four different domestic frameworks. These explications aim at illustrating the shifting balance of power between the state and society in general and between the ministerial bureaucracy and private interest groups in particular. The exercise must combine the findings of a state-centered investigation into the distribution of power between various state institutions (Parliament and the bureaucracy) and among members of the ministerial bureaucracy (Foreign Office, Economics Ministry, Agriculture Ministry) with the findings of a society-centered investigation into the levels of influence exerted by rival private-sector groups (industry, agriculture, commerce, and labor).

Throughout the period under consideration here, German policymakers struggled to frame Eastern trade policies that could accommodate a changing mixture of international, state, and society-based inputs. Constructing an interpretive framework for this issue means offering a supplemental way of viewing the nature of European international system, the character of the German state, and the distribution of power in German society.

Notes

1. For overviews of the problems of East European economic underdevelopment in comparison to the West see Alexander Gerschenkron, *Economic Backwardness in Historical Perspective* (Cambridge, Mass., 1960); Karl Mandelbaum, *The Industrialization of Backward Areas* (Oxford, 1945); P.N. Rosenstein-Rodan, "Problems of Industrialization of Eastern and South-Eastern Europe," *The Economic Journal* 53 (June 1943), 202-11; Nicolas Spulber, *The State and Economic Development in Eastern Europe* (New York, 1966); Daniel Chirot, ed., *The Origins of Economic Backwardness in Eastern Europe: Economics and Politics from the Middle Ages to the Early Twentieth Century* (Berkeley, Calif., 1989). The classic Marxist treatment from the Soviet bloc is Karle Obermann, ed., *Probleme der Okonomie und Politik in den Beziehungen zwischen Ost und Westeuropa vom 17. Jahrhundert bis zur Gegenwart* (Berlin, 1960).

2. Highlighting the uniqueness of different societies has long been a primary purpose of the comparative method. See Marc Bloch's seminal essay "Toward a Comparative History of European Societies," reprinted in translation in Fredric C. Lane and Jelle C. Riemersma, eds., *Enterprise and Secular Change* (Homewood, Ill., 1953); William H. Sewell, Jr., "Marc Bloch and the Logic of Comparative History," *History and Theory* 2, (1967), 208-18. Extrapolating from Bloch's guidelines on the proper units for historical comparison, Sewell explained how the "history of a single nation can be comparative history if comparison is used in formulating problems and if explanations of developments in that nation are tested by the comparative method," 214. Further, comparisons between different societies within a single national history more closely approximate the experimental condition of "all other factors being equal." On the spread of Bloch's comparative ideas into East Central Europe and early attempts to write comparative histories of the region, see Domokos Kosáry, "The Idea of a Comparative History of East Central Europe: The Story of a Venture," in Dennis Deletant and Harry Hanak, eds., *Historians as Nation Builders: Central and South-East Europe* (London, 1988).

3. Jürgen Bellers has called the lack of "coherent, systematic standard works" on German foreign economic policy "astonishing," noting that aspects of German foreign economic policy have been treated in several shorter periods, but that a "comprehensive, historically-oriented study" has yet to be undertaken, "Deutsche Aussenwirtschaftspolitik seit 1918– zwischen Imperialismus und Liberalismus, Globalismus und Regionalismus," *Neue Politische Literatur* XXXIII/3 (1988).

4. One work on German-Soviet relations that purports to have "the necessary historical perspective" for examining "the use of economic power as an instrument of foreign policy" (p. 2) is Hélene Seppain, *Contrasting US and German Attitudes to Soviet Trade, 1917-91* (New York, 1992). Seppain's book is useful for bringing together previously published material but largely reproduces what has already been said about German-Soviet trade and East-West economic relations. For these reasons the book keeps alive a number of misconceptions about German polices that might have been understandable in the pioneering works of earlier authors, but that can now be clarified.

5. Since the revival of foreign economic policy studies in the mid-1970s, this body of literature has grown tremendously. Still indispensable are Peter Katzenstein's "Introduction: Domestic an International Forces and Strategies of Foreign Economic Policy" and "Conclusion: Domestic Structures and Strategies of Foreign Economic Policy" from Peter Katzenstein, ed., *Between Power and Plenty* (Madison, Wisc., 1978); Ronald Rogowski, *Commerce and Coalitions: How Trade Affects Domestic Political Alignments* (Princeton, 1989); Benjamin J. Cohen's review article, "The

Political Economy of International Trade," *International Organization* 44, no. 2 (Spring 1990). Important case studies include Stephen Krasner, *Defending the National Interest. Raw Materials Investments and U.S. Foreign Policy* (Princeton, 1978); Peter Gourevitch, *Politics in Hard Times. Comparative Responses to Economic Crises* (Ithaca and London, 1986); Lars Mjoset, "Nordic Economic Policies in the 1970s and 1980s," *International Organization* 41, no. 3 (Summer 1987); Daniel Verdier, *Democracy and International Trade. Britain, France, and the United States, 1860-1990* (Princeton, 1994).

6. For a brief overview of current approaches to the study of foreign economic policies see G. John Ikenberry, David A. Lake, and Michael Mastanduno, "Introduction: Approaches to Explaining American Foreign Economic Policy," *International Organization* 42, no. 1 (Winter 1988), 1-14.

7. For thoughts on the growing need to relate national experiences to the larger international structures of the international environment such as the prevailing power system or economic regime see Akira Iriye, "The Internationalization of History," *American Historical Review* 94 (February 1989), 1-10.

8. This suggests support for Robert Keohane's arguments that systemic (international) level analysis is a necessary "pre-condition" for other approaches to foreign economic policy, Keohane, "The World Political Economy and the Crisis of Imbedded Liberalism," in John H. Goldthorpe, ed., *Order and Conflict in Contemporary Capitalism* (Oxford, 1984), 16. However, the international level approach can claim only a certain procedural primacy; its claim should be restricted to the order in which various approaches are applied to policy problems, i.e. that the international approach must be applied first. Systemic analysis by itself does not illuminate foreign economic policy decisions more fully than exclusively state-centered or society-centered approaches do.

9. The political and economic consequences of these trade-inspired changes constitute one of the most fascinating areas in international trade theory. The ready admission that concepts such as "the social welfare" or "the national welfare" are pure abstractions provides one of the cornerstone justifications for the existence of trade theory as a field of study distinct from microeconomics.

10. The literature on relations between German private-sector interest groups (the *Verbände*) and successive German regimes is voluminous. For historical overviews one can consult Fritz Balich, *Staat und Verbände in Deutschland zwischen 1871 und 1945* (Wiesbaden, 1979); Dieter Fricke, *Lexikon zur Parteigeschichte: die bürgerlichen und kleinbürgerlichen Parteien und Verbände in Deutschland 1789-1945*, 4 vols. (Leipzig, 1983-1986); Hans-Peter Ullman, *Interessenverbände in Deutschland* (Frankfurt/Main, 1988); Theodor Eschenberg, *Das Jahrhundert der Verbände* (Berlin, 1989). Period-specific literature on the subject will be cited at appropriate points in the text.

11. The classic pluralist writings are David B. Truman, *The Governmental Process* (New York, 1952) and Robert A. Dahl, *Who Governs?* (New Haven, 1961). For a neo-pluralist variant see Grant McConnell, *Private Power and American Democracy* (New York, 1967) and Theodore J. Lowi, *The End of Liberalism: Ideology, Policy, and the Crisis of Public Authority* (New York, 1969). On social corporatism see Phillippe Schmitter, "Still the Century of Corporatism?" *Review of Politics* 36 (1974) and "Modes of Interest Mediation and Models of Societal Change in Western Europe," in Schmitter and Lehmbruck, eds., *Trends toward Corporatist Intermediation* (Beverly Hills, Calif., 1979). For recent Marxist theory see B. Guggenberger, "Okonomie und Politik. Die neo-marxistische Staatsfunktionslehre," *Neue Politische Literatur* 4 (1974); Ralph Miliband, *Marxism and Politics* (New York, 1977) and Nicos Poulantzas, *Political Power and Social Classes* (London, 1973). This classification of democratic theory relies on Eric Nordlinger, *On the Autonomy of the Demo-*

Introduction

cratic State (Cambridge, Mass., 1981) chapter two; additional literature on each of these theories can be found in Nordlinger's notes.

12. John Odell has characterized monetary policies and other actions that "cut across all sectors of international transactions in goods ..." as "inherently macropolicies" that cannot be applied selectively, *U.S. International Monetary Policy* (Princeton, 1982), 219. In contrast, one can think of less-encompassing trade controls (tariffs, quotas, health regulations, etc.) as "micropolicies" that cut across only some categories of international transactions in goods and frequently are applied selectively. On this point and on the issue-area approach more generally, see Joanne Gowa, "Public Goods and Political Institutions," *International Organization* 42, no. 1 (Winter 1988).

13. Kym Anderson and Robert E. Baldwin, "The Political Market for Protection in Industrial Countries: Empirical Evidence," World Bank Staff Working Papers, 1981; Helen Hughes and Jean Waelbroeck, "Foreign Trade and Structural Adjustment – Is There a Threat of New Protectionism?" Hans-Gert Braun et al., eds., *The European Economy in the 1980s* (Aldershot, UK, 1983).

14. The ability of institutional structures to reshape the distributions of power in society was already implied in Marx's characterization of the state as an "imperfect mirror" of society, Karl Marx, [finish this citation]; on the role of organizations in "refracting" private-sector struggles see Peter Hall, *Governing the Economy: The Politics of State Intervention in Britain and France* (New York, 1986), 233; for a general discussion see James March and John Olsen, "The New Institutionalism: Organizational Factors in Political Life," *American Political Science Review* 78 (September 1984). For comprehensive presentations of the institutional structures of Germany's twentieth century regimes see volumes 3-5 of Kurt Jeserich et al., eds., *Deutsche Verwaltungsgeschichte* (Stuttgart, 1983-1986).

15. John Ikenberry has offered the state-centered, institutional approach as a "promising, if as yet poorly elaborated, research program for the study of American foreign economic policy" in "An Institutional Approach to American Foreign Economic Policy, *International Organization* 42, no. 1 (Winter 1988).

16. I indicated the need to explore these issues analytically at greater length in "German Trade Policy in Eastern Europe 1890-1990: Preconditions for the Application of International Trade Leverage," *International Organization* 45, no. 3 (Summer 1991), 343-68.

17. See Nordlinger, *On the Autonomy of the Democratic State*; Michael Mann, "The Autonomous Power of the State: Its Origins, Mechanisms, and Results," in John A. Hall, ed., *States in History* (New York, 1987). For an illustrated notion of "nonexistent, weak, moderate, strong, and dominant" levels of state power see Stephen D. Krasner, *Defending the National Interest. Raw Materials Investments and U.S. Foreign Policy* (Princeton, 1978), 57. Similar thoughts are expressed in "The State Structure Explanation," of Peter Gourevitch's *Politics in Hard Times* (Ithaca and London, 1986), 61-62; Joel S. Migdal, *Strong Societies and Weak States. State-Society Relations and State Capabilities in the Third World* (Princeton, 1988); Metin Heper, ed., *The State and Public Bureaucracies: A Comparative Perspective* (New York, 1987).

TOWARD MANAGED TRADE
The First German-Russian Trade Treaty (1894)

*P*erhaps nothing brought together so many of the critical shifts in the economic and political life of Germany during the watershed years of the early 1890s as did the German-Russian trade treaty of 1894. As the product of an extensive economic and political debate on shaping trade flows through government action, the treaty marked the termination of the free trade era that had characterized European affairs since 1860. Certainly free trade had been eroded by the rising tide of tariffs and protectionism that had spread out from Germany across Europe in the 1880s. Yet the concept of state intervention to manage trade flows in accordance with a national economic program was never so clearly articulated as when Chancellor Leo von Caprivi appealed for Reichstag support of his trade treaties as part of strategy of export growth.[1]

In German domestic politics, Caprivi's trade policies highlighted the dramatic political shifts that accompanied the end of Bismarck's chancellorship. The Russian treaty especially catalyzed the processes of political mobilization among broader masses of the German population. Farmers in particular organized themselves as they never had before to articulate an agricultural economic platform. As part of this process, the treaty drove a wedge between agrarian interests and government policies, producing a political novelty in Imperial Germany – a conservative opposition to the kaiser's government. In another political innovation, the treaty created a new channel of state-society communication as Caprivi brought members of Germany's indus-

Notes for this chapter begin on page 49.

trial and commercial elites into an unprecedented consultation with the government on the future course of German trade policy.

Caprivi's use of the Russian trade treaty in pursuit of larger international diplomatic goals directly repudiated the Bismarckian concept of depoliticized foreign trade relations. After Bismarck's resolute separation of trade and finance from other aspects of international relations, the older Prussian Zollverein tradition of employing trade and tariff pressure in international relations was largely forgotten. Caprivi's use of political arguments to advance trade treaties appeared as a radical innovation to a generation that had matured in Bismarck's shadow. All of these new political developments were characteristic of the Wilhelmian, as opposed to the Bismarckian, Reich. All were products of Caprivi's attempts to settle the unresolved conflicts left behind by Bismarck's trade and tariff policies.

Legacies of the "Great Depression" 1873-1896

State responses to the "Great Depression" of 1873 to 1896 were seminal in the development of European economic policies, especially foreign economic policies, and most especially trade policies. In Germany, Bismarck responded to the economic strains of the period by initiating more active foreign trade policies designed to protect prices in the home market and to increase German exports abroad. As in so many other areas, Bismarck's actions in the field of trade policy were largely a balancing act that temporarily masked the basic incompatibility between ultimately conflicting objectives, in this case, protecting German home markets while boosting German exports into other European national markets. Germany's increasingly antagonistic trade relations with Russia in the 1880s began to reveal the impossibility of committing fully to both trade policy tactics simultaneously.

The chancellor's balancing act was dangerous and shortsighted, not only in relation to Russia and other national trading partners, but also in relation to the larger international trade regime that regulated trade relations between all European states. As other European governments followed Germany's protectionist lead, the cumulative effect of these protectionist responses prevented a renewal of the trade treaty network that had stabilized intra-European trade since the early 1860s. The expiration of that treaty network and the opening of German-Russian trade negotiations revealed the unresolved conflicts contained in Bismarck's strategy of simultaneously defending the home market and attacking foreign markets. Because Russia uniquely combined an underdeveloped economy and Great Power status, it forced Germany to choose between the two goals of Bismarck's trade policy. That choice produced the Trade Treaty of 1894 – a true milestone in the development of Russo-German trade relations and a turning point in Germany's understanding of itself.

German trade policies in the years prior to the 1894 trade treaty with Russia had their origins in the "Great Depression" of 1873 to 1896, a long economic downturn characterized by slow growth and an uneven downward slide in agricultural and industrial prices. The depression affected all of the major European economies and hit Germany with special intensity after 1875.[2] German wholesale prices dropped 40 percent between 1873 and 1886 (Graph 1.1) and economic growth slowed by more than one-third, falling to just 1.9 percent annually for the period 1871/75 to 1881/85.[3]

Many years ago, Hans Rosenberg suggested that the "Great Depression marked the decisive turning point in the nineteenth-century history of the relationship between the state and the economy." He explained how the "social character of the economic processes of production, distribution, and consumption became officially recognized. From this time onwards it tended to be the destiny of the state to function as the supreme agent of economic co-ordination and integration on a national scale."[4] The political necessity of securing farm incomes and maintaining industrial employment brought the state into primitive management of the economy during times of crisis: "The explosive forces released by uneven economic development had widely shown themselves to be too dangerous to be left any longer to the 'invisible hand' of Adam Smith."[5]

But exactly how could the new interventionist state respond to the intractable price declines then underway? A number of political, economic, and ideological forces combined to focus government attention and effort on policies of trade manipulation. For Bismarck, the manipulation of German trade flows fulfilled several purposes simultaneously: it responded to the political demand for protection of his conservative clients in agriculture and industry; it fortified the Reich's financial position by taxing imports; it preserved social stability by securing employment; and, in the eyes of nineteenth century economists and policymakers, it remained the least intrusive and only permissible form of state intervention.

Faced with falling prices at a time of increased international trade, hard-pressed European producers saw tariffs as a direct way of counteracting declining prices by limiting foreign competition. Even during the ascendancy of free trade ideas, there had been dissenters such as Friedrich List who advanced the "infant industries" argument to urge delay in Zollverein tariff reductions.[6] Industrial producers returned to List's arguments in reasserting their earlier demands for protection from foreign competition. The renewed drive for tariff protection inspired the creation of a powerful new industrial interest group, the Central Association of German Industrialists (Centralverband deutscher Industrieller), in 1877. Initially dominated by iron/steel and textile manufacturers, this all-inclusive "super" industrial interest group coordinated and intensified protectionist lobbying efforts for other industrial sectors as well.[7]

More important, the 1870s saw a decisive realignment of private sector interests as German agriculture began moving over to the protectionist camp.[8] As agricultural prices in Germany began falling more sharply than industrial prices, farmers quickly latched onto the idea of supporting agricultural prices via a tariff.[9] Protective tariffs soon became the primary means for alleviating the long-term structural crisis that had begun to envelop German agriculture in the late 1870s.[10] Farmers in the hard-hit grain-growing areas of German agriculture became fixated on the readily visible problem of import competition as the ultimate source of their distress.[11] The unique social and political position of the grain-growing eastern Junkers in the complex compromise of the Reich insured that the devastating economic effects of foreign grain imports on German farm incomes would become a political issue of the first order. This issue, which had been simmering through the 1880s, came to a full boil after 1890 as Germany prepared to negotiate a new round of trade treaties with important East European grain exporters: Austria-Hungary, Rumania, and Russia.

Yet general pan-European shift from free trade to protectionism, a trend in which Germany played the leading role, cannot be explained solely in terms of private-sector demands. Ultimately, the private sector cannot protect itself against foreign competition and must rely on some level of state action.[12] European states had numerous motives of their own for imposing higher tariffs. The most fundamental motive was financial – tariffs produced substantial state revenue, allegedly by taxing foreigners.[13] In Germany, the Reich government had obvious financial motivations for high tariffs. Handcuffed in its powers of direct taxation by Article 70 of the 1871 Constitution, the central government lived a precarious financial existence and could not afford to forego or ignore any direct source of revenue.[14] In the decade after 1879 customs duties provided almost 40 percent of the Reich's normal revenues.[15]

Another powerful motive for state intervention in trade policy arose from the critical role that foreign trade had assumed in the economic life of many European economies. The openness of most European economies from 1850 to 1880 had contributed to a stupendous growth in international trade. Between 1850 and 1880 Russian foreign trade quintupled; Austro-Hungarian and French foreign trade more than quadrupled; and British overseas trade more than tripled.[16] German consumption needs and production possibilities were far in excess of the domestic resource base and market. By 1880 the value of German foreign trade (5,737 million marks) was one-third of the value of the German net national product (NNP) (16,902 million marks); German exports (2,923 million marks) equaled 17 percent of the value of the national product.[17] A massive volume of international trade had become essential to continued economic growth. Yet this opened the German economy to severe disturbances from fluctuations and adverse developments in international trading patterns. Of the major European powers, only Britain, whose trade/gross national product ratio hovered around 50 percent for most of this period, had more cause to worry about foreign trade fluctuations than did Germany.

Much of this growth had taken place in a "free trade" environment as Ricardian theories and liberal trade practices gained widespread acceptance, spreading from Britain across the continent to central Europe. With its liberal tariff of 1818, Prussia had been a continental leader in moving toward free trade. Under Prussian leadership the German customs union (the Zollverein) launched a liberal tariff policy in 1834. By 1865 the Zollverein was following a policy of almost unlimited free trade; the new tariff of that year abolished the last remaining grain duties and radically reduced rates on iron products and livestock. As the Zollverein gave way to the new Reich, duties on imported pig iron were abolished in 1873; placement of iron on the free trade list in 1877 marked the high point of liberal trade policy in Germany.[18]

This period of rapid growth had pushed the importance of foreign trade to a level where responsible national governments could no longer observe earlier policies that left these crucial international exchanges to undirected market forces. "Exports" and "sales" were not merely the abstract visions of economists or self-serving slogans of businessmen, but also the key to employment and hence to social stability in countries like Germany, with large industrial sectors. In a sense the very success of free trade practices helped to bring about a reaction to them. Faced with the stupendous growth of a vital economic activity, few governments could resist the temptation to manipulate this flow of trade in an effort to protect themselves in an era of economic hardship.

A final reason for state intervention specifically in the sphere of foreign trade lay in the conceptual and practical limitations of classical economics. The "dismal science" left nineteenth-century governments with few choices in attempting to steer their economies. An unswerving adherence to the gold standard crippled monetary policy. The fundamental assumptions of classical economics (e.g., Say's Law) precluded the use of an anticyclical fiscal policy. In Germany, the federal nature of the state left a great deal of public spending in the hands of state governments rather than the Reich government, so a centralized fiscal response was hardly practical. According to all contemporary views, "the only remaining sphere within which anticyclical economic policies could operate was that of foreign trade, and Bismarck took this course ..."[19] For these reasons, Bismarck himself assumed control of the Prussian Ministry of Trade and Industry in 1880 and held it until his dismissal in 1890.

In their attempts to reshape international trade flows to suit their interests, European governments could employ essentially two types of trade policies: those that protected prices in the home market, and those that sought economic stimulation through an expanded volume of sales abroad. Protective trade policies were relatively easy to implement. Each state could protect its own home market through unilateral tariff action, subject to the limitations of trade treaties it had signed and the ability of its customs service to enforce more stringent trade restrictions. Expansive trade policies, on the other hand, usually proved more complicated, since they required either the submission or the consent of the government of the "target" market. For these reasons, Germany began its antidepression therapy with a strong dose of protective tariff policies before attempting policies of increasing sales abroad.

The 1879 "rye and iron" tariff marked the beginning of Bismarck's new protectionist strategy.[20] The 1 mark/cwt. (hundredweight [cwt.] = 200 kg.) tariff on grain imports was raised to 3 marks in 1885 and then to 5 marks in 1887.[21] Timber, cattle, and animal products including dairy, fats, and meat were all highly protected. Various branches of the textile industry (Germany's largest industrial employer) also received important increases in protectionist duties in 1881 (woolens) and 1885 (linen, cotton, lace).

Across Europe, price protection for the home market was supplemented by government policies for increasing sales in foreign markets. Private-sector producers, both individually and collectively, and agents of the state saw export offensives as the necessary counterpart to protection of the home market. A "broad ideological consensus" on this point underlay widespread German acceptance of Bismarck's policies of overseas expansion.[22]

In seeking to apply its countercyclical trade policies of protection and export expansion, Germany was forced to confront the economic activities of its immense eastern neighbor – Czarist Russia. Whether in protecting the German domestic market in agricultural goods or in seeking new foreign markets for German manufactures, the Reich could not avoid the pressures coming from a huge and rapidly developing economic rival on its eastern borders. Further, Russia presented German economic strategists with a number of problems that they did not encounter in other parts of the world. These problems arose out of the dual, almost paradoxical, nature of the semideveloped Eastern European economies. On one hand, Russia remained an economically underdeveloped country; with a population of 100 million it loomed as a potentially inexhaustible field for German "overseas" economy activity.[23] On the other hand, Russia shared with its Western neighbors the essential political features of a modern state. Its rivals recognized Imperial Russia as one of Europe's Great Powers, even if this status rested as much on Russia's sheer size as on its level of development. The paradox of the Russian condition was captured in Foreign Minister Prince Alexander Gorchakov's phrase that Russia was "a great powerless country."[24]

After 1870, Russia entered a new phase of economic contact with the West as available Russian railroad track shot from 10,731 km. in 1870 to 53,234 km. by 1890, with similar dramatic increases in ton/km. hauled. As an agricultural producer of the first order, Russia's entry into the world market had profound consequences for commodity supplies, standards of living, wages, and incomes for tens of millions of neighboring Germans. The turbulent effects of this entry were something to which the German economy struggled to adjust in the decades before 1914. In Germany, grain imports had already focused attention on Russia as German landowners sought relief from an avalanche of incoming Russian grain.[25] German tariff increases of 1879, 1885, and 1887 were applied to all grain imports, but under the existing circumstances they appeared directed against the rising tide of Russian wheat and rye. These Russian agricultural exports were the economic base on which the Czarist regime stood: they supported the creditworthiness of the government and the value of the ruble, which in turn allowed the Russian state to borrow extensively to modernize its industry and armed forces as Russia struggled to maintain its position in the ranks of the Great Powers.[26] Between 1880 and 1890 grain accounted for just over half (51.7 percent) of Russian exports, an average of 610 million credit rubles annually.[27] The German market, with its densely packed mass of consumers, absorbed one-quarter of the world's grain exports. It played a central role in the marketing of Russian exports; 40 percent of Russian rye exports went to Germany from 1880 to 1890. In that decade Russia earned 875 million gold marks from the sale of wheat and rye in Germany.[28] Under these circumstances it was obvious that Russia's primary interest in the German tariff lay in a reduction of German agricultural duties.

On the other side, German manufacturers looked to the semideveloped portions of the Russian Empire as an outlet for German exports. The Germans correctly perceived the vast market potential of an industrializing Russian empire. Richer, closer, and more densely populated than the illusionary markets of Africa and Asia, the eastern portions of Europe appeared as a potential gold mine just outside the back door of the Reich. In practical terms, German access to Russia's domestic market required the reduction of Russia's prohibitive tariff rates, which had begun rising sharply with the 1876 ordinance requiring all customs duties to be paid in gold rather than in paper rubles; in effect, this was a 30 percent across-the-board tariff increase.[29] From that point, Russian tariffs soared upward at a truly dizzying pace; a 10 percent increase in 1881, followed by a 20 percent tariff increase in 1885, and yet another increase of 20 percent in 1891. By that date the average rate of the Russian tariff was roughly 35 percent ad valorem or triple what it had been in 1876.[30] Between 1880 and 1891, Russian tariff rates increased from an average of 11.7 percent to 20.5 percent for semifinished goods and from 16.6 percent to 30.1 percent for finished goods.[31] Through the remaining years before World War I Russia maintained the highest average tariff rates of any major European power.

Russian tariffs of the 1880s were particularly effective in curtailing German exports to Russia. Not only were the semifinished imports on which the Russian periphery depended taxed especially heavily, but an extra levy was placed on goods imported over Russia's western land border. Moscow designed the land/sea differential to stifle industrial development in Poland by increasing the costs of imported German materials, especially Silesian coal, which had been duty-free before 1885. Between 1882 and 1891 Russian tariffs were increased dramatically on many German industrial exports: raw iron (up 500 percent!), steel (20 percent to 33 percent), unspecified pharmaceuticals (20 percent), copper products (45 percent), locomotives (42 percent), electrical lighting equipment (21 percent).[32]

Every hike in the Russian tariff increased the number of German products that were unable to compete in the Russian market. Exports of otherwise successful German products such as machines, iron products, and industrial copper manufactures all declined sharply after

1882. The German chemical firm, Bayer, began exporting compressed alizarin to Moscow and completing the manufacturing process there in order to avoid Russian tariffs on dyestuffs that had reached 2,000 rubles/ton by 1891.[33] The Russian "monster tariff" of 1891 abruptly ended any chance of German exports recovering to their earlier level. In the difficult decade from 1880 to 1890, German producers had increased their worldwide exports by 14 percent (up to 3,335 million marks); yet during that same period exports to Russia had declined by 13 percent, or 29 million marks (Graph 1.2).[34] By 1888 to 1890 Germany's share of the Russian import market had fallen to just 34 percent, down from 46 percent in the period 1878 to 1882.[35] The German trade deficit with Russia grew correspondingly (Graphs 1.3 and 1.4). Manufacturers from Silesia to Westphalia peppered the Chancellor's Office, the Prussian Ministry for Trade and Industry, the Reich Office of the Interior, and the Reich Treasury Office with petitions to do something about the soaring Russian tariff.[36]

This dual nature of Imperial Russia – a large, underdeveloped economy with European great-power status – put German trade policy in a quandary that ultimately exposed Bismarck's inability to protect the German home market while seeking increased penetration of neighboring markets. On one side, German exporters looked eagerly to the Russian market as a source of increased foreign sales. On the other side, Russia's strength meant that Germany could not use force to gain access to this market. The strength of the Russian state prevented the type of economic penetration that Germany had been able to practice in other "less developed" countries. The methods the Europeans had employed for seizing control of Africa obviously could not be used. Even the somewhat less barbarous methods used in slicing up the China market were not suitable for the Russian Empire. As a tribute to Russian strength, Germany had to trade for or "purchase" the consent of the Russian government for access to the Russian market.[37]

Bismarck was aware of the desirability of a tariff-stabilizing treaty with Russia; on several occasions in the 1880s he approached the Russians on the subject of trade treaty negotiations. In late 1886 Germany and Russia entered negotiations on the possibility of reducing some Russian tariff rates, or at least eliminating the land/sea differential on coal.[38] For their own financial reasons, the Russians were not yet prepared to sign away their right to further tariff increases and effectively terminated the negotiations in 1887 by replacing Finance Minister Nikolai Bunge with Ivan Vyshnegradski, who immediately ordered a new hike in the Russian tariff rate on imported iron products. The Russian a priori refusal to sign a trade treaty with Germany in the 1880s spared Bismarck the necessity of coming to grips with the hard issues of trade negotiations with Russia. Vyshnegradskii's disinterest in negotiating a treaty with Germany allowed Bismarck to avoid confronting the major difficulty of any trade deal with Russia, namely, that in exchange for Russian tariff reductions, Germany would have to reduce its own tariff on agricultural imports, especially grain. Bismarck avoided the choice between domestic protection and export growth, which meant he avoided choosing between the agricultural and advanced industrial pillars of his conservative political coalition.

Bismarck had already determined that Germany would not offer agricultural tariff reductions in order to obtain a treaty with Russia. Confronted with a similar situation in negotiations with Austria-Hungary, Bismarck consistently refused to budge on German agricultural tariffs. Instead, he allowed a number of German tariff disputes with Austria-Hungary to smolder from 1881 through the end of his chancellorship. Even before entering into preliminary talks with the Russians in 1886, Bismarck "emphasized" to his Prussian ministers and Reich state secretaries that "in no case can we repeal our agricultural duties, as perhaps the Russian side might wish."[39] After his dismissal, Bismarck even considered appearing in the Reichstag to express his opposition to future agricultural tariff reductions.[40]

Not even the desire for stable, nonhostile political and diplomatic relations with Russia could induce Bismarck to lower the German tariff for Russian grain. Bismarck felt no need to support his allies with trade or financial considerations. Indeed, one of Bismarck's unique contributions to this era was the relentless economic pressure he applied to even his closest political and strategic allies.[41] In 1887 Bismarck did not hesitate to pull Russian government bonds off the list of securities usable as collateral at the Reichsbank and he applauded a German court ruling prohibiting the investment of trust funds in Russian bonds, yet at the same time he proposed and signed the Reinsurance Treaty with the Russians and arranged for the czar's visit to Germany in 1887.[42]

Bismarck's refusal to lower the grain tariff lay at the root of two sets of contradictions in German foreign economic policy. One obvious contradiction lay in the discrepancy between Germany's increasingly antagonistic economic relations with Russia and Bismarck's desire for stable, cooperative political relations between the two empires. Throughout the 1880s these strains on German-Russian cooperation were masked by Russia's own refusal to consider a trade treaty with Germany. As long as Vyshnegradskii was unwilling to seek a trade agreement, Bismarck was able to conceal his own unwillingness to make the tariff compromises necessary for an agreement.

A second contradiction could be found in the inconsistency between the Reich's protectionist and export-stimulating trade policies – a disparity that was emerging ever more clearly in light of other countries following Bismarck's protectionist lead.[43]

The desire to protect domestic markets while increasing sales in foreign markets was not unique to German trade policy toward Russia or even to German trade policy in general. Bismarck's shift to protectionism in 1879 signaled the start of a snowballing worldwide trend. Italy shifted to the protectionist track with its tariff of 1882. Austro-Hungarian tariff levels had returned to 15 percent ad valorem by 1888. In the United States, the McKinley tariff of 1890 sent a shock wave of fear through European exporters with its average tariff levels of 48 percent ad valorem. France embarked on a radical protectionist trajectory with the Méline tariff of 1890 as an open renunciation of its recent free trade past. The cumulative effect of these European tariff increases precipitated the dissolution of the European treaty network that had facilitated the rapid expansion of Western and Central European trade in the 1860s, 1870s, and 1880s.[44]

Most of the European trade treaties in force in 1890 had been patterned after the Anglo-French Cobden-Chevalier Treaty of 1860. That agreement had contained the original most favored nation (MFN) clause – a stipulation that each nation would acquire any additional concessions that the other might subsequently grant to a third party. That MFN provision became common in European trade treaties over the next twenty years, thereby linking many European countries in what was, in effect, a multilateral web of MFN clauses. The MFN clause became a particularly important concession when included in tariff treaties that bound future tariff rates at specific and concrete values (e.g., 42 rubles/ton on imported German raw iron brought into Russia). In these cases, the signatory states were granting specific tariff concessions not only to each other, but also to any third parties with whom they had already or would subsequently sign MFN treaties. Specific tariff rates needed be set explicitly by number only once; thereafter the same rates would be extended to all other treaty partners of that country via the MFN clause. In sum, the value to country A of an MFN treaty signed with country B related directly to the size and number of specific tariff concessions that B had granted or would grant to countries C, D, E, and F. In signing long-term tariff treaties of ten or twelve years' duration, states bargained away their unilateral control of their own tariffs in exchange for certainty in the tariffs of their trading partners. Long-term tariff treaties of this type had provided the stability that fostered the revolutionary surge in European international trade between 1840 and 1914.

Betwen 1860 and 1880 an extensive web of French MFN tariff treaties signed with Belgium, Italy, the Zollverein, Switzerland, and later with Sweden-Norway, the Netherlands (including the colonies), Spain, and Portugal served as the central anchor for other sets of trade treaties. For example, Spain's own smaller system of treaties centered upon the Spanish tariff reductions set out in the Franco-Spanish treaty. Germany also participated in the French treaty network. After the Franco-Prussian War, the new Reich had obtained an MFN clause from the French in Article XI of the Treaty of Frankfurt (1871). Thereafter, the French Third Republic continued to sign international treaties that contained both the MFN clause and specific tariff concessions. MFN obligations required France to extend to Germany these additional French tariff concessions granted to other countries.

As a result of the European trade treaty structure during these early years of the MFN clause, it was possible for Bismarck to manipulate the system to German advantage. During this time Bismarck signed only treaties with a general MFN clause, making few concrete concessions on the German tariff. France and other counties that signed general MFN treaties with Germany conceded much more than they received, since Germany made virtually no specific tariff concessions to other (third-party) countries that could rebound to French advantage. Bismarck used this international framework to gain a decided advantage in trade with the many European countries that had signed MFN treaties with Germany: Austria-Hungary, Sweden, Norway, Portugal, Belgium, the Netherlands, Switzerland, Italy, and Greece.

In some cases, Germany even obtained bound tariff rates from other countries (Serbia, Rumania, the Ottoman Empire, China, Korea, Siam, and Zanzibar) without binding its own rates. Between 1883 and 1888 Germany bound only a minuscule portion of its tariff in treaties with Switzerland, Italy, Spain, and Greece, whereas these other countries bound all or most of their tariffs in treaties with each other or with France. Germany extended few concrete concessions but received, via MFN, all the tariff reductions negotiated by the other countries among themselves. Germany had been, in effect a "free rider" on the system, managing to enjoy the best of both worlds. Bismarck's practice also preserved Germany's autonomous control over its own tariff rates so that Bismarck could unilaterally post the German agricultural tariff increases of the 1880s. The tariff rates of many other European countries remained fixed at existing levels by the tariff treaty network so these other countries were largely unable to respond in kind to the German tariff increases of the 1880s. With each German tariff increase, the German advantage from the existing arrangement increased as well. The newly founded Reich had become the chief beneficiary of the elaborate French tariff treaty network. Contemporary economist Walter Lotz understood that Germany's enviable position "was due in the large part to the European treaty system created by France."[45]

In this way, the French treaties established an international framework that benefited the Reich economically and politically through the 1880s. This one-sided arrangement allowed Bismarck to pursue, in the short run, his seemingly contradictory trade policies. Germany was able to increase protection for the German domestic market with little fear of retaliation by most West and Central European countries. In domestic terms this meant Bismarck could satisfy protectionist demands without igniting exporters' fears of foreign retaliation, thereby allowing an unnatural and ultimately unstable political alliance of protectionists and exporters. Throughout his chancellorship, Bismarck relied on Germany's unique position within the "French system" of tariff treaties to help conceal the basic incompatibility of protection at home and increasing exports abroad.

The impending expiration of the French treaty network in February 1892 threatened to terminate Germany's uniquely advantageous position within the international trade regime. "The continuation of the existing commercial pattern was impossible if France were unwilling to renew its comprehensive European treaties after February 1, 1892 …. All the protectionist tendencies in Europe would be given free reign."[46] Even if the MFN treaties were re-negotiated, it would be on the basis of much higher tariff levels, as France's own Méline tariff (1890) had already indicated. As Foreign Office State Secretary Alfred Marschall von Biberstein explained to the Reichstag: "Germany had harvested the fruit of a tree that it had not planted. The danger was imminent that the tree might be felled overnight and the fruit, heretofore free, would be gone."[47]

In Germany's foreign trade relations, more than in any other area, Bismarck's successor, Caprivi, inherited a house of cards on the verge of collapse. With the expiration of the international trade treaty network in 1892 Germany was sure to lose the systemic advantages it had so recently enjoyed; in renegotiating its foreign economic contacts German trading partners would not be as generous as they had been in the past. Yet the Reich still urgently needed exports as a source of the economic stability on which social and political stability were predicated. Bismarck's successor somehow had to maintain access to the markets of Germany's European neighbors. These markets had become even more important since

October 1890, when the prohibitive McKinley tariff virtually closed the American market to European textile and other consumer exports. The task of resolving the inherited conflicts in German trade policy fell to Caprivi, who, like Bismarck, sought a trade treaty with Russia as a means of increasing German exports. Caprivi's success in opening fruitful trade negotiations with Vyshnegradski's successor, Serge Witte, in 1892 exposed the impossibility of maintaining the current array of German policies, including distributive policies of protection at home and growth policies of increasing sales abroad. Treaty negotiations with Russia revealed the German grain tariff as the crux of a problem that would force the Reich to give priority to one or the other conflicting approaches to managing its foreign trade. The public debate over the future course of German trade policy that surrounded the Russian treaty forced industry, agriculture, commerce, consumers, and the government itself to articulate for the first time national and individual interests in the Eastern trade.

Behind the decision of how Germany should proceed around the general impasse in its trade relations stood a complicated bundle of economic and political issues that cut to the core of German social structures and political alliances. Economic theory could not resolve this question. Protective policies and export stimulating policies benefited different types of producers. Agriculture, basic textiles, and those heavy industries that produced primarily for the domestic market stood to gain through a priority of home protection. The growing machine-building, chemical, and electrical sectors that could compete successfully on the world market would gain through a priority of export growth. Prioritizing one or the other aspect of trade policy (price protection at home through high domestic tariffs or increased sales abroad though low foreign tariffs) directly affected the distribution of income across the various economic sectors and geographic regions of Germany. The dual nature of Eastern Europe pointed out unambiguously the impossibility of Germany implementing both protectionist and export growth trade policies simultaneously in that region. Caprivi initially faced this problem when negotiating new trade treaties with Austria-Hungary in 1891 and Rumania in 1893. Yet the sheer size of its economy put the Russian Empire in a category of its own as a trade partner. In terms of both the danger it posed to the German domestic market and its potential as an expanding export market, a trade treaty with Russia was far more significant for the Reich than a treaty with any other European country. The material stakes were higher and the political battles correspondingly more vocal and intense.

"Proto-Corporatism" and Economic Diplomacy

In its international context, the German-Russian treaty of 1894 was the product of long-term changes in the international environment from 1879 to 1892. Shifts in the political economy of Europe, in the international trade regime, and in German-Russian bilateral relations prodded Germany to seek a trade treaty with the Russians. In its German domestic context, the process of negotiating, signing, and ratifying the Russian treaty initiated seminal shifts in the domestic politics and the institutional framework of the Kaiserreich. The debates surrounding the treaty redefined political relations between the Reich's leading social groups. Most immediately, the treaty initiated a strain of agricultural opposition to East European trade that brought farmers into open conflict with export-oriented industrial sectors. Domestically-oriented heavy industry occupied a middle position, as it attempted to hold together the broadest possible agricultural-industrial political alliance. In these rough outlines, this acrimonious political constellation remained the domestic context for German trade policy in the East from the 1890s through the early 1930s. The conflicting economic interests of otherwise compatible political allies and similarly inclined social groups made the Eastern trade issue a particularly vexing problem in German political life.

Equally significantly, the process of negotiating the Russian treaty began to modify the existing institutional structure of the Reich as the government opened corporatist channels of communication to the private sector. Under Bismarck, and initially under Caprivi as well, the Reich government had conducted Germany's trade treaty negotiations on an absolutely confidential basis after briefly soliciting specific written petitions from the German Chamber of Commerce. In 1893 to 1894 Caprivi broke with past practice by arranging for an ongoing dialogue between the Reich's state secretaries and representatives from the leading industrial, commercial, and agricultural interest groups (the Verbände). As the new chancellor formalized the government-private sector dialogue in the Tariff Council (Zollbeirat), the interest groups took a critically important first step in gaining some direct influence over Germany's trade policies.

The Russian treaty's impact on imperial German domestic politics was matched by the treaty's momentous consequences for the future conduct of German foreign policy. A debate on the political consequences of the treaty for German foreign policy and Germany's international position ran parallel to the debate on the economic consequences for various domestic groups in Germany. In foreign policy as well, Caprivi broke with inherited practices – in this case rejecting

Bismarck's separation of commercial policy from the other political, diplomatic, and military aspects of German foreign policy.

In late 1890 the new chancellor joined the Crown Council in considering several alternative responses to the impeding sea changes in European trade arrangements. Friedrich List's old proposal for a central European customs union was reconsidered, with Germany, France, Italy, and Austria-Hungary as members. At the other extreme, the likely Bismarckian response of raising tariffs and fighting out a series of European tariff wars was also reviewed.[48] Caprivi chose a middle option, abandoning Bismarck's insistence on German tariff autonomy and retreating from protection of German agriculture. In 1891 he began to reorient German trade policy by negotiating a series of long-term MFN tariff treaties on the basis of mutual tariff reductions. Trading reductions on its own agricultural tariff rates for reductions on other countries' industrial rates, Germany initiated long-term MFN tariff treaties with Austria-Hungary, Italy, and Belgium in 1891, with Rumania, Serbia, and Spain in 1893, and with Russia in 1894.[49] Caprivi's trade policies, especially the prospect of a treaty with Russia, decisively altered the political relations between the Reich's leading private-sector groups by goading German farmers into an unprecedented flurry of mass-based political activity. The treaties with Austria-Hungary, Italy, and Belgium in 1891 had stretched the Conservatives' instinctive loyalty to the crown to the breaking point. Agrarian opposition to the government grew rapidly from 1891 to 1894, born out of a deep and abiding fear that Caprivi's trade policies would destroy German agriculture. When Caprivi began final negotiations for a Russian treaty in 1893, the agrarian opposition was intense and vocal. German agrarian interests clearly perceived the danger of Russian agricultural exports. The prospect of allowing Russian grain into Germany at the new, lower tariff rates of 3.5 marks/cwt. appeared to German land owners as a blow from which the distressed Junker grain-growing estates might not recover. At the same time, the agrarians were quickly learning to organize themselves and to defend their interests on trade issues. By the time the Reichstag debated the Russian treaty in February 1894, the agrarians were a far more potent political force than they had been just three years previously.

Three large groups served as the focal points of agrarian opposition to Caprivi's trade policies: the Catholic Peasants' League (Bauernverein), the Bavarian Peasants Union (Bauernbund), and most significantly, the Agrarian League (Bund der Landwirte).[50] This latter group developed into one of the most well-known and powerful interest groups in Germany, with a mass organization of 300,000 by 1910, eventually eclipsing agriculture's older representative body, the German Agricultural Council (Deutsche Landwirtschaftsrat). More important, the Agrarian League soon came to dominate the Conservative party, transforming it from "a constitutional party to an agrarian party, from a party of throne and altar to a party for which increased agricultural incomes were the basis of the national welfare."[51] In this way, Caprivi's trade policies created a destabilizing political novelty for Imperial Germany, that is, conservative opposition to the government.

By late 1891 the accelerating deterioration in German-Russian trade relations had escalated into a full tariff war that generated even higher Russian tariff rates on German products.[52] German exporters redoubled their appeals to the government for a German-Russian understanding that would secure some reduction in Russian tariff rates. Poor harvests and soaring grain prices in Germany from 1890 to 1892 spurred Russian hopes that the Reich would reduce the German grain tariff unilaterally, allowing Russia to preserve its own recent tariff increases of 1891.[53] For that reason, the Russians offered no tariff reductions on important German exports (textiles, metal products, chemicals, sugar, hops) when making preliminary contact with the Germans in November 1891 about a resolution of trade issues.[54] Caprivi withstood the domestic political pressure for a reduction in the grain tariff, which peaked in late summer of 1891.[55] Thanks in part to the very high prices for grain still prevailing, Caprivi secured an overwhelming ratification (243 to 48) of the treaty with Austria-Hungary in December 1891. The German Foreign Office returned to the Russian negotiations in August 1892.[56]

Throughout the summer of 1892 German manufacturers and traders flooded the Reich offices with petitions requesting specific reductions in the Russian tariff of 1891. The industrial Centralverband asked Germany to seek a "general reduction of [Russian] tariff rates" on German goods, emphasizing in particular the need for reductions on leather goods, natural and synthetic dyes, textiles, and cast-iron products. Industry-specific interest groups in textiles (Verein der Wollkämmer) and metallurgy (Verband der deutschen Eisenhüttenleute) reinforced these requests with additional petitions, as did individual firms, such as the metalworking firm Felten and Giulleaume. The Chambers of Commerce in the deeply affected northern German commercial cities (Lubeck, Danzig, Königsberg, Memel) urged the government to sign a tariff-reducing treaty with Russia.[57] On the basis of these requests, the Reich government compiled a list of "preliminary suggestions for the Russian tariff," presenting requests for specific tariff reductions on over 200 items. In

November 1892 negotiations with Russia broke down because neither side would make the first commitment on extending MFN status until other third-party negotiations (especially the Russian-French trade talks) were concluded. The Russians continued to seek Germany's new lower agricultural tariff rates via an MFN clause without sacrificing much of their own. Mikhail Murav'yov, the Russian *chargé d'affaires* in Berlin, warned Foreign Office State Secretary Alfred Marschall that Russia would create a new maximum tariff for future application toward countries that did not have MFN relations with Russia.[58] While the two governments made little progress toward a treaty, the downward trend in German manufactured exports to Russia continued.

Germany's recent tariff-reducing treaty with Austria-Hungary raised the question of the Reich signing a similar deal with Russia as a way out of the current trade impasse. In the 1880s only a few brave voices in industrial circles had dared to suggest extending lower agricultural rates to Russia in order to obtain Russian tariff concessions in return. In 1891 heavy industrial interests in the Centralverband still sought to preserve industrial-agrarian unity by declaring that "German industry seeks no advantages [in trade treaties] that can be achieved only at the expense of agriculture."[59] In August 1892 the Chamber of Commerce for Lubeck took the lead by directly suggesting that Germany lower its duties on wheat, rye, barley, oats, corn, and flax. By the end of 1892 most commercial and industrial groups strongly favored this tactic; by 1893 it was the consensus view among manufacturers and traders.[60]

Thereafter, export-oriented business and protectionist agriculture were at each other's throats over tariff and trade policy toward Russia. The trade negotiations with Russia embodied the conflicting interests of German domestic- and export-oriented producers on the grandest possible scale, with the result that the Russian treaty of 1894 became the most serious dispute within the conservative alliance in the imperial era. Agriculture's swing toward protectionism in 1879 had brought agricultural and the dominant industrial interests together for a decade of protectionist cohabitation. Changes in the production profile of German industry during those years now sent a large portion of newer, export-oriented industry and agriculture on different trade policy trajectories. As German engineer-entrepreneurs began translating the scientific discoveries of the late nineteenth century into a second industrial revolution, they created a new generation of industries: chemicals, pharmaceuticals, metalworking, machine-building, electricals, and motor vehicles. After 1890, these sectors were poised to challenge in economic importance the older mining, metallurgy, and basic textile industries that had dominated the German industrial economy in the 1870s and 1880s. By 1890 the metalworking industry employed almost one million workers, roughly equal to mining employment and over four times the work force of heavy metallurgy. Shortly thereafter metalworking overtook basic textiles in its share of the industrial work force, by 13 percent to 11.9 percent The significantly higher production growth rates for these new industries (e.g., 6.2 percent annually for chemicals, 3 percent for textiles, from 1850 to 1913) meant that the economic future belonged to the newcomers. These new, technologically more advanced branches of production made themselves felt in the structure of German exports. By the time the Russian treaty was debated in the Reichstag, machinery (exports of 64 million marks in 1893), finished iron manufactures (93 million marks), and aniline dyes (53 million marks) had assumed positions among Germany's leading exports.[61] Industrialists in these sectors began to assert themselves against the established protectionist coalition in pursuit of a trade treaty that lowered Russian tariffs. Agricultural rejection of lower German grain tariffs in any Russian treaty provoked a bitter split between the two pillars of Bismarck's conservative political alliance, the "landowner-industrial condominium directed against the proletariat," in the words of historian Eckart Kehr.[62]

In January 1893 a number of well-known spokesmen for German agriculture formalized their differences with the majority of the industrial and commercial communities by declaring that they would oppose any treaty that extended lower tariff rates to Russia. Agriculture delivered its message at a four-day conference on the future course of German trade policy toward Russia. The Reich Interior Office organized this meeting to bring together representatives from a number of the leading industrial, commercial, and agricultural interest groups in order to hear their opinions. The deeper significance of this meeting lay in the fact that it took place at all. For the first time the Reich government constructed a forum for the explicit purpose of soliciting private sector opinion on a major policy issue.[63]

Prior to the Russian treaty, the chancellor, the state secretary of the interior, and the Foreign Office had formulated German trade policy and negotiated trade treaties in virtual secrecy. Even within the Foreign Office, career diplomats from the Political Division were given control over treaty negotiations despite the creation of a new Commercial Affairs Division in 1885. Under Caprivi, Foreign Office State Secretary Marschall assumed direction of trade policy within the Foreign Office.[64] Control and execution of trade policy lay in the hands of the chancellor and the most aristocratic and most Prussian division of the most aristocratic and most Prussian of the Reich Ministries, the Political Division of the Foreign Office. The Foreign Office relied on the German Chamber of Commerce's brief solicitation of private sector written petitions as the government's information base for its foreign negotiations. The inadequacies of this superficial recruitment of specific commercial and industrial requests in a time of rapid technological development and growing interest group articulation were increasingly obvious. Caprivi had continued these practices in the negotiation of his first round of treaties with Austria-Hungary, Italy, and Belgium in 1891. Introducing these treaties to the Reichstag, Caprivi actively defended the government's practice of conducting the negotiations on a secret (geheim) basis.[65]

While these practices in trade policy were certainly an outdated reflection of an older, much simpler economy, they were also symptomatic of the continuing high degree of state autonomy in the quasi-democratic Reich. Bismarck's approach to trade negotiations demonstrated how much of the absolutist Prussian state's preconstitutional autonomy had been preserved in the Reich after 1871. With the king's permission, a small number of men (fluctuating around a half dozen) directed the bureaucratic and military apparatus of the Prussian kingdom. In charting the rise of absolutist Prussia, the monarchy had employed this apparatus at various times against every social class.[66] This bureaucratic absolutism was only mildly diluted as it moved from Prussia to the Reich. The autonomy of German kaiser, his chancellor, and imperial bureaucracy was only marginally less than that of the Prussian king, his minister-president, and royal bureaucracy. To be sure, the political realities of the Reich (including a quasi-democratic Constitution, the rise of revolutionary social democracy, and the persistence of an eloquent, if ineffectual, liberal opposition) limited the political maneuvering room for the kaiser's government.[67] Yet there remained few effective institutional checks on the imperial executive in most policy areas. In this "Bonapartist" system, the government and bureaucracy prided themselves on the distance they maintained from civil society.[68]

In trade policy, parliamentary control of the executive via Reichstag and Bundesrat approval of trade treaties (Articles 4 and 11 of the Reich Constitution of 1871) was weakened by the peculiarities of ratification procedures. The German constitutional arrangement allowed proposed trade treaties to be "presented to the Reichstag for ratification as an inviolable whole, so that changes in individual tariff positions could no longer be undertaken."[69] Like Bismarck, Caprivi was able to present the parties in the Reichstag with a completed treaty that reduced parliamentary influence to a single yes or no vote. As long as members of Parliament could not help shape the treaty by altering individual tariff rates, the Reichstag's role would remain incidental. The agrarian leader, Wilhelm von Kardorff, pointed out that the Reichstag's restricted ability only to accept or reject the treaties as they stood meant that the parliament could not "exercise influence in the formation of tariffs."[70] This left the process of formulating tariffs and trade treaties in the hands of the ministerial bureaucracy under the direction of the chancellor, the state secretaries of the interior and treasury, and the Prussian ministers of trade and agriculture.

After the old chancellor departed, both agriculture and industry criticized the government's retention of what they considered an outmoded mechanism for foreign trade negotiations. The Agricultural Association of Saxony complained that "before the conclusion of these treaties [i.e., those of 1891: Austria-Hungary, Italy, and Belgium] no opportunity for expression had been given" to agriculture; this was "all the more lamentable since the negotiations were conducted entirely secretly."[71] Alarmed by Caprivi's trade agreement with the grain-exporting dual monarchy and by the uncertain course of future trade policy, previously content agricultural groups demanded that their newfound voices be heard. While the content of Caprivi's policies encouraged many in the business community, the secretive character of policy formation and international negotiation continued to frustrate their hopes for inclusion in these processes. In the Reichstag, the Westphalian leather manufacturer Theodor Möller (National Liberal), attacked the government for maintaining "absolute secrecy about its goals" while negotiating recent trade treaties. To shouts of "Bravo!" from the floor, Möller blasted the insufficiencies of using only the German Chamber of Commerce to collect industrial and commercial opinion and went on to demand that the government put itself in "direct contact" with industry before negotiating additional treaties. In front of the industrial Centralverband, Möller criticized "a system in which the bureaucracy believes it possible to conclude treaties with only incidental information from the interested parties, while the other side stands in continual, close contact with [its] interested parties." He further bemoaned the "bureaucratic conceptions that rule our state" making direct participation by the private sector in international negotiations impossible.[72]

In this context, the government's decision to recruit a range of industrial and commercial opinions about a treaty with Russia, even on a limited, noninstitutional basis, constituted a radical innovation. The impetus came from Prussian Trade Minister Hans Hermann

Freiherr von Berlepsch (1890 to 1896), a progressive Saxon with maverick political and social views.[73] He had suggested in October 1892 that it might be "desirable to arrange an oral discussion with the leading representatives of the participating industrial sectors" about Germany's demands on the Russian tariff.[74] When the state secretary at the Reich Interior Office, Karl Heinrich von Boetticher, called an interministerial meeting for 10 January 1893 for the purpose of "determining the basic questions of a trade and tariff agreement with Russia," Berlepsch again proposed that the government "hear a limited number of technical experts and industrialists regarding their wishes for a German-Russian trade treaty." Berlepsch even suggested which interest groups the government should invite. The ministers accepted Berlepsch's plan, adding four agricultural experts from the German Agricultural Council as proposed by Prussian Minister for Agriculture Wilhelm von Heyden-Cadow.[75]

Private-sector representatives came together with members from the Reich interior, foreign, and treasury offices and with members from the Prussian trade, finance, and agriculture ministries for four days of meetings beginning on 24 January 1893.[76] The industrialists concentrated their arguments on the need for deep reductions in the Russian tariff, presenting dozens of examples and specific demands.[77] Yet they carefully avoided mentioning what Germany might have to give to the Russians in return. Only on the final, supplemental day of discussions on 30 January did the agricultural representative Count Albrecht Stolberg-Wernigerode (the Oberpräsident of East Prussia) take the bull by the horns, declaring bluntly that the Agricultural Council "must speak out against the elimination of the differential grain duty" (i.e. the higher rate on Russian versus Austro-Hungarian grain). When asked by Boetticher if he would oppose any German-Russian treaty obtained through German tariff concessions, Stolberg-Wernigorode replied only that he would oppose any treaty that made agriculture "suffer in sympathy" with industry during the current unsatisfactory relations with Russia.[78] On the government side, ministerial representatives gave no explicit indications on future German trade policy toward Russia, though they obviously felt the session had produced useful business and technical information, which was hardly surprising in view of their superficial knowledge prior to the meeting. On the basis of these discussions the government made more than sixty changes in the position it had outlined to the Russians in August 1892. These refinements must be seen as concrete results of the bureaucracy's new dialogue with the private sector. More important, this meeting served as the staring point for a process of bringing the voices of commerce, industry, and agriculture into the process of formulating German trade policy.

An exchange of notes between Foreign Office State Secretary Marschall and the Russian ambassador in July and August 1893 cleared the ground for the opening of formal trade treaty negotiations in Berlin on 1 October, with the talks to center on what Russia could offer in exchange for the lower German tariff rates.[79] On 17 August Caprivi named the German negotiating team – Baron Max von Thielmann, the Prussian envoy in Hamburg, to serve as chief negotiator, supported by negotiating assistants and staff from the Foreign Office. In September 1893 the Reich government again turned to the private sector in order to hear its views on trade policy toward the Russians. In his letter to the Reich and Prussian ministers, Caprivi declared that "it might appear useful (zweckmässig) to keep a few representatives from industry and commerce and agriculture ready in an Advisory Council (Beirat) for short-term use." He charged Boetticher with the task of building such a council and reporting its membership to the chancellor.[80]

Boetticher arranged a two-day session with some ninety representatives from agriculture, industry, and commerce, to be held in the Reichstag building on 27-28 September.[81] As chairman, he opened the session with the portentous declaration that the imperial government intended to "remain in constant and close contact with the economic groups of the Reich that are interested in the current negotiations with Russia." The program for the session supported this claim by proposing a general discussion of German trade policy toward Russia and then election of a Standing Council of nine or eleven members. That Standing Council would serve as a "connecting link between agriculture, industry, and commerce on one side and the government on the other side."

This important development in the relations between the imperial government and the private sector was somewhat eclipsed by the intensity of private-sector conflict over the desirability of a German-Russian treaty. The majority of industrial and commercial representatives no longer hesitated to express themselves in favor of extending lower agricultural tariffs to Russia in order to sign a treaty, and to end the damaging tariff war that had reached a new peak in the summer of 1893.[82] Spokesmen from large and small manufacturing sectors -from chemicals and textiles to watchmaking and musical instruments – spoke in favor of a treaty. Members of the chemical and textile industries emphasized the current size and future potential of the Russian market for their exports. Only Westphalian heavy industry discounted the importance of the Russian market for its products. Responding to claims that German industry needed a treaty with Russia, Krupp Director Hanns Jencke declared that "this does not apply to the iron and steel industry of Rhineland and Westphalia. Previously Russia played a large role in [our] sale of railroad materials. This has now completely ceased ... the Russians have developed their own industry."[83]

Commercial groups and urban Chambers of Commerce from cities as diverse as Stettin, Leipzig, Dessau, Nuremberg, Mainz, Posen, Lubeck, and Königsberg repeatedly declared their "unanimous" supported for a treaty. In fact, the harshest antiagrarian opinions came from this quarter, giving the debate something of a town-versus-country character as municipal associations took up the interests of urban consumers and workers, labor having been excluded from any organized representation of their own interests. Municipal Councillor Harkew from Stettin, as the first speaker, bluntly declared that Germany needed a treaty, that a treaty was not possible "if concessions are not made on our side," and that "these can only lie in the agricultural sector." After quickly dismissing agricultural arguments against a treaty, Harkew concluded with the implication that agricultural prices must be reduced, since German industrial competitiveness required "that our population be fed just as cheaply as other populations."

Among the agricultural representatives were the leading names in Prussian land-owning society and conservative politics: von Arnim-Güterberg, von Hatzfeldt-Trachenberg, von Kanitz-Podangen, and von Mirbach-Sorquitten. The group was unanimous in its assessment that agriculture simply could not afford the consequences of a lower tariff on Russian grain. Unrealistically extreme views were expressed particularly by Landrat von Roeder (Ober-Ellguth), Krauss (Königsberg), and von Puttkamer (Freiforst in West Prussia). Roeder denied earlier assertions that Prussia had become an "industrial state" and reminded the group that "agriculture is the first Estate" in the Reich. Similarly, Puttkamer asked imperiously: "How consequential are these petty interests in comparison to the mighty interests of agriculture which are at risk?"

Yet the agricultural representatives correctly sensed that Caprivi had already committed the Reich to a policy of extending the lower rates to Russia in exchange for Russian reductions. Toward the close of the session Puttkamer declared, "I know that the fate of agriculture in this assembly and within the government is sealed, so I will rely on another assembly, the Reichstag, which will better protect the interests of producers." Roeder also promised a battle in the Parliament, declaring that the treaty "is a battle of interests which ultimately will be decided in favor of that party which has the power in the Reichstag." Other agricultural representatives began listing forms of compensation that would make the treaty more palatable to them, especially abolition of the "identity certificates" for tariff rebates on grain exports. Over the next five months, until the ratification of the treaty in early 1894, the split between agriculture and industry played itself out in the press and in public, culminating in the Reichstag debates on ratification in February and March 1894.

Against this background of increasing acrimony, the session concluded with the election of a Standing Council that would remain the point of contact between the government and the private sector. Each "estate" elected three representatives. Agriculture elected their parliamentary champion, Count Hans von Kanitz, as well as von Arnim-Güterberg, and estate owner Reich. Industry elected the long-standing critic of the government's secretive trade policy deliberations, Theodor Möller, along with textile man Hermann Vogel from Chemnitz and the Silesian mining director Paul Wachler (Dönnersmarck-Hütte).[84] Representing commerce were the Chairman of Lubeck's Chamber of Commerce, a vocally antiagrarian Frankfurt grain merchant named Ponsick, and a representative from Königsberg.[85]

The formation of this Standing Council of private representatives was a watershed in state-society, government-business, and bureaucracy-interest group relations in Germany. It produced a significant, though not easily visible, change in German domestic politics by giving the private-sector interest groups a limited role in shaping the Reich's foreign trade policies. Not only had Caprivi brought the private sector into the process of trade policy formulation in Germany, he had institutionalized its voice, even if only in this ad hoc council. Caprivi's actions were an important first step in bringing the private sector into the process of German trade policy formulation. After the Russian treaty of 1894, both the bureaucracy and the interest groups assumed that some form of regular, institutional private-sector participation would remain an integral part of formulating trade policy and negotiating trade treaties. In a longer view, we can see the Standing Council, generally referred to by contemporaries as the "Tariff Council" (Zollbeirat), as the first of the "corporatist" arrangements that thereafter played increasingly important roles in the formulation of Germany's economic policies.

The role of the Tariff Council *(Zollbeirat)* in the upcoming negotiations remained unclear. The industrial and commercial members of the group worked feverishly to get themselves involved in the negotiations on the German side. Caprivi's instructions had mentioned only that a private sector "advisory council" should be kept "ready."

The Interior Office had no plans for this group beyond having this new body serve a point of "contact" between the government and the private sector. Möller, who had long argued for some private-sector input into the negotiation of trade treaties, made the most of this ambiguous opportunity to play an officially sanctioned role in the process. With the support of the industrial Centralverband and the German Chamber of Commerce, Möller organized a common office for the industrial and commercial members of the Tariff Council.[86] After collecting copies of the hundreds of existing petitions concerning the treaty, Möller's office appointed special, industry-specific technical advisers to evaluate requests for changes in the Russian tariff. To lend an official character to these activities, Möller invited members of the Bundesrat to the sessions. Industrial experts delivered oral reports to and were questioned by members of the Bundesrat about private-sector requests for Russian tariff reductions. On this basis, the Tariff Council produced its own report and commentary on the first Russian reply to German tariff requests. H.A. Bueck, as secretary and influential leader of the industrial Centralverband, praised Möller's "extraordinary energy in recommending these requests in the negotiations." However, the influence of the Tariff Council on the government negotiating team and the impact of its opinions on the German negotiating position was probably much less than Möller led others to believe.

There is no direct evidence that any member of the German delegation relied on advice from the Tariff Council. Thielmann's own reports to Caprivi never once mentioned the Council. His insistence on obtaining the maximum possible concessions from the Russians grew primarily out of his own sense of professional diplomatic duty. After a 1 November breakfast meeting with the kaiser at which "His Majesty took the opportunity to express repeatedly his firm will not to back down from our [trade treaty] demands on Russia," Thielmann needed no prodding from commercial circles.[87] Thielmann was a career diplomat in the most prestigious and impermeable organization in the entire Reich/Prussian administration, the Political Division of the Foreign Office. Thielmann appreciated the difficulty of bringing the final document through the Reichstag against known agrarian opposition and the consequent need to secure every possible industrial and commercial vote. At the same time, his obvious lack of interest in the activities of the Tariff Council was typical of the "bureaucratic conceptions" that ruled the Foreign Office and about which Möller complained in vain. The Treasury Office member of the German delegation also made no mention of Möller's group in detailed reports to his office. The files of the Treasury

Office, which stood in intimate contact with the Interior Office on this issue, contain only one passing mention of the Tariff Council.[88] Bueck was surely exaggerating when he claimed that the Tarriff Council "was listened to continually, and was given real influence in the negotiations."[89]

In fact, the 1893 to 1894 negotiations for the Russian treaty still had quite a bit in common with the old practices developed by Bismarck's Foreign Office and largely retained by Caprivi. The central point remains that the government's fundamental policy decision – the decision to offer Germany's new, lower tariff rates to Russia in exchange for Russian tariff reductions – had been made by August 1892 (possibly as early as 1891) without any direct input from any portion of the private business sector. Only six and twelve months later did Caprivi offer industrial, commercial, and agricultural groups unprecedented opportunities for expressing their general opinions on the desirability of a German-Russian treaty and for making specific requests for reductions in the Russian tariff. After German-Russian negotiations began in earnest on 3 October 1893, the decision to accept or reject specific Russian offers and the final judgment as to whether Russian concessions constituted a sufficient basis for signing a long-term treaty rested solely with Thielmann, Caprivi, and Boetticher. The Tariff Council only received reports on the progress of negotiation, Caprivi having decided to break with the old pattern of strict secrecy about negotiations in progress.

Ironically, despite playing almost no role in shaping the Russian-German treaty of 1894, the Tariff Council epitomized Caprivi's New Course approach to trade negotiations. Caprivi broke with the inherited Bismarckian policies and practices as tariff reduction replaced protectionism, long-term treaties replaced tariff autonomy, and dialogue with the private sector replaced secret negotiations with foreign partners. This sort of dialogue between the state and politically or socially estranged groups was central to Caprivi's New Course chancellorship in other areas as well, particularly in his efforts to reach out to the working class. As a rejection of Bismarckian practices, government dialogue with the private sector may have been an end in itself. Yet in matters of trade policy, this dialogue helped secure commercial and industrial private-sector support for lowering agricultural tariffs, support that the new chancellor must have known he would need to overcome both Bismarck's legacy and active agrarian opposition to his policies. Far less secure in his office than Bismarck had been, Caprivi bolstered his position by securing private-sector allies in the face of bitter opposition to the Russian treaty. For several reasons, then, Caprivi's departure from Bismarckian practices required modification of the established institutions and procedures for trade policy formulation.

As the final piece in Caprivi's trade treaty system, the Russian treaty capped a two-year running argument on the wisdom of his trade policies. Both proponents and opponents of the treaty spent as much time attacking and defending the basic direction of Caprivi's trade program – the policy of trading German agricultural concessions for equivalent foreign concessions on manufactured goods – as they did discussing the anticipated effects of specific German or Russian concessions. In this sense, the debate on the Russian treaty was a more sharply expressed continuation of this larger argument, which had begun with the Austro-Hungarian treaty in December 1891 and continued with the Rumanian treaty in December 1893. Industrial groups, commerce, and agriculture had already fully elaborated their positions in the government-sponsored discussions of January and September 1893. Industry in general advanced economic and political arguments in support of a long-term, export-facilitating agreements with the East, emphasizing the need to end the current tariff war with Russia and to avoid the negative impact the treaty might have on German farm incomes. Agriculture continued to insist that it could not bear the commodity price declines that would inevitably result from extending tariff reductions to Rumania and Russia. To this was added an emotional appeal to the Reich's conservative leadership for government support of the "loyal" rural population. These parliamentary debates found parallel expression in other arenas, especially in the press and in extraordinary meetings of the leading interest groups. Commentary in the Conservative *Kreuzzeitung* went hand-in-hand with conservative arguments in the Reichstag, while the pro-treaty forces expressed themselves in *Handelsarchiv, Hamburger Nachrichten,* and *Export.* Discussion of agrarian opposition to the treaty dominated the February 1894 Assembly of Delegates of the industrial Centralverband.[90] The agrarian opposition grew into a general attack on Caprivi's "New Course." The consequences for the Caprivi, Chlodwig Hohenlohe, and Bernhard von Bülow chancellorships were enormous as the Agrarian League became a radical, antimodern movement whose ideas found expression in the new reactionary, anti-Semitic Tivoli Program of the Conservative Party (1892).

In contrast to his predecessor, Caprivi acknowledged the international political content of his trade policies. In dealing with Russia, Caprivi hoped a successful trade treaty could reestablish the harmonious relations that had been soured by Bismarck's tariff policies and had reached a new low after the German decision not to renew the

Reinsurance Treaty in 1890. By introducing noneconomic (i.e., political) considerations into the domestic debate over German trade and tariff policy, Caprivi complicated that debate enormously. Caprivi's political arguments initiated a new era in German foreign policy by awakening subsequent chancellors, beginning with Bülow, to the potential of trade as a foreign policy lever against Russia. However, Bülow's attempts to use that lever failed. The practical limitations of the imperial Reich's import/export controls undermined German ambitions to apply politically motivated trade policies against Russia. The federally organized German customs services proved unable to effectively control trade flows with Russia. Under those conditions there could be no use of trade as a foreign policy lever. In fact, the practical impossibility of placing Russia on less-favorable footing than Germany's other trade partners helped force the passage of Caprivi's treaty in 1894.

Caprivi himself offered clear political arguments in favor of the Russian treaty. Unlike Bismarck, he acknowledged the necessity of coordinating foreign economic policies, particularly trade, with larger foreign policy goals and international relationships. As early as September 1890 he told an interministerial meeting that "an alliance and a tariff war with Austria are incompatible."[91] When presenting the Italian and Austrian treaties to the Reichstag, Caprivi had spoken openly about the "political side of these treaties." Stating plainly the Reich's "interest in strengthening our allies," Caprivi advanced an international political argument for his trade policies. Reichstag member Peter Reichensperger (Center) emphasized exactly these political considerations when he spoke in support of the treaty.[92] The foreign policy argument, especially as it applied to Austria-Hungary, played a significant part in securing Conservative votes for an overwhelming Reichstag majority for the treaties of 1891. Caprivi's logic may have been sound, but his argument caused a small sensation since it so obviously departed from Bismarck's practice of refusing to commit the Reich to the economic support of its allies.[93]

Because Russia was not a direct ally of the Reich, advocates of the treaty recast their political argument. The emphasis now fell on the disastrous diplomatic consequences, including possibly border clashes, that would result if the Reich attempted to exclude Russia from Germany's new trade treaty network. Caprivi warned the Reichstag that St. Petersburg would turn to radical pan-Slavism if Russia were not included in the new German trade treaties. Responding to an old criticism that he had cut the political wire to Russia by allowing the Reinsurance Treaty to lapse in 1890, Caprivi called the new trade treaty a "strong, powerful, new wire to Russia."

Reichstag rejection of the treaty meant cutting all wires to Russia "and you will be responsible for that and not the Government!"[94] Similarly, the industrial Centralverband explained that "for economic and political reasons" it was "impossible" to maintain the old rates on Russian produce when lower rates had been granted to other grain exporters. The *Schlesisches Morgenblatt* had made the same argument since August 1892. Even Bismarck, generally opposed to Caprivi's trade policies, now softened his opposition to the Russian treaty in light of the political argument.[95]

Sensing that this political argument had dangerous potential, perceptive agrarians opposed it, even as it applied to the Austrian treaty. In December 1891 Kanitz had foreseen a Russian treaty as the ultimate political consequence of the Austrian agreement. "Otherwise," he said, "the whole system will culminate in a differential duty directed against Russia," which would be politically intolerable. Kanitz predicted that Caprivi's policies would "force" the Reich to sign a similar treaty with Russia. Kardorff also warned that a Russian treaty would be unavoidable after an Austrian treaty.[96] When Caprivi presented the Rumanian treaty in December 1893, conservative politician Count Limburg-Stirum attacked the government's argument that the Austrian treaty now required a Rumanian treaty; he warned that, together, the Austrian and Rumanian agreements would soon require a Russian treaty. Limburg-Stirum argued passionately against the concept and practice of using trade treaties in support of German foreign policy: "... the worst mistake at that time [1891] was mixing politics and commercial policy ... Gentlemen, it is my opinion – and will always remain so – that this is a false maxim. Commercial policy and politics must be separated from each other .... it is not our opinion that the German Reich is today in a position to [have to] pay anyone for his alliance. (Sehr richtig! on the right)."[97]

Notwithstanding the self-serving nature of this argument, Limburg-Stirum was articulating a genuine concern on the part of conservatives who instinctively clung to Bismarckian practices. They feared the loss of German diplomatic freedom that the political overtones of these long-term trade agreements implied. A preindustrial agrarian worldview could not easily accommodate Caprivi's policy of "strengthening" Germany's allies through trade and economic cooperation. At the same time, Junker belief in German military superiority meant that most Conservatives would not accept the idea that Germany "had to pay for peace" by maintaining harmonious trade relations with its neighbors. "Buying peace! Pfui! – shocking words to every Prussian!" in the opinion of the *Kreuzzeitung*.[98] As some strands of German conservatism took a radical, antimodern twist, agrarians came increasingly to reject the type of economic diplomacy that Caprivi was advancing.[99]

A second, less dramatic, but equally important argument for accepting the Russian treaty was the practical impossibility of Germany effectively discriminating against Russian grain, an impossibility widely recognized in both Germany and Russia. All trade treaty arrangements were limited by the practical problems of implementing adequate import and export controls. The tremendous increase in European trade volume and the rapid changes in trade composition from 1870 to 1914 strained the size and expertise of most continental customs services. In Germany, the problem was once again compounded by the federal structure of the Reich. Article 35 of the Constitution assigned legislative control of the tariff to the Reich, but "levying and administering tariffs" belonged to the reserve rights maintained by many individual states. Duties were levied and collected by the administrations of the individual states under the "supervision" of 15 Reich "plenipotentiaries" and 45 "station inspectors."[100] In theory, customs enforcement was uniform; in practice it was neither uniformly rigorous, nor particularly well-coordinated. German customs outposts did not check all merchandise upon arrival, nor could customs personnel identify the origin of every shipment. Under these circumstances, it was, in fact, impossible for Germany administer a tariff that prescribed two or more different rates of duty on the same commodity, depending on its point of origin.

Kanitz had correctly foreseen this danger when Caprivi proposed the Austro-Hungarian treaty in 1891. During the debate on the Rumanian treaty, the agrarians returned to this argument, with Kardorff warning explicitly that Russian grain would be brought into the Reich at the reduced tariff rate via Rumania. After Germany ratified the Austrian Treaty, Prussian Trade Minister Berlepsch warned Caprivi that Russia could and would "exploit" the difference between the 3.5-mark duty charged on Austro-Hungarian grain and the 5-mark duty imposed on Russian produce.[101]

The Russians were, in fact, exploring the possibility of exploiting the tariff differential. In August 1892 Witte let visiting German railroad directors know that he had recently been in Vienna to arrange for the shipment of Russian grain through Galicia (via Lvov) into Austria-Hungary. Caprivi received reports that Witte was in Vienna seeking "concessions" on railroad rates "that would enable Russia to bring its grain onto the German market via Austria-Hungary." A second report indicated that Russia was preparing to reduce its own domestic rail rates on the lines heading from Kiev to Lvov and from Kiev to Berlin via Alexandrovo.[102] Johannes Miquel, whose Finance

Ministry oversaw the customs service in Prussia, concluded from an inquiry among customs officials at the provincial level that "the possibility of such [Russian] customs evasion is generally recognized; and adequate steps for the effective protection of our customs interests could not be suggested." West Prussian importers confirmed that Russian lumber could be disguised as Austrian in origin if Habsburg officials allowed it to pass as such. The government's own explanatory memorandum on the treaty acknowledged publicly that it was "highly doubtful" whether the Reich could handle Russian grain differentially over the long term.[103]

Both the agrarian opposition and the Reich ministers acknowledged the political and practical impossibility of excluding Russia from Caprivi's new trade treaty network, yet the two sides drew fundamentally different conclusions from this realization. For Caprivi and the Reich government, this fact confirmed the inevitable character of the Russian treaty. In their minds the treaty with Austria-Hungary (and the subsequent treaty with Rumania) had long since made a Russian treaty unavoidable. In the Reichstag, Caprivi called the Russian treaty "a simple consequence of the previous treaties," eliciting cries of "Aha!" from the Conservatives.[104] For the agrarians, the necessity of including Russia in the treaty system meant that the system as a whole must be changed. If earlier treaties now required a treaty with Russia, then these earlier agreements ought to terminated. Kanitz flatly proposed "to annul the Austrian treaty of 1891." The *Kreuzzeitung* went even further, urging Germany "to rip up the trade treaties with Austria and Italy, if necessary" in order to avoid extending similar benefits to the East.[105] The unrealistic conclusion of this line of thought was a maintenance of the old Bismarckian trade practices that had become impossible after the expiration of the French treaty network in 1892.

Caprivi's use of long-term trade treaties with MFN clauses and bound tariff rates meant that Germany had to extend the lower rates contained in the earlier treaties (1891) to Russia as well. Even a basic MFN agreement between Berlin and St. Petersburg would connect Russia to the lower rates granted elsewhere in the German system. This connection ensured that agrarian opposition to lower rates for Russia would eventually require opposition to the Caprivi system as a whole and to the basic tool of that system, long-term MFN treaties. Agrarian opposition had initially been limited to the content of Caprivi's trade policy in the East (i.e., reducing the German grain tariff). The debate on the Russian treaty extended this opposition to the idea of trade policy as foreign policy, and to the form of German trade policy in long-term treaties. Agrarian rejection of the "conventional" and internationally accepted tool for the regulation of foreign trade – the long-term MFN treaty – was another step down a very slippery slope of agrarian radicalism that made political cooperation with the conservatives increasingly strenuous.

Despite its radical energy, agrarian opposition to Caprivi's trade polices failed in the short run. The final vote on 10 March 1894 totaled 200 for the Russian treaty and 146 against, with the Socialists supporting the government and the Conservatives in opposition! With Caprivi and Wilhelm II pushing hard for the treaty and almost all nonagricultural groups in favor, treaty opponents had foreseen defeat.[106] In gratitude, Wilhelm made Caprivi a count, and Czar Alexander III, in one of his last acts, made Wilhelm an admiral in the Russian navy. But the celebrations did not last long. The autonomy of the chancellor's office could insulate Caprivi from immediate political pressures, but it could not protect him indefinitely against the unrelenting agrarian hatred that helped bring him down just seven months after the Russian treaty was signed.[107]

As in so many areas, Caprivi's New Course chancellorship departed from established Bismarckian practices in trade and tariff policy. Most important, the new chancellor terminated the secretive practices of trade treaty negotiation and rejected the dichotomy of economic relations and other aspects of international relations, both key elements of the Bismarck era. Instead, Caprivi included private-sector forces into government trade policy councils and connected trade policy to larger foreign policy goals. Inasmuch as Bismarck's practices had engendered a great deal of private-sector resentment in Germany, had soured relations with Russia, and had brought the Reich's foreign trade policy to a dead end in the face of European changes after 1892, a departure from his methods was both desirable and necessary.

Caprivi's decision to establish a standing Tariff Council legitimated private-sector claims for some voice in trade policy formulation. Bueck told the industrial Centralverband that with government consultation with the private sector "Germany has opened a new path with these negotiations."[108] The new arrangements tantalized the private-sector interest groups by giving them a limited role in shaping the Reich's foreign trade policies. However, in the 1890s Germany stood only at the very beginning of the "new path" to which Bueck referred. The inclusion of a small private-sector voice in government trade policy councils only highlighted the imperial state's high degree of autonomy from civil society.

But the changes instituted by Caprivi's innovations left a number of serious issues unresolved. Many aspects of the New Course were subsequently undone by Caprivi's more conservative successors.

The extent and form of private sector input into the process of trade policy formation had been neither regularized nor institutionalized for the future. Its grip on participation in the policy process was tenuous. The struggle of the private sector to inject itself more fully into the process would soon be renewed in anticipation of a new Russian treaty in 1904.

Perhaps no portion of Caprivi's New Course was ultimately more momentous then his public break with Bismarck's practice of separating trade policy from other foreign policy considerations in the conduct of Germany's international affairs. In doing so, Caprivi greatly increased the potential for German influence in Eastern Europe. Yet by introducing this noneconomic, political thinking into German trade policy, Caprivi made the task of formulating German trade policy that much more difficult. Here, too, the future fate of Caprivi's new practice of trade-based economic diplomacy remained unsure. The conceptual limitations of the preindustrial agrarian/military Junker mentality could not accept Caprivi's argument for Germany's use of economic diplomacy as part of foreign policy. Practical limitations also restricted the use of trade policy in support of foreign policy goals. Neither the European international economy nor the German customs service could yet accommodate a policy that might require extensive import/export controls and documentation. If treaties with Austria-Hungary and Rumania led unavoidably to a treaty with Russia, how could Germany hope to gain political advantages from selective trade policies?

Resolving these complex issues was made more difficult by an agrarian response to the Russian treaty that might best be characterized as obstructionism regarding German trade policy toward the East. Radical conservatives rejected the content of Caprivi's trade policy toward Russia, the underlying economic and foreign policy arguments, and long-term MFN treaties that were the vehicle for the policy. In 1893 German agriculture flatly rejected any trade treaty that would put Russia on equal footing with Germany's other trade partners in Eastern and Western Europe. For the next forty years, German agriculture actively sought to block the conclusion of trade agreements between Germany and its Eastern neighbors with the result that agriculture's input on German trade policy toward the East grew increasingly one-dimensional and negative.

Notes

1. In his remarkable speech of 10 December 1890, Caprivi captured the necessity for a national economic strategy by declaring that "We must export – either export goods or we export people." *Stenographische Berichte über die Verhandlungen des deutschen Reichstages* [hereafter, *Sten. Ber.*], 1890/92, V, 3301 ff.

2. For overviews of German economic development in the nineteenth century, see Helmut Böhme, *Prolegomena zu einer Sozial- und Wirtschaftsgeschichte Deutschlands im 19. und 20 Jahrhundert* (Frankfurt, 1968); Knut Borrchardt, "The Industrial Revolution in Germany," in C.M. Cipolla, ed., *Fontana Economic History of Europe* (London, 1973), vol. 4/1; F.W. Henning, *Die Industrialisierung in Deutschland 1800-1914* (Paderborn, 1993); Walter G. Hoffmann, *Das Wachstum der deutschen Wirtschaft seit der Mitte des 19. Jahrhunderts* (Berlin, 1965); F. Lütge, *Deutsche Sozial- und Wirtschaftsgeschichte*, 3d ed. (Berlin, 1966); Hermann Kellenbenz, *Deutsche Wirtschaftsgeschichte*, 3 vols. (Munich, 1981) vol. 2 *Vom Ausgang des 18. Jahrhunderts bis zum Ende des zweiten Weltkrieges*. For the impact of the depression, see Hans Rosenberg, *Grosse Depression und Bismarckzeit. Wirtschaftsablauf, Gesellschaft und Politik in Mitteleuropa* (Frankfurt, 1976); R. Spree, *Die Wachstumszyklen der deutschen Wirtschaft von 1840 bis 1880* (Göttingen, 1978).

3. Germany's Net National Product (NNP) had grown at an average annual rate of over 3 percent in the period 1861/67 to 1871/75 (1913 prices), calculated from Hoffmann, *Das Wachstum der deutschen Wirtschaft*, Table 1, 14. For price declines, see Alfred Jacobs and Hans Richter, "Die Grosshandelspreise in Deutschland 1792-1934," *Sonderhefte des Instituts für Konjunkturforschung* 37 (Hamburg, 1935).

4. Hans Rosenberg, "Political and Social Consequences of the Great Depression of 1873-1896 in Central Europe," in James Sheehan, ed., *Imperial Germany* (New York, 1976), 47.

5. Hans-Ulrich Wehler, "Bismarck's Imperialism 1862-1890," in James Sheehan, ed., *Imperial Germany* (New York, 1976), 198. Also his "Der Aufstieg des Organisierten Kapitalismus und Interventionstaates in Deutschland," in Heinrich A. Winkler, *Organisierter Kapitalismus. Voraussetzungen und Anfänge* (Gottingen, 1974), 36-57.

6. H.-P. Olshausen, *Friedrich List und der deutsche Handels – und Gewerbeverein* (Jena, 1935).

7. On the Centralverband see the memoir history of Henry Axel Bueck, longtime executive secretary of the Centralverband, *Der Centralverband deutscher Industrieller 1876-1901*, 3 vols. (Berlin, 1902-1905), vol. 1, 105 ff.; F. Hauenstein, "Die ersten Zentralverbände," in F. Berg (hrsg.), *Der Weg zum industriellen Spitzenverband* (Darmstadt, 1956), 1-73; Harmut Kaelble, *Industrielle Interessenpolitik in der wilhelmischen Gesellschaft. Centralverband deutscher Industrieller 1895-1914* (Berlin, 1967), 3-9; Th. Hassler, "Aufzeichnungen über Bismarck und den Centralverband deutscher Industrieller," *Tradition* 7 (1962), 223-33; Ivo N. Lambi, "The Protectionist Interests of German Iron and Steel Industry, 1873-1879," *JEH* 22 (1962), 59-70; H. Nussbaum, "Zentralverband deutscher Industrieller," in *Die bürgerlichen Parteien in Deutschland. Handbuch der Geschichte der bügerlicher Parteien und anderer bügerlicher Interssenorganisationen vom Vormärz bis zum Jahre 1945* (Leipzig, 1970), 850-71; Gerhard Schulz, "Über die Entstehung und Formen von Interessengruppen in Deutschland seit Beginn der Industrialisierung," *Politische Vierteljahresschrift* 2 (July 1961), 124-53.

8. In 1874 Germany moved from a net exporter of wheat to a net importer. Thereafter through the end of the decade Germany imported 4.5 million metric tons (MMT) of wheat, valued at 963 million marks. While Germany had long been an importer of rye, the volume of incoming grain nearly tripled from 1.2 MMT in

1860 to 1865 to 6.4 MMT in 1874 to 1879, *Statistisches Jahrbuch des deutschen Reiches* 2 (1881), 81.

9. From the large body of literature on the role of German agriculture in this, see above all Karl W. Hardach, "Die Haltung der deutschen Landwirtschaft in der Getreidezoll-Diskussion 1878/79," *Zeitschrift für Agrargeschichte und Agrarsoziologie* 15 (1967), 33-48 and the literature cited there; J.C. Hunt, "Peasants, Grain Tariffs, and Meat Quotas: Imperial German Protectionism Reexamined," *CEH* 7 (1974), 311-31. Hardach credits the protectionist turn to the bourgeoisie, arguing that agriculture came to the idea of protective tariffs largely after 1879, a position shared in the literature of the old German Democratic Republic by Hans Mottek et al., *Wirtschaftsgeschichte Deutschlands* (Berlin, 1964 and later), vol. 3, 109.

10. On the problems of German agriculture after 1875 see W. Abel, *Agrarkrisen und Agrarkonjunktur im Mitteleuropa vom 13. bis zum 19. Jahrhundert* (Berlin, 1935); S. v. Ciriacy-Wantrup, *Agrarkrisen und Stockungsspannen* (Berlin, 1936); H.W. Finck v. Finckenstein, *Die Entwicklung der Landwirtschaft in Preussen und Deutschland 1800-1930* (Wurzburg, 1960); Max Rolfes's contribution in Hermann Aubin and Wolfgang Zorn, *Handbuch der deutschen Wirtschafts- und Sozialgeschichte* (Stuttgart, 1976), vol. 2, *Das 19 und 20. Jahrhundert*, 495-526. Contemporary "conservative" economists Karl Oldenberg, Max Sering, Adolf Wagner, and "liberal" economists Lujo Brentano, Johannes Conrad, Theodor von der Goltz, Walther Lotz, and Max Weber were all well aware that German agriculture had entered a crisis state in the 1880s. Von der Goltz, for example, concludes his *Geschichte der deutschen Landwirtschaft* (Stuttgart, 1903) with a chapter on "Die am Ausgang des 19. Jahrhunderts über die deutsche Landwirtschaft hereingebrochene Krise, deren Ursache und Charakter."

11. A view that was supported by contemporary opinion even among liberal economists, Kenneth D. Barkin, *The Controversy over German Industrialization 1890-1902* (Chicago, 1970), 192 ff.

12. Even international cartel agreements designed to provide a type of protection rely on at least the threat of state action, as a number of cases from the cartel-rich interwar period show.

13. Most of the fiscal arguments surrounding German tariff policy before World War I only "show how foolish it is to try to measure a tariff height and capacity for doing harm by the tax revenue it brings in." As for "making the foreigner pay" the tariff, current economic theory considers this possible "for a country large enough to appreciably affect the relative price of the goods it imports" provided the country employs "small, shrewdly gauged tariffs," Paul A. Samuelson, *Principles of Economics*, 9th ed., (New York, 1973), 677-78; Richard E. Caves and Ronald W. Jones, *World Trade and Payments*, 3d ed., (Boston, 1981), 214-17.

14. The text of the constitution in Rudolf Schuster (hrsg.), *Deutsche Verfassungen* (Munich, 1979). For a summary discussion of the Reich's peculiar public finances see Hajo Holborn, *A History of Modern Germany* (Princeton, 1969), vol. 2, 269. For more depth see Paul Laband, *Das Staatsrecht des deutschen Reiches*, 5th ed., 4 vols. (Tübingen, 1914); vol. 4, 376 ff., 405 ff.; Ernst Rudolf Huber, *Deutsche Verfassungsgeschichte*, 5 vols. (Stuttgart, 1963-1978). The most useful explication is Karl Hettlage's contribution in Kurt Jesserich et al. (hrsg.), *Deutsche Verwaltungsgeschichte* (Stuttgart, 1984), vol. 3, 250-63.

15. "Eingangs-Abgabe" as a percentage of "Ordentliche Einnahmen," *Statistisches Jahrbuch*, 11 (1890), 172-73, 176. Rising grain tariffs and a growing demand for imported grain throughout this period caused import duties on grain alone to rise from 10 percent of all customs revenue in 1879/80, to 32 percent in 1888/89, ibid., 179. Hans Rosenberg has even suggested that Bismarck planned to establish "the unassailable financial independence of the Reich and its military

35. Russian statistics show an even more dramatic decline in German exports, down from 274.3 million rubles in 1880 to 114.3 million rubles in 1890, Wittschewsky, "Zoll- und Handelspolitik Russlands," Table II, 437.

36. See e.g. the numerous complaints contained in Bundesarchiv, Reichsschatzamt/file #1688 "German-Russian Trade Relations, Feb. 1880-July 1892" [hereafter BA R 2/1688]. The Geheimes Staatsarchiv Preussischer Kulturbesitz in Berlin-Dahlem now has the Prussian Trade Ministry files on "Initiating a Trade Policy Agreement with Russia" [hereafter GStA PK: I.HA/Rep.120 C XIII, 6 a, Nr. 35, vols. 1-4].

37. See Benjamin Constant's statement that trade "is attempt to obtain by mutual agreement that which one does not hope any longer to obtain by violence," *De l'esprit de conquête et de l'usurpation dans leurs rapports avec la civilisation européenne,* part 1, chapter 2 as cited in Albert O. Hirschman, *National Power and the Structure of Foreign Trade,* (Berkeley, 1945, expanded ed. 1980), 14. John McKay has identified Russia's dual nature as one important reason for the "important and beneficial role" that foreign entrepreneurs played in Russian economic development, *Pioneers for Profit. Foreign Entrepreneurship and Russian Industrialization 1885-1913* (Chicago, 1970), 379, 385 ff.

38. Count Max von Berchem, under-secretary in the German Foreign Office, to Karl Heinrich von Boetticher, state secretary of the interior, 26 August 1886, BA R 2/1688.

39. Under-Secretary for Foreign Affairs Berchem to State Secretary for the Interior Boetticher, 25 August 1886, BA R 2/1688.

40. Sarah Tirrell, *German Agrarian Politics after Bismarck's Fall* (New York, 1951), 114.

41. Bismarck concluded the Dual Alliance in 1879 with only a passing reference to trade issues although he must have known that German tariff rates on grain and linen implemented that very same year were hurting Austria-Hungary, Germany's closest ally and premier trading partner. Johannes Lepsius, Albrecht Mendelssohn-Bartholdy, and Friedrich Thimme, eds., *Die grosse Politik der europäische Kabinette, 1871-1914* (Berlin, 1922-1927), vol. 3, 85 ff. In the 1880s, the Dual Alliance covered over a de facto trade war that had originated with new increases in the German autonomous tariff of 1881.

42. On the growth of economic antagonism between Germany and Russia and its impact on political relations in this period see Helmut Böhme, "Die deutsch-russischen Wirtschaftsbeziehungen unter dem Gesichtspunkt der deutschen Handelspolitik (1878-1894)," in Werner Conze (hrsg.), *Deutschland und Russland im Zeitalter des Kapitalismus 1861-1914* (Wiesbaden, 1977), 173-90; Hans-Ulrich Wehler, "Bismarcks späte Russlandpolitik 1879-1890," now in Wehler, *Krisenherde des Kaiserreiches;* Horst Müller-Link, *Industrialisierung und Aussenpolitik. Preussen-Deutschland und das Zarenreich von 1860 bis 1890,* (Göttingen, 1977); Sigrid Wegner-Korfes, *Otto von Bismarck und Russland* (Berlin, 1990), 133 ff., 158; Andreas Hillgruber, "Deutsche Russlandpolitik 1871-1918: Grundlagen- Grundmuster- Grundprobleme," in Hillgruber (hrsg.), *Deutsche Grossmacht – und Weltpolitik im 19. und 20. Jahrhundert* (Dusseldorf, 1977), 70-90. These all might be placed in the context provided by George Kennan, *Decline of Bismarck's European Order: Franco-Russian Relations, 1875-1890* (Princeton, 1979). A number of Russian documents from the period were published in their original French in "Russian-German Relations," in the Soviet historical journal *Krasnyi Arkhiv* 1, (1922), 5-208. English summaries are available in Louise Boutelle and Gordon Thayer, eds., *A Digest of the Krasnyi Arkhiv (Red Archives) A Historical Journal of the Central Archive Department of the U.S.S.R.* (Cleveland, Ohio, 1947), 1, 1-5.

43. In analyzing German trade polices of 1914, Fritz Fischer has described the "obvious dilemma of an economic policy which was oriented towards the world mar-

ket but at the same time committed to protect German production and agriculture by high tariff barriers ..." *War of Illusions* (New York, 1975), 363. That dilemma was first exposed at the end of the 1880s and, as we shall see, only good fortune allowed successive German chancellors to postpone choosing between these two ultimately incompatible elements of trade policy.

44. On the Méline tariff, see Eugene O. Golob, *The Méline Tariff: French Agriculture and Nationalist Economic Policy* (New York, 1944); more recently on the parallels of French and German tariff policies, Herman Lebovics, *The Alliance of Iron and Wheat in the French Third Republic, 1860-1914: Origins of the New Conservatism* (Baton Rouge, 1988). For European protectionist developments overall, Knut Borchardt, "Protectionism in Historical Perspective," in Borchardt, *Perspectives on Modern German Economic History and Policy* (New York, 1991), 1-15; W.B. Harvey, *Tariffs and International Relations, 1860-1914* (Chicago, 1938).

45. Walter Lotz, "Die Handelspolitik des deutschen Reiches unter Graf Caprivi und Fürst Hohenlohe (1890-1900)," *Schriften des Vereins für Socialpolitik* 91 (1901) vol. 3, 65.

46. Lotz, "Handelspolitik," 65

47. *Sten. Ber.* 1893/94 Bd. I, 18 (23 Nov. 1893). In addition to the expiring French treaties, Spain's treaties with Belgium, Switzerland, Sweden, Norway, and Italy as well as the Swiss treaty with Austria-Hungary were all scheduled for expiration on February 1, 1892. The Portuguese-Italian treaty expired on 24 January, the Swiss-Italian treaty on 14 February. Germany's treaties with Spain and Switzerland expired on 1 February, see Lotz, "Handelspolitik," 62.

48. Barkin, *The Debate over German Industrialization,* 46-8; the best account is Rolf Weitowitz, *Deutsche Politik und Handelspolitik unter Reichskanzler Leo von Caprivi 1890-1894* (Düsseldorf, 1978), 41-48. According to J. Alden Nichols, Bismarck himself "would probably have raised his tariffs further and fought it out" in a series of European tariff wars, Nichols, *Germany After Bismarck* (Cambridge, Mass., 1958), 140; Lotz cites several statements by Herbert v. Bismarck to support the assertion that at the time of Bismarck's departure "the plan existed" to raise tariffs and then negotiate new treaties on the basis of increased tariffs. Lotz, "Handelspolitik," 66.

49. The core of the Austrian treaty lowered German tariff rates on both wheat and rye by 30 percent, from 5 marks/cwt. to 3.5 marks in exchange for numerous Austrian tariff reductions on manufactured and semimanufactured items, *Sten. Ber.*, 1890/92, Anlageband V, 3215 ff. The origins of this strategy remain obscure. In the Reichstag, Caprivi defended the decision as his own, *Sten. Ber.* 1890/92, V, 10 December 1891, 3318. Nichols accepts this, citing Count Lerchenfeld's memoirs in support, although Nichols himself apparently could find no documentary proof in Caprivi's papers, Nichols, *Germany After Bismarck,* 145. Contemporaries, including Bismarck, suspected Caprivi's old friend and new chief of staff in the Reich chancellery, Karl Göring, of initiating the idea, possibly in conjunction with Counselor Hüber from the Reich Interior Office. Waldersee's *Denkwürdigkeiten* (1922) and other memoirs have been cited by Nichols and many others in support of this claim. The Caprivi-Göring-Hüber connection is unraveled without resolving ultimate responsibility in Weitowitz, *Deutsche Politik und Handelspolitik,* 41-48.

50. The organizational growth of "radical" agrarian opposition is well documented in J. Croner, *Die Geschichte der Agrarische Bewegung in Deutschland* (Berlin, 1909); Sarah Tirrell, *German Agrarian Politics after Bismarck's Fall;* I. Faar, "Populism in the Countryside. The Peasant Leagues in Bavaria in the 1890s," in R. J. Evans, ed., *Society and Politics in Wilhelmine Germany* (London, 1978), 136-59; and, above all, in H.J. Puhle, *Agrarische Interessenpolitik und preussischer Konservatismus im wilhelmischen Reich 1893-1914. Ein Beitrag zur Analyse des Nationalismus in Deutschland am Beispiel des Bundes der Landwirte und der Deutschkonservativen Partei* (Hannover, 1966).

51. Thomas Nipperdey, "Interessenverbaende und Parteien in Deutschland vor dem ersten Weltkrieg," now in Hans-Ulrich Wehler (hrsg.) *Moderne deutsche Sozialgeschichte* (Cologne/Berlin, 1966), 380. Similarly, Gerhard Ritter in *Die deutschen Parteien 1830-1914. Parteien und Gesellschaft im konstitutionellem Regierungssystem* (Göttingen, 1985), 77; and in "The Social Bases of the German Political Parties 1867-1920," in Karl Rohe, ed., *Elections, Parties, and political Traditions. Social Foundations of German Parties and Political Systems, 1867-1987* (New York, 1990); also Dirk Stegmann, *Die Erben Bismarcks. Parteien und Verbände in der Spätphase der Wilhelminischen Deutschlands* (Cologne/Berlin, 1970), 20, 37.

52. Prior to the 1891, Russia had been the most significant foreign market for Germany's largest producer of agricultural machines, Heinrich Lanz. During the tariff war these exports "practically ceased," "Der wirtschaftliche Aufstieg des Hauses H. Lanz," provided by John Deere Werke, Mannheim.

53. Berlin wheat prices peaked in May 1891 at 241 marks/ton, well above the London price of 189 marks and above the more normal Berlin trading range of 180 to 200 marks/ton in 1889; Berlin rye peaked in November 1891 at 239 marks/ton, Paris, 175 marks/ton, Berlin in 1889, 150-170 marks, J. Conrad, "Die Stellung der landwirtschaftlichen Zölle in den 1903 zu schließenden Handelsverträgen Deutschlands," in *Schriften des Vereins für Sozialpolitk* 50 (1900), 105-86, tables I and II.

54. For a secondary account of German Russian trade negotiations 1891-1893 see *Reichsanzeiger* 28 July 1893; Great Britain, *Parliamentary Papers*, 1904, Cmd. 1938, "Reports on Tariff Wars between Certain European States." The documents in *Grosse Politik*, VII are summarized in Tirrell, *German Agrarian Politics*, 248 ff. Original documentation can be found in BA R 2/1689-1693.

55. See Lotz, "Handelspolitik," 72-78; Caprivi's statement in the Prussian Landtag on 1 June 1891 (*Sten. Ber.* Haus der Abgeordneten, 1891, V, 2447); *Reichsanzeiger* 14 August 1891.

56. Note from German Foreign Office Under-Secretary Baron Wolfram von Rotenhan to the Russian chargé d'affaires in Berlin, Mikhail Murav'yov, 10 August 1892, BA R 2/1689. Murav'yov served under the very able Russian Ambassador Count Paul Shuvalov (1885-1894). After serving as ambassador in Copenhagen and then as director in the Foreign Office, Murav'yov became foreign minister (1897-1900), a post for which he was "decidedly lightweight," in the estimation of Dominic Lieven, *Russia's Rulers Under the Old Regime* (New Haven, 1989), 198; see also Erik Amberger, *Geschichte der Behördenorganisation Russlands von Peter dem Grossen bis 1917* (Leiden, 1966), 448, 130.

57. For these petitions of August 1892 see BA R 2/1689.

58. Marschall to Caprivi with a copy of the Russian note, 16 November 1892, BA R 2/1689.

59. The declaration appeared in the, Nr. 32, 6 February 1891 as cited in Bueck, *Centralverband*, 451. A similar statement was issued in December 1891 by the heavy industrial Rhine-Westphalian "Langnamverein," cited in Lotz, "Handelspolitik," 96.

60. Müller-Link refers to "isolated voices" urging this course of action in 1887, *Industrialisierung and Aussenpolitik*, 285. Lubeck Chamber of Commerce petition, 25 August 1892, BA R 2/1689.

61. *Statistisches Jahrbuch* 24 (1903), 166-67; Wolfram Fischer, "Bergbau, Industrie und Handwerk," in *Handbuch der deutschen Wirtschafts – und Sozialgeschichte*, vol. 2, tables 4,5,7, 535, 538, 540. For more on the second industrial revolution in Germany see, in addition to the literature cited in note 2, Knut Borchardt, *Die Industrielle Revolution in Deutschland* (Munich, 1972); F.-W. Henning, *Das Industrialisierung in Deutschland 1800-1914*; W. Fischer and Czada, "Wandlungen in der deutschen Industriestruktur im 20.Jh. Ein statistisch-deskriptiver Ansatz," in Ger-

hard Ritter (hrsg.), *Entstehung und Wandel der modernen Gesellschaft* (Berlin, 1970), Wilhelm Treue, *Gesellschaft, Wirtschaft und Technik Deutschlands im 19. Jahrhundert* (Munich, 1970).

62. The problems involved in maintaining the industrial-agricultural conservative alliance on a whole range of issues is the subject of a number of good studies: Barkin, *The Debate over German Industrialization;* J.A. Nichols, *Germany after Bismarck,* 150-51, 293-95; W. Hermann, *Bündnisse und Zerwurfnisse zwischen Landwirtschaft und Industrie seit der Mitte des 19. Jahrhundert* (Dortmund, 1965); James Sheehan, "Conflict and Cohesion among German Elites in the Nineteenth Century," in Sheehan, ed., *Imperial Germany,* 62-92; Fritz Fischer, *Bündnis der Eliten. Zur Kontinuität der Machtstrukturen in Deutschland 1871-1945* (Düsseldorf, 1979); C.G.J. Röhl, *Germany Without Bismarck. The Crisis of Government in the Second Reich* (London, 1967); Dirk Stegmann, *Die Erben Bismarcks;* H.J. Puhle, "Parlament, Parteien, und Interessenverbände 1890-1914," in M. Stürmer, ed., *Das Kaiserliche Deutschland* (Düsseldorf, 1970), 340-77.

63. Here I am referring to an organized session with a group recruited from a broad section of the private sector, something well beyond those rare, confidential meetings between leading industrialists and Prussian/Reich officials, such as the one on 24 November 1890 between some members of the Centralverband Direktorium and the Prussian Trade Minister. See Bueck, *Centralverband,* 446.

64. Weitowitz, *Deutsche Politik und Handelspolitik,* 41.

65. *Sten. Ber.* 1890/92, V, 10 Dec. 1891, 3303.

66. For background on the development of the Prussian and Reich bureaucracies in this sense see, Rosenberg's classic study *Bureaucracy, Aristocracy, and Autocracy: The Prussian Experience 1660-1815* (Cambridge, Mass., 1958); Rudolf Morsey, *Die Oberste Reichsverwaltung unter Bismarck 1867-1890* (Münster, 1957); Fritz Hartung, "Studien zur Geschichte der preussischen Verwaltung," part II, in Hartung, *Staatsbildende Kräfte der Neuzeit* (Berlin, 1961), 248 ff.; John C. G. Röhl, "Higher Civil Servants in Germany 1890-1900," in Sheehan, ed., *Imperial Germany,* 129-52; Bernhard Mann, "Zum Verhältnis von Regierung, Bürokratie und Parlament in Preussen 1867-1918," in Gerhard A. Ritter (hrsg.), *Regierung, Bürokratie, und Parlament in Preussen und Deutschland von 1848 bis zur Gegenwart* (Dusseldorf, 1983), 76-89. For a look at Prussian civil servants as a social group see Tibor Süle, *Preussische Bürokratietradition* (Göttingen, 1989).

67. On the functioning of the regime in light of the constitution of 1871 see Reinhard Mußgnung, "Die rechtlichen und pragmatischen Beziehungen zwischen Regierung, Parlament, und Verwaltung," in *Deutsche Verwaltungsgeschichte,* vol. 3, 109-27.

68. On the concept of Bonapartism as it applies to imperial Germany see Allan Mitchell, "Bonapartism as a Model for Bismarckian Politics," *JMH* 49 (1977), 181-99; Gustav Seeber, "Bonapartismus und Bourgeoisie. Ausgangspositionen und Probleme," in Seeber et al., *Bismarcks Sturz. Zur Rolle der Klassen in der Endphase des preussisch-deutschen Bonapartismus 1884/85 bis 1890* (East Berlin, 1977), 5-34; Ernst Engelberg, "Zur Entstehung und historischen Stellung des preussisch-deutschen Bonapartismus," in Fritz Klein and Joachim Streisand, *Beiträge zum neuen Geschichtsbild* (Berlin, 1956); Winkler's argument that Bismarck's regime was not a dictatorship in *Revolution, Staat, Faschismus* (Göttingen, 1978), 54 ff.; H.-U. Wehler, *Bismarck und der Imperialismus,* 455-504; Michael Stürmer, "Konservatismus und Revolution in Bismarcks Politik," in Stürmer (hrsg.), *Das Kaiserliche Deutschland,* 143-67 and his *Regierung und Reichstag im Bismarckstaat 1871-1880. Cäsarismus oder Parlamentismus* (Dusseldorf, 1974). Other analytic concepts applied to the system include: "krypto-absolutism" (Ernst Rudolf Huber), "bureaucratic absolutism" (Hans Rosenberg), and "semiabsolutist military monarchy" (Roger Fletcher).

69. Complaint of the *Sächische Landwirtschaftliche Zeitschrift*, Nr. 37, 17 September 1892, GStA PK: I.HA/Rep.120 C XIII, 6 a, Nr. 35, Bd.2, Blatt 20.

70. Siegfried von Kardorff, *Wilhelm von Kardorff. Ein nationaler Parlamentarier im Zeitalter Bismarcks und Wilhelms II, 1828-1907* (Berlin, 1936), 244 as cited in Tirrell, *German Agrarian Politics*, 219.

71. *Sächische Landwirtschaftliche Zeitschrift*, Nr. 37, 17 September 1892, GStA PK: I.HA/Rep.120 C XIII, 6 a, Nr. 35, Bd.2, Blatt 20.

72. *Sten. Ber.* 1890/92, V, (23 November 1893) 3418; speech at the Assembly of Delegates of the Centralverband deutscher Industrieller, 19 February 1894, GStA PK: I.HA/Rep.120 C XIII, 6 a, Nr. 35, Bd.4, Blatt 257. Möller was a member of the Langnamverein and would serve as Bülow's Prussian trade minister from 1901 to 1905.

73. For a portrait of this fascinating figure, see Otto Neuloh's contribution to *Männer der deutschen Verwaltung*, (Cologne, 1973), 195-210; for Berlepsch's central role in the important labor legislation of the New Course see Hans-Jörg von Berlepsch, *"Neuer Kurs" im Kaiserreich? Die Arbeiterpolitik des Freiherrn von Berlepsch 1890 bis 1896* (Bonn, 1987); for the minister's own account of this and other projects see his memoirs, *Sozialpolitische Erfahrungen und Erinnerungen* (München-Gladbach, 1925).

74. According to the state secretary at the Reich Interior Office, Karl Heinrich von Boetticher, Caprivi decided to postpone such a decision until after the Russians responded to Germany's most recent note, Boetticher to Berlepsch, 16 November 1892, GStA PK: I.HA/Rep.120 C XIII, 6 a, Nr. 35, Bd.2, Blatt 43.

75. Boetticher to Caprivi, 20 January 1893, BA R 2/1690. Berlepsch had a penchant for proposing extraparliamentary negotiating bodies; his labor legislation proposals contained numerous such suggestions. Commercial and manufacturing representatives were certainly eager for such a body to discuss tariff and trade issues, while heavy industrialists, content with Bismarck's protectionist policies, were worried they might lose influence to the up-and-coming industrial sectors. See Hans Peter Ullmann, *Der Bund der Industriellen* (Göttingen, 1976), 25; Bueck, *Centralverband*, 462.

76. Boetticher's Interior Office had invited the Verein Eisen- und Stahlindustrieller (North-West Group and Upper Silesian Group), Leipzig Fabrikaten Verein, Oberschlesische Berg- und Hüttenmannische Verein, Verein deutscher Messingwerke (Altona/Westfalen), Central Verein deutscher Wollewarenfabrikaten, Central Verband deutscher Industrieller, Verein deutscher Keramischerfabrikaten, and the Chambers of Commerce from Krefeld, Barmen, Eberfeld, and Muënchen-Gladbach. The Landwirtschaftsrat provided the agricultural experts: Count Albrecht von Stolberg-Wernigerode, Gorrez, and Prof. Odelbünk. Boetticher to Caprivi, 20 January 1893, BA R 2/1690, the Treasury Office's minutes of these meetings are contained in that file. On the German Chamber of Commerce see *Findbücher zu Beständen des Bundesarchivs*, Bd. 12 (Koblenz, 1976); D. Schaefer, "Der deutsche Handelstag auf dem Weg zum wirtschaftlichen Verband," in H.J. Varain (hrsg.), *Interessenverbände in Deutschland* (Cologne, 1973). For the Union of German Iron and Steel Industrialists see especially Clemens Klein, *Aus der Geschichte des Vereins deutscher Eisen - und Stahlindustrieller* (1924) and the manuscript "Geschichte des Vereins deutscher Eisen – und Stahlindustrieller 1874-1934," BA R 13I/12 and 13, which was based on more extensive archival material than we possess today.

77. E.g., Upper Silesian industry wanted reductions on raw iron (from the 1891 rate of 35 kopeks/pud to 25 kopeks/pud), on band iron (from 60 kopeks/pud to 45 kopeks/pud), and on railroad rails (from 60 kopeks/pud to 45 kopeks/pud); the textile industry wanted reductions on silks (from 7.50 rubles to 3.75 rubles), on half-silks (from 3 rubles to 1.10 rubles), and on cottons (from 1 ruble to .5 ruble);

chemical exporters sought reductions on tannin (from 6 rubles/pud to 2.40 rubles/pud) and various dyes, BA R 2/1690.

78. In 1895 Stolberg was dismissed from his government post for his support of the Agrarian League in opposition to the government.

79. Marschall's notes of 10 July and 27 July and the Russian responses of 24 July and 5 August in BA R 2/1691. For background on the Russian decision to pursue a treaty, consult Sigrid Wegner-Korfes, "Die Rolle von S.Ju. Vitte beim Abschluss des russisch-deutschen Handelsvertrages von 1894," *Jahrbuch für die Geschichte der sozialistischen Länder Europas* 22 (1978), 119-46.

80. Caprivi to the Reich Interior and Treasury Offices, and to the Prussian ministries of trade, finance, and agriculture, 17 August 1893, BA R 2/1691.

81. Boetticher asked for an undefined, but "limited" number of representatives from the German Chamber of Commerce (DIHT), the Centralverband deutscher Industrieller, and the Landwirtschaftsrat, see Boetticher to Posadowsky, state secretary in the Treasury Office, 2 October 1893 for the full minutes of the session as well as a list of participants, see BA R 2/1691. On negotiations between the Centralverband and the German Chamber of Commerce for selecting industrial and commercial representatives see Bueck, *Centralverband*, 465; Ullmann, *Bund der Industrieller*, 26.

82. In July 1893 Russia initiated a tit-for-tat exchange between the two countries that ended in August after each country had slapped the other's exports with a new 50 percent tariff increase.

83. According to Jencke, sales to Russia from Krupp's steel casting plant in Essen totaled 9 million marks in 1875, but had fallen to only 200,000 marks by 1884 (i.e., *before* the most severe Russian tariff increases of 1885 and 1891), Minutes, 28 September 1893, BA R 2/1691. The Dortmund Chamber of Commerce expressed similar views about the declining importance of the Russian market for heavy industry in a 16 December 1892 petition to the foreign office, GStA PK: I.HA/Rep.120 C XIII, 6 a, Nr. 35, Bd.2, Blatt 66. Similarly, Klein in "Geschichte des VdESI," BA R 13I/12 and 13, 146. The oft-repeated assertion of secondary literature that heavy industry pressed aggressively for a treaty must be treated with caution, see e.g., Stegmann, *Erben Bismarcks*, 60-61; S. Kumpf-Korfes, *Bismarcks "Draht nach Russland"* (Berlin, 1968), 115, 129 (on which Stegmann relies); Ullmann, *Bund der Industriellen*, 26.

84. On the role of the industrial Centralverband in securing these elections, Ullmann, *Bund der Industriellen*, 25-26.

85. After the first, January 1893, government-private sector meeting, the Pforzheim Chamber of Commerce had proposed the creation of a private sector standing council to advise the government on trade matters. Leaders of the Centralverband did not support the effort, preferring to rely on thier own, superior private contacts with the Reich leadership, Bueck, *Centralverband*, 462; Ullman, *Bund der Industriellen*, 25.

86. The following summary of activities is taken from Möller's speech to the Centralverband on 19 February 1894, GStA PK: I.HA/Rep.120 C XIII, 6 a, Nr. 35, Bd.4, Blatt 358 ff; Bueck, *Centralverband*, 469 ff.

87. Thielmann to Caprivi, 1 November 1893. BA Potsdam R 901/10678 Bl. 10 and passim; Lamar Cecil, *Wilhelm II. Prince and Emperor, 1859-1900* (Chapel Hill, N.C., 1989), 193.

88. After Pritsch resigned in December 1893, Thielmann appointed Henle to head the negotiations on customs administration (always a substantial point when dealing with the Russians). Henle later drafted the crucial sections (III A and B, IV, V) of the explanatory memorandum that accompanied the treaty to the Bundesrat. The Treasury files are BA R 2/1690-1695. Speaking to the Reichstag

some years later, Posadowsky cited the Tariff Council as "having performed positive work," *Sten. Ber.* 1897/98, 14 December 1897, reprinted in Penzler, *Graf Posadowsky,* 569.

89. Speech to the Centralverband, 19 February 1894, GStA PK: I.HA/Rep.120 C XIII, 6 a, Nr. 35, Bd.4, Blatt 348. Note Beuck's passive construction, which fails to identify who was allegedly listening to the Tariff Council or granting it influence. More accurate was his subsequent comment that Möller and other members of the council "achieved the most that could be achieved in that position," ibid.

90. Detailed recapitulations of these arguments as they unfolded in the Reichstag and in the press are available in the secondary literature on the 1890s; see especially Sarah Tirrell, *German Agrarian Politics,* chapters IV, V, VII, IX and J. Alden Nichols, *Germany After Bismarck,* 138 ff., 287 ff., both of which recount in great detail the proceedings in the Reichstag; also J.G. Roehl, *Germany Without Bismarck;* Alexander Gerschenkron, *Bread and Democracy in Germany.*

91. Cited in Nichols, *Germany After Bismarck,* 140, although without documentary evidence.

92. *Sten. Ber.* 1890/92, V, 10 December 1891, 3307, 3309-3310.

93. Woodruff D. Smith argues that the reasoning behind Caprivi's low tariff policy was "practically identical" to that behind the more ambitious plans of German economic imperialists (Weltpolitiker) both in and out of office, *The Ideological Origins of German Imperialism,* (New York, 1986), 79. Caprivi's 10 December 1891 Reichstag speech did contain a number of ideas on international economic relations that one might identify as "proto-Weltpolitik."

94. *Sten. Ber.* 1893/94, II, 27 February 1894, 1451

95. Resolution #2 of the Assembly of Delegates of the Centralverband deutscher Industrieller, 19 February 1894, GStA PK: I.HA/Rep.120 C XIII, 6 a, Nr. 35, Bd.4, Blatt 344; *Schlesisches Morgenblatt,* Nr. 187, 12 August 1892; Friedrich Thimme, ed., "Bismarck und Kardorff," *Deutsche Revue,* 42 (II), 150; Kardorff interpreted Bismarck's ambiguous article in the *Hamburger Nachrichten* (9 February 1894) as an indication that Bismarck might even speak out in favor of the treaty, Tirrell, *German Agrarian Politics,* 260.

96. *Sten. Ber.* 1890/92, V, 3315, 10 December 1891; *Sten. Ber.* 1893-94, I, 32-34, 23 November 1893 (Kanitz); *Sten. Ber.* 1890/92, V, 3334, 11 December 1891 (Kardorff).

97. *Sten. Ber.* 1893-94, I, 12 Dec. 1893, 388; *Sten. Ber.* 1893/94, I, 23 Nov. 1893, 16.

98. *Kreuzzeitung,* 23 November 1893 in *Schulthess' Europäischer Geschichtskalander* (1893), 154.

99. Smith, *Ideological Origins of German Imperialism,* 83 ff. for "radical conservative" rejection of the "economic imperialism" that "constituted the core of Weltpolitik."

100. Article 36, "Levying and Administration of Customs Duties and Taxes," granted the right of self-collection to those individual German states that had collected their own customs duties prior to unification, Schuster, *Deutsche Verfassungen,* 80; Hettlage's explanation of the customs administration in *Deutsche Verwaltungsgeschichte,* vol. 3, 256 ff.

101. *Sten. Ber.* 1893/94, I, 76, 25 November 1893 (Kardorff); Berlepsch to Caprivi, 20 February 1893, GStA PK: I.HA/Rep.120 C XIII, 6 a, Nr. 35, Bd. 2, Blatt 115.

102. The oberpräsident of West Prussia to Caprivi, 23 August 1893; unsigned Reich Chancellery memorandum, BA R 2/1691.

103. Miquel to Berlepsch, 1 June 1893, GStA PK: I.HA/Rep.120 C XIII, 6 a, Nr. 35, Bd.2, Blatt 221; the oberpräsident of West Prussia to Caprivi, 23 August 1893, BA R 2/1691; *Sten. Ber.* 1893/94, Anlage, II, Nr. 190, 1005.

104. *Sten. Ber.* 1893/94, II, 27 February 1894, 1450.

105. Kanitz on 23 November 1893, Sten. Ber. 1893-94, I, 32, 34-35; *Schulthess' Europaeischer Geschichtskalander* (1893), 154.
106. The Social Democrats (40), the Radical People's Party (22), the Radical Union (12), and the Poles (15) unanimously supported the treaty. The issue split both the National Liberals (34 for and 16 against), and the Center (45 for and 39 against). The Free Conservatives and Conservatives voted overwhelming against the treaty, although in each case with a few defections. In January 1894 the German Chamber of Commerce wrote to each individual chamber suggesting how they might best influence individual Reichstag members to vote for the treaty. See, e.g., Frentzel (chairman of the German Chamber of Commerce) to the Cologne Chamber, 12 January 1894, Rheinisch-Westfälisches Wirtschaftsarchiv, Cologne (hereafter RWWA) 1-24b-32; petitions of the individual chambers, various other groups such as the "Export Union of the Kingdom of Saxony," and several North German city governments to the Reich Treasury Office in BA R 2/1694.2
107. For more recent accounts of Caprivi's dismissal, see Cecil, *Wilhelm II*, 193-211; Röhl, *Germany Without Bismarck* (Berkeley, 1967), 86 ff.; Nichols, *Germany After Bismarck*. Valuable older works include: Karl Kröger, *Die Konservativen und die Politik Caprivis* (Rostock, 1937), Robert Geis, *Der Sturz des Reichskanzlers Caprivi* (Berlin, 1930); Major von Ebermeyer, "Caprivis Entlassung," *Deutsche Revue* 47 (1922), 193-213.
108. Bueck's speech to the Centralverband, 19 February 1894, GStA PK: I.HA/Rep. 120 C XIII, 6 a, Nr. 35, Bd.4, Blatt 348.

Chapter Two

GERMAN-RUSSIAN TRADE
The Second Round

As early as 1897 the leading economic interest groups began preparing for the renewal of Caprivi's trade treaties in 1903 to 1904. As the treaties approached renewal, so, too, were the domestic political struggles over trade and tariff policy that had surfaced in 1893 and 1894 renewed. The powerful positive and negative effects that Russian trade had exerted on various sectors of the German economy since 1894 intensified the political confrontations surrounding treaty renewal. In the first of these domestic political struggles – that over the content of German tariff policy – Chancellor Bernhard von Bülow reversed the outcome of the Caprivi years by including basic agrarian demands in the new 1902 tariff. Despite the inclusion of agrarian demands, the 1902 tariff did not by itself constitute a defeat for industrial and commercial interests. Tariff reform and treaty renewals would be separated by two years, so the subsequent impact of the new tariff provisions on the upcoming treaty negotiations was not immediately discernable. A second domestic struggle – the private sector's battle to inject itself more forcefully into the trade policy decisionmaking process – ended in an unqualified defeat for the private interest groups. Material differences and organizational rivalries prevented the private-sector from establishing a working coalition of interest groups broad enough to challenge the government.

By 1903 the government had resolved both of these domestic conflicts to its own advantage. At that point, a third struggle – the international contest between Germany and Russia over the content of the new trade treaty – was just beginning. Chancellor Bülow needed a victory in the international arena in the form a satisfactory new treaty with Russia in order to provide the final security for the government's recent victories in the domestic arena.

Economic and Political Developments 1894-1904

The development of German-Russian trade in the decade following the 1894 treaty only confirmed that the political struggles of 1891 to 1894 had not been out of proportion to the material interests at stake in Caprivi's new trade policies. The value of Germany's two-way trade with Russia had almost doubled from its 1893 value when it crossed the one billion mark level in 1898 (Graph 2.1).[1] By 1904 two-way trade topped 1.2 billion marks and was still growing. Imports from Russia rose quickly for five years following the treaty, topping 700 million marks in 1897. By 1903 imports surpassed 800 million, double their value for "normal" years in the pretreaty period, and were still increasing (Graphs 2.7 and 2.8). The treaty also initiated six years of strong export growth to Russia. Just three years after the agreement was concluded, German exports had doubled from the low levels of the 1892 to 1893 years (see Graph 2.3). Despite rising prices for German industrial products, exports to Russia in the second half of the treaty period dwarfed the export levels of the 1880s and early 1890s.[2] Over the long term, the growth of exports to the Russian market outpaced the growth of German exports to the world at large, so Russia continued to gain importance as a market for German products (Graph 2.4 and 2.5).[3]

Further, trade after 1894 no longer exhibited the violent downturns that had characterized the period 1879 to 1894 (Graph 2.2). By binding Russian tariff rates for a ten-year period, the treaty eliminated the type of tariff-induced setbacks that had hampered German exports in earlier years. German producers now had the long-sought "stability" required for an expansion of German exports to Russia. The flattening of export growth for some years after the post-treaty boom of 1895 to 1899 was insignificant in comparison to the dramatic declines of the mid-1880s and the early 1890s. The good German harvest of 1899 reduced German imports from Russia in that year, but that sort of natural fluctuation was only a ripple on a rising tide of trade.

The German commercial community was a major beneficiary of this greatly increased trade volume. The value of goods moving through the port facilities at Bremen on their way to or from Russia had tripled from 32.8 million marks in 1890 to 97.1 million in 1902.[4] Not only the North German shipping and merchant communities, but importers, exporters, distributors, and wholesalers across Germany and their agents in Russia were participating in the expansion of trade.

The treaty benefited a wide array of German exporting producers since Russian demand ranged across a variety of German industrial branches, from consumer textiles to industrial chemicals. As a result of their own industrial progress, Russian buyers concentrated on the more advanced German products. Exports of "instruments, machines and motor vehicles" to Russia more than tripled between 1894 (21 million marks) and 1899 (67 million marks). On the other hand, exports of more basic products that had earlier played important roles in German-Russian trade grew only slowly or remained flat.[5] The structure of German exports to Russia in 1903 (Graph 2.6) shows only one leading item in the unfinished category, a non-German product, (re-exported raw cotton). Only one semifinished item was significant (animal skins). The other leading export commodities were sophisticated finished goods intended for private consumers and industrial buyers. The advanced machinery, pharmaceuticals and dyes, and ironware branches together accounted for almost one-third of German exports. Here again Russian demand was shifting toward the more sophisticated products. By 1903 sales of "fine" ironwares (16.2 million marks) surpassed sales of less finished (grob) iron exports that had dominated in earlier years. Exports of raw iron to Russia were negligible, despite the general expansion of trade.[6] For a number of these sophisticated export items, the Russian market had assumed a critically important place. In 1903 Russia was the premier export market for agricultural machinery (5.5 million marks), sewing machines (6.5 million marks), and miscellaneous industrial machinery (7.9 million marks), and the second most important market for products such as fine ironwares (18.4 million marks) and aniline oil (6 million marks).[7] In 1900 Russia purchased one-fifth of Germany's exports of electrical equipment.

This pattern of exports to Russia in which newer, more sophisticated industrial products assumed the leading role reflected the continuing technological development of the Reich at the turn of the century. In an accelerated continuation of trends just visible at the time of the first German-Russian treaty in 1894, the older, heavier, and more basic industries were eclipsed by the dynamic newcomers in the last two decades before the war. By 1900 the German chemical industry had grown to an annual turnover of 2.4 billion marks. Controlling 30 percent of the world trade in pharmaceuticals by 1914, Germany was on its way to becoming "the world's apothecary," as one leading producer put it.[8] The electrical industry was poised for a similar takeoff in the decade 1904 to 1914. By 1905 employment in the metalworking industry (1.4 million workers) was only slightly behind employment in all of heavy industry (1.8 million).[9] In 1908 machinery surpassed cotton textiles as Germany's premier export item. Even newer products such as telegraph and electric cable now made themselves felt in Germany's export structure, further reducing the significance of established items as a percentage of German exports. Both cotton and woolen textiles declined noticeably, as did basic iron products such as railroad rails; coal exports stagnated.[10]

For German landowners in the Agrarian League, the effects of the 1894 treaty appeared to confirm all of the dire predictions they had made about Russian imports and their impact on farm prices in Germany. The bulk of the increased imports from Russia were agricultural products, especially basic grains. From 1894 to 1904 grain made up 42 percent of German imports from Russia, with wheat, barley, and rye accounting for just under one-third of German imports from Russia in 1903 (Graph 2.9). The steady advance of wheat and barley imports from Russia was one of the most consistent features of the first treaty period.[11]

The Agrarian League blamed Caprivi's treaties for the precipitous decline in agricultural prices from 1891 to 1895 (see Graph 2.10). Grain prices had been unnaturally high in 1891, but when wheat and rye prices reached their lowest levels in memory in the third quarter of 1894, farmers blamed the recently concluded treaties, especially the Russian treaty.[12] Inasmuch as Russian wheat helped satisfy the German consumer's growing preference for wheat over rye, these imports did contribute to the slackening demand and declining price for domestically produced German rye.[13]

The powerful and uneven economic impact of the tremendous increase in German-Russian trade from 1894 to 1904 sparked commensurately powerful and divergent political reactions in Germany's leading economic groups. Agricultural opposition to the kaiser's government did not subside, even after an unrelenting vendetta by agricultural interests helped secure Caprivi's dismissal in 1894. Initially, neither the new chancellor, Prince Chlodwig Hohenlohe-Schillingfürst, nor the kaiser were inclined to give in to agricultural demands, the least of which was a full restoration of the pre-Caprivi tariff rate on grain imports, 5 marks/cwt.[14] In 1895 the government dismissed Count Stolberg, the oberpräsident of East Prussia, for his overly vocal support of the Agrarian League. Agrarian dissatisfaction with the government remained strong in the Prussian provinces east of the Elbe. The alarming gap between agricultural and industrial prices that reopened in 1898 insured that the agrarian opposition would not rest.

Based on their dissatisfaction with trade and agricultural policies, agrarians in the Reichstag and the Prussian Landtag devoted themselves to obstructing virtually every government initiative. Given the parliamentary constellation of the middle Wilhelmine years this was easy to do. The government was unwilling to speak to the Social Democrats or Radicals and unable to rely on support from the Center party after Marschall's departure from the Foreign Office in October 1897. Confronted with conservative agrarian opposition, the government had even fewer parliamentary options. The rivalry-riddled Hohenlohe ministry struggled to arrange a parliamentary majority with each successive piece of legislation. In 1899 Conservative votes help send both the so-called Hard Labor Bill (a personal project of the kaiser's) and the Prussian Canal Bill down to humiliating defeats, the former in the Reichstag, the latter in the Prussian House of Deputies. The government responded by purging the Prussian administration of those members who would not renounce their membership in the Agrarian League. The breach between the government and the agrarian opposition in the Conservative, Free Conservative, and National Liberal parties was total.[15]

Radical agrarian and protectionist proposals that aimed unambiguously at reducing the volume of German-East European trade directly threatened the gains made by commercial groups under the 1894 treaty. Individual members of the merchant community as well as the traditional institutional voice of these interests, the German Chamber of Commerce, had been in the forefront of the Tariff Council and Reichstag battles in favor of the 1894 treaty. German traders were determined to defend their gains when the Russian treaty came up for renewal in 1904. For this purpose they had organized (with the support of liberal allies in the banking community and export industries) both the German-Russian Association for the Care and Development of Mutual Trade Relations (Deutsch-Russischer Verein zur Pflege und Förderung der gegenseitigen Handelsbeziehungen) and the League for the Advancement of Trade Treaties (Handelsvertragsverein) in 1899. The industrial Centralverband condemned this latter group especially as "a rallying point for all free trade interests." Despite this condemnation, many manufacturers supported the league, which presented itself as the leading opponent of radical agrarian demands that Germany abandon conventional trade practices such as long-term trade treaties with MFN clauses.[16]

In their efforts to defend the treaty and expand trade with Russia, the commercial community found allies in those industrial sectors that had benefited from the treaty through increased exports to Russia. Sensing a growing divergence of interests between themselves and the iron and steel interests that dominated the industrial Centralverband, the export-oriented industries began organizing their own industrial interest groups. The chemical industry in the Association for Safe-guarding the Interests of the German Chemical Industry (Verein zur Wahrung der Interessen der chemischen Industrie Deutschlands) had already withdrawn from the Centralverband in 1889.[17] After their experiences with the Russian treaty in 1894, other export-oriented industries also grew dissatisfied with the Centralverband's lingering enchantment with tariff protection and its commitment to finding a modus vivendi with the agrarians. Urged on by the chemical industry, a collection of clothing, machine-building, and wood products manu-facturers established a new "super" industrial interest group, the Union of Industrialists (Bund der Industriellen) in 1895. Claiming to speak for the "finished goods industries," this new body emerged as a direct rival and counterweight to the older Centralverband.[18] As leader of the spurned Centralverband, Bueck played down the impor-tance of the new rival group, but was forced to concede that this "split" (Spaltung) within German industry was "extremely regrettable."[19]

By 1904 one could speak of two loose industrial factions divided by the relative importance of the Russian (and other foreign) markets for their future development.[20] For one group of industries (anchored by machine-building, leather products, and chemicals) Russia had now emerged as a leading, if not the premier, export market. In con-trast stood those older, heavy industries of iron- and steel-making, for which the Russian Empire had generally ceased to be a major market. These two industrial groupings formalized their material differences by creating rival, though not fully mutually exclusive, interest group organizations. With little direct material interest of their own at stake, the heavy goods industrialists might have been inclined to accom-modate the finished goods industries in trade policy. The difficulty lay in the continuing desire of heavy industry to maintain (or renew) a political alliance with its conservative counterparts in agriculture.[21] The collapse of that industrial-agricultural cooperation had split the National Liberal, Free Conservative, and Conservative parties in their votes on the treaty in 1894 and had helped make the Reich very nearly ungovernable in the half-decade since Caprivi's fall.

The Limits to Corporatist Trade Management

The combination of bitter agrarian opposition, a growing split within German industry, and an aggressive spirit of free trade in commercial circles did not auger well for the government's ability to find a viable future course for German trade policy when the Caprivi treaties came up for renewal in 1903 and 1904. The doubling of two-way trade and its powerful positive and negative impacts on various sectors of the German economy threatened to produce a battle royal over future German trade policy toward Russia. The extensive and impassioned German press coverage of a small German-Russian tariff dispute over the importation of live pigs from Russian Poland to Upper Silesia in 1896, and the repeated Conservative attempts to have portions of the treaty altered showed that tempers were still running hot over German-Russian trade issues. In May 1897, Henry Boettinger, chairman of the Board of Directors at Bayer and later at Elberfeld Farbwerke and a leading member of the chemical industry's interest group, warned the directors of the Centralverband that "tough battles" (schwere Kämpfe) would surround the renewal of the treaties.[22]

The experience of the private-sector with the first Russian treaty in 1894 now added an organizational dimension to the struggle over these very real material differences. Based on Caprivi's creation of the Tariff Council for the 1894 Russian treaty, each of the major private economic interest groups counted on the Chancellor's Office to once again employ some organizational link connecting the private-sector with the government. In all probability this (as yet unborn) new body would have at least as much influence as the old Tariff Council and perhaps a good deal more, since the novelty of this consultative practice had been replaced by the widespread assumption that some such private body would have a role to play in the treaty renewal process. Any economic sector or individual interest group that could establish a dominant position within this new organization would ensure for itself a prominent voice in the upcoming treaty deliberations.

With the thought of securing such a dominant position, each of the leading interest groups attempted to organize under their own auspices some type of central private-sector organization for the preparation of trade treaties. The Centralverband sought to preserve the dominant position it had acquired in the Caprivi's Tariff Council. The German Chamber of Commerce launched an offensive to regain its "traditional" position as the primary source of trade information to the government. At the same time the "independent" industrial interest groups, particularly that of the chemical industry, tried to break the monopoly position of these two older and more powerful organizations. By seizing the initiative, the successful group might be able to compose the organizational rules of a new body to accord the initiator a central position in the deliberations. Each of the competing interest groups hoped to set the organizational rules for a broadly based private-sector assembly that might claim to represent the interests of all of the Reich's productive elements (with the continued exclusion of labor).

Despite three years of organizational maneuvering, no single interest group or coalition of groups was able to construct a broadly based private-sector assembly for an effective discussion of trade policy. That failure, and the subsequent need for the government to impose an organizational settlement on the warring interest groups, fatally weakened the private-sector's attempt to inject its voice into the government's trade policy deliberations.

The commercial community, operating through the German Chamber of Commerce, made the first move toward establishing a new organization, even before the old Tariff Council had expired.[23] In November 1893 the Governing Committee of the German Chamber of Commerce discussed the issue of "creating a central office which would prepare the negotiation of future trade treaties by collecting and evaluating the necessary material." The chamber agreed to approach the Centralverband on this issue via the personnel overlaps between the chamber's Governing Committee and the Direktorium of the industrialists' association.[24] In April 1894, the chamber swung over to the offensive, suggesting to the Centralverband that the offices of the chamber be expanded to constitute the new "Central Office" for the preparation of trade treaties. A "commission" of three members each from the chamber and the Centralverband would oversee the business of the Central Office, but the "formal leadership of the entire project must remain in the hands of the German Chamber of Commerce."[25] The German Chamber of Commerce was hoping to use its semiofficial status and its traditional role as the government's primary source of trade information to fortify its position in the upcoming organizational struggle for control of the planned Central Office.[26] The Centralverband, however, hoped to preserve the dominant influence it had achieved within Caprivi's Tariff Council. Centralverband members Möller and Wachler had emerged as the most widely recognized spokesmen for the Tariff Council, which also had used the Centralverband's offices and staff. For these reasons, Centralverband Chairman Theodor Hassler told the German Chamber of Commerce that the industrialists "recognized the importance" of the proposed Central Office, but could not agree to the chamber's claim for "sole leadership" of the agency. Fruitless "oral negotiations" continued between the two great interest groups through the summer of 1894. By November 1894 the chamber concluded that it would not be possible to reach an agreement with the Centralverband that "would leave both parties with the desired freedom" and threatened to press ahead with its own organization.[27]

The stakes in this organizational battle were raised dramatically in January 1896 when the state secretary in the Reich Treasury Office, Count Arthur von Posadowsky-Wehner, told the Reichstag that the government planned to publish an updated tariff schedule. This project emerged as the single most comprehensive revision of Germany's tariff structure between 1869 and 1951. As a codification project it ranks with the creation of the Civil Law code as one of the great organizational achievements of the empire. In the construction of a fully new tariff catalog, the government would require considerable private-sector technical assistance. Manufacturers' participation was essential to any realistic attempt to modernize the outdated "official commodity catalog" (ämtlicher Warenverzeichnis) covered by the tariff. According to Bueck, this meant that "arranging and leading the cooperation of these technical experts would be the first and most pressing task of the Central Office." In fact, the work involved in revising the tariff came to dominate the activities of every private-sector interest group from 1897 to 1902.[28]

In the spring of 1897 the largest of the independent interest groups, the chemical industry, approached the Centralverband with a new plan regarding the "establishment and duties of a Central Office for the Preparation of Trade Treaties." Dismissing the Centralverband as excessively protectionist and the chamber as too free-trade oriented, the chemical group urged the creation of a fully new body. As a first step, this plan called for a "conference of representatives from the various interest groups" under the chairmanship of Adolf Frentzel from the German Chamber of Commerce.[29] As an independent group, the chemical industry's association risked being excluded from (or subordinated within) any body that emerged from a joint project of the industrial Centralverband and the German Chamber of Commerce. On the other hand, a fresh start, with each of many groups on equal footing, would provide independent groups such as the chemical association with their best chance to obtain some voice in the new Central Office. For that very reason the Centralverband opposed the chemical plan and returned to the idea of working with the German Chamber of Commerce. The direktorium charged Bueck with the task of producing a Centralverband plan on this matter.

On 13 June 1897 Bueck offered a pessimistic report to the directors on the options available to the Centralverband. He summarized the obstacles to cooperation between the Centralverband and the Chamber of Commerce as follows: "neither of these two organizations was willing to subordinate itself to the other." Industry of all types did not feel itself well represented by the chamber, since the "influence of free traders" there was too great. On the other side, the chamber members feared the Centralverband's "highly protectionist" reputation. For these reasons, any "joint activity" between these two largest groups was "impractical." The same was true of the proposed cooperation between the Centralverband and the independent industrial groups. In view of the organizational rivalries and material differences within the various factions of Germany's industrial and commercial communities, Bueck concluded that "the idea of establishing a Central Office for the Preparation of Trade treaties from the existing economic organizations must be abandoned." The Direktorium agreed that "a central office for the preparation of trade treaties could not be constructed and maintained through the activity of the interest groups."[30]

The most likely consequence of abandoning private-sector efforts for a central trade treaty office would be a return to earlier practices whereby the ministerial bureaucracy excluded the private-sector from deliberations on tariff and trade policy. Again there would be no institutional voice for private interests in German trade treaty negotiations. This would mean abandoning the small private-sector gains that had been made during the first Russian treaty in the form of the Tariff Council.

Bueck's proposed solution to the problem of private-sector disorganization called for the Reich government to step into the process. Members of the ministerial bureaucracy would participate directly in the new body, laying down the organizational guidelines for the participation of the private-sector. Drawing on the experience of Caprivi's Tariff Council, Bueck told the Centralverband that "only the Reich government can create the basis" for "harmonious activity" by the private-sector. The Central Office would comprise members from both the government (the Reich and Prussian ministries and the individual German states) and from the private-sector (industry, commerce, and agriculture). It would be "necessary" for members of the ministerial bureaucracy to chair meetings of the proposed Central Office, its committees and subcommittees. In addition, the Reich should carry the costs of the offices and staff of the new Central Office.[31]

Bueck's plan wonderfully illuminates the relations between the state and society and this point in the empire. The conflicting material (and therefore organizational) interests between the leading sectors of the German economy precluded the possibility of these groups reaching a consensus among themselves on even the preliminary questions of Germany's future trade policies. These material differences far outweighed the common interest of increasing the role of all private-sector groups in formulating Germany's tariff and trade policies. Bueck's statements were an open admission of this fact by one of the most powerful interest groups. These groups required the strong hand of the Reich government to settle the disputes raging between them. Without that hand, the private-sector had been unable for almost four years to establish a common agency for the expression of its interests. Even with the exclusion of agriculture, neither industry and commerce nor heavy and light industry could agree on a common platform for the discussion of trade issues. This certainly did not bode well for the ability of these groups to reach a compromise when the tough questions of material interest and economic trade-offs should arise in the course of tariff revision and international negotiation. Instead of asserting itself to obtain a larger role in trade policy formulation than the limited one allowed to it by Caprivi, the private-sector subordinated itself to the government by admitting that it could not put its own house in order in the preliminary matters of organization.

The government had its own reasons for establishing the type of mixed government-private forum that the Centralverband was now suggesting. Obviously, the planned reorganization and revision of the tariff classifications would require extensive private-sector participation in some form. More important, a number of conservative ministers, especially Prussian Finance Minister Johannes Miquel, saw Bueck's plan as a chance for bringing agricultural Reichstag deputies back into a positive relation with the government by healing the industrial-agricultural split that had emerged from the battles of 1894. The government's swing back to conservatism had already forced Berlepsch to resign in frustration at the end of 1896. In 1897 the kaiser replaced Marschall at the Foreign Office with the conservative Bernhard von Bülow, and Boetticher at the Interior Office with the agrarian-oriented Posadowsky. The decks were now clear for a drastic change of domestic political course by the kaiser's government.[32] For Miquel, Posadowsky, and the kaiser, all of whom now sought a political rapprochement with the Conservatives, Bueck's call for government help in organizing the private-sector served as the starting point for rebuilding a conservative political alliance.[33]

In July 1897 Miquel met with Bueck, Hassler, and Emil Russel, second vice-president of the Centralverband, to discuss the Centralverband's plan for a government initiative in bringing together the fractious elements of the commerce, industry, and agriculture. Bueck's memorandum had been "confidentially" circulated to Reich offices (interior, treasury, and foreign offices) and the Prussian ministries (finance, trade) in June and July and submitted to the chancellor as a petition (Bitte) on the subject.[34] In recommending the plan to the Ministry of State meeting on 29 July, Miquel explained that the proposed tariff and treaty forum could help the government by "bringing the parties together in the economic field so that political differences would play a less prominent role in the upcoming Reichstag and Landtag elections."[35]

Only Posadowsky-Wehner at the Interior Office expressed serious reservations with the Centralverband plan, even though he sympathized with the goal of restoring good relations with the Conservatives via a tariff understanding.[36] He worried that a mixed government-private body was too great a concession to the private-sector and that the government might lose its "independence" by directly participating in such a forum. He preferred an entirely private consultative body on which the government might draw only when the need arose.[37] On 3 September Bueck met again with Posadowsky, presumably explaining again that the private-sector by itself could not organize such a forum. Bueck emphasized the need for immediate government action in clearing up the organizational problems and initiating the hard work of preparing for the new treaties. Posadowsky appeared to give in on the idea of a "conference" of industrial, commercial, and agricultural representatives for the purpose of reaching an understanding on tariff and trade treaty issues. But before that larger assembly took place he met "confidentially" with members of Centralverband (Hassler, Jencke, Bueck, Möller, Koenig), the German Chamber of Commerce (Chairman Frentzel and others), and the German Agricultural Council (including von Roeder, von Kanitz, von Arnim).[38] That meeting finalized the organizational outlines for the new Economic Committee of the Reich Office of the Interior – the culmination of the private-sector's three-year failure to establish its own functioning Central Office for the preparation of trade treaties.[39]

The members of the Economic Committee envisioned two important tasks for their new organization over the next several years. First, the committee would prepare all aspects of the upcoming revision of the German tariff, including the commodity catalog, the tariff rates, and the law governing customs revenues. In these areas, the Economic Committee played an important, though not readily visible role, in the reorganization of the German tariff. Not only did the committee provide the necessary technical data for a revision of the tariff catalog, it provided a forum for the resolution of numerous private-sector differences on product classification and tariff rates, particularly between industrial factions.[40] In effect, the Economic Committee served as a forum for securing private-sector agreement on many portions of the tariff before the legislation was brought to the Reichstag. The Economic Committee marked an important advance in the private-sector's ability to resolve some of its internal differences. In this way, the Economic Committee was a vastly more important than the earlier Tariff Council had been, and marked the continuing development of corporatist organized capitalism in the German economy. Because the government's subsequent maneuvering of the tariff through the Reichstag involved "one of the most peculiar and complex chapters in German parliamentary history," the importance of the preparatory work of this committee has not been fully appreciated.[41]

Yet the differences between large portions of German industry and commerce on one side and agriculture on the other side prevented the Economic Committee from offering a resolution of the most fundamental questions concerning future German tariff and trade policies.[42] Ultimately, the upper reaches of the Reich and Prussian ministerial bureaucracies provided the answers to these questions on the content of future German policies on agricultural goods and the form of future German trade relations. Just as Caprivi himself had made the fundamental decisions on the future of German trade policy in 1892 to 1894, so too now Posadowsky and Bülow made the final decisions about the form and content of the 1902 tariff. The Centralverband had miscalculated when it assumed that bringing the government into a mixed government-private forum would give the private-sector some "expectation" that the government would discuss matters with it.[43] In fact, the origin and the very structure of the Economic Committee (with government participation and ministerial bureaucrats as Chairmen of every session) were admissions that even the nonagricultural private-sector groups could not present a united front that might challenge governmental autonomy in the management of tariff and trade policy.

The final decision on Posadowsky's plan to raise agricultural rates in order to make peace with the conservatives was made by Bülow himself and cleared with the kaiser in October 1900 as a precondition for Bülow assuming the chancellorship.[44] Bülow himself also resolved the impasse on "double tariff" issue, proposing that minimum rates be set only for the most important agricultural items. The tariff of 1902 subsequently did contain a French-style double tariff for grain.[45] The government reached its other important decisions in the interministerial Kommissarische Berathungen of March 1901. In these sessions representatives from the Reich offices and Prussian ministries worked out the final decisions on the most vital tariff issues without the participation of any private-sector representatives.[46] Here, removed from direct contact the interest groups, the government resolved the basic issue of agricultural tariff rates: the grain tariff would be raised to 7.50 marks/cwt. for wheat and 7.00 marks/cwt. for rye, with absolute "minimum rates" of 5.50/cwt. and 5.00/cwt. Farmers received minimum tariff rates just above the pre-Caprivi levels and the assurance that these rates could not be undone without explicit Reichstag approval. A number of domestically oriented industries also received the increased protection they desired.[47]

Yet the agricultural tariff increases were not necessarily a defeat for industrial and commercial interests. These groups were not concerned primarily with agricultural tariff rates per se, but with the impact of the rate increases on Germany's ability to conclude export-facilitating international trade treaties. Exporters had no concrete cause for complaint since the impact of a German tariff increases on the outcome of the upcoming trade treaty negotiations was not yet clear.[48] The inability to determine the future impact of tariff on international agreements helped defuse opposition to the agricultural rate increases. Also, Bülow ignored the more radical agricultural demands for an end to long-term trade treaties and no use of the MFN clause, both of which were passionately rejected by industrial and commercial groups across the board.[49]

The private sector had foreseen the second important function of the Economic Committee in advising the government on applying the tariff to the upcoming treaty renewal negotiations. Indeed, it was for this purpose, i.e. advancing the voice of the private sector during the 1903 to 1904 trade treaty negotiations, that the various interest groups had begun to plan the formation of some type of Central Office for the Preparation of Trade Treaties in 1894 and 1895. In this second task, the Economic Committee failed decisively, since it could not win an increased voice for these private groups vis-à-vis the government in determining the content of German positions in international trade negotiations.

Bülow's government gave the private-sector less opportunity for active participation in negotiating the Russian treaty of 1904 than Caprivi had a decade earlier. While Caprivi had given the Tariff Council ample opportunity to express itself after its creation in 1893, the Bülow government allowed the Economic Committee to wither after the new tariff was completed in 1902. The new tariff (as part of the successful Miquel/Bülow Sammlungspolitik) had restored the government's base in the Reichstag by bringing the agrarians over in support of Bülow. From this new position of strength, Bülow and

Posadowsky simply failed to convene the Economic Committee even once for consultation on the new treaties (the power of government chairmanship in the committee once again was immensely significant).

Bueck lamented to the powerful Union of Iron and Steel Industrialists (Verein deutscher Eisen- und Stahlindustrieller) that, "With regard to the negotiations for new trade treaties neither the organized representative bodies of industry, nor the Centralverband nor any of the groups belonging to the Centralverband have been in any way employed" by the government.[50] Not even Theodor Möller, serving as Prussian trade minister since 1901, could reverse the Bülow-Posadowsky policy of keeping the industrial and commercial interest groups at arm's length. As a private industrialist in the 1890s, Möller had led the assault on the government's exclusion of private-sector representatives in international negotiations. Now, as part of the Bülow government, he was unable to arrange the type of active private-sector involvement that he felt was really necessary in international trade negotiations.

In preparing for the Russian treaty of 1904, the government outlined Germany's negotiating position and tactics in series of interministerial Kommissarische Berathungen held in 1903 under the chairmanship of Director Paul von Körner, head of the Commercial Affairs Division of the Foreign Office.[51] Körner subsequently led the German negotiating team, which contained only members of the Reich and Prussian ministries. The private interest groups were bitterly disappointed by their exclusion from these processes. Bueck explained, "It is true that the Centralverband had earlier campaigned for the convocation of the Economic Committee: the Association intended mainly to recommend the establishment of a Collegium of experts which would engage in the same type of activity during the [current] treaty negotiations as the so-called Tariff Council had exercised during the conclusion of the treaty with Russia in 1893-94." Bueck "noted with regret that no organization of this type had been established for the negotiations currently in progress." He "felt it his duty, in view of the upcoming negotiations with Russia, to point out the inadequacy of the current arrangement and to recommend the inclusion of recognized representatives from industry." The government responded by assuring Bueck that his "suggestions" would receive a "kind review." Even Westphalian heavy industry, which had supported the government's pro-agrarian position (and which itself had received most of what it asked for in the 1902 tariff), found this situation of exclusion intolerable.[52]

The structure of the Reich gave the government every advantage over the private-sector in this dispute. Despite the precedent of

Caprivi's Tariff Council, the private-sector had no legal claim or "right" to a voice in international trade negotiations. The authoritarian monarchical structure of the regime lent the bureaucratic apparatus more than enough prestige, authority, and discipline to fend off the intrusive inquiries from a badly fragmented private sector. These circumstances reduced the interest groups to appealing to the government via petitions, protests, and offers to "help" in the negotiations.[53] The government welcomed these petitions and in fact used the material in them as the "starting point" for establishing Germany's negotiating position on many commodities. But the private-sector did not view that sort of consideration, in which the interest groups remained dependent on government benevolence, as adequate substitution for a real voice in trade policy deliberations.

By 1903 the government had resolved to its satisfaction the domestic conflicts surrounding renewal of the Russian treaty. In the conflict over the content of German tariff policy, the government had succeeded in modernizing the tariff, raising many tariff rates, and repairing the relations with the agrarian interests in the Reichstag. At the same time, the government had so far managed to avoid giving German commercial and industrial exporting interests a real cause for complaint about trade policy. In a second domestic struggle, Bülow had inflicted an unqualified defeat on the private interest groups, largely by simply ignoring their demands for greater participation in the formation of tariff and trade policy. Despite the creation of a new government/private-sector Economic Committee, the upper levels of the Reich and Prussian administrations, particularly the chancellor and Interior Office State Secretary Posadowsky, continued to make the most important decisions on the form and content of the German tariff. Preparations for trade treaty negotiations with the Russians and the negotiations themselves remained exclusively in the hands of the state bureaucracy. In this case, control was concentrated chiefly in the persons of Chancellor Bülow and Foreign Office Director Körner. By granting the agrarians a portion of their tariff demands and by excluding the business community from treaty preparations, Bülow had reestablished governmental authority, if not popularity, vis-à-vis dissatisfied private-sector elements.

Yet Bülow's successful assertion of governmental authority in the these domestic struggles would be for nought if the Reich government failed in the international struggle that was just beginning between Germany and Russia over the content of the new trade treaty. For Bülow the stakes were high. Only a successful renewal of the Russian treaty could confirm and legitimize the government's actions in the domestic struggles of 1901 to 1903. Conversely, an unsatisfactory outcome of the treaty negotiations would immediately reopen the domestic conflicts and threaten the settlements that the government had managed to impose on the business community.

Trade and High Politics:
Treaty Renewal and the Russo-Japanese War 1903-1904

Chancellor Bülow needed a victory in the international arena (in the form a satisfactory new treaty with Russia) in order to provide the final security for the government's recent victories in the domestic arena. A satisfactory treaty would prove that higher protection for agriculture did not endanger German industrial exports. Consequently, a renewed Russian treaty would serve as a major link in the chancellor's domestic Sammlungspolitik.[54] At the same time, by securing a treaty renewal the government could demonstrate the ability of the ministerial bureaucracy to negotiate successfully without the type of direct private-sector participation that the interest groups had insisted was necessary. On the other hand, the government's failure to secure a treaty on the basis of the 1902 tariff would certainly cause industrial exporters to blame the impasse on the Reich's new "minimum rates" on Russian grain. An industrial-commercial assault on the agricultural portion of the tariff, on the agrarians' intransigence, and on the government's pro-agrarian stance would be unavoidable. Further, Bülow's mismanagement of the treaty renewal would cause the whole of the commercial and industrial communities to blame the debacle on the government's failure to adequately include private-sector opinion in its deliberations. Bülow's conservative domestic program and his personal standing as chancellor were at stake in the upcoming negotiations. He himself described "the vital importance for us of coming to a commercial understanding, especially with Russia."[55] Unfortunately for the chancellor, the Russians were not in a cooperative frame of mind.

The 1894 treaty had produced a good deal of dissatisfaction among the manufacturing interests in Russia. Reports coming back to the German Foreign Office from Consul Maron in St. Petersburg and from the consulate in Moscow showed a cool response by Russian industry to the 1894 treaty. The textile industry, especially woolens, strongly opposed the treaty. They were supported by the extreme nationalist *Moscow Gazette (Moskovskaia Vedomosti)*. The iron, coal, and steel industries only hesitantly accepted the need for the treaty. This position was reflected in the pages of the *Citizen (Grazhdanin),* the Finance Ministry's own *Financial Herald (Vestnik Finansov),* and St. Petersburg's *New Times (Novoe Vremia)* all of which "at the moment are supporting the Finance Minister."[56] Despite the steadily increasing Russian exports to Germany and Russia's large positive balance of trade with the Reich, Russian judgments of the treaty become increasingly negative as time wore on. Already in December 1894, Maron noted on "the repeatedly expressed opinion that Russia had obtained no advantages from the treaty."[57]

By July 1897 Russian attention had turned to the issues of treaty renewal and the tone in the press had become openly hostile. The *Son of the Fatherland (Syn Otchestva)* warned that a "tough battle of interests will be forthcoming" in the treaty renewal and that "we must prepare seriously and in advance in order to defend our interests" so that Germany does not "claim all the advantages for itself and push all the disadvantages onto Russia."[58] Ambassador Friedrich Alvensleben reported from St. Petersburg on the greatly increased Russian governmental and private-sector activity in preparation for the treaty renewal. This activity coincided with the publication of the 1902 German tariff, with its increased rates for agricultural imports. The *New Times* was confident that these rates would be reduced in the course of German-Russian negotiations: "It is to be expected that Germany will show itself to be more generous in the negotiations than it is now in its words." Similarly, the Warsaw chapter of the Society for the Advancement of Russian Industry and Trade was counting on the Russian government being able to obtain "at least a partial reduction of these immoderately high and oppressive [agricultural] tariff rates."[59] In February 1903, Germany and Russia exchanged preliminary notes about negotiations for a new treaty. A month later, Alvensleben warned Bülow that Russian Finance Minister Witte "is in difficult position with the representatives of [Russian] agriculture in regard to new trade treaties" because the 1903 Russian tariff had increased duties on imported agricultural machinery. Witte would try to extract himself from these difficulties by pressing hard for increased animal and grain exports.[60]

This combative Russian attitude could create a difficult situation for the Bülow government. The German delegation seemed confronted with the impossible task of negotiating a treaty that would secure roughly the same Russian tariff rates as the 1894 treaty had, yet in return Germany would offer only its new "minimum rates" on imported wheat and rye, although these were one-and-one-half times the 1894 rates. In other words, Germany sought to retain the increases in its own new 1902 tariff while forcing reductions in the Russian 1903 tariff.[61]

The Russians would certainly insist on a reduction of the German grain tariff, probably even to levels below the "minimum rates." A

German concession on that point was out of the question since it would mean both driving the agrarians into the opposition again and relying on Socialist and Radical votes in the Reichstag for approval of the necessary legislation, all of which ran directly counter to Bülow's conservative domestic program. However, if Germany refused the Russian demand, Witte might allow the 1894 treaty to expire. He could then let the new Russian tariff raise the duties on German goods in the hopes of subsequently renewing negotiations, with the same Russian demands, from a stronger position. In that case, Bülow's inability to secure a renewal would cause an unraveling of the settlements imposed by the government on the domestic disputes of 1902 to 1903.

Even before the opening of formal negotiations on 5 August 1903, German and Russian statements indicated that the two countries were digging in their heels on positions that were still far apart. In February 1902 the German Foreign Office sent a confidential message to Witte that Germany "could not reduce" the 5.00/5.50 tariff rates on grain in the upcoming treaties.[62] At the end of the year, Bülow warned the world in a Reichstag speech that Germany would not make major concessions on the new tariff rates in order to reach international agreements that, in his opinion, Germany's trade partners needed more than the Reich did.[63] Despite these warnings, the Russians submitted a preliminary written list of "suggestions for changes in the German-Russian trade treaty" that asked for significant tariff concessions on a number of crucial agricultural items. The Russians declared flatly that they could "enter into only that type of treaty with Germany which grants Russia at least the same tariff reductions as the current treaty." With regard to grain, the Russians wanted a continuation of the current rates (3.50 marks) on wheat and rye, or at least something under the "minimum rates" of 5.50 marks/cwt. and 5.00 marks/cwt. An internal comment of the German Treasury Office indicated that "in the most extreme case, the minimum tariff rates might be granted." On a variety of other items (e.g., timber, pork, butter, poultry) the Russian "suggestions" were far in excess of the positions arrived at in German internal deliberations. The Russian demand that Germany end its veterinary sanctions against live animal imports from Russia was, in the Treasury Office's opinion "unacceptable."[64]

When formal negotiations opened in St. Petersburg on 5 August 1903 both sides were firmly committed to positions on the grain issue that were far apart. The head of the Russian delegation, Vasili Timiriazev, the ministerial aide for trade and industry in the Finance Ministry, told Körner that the "decisive point" was reducing Germany's grain rates below the "minimum" levels. Two weeks later, Körner was still explaining that a reduction below 5.5 marks/cwt. for wheat and 5 marks/cwt. for rye was impossible. Witte himself told Körner that Russia could accept Germany's minimum rates only if the Reich promised that these same rates would not be given for American grain.[65]

The two countries also remained far apart on the important issues of Russian tariff rates for industrial imports from Germany. According to the Russians, many of their new 1903 rates could not be reduced back to the 1894 levels. Körner characterized the preliminary Russian offers in this area as "in general ... pretty paltry." Further, there remained the problems of the Russian land/sea tariff differential, which had been reintroduced in the 1903 tariff, and the importation of live animals from Russia into the Reich. After eighteen negotiating sessions had produced almost no progress, both sides agreed to break off the talks for a month of reconsideration.[66]

Back in Berlin, government deliberations produced a "unanimous opinion" that Germany could not go below the 1902 minimum tariff rates on wheat, rye, and oats. On barley, only the Treasury Office and the Prussian Trade Ministry would agree to the Russian demand for a 2-mark duty; on pork imports, the Treasury Office position of 8 marks (all other ministries held the line at 12 marks) did not even come close to the Russian demand for a 5-mark duty. On two other import agricultural items in German-Russian trade, butter and eggs, the Russian demands remained beyond what Germany was prepared to grant. Yet the Reich was still insisting on further reductions in the Russian tariff. In the German view, the reductions offered by Russia so far were not sufficient compensation, even for Germany's 5.00/5.50 grain rates. The Germans were determined to "stick to" their original demands especially on chemicals (tannin, white lead, zinc white), iron, steel, and copper products, and a wide variety of machines (from threshers to gas meters).[67]

In a series of written questions to the Treasury Office, Bülow began searching for alternative means for reaching an agreement with Russia, either through compromise or through increased pressure: Could Germany grant Witte's request to give Russian grain some type of preference over American grain? Could the Reich annul the existing trade treaty as a way of exerting more leverage on Russia? Would the Reich be sufficiently well served by the 1902 tariff in the event of a tariff war with the Russia? Treasury responses offered little help for the German position. As in 1892 to 1894, the difficulty of effective, discriminatory customs control made preferential or discriminatory treatment of Russian grain impractical.[68] As a result, Bülow could not pursue the anti-American compromise suggestion. On the other hand, the Reich was not in a position to adequately defend itself should negotiations collapse and a tariff war break out while treaties remained in force with other agricultural exporters. Some form of negotiated agreement had to be found. Yet the Russians showed no sign of yielding.

While the Germans were reaffirming their determination to stick to their earlier demands, Russian industry and agriculture were urging the czar's government not to soften its demands on Germany. In October 1903 the St. Petersburg Forestry Society renewed its call on the Russian negotiators to get some reduction in the German timber tariff. The largest Moscow paper, *Russkoe Slovo,* which represented the opinions of the "big industrialists," according to the German consulate in Moscow, insisted that Russia obtain some concessions on the shipment of live cattle and fresh meat into Germany.[69] These statements only confirmed the extent of the differences between the two countries. A second round of negotiations began in November 1903. Despite extensive contact (five sessions on veterinary questions, six sessions on other tariff aspects of the treaty, and extensive work by the new Sub-Commission on Customs Administration), the month generated no significant progress.

As far back as 1900 the Foreign Office had warned the government about the difficulty of concluding new trade treaties, and especially a treaty with Russia, once German "minimum" tariff rates were in place. As state secretary in the Foreign Office, Bülow himself had penned an objection to the creation of a double tariff based on the difficulties of negotiating and reaching international agreements with minimum rates in place.[70] Posadowsky (the real force behind tariff reform in the final days of the Hohenlohe chancellorship) had ignored these concerns. The Union of German Iron and Steel Industrialists, with Bueck in the lead, had also warned the government that the minimum rates would "endanger or even make impossible the conclusion of trade treaties."[71] Based on the written and oral negotiations conducted with the Russians over the course of 1903, these prophecies now seemed horribly prescient.

In early 1904 Bülow's position was suddenly rescued by the outbreak of the Russo-Japanese War. The situation in the Far East had deteriorated rapidly since November 1903. The Japanese were determined to use force if necessary in order to compel a Russian withdrawal from Port Arthur, in compliance with earlier promises. On the Russian side, Interior Minister Vyacheslav Plehve and the military were determined to hold on to Russia's recent acquisitions, accepting war as the consequence. Beginning with the Japanese attack on the Russian fleet at Port Arthur on 8 February 1904, the Russians suffered a quick series of naval and land defeats, culminating in Admiral Togo's victory over Admiral Makarov and the destruction of the Russian Pacific Fleet on 13 April 1904.[72]

This disastrous course of events in the opening round of the conflict with Japan put Russia at the mercy of the German policy, both strategically and financially. Neither of the Franco-Russian military agreements (1894, 1902) were binding on France in this non-European war, and the French signaled their intention to remain neutral. In January 1904 Bülow and Wilhelm II had agreed that Germany should remain neutral in the impending conflict. The kaiser's personal declaration of "benevolent neutrality" initiated a period of "especially hearty and intimate relations" between the kaiser and the czar.[73] As additional troops were shifted from European Russia to Far East in the early months of 1904, the western border of the czar's empire was left increasingly vulnerable. Russian security now depended on the continued benevolence of the German Reich. As Witte exclaimed to War Minister Aleksei Kuropatkin: "If they [the Germans] were to attack now! I am convinced that in less than a month and a half, they would occupy a line from Smolensk through Kiev to Nikolaev." In addition, the impoverished Russian government was "in sore need of foreign loans" and sought these in both France and Germany.[74]

As Russia's military and financial position deteriorated during the spring of 1904 and the conventional *do ut des* of international negotiation showed no promise of producing an acceptable German-Russian trade treaty, Bülow decided to use Russia's military and financial dependency on Germany for increased leverage in the stalled trade treaty negotiations.[75] With the approval of Bülow and the Foreign Office, Kaiser Wilhelm II sent a personal letter to Czar Nicholas on March 29 in which he mentioned that "... I see from the papers that our treaty of Commerce seems to have come to a deadlock ....After all one cannot wait for ever considering the many months that have already been wasted." Wilhelm went on to suggest that Nicholas "send some person of importance to Berlin straight to Bülow to finish the game off with him personally; a man of first rate capacity and well versed in such matters; that would do much good."[76]

In St. Petersburg, a "special conference of statesmen" under Witte's chairmanship quickly concluded that "in order to avoid a break with Germany, we must submit to her demands" on the trade treaty. Despite whimpering about the German position on the agricultural question ("the greatest difficulty lies only in our common agreement upon the "minimal" duty on corn, wheat, etc."), the czar agreed to send to Witte to Germany to negotiate the treaty directly with Bülow. Nicholas assured the Germans that "Witte is ready to proceed quickly with this affair," stating openly that "I have given directions to Witte to meet the German proposals as far as possible."[77] Under these circumstances, even the resourceful Witte was powerless as a negotiator. Not only did Russia desperately need an agreement, but Witte himself needed a successful conclusion of his assignment in order to bolster his eroding position within Nicholas's inner circle.[78] Witte's unpleasant task was to trade Russian agreement to German tariff rates for unwritten understandings on continued German "benevolent neutrality" and Russian access to the German financial market.

In July 1904 a small Russian delegation travelled with Witte and Timiriazev to the East Frisian vacation island of Norderney for direct negotiations with a powerful and compact German delegation consisting of Bülow, Posadowsky, and Körner.[79] According to Witte, Bülow "felt sure that I would make all the concessions that were demanded of us ... He must have been informed from St. Petersburg that I had received instructions to bring the parley to a peaceful end at any price." Within a few days Witte had conceded the grain tariff, on the "explicit orders" of Nicholas.[80] On other agricultural items as well (eggs, butter, wood, pork, poultry, fresh meat) Witte was forced to accept the recent German tariff increases and veterinary restrictions. For some of these items (pork, fresh meat) the tariff rates now imposed by the Germans were well above the levels Körner had been prepared to offer in the earlier conventional negotiations.

Equally important, the Germans managed to eliminate or minimize many of the scheduled increases in the Russian tariff. The Germans did not accept the full 1903 Russian tariff increases on one single chemical, metal, or machine item. On machine exports, a "highest priority" item for German negotiators, Russian tariff increases were kept well below both the published rates of January 1903 and the concessionary rates offered by the Russians in the October 1903 negotiations. On the seven categories of machinery designated in the new treaty, the Germans were able to reduce Russian rates from the 1894 level on one category; to hold rates steady on three categories; and to accept small increases on three categories. On none of the machine exports did the Germans accept the Russian offers of October 1903. On seven different chemical products, two were held steady and five increased slightly; of eleven categories of metal products, six were held steady and five increased. In just three weeks of negotiation, the Germans had forced Witte to abandon all of the major material positions that the Russian negotiators had stubbornly held for over a year.[81]

The treaty is as significant for the manner and circumstances of its negotiation as it is for its content. By implicitly linking the treaty to other, nontrade issues, Bülow had taken a quantum leap forward in politicizing German-Russian trade. The connection of the trade treaty not only to a German loan, but also to Germany's "benevolent neutrality" in the Russo-Japanese war brought the trade into the same arena with the classic issues of high politics. The use of a private letter from the kaiser to the czar, and the chancellor's personal negotiation of the treaty reinforced this. Bülow had added a new dimension to German-Russian trade disputes. Even during the tariff "war" of 1893, neither side had employed nontrade weapons. That conflict had originated, had been fought out, and had concluded in the realm of tariff and trade measures. Now, by linking the new treaty to Germany's financial and military posture during the war, Bülow dramatically expanded the playing field on which international trade conflicts could be contested, and qualitatively changed the types of weapons that might be employed.

Trade and Politics 1904-1914

The 1904 treaty resolved the commercial conflict between Russia and Germany unambiguously in Germany's favor. As a clear victory for the Reich over the Russian Empire, the treaty had profound consequences for the future development of German-Russian political and economic relations. On one hand, the treaty fostered another decade of surging growth in two-way trade; in 1913 the value of trade was two-and-a-half times the trade value of 1900. On the other hand, German use of political pressure to impose the treaty on Russia had a disastrous effect on subsequent political relations between the two countries.

The treaty of 1905 provided the basis for another tremendous period of growth in German-Russian trade.[82] In less than a decade, the treaty fostered a near doubling of total trade, from 1.2 billion marks in 1904 to over 2.5 billion marks in 1913 (Graph 2.11). Graph 2.12 shows the positive development of trade in the treaty era (i.e. since 1894) in comparison to the pre-treaty years. The 1894 treaty had lifted German exports from the 100 million to 200 million mark level to the 300 million to 400 million mark level (Graph 2.13). By 1907 the dislocation of the 1905 revolution had subsided and the 1906 French loan of Fr. 2.25 billion had stabilized the Russian regime financially. Thereafter, German exports exhibited phenomenal increases as the Russian economy surged in the czarist regime's final attempt to modernize the empire's infrastructure. In 1913 exports to Russia were 1010 million marks; the value of machine exports alone (130 marks) nearly equaled the value of all German exports to Russia in 1887. Russia was absorbing 8.7 percent of Germany's total exports, making it Germany's third-largest export market behind Britain and Austria-Hungary and the only market of these three that was still expanding. Trade emerged as the most significant form of economic contact between the two empires, far surpassing the value of German investments in Russia.[83]

Despite relatively high industrial prices in Germany, export growth was strongest among industrial finished goods, which now made up two-thirds of German exports to Russia (Graph 2.15). Raw materials such as rye, wool, and coal made up only one-quarter of German exports to Russia; finished and semifinished goods made up the other three-quarters. A half-dozen categories of advanced finished products made up more than 50 percent of German exports to Russia. German exports took off in exactly those areas where the new treaty had rolled back or significantly reduced the planned Russian tariff increases of 1903, especially on a wide variety of leather products, chemicals, metalwares, and machines. In 1913 the Russian market purchased 19.2 percent of all German exports of electrical equipment (34.5 million marks); 19.1 percent of all machine exports (130 million marks); 25 percent of private motor vehicles (18 million marks)![84]

This expansion of exports was certainly a boon to the German economy. Assuming a 20 to 25 percent average rate of profit on German industrial products, German manufacturers and exporters earned 700 million to 800 million marks in profits from the Russian market in the final five years before the war.[85] For Germany this golden era of trade with the East left a powerful impression on the minds of the business community as the Russian market began to reveal for the first time its vast capacities. For years after the Bolshevik revolution, both the private-sector and Weimar governments chased the memory of this level of trade.

More problematic than estimating the scale of the treaty's benefits for the Reich is determining whether Russia also benefited from the growth of German-Russian trade as it developed under the 1904 treaty. By thwarting Russia's planned tariff increases, Germany deprived Russian industry of what had traditionally been an effective form of protection and insured that the Russian market would remain open for German manufactured exports. The experiences of the period 1880 to 1904 had shown that the Russian tariff could exercise a decisive influence on German exports. By rolling back and holding down Russian tariff increases, the 1904 treaty created the conditions for an unprecedented German export boom.[86] The new treaty, combined with the impressive performance of German manufacturing industries, produced 5.75 billion marks in German exports to Russia from 1905 to 1913.

On the other hand, Witte, among others, argued that the conditions of 1905 to 1914 were not those of the 1880s. Russian industry's own inability to supply the country with sufficient amounts of the materials needed for large-scale industrialization and rearmament from 1910 to 1914 meant that imports of foreign equipment were sure to increase even if the Russians raised their tariffs substantially.[87] The most advanced German industries would certainly have seen growth in the energetic Russian market after 1909 even if the 1904 treaty had been less one-sided. Under these circumstances one must be very cautious in making the argument that if the Russians had secured a more favorable treaty, the empire might have reduced its imports from Germany significantly.

Did this greatly increased volume of trade make a positive contribution to Russian economic development in the years before World War I? A global assessment cannot be accurate for every sector of the Russian economy. With that in mind, one can still venture to say that, despite the circumstances surrounding the treaty, Russia acquired significant benefits from the pattern of German-Russian trade after 1905. It is now widely accepted that the importation of advanced foreign technology was crucial to the rapid industrial progress made by Russia in the final years before the war.[88] In this context, massive Russian imports of German machinery, electrical equipment, and motor vehicles must be counted a positive contribution to the infrastructure and economic performance of the czar's empire. The 700 million to 800 million marks in profits that accrued to German producers as a result of these valuable imports were only 6 to 7 percent of the 11,664 million marks the Russians paid out from 1898 to 1913 in interest on its public and private foreign debt.[89]

Equally positive for Russia, the higher 5.00/5.50 tariff rates for Russian grain that Bülow had preserved in the treaty did not reduce the rising volume of grain imports from Russia.[90] Sales of Russian wheat and barley especially continued to increase; German imports of Russian wheat averaged 767,100 tons annually from 1902 to 1904, but 1,279,600 tons annually from 1909 to 1911. For that reason, the 1904 treaty did not reduce the German trade deficit with Russia, which totaled 6.5 billion marks from 1905 to 1913 (Graph 2.14). By exporting food and raw materials to Germany, Russia produced a trade surplus that brought almost 11 billion marks to the czar's empire from 1894 to 1913. Russia found its largest foreign market in neighboring

Germany, which took 30 percent of Russia's total exports in 1913.[91] The German market for Russian food and raw materials played an irreplaceable role in Russian economic progress.[92]

Russian dependence on agricultural exports and raw materials to achieve these surpluses was not a consequence of the recent treaty. Nor was this Russian strategy and pattern of exports and unique to the period after 1905; both Vyshnegradski and Witte had encouraged agricultural exports. In using export earnings to finance additional loans and to import capital equipment, Witte had pursued a classic strategy for economic development. After 1905, agricultural and raw material exports continued to provide the basis for Russia's industrial, military, and financial modernization. Commerce Minister Timiriazev repeatedly pointed out to Russian business circles that "the Russian domestic market cannot replace the foreign market for Russian agriculture," and that even if this replacement were possible, "the export of agricultural products [would remain] absolutely necessary on account of the balance of payments."[93] The important strides made in Russian industrialization and economic modernization in the years just before 1914 show that this strategy was not a dead end for Russia.[94]

A more ominous development from the Russian view was the controlling position in Russian foreign trade assumed by Germany in the decade from 1904 to 1914. In 1894 Germany and Britain had each provided about one-quarter of Russia's imports. The Caprivi treaty helped Germany gain 35 percent of the Russian market (to Britain's 17 percent) by 1902. The new treaty intensified that trend so that by 1913 the highly productive German economy had captured 45 percent of the Russian import market and 30 percent of the Russian export market. Yet these figures represented "only" 9 percent of German total exports and 14 percent of total imports. By 1913 the British share of the Russian import market had fallen to just 12 percent, with France and other European countries supplying the difference. The quantitative inequality was further exacerbated by the fact that few other, or in some cases no other, countries could deliver the advanced chemical, electrical, and machine exports that Germany sent to Russia while a number of other countries might serve the Reich quite well as alternative sources for Russian agricultural exports.

The Russian *Revue Contemporaine* did not hesitate to blame the 1904 treaty for the German "conquest of the Finnish market" and for the fact that "half of Russian foreign trade is in German hands."[95] By holding down Russian tariff increases and providing long-term stability to all aspects of trade relations, the treaty undoubtedly contributed to a growing German presence in the Russian import market. But a number of other well-known factors -market knowledge, quality products, prompt delivery, expert installation, and reliable service -also contributed to German export successes in Russia and elsewhere around the world.

Contemporary Russian opinion almost certainly overestimated the economic disadvantages produced by the 1904 treaty. Nonetheless, the Russian perception of the 1904 agreement as an economically damaging treaty that Russia would not renew emerged as a major source of Russian-German friction in the decade before World War I. Beyond the economic terms of the treaty, the manner in which Bülow had pressed the Russians for an agreement poisoned future relations between the two empires. In short, the process was as important as the product in provoking Russian resentments.

By exploiting Russia's weakened condition in order to obtain a new German-Russian trade treaty in 1904, Bülow engendered broad Russian antipathy toward Germany. Among intelligentsia, industrial leaders, and agricultural representatives, as well as within the Russian imperial bureaucracy, the feeling was widespread that the Reich had done the Russians a great injustice with the 1904 treaty. Instead of diminishing over time, attacks on the treaty, as a symbol of the German economic "yoke," became more vitriolic as German-Russian trade increased from 1905 to 1913.[96] By the spring of 1914, charges and countercharges concerning the treaty and other trade practices had reached dangerous levels on both sides.

As early as January 1905 the large St. Petersburg newspaper, the *Berzhevye Vedomosti,* explained that undoubtedly Germany would have been forced to make concessions in the treaty if Russia had not been involved in a war with Japan.[97] The Russian government did not explicitly deny that German political pressure had played a role in the 1904 treaty. Rather, the ministerial bureaucracy sought to deflect attention away from this point and to focus it instead on the need for extensive and thorough preparation in advance of the 1917 treaty renewal negotiations. As part of the bureaucratic reorganization of 1905, the government elevated the Finance Ministry's department of trade and industry to the status of a new, independent Ministry of Trade and Industry. Vasili Timiriazev, who had led the Russian delegation in the early rounds of German-Russian negotiations in 1903 to 1904 and had accompanied Witte to the final sessions in Norderney, assumed the post of trade minister.[98] As a participant in the Norderney negotiations, Timiriazev understood the strategic and financial background to the 1904 treaty. Still, in his lectures to various business groups he preferred to emphasize the need for better private-sector information and government preparation as the keys to obtaining a better treaty in the future. Timiriazev even asserted that Russia had signed the 1904 treaty not because of the war with Japan, but rather out of fear of being closed out of the German market for agricultural imports.[99] More honestly, Witte himself spoke of "burdening ourselves for ten years with a disadvantageous treaty" and subsequently described Bülow's actions as "unscrupulously taking advantage of our unfortunate situation [to] extort from us highly important concessions which we should never have yielded ... under normal conditions."[100]

As the Russian economy stabilized after the revolutionary disturbances of 1905 to 1906 and then began a new period of growth in 1910, the perceived unfairness of the treaty inspired increasingly direct anti-German agitation in the economic sphere. Ironically, Russian industrialists tried to dampen public outrage over the treaty, despite their own dissatisfaction with the agreement. They feared that an obsession with Germany's minimum rates on wheat and rye would drive Russia to "pay any price" in industrial tariff concessions in order to get some German agricultural concessions when the treaty expired in 1917.[101] Moderate voices on both sides, including Russian Trade Minister Timiriazev and Foreign Minister Sergei D. Sazonov and the German ambassador in St. Petersburg, Friedrich von Pourtales, were overwhelmed by a rising chorus of hostile recriminations from Russia and fearful reaction from Germany.

Russian agriculture strongly resented the German "minimum rates" on grain that became symbols of the unjust treaty. Further, the Reich government's hidden subsidy for German grain exports had fueled a steady increase in shipments of German rye to Finland and the Polish territories of the czar's empire, gradually displacing Russian grain in the Finnish market and provoking further Russian resentments against German trade practices perceived as unfair.[102]

Russian economists such as I.M. Goldstein reminded the readers of the *Financial Herald* that Russia had been "forced" into a disadvantageous tariff treaty with Germany because of the Japanese war. He urged the government to declare in advance that the 1904 treaty "cannot be renewed with such unfavorable conditions for Russia."[103] Even the *Revue Contemporaine,* considered by the German Consulate in St. Petersburg as "close to the government," admitted to "the state of inferiority in which the present treaty has placed us."[104] Other papers were prepared to go much further in their denunciations of the treaty. By 1911 the *European Herald (Vestnik Evropy)* reminded readers of the (unspecified) "heavy losses" caused by the treaty. As early as 1912 the *Financial Herald* began ruminating on how Germany could be hurt in a future German-Russian tariff war. By the spring of 1914 the usually responsible *New Times* spoke bluntly of "robbery" in connection with the 1904 agreement.[105] Duma Deputy Shingarev called the treaty "a worse defeat than the Japanese war."[106]

This ongoing dispute over the fairness of the 1904 treaty was inflamed further by a number of unilateral Russian actions on customs administration that were perceived by the Reich government as harassment of German exporters. In the spring of 1912 the Reich Interior Office was searching for appropriate "retaliatory measures" in response to Russian customs procedures that were restricting imports of German agricultural machinery and other groups of industrial products.[107]

By 1914 the accumulation of Russian invective against the 1904 treaty began to bring on sharp German reactions. Inside the Reich, some of the energy previously expended in domestic struggles over trade policy now was vented externally in an effort to convince the Russians that Germany would insist on treaty renewal in 1917 without substantial modification. In a major Reichstag speech of January 1914, Interior State Secretary Clemens von Delbruck signaled to German and Russian audiences the future course of German trade policy: "The government therefore remains of the opinion that our present tariff protection is generally adequate, that it must be maintained, and that our policy in concluding agreements must essentially remain the same. In particular we must allow our agriculture to continue to enjoy the existing tariff protection."[108]

Commercial antagonism helped set the stage for the particularly bitter and dangerous German-Russian "press war" in the spring of 1914, in which trade issues played a central role.[109] In April 1914 the Russian Duma moved to place a tariff on imported grain, a measure that affected Germany almost exclusively. Germany's East Elbian estate owners stood to lose the most from this new Russian measure. Conservative forces in the Reichstag, among the interest groups, and in the press expressed their outrage immediately and forcefully. Even left-liberal elements of the German press that previously had been generally unsympathetic to Junker economic interests now criticized the Russian government for a new round of tariff chicanery designed to make a renewal of the existing treaty impossible. Across the political spectrum, the German press employed the phrases "trade war," "tariff war," and "economic war" in analyses of German-Russian relations that spring. The vast majority of these expressed opinions expected hostile economic relations to exert considerable negative impact on the overall relationship between the two states.[110]

German economists and historians have offered a wide range of assessments of the importance of the 1904 treaty in driving German-Russian relations to the breaking point in 1914. Writing in the *Österreichische Rundschau* in 1915, the liberal economist Lujo Brentano put a good deal of the blame for the war with Russia on the treaty. Economist Friedrich Aereboe did the same a decade later in his *Agrarpolitik*. Historian Eckart Kehr declared that the German agricultural policies embodied in the 1902 tariff and 1904 treaty made a German-Russian political understanding "impossible."[111] More recently, Fritz Fischer, Klaus Wernecke, and Volker Berghahn have all discussed the German trade policies and the resulting German-Russian commercial tensions as contributing factors in German foreign policy on the eve of World War I.[112] These assessments are supported by data reminding us that direct trade between Germany and Russia far outweighed the trade between these two European powers and any of the less-developed countries in which German-Russian imperialist and commercial rivalries played themselves out, for example in Turkey and Iran.[113]

When German and Russian negotiators did eventually meet to discuss renewal of the 1904 treaty, it was under circumstances that neither party had foreseen in 1914 – the German-Russian peace negotiations of 1917-1918 at Brest-Litovsk. By that time militarism had replaced mercantilism and conquest had superseded commerce as the primary tools of German foreign policy toward Russia. By the end of 1917 Germany had developed grandiose ambitions in the East. German war aims of 1917 were revealed by the staggering territorial terms demanded of exhausted Russia. All of Russia's western provinces were to fall under direct or indirect German control, including Poland, Lithuania, Courland, Livonia, and Estonia; newly independent Finland and the Ukraine would experience strong German influence; six billion marks in compensation from the remaining Russian territories were to follow. These fundamental territorial revisions largely eclipsed the trade negotiations at Brest-Litovsk.[114]

As early as 11 December 1917 State Secretary Hans Karl Freiherr von Stein set out plans for an interministerial "Standing Committee for Commercial Relations with Russia" that would include both civilian and military officials. By the end of January 1918 Stein had brought together a staff of 350 for the purpose of "resuming trade relations with Russia."[115] Prior to the start of negotiations with the Russians, discussions among the German civilian ministries had revealed a broadly based consensus that "the hitherto existing German-Russian trade treaty had exerted a very positive effect on the Germany economy." Although the German government noted its intent to "modify the trade treaty at individual points of greater or lesser importance," the German delegation entered trade negotiations at Brest-Litovsk with the "primary goal of reactivating the [1904] treaty in its entirety" as the basis for future economic relations.[116] Subsequent negotiations with the new Russian government centered on the German demand for a formal renewal of the 1904 treaty and steadfast Bolshevik insistence that the old treaty could not be renewed and that a new treaty must be negotiated, even if it were to contain the same provisions as the 1904 agreement. On 27 January 1918 the German government agreed to the Bolshevik suggestion that the modified terms of the 1904 treaty be appended to the Peace of Brest-Litovsk. The decision was communicated to chief German economic negotiator Paul von Körner at Brest-Litovsk that same day.[117] The issue was resolved as Article XI of the Peace Treaty of Brest-Litovsk, which stated that Russian-German economic relations would be determined by the regulations set out in Appendix II to the treaty.[118]

The Imperial Legacy

Despite the zig-zag nature of German tariff policy and trade policy toward Russia, the experiences of the imperial era handed down several enduring and identifiable legacies in these issue areas. These imperial legacies were largely those of unresolved domestic conflicts and highly politicized foreign trade policies. They proved to be a heavy burden for future German regimes.

Bülow's stunning success in the second German-Russian trade treaty in 1904 had profound consequences for the German domestic processes of framing trade policies. Bülow had produced a treaty that satisfied protectionist agriculture and heavy industry as well as export-oriented light industry and commercial circles – a feat widely considered impossible in Germany at the start of the negotiations. His achievements in the international trade arena legitimized both the content of his negotiating position and the manner of his internal preparations for the treaty.

Like Bismarck, Bülow successfully exploited a weak point in the international system in order to avoid a cluster of divisive domestic trade issues. Through sudden and unforeseen good luck, the government was able to adjourn a painful debate that had divided German industry and pitted agriculture against the commercial community. The Russian-Japanese War allowed Germany to postpone some difficult trade policy decisions. However, the fortuitous circumstances surrounding the 1904 treaty could not be expected to repeat themselves. Unfortunately, the burden of addressing these unresolved issues fell to the overmatched Weimar Republic.

Most immediately, Bülow's treaty success guaranteed the integrity of the 1902 German tariff as the resolution of the turn of the century tariff struggle. The Russian treaty managed to maintain increased protection for German agriculture without reciprocal harm to German exports. By legitimizing the tariff, the treaty anchored Bülow's conservative domestic Sammlungspolitik. Yet this success had allowed Bülow and the Reich as a whole to avoid making the tough choice between prioritizing either domestic protection or export expansion. The Reich had not resolved its internal differences over the content of future trade policy. Like Bismarck, Bülow left behind an ambiguous trade policy legacy that could not be perpetuated. International pressures would eventually expose the incompatibility of domestic protection and export expansion, just as they had after Bismarck's departure. For this reason, a third round of German political struggles over trade issues anticipated the trade treaties to be renewed in 1916 to 1917. The formation of an avowedly antiagrarian commercial-industrial alliance in the Hansa-Bund (1909) promised another bitter confrontation over German trade policies. Since the Hansa-Bund itself struggled to control the "divergent interests" within it, a clean and quick victory resolution of these questions appeared impossible.[119]

Bülow's treaty also vindicated the "closed-door" manner in which imperial governments had prepared for and negotiated their trade treaties. Private-sector claims that it would be impossible to gain an advantageous treaty without their direct expert participation now appeared groundless, even ridiculous. Bülow, Interior Secretary Posadowsky, and Foreign Office Director Körner had produced an unexpectedly advantageous treaty by themselves, thereby reinforcing the government's autonomous control over trade policy. This autonomy underlay the radical changes in the content of German trade policy that accompanied the transitions from Bismarck's protectionism to Caprivi's treaties and from the Caprivi treaties to the Bülow tariff. The Bonapartist nature of the German political system enabled one chancellor to reverse the trade and tariff policies of his predecessor, limited only by his ability to obtain a single majority "yes" vote in the Reichstag. Caprivi directed the autonomous bureaucracy against the interests of the Junkers by reducing Bismarck's agricultural tariffs. For this he paid the price of unrelenting agrarian hatred, which brought him down in 1894.

Throughout the imperial era, the issue of how private-sector voices and state agents might cooperate to formulate and execute

German trade policies together remained unresolved. The ministerial bureaucracy enforced the state's claim to its dominant role in tariff policy and its exclusive control of foreign trade negotiations. Yet
the same high level of material stakes that perpetuated private-sector
conflict over the direction of German trade policy also kept alive the
private-sector's struggle to gain some regular and effective form of
participation in the decisive deliberations on these issues.[120]

The linkage of German-Russian trade to larger political issues provides one of the few points of continuity in German trade policy
from Caprivi to Bülow. Caprivi argued for the use of trade to influence nontrade portions of the German-Russian relationship; Bülow
did the reverse, i.e., he used nontrade portions of the relationship to
influence German-Russian trade. Caprivi had thought of expanding
trade as a means toward his end of better political relations with Russia. For Bülow, satisfactory trade relations had become an end in
themselves to be pursued by diplomatic and financial means. Despite
the reversal of means and ends in the two treaties, both outcomes
ultimately revealed that attempts to manipulate intra-European trade
flows were very limited ways of affecting international relations
before 1914. The German state structure and the nature of the European international economy restricted the Reich's powers of trade
regulation and its ability to manipulate international trade flows. As
the Prussian Finance Ministry explained to Caprivi in 1984 and the
Reich Treasury Office explained to Bülow in 1903: Germany did not
possess the effective import/export control mechanism required to
discriminate against Russian products in an MFN system. Even after
the Germans had obtained a controlling position in Russian foreign
trade, the German administrative structure and Russian participation in an European international trade system of long-term MFN
treaties made it virtually impossible for Germany use this trade
advantage for political or diplomatic gain. Those limitations on trade
politicization were swept aside by the events of 1914 to 1918.

Since Bülow could not manipulate trade in order to gain a new
German-Russian trade treaty, he employed other financial, diplomatic, and strategic weapons in order to obtain a treaty that produced tremendous commercial benefits for Germany.[121] In this area,
the imperial German legacy of politicized trade went far beyond the
resulting Russian political hostility of 1905 to 1914. Bülow's actions
anticipated a new era in European trade politicization that would follow World War I. In defense of the burdensome commercial clauses
imposed on Germany as part of the Versailles settlement, the Allies
could well have cited German actions in the trade negotiations of
1904 and 1918.

Notes

1. Based on data contained in *Statistik des deutschen Reichs*, N.F., vol. 158.1, V, 1-73; ibid., vol. 182.1, V, 1-87; *Statistiches Jahrbuch für das deutsche Reich*, various volumes, and the sources cited in chapter one. Values in all graphs exclude precious metals.
2. This despite an 1897 revision of German trade statistics to exclude exports to Finland from the export statistics on Russia. Prior to 1896 exports to Finland had been included in the German statistics on exports to Russia.
3. In the turbulent 1880s, Russia had taken an annual average of 5.7 percent of Germany's total exports. In the treaty period this rose to 8.2 percent and the Russian market had shown the capacity in some years to absorb more than one-tenth of Germany's total exports.
4. Handelskammer zu Bremen, *Statistische Mitteilungen betreffend Bremens Handel und Schifffahrt*, 1890, 11; 1902, 15.
5. Exports of wool and woolens to Russia increased from 15 million marks in 1894 to 22 million in 1899; exports of animal skins were almost stagnant at 15 million marks in 1894 and 18 million in 1899, *Statistik des deutschen Reichs*, N.F., vol. 135.1, V, 5.
6. *Statistik des deutschen Reichs*, N.F., vol. 182.1, V, 30 ff.
7. *Statistiches Jahrbuch für das deutsche Reich*, 28 (1905), 133, 136, 106, 96. The data cited here on exports of fine ironwares to Russia is at variance with the data published in *Statistik des deutschen Reichs* and cited in note 7. For Germany's largest producer of agricultural machinery, Heinrich Lanz, the "trade treaties with Russia, Serbia, and Rumania in 1894 expanded exports to those countries considerably," "Der wirtschaftlicher Aufstieg des Hauses H. Lanz," manuscript provided by John Deere Werke, Mannheim.
8. Hermann Kellenbenz, *Deutsche Wirtschaftsgeschichte*, vol. 2, 261; Knoll AG (hrsg.), *100 Jahre im Dienst der Gesundheit 1886-1986* (manuscript), 50.
9. Wolfram Fischer, "Bergbau, Industrie, und Handwerk," in *Handbuch der deutschen Wirtschafts - und Sozialgeschichte*, vol. 2, table 4, 535.
10. *Statistisches Jahrbuch für das deutsche Reich*, various years, especially vol. 31 (1910), 218, Table 7.b.2.
11. On these developments see J. Conrad, "Die Stellung der landwirtschaftliche Zölle in den 1903 zu schließenden Handelsverträgen Deutschlands," *Schriften des Vereins für Sozialpolitik* 90 (1900); Heinrich Dade, "Die Agrarzölle," *Schriften des Vereins für Sozialpolitik* 91 (1901); Friedrich Beckmann, "Die Entwicklung des deutsch-russischen Getreideverkehrs unter den Handels-Verträgen von 1894 und 1904," *Jahrbücher für Nationalökonomie und Statistik* 101 (1913), 145-71.
12. At 116.9 marks/ton in 1894, German wholesale prices for rye were down 45 percent from their high of 209.9 marks/ton in 1891; at 131.5 marks/ton in 1894, wheat was down 38 percent from 213.9 marks/ton in 1891. For the five-year period 1894 to 1898, wholesale rye prices averaged 131 marks/ton or 18 percent lower than the 159 mark/ton in the last five-year period before Caprivi's treaties, 1887-1891; wheat prices were 10 percent lower, averaging 162 marks/ton from 1894 to 1898 and 181 marks in 1887 to 1891, *Statistisches Jahrbuch für das deutsche Reich* 16 (1895), 130; ibid. 26 (1905), 210.
13. In Bremen, a major grain entrepôt, wholesale prices for rye fell to 76 marks/ton in October 1894, Conrad, "Die Stellung der landwirtschaftliche Zölle in den 1903 zu schließenden Handelsverträgen Deutschlands," *Schriften des Vereins für Sozialpolitik* 90 (1900), table II.
14. More extreme agrarian demands included immediate termination of Caprivi's Eastern trade treaties, an end to the practice of signing long-term tariff treaties, no

use of the MFN clause, and a government monopoly on importing grain, see Sarah Tirrell, *German Agrarian Politics After Bismarck's Fall*; Pühle, *Agrarische Interessenpolitik*, 73 ff., 227 ff.

15. On these developments see J.C.G. Röhl, *Germany Without Bismarck; The Crisis of Government in the Second Reich* (London, 1967), 135 ff., 246 ff., 262 ff.; Tirrell, *German Agrarian Politics*; Pühle, *Agrarische Interessenpolitik*, 165 ff.; 213 ff.

16. H.A. Bueck, *Der Centralverband deutscher Industrieller 1876-1901* (Berlin, 1902), vol. 1, 571; on the Trade Treaty Association see Dirk Stegmann, "Linksliberale Bankiers, Kaufleute, und Industrielle 1890-1900. Ein Beitrag zur Vorgeschichte des Handelsvertragsverein," *Tradition* 21 (1976); L. Elm, "Handelsvertragsverein," in *Die Bürgerlichen Parteien in Deutschland*, Bd. 2, 197-200; Helga Nussbaum, "Die Bildung zweier Lager in der Industrie. Der Handelsvertragsverein," in Varain, *Interessenverbände in Deutschland*, 204-15.

17. R. Sonnemann, "Der Verein zur Wahrung der Interessen der chemischen Industrie Deutschlands," in *Wissenschaftliche Zeitschrift der Friedrich Schiller Universität Jena* 14 (1965), 275-77; Kaelble, *Industrielle Interessenpolitik*, 174 ff. On the "independent" interest groups and their relations to the suprasectoral "Dachverbände" see Helga Nussbaum, *Unternehemenr gegen Monopole. Über Struktur und Aktionen antimonopolistischer bürgerlicher Gruppen zu Beginn des 20.Jahrhunderts* (Berlin, 1966); Pierenkemper, "Trade Associations in Germany in the Late Nineteenth and Early Twentieth Centuries," in H. Yamazaki and M. Miyamoto, eds., *Trade Associations in Business History* (Tokyo, 1986), 233-67 and the literature cited there. Useful older literature includes H.E. Krueger, "Historische und kritische Untersuchungen über die freien Interessenvertretungen von Industrie, Handel und Gewerbe in Deutschland insbesondere die Fach- Zweck-und Zentralverbände gewerblicher Unternehmer," in *Schmollers Jahrbuch für Gesetzgebeung, Verwaltung und Volkswirtschaft* 32 (1908), 325-58 and 33 (1908), 189-240; F. Schomers, "Die freien Interessenverbände für Handel und Industrie und ihr Einfluss auf die Gesetzgebeung und Verwaltung," in *Schmollers Jahrbuch* 25 (1901), 57-138.

18. U. Merkel, "Der Bund der Industriellen," in *Die Bürgerlichen Parteien in Deutschland*, vol. 1, 117-26; S. Pausewang, "Zur Entstehung des gesellschaftsbildes mittelständischer Unternehmer. Inhaltsanalyse der Zeitschrift "Deutsche Industrie" des Bundes der Industriellen" (Ph.D. diss., Marburg, 1967); Hans-Peter Ullman, *Der Bund der Industriellen. Organisation, Einfluss, und Politik klein- und mittelbetrieblicher Industrieller im Deutschen Kaiserreich 1895-1905* (Göttingen, 1976).

19. Bueck, *Der Centralverband deutscher Industrieller 1876-1901*, vol. 1, 269.

20. This two-sector model has often been pushed too far as an explanation for almost all aspects of German industrial politics after 1890. See Harmut Pogge von Strandmann's discussion of these efforts and his cautions on "applying the simple two-sector thesis" "Wiedersprüche im Modernisierungsprozess Deutschlands," in Dirk Stegmann, et al. eds., *Industrielle Gesellschaft und Politisches System. Beiträge zur politischen Sozialgeschichte* (Bonn, 1978), 230 ff. Peter Hayes's short and forceful rejection of "the chimera of an industrial two-party system" still awaits equally forceful documentation, "Industrial Factionalism in Modern German History," *CEH* 24, no. 2 (1991), 131. Using the debates over German trade policies in Eastern Europe as one lengthy test case for the two-sector model reveals that we do not yet have a more fruitful approach for analyzing the heated wranglings generated by Eastern trade issues between 1890 and 1930.

21. A major industrial figure in this effort was the glass industrialist Richard von Vopelius, Hentschel, *Wirtschaft und Wirtschaftspolitik*, 187; Stegmann, *Erben Bismarcks*, 25, 71 ff.; Pühle, *Agrarische Interessenpolitik*, 155 ff.

22. Press reports in BA R 2/1695 and 1696; Boettinger's statement of May 1897 in Bueck, *Centralverband*, vol. 1, 515.

23. The Tariff Council continued in existence through 1895, participating in the treaty negotiations with Portugal and Japan.

24. H.A. Bueck, *Centralverband*, vol. 1, 509-10. Bueck, along with the chairman of the Central Association, Theodor Hassler, and second Vice-chairman, Emil Russel (Disconto-Gesellschaft), were members of both the Central Association's direktorium and the Governing Committee of the German Chamber of Commerce.

25. Bueck, *Centralverband*, vol. 1, 510 ff. This preceded the Chamber of Commerce committee meeting of 16 November 1896 which Stegmann uses as the beginning of chamber preoccupation with this issues, *Erben Bismarcks*, 69.

26. The individual chambers were not "free" associations, but rather were chartered and regulated by law. In Prussia, for example, by the 1870 Law on Chambers of Commerce (Gesetz über die Handelskammern), see Klara van Eyll, "Berufsständische Selbstverwaltung," in *Deutsche Verwaltungsgeschichte*, vol. 3, 71-84 and the literature cited there.

27. Bueck, *Centralverband*, vol. 1, 510.

28. H.A. Bueck, *Centralverband*, vol. 1, 520. In 1879 the German tariff contained two commodity classifications for chemical products with a total of eleven individual tariff rates; the revised tariff of 1902 contained 123 commodity classifications with 140 individual rates, Karl Dammann, "Zollpolitik und Chemische Industrie," 682, Bayer-Archiv Leverkusen 62/22.3 For a portrait of the subsequently immensely influential Posadowsky, see the contribution by Karl Erich Born in *Männer der deutschen Verwaltung* (Köln, 1963), 211-28; Martin Schmidt, *Graf Posadowsky. Staatssekretär des Reichsschatzamtes und des Reichsamtes des Innern 1893-1907* (Halle, 1935); his speeches collected in Johannes Penzler, ed., *Graf Posadowsky als Finanz-, Sozial, und Handelspolitiker*, 3 vols. (Leipzig, 1907).

29. Bueck, *Centralverband*, vol. 1, 512-13.

30. Bueck, *Centralverband*, vol. 1, 523-24, 527. A final attempt by the private sector to build some type of Central Office failed when the industrial Centralverband rejected a July 1897 initiative by the German Agricultural Council for these two organizations to hold preliminary discussions. The Centralverband would not proceed without the participation of the German Chamber of Commerce, a condition the Agricultural Council rejected. Bueck, *Centralverband*, vol. 1, 528 ff.; *Deutsche Volkswirtschaftliche Correspondenz*, 30 July 1897 as cited in Stegmann, *Erben Bismarcks*, 70 note 65.

31. Bueck, *Centralverband*, vol. 1, 527-28 passim.

32. On the consequential changes in the Reich offices and Prussian ministries that left Miquel the dominant force in domestic political strategy 1897-1901, see Lamar Cecil, *Wilhelm II*, 257 ff.; Roehl, *Germany Without Bismarck*, 229 ff.; on Miquel see Siegfried Heincke in *Männer der deutschen Verwaltung*, 167-80.

33. Indeed, the kaiser's "Bielefeld speech" of 18 June 1897 and Miquel's own speeches on 15 July in Solingen and on 23 July in the Prussian House of Deputies announcing its new, conservative Sammlungspolitik, came just as the Centralverband provided the government with an opportunity to begin realizing this political strategy.

34. Bueck, *Centralverband*, vol. 1, 527. In light of this evidence, Volker Hentschel's assertion that origins of the initiative for the consultative body "cannot be exactly determined" should be dismissed; Hentschel, *Wirtschaft und Wirtschaftspolitik im wilhelmischen Deutschland. Organisierter Kapitalismus und Interventionsstaat* (Stuttgart, 1978), 184.

35. Roehl has used documents previously located in the Zentrales Staatsarchiv Merseburg of the GDR and now in the Geheimes Staatsarchiv Preussischer Kulturbesitz, Berlin-Dahlem on the Ministry of State meetings to explain the government's motives in agreeing to Bueck's plan, *Germany Without Bismarck*, 246 ff.

36. In January 1896 Posadowsky, then still state secretary in the Reich Treasury Office, told Chancellor Hohenlohe that after the Caprivi treaties expired, the government must rewrite the tariff with higher agricultural duties and that "until then the agrarians would have to be patient," Hohenlohe, *Denkwürdikeiten der Reichskanzlerzeit*, 3 vols. (Stuttgart/Berlin, 1931), vol. 3, 156, cited in Stegmann, *Erben Bismarcks*, 64.

37. Bueck, *Centralverband*, vol. 1, 527-28; Roehl, *Germany Without Bismarck*, 246, footnote 3; Schmidt, *Graf Posadowsky*, 64-65.

38. Bueck, *Centralverband*, vol. 1, 533-34; Roehl, *Germany Without Bismarck*, 246, footnote 3; Schmidt, *Graf Posadowsky*, 64-65.

39. Chancellor Hohenlohe announced the formation of this "Wirtschaftlicher Ausschuss beim Reichsamt des Inneren" on 15 November 1897; its activities are recorded in detail in BA R 2/10344. On government relations with the committee, BA R2/24449-24462 and Posadowsky's explanation of the Economic Committee to the Reichstag on 14 December 1897, *Sten Ber.* 1897/98, reprinted in Penzler, *Graf Posadowsky*, vol. 1, 558-565. Valuable secondary studies that investigate its work are Stegmann, *Erben Bismarcks*, 70 ff.; Hentschel, *Wirtschaft und Wirtschaftspolitik*, 184 ff.

40. These files are wonderfully informative of the way in which individual tariff questions created divisions and coalitions in the business community, e.g. between spinners and weavers in the textile industries, BA R 2/10344. Posadowsky insisted to Thielmann, now in the Reich Treasury Office, that the information from these hearings be carefully considered when deliberating on the form of the tariff, 8 March 1899, BA R2/24449.

41. Barkin, *The Controversy over German Industrialization*, 237.

42. Posadowsky's comments to Thielmann on the report (Gutachten) issued by the Economic Committee, 13 July 1900, BA R2/24458.

43. Director Jencke's speech to the governing committee of the Central Association of German Industrialists from 18 October 1897 in Bueck, *Centralverband*, vol. 1, 539-41. Bueck had argued in 1897 that "the Central Office will be able to complete its important tasks only if its stands in close contact with the competent authorities, and for this the continual participation by these authorities is an absolute precondition," ibid., 527.

44. Bernhard von Bülow, *Memoirs of Prince von Bülow*, vol. 1, 441-42. Lerman on Bülow's active role in shaping the tariff, *The Chancellor as Courtier*, 51 ff., 76.

45. Bülow's decision apparently on 27 October 1900, Thielmann to Bülow from 4 April 1901, BA R2/24461; Adolf Wermuth (director of the new Commercial Affairs Department of Interior Office), *Ein Beamtenleben* (Berlin, 1922), 223; Lerman, *Chancellor as Courtier*, 52 and her statement that Bülow had decided on a "middle of the road tariff policy" in May 1901, 72. The double tariff for grain had been an a demand of the German Agricultural Council since February 1898, Peter Christian Witt, *Die Finanzpolitik des deutschen Reiches von 1903 bis 1913. Eine Studie zur Innenpolitik des Wilheminischen Deutschland* (Hamburg, 1970), 66. By 1901, the "agrarian-conservative" members of the Reichstag had raised this demand "to an issue of the first order," Treasury Office report to Bülow, 4 April 1901, BA R2/24461. The Direktorium of the Centralverband had been unable to agree on a position on this issue at its meeting on 19 September 1900, but spoke out against the minimum rates for grain on 9 August 1901 in a resolution approved by the full association on 1 October, Bueck, *Centralverband*, vol. 1, 570, 586. Other leading industrial and commercial groups also spoke out against minimum agricultural rates: the Union of German Industrialists on 16 September 1901, the Union of German Iron and Steel Industrialists, though not as forcefully as Bueck had urged, on 3 October 1901, Ullmann, *Bund der Industriellen*, 188 ff.; Klein, "Geschichte des VdESI," BA R13I/12, Bl. 205.

46. Minutes of the March Berathungen in BA R 2/24466. Paul von Körner, director of the Foreign Office's Commercial Affairs Department, and members of the Treasury Office consistently argued against the highly protectionist measures in the tariff (i.e., against double tariff minimum rates for agriculture and high levels of agricultural and industrial protection). The Prussian Trade Ministry, with the Theodor Möller replacing Ludwig Brefeld in 1901, occupied a neutral middle position. On the protectionist side in both issues sat the Reich Interior Office (Posadowsky), the Prussian Agricultural Ministry (Hammerstein, succeeded by Victor von Podbielski), and the Prussian Finance Ministry (Miquel, succeeded by Georg von Rheinbaben), BA R2/24461-24466.

47. Virtually all of German industry was willing to concede some upward revision of agricultural tariffs, but opinions differed widely as to what a necessary, fair or tolerable revision meant in real terms, Stegmann, *Erben Bismarcks*, 65; Hentschel, *Wirtschaft und Wirtschaftspolitik*, 185 ff.

48. Within the exporters' camp, opinions on this subject diverged. The chemical industry felt that the minimum tariff for agricultural goods "endangered" or "made impossible the conclusion of trade treaties," resolution of the Association for Safeguarding the Interests of the Chemical Industry in Germany, 19 September 1901, cited in Dammann, "Zollpolitik und Chemische Industrie," 684, Bayer-Archiv Leverkusen 62/22.3. At the same time, the Union of German Industrialists felt that "the possibility of concluding long term trade treaties is by no means precluded by the published draft of the tariff," *Jahrbuch des Handelsvertragsvereins* (1901), 104, cited in Hentschel, *Wirtschaft und Wirtschaftspolitik*, 188, note 50; Ullmann, *Bund der Industriellen*, 188 ff.

49. On this controversy, see Stegmann, *Erben Bismarcks*, 77 ff.; Hentschel, *Wirtschaft und Wirtschaftspolitik*, 186 ff.; Ullmann, *Bund der Industriellen*, 175 ff.; private-sector petitions in BA R2/24459; *Jahresbericht der Handelskammer zu Hamburg*, 1900, 18; 1901, 18. The Foreign Office and Treasury Office were strongly in favor of retaining long-term tariff treaties with MFN clauses, Bülow to Thielmann and Posadowsky, 5 July 1900, BA R2/24458.

50. Bueck's report on commercial policy at the executive board meeting of the Union of Iron and Steel Industrialists, 29 September 1903, Klein, "Geschichte des Vereins deutscher Eisen-und Stahlindustrieller 1874-1934," BA R 13 I/12, Bl. 215.

51. BA R2/1697-1699.

52. Bueck's report on commercial policy at the executive board meeting of the Union of Iron and Steel Industrialists, 29 September 1903, Klein, "Geschichte des VdESI," BA R 13 I/12, Bl. 215-216.

53. The Treasury Office files on the negotiations with Russia contain petitions and requests from the electrical industry, brown coal industry, chemical industry, the Central Association, and numerous Chambers of Commerce, BA R 2/1696-1700; five petitions from the Union of Iron and Steel Industrialists cited in Klein, "Geschichte des VdESI," BA R13I/12, Bl. 215.

54. On the significance of the Reichstag tariff vote for the future of Wilhelmine politics see Eckart Kehr, *Schlachtflottenbau und Parteipolitik. Versuch eines Querschnitts durch die innenpolitischen, sozialen, und ideologischen Voraussetzungen des deutschen Imperialismus* (Berlin, 1930); Stürmer, *Erben Bismarcks*, 80 ff.; Volker Berghahn, "Flottenrüstung und Machtgefüge," in Stürmer, ed., *Das Kaiserliche Deutschland*, 378-96. More skeptical are Pühle, *Agrarische Interessenpolitik*, 240 ff.; Geoff Eley, "Sammlungspolitik, Social Imperialism, and the Navy Law of 1898," *Militärgeschichtliche Mitteilungen* 15 (1974); Volker Hentschel, *Wirtschaft und Wirtschaftspolitik*, 184; Lerman, *The Chancellor as Courtier*, 75 ff.

55. Bülow's margin comments from 17 March 1903 on a report from Ambassador Friedrich Alvensleben, *Grosse Politik*, vol. 18, Nr. 5404. On the day of his appoint-

ment as Chancellor, Bülow had given the kaiser "the assurance that, as I confidently hoped, even if we did increase agricultural duties, we should be able to conclude advantageous commercial treaties with Russia, Austria, Rumania ..." Hearing of this "assurance," Herman von Lucanus (chief of the kaiser's Civil Cabinet) told Bülow to "above all, see to it that we conclude commercial treaties." Bernhard von Bülow, *Memoirs of Prince von Bülow*, vol. 1, 442-43. Lerman also mentions "Bülow's particular stake in securing the successful renegotiation of the treaties ...," *Chancellor as Courtier*, 111.

56. The German imperial consul in St. Petersburg (Maron) to the Foreign Office, 17 February 1894, BA R2/1695. For an introduction to the politics of the Russian press see Christoph Schmidt, *Russische Presse und Deutsches Reich 1905-1914* (Köln/Wien, 1988), 12-38.

57. The German imperial consul in St. Petersburg (Maron) to the Foreign Office, 4 December 1894, BA R 2/1695.

58. As reprinted in the *Münchener Allgemeine Zeitung*, 29 July 1897, BA R 2/1696.

59. Ambassador Alvensleben to the Foreign Office, 1 August 1901, BA R 2/1696; the General Consulate in Warsaw (Haxthausen) to the Foreign Office, 18 December 1902, BA R 2/1697.

60. Alvensleben to Bülow, 25 March 1903, BA R 2/1698. On Russian political struggles over tariffs on agricultural machinery see Carl Allen Goldberg, *The Association of Trade and Industry 1906-1917: The Successes and Failures of Russia's Organized Businessmen* (Ann Arbor, 1974) 286 ff.

61. The Russians had raised duties on a number of goods that were important German exports, such as chemicals, metalwares, and machinery. The increases on ten different categories of machinery, for example, ranged from 20 percent to 120 percent over the rates contained in the 1894 treaty.

62. The message went via an unnamed "third party," Memorandum by the Under State Secretary in the Foreign Office (Otto von Mühlberg), 18 February 1902, *Grosse Politik*, vol. 18, Nr. 5404, note ***.

63. *Sten. Ber.* 1900/1903, III, 14 Dec. 1902, 7154-64.

64. Summary of the Russian note, Foreign Office to the Treasury Office, 27 June 1903 and Meuschel's marginal comments, BA R 2/1699.

65. The Prussian Agriculture Ministry's member of the delegation, Wolfgang Kapp (the putschist of 1920!), still insisted that Germany could not offer anything below 6 marks for wheat and 5.50 marks for rye, Körner to Bülow, 7 August 1903 and 16 August 1903, BA R 2/1699.

66. Körner to Bülow, 28 August 1903, BA R 2/1699.

67. Foreign Office and Treasury Office notes from the interministerial meeting held in the Foreign Office on 2 November 1903, BA R 2/1700.

68. Bülow's questions from 26 October and the Treasury Office's replies, BA R 2/1700.

69. Reports from the counsel in St. Petersburg and the consulate in Moscow, 4 November and 14 November 1903, BA R 2/1701.

70. Bülow to Posadowsky and Thielmann, 15 July (composed at the "end of May") 1900, BA R2/24458. Körner had renewed these Foreign Office objections in the Kommissarische Berathungen of March 1901, submitting a report warning the government that the existence of "minimum" rates would put Germany in an impossible position when negotiating with Russia. The Foreign Office claimed that it was "urgently required that the possibility of making a meaningful concession [on Russian rye] be held open," BA R 2/24466.

71. Bueck's warning was expressed at the general assembly of the Union of German Iron and Steel Industrialists, 3 October 1901, Klein, "Geschichte," BA R 13 I/12.

72. On the origins of the war see, Andrew Malozemoff, *Russian Far Eastern Policy 1881-1904* (New York, 1958); Ian Hill Nish, *The Origins of the Russo-Japanese War* (London and New York, 1985). On the military effort see Great Britain, Committee of Imperial Defense, *Official History of the Russo-Japanese War* (London, 1910-1920); Ogawa Gotaro, *Expenditures of the Russo-Japanese War* (New York, 1923); R.M. Connaughton, *The War of the Rising Sun and the Tumbling Bear: A Military History of the Russo-Japanese War 1904-05* (London and New York, 1988). A good overall study is J.N. Westwood, *Russia against Japan: A New Look at the Russo-Japanese War* (Albany, NY, 1986).

73. *Grosse Politik*, vol. 19, Nrs. 5943 and 5931; *Grosse Politik*, vol. 19, Nr. 6028, note *; Walter Goetz, *Briefe Wilhelms II an den Zaren 1894-1914* (Berlin, 1920); Issac Don Levine, *Letters from the Kaiser to the Czar* (New York, 1920).

74. Cited in Alfred Klein, "Der Einfluss des Grafen Witte auf die deutsch-russischen Beziehungen" (Ph.D. diss., Münster, 1932), 17; Serge Witte, *Memoirs of Count Witte* (Garden City, NY, 1921), 413.

75. The idea of connecting German loans to Russian trade concessions had been aired before. As a condition for facilitating the 390 million mark loan the Russians were negotiating with the German banking house of Mendelssohn in 1902, Bülow and Alvensleben had considered requiring the Russians to give written assurances that they would agree to the 5.00/5.50 grain rates. The plan was abandoned when German "financial circles" told the chancellor that any conditions attached to a German loan would drive the Russians to the ready French market, *Grosse Politik*, vol. 18, Nrs. 5404-5407.

76. *Grosse Politik*, Nr. 6034, note *; Goetz, *Briefe Wilhelms II and den Zaren*, 339; see also Levine, *Letters from the Kaiser to the Czar*. Bülow claimed that the kaiser's letter was preceded by a feeler sent to Witte through the German banker Ernst Mendelssohn. Bülow, *Memoirs*, vol. 2, 46.

77. Witte, *Memoirs*, 413; Nicholas II to Wilhelm II from 1 June 1904, *Grosse Politik*, vol. 19, Nr. 6034.

78. The consequences of Witte's personal position were pointed out to Bülow by the state secretary in the Foreign Office, Oswald von Richthofen, in early July 1904, *Grosse Politik*, vol. 19, Nr 6042.

79. Bülow's arrangements for the Norderney meetings reveal his determination to use this occasion to obtain the desired trade treaty. In this final phase of negotiations Bülow took no chances on an outside disruption; private sector representatives were ignored, the kaiser was tricked into staying away, and the Prussian ministers were bluntly excluded from the sessions, Lerman, *Chancellor as Courtier*, 92, 105.

80. Witte, *Memoirs*, 414; Bülow to Wilhelm II from 15 July 1904, *Grosse Politik*, vol. 19, Nr. 6043.

81. The agreement, in the form of a supplementary treaty to the treaty of 1894, was signed in Berlin on 28 July 1904; it is available as Nr. 543 in *Sten. Ber.* 1903/05, Anlageband VI and VIa. Internal discussion of the German negotiating position in BA R 2/1699 and 1700.

82. The following discussion is based on data contained in *Statistik des deutschen Reiches*, N.F. Bd. 271, V, 1 ff. as well as the sources cited earlier.

83. There is no definitive data on the value of German direct investment in Russia prior to 1914. Both the Leo Pasvolsky/Harold Moulton study, *Russian Debts and Russian Reconstruction* (New York, 1924), 21-22, 181-82 and Lyashchenko's *History of the National Economy of Russia*, 715-16 rely on the data complied by P.V. Ol' in his work on foreign capital in Russia, *Inostrannye Kapitaly v Rossii* (Petrograd, 1922). Ol' puts German direct investment in the private enterprises of Russia at 953.6 million marks or 19.7 percent of the total foreign investment. M.W. Shoe-

maker has recently offered an estimate of 1,030 million marks, *Russo-German Economic Relations 1850-1914* (Ph.D. diss., Syracuse University, 1981) cited in Brigitte Lohr, *Die "Zukunft Russlands": Perspektiven russischer Wirtschaftsentwicklung und deutsch-russische Wirtschaftsbeziehungen vor dem Ersten Weltkrieg* (Wiesbaden, 1985), 128. At roughly 1,000 million marks, German investment for the entire prewar period was just one-fifth the value of German exports to Russia under the second treaty 1905-1913 (4,816 million). On the difficulties in determining the value of German investment see, Bernd Bonwetsch, "Das ausländische Kapital im Russland. Bemerkungen zum Forschungsstand," *Jahrbücher für die Geschichte Osteuropas* 22 (1974), 412 ff.; Lohr, *Zukunft Russlands,* 128 ff.

84. Calculated from *Statistik des deutschen Reiches,* N.F. Bd. 271, V, 1; *Statistisches Jahrbuch für das deutsche Reich* 35 (1914), 252.

85. Kirchner cites profit rates of 5 percent to 42 percent depending on the industry, *Deutsche Industrie und die Industrialisierung Russlands,* 341-42 (St. Katherinen, 1986). Russian sales of pharmaceutical giant Knoll AG had risen to one-third of all Knoll's foreign sales, equal to half the turnover in Germany itself. Bayer built the "largest foreign operation in the German dyestuffs industry," with 414 employees in Russia, Knoll, *100 Jahre im Dienst der Gesundheit 1886-1986,* 50; *Bayer Review,* 3/1988, 14.

86. Focusing on secondary issue of German industrial investment and operations in Russia and on nontariff barriers to German sales there, Walther Kirchner has argued for the relative unimportance of tariffs in the totality of German-Russian economic relations, "Russian Tariffs and Foreign Industries before 1914: The German Entrepreneur's Perspective," *JEH* 41 (1981), 361-79; *Die Deutsche Industrie und die Industrialisierung Russlands 1815-1914.* This work should be approached with extreme caution. Kirchner overestimates the importance of investment relative to trade, ignores the intense political lobbying on tariff questions conducted by the German interest groups (and the fine body of historical work that has been assembled on that question), and at several points he contradicts himself by citing German entrepreneurs' concerns with tariff questions. Further, the book contains numerous glaring factual errors that bear directly on the larger argument. For example, in claiming on 310, note 10, that the declines in German exports to Russia "in the years 1883-1887 did not follow tariff increases," he appears fully unaware of the roughly 20 percent Russian tariff increase of 1885!

87. Lohr, *Zukunft Russlands,* 157 ff.; Bernd Bonwetsch, "Handelspolitik und Industrialisierung. Zur aussenwirtschaftliche Abhängigkeit Russlands," in Dietrich Geyer, ed., *Wirtschaft und Gesellschaft im vorrevolutionären Russland* (Köln, 1975), 289 ff. Director Ewald Hilger made the same point to the VdESI's Trade Policy Committee, BA R131/146.

88. The "implantation of advanced techniques" and use of "advanced technology" was one of the key aspects of the "important and beneficial role" that foreign participants played in Russian industrialization, John McKay, *Pioneers for Profit. Foreign Entrepreneurship and Russian Industrialization 1885-1913* (Chicago, 1970), 379, 381 ff., an assessment grudgingly accepted by Olga Crisp in "Foreign Entrepreneurship and Russian Industry," reprinted in Crisp, *Studies in the Russian Economy before 1914* (London, 1976), 189-96.

89. Calculated from Lyashchenko, *History of the National Economy of Russia,* 718.

90. Although they did accomplish their primary purpose – bolstering domestic grain prices in Germany. Rye prices averaged 173 marks/ton 1905 to 1912 or 25 percent above the 1894 to 1898 average of 131 marks. Wheat at 211 marks/ton 1905 to 1912 was 24 percent above the 1894 to 1898 average of 162 marks, *Statistisches Jahrbuch für das deutsche Reich,* 26 (1905), 210; 35 (1914), 306. German consumers' determination to buy Russian wheat despite the increased costs brought on by a

tariff of 23 percent ad valorem also supports the argument that Russian industrialists would have continued to buy the German industrial equipment they urgently desired even in the face of cost increases brought on by the Russian tariff.

91. Timiriazev stated openly that "it can not be in our interest to exchange the German market for other markets," German Embassy in Moscow (Friedrich Pourtalès) to Bethmann-Hollweg, 8 March 1914, BA Potsdam, R 901/6274, Bl. 47.

92. Following in the footsteps of Paul Gregory, Arcadius Kahan, and James Simms, Heinz-Dietrich Löwe has recently offered a study describing the substantial improvement in the living standards of the Russian peasantry precisely during the time when grain imports to Germany began on a truly massive scale, *Die Lage der Bauren in Russland 1880-1905: Wirtschaftliche und soziale Veränderungen in der ländlichen Gesellschaft des Zarenreiches* (St. Katherinen, 1987). For a statistical discussion of foreign demand factors in raising grain prices in Russia see B.N. Mironov, *Khlebnye tseny v Rossii za dva stoletiia (XVIII-XIX vv.)* (Leningrad, 1985).

93. German consulate in Moscow (Kollhaas) to Bethmann-Hollweg, 12 March 1912, BA R 2/1702.

94. For an introduction to the problems of evaluating Russian economic development before the revolution see the summary discussion in Paul R. Gregory and Robert C. Stuart, *Soviet Economic Structure and Performance*, 2nd ed. (New York, 1981), 15-36 and the literature cited there.

95. German consulate in St. Petersburg (Trautmann) to Bethmann-Hollweg, 15 August 1911, BA R 2/1702.

96. The "yoke of German trade" was frequently used during the war to rally anti-German sentiments in Russia, Handelsvertragsverein to Bethmann-Hollweg, 29 September 1915, BA Potsdam, R 901/6275, Bl. 235.

97. Cited in Schmidt, *Russische Presse und Deutsches Reich 1905-1914*. Schmidt characterizes this view as "widespread" in Russia, 108.

98. Amberger, *Geschichte der Behördenorganisation Russlands*, 204 ff., 227 ff. In his 1908 book, "Our Economic Situation and the Tasks of the Future," the head of the Industrial Section of the Ministry for trade and industry, V.P. Litvinov-Falinsksy, discussed at some length the unfavorable outcome of the 1904 negotiations, Goldberg, *The Association of Trade and Industry 1906-1917*, 290.

99. German consulate in Moscow (Kollhaas) to Bethmann-Hollweg, 12 March 1912, BA R 2/1702.

100. Witte's comment cited in Alfred Klein, *Einfluss Witte*, 18; Witte, *Memoirs* 72.

101. Report from the consulate in St. Petersburg to the Bethmann-Hollweg, 15 August 1911, BA R 2/1702. On Russian industrial interests and the politics of the Russian tariff see, Goldberg, *The Association of Trade and Industry 1906-1917*, 279 ff. For readers of Russian, both Goldberg's work and the earlier study by Ruth Roosa, "The Association of Industry and Trade 1906-1914: An Examination of the Economic Views of Organized Industrialists in Pre-revolutionary Russia," (Ph.D. diss., Columbia University, 1967) have been supplemented by L.E. Shepelev, *Tsarizm i burzhuaziia v 1904-1914 gg. Problemy torgovo-promyshlennoi politiki* (Leningrad, 1987) and Susan P. McCaffray, *The Politics of Industrialization in Tsarist Russia. The Association of Southern Coal and Steel Producers 1874-1914* (DeKalb, Ill., 1996).

102. Consulate in St. Petersburg (Biermann) to the chancellor on Russian measures proposed to counter subsidized German rye exports, 04 March 1912, BA R 2/1702.

103. The trade attaché at the German consulate in St. Petersburg (Wossidlo) to Chancellor Bethmann-Hollweg, 23 September 1912; report from the consulate in St. Petersburg (Biermann) to the chancellor, 15 March 1912, BA R 2/1702.

104. Reports from the German consulate in St. Petersburg to the chancellor, 13 March 1912 and 15 August 1911, BA R 2/1702.

105. Cited in Schmidt, *Russische Presse*, 116, 118.
106. Cited in Barkin, *The Controversy over German Industrialization*, 249.
107. Interior Office to the Treasury Office, 1 February and 27 March 1912, BA R2/1702. Russian administrative restrictions on German railroad equipment for private lines in Russia also aroused the German government. The Russians had long been notorious for their use of what today we would call "nontariff barriers" (NTBs) to trade.
108. *Sten. Ber.*, vol. 292, 6637 ff. Delbruck's speech is also analyzed by Fischer, *War of Illusions*, 362 ff.
109. The term Pressfehde is Klaus Wernecke's, *Der Wille zur Weltgeltung. Aussenpolitik und Öffentlichket im Kaiserreich am Vorabend des Ersten Weltkrieges* (Dusseldorf, 1970), 268 ff.
110. On all these developments, Wernecke, *Wille zur Weltgeltung*, 268 ff. and Fritz Fischer, *War of Illusions. German Policies from 1911 to 1914* (New York, 1975), 362 ff.
111. Barkin, *The Controversy over German Industrialization*, 249; Kehr, "Englandhass und Weltpolitik," in *Primat der Innenpolitik* (Berlin, 1965), 171.
112. In addition to the previously cited works by Fischer and Wernecke, see also Volker Berghahn, *Germany and the Approach of War in 1914* (New York, 1973).
113. In 1913 German exports to Russia were 1,011 million marks, German exports to "Persia" were less than 5 million. Fischer's earlier book, *Griff nach der Weltmacht* (Dusseldorf, 1961) focused on German-Russian commercial rivalry in non-European territories and third markets and did not consider extensively the flow of trade between the two great powers themselves as a possible source of tension, 23-26.
114. The classic and still unsurpassed account of Brest-Litovsk is John Wheeler-Bennett, *The Forgotten Peace: Brest Litovsk* (London, 1938). Also important is Fischer's discussion in *Griff nach der Weltmacht*, chapter 18.
115. Stein to the Treasury Office, 14 January 1918; Stein memorandum on "State of Organization Regarding Resumption of Trade Relations with Russia," 26 January 1918, both in BA R 2/1703. Revealingly, the two largest bureaucratic suppliers of staff for this group were the War Ministry (47 persons) and the Supreme Command (68 persons).
116. Minutes of the Streng geheim interministerial meetings of 4-5 December 1917 concerning "Terms of the German-Russian Peace Treaty," BA R 2/1703. Proposed German modifications centered on reducing or eliminating Russian export tariffs on minerals and ores and expanding the possibilities for transit trade through Russian territory.
117. Minutes of the interministerial discussions held in the German Foreign Office, 27 and 28 January, 1918, BA R 2/1703.
118. On the economic aspects of German policy toward Russia 1917-1918 see Hartmut Pogge von Strandmann, "Grossindustrie und Rapallopolitik," *HZ* 222 (1976), 265-341, in particular 272 ff.; Winfried Baumgart, *Deutsche Ostpolitik 1918. Von Brest-litovsk bis zum Ende des Weltkrieges* (München, 1966).
119. Siegfried Mielke, *Der Hansa-Bund für Gewerbe, Handel, und Industrie 1909-1914* (Göttingen, 1976), 34 ff., 146, 182; Stegmann, *Erben Bismarcks*, 176 ff.
120. Stegmann, *Erben Bismarcks*, 236 ff.; 328 ff.
121. Fifty years ago Albert Hirschmann noted how "frequently the adoption of certain economic policies leading to greater power for a given nation is possible only if there already exists an initial power disequilibrium in favor of that nation," *National Power and the Structure of Foreign Trade* (Berkeley and Los Angeles, 1945), 13.

Chapter Three

STRUCTURES OF GERMAN TRADE
POLICY IN THE WEIMAR REPUBLIC

Economic Warfare after 1918: The Versailles Framework

*T*he intensity and duration of the great conflict of 1914 to 1918 gave the combatants on both sides unprecedented opportunities to pursue various strategies of economic warfare.[1] Economic warfare began almost immediately in 1914 as both sides adopted commercial strategies to support of their battlefield efforts against the enemy. Initial British and German measures – export controls by both sides, the Royal Navy's restricted blockade, and early German guidelines for submarine commanders – all fell loosely within the bounds of international agreement as embodied in the Declarations of Paris (1856) and London (1909). Yet international institutions in this field were notoriously weak. The British Parliament had never ratified the London declaration and belligerents on both sides had flouted its provisions during the Balkan wars of 1912 to 1913. By the early spring of 1915, practices by both Entente and Central powers exceeded those allowed under existing international law. In February the Germans initiated their first, brief round of unrestricted submarine warfare.[2] The Allies responded with an unrestricted blockade of Germany, a tighter definition of "German origin" (25 percent of a commodity's content), an extended concept of "continuous voyage," and increased pressure on the Reich's neutral neighbors.[3]

Beyond winning the war, both sides were already attempting to win the peace by inflicting long-term economic damage on the opponent.

Notes for this chapter begin on page 137.

The Reich sought to secure future overseas markets for advanced German exports by banning the export of machines and machine parts that could be used to build competing industries abroad. The British blacklist system clearly "had the secondary aim of causing lasting damage to German business interests overseas."[4] From these actions it was only a small step to the notion that the some aspects of economic and commercial warfare would be continued even after the military conflict had been concluded. The May 1917 Paris Economic Conference of the Allied powers provided an ominous preview of how the Entente planned to use its military victory to secure long-term commercial advantages over Germany. Two years later, the Treaty of Versailles imposed many of these economic penalties on Germany.

Virtually every aspect of the settlement with Germany – the territorial revisions, the material confiscations and reparations, and the explicit commercial restrictions – can be seen as a continuation of economic warfare after 1918. One did not have to be a German nationalist to understand Versailles as "the continuation of economic warfare with other means."[5] Beyond the size of the territorial and population losses (13 percent and 10 percent of the respective totals), the new borders destroyed the economic structure of the Reich as it had developed from 1871 to 1918. Without these territories, Germany lost 15 percent of its arable land, 12 percent of livestock, 19 percent of iron and steel production ability, 68 percent of zinc reserves, 75 percent of iron ore reserves, and 26 percent of hard coal reserves.These adjustments came to a Germany already exhausted by the struggle of 1914 to 1918. In the course of the war and defeat, Germany had consumed almost three-quarters of its property and investments abroad. As part of the Versailles treaty, Germany lost all of its colonies and 90 percent of its merchant fleet. Even in the conduct of its postwar trade and tariff policy, Germany was severely limited by Part X (Economic Clauses) of the Treaty of Versailles. Articles 264 to 267 enforced a one-sided extension of MFN status by Germany to the "Allied and associated powers" (including Poland and Czechoslovakia) for a five-year period through 10 January 1925. Article 269 imposed a six-month (i.e., until 10 July 1920) rollback and freeze for all German tariff rates on Allied goods at "the most advantageous rates" in effect on 31 July 1914. That tariff reduction was extended to thirty-six months for basic agricultural goods, lumber, and some textiles. Article 270 empowered the victors to apply a "special customs regime" to Germany for five years. In addition, French and Polish exports to Germany enjoyed special benefits. Article 268(b) allowed Polish exports from former German territories to enter Germany duty-free for three years.[6]

Even after the treaty had been signed in June 1919 and the "final" amount of reparations had been set in April 1921, the Allies continued to impose a wide variety of commercial penalties as means of discriminating against Germany. In the economic field especially, it was an "illusion ... to equate the cessation of fighting with the restoration of peace."[7] The British maintained their blockade until June 1919 and even thereafter German ships were excluded from the ports of some countries, such as Australia. In January 1921 the British agreed to a French plan calling for the Germany to pay 26 percent of its export proceeds over the next forty-two years as part of reparations. The Allies' London Ultimatum forced the Germans to begin payment on these terms. As part of the Rhineland occupation, the Allies impounded the customs revenues of the occupied territories in the spring of 1921. High tariffs directed against (commercially defenseless) Germany and outright bans on imports of German coal and some chemical products remained part of Allied policy through 1924.

The tremendous costs of the war and the peace settlement placed unbearable new burdens on German trade and tariff policy.[8] In the diminished Reich, "the fate of German economic life would in the future depend more than ever on foreign trade" as most Germans grudgingly realized and Economics Minister Edward Hamm stated in 1924.[9] The new Germany required a dramatic increase in exports to compensate for the loss of income from its foreign holdings and its merchant fleet, now either consumed or confiscated. In the decade before 1914 these assets had generated an invisible surplus of 2.1 billion marks annually, which had covered the Reich's merchandise trade deficit. After 1919 Germany required a positive trade balance not only to support its overall payments balance but also to generate the payments for reparations, set in April 1921 at 132 billion gold marks. As Hamm explained in 1924, "to meet these heavy obligations Germany has at present nothing but the value of her exports."[10] At the same time, imports would have to increase. The loss of valuable agricultural areas meant greater German dependence on imported food. The detachment of major iron and coal deposits dramatically weakened the position of German heavy industry in the German domestic market vis-à-vis European competitors.

Weimar policymakers faced the task of finding a commercial strategy that could promote export growth, accommodate increased imports, and protect the remaining domestic producers in agriculture and basic industries. In essence, the republic inherited an updated and sharpened version of the earlier tariff policy conflicts that had raged between primary producers and other German manufacturers and consumers – a conflict for which the imperial Reich had never found a genuine solution.

More troublesome still for the resolution of these issues was the transformation of the international economic environment in this period. The war destroyed Europe's old liberal, multilateral trade regime of long-term MFN treaties. After 1918, the legacy of combat and the rancors of peace worked against the re-creation of a smoothly functioning European international economy. For both material and political reasons, "international trade never regained its former momentum in the interwar years" and European trade growth in this period lagged far behind the impressive growth rates of 1880 to 1913.[11] Slow growth rates inspired protectionist policies that, in turn, made international trade negotiations more pointed and the conclusion of international agreements more difficult.[12]

The peace settlement's politicization of trade in the postwar world greatly exacerbated the economic difficulties of restoring Europe's prewar liberal trade regime. Across Europe from London to Moscow, and in Germany from the Ruhr to Upper Silesia, political and economic issues were now inextricably entangled. The under-secretary for commercial affairs in the new Reich Economics Ministry, Hans Posse, described the situation in Europe in 1924 as one in which "political questions hide behind economic facades" and vice versa. The war guilt, reparations, and commercial clauses of Versailles combined to produce a European mentality in which "economics was confused with ethics."[13] The intimate linkage between economic and political demands in Europe produced jumbled bundles of intractable international politico-economic problems. The prospects for untangling the most difficult international issues and resolving them in a step-by-step approach appeared hopeless.

Nowhere were Germany's economic and political problems more difficult to resolve than in Eastern Europe.[14] Here, the "war and pre-war events had left bitter memories in the minds of many nations, and they were now carried away by the longing for full national independence and for national aggrandizement and prestige."[15] As part of this longing, a spirit of economic nationalism directed against Berlin and Vienna gripped Eastern Europe. A number of countries that enjoyed substantial commercial benefits as a result of the Versailles settlement did not negotiate long-term trade agreements with Germany during this period. Instead of using the period 1920 to 1925 as an opportunity to trade an early renunciation of their special privileges for some German concession as the basis for a long-term treaty, these countries preferred to make full use of their advantages under the Versailles settlement. This caused trade problems to fester and German resentment to build, making treaty negotiations after 1925 much more difficult.[16]

Because of their low overall productivity, large agricultural sectors, and lack of domestic capital, most Eastern European states felt themselves vulnerable to external commercial and financial pressure. To offset this perceived vulnerability, almost all Eastern European governments adopted policies designed to increase their national economic independence from their neighbors, both large and small. With hard economic times and political uncertainty at home, each government felt obliged to ease domestic problems by wringing advantages from its trading partners. The ability to gain such advantages could be a form of legitimization for new governments. This thinking, which was often based more on nationalist emotions than on economic logic, exacerbated the already difficult material issues involved in trade negotiations in Eastern Europe. "Economic nationalism" and "the understandable but nevertheless irrational craving for state autarky" including "government fiscal, tariff, and investment policies" aggravated economic problems across the area.[17] East Europe states generally had higher tariffs and more numerous nontariff barriers to trade than their counterparts in Western Europe, North America, and other areas of the world. As a result, East European trade had difficulty regaining its prewar significance; as late as 1925 it had recovered only three-quarters of its 1913 level.[18]

Despite the many obvious limitations that the peace settlement imposed on German foreign policy, the new era of trade politicization did contain some advantages for the defeated Reich. In February 1919 Reich President Friedrich Ebert had lamented to German Foreign Minister Count Ulrich von Brockdorff-Rantzau that "actually at present [Germany] cannot pursue any foreign policy at all."[19] But Ebert was wrong. Politicized trade offered the Reich a way to use its still considerable economic potential for political gain. Even after the territorial reductions of the Versailles treaty, Germany possessed tremendous productive and export power and remained the largest consumer market in Europe. Politically outcast and militarily stripped, Germany naturally sought to employ its economic resources in the service of foreign policy. In the Economics Ministry, Under-Secretary Posse was blunt: "For a weakened state like Germany, which must, for all practical purposes, do without any military protection, the only remaining means of repelling unjust foreign interests is its trade policy."[20] A German émigré group from Russia understood the situation as early as 1919, noting that "under the pressure of the circumstances, our foreign policy can only be economic policy for the immediate future."[21]

The new rules of international trade – embodied in the Allies' treatment of Germany, in the extensive government economic controls in nearly every European country, and in the autarkic policies of new East European governments – allowed the use of commercial and financial weapons in the pursuit of political foreign policy goals. Equally important, the unprecedented degree of state economic regulation of foreign trade and exchange during the war provided postwar governments with the legal and administrative means to control and direct trade flows in accordance with other foreign policy objectives. Even in the relatively normal years of 1925 to 1929, many state economic controls did not disappear. In Germany, for example, imports and exports of coal remained subject to strict state controls. This newfound ability to control trade, which had been unthinkable before the war, made dramatic alterations of trade flows by postwar governments a realistic possibility.

These circumstances of politicized trade provided the ideal operating environment for Gustav Stresemann, German foreign minister from 1923 to 1929, who had long argued for an active integration of international economic and political concerns. As a product of the Saxon industrial environment, Stresemann was keenly aware of Germany's intensive and extensive trade connections. Stresemann had founded the Association of Saxon Industrialists in 1902 and attached his group to the export-oriented Union of Industrialists on the Reich level. In 1907 he entered the Reichstag as a moderate member of the National Liberals; ten years later he was chairman of his party's parliamentary delegation. In a truly visionary Reichstag speech on The World Economy and Foreign Policy given in 1910, Stresemann informed the government that "international policy today is primarily world economic policy." Sharpening traditional German business complaints, he criticized the aristocratic Foreign Office for divorcing "politics" from "economics" and went on to point out that the "consuming power" of Germany's sixty-million-strong domestic market could be "thrown onto the scales for our interests."[22]

As foreign minister and leader of the new German People's Party (DVP), Stresemann remained convinced that Germany could use its economic strength to advance its foreign policy interests. In 1927, at a meeting of the machine industry's interest group, which was closely connected to the DVP, Stresemann repeated his old idea that "other" European states depended on the German market for the sale of their goods. Always critical of a "useless Prestigepolitik," he understood how to use Germany's strengths in the new European system: "I believe that today any Foreign Minister must solve the task of making foreign policy by using world economic circumstances and the one area in which we are still a great power – our economic power."[23]

Yet the new use of trade and tariff treaties as foreign policy tools only further increased the difficulties of reaching a domestic consensus on the content of trade and tariff policy. In contrast to the prewar period, German trade agreements now had to perform double duty, producing political as well as economic concessions abroad. Even without these political burdens, imperial German governments had not been able to produce a coherent tariff and trade strategy since it had proved to be impossible to construct a common economic platform out of essentially incompatible material interests. For Weimar governments, the construction of an economically acceptable trade policy would complete only one-half of the job. It still remained for Stresemann and other German politicians to balance the nation's economic interests in trade with a variety of other foreign policy considerations – diplomatic, military, and ethnic. Ernst Trendelenburg, state secretary in the Economics Ministry from 1923 to 1932, explained in 1925 that German trade treaties had to "protect" three German interests simultaneously: "pure foreign policy, economic policy, and financial policy." The imperial era had left an ambiguous legacy of regarding the use of politicized trade as a foreign policy tool. Trendelenburg warned that the "greatest potential for friction" in mapping out a trade strategy lay in the conflict between "economic and foreign policy interests."[24] In this, he captured the essence of Weimar's future trade policy failures.

The burdens that the international system placed on German trade policy in the 1920s might have been overwhelming even under the best of domestic political circumstances. Unfortunately, the structure of domestic politics in Weimar seemed only to magnify the republic's international difficulties. The task of producing new trade agreements fell to a fractured regime that lacked the strength and authority to arbitrate between competing and conflicting economic groups. Precisely at the time when German governments most needed to secure trade treaties that could strengthen Germany's international economic and financial position, domestic strife about the economic costs of increased foreign trade paralyzed German trade policy and repeatedly prevented the republic from effectively employing what many thought could be its most effective international tool.

The Difficulties of Corporatist Trade Policy

Just as the war and peace settlement profoundly altered the international framework and climate for trade negotiations, so too, did the years 1914 to 1920 transform the German domestic framework for establishing and executing trade and tariff policy. Between 1914 and 1924, the prewar system that had concentrated the state's autonomous control over trade policy in the hands of the leading men in the chancellery and the Foreign Office disappeared. In its place evolved a system that spread control over trade policy across a changing number of different government and private-sector actors. The diffusion of authority within the government and the sharing of control between the state and the private-sector produced an extremely cumbersome and unwieldy means for planning German trade strategy and tactics.

This new, extensive, and ragged mechanism had great difficulty reaching and executing trade policy decisions. Indeed, this corporatist mechanism was largely incapable of resolving the difficult choices and bitter divisions involved in articulating Germany's postwar trade policy. This inability was soon apparent as successive German governments lurched from one last-minute decision and short-term policy to the next. By taking months to reach short-term solutions to tariff problems, the government fostered a constant political agitation over tariff issues. This tariff uncertainty frequently prevented Germany from taking the sort of definite action required to conclude meaningful trade agreements with its Eastern neighbors.

The scope, intensity, and length of the Great War of 1914 to 1918 forced the Reich to institute unprecedented controls on German foreign trade, but the government itself was not yet capable of overseeing and enforcing such control. Thus the Interior Office turned to the private interest groups for help in processing the mountains of paperwork required by the new import/export regulations. As the war went on, the imperial bureaucracy surrendered an increasing portion of its previously exclusive control over trade policy to the private-sector. The postwar problems of economic dislocation from 1918 to 1923 required even greater private-sector involvement in trade control. With private-sector participation, Weimar gained an effective administrative mechanism for trade control – something imperial Germany had never had. As the price for this new mechanism, Weimar, with its porous, diffuse, and democratized state structure, allowed the private-interest groups to influence trade policy formulation in a way that had never been possible under the more compact, more dense, and more authoritarian imperial state.

The general failure of the Reich (along with other powers) to prepare in advance for the economic aspects of World War I has been described often enough to make a recounting here unnecessary.[25] In sum, the Reich entered the war without adequate plans for the long-term economic mobilization that the war required, especially the problems of labor allocation and foreign trade regulation. The Reich's management of all aspects of the war economy in 1914 and 1915 "was characterized by sporadic and uncoordinated measures." In no area was this more true than in foreign trade regulations, where import and export controls were "not measures of a previously prepared systematic plan, but rather a multiplicity of hasty and incomplete laws and ordinances (Gesetze und Verordnungen) which were fashioned in the hour of need."[26] Throughout the war and the postwar period of adjustment, the Reich groped its way toward increasingly comprehensive solutions for the critical problem of managing foreign trade.

The government took its first steps toward regulating Germany's wartime trade on 31 July 1914, one day before the general military mobilization. Using Article 2 ("extraordinary provisions") of the 1869 Tariff Law, the government promulgated eight imperial ordinances designed to ensure adequate supplies for Germany's war economy by forbidding the export of animals, animal fodder, motor vehicles, weapons and munitions, railroad materials, raw materials for military stores, medical supplies, and carrier pigeons. Article 2 of each ordinance empowered the chancellor both to publish a catalog of the specific items covered and, in specific cases, to grant exemptions to the export prohibitions.[27] As shortages grew, the War Ministry's new Raw Materials Section (KRA) added many additional items to these lists. A second set of export controls attacked the Entente by prohibiting exports of goods that might contribute to the enemy's war economy even if these were not in short supply in Germany (e.g., chemical dyes). Finally, a third category of ordinances was designed to protect the future overseas market for German exports by banning the export of machines and machine parts that might be used to build competing industries abroad. On 31 July 1914 the first list of almost 100 export-controlled items appeared in the *Reichsanzeiger*. By October 1915 a compilation of the export-control ordinances and a catalog of corresponding items ran to sixty-nine pages. Shortly thereafter the Reich found it more expedient to publish a list of those items that were still free for export since this would be "substantially smaller and handier" than a list of controlled items.[28]

In contrast to exports, which came under state control immediately in July 1914, imports were not restricted until 1916. Throughout 1914 and most of 1915 the government did everything possible to facilitate increased imports for war consumption. The Law on Temporary Import Facilitation of 4 August 1914 granted the Bundesrat the power to reduce or abolish import duties for the duration of the war. The first such reductions on forty-nine food and fodder items appeared that same day. On 8 March 1915 a Decree on Temporary Import Facilitation abolished the import duties on another forty-nine items, mostly industrial raw materials. A half-dozen similar tariff reductions followed in 1915.[29] At that time imports of luxury goods and certain critical raw materials were "centralized" for the purpose of rationing. By 1916 the declining value of the mark abroad caused the Reich to restrict nonessential imports as a means of improving Germany's balance of payments in order to support its currency abroad. An ordinance of 25 February 1916 gave the Chancellor's Office the power to prohibit imports of "nonessential goods." A year later, a new Ordinance on Regulating Imports radically expanded this control with a blanket prohibition of all imports not specifically licensed. By 1917, Germany had reached a state of almost total foreign trade control. Every import shipment and virtually every export shipment required a Certificate of Permission (Bewilligung or Genehmigung), which could be obtained only by filing the appropriate import/export application (Antrag).[30]

These comprehensive trade regulations had long since surpassed the level of real control that the Reich administration could oversee and enforce. The Reich Interior Office established a new subdepartment IV C for Import and Export Licensing in August 1914 to enforce the first round of export regulations.[31] But the Interior Office bureaucracy could not possibly provide systematic documentation for every shipment in the large volume of trade entering or leaving the Reich. In October 1914, i.e., less than two months after the effective date of the original eight export ordinances, the Interior Office was forced to admit that it could not and would not be able to cope with the flood of export applications it was receiving, some six thousand to seven thousand in November alone.[32]

The enormous size of the export control task forced the Interior Office to turn to the private-interest groups for help in processing the mountains of paperwork required by the new trade controls. Beginning with the chemical industry in mid-October 1914, the Interior Office established private interest groups as the nuclei for establishing industry-specific Central Agencies for Export Permission. By November 1914 the Interior Office had established Central Agencies for the following industries: chemicals, iron and steel, tannin, skins and pelts, leather, glass, rubber, machine building, opticals, paper, woolens, and sugar. The Interior Office transferred some of the duties of export control onto these agencies by authorizing them to collect the export applications, to weed out clearly unacceptable exports, and to "recommend" approval of the remaining applications, which the agency then passed along to the Interior Department for final certification. Each agency was headed by an confidential agent (Vertrauensmann), usually nominated by and often a member of the leading interest group in that field.[33]

By 1917 the central agencies had virtually replaced the Interior Office as the real source of export control, despite the creation of a new Reich Commissar for Import and Export Permission as a special agent of the Interior Office. From November 1914 to November 1915 the central agency for iron and steel exports collected and evaluated over sixty-two thousand export applications, weeding out almost one-third and recommending approval of the other forty-two thousand. Interior Office approval had become largely a formality; recommendation by a central agency "almost always" led to approval of the export application in the Interior Office. As the scope of trade regulation increased after 1914, the central agencies acquired increased powers to control exports. In 1916 the central agencies assumed the important new task of approving export prices.[34]

In order to fulfill these functions, the agencies generated large administrations of their own. By 1916 the central agency for iron and steel employed twelve officers, eight price researchers, two agents abroad, and a staff of seventy. Estimating the size of other central agencies (for which the data are not readily available) on the basis of these numbers indicates that in two years the private-sector had built a fragmented bureaucracy of 144 officers, 96 price researchers, 24 agents abroad, and a staff of over 800 persons in order to support government regulation of Germany's twelve leading export industries.[35] The operations must have been considerable since the Interior Office allowed the central agencies to charge a processing fee on export applications in order to support these growing private-sector bureaucracies. On the import side, parallel structures to the central agencies were established in the form of Aid Committees (Hilfsausschusse) that reviewed import applications after 1916. At the same time, both the military and the civilian arms of the government kept a tighter rein on the state's powers of regulating and rationing imports than they had on controlling exports.[36]

By the end of 1917 a number of industrialists and government officials concluded that at war's end a substantial degree of wartime economic regulation would have to be extended through the period of demobilization. In early 1918 Jakob Reichert, a leading figure in the steel industry, pointed out that Germany must maintain export controls on raw materials in short supply during the initial postwar period. In fact, the economic and political chaos that engulfed the Reich in the wake of military defeat greatly increased the need for import and export controls. The declining value of the mark stimulated exports and exacerbated domestic shortages. A brief experiment with relaxed export controls in 1919 led immediately to a dangerous depletion of Germany's remaining inventories and a widespread recognition in industry that controls must be maintained.[37] At the same time, efforts to strengthen the mark by improving the balance of payments required continued import controls as a brake on unnecessary imports.

The conditions of the armistice and the Treaty of Versailles forced Germany to generate a new set of even more comprehensive trade regulations. In their occupation of the Rhineland, the Allies had expelled Reich Economic Office officials responsible for overseeing Germany's wartime trade regulations and had declared those regulations void. These Allied actions created a "hole in the West" (Loch im Westen) through which unnecessary luxury imports flowed unrestricted into Germany. Articles 264 to 267 and 269 of the Versailles Treaty prevented Germany from using high import and export tariffs (which would have signaled a return to more traditional forms of regulation) to control trade.In March 1920, Germany responded to the Allied occupation by modifying its import regulations of 16 January 1917. The new rules confirmed the blanket control over all imports and provided for enforcement of import controls at points inside the border, making it possible to control imports as they crossed from the occupied Rhineland into the rest of Germany.[38] Continuing control over exports had already been reaffirmed by the Economics Ministry's November 1919 Ban on the Export of Vital Commodities and the 20 December 1919 Ordinance on Foreign Trade Controls. These regulations sought to halt the flow of goods out of Germany that was producing shortages and home and leading to charges of German "dumping" abroad.[39]

In the context of gradually renewed European commercial activity after 1920, these extended controls now generated a greatly increased number of import and export applications. In 1915 manufacturers and traders had filed 62,000 export applications for German iron and steel products. By 1922 applications had soared to 187,000, or 512 export applications per day for this industry alone. According to Ernst Trendelenburg, Reich commissar for import/export permission from 1919 to 1923, the extensive scope of German trade controls in 1920 required checking on twenty thousand to thirty thousand individual subjects per day.[40] When explaining the proposed new regulations in November 1919, Under-secretary Julius Hirsch in the Economics Ministry stated plainly to representatives from various ministries that the new regulations would require "a greatly expanded apparatus."[41]

The increased workload forced the limited state administration to transfer an even greater portion of the real control function to the private-sector groups. As Trendelenburg explained: "It is immediately clear that a state bureaucracy is not capable of mastering such an enormous task. Within the limits of the official bureaucracy it would be completely impossible to have at our disposal such a number of number of persons with sufficient technical expertise. For that reason the organization of foreign trade controls is constructed on the basic principle of state supervised economic self-administration."[42]

Comfortable with a reliance on private-sector enforcement of trade controls, the Economics Ministry released a new set of regulatory statutes on 8 April 1920 that radically expanded the role of private-sector agents in controlling import and exports.[43] The remaining old wartime private-sector agencies for exports (central agencies) and imports (aid committees) were merged and renamed Foreign Trade Offices (Aussenhandelsstellen).[44] These Foreign Trade Offices served as the centerpieces of the Reich's system of "state supervised economic self-administration."[45] Each such office was headed by "Reich plenipotentiary" (Reichsbevollmächtigter) who in many cases was the executive secretary of the corresponding private interest group.[46] The regulatory statutes of 8 April allowed the Reich commissar to transfer most of the trade control duties to the Foreign Trade Offices with the result that these private offices assumed the functions of the state to a far greater degree that the private agencies and committees of 1914 to 1919 had done. Trendelenburg delegated to the Foreign Trade Offices the formal right to grant export and, later, import licenses. Whereas the old central agencies had the legal right only to make recommendations to the Interior Office, the new Foreign Trade Offices had both the substantive and formal right to issue licenses. In addition to reviewing and approving minimum export prices, the new offices now acquired the power to review both the volume and price of imports.[47]

By extending and formalizing the role of the private-sector in controlling imports and exports, the new rules of 1919 and 1920 diverted some of the power to set trade policy away from the state organs and toward the private-interest groups. The privately based Foreign Trade Offices expanded rapidly to accommodate their increased powers; by 1922 the Office for Iron and Steel Products employed almost 200 persons, or twice the number of 1916. By April 1920, forty-two Foreign Trade Offices with the participation by over 100 specialized interest groups were controlling Germany's imports and exports.[48]

The important role of the private-sector agencies in trade control was apparent to the interest groups themselves. Since 1917 the private-sector control agencies for many industries had been in "loose contact" with each other. In July 1920 these men met together, demanded, and obtained from the government certain modifications in the new export "tax." In the spring of 1921 the Reich plenipotentiaries for many industries joined together to establish a permanent office "for the purpose of managing the common matters of trade control vis-à-vis the [state] authorities ...." The group soon established its own secretariat and publication, Deutschen Aussenhandels-korrespondenz.[49] In its 6 March 1921 meeting the Executive Committee (Hauptvorstand) of the iron- and steelmakers' interest group maintained that a continuation of export controls "could be executed effectively only on the basis of voluntary cooperation of tightly bonded interest groups (festgefügten Verbänden)."[50] Increasingly aware of their own irreplaceable function in the trade control system, some private-sector groups began considering the future possibility of eliminating the state's involvement altogether and instead controlling trade exclusively by agreements within and among private-sector groups.[51]

Trendelenburg's statements about the inadequacy of the government bureaucracy and the indispensable role of the privately based Foreign Trade Offices were not lost on the private-interest groups. These groups now saw clearly the weaknesses of the state administrations, both imperial and republican, when confronted with unprecedented tasks of economic regulation. Even after extensive trade controls were relaxed in 1924, the most powerful economic groups sought to maintain in the new political system the influence over trade policy that they had acquired since 1914. Weimar governments could not undo the "growing osmosis of state and society."[52] In Germany more than elsewhere, the gigantic tasks of 1914 to 1918 had compelled a quietly revolutionary cooperation between state agents and private interests. The terms of Versailles and the economic problems of 1918 to 1923 only heightened awareness on both sides of the continued need for this type of cooperation. By the time economic normalcy returned to Germany in 1925, there could be no return to the pre-1914 gulf that had separated private-sector interests from upper levels of the bureaucracy in the Reich Interior Office and Foreign Office. Throughout the Weimar era, the most powerful economic interest groups asserted themselves forcefully on trade issues, either by engaging the ministerial bureaucracies directly in order to secure administrative action or by working through a political party when parliamentary decisions were required.

A number of critical changes in the German political system from 1914 to 1920 allowed private economic groups to bring their newfound influence to bear on the state administration. Between 1917 and 1925, ministerial reorganization, military defeat, and political democratization combined to destroy the old impermeable character of the pre-1914 Reich/Prussian ministerial bureaucracy. In its place appeared a porous state structure that diffused authority both across and within branches of government. With the full parliamentarization of the government in February 1919, a greatly increased number of ministers were responsible to the Reichstag. As a result, the top bureaucratic posts (ministers and sometimes state secretaries) were occupied by leading figures of the governing political parties. Inasmuch as the political parties served largely as the parliamentary agents or proxies of the largest economic groupings, the increased Reichstag control over the bureaucracy served, in effect, as another channel for interest group influence on the state.[53]

An important structural precondition for the private-sector's ability to gain influence over the bureaucracy was the crumbling of the old compact imperial bureaucracy that had helped preserve a quasi-authoritarian control over trade policy exerted by a small number of Foreign Office and Interior Office officials. The progressive diffusion of responsibility for trade policy across several government organs created a broader target with new openings for private-sector pressure on state agents. Beginning with the creation of a new Reich Economics Office in 1917 and culminating in the establishment of an interministerial Trade Policy Committee in 1925, successive German governments spread control over trade policy across an increasing number of governmental institutions. Policies that once had been formed by relatively small group of bureaucrats were, by the 1920s, being formed by numerous politicians.

The fragmentation of government responsibility for trade policy control began with the Imperial Edict for the creation of a new Reich Economic Office on 21 October 1917.[54] For years, the commercial community had advocated the creation of either an Economics Office or a Commerce Office at the Reich level. The war made such an office even more necessary, both to handle the problems of economic mobilization and to defend civilian economic and commercial interests against intrusions from the military. With Bismarckian logic, Interior State Secretary Karl Helfferich refused to allow the separation of economic policy from other aspects of domestic and social policy, or what he termed the "vivisection" of his Interior Office. Only as a concession to the bourgeois parties in the Reichstag, did a separate Reich Economics Office finally emerge as part of the solution to the crisis surrounding Chancellor Bethmann Hollweg's resignation in July 1917. On 31 October 1917 the government of new Chancellor Georg Michaelis transferred the management of trade, trade policy, trade treaties, tariff questions, and import/export controls from the Interior Office to the new Economics Office. Coming as a concession to the Reichstag, the transfer weakened the authority of the bureaucracy vis-à-vis the Parliament.[55] The creation of a new Reich level office to handle trade policy questions also weakened each of the two traditionally most powerful Reich offices – the Interior Office and the Foreign Office.[56]

A number of other wartime developments were already eroding the authority and prestige of the Foreign Office. The commercial community was furious over the Reich's combination of military strategy and foreign policy that alienated one neutral country after the other without regard for the economic and commercial consequences.[57] The most important neutrals (United States, Argentina, Sweden) had been alienated by Foreign Office blunders such as the Zimmermann Telegram rather than by premeditated and deliberately pursued policies. By the spring of 1918 business demands for a thoroughgoing reform of the Diplomatic Service and the Foreign Office had reached the point that both a Reichstag delegation and the state secretary in the Foreign Office, Richard von Kühlmann, traveled to Hamburg to respond to commercial complaints. This unprecedented action signaled how far the erosion of imperial bureaucratic autonomy had already progressed.[58] In addition to these attacks by an insistent private-sector, the primacy of the Foreign Office was threatened from within the ministerial structure by the ambitious plans of Hans Karl Freiherr von Stein, the new state secretary in the Economics Office from November 1917 to November 1918. Stein's December 1917 organizational plan for the Economic Office created departments to handle trade, trade policy, imports/exports, and trade treaties (Department IA), and economic reporting and information, including foreign trade promotion (Department IC). Department IA would contain individual country "desks" (referate) for "economic relations with individual foreign countries."[59] When Stresemann's impassioned demand for reform of the Foreign Office (Reichstag speech of 25 June 1918), failed to elicit any meaningful government response, members of Germany's commercial and industrial circles began to pin their hopes on the Economics Office, where private-sector interests were being allowed to express "a strong influence" on affairs.[60]

Confronted with an unprecedented threat to its jurisdiction and authority, especially in the area of trade policy, the Foreign Office accepted many of the business suggestions for reform. The so-called Schuler Reforms of 1918 to 1920 were designed specifically to meet business demands for a new Foreign Office structure that would integrate economic factors with other foreign-policy considerations.[61] Fortified by these reforms, the Foreign Office began to reassert itself in the bureaucratic infighting over control of trade policy. In March 1919, the Foreign Office managed to pry the economic reporting and information service for foreign countries away from the Economics Ministry and helped deflect State Secretary Hirsch's plan for an aggrandizement of the Economics Ministry at the expense of its rivals. But the Economics Office remained influential via the commissar for import/export permission who served there. After a year-long battle between the two ministries, the Foreign Office emerged with a cabinet confirmation of its position as the primary ministry for conducting international trade and negotiations.[62] The cabinet had confirmed the central role of the Foreign Office in representing the German position in international negotiations. But that assurance did not prevent other ministries from involving themselves in determining the content of German trade policies, i.e. in shaping the substantive positions that the Foreign Office would represent.

The creation of several new Reich Offices from 1917 to 1920 (renamed "ministries" as of March 1919) meant that, in addition to the Foreign Office, at least six ministries felt they should have some voice in trade policy formulation. The ministries for economics, transportation, finance, agriculture, economic demobilization, and reconstruction would not abandon their claims to participate in trade policy decisions. In the spring of 1920 both the Finance Ministry and the Ministry for Reconstruction were demanding a voice in setting trade control policy.[63] In September 1924 Economics Minister Hamm listed seven different Reich ministries as the "main participants" in the trade talks with France (economics, finance, labor, agriculture, interior, foreign office, and the Ministry for Occupied Territories). The situation did not improve over time. When Julius Curtius of the German People's Party (DVP) took over the Economics Ministry in 1926, he realized that the "splintering of the economic policy responsibilities in the Reich urgently required a consolidation." He planned to consolidate these duties in the Economics Ministry as an Economic General Staff. This, too, was blocked by his cabinet rivals.[64] A 1930 critique of Reich economic policy complained that "there are no fewer than five economics ministries" that the Economics Ministry itself "is not what it should be . . . the central office from which the Reich's economic policy is directed."[65]

The tendency of certain economic groups and the corresponding political parties to associate themselves with particular ministries added real material substance to these bureaucratic rivalries. Trendelenburg understood that "behind the unavoidable frictions are hidden not so much personal conflicts and departmental interests as extraordinarily weighty conflicts of interest …."[66] Chancellor Hans Luther described how certain parties became "closely connected with" (nahestehend) with particular ministries.[67] The protectionist elements of agriculture and heavy industry generally concentrated themselves in the German Nationalist Party (DNVP) and established a stronghold in the agriculture and finance ministries.[68] The most influential interest groups of these sectors, the new Reich Land Union (Reichslandbund) in agriculture and the Union of German Iron and Steel Industrialists, argued for the primacy of the domestic market and a restriction of imports as the best way for Germany's to achieve its necessary trade surplus.[69] In this they were seconded by the DNVP, which staked out the most protectionist party position.[70]

These protectionist groups opposed the more liberal trade policies of the commercial communities and the export-oriented industries generally associated with the German Democratic Party (DDP) and Stresemann's People's Party (DVP). Stresemann himself rejected protectionist policies; senior officials in Foreign Office were eager to use trade agreements as tools of foreign policy, which implied some loosening of protectionist restrictions.[71] The electro-technical and machine-building industries were especially vocal in urging a priority for exports and a corresponding policy of low tariffs.[72] After the Socialists (SPD) withdrew from the government in November 1923, the Labor Ministry continued to consider the trade policy interests of workers, consumers, and the urban population under the Christian trade-union representatives of the Catholic Center Party.[73] These conflicting interests remained somewhat muted through 1923 because of Germany's restricted trade and tariff policy sovereignty. With those restrictions slated to expire in January 1925, the Reich faced the important task of negotiating a battery of new trade treaties over the upcoming year.[74]

In early 1925, protectionist agricultural groups launched an all-out frontal assault on the special prerogatives of the Foreign Office in controlling trade negotiations. The protectionist groups benefited from the German Nationalist gains in the elections of December 1924 and the assignment of the Economics Ministry to Albert Neuhaus and the Finance Ministry to Otto Schlieben (both DNVP) in the first Luther cabinet. These gains then strengthened the position of "DNVP-associated" Gerhard Kanitz at the Agriculture Ministry. Taking advantage of this position, Kanitz encouraged the ministerial jealousies of finance and transportation to undermine Foreign Office control over trade negotiations by insisting that the government require the Foreign Office to conduct all trade negotiations in Berlin so that other ministries could participate more fully. The Transportation Ministry seconded this idea and the issue came to cabinet discussion twice in February 1925.[75] At the same time the leadership of the largest agricultural interest group, the Reich Land Union, met with Chancellor Luther to express their distrust of both Stresemann's Foreign Office and the under-secretary for commercial affairs in the Economics Ministry, Hans Posse. The Reich Land Union demanded that Luther shift control over trade policy and trade treaty negotiations away from the Foreign Office to a new interministerial "central office" connected directly to the Chancellery.[76]

In a losing effort, Stresemann sought to resist all encroachments on the Foreign Office's exclusive position in trade negotiations. Aside from the Foreign Office, only the Labor Ministry supported the existing system in the hope of preventing agriculture from gaining a larger voice in trade policy. When the ministers met to discuss the matter at a Chefbesprechung on 23 February, Stresemann met the agricultural challenge head-on by acknowledging the need "to bring about a clarification of who in fact was to represent the economic interests [of Germany] in trade treaty negotiations." He defended the existing arrangement by repeatedly claiming that the "business community" trusted the Foreign Office and that "the parties" in parliament did not desire a change. Economics Minister Neuhaus offered a compromise plan by which the state secretary in the Economics Ministry would become (ex officio) the commissar for trade treaty negotiations, responsible to the Foreign Office and Economics Ministry jointly, with his office attached to the Foreign Office – a situation Stresemann described as "impossible." Luther bent toward Stresemann by suggesting the creation of an interministerial Trade Policy Committee located within the Foreign Office.[77] On 9 March the cabinet empowered the chancellor to "solve the organizational questions of trade treaty negotiations in conjunction with the finance, economics, agriculture, and foreign ministers."[78] From this directive and the chancellor's earlier suggestion emerged the interministerial Trade Policy Committee (Handelspolitischer Ausschuss) on 19 March 1925. The Foreign Office held the chairmanship and provided the secretariat for the new body, which contained members from the finance, economics, agriculture, and foreign ministries. The committee's decisions, taken initially at the level of department heads, were not binding; dissenters could appeal to the four state secretaries, and then to the cabinet for final decisions.[79] The Trade Policy Committee institutionalized the right of four distinct ministries to participate fully, directly, and equally in trade policy formulation and trade treaty negotiations. The committee embodied the state's diffusion of trade policy responsibility horizontally across several ministries and vertically through multiple levels of government. This fragmentation and the newly revealed weakness of the state's own trade control apparatus combined to produce an especially porous state structure in the field of trade policy. Permeability and fragmentation, in turn, enabled particular interest groups and their corresponding political parties to colonize particular ministries: agricultural and heavy industrial interests in the German Nationalist Party gained a foothold in the agriculture and finance ministries; labor/consumer/urban interests held the Labor Ministry; and export-oriented finishing industries and the People's Party defended their views in the Foreign Office and at the second level of the Economics Ministry.

Private-sector representatives intruded even further into trade policy formulation by participating directly in international trade negotiations as "experts" attached to German delegations. This practice fulfilled a long-standing desire of the German business community, dating back to Theodor Möller's criticisms of Bismarck and Caprivi in the 1890s. Despite the assertion of Foreign Office Under-Secretary Karl Ritter that private-sector participation was not the rule, the practice was quite common. Only the representatives of organized labor were denied the right to participate. Commerce and industry were bitterly opposed to labor participation. With business support, the Foreign Office was able to fend off two major efforts by labor in 1924 and 1925 to gain some representation in Germany's trade delegations.[80] From 1920 to 1925 private businessmen participated extensively in German trade negotiations with France, Rumania, Soviet Russia, and Czechoslovakia. At various times industrial commercial and agricultural representatives negotiated directly with their foreign counterparts or with foreign governments, since private international trade agreements and cartel arrangements often went hand-in-hand with official treaties.

In this way, the Weimar political system encouraged the interest groups to carry their trade policy differences into the Reichstag and, more significantly, directly into the cabinet, the ministerial bureaucracy, and on occasion even inside Germany's trade delegations. The unstable multiparty coalitions that characterized Weimar were thus reproduced at four different levels, and firm trade policy decisions required the approval of several interest groups at all these levels.[81] The structure of decisionmaking was very fragile since any one of the major economic groupings at any level could obstruct trade policy. The porous state deprived its agents of sufficient stature to stand above or beyond these disputes. They could not impose a set-tlement on the conflicting interest groups in the heavy-handed man-ner of Bülow and Posadowsky. When the economic interests could not generate a private-sector consensus, as was often the case, Ger-man trade policy ground to a halt. Even under the best of economic and political circumstances, the Trade Policy Committee would have been an extremely cumbersome mechanism for conducting foreign trade relations. Under Weimar circumstances – extensive coalition governments confronting difficult and painful trade policy choices – policy by committee produced paralysis.

Given the unprecedented range of trade policy problems that Weimar faced, it is hardly surprising that the major economic actors in Germany should have deep, substantive differences over how best to tackle those problems. The new republic inherited several divisive trade and tariff issues that had been left unresolved by Germany's last prewar round of trade treaties in 1904 and 1905. The peace settle-ment produced new, additional international political and economic strains that exacerbated these problems. Corporatist stalemate and turbulent economic conditions extended the debate over decontrol-ling Germany's foreign trade through 1924. That issue was followed immediately by a vicious renewal of the tariff debate, in which the old slogans of Agrarstaat versus Industriestaat were modernized as "primacy of export" versus "primacy of domestic market strength" in accordance with the structural changes imposed by Versailles. Weimar corporatism was largely incapable of resolving the funda-mental debates over the form and content of German tariff policy. As a result, recurring, unsettled trade and tariff problems nagged the regime from 1923 through 1933 and undermined Germany's ability to conclude meaningful treaties with trade partners in the East.

The first major trade policy issue confronting the Reich centered around the economic "demobilization" of Germany's foreign trade. Charting a path away from trade controls and toward the free circu-lation of goods became a six-year ordeal as political stalemate ham-pered efforts to end trade controls and put a new tariff in place. As early as November-December 1918 the issue of how and when to proceed with trade deregulation produced sharp divisions disagree-ments between industrial interest groups, and on some occasions even within certain industries. A meeting of all sectors of the iron industry with the Reich Economics Office in November 1918 revealed widely divergent views on the issue of future controls. Con-trols of raw materials would of course remain for the foreseeable future; beyond that, however, the question was open. Heavy indus-trialists such as Bruhn (Krupp) for the Raw Iron Association

(Roheisenverband), Hugo Stinnes, and Stinnes's Managing Director Albert Vögler favored immediate abolition of price and export controls. Eugen Leidig for the Pipe Association (Röhreverband) spoke out for the continuation of export restrictions. In the iron finishing and processing industries the situation was even more confused: the producers of "small iron and steel wares" demanded the "maximum possible [export] freedom"; the motor vehicle industry favored continued controls; and the critically important machine-building and electrical industries could not even offer opinions due to "widely divergent views" and a "lack of unity."[82]

A meeting of the German Industrial Council (Deutsche Industrierat) in December 1918 also revealed widely divergent views. Members of the textile industry took the lead in arguing for an end to trade controls, while others argued that import restrictions must remain "at least for the immediate transition period."[83]These industrial views conflicted with consistent, if not particularly helpful, demands by the commercial community that all import and export controls be phased out beginning immediately. Even as the inflation began to reach previously unimaginable proportions in mid-1922, groups such as the Hamburg Committee for the Freedom of Foreign Trade could find no sympathy for the trade control mechanisms.[84]

The position of the industrial interest groups within Germany's new trade control structure meant that trade deregulation required an industrial consensus. Commissar Trendelenburg understood that these differing opinions were caused by "extraordinarily weighty conflicts of interest, namely those between big business (Grossindustrie) and small producers (Kleingewerbe) and between export industries and exporters." He went on to scold the "leading economic groups" for their lack of "national unity ... in these times of emergency."[85] Without that unity, the absence of industrial consensus for a change preserved the tightly regulated status quo. Shortly thereafter, the economic problems of 1919 (inflation, shortages, "hole in the West") overtook Germany, effectively ending any chance for decontrol in the near future.

Two years later an industrial consensus still had not emerged. In the spring of 1921 an improving economic situation again briefly opened the possibility of relaxing some export controls. The mark had regained a good portion of the value lost during 1919; in January 1921 it had recovered to almost exactly where it had been one year earlier, at 65 marks to the dollar. In March 1921 Economics Minister Ernst Scholz (German People's Party) presented a program that would drop the existing export controls on most finished goods, retaining controls only on raw materials and food. The commercial community enthusiastically supported Scholz's proposal. Once again the heavy industrial community split on the deregulation issue. Within the Union of Iron and Steel Industrialists, ten producers' groups (Wirtschaftsgruppen) voted for complete export freedom; three voted for price deregulation with continuing export restrictions; and twelve favored continuation of the existing controls. This indecision, combined with stiff opposition from the labor unions and the SPD (led by former Economics Minister Wissel) blocked implementation of the plan. The mark began to drop sharply in the second half of 1921 so that another chance for deregulation would not appear until after the currency reform of November 1923.[86]

Far more consequential than these earlier bouts of policy deadlock was Weimar's recurrent inability to achieve strategic clarity in its tariff policy. Beginning in 1924, political deadlock over the future of German trade policy prevented the Reich from generating a new tariff promptly. Because of the political paralysis, Germany could not respond in January 1925 to the end of the Versailles commercial restrictions and the return of German trade and tariff policy sovereignty. Although Germany had had over four years to prepare for this date, interest-group conflict over trade policy prevented timely action. Deep differences between agriculture and industry over agricultural tariffs and between heavy and light industry over the raw iron tariff forced the postponement of a new tariff until August 1925. The tariff delay held up Germany's most important foreign trade negotiations for over a year, during which trade relations with a number of countries, particularly Poland, deteriorated badly. Further, the tariff legislation finally approved by the Reichstag in August 1925 was not the comprehensive, long-term settlement of tariff issues that its 1902 predecessor had been. Rather, the new tariff legislation dissected the tariff problem into a number of component issues, each with a short-term solution – a tactic that was crucial for gaining government approval and a parliamentary majority. In addition, the tariff legislation as a whole required renewal after just two years. As a result, the tariff issue received no long-term solution in Weimar. From 1924 through the 1932 the cabinet and the Reichstag faced a steady stream of tariff issues at six- and twelve-month intervals. This tariff uncertainty facilitated the agrarians' obstructionist tactics and provided no respite for Weimar's fragile coalition governments. Together with the difficult international trade issues of the 1920s, these domestic weaknesses prevented Weimar from reaching meaningful trade agreements with its Eastern neighbors.

By early 1924, the new currency had proven its stability, and the basic economic preconditions for trade deregulation were at hand.

In early 1924, the government of Chancellor Wilhelm Marx began formulating plans for removing the decade-old import/export controls. Virtually the entire agricultural, industrial, and commercial communities longed for a return to a "normal" trade regime in which the tariff and treaties, not licenses and price controls, would govern German foreign trade. Deregulation required that Germany revise its outdated tariff rates (those of 1902) in accordance with the new conditions of the 1920s. The mixed government-private Customs Tariff Committee had already modernized the commodity classifications; it now remained to set the new tariff rates. The prospects for resolving these thorny tariff issues under Chancellor Marx were not promising. His minority government was a bourgeois coalition of the Center, the Democrats, and the German People's Party, augmented by selective participation of the Bavarian People's Party (BVP), unsteadily tolerated by the Socialists on the left and generally opposed by the German Nationals on the right.

In January 1924, Economics Minister Hamm (German Democrats) urged the cabinet to "accelerate" the tariff revision.[87] Germany required a new tariff first and foremost in order to proceed with trade deregulation (especially of imports). In addition, the Reich needed a new tariff in order to begin trade treaty negotiations once Germany recovered its trade sovereignty in January 1925. Without a tariff in place or in the wings, Berlin would have no capacity to bargain with potential trade partners. On 11 January the Economics Committee of the cabinet approved a joint Economics Ministry/Foreign Office plan to proceed "confidentially" and "with all possible speed" toward completing a tariff revision that could remain in force "for a short time" while a larger revision was undertaken. The government also sought an extension of the 1922 Enabling Law, which gave the government the power to alter tariff rates by decree, subject to the consent of both chambers of Parliament.[88] When the tariff revision was still not completed by mid-June, Hamm and Finance Minister Hans Luther proposed using the final days of the Enabling Law for an ordinance that would increase duties 30 percent to 80 percent on a wide variety of manufactured items. The new rates could be in place before the conclusion of the politically important trade treaty with Austria.[89]

At this point Agricultural Minister Kanitz (officially an independent, but in fact "associated" with the German Nationals) insisted that some tariff protection be extended to agriculture as well. Agricultural goods had entered Germany duty-free for almost a decade, i.e. since the old 1902 tariff duties had been suspended with the outbreak of war in 1914. Kanitz proposed a blanket reinstitution of the pre-war agricultural tariff; if necessary, the government could then use its decree powers to reduce certain of these duties.[90] Both the Union of German Farmer's Associations (Vereinigung der deutschen Bauernvereine) and the Reich Land Union made clear to the government that they would not accept tariff increases for industry while farmers remained unprotected. In view of the already alarming gap between agricultural and industrial prices in Germany, farmers insisted on receiving the "same protection" as industry.[91] Chancellor Marx, Finance Minister Luther, Interior Minister Karl Jarres (German People's Party) and even State Secretary K. J. Hermann Geib in the Labor Ministry readily conceded the distressed financial position of many German farmers, both large and small, in both Prussia and South Germany.[92]

A considerable portion of heavy industry supported agricultural demands for reinstituting the prewar tariff. The industrialists' immediate motive was to secure agricultural allies for their own struggle to obtain a 1 or 1.50 mark/ton tariff on raw iron imports. The manufacturing sectors in Germany (joined together in the Working Group of the Iron Finishing Industry, or AVI from its German initials) vigorously opposed a raw iron duty. The threat of a "low tariff insurrection" by the iron finishing industry, which hung in the air through 1924, muddied the tariff waters further.[93] AVI arguments about the resulting increased costs of German products and the loss of international competitiveness appeared strong enough to rally the export interest in the DVP and virtually all of the Center, DDP, and SPD in opposition to an iron duty. In their bid for protection, heavy industry's only possible allies lay in the agricultural groups.[94] The immediate material motives for heavy industry supporting agricultural tariffs reinforced a larger ideological commitment by heavy industry to renew the traditional alliance between these two still powerful pillars of conservative politics in Germany.[95]

Kanitz's insistence on agricultural tariffs put the coalition cabinet in a difficult position just at the time when the government was seeking both Socialist and some German National support for the Dawes Plan legislation and rescheduled the reparations payments placed on Germany by the Treaty of Versailles. (Since the Germans pawned the national railway receipts as a guarantee of future reparations payments, the Dawes proposals required not just a simple majority, but two-thirds approval of the Reichstag.) Marx warned that the reintroduction of agricultural duties would be "flatly refused" by the Socialists.[96] Government advocacy of such a plan might drive the SPD into opposition at a time when their votes were needed for ratification of the Dawes Plan. In the worst case, the Socialists might support the "no confidence" measure that the Communists would surely advance when new tariffs were proposed. On the other hand, as Kanitz pointed out, agricultural protection would "take the wind out of the sails of the German Nationals on the agrarian question" and might bring them out of their "stubborn opposition" to the Dawes Plan.[97] The Reich Land Union had assured Kanitz that it could keep about half of the German Nationals from voting no confidence over Dawes in exchange for restored agricultural duties.

Labor Minister Heinrich Brauns (Center) opposed agricultural duties as both politically inopportune and counter to the government's program of lowering industrial production costs; he was supported in this by Economics Minister Hamm. Chancellor Marx and Stresemann offered various plans for agreeing with the idea of revived agricultural duties yet delaying actual implementation. Kanitz insisted that any industrial tariff increases be accompanied at that time by the restoration of agricultural duties and threatened to quit the cabinet unless this condition was met. Since the loss of Kanitz would have fully alienated the not only the German Nationals, but a good portion of Stresemann's own German People's Party, the cabinet had no choice but to accept Kanitz's plan.[98]

The resulting situation was not atypical for Weimar coalition politics. Kanitz, the German Nationals, and the agricultural lobby had sufficient political leverage to block Hamm's plan for tariff increases on industrial goods only. On the other hand, Socialist, labor union, and some bourgeois opposition could easily block passage of tariff legislation that renewed agricultural duties. Socialist leader Rudolf Hilferding told Marx that the agricultural tariff would be "difficult to bear" for the Socialists; the chairman of the SPD Reichstag group, Hermann Müller, was even less accommodating.[99] With the most immediate pressure being Kanitz's insistence that the government present agricultural as well as industrial tariff increases to the parliament or face his resignation, the cabinet approved such a bill on 2 July and presented to the Reichsrat (upper house) the next day.[100] In a meeting with trade union leaders on July 15, Kanitz failed to gain their support for agricultural protection. Representatives from the General Federation of German Unions (ADGB) said the time had come to "pay back the farmers for what they had done to the workers during the war" on the food issue.[101] The divided coalition government had only reluctantly agreed to advance the idea of renewed agricultural duties. Kanitz soon discovered he did not have sufficient support within the cabinet to ensure that his ministerial colleagues, their political parties (Center, Democrats, and German People's Party), and the commercial and industrial interest groups associated with them would genuinely support the government's proposed tariff in parliament.[102] Just three weeks after the legislation was presented to the Reichsrat, Kanitz complained to Marx that "it is an open secret that some of the ministers have expressed fairly openly to circles of their political friends that the proposed tariff is [already] now a failure." Kanitz also accused the state secretary in the chancellery, Franz Bracht, of urging Prussia's Reichsrat deputies to vote against the tariff. Marx responded that the cabinet was "holding tight" to the agreed-on draft, but acknowledged that "a certain difference of opinion among the governing parties exists at this time." Indeed, some of the commercial interest groups, such as the Foreign Trade Association (the old Trade Treaty League renamed), were leading the campaign against renewed agricultural tariffs.[103] In the cabinet meeting of 21 August, the Democratic Ministers Hamm (Economics) and Rudolf Oeser (Transportation) urged the government not to present the tariff bill to the Reichstag since the issue might split the governing coalition. Although Marx admitted that he "considered it a mistake to present the draft to the Reichstag at this time," the Center and German People's Party ministers felt the cabinet must keep its promise to the farmers. The government presented the draft to the Reichstag on 22 August. Four days later Hamm warned the cabinet that "because of the special difficulties associated with the question of agricultural tariffs, it is not to be expected that this law will pass the Reichstag in current legislative period." Despite this warning and the obvious danger of the tariff not passing, the cabinet was unable to reach a decision on a tariff backup plan presented by Hamm.[104]

The government managed to delay Reichstag debate on the tariff bill until Saturday, 30 August – the last day of session before recess and one day after the Dawes Plan legislation had been ratified. When the bill was introduced the Socialists moved that it be stricken from the agenda. Instead of voting against this motion, the Democrats, with Economics Minister Hamm on the floor, presented their own motion to refer the bill back to committee. Kanitz insisted the Reichstag consider the tariff bill. At that point, the Socialists withdrew from the chamber and the parliament lost its quorum. After an extensive rules debate and another failed attempt to produce a quorum, parliament adjourned for autumn recess without having considered the tariff and was subsequently dissolved for new elections on 20 October.[105] Divergent tariff interests among Germany's leading economic groupings were reflected in coalition politics that produced tariff policy paralysis in both the Reichstag and the cabinet.

Consensus was widespread in both government and the private-sector that in failing to secure a new tariff before the Reichstag dissolution, Germany was courting international disaster.[106] Preliminary trade negotiations were already either scheduled or underway with France, Belgium, Italy, Japan, and Poland. Parliamentary paralysis on the tariff issue forced the Foreign Office to ask for an Enabling Decree (Ermächtigungsgesetz) to put international economic agreements into force pending Reichstag review. With the Reichstag fragmented over the tariff issue in the summer of 1924, the government had used the president's Article 48 emergency powers (yet a further diffusion of power) to put the German-Austrian treaty of 12 July 1924 into force. Since that time the Reich had lost some trade advantages already negotiated because it could not fulfill promises to put the agreements into effect immediately.[107]

The lack of a valid tariff as the basis for international negotiation placed German negotiators in impossible situations once the Reich recovered its trade policy sovereignty on 10 January 1925. Stresemann received a steady stream of disastrous reports from German negotiators abroad: from Ulrich Rauscher in Warsaw, Trendelenburg in Paris, and Karl Edler von Stockhammern in Rome.[108] Stresemann considered the possibility of using the president's emergency powers under Article 48 to restore the government's tariff-setting powers, which had expired in June 1924.[109] Problems reached a crisis point in March 1925 when Italy broke off negotiations. Sweden and the United States threatened reprisals if Germany did not finally end its extensive import/export controls.[110] Returning from Paris in early May 1925, Trendelenburg told his colleges at the Economics Ministry that "to one such as I, who has been absent from domestic political life for six months, it is barely conceivable that in this time it has not been possible to establish some clarity in our tariff policy."[111]

The German industrialists such as Karl Lange (chairman of the powerful Union of Machine Building Institutes) who participated in Germany's trade negotiations were well aware of the difficulties caused by the lack of an updated tariff. Just two weeks after the Reichstag dissolution, the Executive Committee of the industrial Reichsverband urged the government to use Article 48 to get an industrial tariff in place. In March 1925, the chairman of the German Chamber of Commerce, Felix Mendelssohn, and the executive secretary of the Reichsverband, Ludwig Kastl, wrote to the Foreign Office urging the government to seek a new Enabling Decree in order to impose new industrial tariff increases. The accompanying Reichsverband resolution warned explicitly about the danger to Germany's attempted international negotiations. Karl Lange and Hans von Raumer, a leader in the electro-technical industry, seconded this idea.[112] The liberal *Vossische Zeitung* ran stories on 11 March and 27

March asking "Where is the New Tariff?" Even the generally recognized urgent need for a tariff could not overcome the deep differences of opinion on how that tariff should be constructed. After Hans Luther put together a right-center majority government in January 1925, it still required another eight months of tough bargaining before the government produced a new tariff – one that did not solve the basic conflicts, but rather diffused them over time.

In the spring of 1925, Luther's new coalition cabinet of German Nationals along with the Center and People's parties approached the stressful tariff issue.[113] The inclusion of the German Nationals in the cabinet, with Neuhaus and Schlieben as economics and finance ministers, meant that the government could not possibly construct a so-called "small tariff" (i.e., one that raised industrial duties but did not include increased protection for agriculture) as the Chamber of Commerce, industrial Reichsverband, electro-technical, and machine-building industries were urging. On 12 March, Kanitz warned his cabinet colleagues that German farmers were "in an evil mood" and would defeat any proposed tariff that did not contain increased agricultural duties.[114] At a meeting of party leaders on 18 March, Thomsen (German Nationals) demanded immediate presentation of a new tariff containing agricultural protection.[115] In the first half of 1925, agricultural agitation surpassed anything that Imperial Germany had known. The Reich Land Union mobilized its provincial organs nationwide and each of the independent state Agricultural Chambers mobilized their provincial and local members. The result was a flood of angry petitions to the government demanding tariff increases equal to those granted to industrial products and the establishment of "minimum rates" on some products, as the 1902 tariff had provided.[116] In June, Neuhaus informed his cabinet colleagues that the DNVP would not approve any MFN trade treaties (several were under negotiation) until agriculture had some "certainty" about future tariff rates.[117]

On the other hand, the Christian trade unions opposed new agricultural duties and the large labor component of the Catholic Center Party was unlikely to support such legislation. On 11 April Christian labor leader Adam Stegerwald told Chancellery State Secretary Franz Kempner that he would not attend a coalition meeting on the tariff scheduled for 21 April.[118] Indeed, the Center's desire to continue postponing any action on the tariff question played a major role in delaying the new legislation.[119] Kempner summed up the impasse by saying that if the new tariff did not contain agricultural protection the German Nationals would vote against it "which might produce some unpleasant effects on the cabinet." On the other hand, if the tariff did contain agricultural protection "at least a large portion of the Center will vote against it, so that the legislation would be in danger."[120]

The export-oriented, light industry interest groups remained opposed to agricultural duties. Karl Lange, who served as the executive secretary for a powerful interest group representing the principal users of iron and steel in manufacturing, informed the government that "under the current conditions the great majority of the German finished goods industries thoroughly reject the demand for grain duties." This opposition was offset by the obvious and pressing need to get a tariff in place as soon as possible so that trade treaties might be concluded. Under these conflicting pressures, Stresemann's own German People's Party (DVP) remained undecided on the tariff issue through April 1925.[121]

By June, an unstable, ad hoc coalition of agriculture, heavy industry, Foreign Office and foreign trade interests had emerged that for the moment favored immediate passage of a new tariff with agricultural concessions. The overall situation had been made easier by an agreement between heavy industry and the Working Group of Iron Finishing Industries (known as the AVI group) for an export subsidy that resolved the issue of the raw iron tariff. The agreement gave both parties some incentive to work for tariff legislation that would secure their privately negotiated agreement by putting the tariff issue to rest.[122] Yet any agricultural tariff still faced serious opposition within the government; most especially from the labor wing of the Center, but also from export and commercial interests that had not yet committed themselves to agricultural duties as the price for securing the tariff legislation needed to proceed with international trade negotiations.

With a compromise on a genuine solution of the tariff issue still out of reach, the government began working toward a less-than-genuine solution by modifying the proposed legislation to spread out the toughest decisions over a period of time. At a series of interministerial meetings in late April, the ministers managed to agree (or as Kempner's notes insightfully show "no objections were raised") to a new "basis of discussion." The plan provided the long-needed increase in industrial rates and restored the tariff on agricultural goods at the 1902 to 1914 autonomous tariff level (i.e., on the basis of 7.50 marks/cwt. for wheat and 7.00 marks/cwt. for rye). These rates exceeded the 1902 to 1914 "treaty levels" (5.50 and 5.00) that had, in fact, been the effective rates from 1902 to 1914. "Minimum rates" for numerous agricultural products were also restored. Together, these provisions satisfied the most urgent agricultural demands. The plan was made palatable to reluctant elements of industry and labor in the

DVP and the Center by the introduction of greatly reduced "transition rates of duty" for thirty of the most important agricultural products. These much lower rates, based on duties of 3.50 and 3.00 marks/cwt. for wheat and rye, would run initially through July of 1926.[123] In other words, the most unpleasant agricultural duties would be introduced at a later date.

By the time the plan emerged from an interparty meeting on July 20, it was little more than a short-term framework for transferring the tough decisions from the parliament back to the ministerial bureaucracy and for deferring most of these decisions to a later date.[124] The advantage of this vacuous legislation lay in its inability to arouse opposition. The Christian trade unions agreed to it in exchange for a sales tax reduction and the use of agricultural tariff revenue for social welfare purposes. The industrial Reichsverband agreed only because "a speedy passage of the tariff revision was a pressing need for the trade treaty negotiations currently underway." Similarly, the German Chamber of Commerce agreed to it and asked its local members to "make passage possible," but would not support it publicly.[125] This unenthusiastic support secured the votes of the Center, the German People's Party, and the industrial wing of the German Nationals. Kanitz's support for it as the best obtainable brought the agrarian wing of the German Nationals along. These groups maneuvered their project through the Reichstag not by persuading the opposition of its merits, but rather by gutting the legislation so that its immediate effects were not objectionable. The Law on Tariff Changes received final approval on 17 August 1925.[126]

Since the legislation did not resolve the basic issues that divided Germany, it did not provide the country with a respite from tariff conflict. Section 10 gave the entire legislation a life of less two years (to 31 July 1927), so that even without any intervening disputes, Germany would have a respite of perhaps one year before the tariff battle was renewed. Section 10 also empowered the Finance Minister to phase in the agricultural tariff increases for various products as he saw fit between August and October via ministerial order. As soon as the legislation passed, Finance Minister Schlieben was under intense pressure from farmers, who wanted immediate implementation to cover this year's harvest, and from labor and consumers who wanted one more duty-free season. That conflict lasted throughout August and September 1925.[127]

A key element in the 1925 compromise was the "transition duties" for the most important agricultural imports. The legislation set these rates to expire on 31 July 1926. By March 1926 the battle was already in full force over whether these lower rates should in fact be allowed to expire and the 7.00/7.50 rates be allowed to take effect. Agitation on both sides was fierce. Stresemann called this decision "one of the most important domestic political questions of the upcoming months."[128] In a series of cabinet meetings running from April to June 1926, the cabinet decided to prevent implementation of the 7.00/7.50 autonomous rates by creating a new five-month "transition autonomous rate" at 5.00 marks/cwt. for both wheat and rye, to run through 31 December 1926. The Foreign Office expected that rate to be reduced soon in a trade treaty with Poland.[129] The tariff situation had become so confused that a good many German Missions and Consulates abroad did not know which rates applied to which commodities for which periods.

When a Polish treaty did not materialize in 1926, the Marx cabinet approved an extension of the 5.00 rates for another three months, through 31 March 1927. On 4 March 1927 the cabinet approved another three-month extension through July 1927, when the tariff law of 1925 expired.[130] After extensive cabinet discussions in 1927 the lower rates were included in the renewed tariff legislation scheduled to run to 1930. That tariff, however, was cut short by the crisis of German agriculture in the summer of 1929.[131] Between October 1924 and the summer of 1929, successive German coalition governments confronted the issue of agricultural tariffs six different times in five years!

In addition to these frequent confrontations with the agricultural tariffs, the Finance Ministry experienced a nonstop flow of petitions requesting changes in individual rates on all types of commodities. Section 4 of the 1925 tariff law invited this pressure by empowering the government to alter individual tariff rates "in the event of a pressing economic need," subject to the consent of the Reichsrat and a Reichstag committee. On scores of items ranging from chemical products to Oriental rugs, interest groups both large and small on both sides of every issue pestered the government for changes. With every attempt by the government to accommodate a just complaint of producers or consumers, the commercial community complained that "tariff uncertainty" was ruining their ability to conduct import/export business.

The contrast between the tariff legislation of 1925 and Caprivi's ten-year treaties or Bülow's comprehensive tariff of 1902 is obvious. For better or for worse, both Caprivi and Bülow had managed to impose long-term tariff settlements on Germany's conflicting economic interests. The 1925 legislation, by contrast, produced neither tariff stability nor a political respite from tariff quarrels. Between 1925 and 1929, successive coalition governments faced an unending series of tariff policy decisions, each one accompanied by bitter interest group and political party conflict. In sum, Weimar's corporatist political-economic system could not resolve the serious tariff policy disputes that divided Germany in the 1920s. Wracked by the irreconcilable differences between the domestically oriented agricultural and heavy industrial interests on one side and the export-oriented commercial and light industrial interests on the other side, successive coalition governments were unable to formulate functioning policies, first on the issue of deregulating foreign trade and subsequently on the tariff issue.[132] Goaded into action by the external necessity of having some tariff in place, the corporatist system shook off its paralysis only to lurch unsteadily from one painful short-term or ad hoc decision to the next.

Notes

1. For an introductory discussion of these issues see Gerd Hardach, *The First World War, 1914-1918* (Berkeley and Los Angeles, 1977), 11 ff., 35 ff. and the literature cited there.

2. For the German perspective on these developments see A. Spindler, *Der Handelskrieg mit U-Booten. Der Krieg zur See 1914-1918*, 5 vols. (Berlin and Frankfurt, 1932-1966); Bernd Stegmann, *Die deutsche Marinepolitik 1916-1918* (Berlin, 1970).

3. On the Allied blockade see the official British history by A.C. Bell, *A History of the Blockade of Germany, Austria-Hungary, Bulgaria, and Turkey, 1914-1918* (London, 1924); Louis Guichard, *Histoire du Blocus Naval 1914-1918* (Paris, 1929); Marion Siney, *The Allied Blockade of Germany 1914-1916* (Ann Arbor, Mich., 1957). On the political consequences for neutrals see Ernest May, *The World War and American Isolation* (Cambridge, Mass., 1963).

4. Hardach, *The First World War*, 25. On British plans to restrict German trade after the war see Robert E. Bunselmeyer, *The Cost of the War 1914-1919: British Economic War Aims and the Origins of Reparation* (Hamden, Conn., 1975).

5. "Die deutschnationale Zoll- und Handelspolitik," Jakob Reichert to DNVP industrialists in Cologne, 9 September 1926, BA R 131/101.

6. *The Treaty of Peace between the Allied and Associated Powers and Germany* (London, 1920). For an explanation of the terms, D. Thomson, *Europe since Napoleon* (London, 1966), 623 ff.; R. Butler, "The Peace Treaty Settlement of Versailles, 1918-1933," in C.L. Mowat, ed., *The Shifting Balance of World Forces, 1898-1945* (Cambridge, 1968); summary in Derek Aldcroft, *From Versailles to Wall Street, 1919-1929* (Berkeley and Los Angeles, 1977), 22 ff. The terms have been the subject of a number of critical analyses, among them, J.M. Keynes, *The Economic Consequences of the Peace* (London, 1919); E. Mantoux, *The Carthaginain Peace or the Economic Consequences of Mr. Keynes* (London, 1946). Consult also Max Gunzenhäuser's bibliography, *Die Pariser Friedenskonferenz und die Friedensverträge 1919-1920* (Frankfurt, 1970).

7. Rene Albrecht-Carrié, *The Meaning of the First World War* (Englewood Cliffs, N.J., 1965), 110. On the restive nature of the European interwar order see Albrecht-Carrié, *Diplomatic History of Europe since the Congress of Vienna* (London, 1965) 360 ff.; R.J. Sontag, *A Broken World, 1919-1939* (New York, 1971); Hans Gatzke, ed., *European Diplomacy between the Two Wars, 1919-1939* (Chicago, 1972); G. Ross, *The Great Powers and the Decline of the European State System 1914-1945* (London, 1983); Sally Marks, *The Illusion of Peace: International Relations in Europe 1918-1933* (London, 1976).

8. On Germany's position in the international economy from 1920 to 1933 begin with Wolfram Fischer, "Die Weimarer Republik unter den weltwirtschaftlichen Bedingungen der Zwischenkriegszeit," in Hans Mommsen et al., eds., *Industrielles System und politische Entwicklung in der Weimarer Republik* (Dusseldorf, 1974), 26-51 and the literature cited there.

9. "German Tariff Proposals," *London Times*, 23 July 1924. Several members of the ministerial bureaucracy produced lengthy essays on the importance of trade and trade policy for Germany's economic future. See, e.g., Hans Ernst Posse (under-secretary for Commercial Affairs in the Economics Ministry 1925-1933, state secretary 1933-1941), *Grundlagen der künftigen deutschen Handelspolitik* (Berlin, 1924); Kurt Wiedenfeld, *Deutschlands Handelspolitische Aufgaben* (Leipzig, 1925); Ernst Trendelenburg (Reichskommisar for Import/Export Permission 1919-1923, state secretary in the Economics Ministry 1923-1932), "Deutsche Aussenhandelspolitik. Grundlagen Ergebnisse, und Ausblicke," in *Wirtschaftsdienst* 10 (1925), 51, 1091-93; 52, 1937-39. It is revealing that from 1923 to 1941 the Economics Ministry's top bureaucratic post (state secretary) went to two men (Trendelenburg and Posse) with primary expertise in foreign trade matters.

10. "German Tariff Proposals," *London Times*, 23 July 1924. The Versailles reparations literature is voluminous. The outstanding studies include Charles S. Maier, *Recasting Bourgeois Europe. Stabilization in Italy, France, and Germany in the Decade after World War I* (Princeton, 1975); Steven Schucker, *The End of French Predominance In Europe: The Financial Crisis of 1924 and the Adoption of the Dawes Plan* (Chapel Hill, 1976); Jacques Bariety, *Les relations franco-allemandes apres la Premiere Guerre mondiale, 10 novembre 1918 – 10 janvier 1925: de l'execution a la negociation* (Paris, 1977); Marc Trachtenberg, *Reparation in World Politics: France and European Economic Diplomacy 1919-1923* (New York, 1980). Also informative is Sally Marks, "Reparations Re-Considered: A Reminder," *Central European History* 2, no. 4; David Felix, "Reparations Re-Considered with a Vengeance," ibid. 4, no. 2. Recent studies of note include Bruce Kent, *The Spoils of War: The Politics, Economics, and Diplomacy of Reparations 1918-1932* (New York, 1989); Hans Otto Schötz, *Der Kampf um die Mark 1923/24: Die deutsche Währungsstabilisierung unter dem Einfluss der nationalen Interessen Frankreichs, Grossbritaniens und der USA* (New York, 1987).

11. Aldcroft, *From Versailles to Wall Street*, 305. On world trade in the interwar period, see Aldcroft's summary discussion. More detailed secondary studies include A. Maddison, "Growth and Fluctuation in the World Economy 1870-1960," *Banca Nazionale del Lavoro Quarterly Review* 15 (1962), 185 ff.; W.S. and E.S. Woytinsky, *World Commerce and Governments* (New York, 1955); Maizels, *Industrial Growth and World Trade* (Cambridge, 1963); P.L. Yates, *Forty Years of World Trade* (London, 1959).

12. According to Posse, interwar governments typically placed so many limitations on MFN agreements that the MFN clause had become a "only a shell without a seed," *Aus der Werkstatt der Handelspolitik* (Stuttgart/Cologne, 1949), 18. Several League of Nations reports documented the role of protectionist trade policies in inhibiting a full revival of European commercial relations in the 1920s, see e.g., *International Economic Conference: Final Report of the Trade Barriers Committee of the*

International Chamber of Commerce (Geneva, 1927); *Tariff Level Indices* (Geneva, 1927); *Commercial Policy in the Interwar Period* (Geneva, 1942).

13. "Denkschrift zur Handelspolitik der Regierung," (manuscript 1924-1925), BA Nachlass Posse/2; Rene Albrecht-Carrié, *The Meaning of the First World War*, 114 ff..

14. On economic developments in Eastern Europe between the wars see Ivan T. Berend and György Ranki, *Economic Development of East-Central Europe in the 19th and 20th Centuries* (New York, 1974); Zdenak Drabek, "Foreign Trade Performance and Policy," in M.C. Kaser and E.A. Radice, eds., *The Economic History of Eastern Europe 1919-1975, Economic Structure and Performance between the Two Wars* (New York, 1986), vol. 1, 379-466; Gy. Ranki and J. Tomaszewski, "The Role of the State in Industry, Banking and Trade," in Kaser and Radice, eds., *The Economic History of Eastern Europe 1919-1975,Interwar Policy, the War, and Reconstruction* (New York, 1986), vol. 2, 3-48; Nicholas Spulber, *The State and Economic Development in Eastern Europe* (New York, 1966); Ranki, "The State and Society in East Central Europe after the First World War," in Soloman Wank et al., eds., *The Mirror of History: Essays in Honor of Fritz Fellner* (Santa Barbara, CA, 1988).

15. Friedrich Hertz, *The Economic Problem of the Danubian Countries*, (New York, 1970), 56. On the evolution of these thoughts see e.g., Rudolf Jaworski, *Handel und Gewerbe im Nationalitätenkampf: Studien zur Wirtschaftsgesinnung der Polen in der Provinz Posen (1871-1914)*, (Göttingen, 1986); Wiktor Sukiennicki, *East Central Europe during World War I*, 2 vols. (Boulder, Col., 1984); Josef Chlebowczyk, *Miezdy dyktatem, realiami, a prawem do samostanowiennia: Prawo do samookreslenia i problem granic we wschodniej Europe Srodkowej w pierwsej wojnie swiatowej oraz po jej zakonczeniu* (Warsaw, 1988).

16. On German foreign economic policy toward East European areas not covered in this study see György Ránki, *Economy and Foreign Policy: The Struggle of the Great Powers for Hegemony in the Danube Valley, 1919-1939* (Boulder, Colo., 1983); the contributions of Marie-Luise Recker and Merja-Liisa Hinkkanen-Lievonen in Recker, ed., *Von der Konkurrenz zur Rivalität: Das britisch-deutsche Verhältnis in den Ländern der Europäischen Peripherie 1919-1939* (Wiesbaden, 1986).

17. Joseph Rothschild, *East Central Europe between the Wars* (Seattle, 1974), 15, 22. These developments have received the most attention in the successor states of the old Austro-Hungarian Empire, see Leo Pasvolsky, *Economic Nationalism of the Danubian States* (New York, 1928); Frederick Hertz, *The Economic Problem of the Danubian Countries* (New York, 1970). For a defense of these policies see Jan Kofman, "Economic Nationalism in East-Central Europe in the Interwar Period," in Henryk Szlajfer, ed., *Economic Nationalism in East-Central Europe and South America, 1918-1939* (Geneva, 1990), 191-249, particularly 240 ff.

18. Maddison, "Growth and Fluctuation in the World Economy, 1870-1960," as cited in Aldcroft, *From Versailles to Wall Street*, 101, 119.

19. Cited in Peter Grupp, *Deutsche Aussenpolitik im Schatten von Versailles 1918-1920: Zur Politik des Auswärtigen Amts vom Ende des Ersten Weltkriegs und der November-Revolution bis zum Inkrafttreten des Versailler Vertrags* (Paderborn, 1988), 8. Grupp argues that the arrival of Wilson and Lenin on the European diplomatic scene afforded Germany new diplomatic options, even in the difficult circumstances of defeat, but that the old bureaucrats of the Foreign Office were incapable of recognizing these new opportunities. By the time the Versailles treaty was signed, a number of significant German-Polish economic agreements with political overtones had already been concluded (see Chapter four).

20. "Denkschrift zur Handelspolitik der Regierung," (manuscript 1924-1925), BA Nachlass Posse/2.

21. Governing Committee for German Expellees from Russia to the Foreign Office 12 December 1919, BA R 43I/1192. On Germany's struggle to find its place in the

interwar order see Werner Conze, "Deutschlands weltpolitische Sonderstellung in den zwanziger Jahren," *VfZ* 9 (1961), 166-77; Gerhard Weinberg, "The Defeat of Germany in 1918 and the European Balance of Power," *CEH* 2 (1969); J. Hiden, *Germany and Europe 1919-1939* (London, 1977). Peter Krüger's *Die Aussenpolitik der Republik von Weimar* (Darmstadt, 1985) may be the best of the recent studies; Marshall Lee and Wolfgang Michalka, *German Foreign Policy 1917-1933: Continuity or Break?* (London, 1987); Christoph Kimmich, *Germany and the League of Nations.* For secondary sources on all aspects of German foreign policy consult Christoph Kimmich, *German Foreign Policy, 1918-1945: A Guide to Research and Research Materials,* 2nd ed., (Willmington, Del., 1991).

22. Reprinted in Gerhard Zwoch, ed., *Gustav Stresemann, Reichstagsreden,* (Bonn, 1972) 20-42. In addition to the Zwoch collection, subsets of Stresemann's papers are variously available in Henry Bernhard, ed., *Gustav Stresemann: Vermächtnis. Der Nachlass in drei Bänden* (Berlin, 1932-33); Eric Sutton, ed., *Gustav Stresemann. His Diaries, Letters, and Papers,* 3 vols. (New York, 1935-40); Arnold Harttung, ed., *Gustav Stresemann: Schriften* (Berlin, 1976). The earlier collections should be consulted in conjunction with Hans Gatzke, "The Stresemann Papers," *JMH* 26 (1954); the full Nachlass is available at the PAAA, Bonn and on microfilms of the T-120 series as cataloged in George Kent, *A Catalog of Files and Microfilms of the German Foreign Ministry 1920-1945,* 4 vols. (Stanford, Calif., 1962-1972), vol. 2 (1964), 987 ff., 1162 ff.

23. Meeting of the Union of Machine Building Institutes (VDMA), 28 April 1927, BA R 13I/252; Stresemann to the Central Committee of the DVP, 22 November 1925, reprinted by Henry Turner in *VfZ* 15 (1967), 434. Important secondary studies of Stresemann's policies as foreign minister include Hans Gatzke, *Stresemann and the Rearmament of Germany* (Baltimore, Md., 1954); Robert Grathwol, *Stresemann and the DNVP: Reconciliation or Revenge in German Foreign Policy* (Lawrence, Kan., 1980); Henry Turner, *Stresemann and the Politics of the Weimar Republic* (Princeton, 1983). For full biographies see Felix Hirsch, *Stresemann. Ein Lebensbild* (Göttingen, 1978); Wolfgang Stresemann, *Mein Vater Gustav Stresemann* (Berlin and Munich, 1979); Kurt Koszyk, *Gustav Stresemann. Der kaisertreue Demokrat. Eine Biographie* (Cologne, 1989); Wilhelm von Sternburg, *Gustav Stresemann* (Frankfurt, 1990). Earlier literature is accessible through Martin Walsdorff, ed., *Bibliographie Gustav Stresemann* (Dusseldorf, 1972).

24. Speech on German foreign trade policy to the Hamburg chapter of the Central Association of German Wholesalers, 4 December 1925, carried by Wolff's Telegraphisches Buro, Nr. 2189-2190, BA R 43I/1085. Despite the central role of foreign economic policies in Weimar's overall foreign policy, there exist almost no studies of Weimar foreign economic policy that focus on domestic economic interests as reflected in foreign policy. Notable is the work of Karl Pohl, particularly *Weimars Wirtschaft und die Aussenpolitik der Republik, 1924-1926: Vom Dawes-Plan zum Internationalen Eisenpakt* (Dusseldorf, 1979). Also exceptional is Maier, *Recasting Bourgeois Europe,* especially 516 ff. although this is not a study of foreign policy per se. The contributions by Dirk Stegmann and Alan Milward in Mommsen et al., eds., *Industrielles System,* explore German economic interests without explicitly connecting these to specific foreign policy actions.

25. Arthur Dix, *Wirtschaftskrieg und Kriegswirtschaft* (Berlin, 1920); O. Korfes and W. Dieckmann, "Die Weltwirtschaftliche Abhängigkeit Deutschlands vor dem Kriege," in *Archiv für Politik und Geschichte* 5 (1925), 1 ff.; Reichsarchiv, ed., *Kriegsrüstung und Kriegswirtschaft. Die militärische, wirtschaftliche und finanzielle Rüstung Deutschlands von der Reichsgründung bis zum Ausbruch des Weltkrieges* (Berlin, 1930); Gerald Feldman, *Army, Industry, and Labor 1914-1918* (Princeton, 1966); Lothar Burchardt, *Friedenswirtschaft und Kriegsvorsorge. Deutschlands wirtschaftliche*

Rüstungsbestrebungen vor 1914 (Boppard, 1968); Militärgeschichtliches Forschungsamt Freiburg, *Handbuch zur deutschen Militärgeschichte 1648-1939* (Frankfurt/Main, 1968), vol. 5; Reinhold Zilch, "Zur wirtschaftlichen Vorbereitung des deutschen Imperialismus auf den ersten Weltkrieg. Das Protokoll der Sitzung des 'Wirtschaftlichen Ausschusses' bei der 'Ständigen Kommission für Mobilmachungangelegenheiten' vom Mai 1914," in *ZfG* 24 (1976), 202 ff. Revealing memoirs include Joachim Delbrück, ed., Clemens von Delbrück, *Die wirtschaftliche Mobilmachung in Deutschland 1914* (Munich, 1924); Eliza von Moltke, ed., Helmuth von Moltke, *Erinnerungen, Briefe, Dokumente 1877-1916* (Stuttgart, 1922).

26. Friedrich-Wilhelm Henning, *Das industrialisierte Deutschland 1914 bis 1972* (Paderborn, 1974), 50-51; Günther Haberland, *Elf Jahre Staatliche Regelung der Ein-und Ausfuhr. Eine systematische Darstellung der deutschen Aussenhandelsregelung in den Jahren 1914-1925* (Leipzig, 1927), 4.

27. The ordinances themselves are contained in *Reichsgesetzblatt* [hereafter *RGBl.*] 1914, 259.

28. Haberland, *Elf Jahre Staatliche Regelung*, 6 ff., 14; Arthur Dix, *Wirtschaftskrieg und Kriegswirtschaft. Zur Geschichte des deutschen Zusammenbruchs* (Berlin: Ernst Siegfried Mittler, 1920), 341. On the KRA see Feldman, *Army Industry and Labor*, 45 ff.; Ehlert, *Zentralbehörden*, 38 ff.

29. *RGBl.* 1914, 352; *RGBl.* 1915, 135.

30. Haberland, *Elf Jahre Staatliche Regelung*, 16 ff.; Dix, *Wirtschaftskrieg und Kriegswirtschaft* 343.

31. On the evolution of the Interior Office 1914-1917 see Friedrich Facius, *Wirtschaft und Staat. Die Entwicklung der staatlichen Wirtschaftsverwaltung in Deutschland vom 17.Jh. bis 1945* (Boppard, 1959) 235, 239; Haberland, *Elf Jahre*, 28 ff.; Walther Hubatsch, *Entstehung und Entwicklung des Reichswirtschaftsministerium, 1880-1933* (Berlin, 1978), 15 ff.; Hans Gotthard Ehlert, *Die wirtschaftliche Zentralbehörde des deutschen Reiches 1914-1919* (Wiesbaden, 1982), 53 ff.. Summary discussion in Hans Fenske, "Die Verwaltung im Ersten Weltkrieg," in Jeserich et al., eds., *Deutsche Verwaltungsgeschichte*, vol. 3, 892-93.

32. Executive Secretary of Union of German Iron and Steel Industrialists Jakob Reichert to all member groups, 31 October 1914, BA R 13I/181. Based on Haberland's figure of 27,500 export applications filed with the Interior Office between August 1914 and January 1915. Haberland, *Elf Jahre*, 29.

33. Haberland, *Elf Jahre*, 31; Dix, *Wirtschaftskrieg und Kriegswirtschaft*, 342-43. For example, Jakob Wilhelm Reichert, Bueck's successor as executive secretary (Geschäftsführer) of the Union of German Iron and Steel Industrialists, served as the Agent for the Central Agency covering iron and steel products. Although the Central Offices became channels for unprecedented private sector influence on government trade policy, Ehlert is wrong to imply that the offices "were created by export-oriented industrial sectors ... for the purpose of influencing state controlled foreign trade," *Wirtschaftliche Zentralbehörde*, 295. The impetus came from the Interior Office as a way of alleviating the administrative burden on the government bureaucracy.

34. Klein, "Geschichte des VdESI" BA R 13I/13; Haberland, *Elf Jahre*, 31.

35. Data for the Iron and Steel Central Agency in Klein, "Geschichte des VdESI" BA R 13I/13, Bl. 25. By comparison, the Reich Economics Office employed forty upper-level officers (Beamte) and had a total size of 153, including servants and doormen, Hubatsch, *Reichswirtschaftsministerium*, 21; the entire Reich Interior Office employed only 192 officers in 1914.

36. Haberland, *Elf Jahre*, 31. The Raw Materials Section (transferred from the Prussian War Ministry to the Reich War Office in 1916) continued to play an important role along with the specific Kriegsgesellschaften and government-dominated Zen-

tral-Einkaufs-Gesellschaft established in 1915 by the Interior Office. The deputy commanding generals (stellvertretende Generalkommandos) used their extensive powers under the 1851 Prussian Law of Siege (invoked at mobilization) to make arbitrary seizures of shipments they considered suspicious, see Klein, "Geschichte des VdESI" BA R13I/13 and BA R13I/181.

37. Reichert with a view from heavy industry, in Klein, "Geschichte des VdESI," BA R 13I/13, Bl. 26. For agreement in the finishing industries on the continued need for trade controls see, e.g., the comments by AEG Direktor Felix Deutsch in the *Vossische Zeitung*, 9 November 1919, cited in Haberland, *Elf Jahre Staatlicher Regelung*, 52.

38. Haberland, *Elf Jahre*, 38-44; *RGBl.* 1920, 334.

39. The first new compendium of goods covered by the intensified 1919 export controls appeared in April 1920. *RGBl.* 1919, 1919, 2128; Haberland, *Elf Jahre*, 50.

40. Klein, "Geschichte," BA R 13I/13; Ernst Trendelenburg, "Weltwirtschaftskrise und Aussenhandel" (Lecture presented at the Deutsche Hochschule für Politik in Berlin on 26 January 1921), 30.

41. Hirsch to an interministerial group in the Economics Ministry, 18 November 1919, BA R 43I/1172. Hirsch had been professor at the Handelshochschule in Cologne, 1917-1919; a department head in the Reich Food Ministry, March-August 1919; and served first as Under-secretary, August 1919-March 1920, and then state secretary, April 1920-March 1923, in Reich Economics Ministry.

42. Ernst Trendelenburg, "Weltwirtschaftskrise und Aussenhandel," 30. In contrast to Eckart Kehr's view that the war economy "made the bureaucracy conscious of its gigantic intervention potential," the regulation of trade between 1914 and 1920 did more the opposite, i.e., it made the bureaucracy aware of its own limited abilities for intervention and the need to rely on voluntary cooperation with the private sector, Kehr, "Die Diktatur der Bürokratie," in Wehler, ed., Kehr, *Die Primat der Innenpolitik* (Berlin, 1965), 250.

43. *RGBl.* 1920, 500. These new regulations were based on the export and import ordinances of December 1919 and March 1920.

44. That these new offices had the same designation as the new foreign trade department (Außenhandelsstelle) in the Foreign Office, later renamed Department X, only highlights the chaotic state of German trade control bureaucracy at this time.

45. The concept of "economic self-administration" has been central to the development of German corporatism over the past 80 years. Rudolf Wissel (SPD), Economics Minister (February-July 1919) set out his early thoughts on the subject in "Wirtschaftliche Selbstverwaltung – zwei Kundgebungen des Reichswirtschaftsministeriums," in *Deutsche Gemeinwirtschaft* 10 (1919). In April 1919 Wissel had begun to develop the idea of the Aussenhandelsstellen as part of his larger concepts of self-administration and Gemeinwirtschaft. See Ehlert, *Wirtschaftliche Zentralbehörden*, 300 ff.

46. Haberland, *Elf Jahre*, 58 ff.; Wilfried Berg, "Reichswirtschaftsministerium," in *Deutsche Verwaltungsgeschichte*, vol. 4, 169, note 7.

47. The Reich plenipotentiary was considered a civil servant in both public and criminal law. Article 7 of the 8 April 1920 regulations formalized the power of the central offices both to collect the new export tax for the government and to charge their own fees for processing import/export applications.

48. Klein, "Geschichte," BA R13I/13, Bl. 25; report of the Economics Ministry to the Chancellery, 20 May 1920, BA R 43I/1172.

49. Wolff's Telegraphische Buro [hereafter "WTB"] report no. 1235, 15 July 1020, BA R 43I/1172; Klein, "Geschichte," BA R 13I/13, Bl. 87-88.

50. BA R13I/196.

51. The Executive Committee of the Union of German Iron and Steel Industrialists discussed this possibility at its 21 October 1921 meeting, Klein, "Geschichte des VdESI" BA R13I/13 Bl. 91. However, that type of regulation would have required an extraordinary degree of consensus among the various private-sector groups. As the trade policy conflicts of 1924 to 1925 would soon demonstrate, that degree of consensus did not exist.

52. Ernst Wolfgang Bockenförde, "Der Zusammenbruch der Monarchie und die Entstehung der Weimarer Republik," in *Deutsche Verwaltungsgeschichte*, vol. 4, 17. In similar language, Richard Teichgraeber has recently referred to "the distinctly German view that economics must focus on a self-evident symbiosis of state and economy," book review of Keith Tribe, *Governing the Economy, AHR* 95, no. 5 (1990), 1567.

53. For an analytic narrative of these corporatist developments (and parallel evolutions in Italy and France) 1919-1925 see Maier, *Recasting Bourgeois Europe.*

54. *RGBl.* 1917, 963.

55. On these developments see Fenske, "Verwaltung im Ersten Weltkrieg," *Deutsche Verwaltungsgeschichte*, vol. 3, 892-93; Facius, *Wirtschaft und Staat*, 84-93; Hubatsch, *Reichswirtschaftsministerium*, 19 ff.; Ehlert, *WirtschaftlicheZentralbehörde*, 54-72.

56. This, even though Helfferich had stated at the creation of the Economics Office in March 1917 that the "conclusion of trade treaties" would remain the responsibility of the Foreign Office, cited in Hubatsch, *Reichswirtschaftsministerium*, 50.

57. On this see especially Kurt Doss, *Das deutsche Auswärtige Amt im Übergang vom Kaiserreich zur Weimarer Republik* (Dusseldorf, 1977).

58. As Doss points out: "An imperial State Secretary was not receiving "penitents" submitting requests or suggestions at his office, but rather he had travelled to the home of an insistent "Lobby" that demanded nothing less than the reform of the office which he held by the grace of the Chancellor and his Sovereign …. The visit by members of the Reichstag was in the same sense an unprecedented event," *Das deutsche Auswärtige Amt*, 145.

59. Facius, *Wirtschaft und Staat*, 91; Hubatsch, *Reichswirtschaftsministerium*, 19-20.

60. *Sten Ber.*, Bd. 313, 1914/18, 5657 ff.; Doss, *Das Auswärtige Amt*, 171. On private interests and the new Economics Office see Friedrich Zunkel, *Industrie und Staatssozialismus. Der Kampf um die Wirtschaftsordnung in Deutschland 1914-1918* (Dusseldorf, 1974), 142 ff. as cited in Fenske, "Verwaltung," 893.

61. Although the reforms as implemented did not include all of Schuler's original proposals, they did satisfy long-standing bourgeois reform demands such as increased economic training, merging the consular and diplomatic services and abolishing the departmental distinction between political and commercial affairs in favor of an integrated approach in geographically organized departments, Heinz Günter Sasse, "Zur Geschichte des Auswärtigen Amtes," in Auswärtiges Amt, ed., *100 Jahre Auswärtiges Amt* (Bonn, 1970), 34 ff. The successes and limits of the reforms are treated in detail in Doss, *Das Auswärtige Amt.* Jost Delbrück has noted how "despite the reforms, the special esprit de corps of the foreign service remained intact," "Auswärtige Angelegenheiten," in *Deutsche Verwaltungsgeschichte*, vol. 4, 153. Peter Grupp argues that the increased influence of "economic experts" within the Foreign Office after 1918 meant simply that "liberal economic and financial imperialists replaced autocratic military imperialists without questioning [German] imperialism per se," an analysis that echoes Woodruff Smith's division of German foreign strategists into economically oriented "Weltpolitiker" and the "conservative Lebensraum imperialists," Grupp, *Deutsche Aussenpolitik*, 45; Smith, *Ideological Origins of Nazi Imperialism*, 52 ff., 83 ff.

62. Cabinet meeting of 10 April 1920 in BA R 43I/1172. On the dispute over the Information and Reporting Service (which dragged on in muted form through

1927) see Ehlert, *Wirtschaftliche Zentralbehörde*, 201-12. Correspondence between the Foreign Office and the Economics Ministry on that issue, BA R 43I/1198. On the Foreign Office during Weimar see Sasse, *100 Jahre Auswärtiges Amt 1870-1970*, Kurt Doss, "The History of the German Foreign Office," in Zara Steiner, ed., *The Times Survey of Foreign Ministries of the World* (London, 1982); Herbert von Hindenburg, *Das Auswärtige Amt im Wandel der Zeiten* (Frankfurt, 1932).

63. See the appeals by these ministries 13 Feb and 19 March in BA R 43I/1172. Fortunately the Economics Ministry never carried out its plans to call on the constitutionally established Reich Economic Council to "advise the government in all basic questions of foreign trade control," Economics Ministry draft of Foreign Trade Regulations 3 March 1920, BA R 43I/1172.

64. Hamm to the Chancellery State Secretary Franz Bracht, 24 September 1924, BA R 43I/1085. Curtius considered the trade department to be "the core of the Economics Ministry," Julius Curtius, *Sechs Jahre Minister der Deutschen Republik* (Heidelberg, 1948) 19, 20 ff.

65. Günther Stein in the *Berliner Tagblatt und Handelszeitung*, 20 May 1930, cited in Wilfried Berg, "Reichswirtschaftsministerium," in *Deutsche Verwaltungsgeschichte*, vol. 4, 169, note 6.

66. Ernst Trendelenburg, "Weltwirtschaftskrise und Aussenhandel," 31.

67. Luther cites the example of the DNVP and the Finance Ministry, *Politiker Ohne Partei* (Stuttgart, 1960), 316. Just as one must be careful not to portray the correspondence between economic interest groups and political parties too strongly, so, too, one must not suggest a mechanistic control of entire Weimar ministries by either the interest groups or the parties. For thoughts from another context on how private interests might "capture" portions of the bureaucracy see the sources cited in Stephen D. Krasner, *Defending the National Interest. Raw Materials Investments and U.S. Foreign Policy* (Princeton, 1978), 61, 63.

68. After the elections of 1924, the DNVP Reichstag faction (111 members) contained fifty-two members of the Reichslandbund and thirty-nine active farmers. By comparison, the next largest group of agrarians were located in the Catholic Center Party (sixty-nine parliamentary deputies), four Landbund members and thirteen active farmers, Stürmer, Koalitionen und Oppositionen," in Stürmer, ed., *Weimarer Republik*, 251, note 10, 252 note 14. "The vocation on which all of fates hang is agriculture," "Principles of the DNVP, (undated, 1925), Bayer Archiv, Leverkusen, 62/10.3, Bd.1. On the DNVP in Weimar see Werner Liebe, *Die DNVP 1918-1924* (Dusseldorf, 1924); L. Hertzmann, *DNVP. Right-wing Opposition in the Weimar Republic 1918-1933* (Lincoln, Neb., 1963); Klemens von Klemperer, *Konservative Bewegungen zwischen Kaiserreich und Nationalsozialismus* (Munich, 1962).

69. At a meeting with the chancellor on 19 March 1925, Reich Land Union leaders Eberhard von Kalckreuth, Karl Hepp, and Prätorius von Richthofen told Luther that "One must above all prevent the importation of non-essential goods." Chancellery Office memorandum BA R 43I/1085. General-Director Albert Vögler (Dortmund, United Steel) summed up the position of heavy industry in a speech to the iron industrialists (Eisenhüttentag) on 30 November 1924: "The revival of the domestic market is economically and politically far more important than the promotion of exports. We can bring our balance of trade in order better by limiting imports rather than by strengthening exports." BA R13I/346.

70. The DNVP advocated efforts to "preserve or if possible increase the ability of the internal market to absorb domestic products." The German Nationals were also the only party not to shy away from the term "protectionism" (Schutzzollpolitik) and proudly proclaimed that "no other party has so energetically emphasized the need to tackle the [trade balance] problem not only through increasing exports but also by controlling imports." The DNVP also attempted to associate export-

oriented policies with "the left-wing parties," Executive Secretary of the Union of German Iron and Steel Industrialists and DNVP Reichstag Deputy Jakob Reichert's speech on German National Tariff and Trade Policy to a group of DNVP industrialists in Cologne, 9 September 1926, BA R13I/101. The foregoing material on heavy industry and the DNVP is not immediately compatible with Peter Hayes's view that earlier "internecine quarrels over tariffs were not repeated under Weimar" and that "heavy industrialists ... resisted all forms of protectionism," "Industrial Factionalism," *CEH* 24, no. 2 (1991), 126.

71. Stresemann repeatedly warned against overemphasizing protection for the domestic market: "Industries in various countries do not have an exclusive right to the domestic market and it wrong to think that the government's sole responsibility is to secure the domestic market with import bans, quotas, and tariff barriers." Speech to a meeting of the Union of German Machine Building Institutes, Berlin, 28 April 1927, BA R 13I/252.

72. Hans von Raumer (AEG, a leading representative of the electro-technical industry, and economics minister in the Stresemann cabinet, August-October 1923) told the Central Association of the German Electro-Technical Industry on 20 June 1924 that "We must proceed from the principle that Germany's economic future rests on the export of finished goods, which means that the tariff should not increase the production costs of the German finished goods industry." BA R 13I/346. Similarly in Principles of the DVP, Bayer Archiv, Leverkusen 62/10.3, Bd. 1.

73. Within the Center, agrarian interests were frequently offset by the party's labor wing. On the dilemmas of the Center Party during Weimar see above all the work of Ralph Morsey: *Die Deutsche Zentrumspartei 1917-1923* (Dusseldorf, 1966); "Die deutsche Zentrumspartei," in Morsey and Matthias, eds., *Das Ende der Parteien* (Dusseldorf, 1960), 281-453; Morsey, ed., *Die Protokolle der Reichstagsfaktion der deutsche Zentrumspartei*, 2 vols. (Mainz, 1969, 1981).

74. The fragmentation of bourgeois interests in Weimar Germany has been discussed in a larger political context by Larry E. Jones, "'The Dying Middle': Weimar Germany and the Fragmentation of Bourgeois Politics," *CEH* 5 (1972), 23-54; and as a social phenomenon by Hans Mommsen, "The Decline of the Bürgertum in Late Nineteenth-and early Twentieth-Century Germany," reprinted in translation in Mommsen, *From Weimar to Auschwitz* (Princeton, 1991), 11-27.

75. Kanitz to the state secretary in the Reich chancellery, 9 February 1925; Transportation Minister Rudolph Krohne to the chancellery, 18 March 1925, BA R 43I/1085.

76. Chancellery Office memorandum on a meeting of the Reich Land Union (Eberhard von Kalckreuth, Hepp, von Richtofen) and Reichstag member Walter Stubbendorf with the chancellor on 19 March 1925. Hepp rejected Posse as director of the proposed central office as he "tended to put export interests in the foreground," BA R 43I/1085.

77. Minutes of the Chefbesprechung, 23 February 1925, BA R 43I/1085.

78. Karl Dietrich Erdmann and Hans Booms, eds., *Akten der Reichskanzlei. Die Kabinette Luther I und II*, (Boppard, 1977) [hereafter: "*Akten Luther*"], 153.

79. Government resolution of 19 March 1925 on the creation of and the standing orders for the Trade Policy Committee, BA R 43I/1079. Stresemann gained a small victory within a large defeat by securing Foreign Office chairmanship of the new committee under Karl Ritter, Director of the Foreign Office's own Special Office for Economics (Sonderreferat Wirtschaft) when earlier discussions had all favored Economics State Secretary Trendelenburg as chairman.

80. Typical of business opposition was the Altona Chamber of Commerce to State Secretary Ritter 16 January 1925. See also Ritter's report on a meeting with labor

representatives 5 December 1924 and his letter to the major labor unions and employee associations 30 December 1925, all in BA R 43I/1085.

81. Still unsurpassed in its analysis of Weimar governmental (in)stability is the work of Michael Stürmer, *Koalition und Opposition in der Weimarer Republik, 1924-1928* (Dusseldorf, 1967); summarized as "Koalitionen und Oppositionen: Bedingungen parlamentarischer Instabilität," reprinted in Stürmer, ed., *Die Weimarer Republik. Belagerte Civitas* 2nd ed., (Königstein, 1980), 237-253.

82. Minutes by Jakob Reichert (Union of German Iron and Steel Industrialists) of a meeting between a "large number of representatives of the iron producing and processing industries" and members of the Reich Economics and Foreign Offices, 8 November 1918, BA R13I/189.

83. Meeting on 19 December 1918, BA R13I/189. The German Industrial Council (Der deutsche Industrierat) met for the first time in February 1918 as the continuation of the War Committee of German Industry (Kriegsausschuss der deutschen Industrie) formed in 1914 to encompass both of the prewar industrial Dachverbände, the Central Association of German Industrialists and the Union of Industrialists. On these organizational developments and the creation of a new industrial Reichsverband der Deutscher Industrie in 1919, see Friedrich Zunckel, "Die Gewichtung der Industriegruppen bei Etablierung des Reichsverbandes der Deutschen Industrie," in Mommsen et al., eds., *Industrielles System*, 637-47; M. Metzner, "Der Reichsverband der Deutschen Industrie. Gründung und organisatorischer Aufbau," in Berg, ed., *Der Weg zum industriellen Spitzenverband*, 118-143; R. Tross, "Die Wirtschaftspolitik der Reichsverband der deutschen Industrie," in ibid., 144-225.

84. Hamburg Committee for the Freedom of Foreign Trade to the chancellor, 13 July 1922, BA R 43I/1172. Similar or overlapping groups, such as the Hamburg Committee for the Return to a Peace Economy, existed in other North German cities as well.

85. Ernst Trendelenburg, "Weltwirtschaftskrise und Aussenhandel," 31.

86. Scholz presented his plan to the Reich Economic Council (Vorläufiger Reichswirtschaftsrat) on 16 March 1921. Meeting of the Main Committee (Hauptausschuss) of the VdESI, 6 May 1921, BA R 13I/196. For the economic context of these debates consult Gerald D. Feldman, The Political Economy of Germany's Relative Stabilization during the 1920/21 Depression," in Feldman et al., eds., *The German Inflation* (Berlin, 1982), 180-206.

87. *Akten der Reichskanzlei. Die Kabinette Marx I und II* (Boppard, 1973) [herafter "*Akten Marx*"], 187-89. On German tariff efforts in 1924, particularly in connection with reaching a trade agreement with France see Maier, *Recasting Bourgeois Europe*, 516 ff.; Karl Heinrich Pohl, *Weimar's Wirtschaft und die Aussenpolitik der Republik 1924-1926* (Dusseldorf, 1979), 44-49, 51-53, 55-58. Also Dirk Stegmann, "Deutsche Zoll- und Handelspolitik 1924/25-1929 unter besonderer Berücksichtigung agrarischer und industrieller Interessen," in Mommsen et al., eds., *Industrielles System*, 499-513; Michael Stürmer, *Koalition und Opposition in der Weimarer Republik, 1924-1928*, 47 ff.; Arno Panzer, *Das Ringen um die deutsche Agrarpolitik von der Währungsstabilisierung bis zur Agrardebatte im Reichstag im Dezember 1928* (Kiel, 1970), 7 ff.

88. *Akten Marx*, 227-28. The Enabling Law of 5 August 1922 (*RGBl.*, I, 709) was due to expire on 30 June 1924.

89. Cabinet meeting of 19 June 1924, *Akten Marx*, 717.

90. Cabinet meeting of 19 June 1924, *Akten Marx*, 717-722.

91. Reich Land Union to the government, 21 June 1924, *Akten Marx*, 729; Executive Committee of the Union of German Farmer's Associations (August Crone-Munzebrock) to the Chancellor 17 June 1924 in BA R 43I/1216. An index of

German industrial prices stood at 146 in 1924, while the corresponding agricultural price index stood at just 112 (1913 = 100), Jacobs and Richter, "Grosshandelspreise," 83.

92. Cabinet meeting of 19 June 1924, *Akten Marx*, 717-722.

93. Maier, *Recasting Bourgeois Europe*, 526-27. On relations between the heavy iron producers and the AVI iron consumers and the consequences for German tariff legislation see Ulrich Nocken, "Inter-Industrial Conflicts and Alliances as Exemplified by the AVI Agreement," in Mommsen et al., eds., *Industrielles System*, 693-704; Stegmann, "Deutsche Zoll-und Handelspolitik," in ibid., 508-9; Maier, *Recasting Bourgeois Europe*, 526 ff.; Pohl, *Weimars Wirtschaft*, 47 ff., 53-55.

94. Evidence on this point abounds, see e.g., Vögler's essay in *Eisen und Stahl* 44 (1924), 1608 ff.; Reichert's margin comments expressing frustration at an RdI memo of 10 July 1924 and its "caution" in not supporting agricultural tariffs, BA R13I/351; Krohn describes a "tariff alliance of industry and agriculture," *Stabilisierung und Ökonomische Interessen*, 174 and ff.; Stegmann outlines the revival of "solidarity protectionism" 1924-25," in Mommsen, ed., *Industrielles System*, 506.

95. Gessner, *Agrarverbände*, 68 ff.; the point is made most forcefully by Pohl, *Weimars Wirtschaft*, 115 in explicit rejection of Panzer's assertion that there remained only a "very weak political-ideological band that carried the cooperation between agriculture and industry," *Ringen um Agrarpolitik*, 43.

96. Cabinet meeting, 19 June 1924, *Akten Marx*, 721.

97. Cabinet meeting, 19 June 1924, *Akten Marx*, 721.

98. Cabinet meetings, 19 and 26 June 1924, *Akten Marx*, 717-22, 743-47.

99. Cabinet meeting, 26 June 1924, *Akten Marx*, 743.

100. Cabinet meeting of 2 July 1924, *Akten Marx*, 717; Reichsrat-Drucksache, 1924, Nr. 104.

101. *Akten Marx*, 888, note 14.

102. E.g., the German Chamber of Commerce's Governing Committee passed a resolution on 23 September 1924 accepting a "provisional change" in the tariff rates, including the 1914 grain rates, but did nothing to campaign for passage of the new tariff in the Reichstag, PAAA, Zollwesen 4, Bd. 3.

103. Kanitz to Chancellor Marx, 25 July 1924, Marx to Kanitz, 31 July; Foreign Trade Association to the chancellor, 14 July, all in BA R 43I/2416. Prussian, Saxon, and Hansa-city delegates did vote against the tariff, which passed the Reichsrat on 8 August, 35 to 26 with 5 abstentions.

104. Cabinet meetings of 21 and 26 August 1924, *Akten Marx*, 995-96, 1001-1002; Hamm to Chancellery State Secretary Bracht, 26 August 1924, BA R 43I/2416.

105. *Sten Ber.*, Bd. 381, 1143 ff.; Gessner, *Agrarverbände*, 70; Panzer, *Ringen um Agrarpolitik*, 14-15; Stürmer points out that fifty-eight members of the bourgeois middle parties were also absent, *Koalition und Opposition*, 57.

106. Years later, Curtius recalled how "conflicts with Agriculture Ministry over exports and the domestic market had badly damaged the 'Gesamtpolitik' of the Reich," Julius Curtius, *Sechs Jahre Minister der Deutschen Republik* (Heidelberg, 1948), 20.

107. Ritter (Foreign Office) to the other members of the Trade Policy Committee, the Justice Ministry, and two Prussian ministries, 13 November 1925, BA R 43I/1085.

108. Rauscher to the Foreign Office, 11 December 1924, PAAA, Zollwesen 4, Bd. 3; Stockhammern to the Foreign Office, 10 February 1925, BA R 43I/2427.

109. Stresemann to the state Secretary Bracht in the chancellery and to the economics, finance, agriculture, interior, and justice ministries, 28 November 1924, BA R 43I/2417.

110. Report from Rome to the Foreign Office 4 March 1925, BA R 43I/2417; Karl Ritter (Foreign Office commissar for economic negotiations) to Stresemann, 6 March 1925, PAAA, Zollwesen 4, Bd. 3.

111. Trendelenburg to the Economics Ministry, 9 May 1925, BA R 43I/2417.
112. Executive Committee of the industrial Reichsverband to Economics Minister Hamm, 17 November 1924; Karl Lange to the Foreign Office, 4 March 1925; Mendelssohn and Kastl to Stresemann, 16 and 17 March; von Raumer, 27 March, all in PAAA, Zollwesen 4, Bd. 3.
113. The tariff legislation of 1925 has received a great deal of attention, see Pohl, *Weimars Wirtschaft*, 113 ff.; Stegmann, "Deutsche Zoll- und Handelspolitik 1924/25-1929," in Mommsen, ed., *Industrielles System*; Stürmer, *Koalition und Opposition in der Weimarer Republik, 1924-1928*, 97 ff.; Dieter Gessner, *Agrarverbände in der Weimarer Republik*, 46 ff., 70 ff.; Claus Dieter Krohn, *Stabilisierung und Ökonomische Interessen. Die Finanz Politik des deutschen Reiches 1923-1927* (Dusseldorf, 1974), 174 ff.; Panzer, *Das Ringen um die deutsche Agrarpolitik*, 24 ff.
114. Minutes of a interministerial meeting on 12 March 1925, BA R 43I/2417. The long delay in decontrolling agricultural prices and trade after the war and the failure to reinstitute agricultural tariffs in 1924 had already irreparably eroded support for the Weimar Republic among German farmers, both large and small, see Jens Fleming, *Landwirtschaftliche Interessen und Demokratie* (Bonn, 1978); Martin Schumacher, *Land und Politik* (Dusseldorf, 1978); Robert Moeller, *German Peasants and Agrarian Politics, 1914-1924: The Rhineland and Westphalia* (Chapel Hill, 1986).
115. Minutes of a meeting of party leaders, 18 March 1925, BA R 43I/2417.
116. See e.g., Bavarian Land Union to the chancellor, 16 June 1925, BA R 43I/2418; Anhalt Land Union 22 June, Koslin County (Pommerania) Land Union 2 July, Agricultural Chamber of Silesia to the chancellor 6 June, Agricultural Chamber of East Prussia 25 June and numerous local chambers, BA R2/24401.
117. Cited in Stürmer, *Koalition und Opposition*, 102; Ministerbesprechung, 20 June 1925, *Akten Luther*, 354.
118. Kempner's notes, 11 April 1925, BA R 43I/2417.
119. On the Center's difficult position in these months, Stürmer, *Koalition und Opposition*, 103-105; Pohl, *Weimars Wirtschaft*, 117.
120. Kempner's notes, 10 March 1925, BA R 43I/2417.
121. Working Group of Iron Finishing Industries (known as the "AVI group") to Economics Minister Neuhaus 6 May 1925; Hamm told the Chancellery that "industry was moving away from the earlier view that industrial and agricultural tariffs had to be resolved simultaneously," 17 March 1925, BA R 43I/1085; Carl Duisburg's attempt to smooth relations between industry and agriculture in his soothing "Tischrede" at the Industrie-Club in Dusseldorf, 7 March 1925, Bayer Archiv Leverkusen 3/039; Center Party industrialist Clemmens Lammers to Luther on the DVP, 15 April 1925, BA R 43I/2417.
122. Nocken, "Inter-Industrial Conflicts and Alliances as Exemplified by the AVI Agreement," in Mommsen et al., eds., *Industrielles System*, 693-704; Stegmann, "Deutsche Zoll-und Handelspolitk," in ibid., 508-9; Maier, *Recasting Bourgeois Europe*, 526 ff.; Pohl, *Weimars Wirtschaft*, 47 ff., 53-55.
123. Finance Minister Schlieben to Kempner 27 April; Kempner's notes 28 April; Schlieben to Kempner 29 April; Kanitz, Schlieben and Neuhaus to Kempner, 1 May 1925, all in BA R 43I/2417. Transition rates would apply to the major grains, flour, cattle, sheep, pigs and pork products, beans, peas, butter, cheese, eggs, sugar, and molasses.
124. *Akten Luther*, 448-49. Even so, the parliamentary passage of the bill made it qualitatively different from earlier plans to raise tariffs via bureaucratic action without any Reichstag participation – a plan that had been rejected by the Center on 21 February 1925, Stürmer, *Koalition und Opposition*, 99; *Akten Luther*, 101-2.
125. Minutes of a meeting of the government and party leaders, 30 July 1925; German Chamber of Commerce (Mendelssohn and Hamm) to Luther, 17 June

1925, BA R 43I/2418; German Chamber of Commerce memorandum, 29 May 1925, RWWA 20-1131-2; Union of Iron and Steel Industrialists, 24 August 1925, RWWA 20-1131-7.

126. *RGBl* 1925, I, 261.

127. See e.g., the Prussian Agriculture Minister to Schlieben 5 September 1925 and the petitions of the Reich Land Union (31 August), the Potato Grower's Society (5 September) and the Reich Market-Garden Association (29 August) in BA R2/24403.

128. Stresemann to Kempner, 17 April 1926, BA R 43I/2419.

129. Foreign Office to the chancellery, 17 April 1926; cabinet meeting of 21 April 1926; Stresemann to Kempner, 28 May 1926, BA R 43I/2419.

130. Chancellery Assistant Secretary Fessler note 22 November 1926; minutes of 4 March 1927 Cabinet meeting, BA R 43I/2419.

131. In 1927 Rhine-Westphalian industrial and commercial groups lamented the continuing tariff instability, noting that as late as 10 June 1927 the "fate of the agricultural duties [in the tariff renewal] remains uncertain." Memo by the Berlin-based information service established jointly by many Rhine-Westphalian Chambers of Commerce and industrial interest groups ("Zweckverband Nord-Westdeutscher Wirtschaftsvertretungen, e.V.") [hereafter "Zweckverband"], RWWA 20-1131-2.

132. Eckert Kehr may have been the first to identify "paralysis of the class forces" as a central characteristic of Weimar, "Die Diktatur der Bürokratie," in *Primat der Innenpolitik*, 244, 250.

Chapter Four

GERMAN TRADE POLICY IN EASTERN EUROPE FROM WORLD WAR I TO THE GREAT DEPRESSION

The economic pressures and political problems that caused the Reich such difficulty in reaching a consensus in the trade deregulation and tariff debates of 1919 to 1925 had an even greater disabling effect on the Reich's ability to negotiate international trade agreements with Poland, Czechoslovakia, and the Soviet Union. As in the tariff debate, Weimar's corporatist structure required that conflicting economic interests reach a working agreement on trade policy in each of several different forums: in direct negotiations between the leading private-sector interest groups, in the factional alliances on the floor of the Reichstag, in the governing coalition in the cabinet, and in the interministerial meetings of the ministerial bureaucracy for foreign economic policy.

Formulating policy for trade treaty negotiations proved to be even more difficult than producing a tariff had been. Consensus within yet another body, the German negotiating delegation, was often elusive, since private-sector members of the team brought their economic differences into the group. In addition, Stresemann's plans to apply commercial policy toward larger foreign policy goals required some level of agreement between the Foreign Office and various private-sectors about the desirability of trading German economic sacrifices for political gains. Beyond these domestic hurdles, there remained the essential problem of coming to an agreement with foreign counter-

Notes for this chapter begin on page 197.

parts on difficult material issues. Even when a common German negotiating position emerged from the domestic filtration process, it could not serve as the basis for international agreement unless it accommodated some essential concerns of Germany's trade partners.

In the give-and-take of international trade negotiations, the German side was crippled by the need to pass each substantive change in its negotiating position through the veto-laden labyrinth of corporatist trade policy formulation. Since, in Stresemann's words, the Reichstag had already "mobilized its last physical strength" for passage of the relatively simpler tariff legislation of August 1925, it is not surprising that further achievements in trade relations – i.e., concluding meaningful trade agreements with the East – lay beyond the bounds of Weimar's political abilities.[1]

Poland

Although the interwar years opened a new chapter in the long history of German-Polish relations, they did not provide a fresh start in relations between the two peoples.[2] Continued German chauvinism and natural Polish resentment of it made every aspect of relations difficult.[3] To this was added the Polish elite's own unrealistic overestimation of interwar Poland's diplomatic, economic, and military abilities, which would prove to be so tragic in the following decade. The rebirth of Poland had been possible only with the Entente defeat of Germany.[4] A new Polish state on formerly "German" territory was to many Germans an unpleasant reminder of the lost war. The broadly based German consensus for the need to revise the terms of Versailles as they applied to Poland ran across the political spectrum.[5] For those Germans who hoped for Germany's return to Great Power status, the existence of a genuinely independent Polish state in any borders was as intolerable in 1920 as it had been throughout the nineteenth century.[6] Yet as long as the Versailles order remained intact the two nations would share a lengthy land border. The Reich would have to find some form of coexistence with its unwelcome new neighbor.

By imposing dramatic territorial changes in East-Central Europe, the Versailles Treaty created a myriad of practical problems along the new German-Polish border to which the Western Allies expected subsequent German-Polish negotiations to find workable solutions. Despite hostility and suspicion on both sides of the new border, the pressure of Allied expectations induced the two parties to find solutions to many of the practical problems involved in transferring formerly German territory to the new Polish state. Over sixty major and minor bilateral agreements were signed by the two governments between 1919 and 1926, although the thorniest issues required years for resolution. Chief among these difficult questions were the "optants issue" (establishing the terms for choice of citizenship by Germans who now found themselves living in Poland according to Article 91 of the Versailles Treaty) and the "liquidation issue" (Poland's right to liquidate the property of German nationals according to Article 297(b) of the treaty).[7] An additional problem was the German perception of a cultural and legal "minority rights issue" in western Poland.[8]

The centrality of these Eastern border issues within Germany's larger diplomatic agenda inspired the Reich to bring every available resource to bear on the problem. Chief among these resources for most of the interwar period was Germany's still considerable economic power. The German Foreign Office in particular did not hesitate to use trade and, to a lesser extent, financial pressure in repeated efforts to obtain Polish concessions on optants, liquidations, and even on the border itself. Only an initial period of German-Polish economic cooperation from November 1918 to June 1920 remained free of these larger political motivations. Thereafter, numerous agents on the German side, including Stresemann himself, began connecting German trade policy toward Poland with the resolution of German political demands.[9] From 1920 to 1926 German-Polish trade relations were inextricably bound up with political issues. When direct trade pressure failed to bring any Polish concessions, Stresemann shifted foreign trade strategies toward Poland at the end of 1926. With an eye to improving German relations with the West as a means of weakening the Polish strategic position, the Reich sought to end its economic hostility toward Poland and to normalize commercial relations. Yet even after the German side dropped any overt connection between trade and outstanding political issues, Germany failed to reach a commercial understanding with Poland. In these efforts, Stresemann was thwarted by the economic interests and political structures of German corporatism because the Foreign Office was unable to pursue its foreign policy strategy in the face of agrarian opposition to an economic understanding with Poland.

In the initial period of postwar dislocation, both private industry and the Reich government entered into numerous cooperative economic relationships with their Polish counterparts. Between February 1918 and July 1920, private-sector groups, local German governments, and eventually even the Reich government itself concluded substantial trade exchanges with Poland without including political (i.e., noneconomic) terms or conditions in these deals. In the confusion along the still undefined German-Polish border during the winter of 1918 to 1919, local authorities and private businesses took the lead in arranging barter exchanges where practicable in order to alleviate critical shortages on both sides. The German government in Thorn and the Polish county of Lipno arranged an exchanged of German sugar, ironwares, lime, coal, and machine oil for Polish potatoes, clover seeds, and lupines. Similarly, the most influential private-sector association of German industrialists in Upper Silesia (The Upper Silesian Mining and Metallurgical Association) organized an exchange of German ironwares, shovels, tip-carts, and chloride explosives for Polish ores and pit-props. Other deals featured exchanges of German salt for Polish meat and German leather for Polish eggs.[10]

In March 1919 the participating members at a German interministerial meeting on relations with Poland (Prussian Trade Ministry, Reich Economics Ministry, Foreign Office, and Labor Ministry) approved these practices, noting that "secret private agreements such as those already in progress can certainly be concluded" even as "diplomatic negotiations with the Poles are completely out of the question at this time." The following week the Economics Ministry confirmed a German policy of allowing barter exchanges as long as these took place on a private basis and did not imply recognition of the Polish government.[11]

Increasingly acute food shortages in eastern Germany forced the Reich to abandon its reserve and enter into official negotiations with the Poles in the spring of 1919. On 2 May, the German Armistice Commission, chaired by Matthias Erzberger, signed a deal with the Polish government exchanging thirty thousand tons of German coal for ninety thousand tons of Polish potatoes. Another deal exchanging German sugar for various Polish products, this time between the new Reich Agriculture Ministry and the Polish government was concluded on 28 July.[12] On 15 August 1919, full and formal economic negotiations between the two countries opened in Berlin, with Karl Edle von Stockhammern of the Foreign Office chairing the German side and Herman Diamand, a leading Polish Socialist Party (PPS) politician, heading the Polish team. On 23 October the delegation chairmen signed a "provisional economic agreement" that arranged another massive coal-for-potatoes exchange (including a 5 million mark credit line for Polish use in ordering German coal), an exchange of German chemical fertilizer and seeds for Polish grain, and a German leasing of critically needed railroad equipment to the Poles.

More significantly, the agreement regulated the border crossings for railroad traffic and established German rights to navigate the Vistula.[13] That agreement marked the high point of German-Polish economic cooperation between the wars.

Shortly thereafter, the Western Allies in Paris apparently grew concerned about the extent of Polish-German economic cooperation, especially where this cooperation went beyond simple barter exchanges and began to touch on areas that would be regulated by the almost completed Versailles Treaty, such as railroad traffic and river navigation. The Allies called the Poles to Paris in November and forced Polish cancellation of the October economic agreement.[14] That cancellation and the publication of the Versailles terms, both in January 1920, signaled the end of that brief period of exceptionally productive nonpoliticized German-Polish economic cooperation. Between January and July 1920 a number of serious problems arose in German-Polish relations. Polish attempts to restrict traffic across the (new) border brought German resentment. The Germans claimed that Poland was already violating Article 89 of the Versailles Treaty by unfairly interfering with traffic across the "corridor" to East Prussia. After the March 1920 Spa Conference announced the very unpopular terms of the upcoming plebiscites in East Prussia and Upper Silesia, tensions in those two areas began rising.[15]

In 1920 Germany confronted the hard issues of postwar trade politicization for the first time. The possibility of using trade sanctions to retaliate for Polish actions along the border and in the new Polish territories was obvious. The governor (Oberpräsident) of East Prussia and the Prussian Ministry of Culture joined German émigrés in urging the Reich to connect any trade talks with Poland to progress on the liquidation, transit traffic, and minority rights questions.[16] On the other hand, Germany still needed food imports from Poland, as Economics Minister Robert Schmidt (SPD) told the Foreign Office in February 1920. Between February and June 1920, the Economics Ministry used its restrictive licensing system to steadily reduce German shipments to Poland as a "response" to Polish traffic restrictions along the new border.[17] Yet at the highest levels of government, Germany policy lacked any direction beyond the use of ad hoc economic reprisals for Polish practices perceived as unjust. Neither Schmidt at the Economics Ministry nor Chancellor and Foreign Minister Hermann Müller (SPD) had a clear strategy for manipulating German trade flows in order to achieve particular noneconomic demands. No coherent plan was in place when Müller's SPD-Center-DDP coalition cabinet (March-June 1920) prepared to accept the Polish offer to negotiate a new economic agreement.

After Walter Simons, who belonged to no party, assumed control over the Foreign Office as part of Chancellor Konstantin Fehrenbach's new centrist coalition (Center-DDP-DVP) Germany moved to a policy of explicitly connecting progress on trade issues to progress on other political matters. Simons told a 2 July 1920 meeting of Foreign Office officials that "until Polish encroachments in the political sphere" were stopped, he "would not even consider" engaging in economic negotiations. In the meantime, German economic "reprisals" would continue. A follow-up meeting of Foreign Office, economics, and agriculture ministry officials the next day insisted on creating a "linkage" (junctim) between the corridor negotiations in Paris and any economic negotiations. One month later, the Economic Ministry began a de facto ban on exports to Poland.[18] When German and Polish negotiators met in Berlin in early November, the Germans stated plainly that they would not negotiate on substantive economic issues unless parallel negotiations on German optants, property liquidation, and minority rights began at the same time.[19]

Although the furor surrounding the plebiscite in East Prussia and especially in Upper Silesia prevented any serious negotiations for much of 1921, the Reich did manage to insist that many practical problems along the border be negotiated. The Geneva Agreement (over 600 articles) of 15 June 1922 reestablished livable conditions in Upper Silesia. The climate improved further after both sides promised in the Warsaw Declaration (20 July 1922) to resume negotiations in September on a host of border problems. Relations once again approached a state of normalcy as the Reich ended its export ban on 22 July. Over the course of 1922 to 1924 German Polish negotiators working in Dresden, Vienna, and other cities produced thirty-eight minor agreements covering secondary issues such as visas, passports, postal service, legal procedures, transportation, and arbitration procedures. The resolution of one of the major outstanding issues – the future of German optants in Poland -with the Vienna Protocol of August 1924 was regarded by both sides as a major achievement.[20]

On 3 September 1924 the Polish Envoy in Berlin, Kazimieriz Olszowski, approached Erich Wallroth, head of the Eastern European Department (IVa) at the Foreign Office about the possibility of entering into economic negotiations soon.[21] Polish trade demands on Germany centered on a half-dozen key commodities: coal, live and slaughtered pigs and cattle, pork, beef, potatoes, and timber. Poles demanded that Germany relax its import ban on coal to allow a negotiated monthly quota of Polish coal into Germany. Articles 268(b) of Versailles and 224 of the Geneva Agreement had granted

Poland a monthly quota of 500,000 tons of Silesian coal that could be exported duty-free into Germany. These provisions were set to expire in June 1925 and the Poles were aiming for a negotiated extension of 350,000 to 450,000 tons/month. Poland also demanded modification of German veterinary regulations that were being used as a non-tariff barrier to obstruct Polish access to the German market for live and freshly slaughtered pigs and cattle. On timber, the Poles sought a reduction in the German tariff on sawed timber from 1 mark/cwt. to .70 marks/cwt. In principle, the Reich was willing to make concessions on these items in exchange for radical, across-the-board reductions in prohibitive Polish tariffs on many finished and semifinished goods. Both parties expected reciprocal MFN clauses to be part of any treaty.[22]

Virtually every member of the Polish policymaking group within the German Foreign Office considered Olszowski's approach to be Germany's best opportunity to date for exerting leverage on Poland through trade negotiations.[23] Stockhammern (now the Foreign Office's "commissar" for trade treaty negotiations) along with Erich Zechlin and Wallroth in the East European Department also insisted on connecting non-trade issues to the trade negotiations. At least the right of German nationals to settle in Poland should be connected to trade concessions. Zechlin told the Finance Ministry that "most likely … the other points of the negotiating program established previously in Warsaw [i.e., the Warsaw Declaration of June 1922] will crop up as well" in the context of any upcoming trade negotiations.[24] The German consul in Poznan, Hentig, presented a list of political "angles" (admission of German teachers to German schools, limitations on liquidations and confiscations, parity in civil procedure) that he felt should be broached in the course of trade negotiations.[25] Even the German envoy in Warsaw, Ulrich Rauscher, a Social Democrat who genuinely hoped for an economic agreement, argued the Foreign Office position that "we will not allow the opportunity to achieve political advantages to pass by." He thought about an end to Polish liquidations or "at least demanding substantial relief in this area."[26] A March 1925 memorandum from the files of Herbert von Dirksen, Wallroth's assistant at the East European Department, repeated Rauscher's earlier thoughts that Germany could somehow use the coal question to force Polish abandonment of further liquidations.[27]

The Foreign Office and Economics Ministry concurred that Germany's economic position was "very strong" vis-à-vis Poland and "will become evermore favorable in the next few months."[28] For these reasons, the Foreign Office urged a policy of postponing negotiations until at least 10 January 1925, when Germany would recover its tariff sovereignty and could terminate the Versailles-imposed unilateral extension of MFN to Poland. Stresemann, who, like most Germans, felt Poland needed a trade agreement more than Germany did, approved the plan for politicized trade negotiations to begin in January 1925.[29] When negotiations opened in Berlin on 13 January 1925, the German Foreign Office was convinced that the Reich could use the coal import quota to extract some Polish concessions on the settlement and liquidation issues. The Germans felt no regret when negotiations broke down in April over the coal issue, specifically over the German refusal to extend the Geneva Agreement guarantee for Polish coal exports into Germany. Negotiating after the expiration of the Geneva Agreement on 14 June 1925 would only enhance the German position.[30] Stresemann had genuinely hoped to avoid "an economic break" with Poland, as his diary entries for June 1925 make clear. Yet he was determined to restrict Polish coal exports into the Reich in order to protect the troubled German coal industry during the current "coal crisis." He noted grimly in his diary that "a way out of this impasse will certainly be extraordinarily difficult to find."[31] The difficulties between the two countries proved insurmountable in the short run. The coal impasse quickly sparked a series of "retaliatory" import restrictions and punitive tariff increases by both sides in June and July 1925 that snowballed into a full-scale tariff war.[32]

While the foreign policy consequences of the tariff war strategy remained at first unclear, the punitive policy had the advantage of immediately satisfying a number of Germany's most important economic interest groups. Since the first formal discussion for German-Polish trade treaty in late 1924, a number of economic groupings had opposed a trade deal with Poland on purely economic grounds. For these elements – heavy industry and agriculture – the political argument for withholding a trade treaty from Poland only reinforced their own immediate material interests.[33]

In the German coal industry, both owners and labor opposed extensive coal concessions to Poland. Coal and coke suppliers in Silesia and Westphalia were advocating an import allotment of just 100,000 tons monthly. In October 1926 a speaker for German Silesia's most important heavy industrial interest group, Heinrich Stähler, cited 120,000 tons as the maximum possible concession.[34] Iron and steel producers had their own worries about Polish competition in basic steel. Aggressive Polish underbidding in the European market and an initial unwillingness to cooperate in the major international cartel agreements heightened these anxieties.[35] It is little wonder that German heavy industry took up the political argument against a Polish treaty.[36]

German agriculture adamantly opposed accommodating the Polish demands, either on live animals, fresh meat, or timber. By 1926 the Reich Land Union had taken the lead in the campaign against allowing any live pig imports from Poland.[37] At the same time, interest groups for the German timber growers and some saw mills rejected plans to offer a tariff reduction on sawed timber. The largest of these groups, the Reich Forestry Council, was actively campaigning for an increase in the sawed timber tariff from 1 mark/cwt. to 2.50 marks/cwt.![38]

Labor interests were divided by the Polish treaty, torn between the desire for lower food prices that would come with a treaty and a fear of higher unemployment for German coal miners. Even before formal negotiations with Poland opened in 1925, miners had approached the German government in opposition to an extensive coal allowance for Poland. In August 1925 the miners' group Arbeitsgemeinschaft der Bergarbeiter protested to Chancellor Luther about a rumored 300,000-ton concession to Poland. With sixty thousand miners unemployed in Germany in 1926, labor asked for "minimal" coal concessions, but urged concessions on agricultural items.[39]

On the other side, commercial groups and export-oriented manufacturers were concerned about the impact of the tariff war on German exports. German export interests had only reluctantly supported Germany's various economic sanctions against Poland from 1920 to 1924.[40] Despite the economic sacrifices that Germany policy imposed on Germany exporters, particularly in Silesia, these private-sector groups refrained from criticizing the German drift into tariff war in 1924 to 1925.[41] In June 1926 the industrial Reichsverband would go only as far as reminding Curtius that all sectors of German industry desired the speedy conclusion of a treaty with Poland.[42]

As the tariff war gained emotional intensity in both countries, German political demands grew fantastic. Reichsbank President Hjalmar Schacht stated repeatedly that "an outright return of the Corridor and Upper Silesia" must precede any economic agreement with Poland.[43] As the financial and political stability of Poland declined precipitously in late 1925, even the normally cautious Stresemann began to envision the imminent financial and economic collapse of the Polish state, which would open the way for a revision of Versailles's Eastern terms. In this context, German policy naturally sought to maintain Poland's economic distress.[44] This meant maintaining the German ban on Polish coal and fighting out the resulting tariff war. The Germans allowed negotiations to remain mired in an opaque concoction of trade and nontrade issues as Poland teetered on the brink of financial ruin and political chaos in early 1926.[45] The

material aspects of the trade negotiations remained intimately connected to negotiations on the right of Germans to enter into and settle in Poland ("right of domicile"). This settlement issue, in turn,
remained tied to the outcome of the still unresolved and emotional
liquidation negotiations going on in Warsaw.

Yet throughout the initial period of tariff war, the Foreign Office
never developed a tactical plan that related in concrete terms how
Germany would use trade concessions to achieve its other political
aims.[46] By 1925 both the Germans and Poles had come to assume
some general connection between the two areas of negotiation, but
the specifics of the German linkage remained undefined. As a result,
German negotiating tactics were confused and confusing. The German chief negotiator, Theodor Lewald, insisted on raising political
issues, but never put forward specific demands or indicated what Germany could offer in the economic sphere in exchange for the some
accommodation on the political side. Wojciech Korfanty, an influential member of the Polish Christian Democrats' parliamentary group
and recognized "German expert" to the Polish government, warned
Stresemann that these issues could not be handled on a general level,
but rather that the remaining questions must be treated in details and
specifics.[47] Intent on achieving a full Polish capitulation, the Foreign
Office bureaucracy never developed a negotiating position that oper-
ationalized German strategy by integrating Germany's political and
economic demands in a tit-for-tat manner.[48] After almost a year of
negotiations, Polish Foreign Minister Aleksander Skrzynski confessed
to State Secretary Carl Schubert in December 1925 that Poland "was
still uncertain what Germany's real demands were."[49]

Despite direct German trade pressure and German attempts to
obstruct international financial assistance for the crumbling zloty,
the fortunes of the Polish state turned sharply and unexpectedly
upward in the spring of 1926. General Josef Piłsudski's coup d'état of
12 to 14 May ousted Poland's fourteenth cabinet since November
1918 (Weimar Germany was in its fifteenth cabinet at this point) and
ended eight years of parliamentary instability. At the same time, the
British coal strike of May to December 1926 opened Scandinavia
and other European markets to the Polish coal that had been shut
out of Germany, exerting a stabilizing effect on the entire Polish
economy.[50] The expanding economy nearly doubled government
tax revenues, allowing a balanced budget by July 1926. Relative
prosperity lured Anglo-American capital back to Poland in 1927
with loans of £2 million and $62 million.[51]

Germany's immediate political aims in Poland now appeared
unattainable in the context of a trade treaty. By the final months of

1926, perceptive members of the Foreign Office such as State Secretary Schubert and Assistant Director of the Eastern Department Dirksen saw that the chance for success in the tariff war had passed.[52] Stresemann began advocating a policy of depoliticizing German-Polish trade issues and concluding an economic agreement with Poland.[53] An economic understanding with Poland would improve Germany's post-Locarno standing with the Western powers and reduce tensions in the East – two developments that might weaken the French support for its Polish ally.[54] In exchange for an improvement in the larger political (and possibly the strategic) situation, Germany would forego its current (and unsuccessful) attempt to extract some concessions from the Poles via punitive trade policies.

In the course of 1927, the Germans embarked on this new tactic of separating German trade interests from other, non-trade issues in negotiations with Poland. When the Polish government expelled four German industrial managers in early 1927, the German Foreign Office and the Economics Ministry sought to prevent a "political reaction" from affecting the trade negotiations despite cries of outrage from the German press. At the end of March the cabinet approved Stresemann's suggestion that the new negotiations on the settlement issues should "remain strictly separated from the trade treaty negotiations." Rauscher would open "diplomatic negotiations on only the settlement questions" in Warsaw. On 5 May 1927 Economics Minister Curtius urged the cabinet to radically scale back German demands in the settlement negotiations so that a trade agreement could be reached.[55]

In the course of 1927 to 1929 the two countries managed to reach agreement on many of the political issues they had previously attached to the trade negotiations. In July 1927 Rauscher negotiated a provisional agreement with the Jozef Lipski, chief of the German Section at the Polish Foreign Ministry, regulating the settlement issue on the more modest basis suggested by Curtius in May. In November 1927 agreement between the two countries was reached on the immigration and social insurance for the roughly 110,000 Polish seasonal agricultural laborers in Germany. Finally on 31 October 1929, Rauscher and Lipski reached agreement on the liquidation questions that had burdened German-Polish relations since the terms of the Versailles settlement had been announced in 1920. One by one, these agreements resolved the political issues that had been associated with the trade talks since 1922.[56] Both the German Foreign Office and Economics Minister Curtius expected the progressive disengagement of political issues from economic problems to facilitate the conclusion of a commercial agreement with Poland. Successful resolutions of the settlement, migratory labor, and liquidation issues strengthened this expectation since the two governments were able to focus their efforts on the material trade issues alone. Yet even as the two countries negotiated trade issues in isolation from other complicating matters, they could not reach a workable agreement.

Although Stresemann's new trade strategy toward Poland made sense in the larger of context of European international relations and in the context of German-Polish bilateral relations, it did not conform to the realities of domestic politics and economic interests in Germany itself. In every area, Weimar's multilevel corporatist policy structure tended to stifle initiatives and produce instead policies of minimal action. Regardless of its ultimately malevolent purpose, an active and positive German policy based on concluding an economic agreement with Poland was inherently much more difficult to execute than a passive and negative policy based on the continuing refusal to cooperate with the Poles. Weimar's general structural constraints on an activist policy were even tighter in the case of a trade treaty where immediate material motives energized private-sector groups to fully exploit the system's opportunities for obstruction. In the search for some common ground upon which to build a commercial agreement with Poland, Stresemann's Foreign Office was repeatedly thwarted by German agricultural groups and coal interests that frantically opposed a German treaty with Poland. The corporatist structures of German politics allowed this economically motivated opposition to successfully obstruct the conclusion of a trade treaty with Poland.

Inability to obtain a trade treaty with Poland, in turn, set limits on Stresemann's revisionist strategy. Without some end to economic hostilities with Poland, German could not expect a full reconciliation with France. Continued German-Polish hostility also kept the Reich dependent on the Soviets in the East. Ironically, in the years 1927 to 1931 when the Foreign Office, Economics Ministry and the vast majority of German industrial interests genuinely sought to reach a trade agreement with Poland, the Reich could not do so because of economically motivated opposition that Weimar's weak coalition governments and corporatist structure could not overcome.[57]

The shift from an anti-treaty policy of confrontation to a pro-treaty policy of economic cooperation meant the end of the broad-based coalition of economic interests that had supported the tariff war in 1925 and 1926, even if some elements had done so reluctantly. Initial supporters of the idea of economic rapprochement with Poland included only those commercial and manufacturing interests that had been reluctant supporters of the tariff war, with the critically affected Silesian manufacturing interests in the lead. Like the Foreign Office, they had by mid-1926 come to see the futility of connecting a trade agreement to other highly-charged political issues. In April 1926, the *Ostdeutsche Wirtschaftszeitung,* published in Breslau by the Silesian Chambers of Commerce, ran a story on the "Delay in German-Polish Economic Negotiations" that criticized Chancellor Luther's coalition governments for believing that an economic agreement with Poland is possible only after "all the legal questions had been cleared up." The paper stated plainly that "continuing to connect the trade treaty question with the liquidation question appears in the long run to be evermore inexpedient."[58] Frustrated by the lack of progress in both the economic and political spheres, Bernhard Grund, president of the Breslau Chamber of Commerce and a private-sector representative in the German negotiating team, urged "the complete separation of the political questions from the economic negotiations."[59]

Unlike the earlier strategy of economic confrontation, the new strategy of cooperation had very vocal opponents. The opposition was particularly active in those economic sectors that would feel the negative impact of a treaty that opened Germany to Polish coal, steel, agricultural produce, and forestry products. In August 1925 the miners' group Arbeitsgemeinschaft der Bergarbeiter had challenged Stresemann directly on foreign economic policy, warning that they would not tolerate "an end to the hostilities with Poland concluded on the backs of the miners."[60] Echoing the miners' criticism of Stresemann's foreign policy ambitions, the Bavarian Land Union declared that agriculture would not tolerate trade concessions "used to reach foreign policy goals."[61]

The corporatist practice of including interest groups members in international trade treaty negotiations allowed these groups to bring their differences directly inside the German negotiating delegation. By October 1926, an open rift had developed between two groups of private-sector members within the German negotiating delegation, pitting the private representatives of agriculture (Walter von Hippel), the coal industry (Heinrich Stähler), and the miners (W. Eggert) against Bernhard Grund, the spokesman for commercial and manufacturing interests.[62]

Weimar Germany's coalition cabinets reflected the conflicts of the pro-treaty and anti-treaty groups in the private-sector. The third Marx cabinet (May to December 1926) included substantial agricultural interests in both the Center party and the Bavarian People's Party. The Agriculture Ministry under Heinrich Haslinde (Center) was unwilling to risk further hardship for Germany's already struggling farmers. Stresemann regretfully acknowledged that the "cata-strophic" economic conditions of small- and medium-sized farms in East Prussia limited Germany's negotiating ability.[63] The Agriculture Ministry acted as a deadweight on this issue, preventing the cabinet from timely and energetic pursuit of an agreement. The Labor Ministry was torn between the conflicting duties of protecting German miners from Polish coal and seeking to reduce food costs by allowing imports of Polish meat and potatoes. On the other side, the People's Party Ministers, Stresemann at the Foreign Office and Curtius at the Economics Ministry, had both political and economic reasons for advancing a treaty that would normalize Germany's trade relationship with Poland. Curtius estimated the 1926 losses to German exporters from the tariff war with Poland at 300 million marks. Even more disturbing was the decline in Germany's share of the Polish import market. In 1924 the Reich had supplied almost 35 percent of all Polish imports; two years later the figure was just 24 percent.[64]

In the face of agricultural opposition to significant concessions on the key trade issues, the German government was incapable of offering Poland sufficient incentives to conclude a trade deal. Germany's leading economic groups, the cabinet, and the negotiating team were badly divided over the size and type of concessions that Germany could afford to offer the Poles in the trade negotiations. The chief German negotiators including German delegation Chairman Lewald and Under-secretary Ernst from the Finance Ministry, who led the German subdelegation in the committee negotiating tariff issues, had realized the insufficiency of Germany's trade offers by the summer of 1926. Ernst and Lewald told the interministerial meeting on 1 October that the negotiations with Poland "can be advanced only" if the German delegation were authorized to make concessions on coal and cattle. After another week of intensive interministerial negotiation, the cabinet authorized the following offer to Poland on 15 October 1926: Germany would accept 200,000 tons of coal monthly, 1,000 freshly slaughtered pigs weekly (to be marketed in Upper Silesia only), an unlimited amount of prepared pork, and would reduce the sawed timber tariff from 1 mark/cwt. to .90 marks/cwt. In other words, Germany would allow only a minuscule number of freshly slaughtered pigs, no live pigs, no cattle (live or freshly slaughtered), and a small reduction in the timber tariff. Ernst had already characterized the timber reductions as "not sufficient," and now correctly predicted to the cabinet that this offer was not sufficient "to get promising negotiations going."[65]

Prospects for a treaty worsened considerably in January 1927 since the fourth Marx cabinet included four ministers from the German Nationals. This conservative/nationalist party with major constituencies in heavy industry and agriculture was disinclined for both political and economic reasons to sign a trade treaty with the Poles. Their agriculture minister, the energetic Martin Schiele, forcefully advocated the concerns of German farmers and foresters about the damaging effects of agricultural concessions to Poland, claiming that Polish exports had the ability to "fully destroy the basis of profitability of German agriculture."[66] The Agriculture Ministry became the stronghold of the anti-treaty forces within the government and worked closely with agricultural interest groups to oppose any significant concessions. Inside the cabinet, Schiele argued for a reduction in the agricultural concessions offered to Poland the previous October. The strong position of the German Nationals in the governing coalition and Schilele's threat to resign kept the cabinet tied up over this question through November 1927.[67] In doing so, he effectively prevented the Reich from reopening negotiations with Poland, since the government was incapable of issuing instructions to its negotiators.[68] Both Stresemann and Rauscher spent most of 1927 evading Polish inquiries about a resumption of negotiations.

As long as the German Nationals were present in the German cabinet, the two countries would remain far apart on both the coal and agricultural issues. Even when negotiations resumed in Warsaw in December 1927, the German Nationals managed to prevent real progress by limiting Germany's offers to levels below the October 1926 offer.[69] The appointment of leading agricultural spokesman and former Finance Minister Andreas Hermes as the new chairman of the German delegation strengthened the institutional basis for agricultural opposition.[70] Even an attempt at moving the negotiations forward via confidential, nonpolitical private-sector consultation failed since talks between joint German-Polish private-sector commissions for industrial and agricultural issues could not achieve any breakthrough.[71]

The increasing cabinet acrimony brought on by Schiele's obstructionism and the obvious dead end reached in the negotiations in 1927 were reflected in the growing divergence between agricultural and industrial interest groups over a Polish treaty. As the issue of Polish hog exports became a central point of the trade negotiations in 1927, the Land Union mobilized its local chapters in support of a "resolution against the planned accommodation of Poland in the import of pigs and pork." Rauscher complained of negotiating under a "barrage of negative resolutions by our agricultural interest groups."[72] Inside the industrial Reichsverband, export interests urged that "everything be done" to get Germany back into normal trade relations with Poland.[73] Both the Reichsverband and the German Chamber of Commerce issued general calls for a trade agreement with Poland.[74] In August 1927 members of the Reichsverband met with leading agricultural associations to discuss the German trade offers to Poland. The agricultural groups resisted industrial pressure for reductions in the potato and timber tariff and the two groups were unable to agree on a negotiating platform that could induce Poland to make substantial tariff reductions of its own.[75]

After another year in which the two countries could manage no significant progress on the material trade issues, relations between German industry and German agriculture began to break over the content of the Polish negotiations.[76] Renewed negotiations between the two groups on 7 and 8 November 1928 "did not lead to an understanding." Reporting to the presidium on these discussions, the chairman of the Reichsverband's Trade Policy Committee, Ernst von Simson (I.G. Farben), felt industry "could no longer support" agricultural demands for a 200,000-cwt. limit on Polish hog exports to Germany. Kastl pleaded that a break with agriculture be avoided, but acknowledged that "there is no [other] treaty that can bring an expansion of trade volume such as the Polish" treaty can. Even the influential Paul Reusch, head of the Gütehoffnungshütte, who continued to work hard for cooperation between industry and agriculture acknowledged that "We want to get the Polish treaty in agreement with agriculture. If that is not possible, then we will go our own way."[77] Relations between the two groups were temporarily repaired by a Reichsverband offer to put up RM 7 million for a private-sector organization that would purchase all imports of Polish pork and market them in a manner that reduced the burden on East Prussia.[78] Yet by late 1929 a final break between the two sectors had become unavoidable. The Reich Land Union had gone over to asserting that Germany could sign no treaty with Poland until the overall financial position of German agriculture improved, while the Reichsverband insisted that it still urgently desired a treaty.[79]

The divergence of agricultural and industrial interests in a Polish treaty played themselves out in the cabinet and Reichstag as well. After the elections of May 1928, the German Nationals were excluded from Müller's Great Coalition government (SPD-Center-DDP-DVP and Bavarians) of June 1928 to March 1930. The great "agricultural debate" in the Reichstag on 3 and 4 December 1928 demonstrated clearly that the increasingly radical demands of agricultural groups would find no support in other economic sectors.[80] Unable to maintain his material positions without the Nationals in the cabinet, Hermes eventually resigned as delegation chairman in September 1929. Rauscher himself took over the final phase of negotiations.[81]

The Müller cabinet had already begun to move toward an understanding with Poland. In the cabinet meeting of 10 November 1928, Stresemann, Curtius, and Hilferding (Finance) called for Hermes's resignation if he continued to balk at cabinet instructions for further concession on Polish pork exports. On 23 November 1928 the interministerial Trade Policy Committee authorized an offer of 350,000 tons/month on the coal question. By mid-December the German offer was 350,000 tons on coal and 11,000 live or freshly slaughtered pigs weekly (of which 5,000 would be reexported). Rauscher was encouraged but felt that "we are not yet far enough."[82] Progress toward a treaty was given another boost by a private-sector agreement on steel exports concluded between key members of German and Polish heavy industry in December 1928.[83] Two months later a new private-sector effort to reach an across-the-board understanding with Polish industry also brought the two closer together.[84]

On 24 October 1929 the Trade Policy Committee overrode Agricultural Ministry objections and recommended an offer of 300,000 tons of coal monthly and 200,000 freshly slaughtered pigs, increasing to 275,000 the next year and 350,000 the year after. Chancellor Müller provided the tie-breaking vote of approval at a cabinet meeting later that day.[85] On the basis of this offer Rauscher managed to sign a deal with Poles in March of 1930 that gave Poland a 320,000 ton monthly coal allowance, and an annual allowance of 275,000 (increasing to 350,000) of freshly slaughtered pigs. The agreement formally included the earlier private-sector guarantee on scrap iron exports to Poland (appendix 5) and informally included the industrial Reichsverband's promise that the full quota of Polish pigs would be purchased at market prices. In exchange, German manufacturers received quotas for the export to Poland of a wide range of goods that had been prohibited by the Polish decrees of 10 February 1928 and 28 December 1929. Tariff rates were not bound since that level of agreement appeared unreachable. Both sides extended MFN status to the other with, each side terminating its specially directed punitive tariff measures. The Rauscher-Lipski 1927 provisional agreement on German entry into and settlement in Poland was incorporated into the agreement as well.[86]

The signed agreement still required Reichstag ratification. While the treaty was pending, economic developments in Germany and their political consequences combined to obstruct final approval. As negotiations entered their final phase in late 1929, the chronic crisis of German agriculture became acute. The German agricultural price index (1913 = 100) skidded from 132 in 1928 to 110 in 1930 and 101 in 1931. Livestock prices fell particularly sharply; by 1931 they stood at just 82 percent of the prewar level.[87] In their precarious economic and financial position, many German farmers felt treaty ratification would be "the death" of agriculture, especially in eastern Germany. The fear of Polish exports driving German agricultural prices down even further goaded German farm organizations into a frenzy of agitation against the treaty.[88] Equally important was the disastrous downturn affecting the German coal mines in 1930. According to the coal industry group in the industrial Reichsverband, German coal production declined 19 percent in 1930 with a corresponding loss of 130,000 jobs. The major coal industry interest groups from western, middle, and eastern Germany vigorously opposed the agreement with its 320,000 ton monthly import allotment.[89]

On the political side, the Müller cabinet of the Great Coalition, which had gone so far to reach an understanding with Poland, collapsed and resigned on 27 March 1930, i.e., just ten days after Rauscher had obtained Polish consent to the agreement. In the new cabinet under Chancellor Heinrich Brüning (Center), Martin Schiele, the well-known opponent of agricultural imports from Poland, returned to the Agriculture Ministry on the recommendation of President Hindenburg himself.[90] The return of Schiele gave the farmers' groups an active advocate inside the cabinet for their anti-treaty position. In addition, Brüning's minority cabinet was generally incapable of commanding a Reichstag majority. For that reason, the government delayed presentation of the treaty to the Parliament – a tactic Curtius belatedly recognized as a mistake.[91]

Curtius at the Foreign Office (having replaced Stresemann upon the latter's death in October 1929) was determined to present the treaty to the Reichstag for ratification. On 25 June 1930 a first reading gained a narrow majority after stormy debate along predictable lines of economic interest. Curtius argued the economic advantages for Germany – export growth and a preservation of tariff autonomy in a general MFN treaty. Other members of the People's Party continued Stresemann's political argument for the treaty, asking for an economic understanding in pursuit of the larger foreign policy goal of international political reconciliation. For the Nationals, Walter Stubbendorff vowed that agricultural groups "will fight the Polish trade treaty to the last; both inside and outside of this house, will every available means." The text was returned to committee for minor modification between readings. The revision process was overtaken by the Reichstag dissolution in July and the new elections of September 1930.[92]

After September 1930, the parliamentary gains of anti-treaty forces (Nazis, Communists, and the various new purely agricultural parties) effectively precluded treaty ratification by the new Reichstag.[93] Yet Brüning continued the fiction that the treaty might yet come through.[94] Even the *Berliner Börsen-Zeitung,* which had consistently been in favor of an agreement with Poland, opined that under the present economic circumstances "it would be better if the trade treaty concluded with Poland last year remained unratified."[95] By late spring of 1931, the Foreign Office was sure that the March 1930 agreement would never be ratified in its current form. When the new Polish Envoy, Alfred Wysocki, visited the Foreign Office on 9 April 1931, Ernst Eisenlohr (Special Economics Department) was already feeling him out about the possibility of renegotiating the deal, a suggestion Wysocki termed "impossible."[96] Since renegotiation appeared impossible, Brüning let the agreement sit unratified while the cabinet struggled with other issues in the summer of 1931, seeking to avert Germany's complete economic collapse. In September the Foreign Office responded to an inquiry from the Saxon government by calming stating that "the question of putting the German-Polish trade treaty into force is not a current issue at this time."[97] When German interest in arranging some type of trade deal revived in the spring of 1932, the negotiations took place under radically different economic and political conditions from those that had surrounded the negotiations leading up the ill-fated 1930 agreement.

Czechoslovakia

The vexing political questions that complicated the early phases of German-Polish trade relations were largely absent from German trade relations with Czechoslovakia during the Weimar period. The establishment of a new Czechoslovak Republic on the territory of the former Habsburg Empire engendered no particular rancor in Germany. The Sudeten lands and their German population had never belonged to the Bismarckian-Wilhelmian Reich. The Versailles peace settlement did not require Germany and this new neighbor to negotiate on a host of unpleasant issues affecting the transfer of these territories and peoples.[98] Other issues (such as the liquidation of German national property) did arise from the Versailles settlement and Czechoslovakia's status as an "associated power" of the victorious Allies. Even these matters were much smaller affairs than the corresponding problems in German-Polish relations and were comparatively quickly resolved by the two countries. Not until the sudden German proposal for a German-Austrian customs union in March 1931 did a first-rate political conflict confound relations between the two states.[99]

Despite the general lack of political rancor between Germany and Czechoslovakia from 1920 to 1931, the two countries could not come to terms on a meaningful trade treaty. The intractable impediments to a treaty were clearly economic, not political, in nature. The major obstacle to a German-Czechoslovak trade agreement was the intense and vocal agricultural opposition to any concessions that might increase Czechoslovak farm exports to Germany. As in the Polish case, Weimar's corporatist state structure could not impose a treaty on economic groups that were determined to resist a commercial agreement. In the absence of any obfuscating international political issues between the two countries, German-Czechoslovak trade negotiations reveal the fundamental weakness of the Weimar domestic system in this area with even greater clarity than do the German-Polish negotiations.

Among the "allied and associated powers" of Europe, Czechoslovakia was unique in its determination to enter into a constructive economic relationship with Germany as soon as possible.[100] Resisting Allied (especially French) pressure to join in the economic blockade of Germany, the Czechoslovak government signed a number of economically and politically significant trade agreements with the defeated Reich between 1918 and 1920.[101] The first of these economic agreements came almost immediately after the end of hostilities in 1918. On 7 December 1918 Stockhammern from the German Foreign Office signed an agreement with representatives of the new Checoslavak Republic authorizing an exchange of German anthracite and Czechoslovak brown coal. The parties also agreed to allow exports of some other tightly controlled commodities particularly desired by the other side: Czechoslovakian lumber, kaolin, graphite, and food would go to Germany while German machines, chemicals, electric lights, and fuses would be available for Czechoslovakia. Entente objections delayed, but could not prevent, Czechoslovak approval of the agreement.[102]

Relations continued to develop smoothly in 1919 as the new German envoy, "affable and unprofessional" Professor Samuel Sänger, arrived in Prague in April.[103] Almost immediately the state secretary in the Czechoslovak Commerce Ministry approached him about the possibility of opening talks in Berlin "on the whole range of commercial questions." Schuster sought to establish an negotiating framework (perhaps a "commission") "out of which a trade treaty might grow." In January 1920 Sänger replied that Germany was willing to open negotiations for "a trade treaty or whatever you wish to call it."[104] After Schuster visited Berlin for preliminary discussions in February, negotiations opened in Berlin in late April and culminated in agreements on economic relations, liquidation, and optants (i.e., the same issues that proved so vexing in German-Polish negotiations) signed in Prague on 29 June 1920.[105]

The Economic Agreement went as far as possible in normalizing commercial relations between the two countries at a time of extensive trade controls in both countries. Most significantly, the agreement established mutual MFN relations between the two countries in all commercial affairs. In the context of 1920 this meant a "general" MFN agreement that did not bind tariff rates or restrict the use of administrative import/export controls. Appendices B and C listed those otherwise restricted goods that each side especially desired to obtain from the other. Appendix D set the terms of coal exchanges between the two countries. Over the following six months, the German government would authorize the export of 654,000 tons of anthracite and coke to Czechoslovakia and allow the import of 1.3 million tons of Bohemian brown coal and 24,000 tons of anthracite.[106] In the liquidation agreement, the Czechoslovaks virtually renounced their right to liquidate German property by promising to limit liquidations to the railroad, mining, and hospital sectors and only in cases required by "the general economic and social interest of the state." Czechoslovakia would present to Germany list of these few properties within one month.[107] With these three agreements, the potentially most difficult political issues between the two countries were already resolved.

The rapidity with which the defeated German Reich and the new Czechoslovak Republic normalized their bilateral relations was rightly perceived as a blow to the French policy of ostracizing Germany. A setback for the French was necessarily a political gain for the Germans. Indeed, for Germany, the package of three agreements was more important politically than economically. From the German view, the major political gains sprang from the terms of the economic agreement.[108] The Prussian Trade Ministry considered the agreement a "great success" since "for the first time we have succeeded in obtaining the broadest possible MFN concessions from a state that already possessed these rights as part of the peace treaty." The Foreign Office evaluated the agreement similarly.[109] Just a year and a day after signing the peace terms at Versailles, Germany had begun its diplomatic rehabilitation by resolving a number of potentially difficult problems and entering into a fully normal relationship with its new neighbor. In addition, the agreement had cost the Reich nothing in substantive trade concessions; Germany had neither bound its tariff rates nor sacrificed the right to restrict foreign trade in accordance with domestic economic requirements.

After the general agreement of June 1920, both governments sought to increase trade in those sectors for which exchanges could be mutually advantageous (i.e., those sectors indicated by the commodity lists appended to the June 1920 agreement). Because of the restrictive trade controls that both sides maintained through 1924 and the dominant role of German private-sector groups in the regulation of German foreign trade at this time, the two sides employed an interlocking combination of public and private agreements to regulate merchandise flows between the two countries. Bilateral negotiations with mixed government-private delegations on each side in January and February 1921 produced a confidential "exchange of notes" covering a wide variety of industrial raw materials and finished products.[110] Both sides promised a generally "favorable" (wohlwollend) treatment of applications to import goods from the other side. In addition, sector-specific arrangements for the most important items (coal, machines, chemical salts, hops, malt, and chemicals) were set by agreement between the leading private-sector interest groups in each country. The role of the two governments in these cases was simply to provide the external conditions for fulfillment of the private agreement. For example, the amounts, types, and prices of chemicals to be exchanged between the two countries had been set on 8 February in an agreement signed by General Director Plieninger of the Chemie-Fabrik Greisheim-Elektron in Frankfurt and Benes, a representative of the dominant Czechoslovak Association for Chemical and Metallurgical Production (Spolek pro chemickou a hutni vyrobu) in Aussig. The provisions of the government note covering chemicals stated only that "the industrial groups on both sides have concluded an agreement of 8 February, the contents of which both governments have noted. The two governments declare their intention to adjust their issuance of import and export certificates such that both industrial groups can fulfill the agreement."[111] Private groups had determined the pattern of trade; government action would confirm it. Parallel private agreements were negotiated for chemical salts between the German Salt Exporting Company and the Czechoslovak Association for Chemical and Metallurgical Production; for hops between the German hops interests and the Saazer Hops Traders; for malt between the German Brewers' Association and the Czechoslovak Malt Commission; for machinery between the Union of German Machine-Building Institutes, the Central Association of the German Electrical Industry, and the Foreign Trade Office of the German Motor Vehicle Industry on one side and the Czechoslovak Metal Syndicate on the other. The coal agreement of June 1920 was renegotiated with government and private-sector participation from both sides.[112] Where private agreements had not yet been arranged, on lumber exports from Czechoslovakia to Germany for example, the two governments called for a meeting of the "German lumber interests and the Czechoslovak lumber industry" in order to get a price agreement in place.

The two countries employed these corporatist methods of trade management more widely in 1922. New privately-based agreements on machines and dyes were concluded as part of the German-Czechoslovak negotiations running from 21 March to 10 April. The coal agreement was extended once again. In February 1924, Stockhammern and the Commercial Attache at the Czechoslovak Legation in Berlin signed a confidential protocol in which both sides increased their import quotas for a range of commodities and promised "favorable treatment" of import applications for many new items.[113] Finally, on 31 July 1924 the two governments signed another confidential protocol covering more than seventy German items exported to Czechoslovakia and ninety-two Czechoslovak commodities headed for Germany. The protocol either promised "favorable treatment," or granted import quotas, or contained private agreements on the volume and value of commodity exchanges. For many important industrial raw materials and finished goods (such as lime, kaolin, flax, film, porcelain, automobiles, tractors, chemicals, printing inks, prepared paper, and machines) private agreements were concluded or renewed. In most of these cases, the two governments promised to "recognize the agreement reached or to be reached by industry on both sides and to place no obstacles in the way of executing" that agreement. In other cases, the governments promised to "arrange for industrial groups on both sides to reach an agreement beyond the existing controls."[114]

In light of the many obstacles to trade persisted in Central Europe from 1921 to 1924, these (confidential, privately based, and government-supported) corporatist methods of trade management worked well in shaping productive exchanges across the German-Czechoslovak border. As essentially private agreements reinforced by confidential protocols, the terms of each arrangement remained secret. Their confidential nature allowed Germany to offer explicit and implicit import allowances to Czechoslovakia that could not have been extended to the many other countries with Versailles-based MFN claims on Germany.[115] The sector-specific, private basis of the agreements assured that the negotiated outcomes would be accepted by the private-sectors on both sides. The Foreign Trade Committee of the German Chamber of Commerce noted at its 9 December 1927 meeting that "the direct industry-to-industry agreements in German-

Czechoslovak trade treaties [sic] had brought many advantages and had removed a number of difficulties from the official negotiations beforehand."[116] In addition, each sector-specific bilateral agreement functioned independently of agreements (or lack thereof) in other sectors. This allowed quick implementation of each deal and renegotiating flexibility. During a period of rapidly changing economic circumstances in which Germany lacked a functioning tariff, these voluntary agreements were arguably the best tool Germany had for regulating foreign trade. The extensive state regulation of trade that persisted in both countries through mid-1925 gave the two governments unprecedented abilities to enforce the terms of these private agreements. Because of the extensive licensing controls then in place, each government could virtually guarantee that goods would enter the country only under previously arranged terms on price, volume, quality, and type. The important role played by private interests groups in administering most of Germany's trade controls made compliance that much more certain. As conegotiator and coenforcer, the German government could use its powers both to encourage German private-sector participation in the process and to support the German interest groups in their negotiations with Czechoslovak counterparts.[117]

In addition to these bilateral understandings, German and Czechoslovak producers were both members in a number of larger multilateral cartels that helped regulate European merchandise flows in the period after government trade controls were dropped in 1924 to 1925. In 1927 Czechoslovakia joined the international steel cartel as part of the "Central European Group" (ZEG) that included Czechoslovakia, Austria, and Hungary with a group production quota of 7.272 percent (2.14 million tons). As agent for the ZEG, the Sales Corporation of United Czechoslovak Steelworks negotiated additional protective agreements with German producers. ZEG firms agreed not to compete against German producers in the German market and in exchange received assurances that the Germans would not export to the ZEG countries, Albania, Bulgaria, Yugoslavia, Romania, Trieste, and Fiume. Either as part of the ZEG unit or as an "associated national group," Czechoslovakia also participated in at least fourteen export sales comptoirs such as the International Rail Makers' Association (IRMA), International Wire Export Company (IWECO), and the International Tube Convention.[118]

Throughout the Weimar years, German and Czechoslovak industrial producers in many sectors were able to organize the movement of products across the border, in most cases on the basis of voluntary agreements by key producers on both sides supported by their governments. One reason for those successes was the "similar economic structure" of the two states. Concentrated industrial centers and a high degree of internal cartelization on both sides facilitated the conclusion of private international private-sector agreements.[119] Yet the similarity of economic structure also encompassed nonindustrial sectors; both countries had "extensive and productive agricultural areas." Trade in the products of those regions did not lend itself to the type of private international organization or management in the way that many industrial exports did. After 1925 the attention of the two governments became increasingly focused on the (ultimately insurmountable) difficulties of reaching mutually acceptable solutions for regulating agricultural trade between the two countries. The ability to shape industrial trade flows by ad hoc private agreements stood in sharp contrast to both parties' inability to conclude a full trade treaty that would cover agricultural produce as well as industrial commodities.

Despite the high level of bilateral cooperation achieved by the two countries from 1920 to 1924, the Reich still felt the need to obtain a full, long-term tariff treaty with Czechoslovakia. As both countries began to deregulate trade in 1924, the state enforcement power behind the private trade-controlling agreements began to disappear. In the future, private agreements would be possible only in well-organized industries such as steel, and even then not for every portion of the product range. Some industrial products had never been covered by such private arrangements and now were governed only by the Czechoslovak tariff subject to the 1920 general MFN agreement with Germany. The German Iron and Steel Wares Association complained bitterly that unbound MFN tariff rates did not guarantee access to the Czechoslovak market for a wide variety of German manufactured goods.[120] Commercial groups always disliked unbound MFN rates since they provided no stability for the import/export business. Finally, the two countries had not reached any agreements on agricultural questions. Tariff rates on both sides remained unsettled for the most important agricultural items in German-Czechoslovak trade: rye, barley, malt, hops, peas, beans, timber, and onions.

The German Foreign Office had originally hoped to open trade treaty negotiations with Czechoslovakia in the summer of 1924, as German trade controls wound down.[121] However, the failure to get a new German tariff in place in September to October 1924 postponed the negotiations until after passage of the German tariff in August 1925. The November 1925 parliamentary elections in Czechoslovakia postponed the starting date again, so that it was not until late March 1926 that the Czechoslovaks indicated their readiness to proceed. The

German cabinet approved an interministerial delegation chaired by the Foreign Office for negotiations to begin in August 1926.[122]

The character and pace of the German-Czechoslovak trade negotiations deteriorated from "normal" in early December 1926 to "slow" by late January 1927.[123] By October 1927 the talks had reached a dead end. The two countries had reached accommodation on reducing tariffs for a number of manufactured items (textiles, leather goods, paper products, ironwares, glass, and ceramics), but had not been able to agree on Czechoslovak demands for German agricultural concessions.[124] Negotiations ground to a halt as the Germans refused to make tariff concessions on a number of agricultural items, especially barley, malt, hops, pears, sawed timber, cheese, and ham. The Czechoslovaks felt that further negotiations on German tariff requests could not continue until the German side had given a positive response to the question of whether "it will be possible for you to negotiate at all about tariff reductions or [other] positive solutions" to the agricultural questions.[125]

The political and economic forces in Germany that combined to produce the impasse in German-Czechoslovak trade negotiations were the same as those that were also preventing a German-Polish trade agreement. Agricultural interest group opposition to tariff reductions for Czechoslovak produce was as vocal and intense as opposition to concessions for Poland. The coalition politics of the fourth Marx cabinet had forced German negotiators to rule out any possibility of future German concessions on these items. Within the cabinet, the German Nationals, especially Agriculture Minister Schiele, again took the lead in opposing tariff concessions and again tried to negatively revise some of the offers already made to Czechoslovakia (e.g., on malt).[126] The geographic position of Czechoslovakia as well as the commodities at issue (especially hops) meant that not only the Prussian agricultural interests opposed concessions, but also that South German governments and agricultural associations in Bavaria and Württemberg expressed their opposition.[127]

In the interministerial Trade Policy Committee, Schiele's Agriculture Ministry stood alone, labeling any agricultural concessions beyond a minute reduction of the hops duty as "impossible." On the other side, the Foreign Office, Finance Ministry, and Economics Ministry all favored an agreement with Czechoslovakia and understood that "obtaining the necessary concessions for German exports and concluding any treaty at all will be possible only if we accommodate Czechoslovakia's primary demands in the agricultural sector." Stresemann appealed to the cabinet for additional concessions, asking for authorization to offer substantial tariff concessions on barley, malt, hops, ham, timber, and beer.[128] Predictably, the Marx government was unable to force a resolution of the issue. The unresolved problem of how to proceed with the Czechoslovak trade negotiations appeared on the cabinet's agenda several times between November 1927 and February 1928; each time the discussion was shelved (vertagt).[129] By the spring of 1928, the Germans were grateful for a chance to postpone further trade negotiations and to shift their attention to talks on how Czechoslovakia's new legislation on the revalorization of pre-1914 Austro-Hungarian debts would affect German bondholders.[130]

When the revalorization issue faded in February 1929, attention returned to trade talks. Yet a resumption of the negotiations required that the German cabinet finally take a stand on the important agricultural questions that had been left unanswered since November 1927. Now that Chancellor Müller's "Great Coalition" government excluded the German National Party, some industrial interest groups saw in the composition of the new cabinet "the possibility of laying down a new basis [for negotiations] in the agricultural sector which is so important to the Czechs." The *Berliner Börsen Zeitung* was less optimistic, noting that if the Czechs maintained their agricultural demands "it is to be expected that the trade treaty negotiations will be adjourned again" since "the political situation in Germany will hardly allow the Czechoslovak demands to prevail."[131]

The Trade Policy Committee's attempt on 19 June 1929 to iron out a new German position for renewed negotiations with Czechoslovakia was a miserable failure. Stresemann and Finance Minister Hilferding (Socialists) were determined to ask the cabinet to approve the concessions under consideration since November 1927. However, in light of the deteriorating economic position of German agriculture, the moderate Agriculture Minister Hermann Dietrich (Democrats) "begged that these questions not be presented to the cabinet" until after the "larger agricultural tariff questions" had been resolved. Even Economics Minister Curtius sought a postponement of the decision to "autumn."[132] The very next day, Stresemann wrote to the chancellery explaining that the cabinet "must take a position on the controversial agricultural tariffs in order to make a resumption of the negotiations possible." One week later the Agriculture Ministry offered a diametrically opposed view in a Reply to the Submission of the Foreign Office. Dietrich stated baldly that "it appears to me impossible at this moment to conduct economic negotiations with the goal of reducing tariffs on German agricultural products." Inside the chancellery, the economics desk officer, Othmar Fessler, and Assistant Secretary Victor Hagenow recommended that negotiations be delayed: "In view of the opposition from the Agriculture Ministry and an abstention by the Economics Ministry, the cabinet will hardly be in any position to decide on accommodation, even on the less important Czechoslovak tariff requests." The government was still irreconcilably divided in the ministers' discussion of 2 July 1929 and could think of nothing more creative to do than to refer the matter back to the Trade Policy Committee for a reexamination of the "individual suggestions" made by the Foreign Office.[133]

Not only was Germany unable to offer any tariff reductions to Czechoslovakia, but the increases in the German tariff that had taken place between November 1927 and July 1929 led to a negative revision of many earlier German offers. Not surprisingly, the Czechoslovak delegation returned empty-handed from the first round of new treaty negotiations in Berlin.[134] The German press reported that on many items the differences separating German and Czechoslovak positions "had become even greater" than they had been in earlier negotiations. In October 1929 the Reichsverband's Trade Policy Committee noted that the July negotiations had "made no progress ... because the German delegation was not in a position to fulfill the primary Czechoslovak requests in the agricultural sector." The failure of either side to suggest a date for resuming the talks was recognized in Germany as pushing the possibility of any trade treaty with Czechoslovakia into the distant future.[135] With this bout of governmental paralysis in July 1929, republican Germany unknowingly passed up its last opportunity for concluding a full trade treaty with Czechoslovakia.

The failure of treaty negotiations in the worsening economic climate of late 1929 had significant consequences for the future. Both governments responded to these setbacks by reverting to the earlier practices of encouraging private-sector agreements to regulate trade in the most important commodities. The German press seemed to endorse the idea by pointing out that the practice had "proven itself" during the economic turbulence of 1920 to 1924.[136] In December 1929 the Czechoslovaks suggested that private-sector groups on both sides open negotiations on Czechoslovak shoe and malt exports. The interministerial Trade Policy Committee expanded on the Czechoslovak suggestion by promoting private talks for textile interests and hops growers on both sides.[137] When private negotiations on the malt trade began in February 1930, they were part of a new era in German trade practices in Eastern Europe.

Soviet Russia

German trade policy toward Soviet Russia never experienced the extended paralysis that plagued German policy toward Poland and

Czechoslovakia. Throughout the period, commercial policy played an important role in defining Germany's with the largest of its Eastern neighbors. As early as 1921, Weimar Germany signed the first of several economic agreements that established, supported, and improved German political relations with the Soviet government.[138] German successes in these efforts were rooted in the nature of the German-Soviet economic relationship in the Weimar years and in the character of the trade and financial agreements concluded between the Reich and Soviet Russia.[139]

As a result of the fundamental changes in Russia after 1917, Soviet trade would not recover the prewar levels of the Czarist Empire at any point from 1918 to 1939.[140] Under these conditions, German trade with the new Soviet Russian state could never recover its prewar importance. Most important for Germany's foreign economic policy, Russia no longer exported agricultural produce on the prewar scale. Not until the forced exports of 1930 to 1931 did the Soviet Union (re)appear as a major player on the international grain market.[141] For hard-pressed German farmers, the absence of large supplies of Soviet agricultural exports on the world market was one of the few favorable developments of the 1920s. Since "Russia" no longer displayed the ability to damage German farm incomes with exports, German agricultural interests no longer bitterly opposed trade agreements with the "Russian" state. Fully preoccupied with real and immediate problems of agricultural competition from Czechoslovakia, Poland, the Baltic countries, Denmark, the Netherlands, and France, agricultural interests in Germany were content to let economic agreements with the Soviets pass without significant opposition.[142]

On the other side, German commercial and industrial exporters initially hoped that some of the massive prewar Russian market might be recovered. The electrical and machine tool industries especially supported renewed economic ties with the Soviets. But exports to Soviet Russia generally failed to reach expectations in terms of both volume and profitability. Particularly in the early Weimar years, the "Russian business" (Rußlandgeschäft) showed no sign of recovering its former splendor.[143] Frustration with the sharp terms and cumbersome workings of the Soviet state monopoly on foreign trade reinforced German feelings that, in general, substantial profits could not be made in Soviet Russia under the circumstances prevailing in the 1920s. Certainly memories of earlier bounty continued to animate hopes for a return to better days in the Russian market. Industrial groups remained interested in the prospect of expanding trade with the Soviets and they never stopped urging the government to do everything possible in this regard. At the same time, those industrialists who had tested the Soviet waters generally understood that German interests were blocked first by the physical state of the Soviet economy and subsequently by the economic policies of the new Soviet government.[144] By 1925 industrialists had largely given up on the prospect of greatly expanded trade with the Soviets in the immediate future. Instead the leading interest groups devoted the vast majority of their political efforts to trade partners and commercial issues where real or more easily realizable profits were at stake.[145]

Not since Bismarck's days had the foreign trade of the Russian or Soviet state meant so little to the German economy. From the economic perspective, trade relations with the Soviets fell from the first circle of German trade policy issues to a distant second or even third level of importance. The removal of German-Soviet trade relations from the list of pressing economic issues facing the Reich provided the German Foreign Office with some freedom from the intrusive interference of the domestic interest groups. Thus, by default, rather than by its own ability to establish an autonomous area of operation, the Foreign Office gained the ability to conduct foreign economic policy toward the Soviets with more consideration for German foreign policy and European international affairs and less concern for domestic political economy than was the case in either German-Polish or German-Czechoslovak relations.[146]

The ability to conclude or to withhold economic agreements from the Soviets served German foreign policy well in both the tumultuous early years and the more stable middle years of the Weimar republic. During the period 1919 to 1923, in which the Reich had seven different foreign ministers, Germany did not pursue a grand strategic plan for a rapprochement with Soviet Russia. On the contrary, several widely divergent and competing views of the Soviet Union coexisted within the foreign policy establishment. A mixture of domestic politics and foreign policy concerns, and economic and strategic motives combined to produce a stop-and-go policy toward the Soviets during this time. Not until Stresemann began to provide a steady strategic concept for German foreign policy did the Reich begin to pursue a conscious policy of balancing its Eastern and Western rivals with a string of alternating and carefully timed economic and political agreements that included the German-Soviet trade treaty of October 1925.

When the Soviet government declared the Treaty of Brest-Litovsk void on 11 November 1918, German-Soviet economic relations entered a limbo from which they did not emerge until May 1921. For a variety of economic and political reasons the Reich government declined to authorize with the Soviets the types of formal trade exchanges it encouraged with Poland and Czechoslovakia from 1919 to 1920. In April 1919 an interministerial meeting chaired by Stockhammern on the subject of "private attempts to resume trade relations with Russia" produced a policy statement on these issues. The group acknowledged that "from an economic standpoint the resumption of trade relations would be desirable," but added that "the situation in Russia cannot be viewed as one in which we can expect any [economic] benefit" for the Reich. Recalling the failure of Soviets to deliver promised goods in the past, the group noted the still overwhelming practical impediments to trade: the "disrupted railroad situation in Russia," government "barriers to free trade," food shortages, and a lack of industrial raw materials. German exporters would insist on payment in neutral or Entente currencies for any German goods, and Soviet foreign exchange reserves were known to be inadequate. Most basically, the Bolsheviks did not reliably control large portions of the country, so that "the government in Moscow, even with the best intentions, is not always in a position to fulfill the obligations it has agreed to." In sum, the economic considerations were secondary for the time being since no significant trade could be conducted. Germany could gain nothing economically by pursuing trade relations with the Soviets and was losing nothing by doing nothing. "Meanwhile, purely political factors are decisive," according to Stockhammern, who explained that the German government was not prepared for the "military and diplomatic consequences" of full trade relations with the Soviets. That rejection was based on both a fear of the Bolshevik "radical communist goal of world revolution," and the need "to avoid fueling Allied suspicions" before the peace terms were settled. The meeting closed with the determination that "all attempts by individual German businesses to concluded deals with the Russian [sic] Government are unwelcome [unerwünscht] until further notice."[147]

The very limited possibilities for trade with Soviet Russia had not improved much when the Foreign Office again reviewed the question in February 1920. Even those influential industrialists such as Walter Rathenau, who argued that "the current waiting posture vis-à-vis the eastern problem is no longer maintainable [ist nicht mehr aufrecht zu erhalten]," had to admit that "Russia is poor and plundered. Reports of existing food and raw material stockpiles are obviously fairy tales."[148] At a confidential meeting of Foreign Office and private-sector representatives, the commercial and industrial circles expressed their interest in the export business to Soviet Russia only if raw materials could be obtained in exchange.[149] However, the continuing practical problems (no proof of exportable Soviet surpluses, disrupted transport, lack of German transit treaties with the Baltic countries) precluded any large shipments in either direction. In view of the economic situation, the private-sector was "almost unanimous" in the view that the German government should continue to avoid entering into official trade relations with the Soviet government.[150] Stockhammern discouraged the business groups' idea of sending a private study commission to tour Soviet Russia as "premature," but he withdrew Foreign Office objections to individual firms signing contracts with the Soviet government.[151]

A primacy of political over economic considerations had heretofore allowed Germany to bide its time in trade policy with the Soviets. After the Versailles Treaty was finalized, political considerations required that Germany make some decisions on relations with Soviet Russia. In February 1920 Foreign Office acknowledged that "for political reasons we cannot take a completely negative stand toward Russian attempts to trade with us, despite the uncertain [economic] prospects."[152] The new Fehrenbach government (June 1920 to May 1921) could not remain immune to the mounting political and diplomatic pressures forcing Germany to adopt some policy toward the Soviets, even if only to respond to Soviet initiatives. In answering an interpellation by the Independent Socialists, Foreign Minister Simons admitted in the Reichstag on 21 January 1921 that Germany "was not in a position to simply ignore" the possible resumption of relations with the Soviets.[153]

Equally important for the future of German policy was the ongoing reform of the Foreign Office. The reorganization plan liquidated the old Commercial Affairs Department and sent the obstructionist Stockhammern over to the new Southeast European Department in March 1920. With Stockhammern out of the way, the "Easterners" in the Foreign Office (Gustav Hilger in Moscow, Moritz Schlesinger of the Reich Office for Civilian Prisoners and Prisoners of War, and "Ago" von Maltzan at the Foreign Office Russian desk) began to activate German policy toward Russia.[154] They obtained Simons's permission to meet the Soviets for further negotiations on the prisoner issue and thereafter on trade matters.[155] On 18 February 1921 Hilger and Schlesinger, Viktor Kopp and Ignaz Jakubovich (future first secretary of the Soviet Embassy in Berlin) initialed a supplemental agreement to an earlier prisoner exchange agreement of April 1920 and approved a draft agreement "to extend the sphere of activity" of the delegations currently negotiating on the final prisoner issues. This latter agreement allowed the existing delegations in Moscow and Berlin to assume the functions of foreign trade offices, and to be suitably expanded.[156] As a result of the revolutionary "March Action" staged by German Communists in Saxony and Thuringia, the cabinet refused to allow an expanded Soviet presence in Berlin as a source of Bolshevik agitation in Germany. The new agreements languished without final German approval.[157] When on 3 May 1921 the Fehrenbach cabinet expressed its intention to resign at the next suitable opportunity rather than accept the Allies' "London Ultimatum" on reparations, the "Easterners" again seized the initiative. Using the cabinet crisis of May 3 to 10 as an excuse for independent action, Maltzan and Gustav Behrendt, head of the East European department in the Foreign Office, signed the two recent German-Soviet agreements without cabinet approval and against President Ebert's will.[158] A month later, in calmer circumstances, the new cabinet of Chancellor Joseph Wirth (Center) approved the agreements without substantive discussion.[159]

Although Germany gained little economically from the agreements, it also cost the Reich nothing economically to improve German-Soviet relations by allowing functioning trade offices. The ravaged state of Soviet Russia and the continued trade controls in Germany ensured that Soviet exports would cause no problems for German producers. In fact, the economic results of allowing expanded trade contacts were minimal in 1921 and 1922. The deeper significance of the agreements lay in the political sphere. The 6 May agreement completed Germany's de jure and de facto recognition of the Soviet government.[160] That fact greatly simplified the resumption of full formal diplomatic relations with the Soviets and was one advantage that Germany possessed over the Western allies one year later at the Genoa Conference.

The 6 May 1921 agreement is especially revealing for the manner in which the Reich concluded it. Despite the fact that a handful of upper-level diplomatic officers strongly favored the agreements, the cabinet as a whole was ambivalent and unenthusiastic about improved economic contacts with the Soviets.[161] The highly unusual and somewhat questionable manner in which the agreements received final signatures was characteristic of the willy-nilly approach to Soviet relations that successive German governments had taken since 1919.[162] Among Germany's leading political figures there was no consensus on improving relations with the Soviets for either economic or political reasons and certainly no conscious policy of "playing the Soviet card" against the Western powers. That strategy was something the Germans would employ first in Genoa.

The Genoa Conference of April 1922 grew out of British Prime Minister Lloyd George's idea to "link a [reparations] moratorium for Germany with the impending [economic] negotiations with Russia." The Entente hoped to arrange an international agreement for European economic reconstruction that could somehow accommodate both the Soviet offer of 28 October 1921 (recognition of czarist debts in exchange for continued famine relief, future reconstruction aid, and a final peace treaty) and the German request of 14 December 1921 for a reparations moratorium.[163] As the possibility of the conference easing the reparations burden on Germany faded away in the spring of 1922, the possibility that reparations might be worsened by an Entente-Soviet deal appeared to grow more real.[164]

Any discussion of Russian debts and a Russian peace treaty left open the possibility of the Soviets paying off czarist debts to the West in exchange for the right to collect reparations from Germany – a right that had been left open to a future Russian government under Article 116 of the Versailles Treaty.[165] In January 1922 Karl Radek, the Bolshevik troubleshooter for German questions, told Maltzan that the French had made such an offer to the Soviets.[166] The Anglo-French London Report of March 1922 also suggested that the Entente would pursue a policy along these lines. Faced with this potentially disastrous worsening of the reparations issue, Wirth began to expound a deliberate policy of improving German-Soviet relations in the hope of "alleviating Western political pressure" on Germany.[167] Foreign Minister Rathenau was well aware that one of Germany's few advantages over the Western powers lay in the expanded German-Soviet relations based on the May 1921 agreements: "Lloyd George intends to place the Russian problem in the center of the conference … Between us and Russia things are different: we have recognized Russia de jure and de facto and are in good economic relations with it; for us the Russian problem is not pressing, we are in the superior position with Russia."[168] The Germans hoped to use their "contacts" with Soviet Russia to prevent the Reich's "isolation" at the conference, "without, however, allowing ourselves thereby to be driven into conflict with the Western powers."[169] As part of that ambiguous policy, Rathenau and Maltzan held extensive discussions from 1 to 3 April in Berlin with Soviet Foreign Minister Georgi Chicherin and the rest of the Soviet delegation on its way to Genoa. Rathenau declined to sign a bilateral agreement with the Soviets before the conference despite the fact that the Soviets "declared their readiness" to do so.[170]

Rathenau still clung to his own idiosyncratic belief that German participation in a mixed government-private international "consortium" for the reconstruction of Russia could bring the Soviets, the Germans, and the Western powers together in an economic and political understanding.[171] Other important German industrial interests focused instead on the upcoming negotiations with the Western countries at Genoa and not at all or very little on economic relations with the Soviets. The industrial Reichsverband's Genoa Committee prepared almost exclusively for international commercial issues that would be discussed with the Entente, never once mentioning negotiations with the Soviets.[172] The Governing Committee of the German Chamber of Commerce scarcely mentioned economic relations with the Soviets in its preparatory discussions.[173]

At Genoa, conference developments quickly reached a critical point for Germany. On 14 April the German delegation became convinced that an Entente-Soviet deal was close at hand.[174] Rathenau, urged on by Maltzan and then Wirth, reluctantly began to consider the possibility of signing an agreement with the Soviets before Germany came to an understanding with the West. Rathenau spent the next two days "completely paralyzed by the prospect of the impression our understanding with the Soviets would make on the Western powers, particularly on Lloyd George." Finally on Sunday, 16 April 1922, Rathenau signed a slightly revised version of the German-Soviet agreement he had passed up in Berlin two weeks earlier.[175]

Although none of the individual economic or political provisions of the agreement were particularly extraordinary, the Treaty of Rapallo irrevocably altered the European diplomatic landscape for the next decade.[176] Rapallo has been seen alternatively as the centerpiece of an "unholy alliance" or as the product of more traditional "balance of power thinking."[177] In both views, Rapallo was a crucial step in Germany's regaining genuine diplomatic autonomy after Versailles.[178] The autonomy obtained from a diplomatic agreement with Soviets provided the base upon which Stresemann subsequently built his revisionist strategy of alternating economic and political agreements with Germany's Western and Eastern neighbors.[179]

The earlier economic agreement of 6 May 1921 had positioned German foreign policy for this bold political step. The earlier agreement had normalized commercial relations between the two countries so that the next logical step in improving these contacts was a general MFN relationship, as contained in Rapallo. Without the de facto and de jure recognition implied by accepting Soviet economic representatives in the earlier agreement, the Reich government (especially the hesitant Rathenau) might well have balked at moving in one step from a state of broken commercial and diplomatic relations to MFN status and full recognition. Within the Rapallo treaty itself the economic clauses provided support for renewed political relations. For the materially oriented Bolsheviks and the economically needy Soviet state, the economic portions of Rapallo were vital prerequisites for a political understanding. For the Soviets, the MFN clause meant the end of the nightmare prospect that Soviet Russia would be permanently discriminated against or even excluded from the foreign trade of the capitalist countries. A written pledge from the Reich government that it would do everything possible to facilitate the contracts signed by German producers was invaluable to the Soviets' New Economic Policy of reconstruction. Establishing the framework for economic relations was as important to the Soviets as reestablishing formal diplomatic relations.[180]

Although the economic provisions were vital to the conclusion of an agreement with the Soviets, Germany had again made trade concessions that were largely formal rather than substantive. The extension of MFN rights cost the Reich nothing in real material terms since the costs and benefits of MFN could be calculated only after Germany put a new tariff and tariff treaties in place. For this reason there could be no economic objections to the treaty during the Reichstag ratification debate of 30 May 1922.[181] The immediate and widespread political impact of Rapallo has largely obscured the nature of the agreement as the starting point for further substantive negotiations on all aspects of normalizing relations. The Rapallo Treaty explicitly called for a subsequent consular agreement, and the German Foreign Office reminded other Reich ministries that "it still remained for a supplementary agreement to settle all individual questions."[182] The bulk of these questions centered on reviving economic relations. At issue were both routine matters (copyrights, patents, taxation, international terms of payment, shipping rights, fishing rights, and the legal status of German citizens in Soviet Russia) and special questions such as the status of German-owned property not yet nationalized by the Bolsheviks. The proper development of trade relations still required agreements on standard issues such as tariff rates, trade offices, property acquisition, and customs administration. The German business community especially was quick to point out that an additional commercial agreement was needed. Without formal legal guarantees, every German businessperson in Soviet Russia remained exposed to the "bureaucratic arbitrariness of low-level officials" on matters of entry visas, residency permits and personal safety.[183]

Beyond all other matters, the Soviet government's claim to a "foreign trade as a monopoly of the state" stood as the major issue requiring clarification.[184] Before 1922, the state monopoly had not been a major concern of German business. No one had been quite sure what Bolsheviks meant by a state monopoly in trade, or whether they could actually introduce such a thing, or even whether the communists would prevail in the civil war. In the prevailing chaotic conditions of

1919 to 1921 no real trade was being conducted anyway. But by early 1922, the Soviets began soliciting bids from German industry for large orders for the reconstruction of the country (e.g. rebuilding the municipal electric works of Kiev, rebuilding the port facilities at Petrograd). It became clear that the Soviet Foreign Trade Office in Berlin (the Handelsvertretung, under direction of General Secretary J. A. Pieper and Boris Stomoniakov), which handled all these commercial negotiations, was using its monopsonist position as a means of seeking unusually generous prices and credit terms from many of Germany's largest industrial enterprises. In June 1922 Hans v. Raumer (AEG) complained to Hermann Bücher (VdESI, RdI) that the Russians were asking for credit terms beyond what AEG gave to its best customers! Raumer noted how "by being played off against each other, the firms negotiating with Russia were being driven down." This came precisely at a time when most of German industry was "not in a position to give any type of credit," as Paul Reusch noted for his own metallurgic firm, the Gütehoffnungshütte.[185] The state trade monopoly also undermined the Soviet concessions made on MFN since "as long as the Russian foreign trade monopoly is strictly enforced the MFN clause will have relatively little meaning for us, since Russia can make MFN rights worthless by transferring the bulk of its trade [away from Germany] or by some other foreign trade rules."[186]

Erich Wallroth oversaw the German preparations for extensive substantive negotiations with the Soviets from their beginnings in August 1922 through February 1923 when he was elevated to the directorship of the East European Department, replacing Maltzan who moved up to state secretary (December 1922 to December 1924). Wallroth was succeeded by Paul Ernst von Körner, the former director of the old imperial Foreign Office's Commercial Affairs Department (II), who had negotiated most of the 1904 treaty with the Russians and had headed the German trade negotiations at Brest-Litovsk in 1918. Now, at age 73, Körner emerged from retirement to take charge of the important upcoming negotiations with the new Soviet regime.[187]

Negotiations for a consular agreement opened in Moscow on 23 June 1923.[188] Over the next six months progress on a number of formal and secondary issues (consulates, shipping, legal aid, inheritance) came quickly. Negotiations continued on various topics through early May 1924, when they were broken off as a result of the "Botzenhardt Incident" at the Soviet trade office in Berlin.[189] When the substantive economic negotiations opened in Moscow in November 1924 both countries had political motives for reaching an economic agreement.

The Germans had completed a comprehensive financial settle-ment with the Western powers in the Dawes Plan of August 1924. Stresemann in particular hoped to complement that achievement with a German-Soviet economic agreement, so that success in the West could be balanced by success in the East. Just three weeks after the Dawes Plan had been ratified in the Reichstag, the Foreign Office planned to send a note "immediately" offering to negotiate (again in Moscow) as early as next month on trade and settlement issues. The Germans sought to resume negotiations as "soon as possible in order to find out if we can bring the Russians to sign with us in the fore-seeable future."[190] The Soviets also had diplomatic reasons to come to terms with Germany; they sought to offset their rapidly deterio-rating relations with Britain and their continuing estrangement from France by concluding an important agreement with the Reich. Ger-man delegation members from the Prussian Trade Ministry and the Economics Ministry reported shortly after negotiations began that one lower-level Soviet negotiator had let slip that "for us it is less important to settle economic relations in this treaty than for political reasons to come to some positive result."[191]

Yet the path to a substantive German-Soviet economic agreement remained blocked by the fantastic demands that both sides to the table in November 1924. The core German demands amounted to a de facto termination of the Soviets state's foreign trade monopoly. The open or veiled "penetration" of the state trade monopoly had been at the heart of German Foreign Office, Economics Ministry, and private-sector demands since the start of German negotiation preparations in August 1922. Those demands were embodied chiefly in the German draft agreement's Article 20, "Acquisition Rights," which would have allowed unregistered German firms direct contact with Soviet producers and end users. In addition, the Germans demanded that the Soviets bind themselves to specific levels of future purchases in Germany and allow specific quotas of German exports, many of which were luxury and consumer goods, into the Soviet Union. The chairman of the Soviet Delegation, Jakob Ganetzski, told German Ambassador Ulrich von Brockdorff-Rantzau at the second negotiating session that the Soviet government was "nothing less than horrified" at the major German demands, which were rejected imme-diately and unequivocally. German secondary demands included free freight transit though the Soviet Union.[192] On their side, the Soviets were most interested in a loan of 200 million marks from the German government, an idea rejected by the Germans as "not feasible." In addition, the Soviets demanded both a veterinary agreement allowing live animal imports from the Soviet Union, and a German promise to maintain the current duty-free status of German grain imports. No German government could promise duty-free imports of Russian grain; via MFN clauses in German treaties with other countries, this would have amounted to opening Germany to grain imports from all agricultural producers. Finally, the Soviets sought to limit the MFN rights they already extended to Germany to only the European portions of the Soviet Union.[193]

After nine sessions in which virtually no progress was made, the German delegation adjourned to Berlin on 17 December.[194] In the course of January 1925, the Reich ministries met repeatedly with private-sector representatives to review the situation. The leading Foreign Office members of the German delegation, Körner and Georg Martius, urged that Germany reconsider some of its earlier demands, especially as these concerned the Soviet foreign trade monopoly and the permissible activities of German businessmen in Soviet Russia. Körner's assertion on 30 December that "a bad treaty is still better than no treaty at all" was angrily rejected by members from the Chamber of Commerce who stated bluntly that it was "better not [to have] a treaty at all than a bad trade treaty." The Westphalian Chambers of Commerce seconded this latter view and subsequently warned their members that "substantial forces are working on the conclusion of a German-Russian trade treaty for political reasons even if that treaty contains no consideration of the basic economic demands that must be raised by Germany."[195] The leading private-sector groups (industrial Reichsverband, German Chamber of Commerce, German Agricultural Council, Central Association of German Wholesalers) insisted on pressing Germany's major demands. At a meeting with ministerial representatives, Karl Fehrmann (Reichsverband) laid out the private-sector demands: "German parity with the state economic organs in Russia as absolutely necessary (a *sine qua non*) for a treaty; acquisition and entry rights "as suggested"; and if specific import quotas could not be obtained from the Soviets, then "security in some form that Germany receives an appropriate portion of the Russian import market." In discussing a compromise formula on acquisition rights in the proposed Article 20, another group of "commercial and industrial representatives" told the Martius that "if the Russians cannot accommodate our wishes that traveling commercial representatives, etc. can be active in Russia without prior registration, then the private-sector has no interest in this article and generally no essential interest in the trade treaty." Nor was the private-sector particularly forthcoming in regard to Soviet demands. The commercial groups were "strongly averse" to providing credit to the Soviet state. Industry was "more in favor," but did not want that issue included in the trade treaty proper.[196]

With the German position unchanged and bearing the same demands, the German delegation returned to Moscow in February for a predictably unsuccessful second round of negotiations. The Soviets were determined to preserve the state foreign trade monopoly in strict form and categorically refused to grant either import quotas or percentage guarantees of the Soviet import market to Germany. The Germans, operating without a tariff, could not yet make any promises on grain tariffs, repeatedly dodged a veterinary agreement, and were not forthcoming on the credit question. Körner returned again to Berlin in early May 1925 no closer to an agreement.

By the spring of 1925 Germany's diplomatic position urgently required that the Reich manage some positive conclusion to its negotiations with the Soviets. Since December 1924 Stresemann had been evading Russian offers for much closer diplomatic coordination between the two countries. In January to February 1925 he had moved closer to the West by launching the initiative that would result in the Locarno Conference and the Treaty of Mutual Guarantee renouncing the use of force along the Rhine. Stresemann still hoped to "combine this Locarno policy with a consolidation of our relations with Russia, if at all possible." Since he was determined to avoid any political agreement with the U.S.S.R. until after the Western negotiations were brought to a close, Stresemann could offer only an economic agreement to reassure the Soviets. Under these circumstances, Körner could not allow the German-Soviet economic negotiations to collapse completely despite six months of deadlock and no realistic hope for movement.[197]

Yet the private-sector representatives on the negotiating delegation were not making the conclusion of an agreement easy. At a meeting with Körner at the Foreign Office, they demanded that the negotiations be moved to Berlin and repeated their view that "if the Russians do not want to agree to our demands then the conclusion of an economic agreement must be refused." Wallroth responded gently that both Brockdorff in Moscow and the Foreign Office in Berlin saw "very important political reasons" for continuing the negotiations in Moscow in order to avoid the impression that "the negotiations would not make progress." He also predicted that even if an economic agreement could not be reached a treaty would still be signed composed of the other, "secondary" agreements such as those on consular rights, legal aid, and shipping. Other delegation members added the opinion of Economics Minister Neuhaus that "for political reasons a breakdown in the negotiations must be avoided" and that if necessary Germany could sign an empty economic agreement that would "prepare the soil for future discussions."[198]

By the time Körner departed Moscow on 29 June 1925 after a fruitless third round of negotiations, the situation had become critical. A German attempt to postpone further negotiations until autumn had "failed because of the Soviet government's mistrust, heightened to an extreme by Germany negotiations with the West." Further, the Soviets had interpreted the postponement suggestion as a "turning of German policy away from Soviet Russia and toward the West." The Soviets then insisted on "immediate conclusion of the entire treaty package, including the Economic Agreement," thus short-circuiting Wallroth's idea of signing only the secondary agreements.[199] Brockdorff warned from Moscow that the Soviets would consider a treaty failure to be "a political act by Germany" and would draw "the appropriate political and economic consequences" therefrom.[200]

Brockdorff and Dirksen, who had assumed control of the negotiations in Moscow after Körner's departure, suggested Germany undertake a final attempt at reaching an agreement with the Soviets. In the event of another failure, the Reich would then offer to sign a limited "temporary economic agreement" of eighteen months.[201] When Brockdorff informed Berlin that Dirksen's meetings with Ganetzski on 14 and 15 July had produced no agreement, Stresemann presented to the cabinet the plan for a temporary agreement. Stresemann laid out the larger political arguments in plain terms, pointing out that "a breakdown in the German-Russian negotiations at this time, especially in view of the still pending guarantee negotiations with the West, would have the most serious political consequences." In the current situation, the Soviets would view "even an attempt at delay" as "a decisive break by Germany from its previous policy, as a turn away from Soviet Russia and toward the West." Stresemann argued in addition that "even a superficial understanding with Soviet Russia" could help Germany's stalled treaty negotiations with France and Poland.[202] Under the diplomatic pressure of his upcoming conference with the Western powers, Stresemann abandoned virtually all of Germany's substantive economic demands in the hope of quickly reaching an agreement with the Soviets. Long-standing German demands on acquisition rights, a set share of Soviet foreign trade, consignment facilities, parcel post delivery, and coastal fishing were not covered. Stresemann reduced German demands to protection against economic espionage, protection against administrative deportation, and a fishing concession on the coast of Murmansk. The Soviets would receive full extraterritoriality for the Berlin Trade Office and the right to ship 800 live hogs weekly to Germany.[203]

On 3 September the Soviets radically reduced their own demands, abandoning their earlier positions on obtaining fixed German tariff rates, the right to export cattle to Germany, and restricting MFN to European Russia.[204] A final month of wrangling over secondary economic issues (veterinary regulations, patent rules, and the German fishing concession) brought the negotiations to the point of collapse on several further occasions. A complete breakdown was avoided only by removing even more substance from the agreement.[205] Parallel negotiations offering the Soviets a small (75 million marks) short-term credit completed the deal.[206] The final treaty text was presented to and approved by the German cabinet on 1 October 1925, just five days before the opening of the Locarno Conference. The agreement was announced in Berlin on 2 October and signed in Moscow along with the other agreements by Brockdorff and Körner for the Reich on 12 October – precisely while Stresemann was negotiating with the Western powers at Locarno.[207]

Although the Foreign Office expressed its satisfactions with the successful, last-minute conclusion of an economic agreement with the Soviets, Germany's industrial and commercial groups received the terms of the deal unenthusiastically. Stresemann conceded that the "material importance of the economic agreement" lagged behind the accomplishments of the various other agreements overall. German desire for free access to the Russian market had run aground on the "immovable objects" of the Soviet "state economy and its foreign trade monopoly." Since it proved impossible for the Germans to "break through the Russian economic system," the major German demands remained unfulfilled. On the other hand, "from the political perspective" the treaty "will be of decisive importance in shaping German-Russian relations, precisely at the present moment when [Germany's] West negotiations are underway and Soviet Russia deeply fears that Germany is beginning to turn away from Russia and from Rapallo."[208]

Organizations more disappointed with the material terms of the economic agreement expressed themselves more directly. The Prussian Trade Ministry bluntly labeled the deal as "completely worthless for Germany" and told the Foreign Office so. Westphalian industry quite correctly saw the agreement as one "concluded for political reasons" and one that had "abandoned all German economic demands." In the opinion of the Westphalian industrial information office in Berlin, Germany "receives practically nothing" beyond what the current situation already offered.[209] The German Chamber of Commerce told its members in confidence that "since the main [German] demands ... have not been fulfilled, there is no reason for the private-sector to cheer the conclusion of this trade treaty." The chamber went on to explain that "... the conclusion of the treaty at this exact moment is obviously attributable essentially to political rather than economic factors." In explaining its planned public reaction to the treaty, the chamber noted that, "It is not considered a matter for the private-sector to decide in this time of great political disputes whether or not the conclusion of a trade treaty with Russia is necessary for foreign policy reasons and what the consequences of a [treaty] rejection would be. Accordingly, Chamber President Hamm urged the business community to "temporarily put up with the treaty as an introduction to the creation of future friendly economic relations."[210]

Despite questions about its economic value for Germany, the Economic Agreement of 12 October 1925 and the 75 million-mark credit played crucial and irreplaceable roles in the development of Stresemann's foreign policy. The agreement fulfilled at least three functions simultaneously for Stresemann. First and most crucially, it allayed Soviet fears about German accommodation with the Western powers. The Soviets genuinely feared that Germany would be turned onto an anti-Soviet path by the Western powers after joining the League of Nations.[211] Stresemann explained to meeting of the German minister-presidents that "for that reason, the Reich government intends to conclude the German-Soviet trade treaty, in order to show to the Russians with all possible clarity that Germany does not intend to orient itself exclusively toward the West."[212] Meeting Chicherin in Berlin in September, Stresemann reassured the Soviet foreign minister that Germany "had no intention of being used for such a purpose [as a] war against Russia." Stresemann insisted that economic agreement demonstrated that Germany was not "now setting [its] policy towards the West" and that he personally "would make a point of getting the treaty adopted if only to dispose of this legend."[213] Chicherin later accepted the economic agreement as "proof of Germany's desire not to be diverted from the Rapallo treaty."[214]

Second, the German-Soviet economic agreement protected Stresemann's Locarno policy from domestic criticisms by shortsighted German nationalists that Germany was selling out to the West. Foreign Office State Secretary Carl Schubert noted the "serious domestic political incrimination" that could result from the perception that Germany's Locarno policy was hurting relations with the Soviets. Stresemann skillfully used the fact "that we are perfectly willing to come to an understanding with the Russian State," to rebuff attacks by the German Nationals that "we are selling ourselves to the West."[215]

Finally, the October economic agreement and 75 million-mark credit provided the starting point for a more significant political understanding with the Soviets. In February 1926, the Reich took the unprecedented step of guaranteeing 300 million marks in export credits to the Soviet government.[216] In positively assessing the credit project, Dirksen noted that Germany must "use both trumps, the economic and the political" to overcome residual Soviet "mistrust of Germany's entry into the League of Nations." Moritz Schlesinger, now a special adviser to the Foreign Office on Russian affairs, explained that "if our policy in the East is to be extended, then politics and economics must go together."[217] Having advanced the political argument repeatedly on behalf of the October 1925 economic agreement with the Soviets, Stresemann now chose to emphasize economic arguments in support of the loan plan. Together with Curtius he persuaded the cabinet that German industry required state-guaranteed credit in order to reverse its declining share of the Soviet import market.[218] In assuming the state guarantee, the Reich put an end to any possible international financial boycott of the communist regime.

With the economic agreement of October 1925 and the new credits of 1926, Germany had fully prepared the ground for an important defensive political agreement with the Soviets.[219] Stresemann himself did not hesitate to point out publicly the role of both the October 1925 economic agreement and the new loans in "strengthening the view ... that Germany was anxious to maintain the freedom of good and friendly relations with Russia."[220] German economic reassurances to Russia culminated in the 24 April 1926 Treaty of Berlin, covering both nonaggression and neutrality between the two countries, including nonparticipation in "an economic or financial boycott" of the other party (Article 3).[221] When negotiations between the German banks and the Soviets became stuck over the discounting costs for Soviet repayments, Stresemann pointed out to Curtius that the Soviets would interpret failure to reach a working trade credit agreements as an act with economic and political consequences.[222]

The Treaty of Berlin completed Stresemann's policy of balancing first economic agreements with the West (Dawes) and the Soviets (12 October 1925), and then defensive political agreements with the West (Locarno) and the Soviets (Berlin Treaty). The German practice of balancing East and West with economic and political agreements had been underway since 1921, as the economic agreement of that year and Rapallo a year later helped restore German diplomatic autonomy and open the way for an economic understanding with the West. By occupying a central position between Dawes and Locarno, the German-Soviet economic agreement of October 1925 had an indispensable function in allowing Stresemann's carefully timed, step-by-step restoration of German strength to proceed.

The political successes of both the 1925 economic agreement and the trade credits program launched in 1926 were tarnished by the failure of either action to stimulate a substantial increase in German-Soviet trade. Despite the 300 million marks in credits, trade with the Soviets languished from 1925 to 1929, largely confirming the pessimistic private-sector assessments of business prospects under the terms of the 1925 agreement.[223] Even with the four-year export credits, German exports to the Soviet Union were just 403 million marks in 1928; a mere 3.3 percent of the Reich's total foreign sales. In 1929 these figures dipped to 354 million marks and 2.4 percent. Even more disturbing was Germany's inability to expand its share of the Soviet import market. Total Soviet imports increased 26 percent between 1927 and 1928, but imports from Germany increased by only 24 percent so that Germany's share of the Soviet market actually dipped slightly to 28 percent.[224] At two meetings in the Foreign Office with the "leading economic interest groups" in October 1927 these groups "pointed out with great emphasis the unsatisfactory development of German exports to Russia, which despite the 300 million-mark credit had not experienced an increase." Three months later, the German Chamber of Commerce released its own data confirming that Germany had actually lost a portion of its Russian market share between 1925 and 1926 (25.6 percent) and 1926 and 27 (25.2 percent) despite the 300 million-mark credit.[225] In early 1928 the Union of German Iron and Steel Industrialists noted with resigned disappointment that "German-Russian trade over the past years has not shown the development expected by the German side."[226]

Equally discouraging were the low profit margins on the trade that was taking place. The Soviet Foreign Trade Office in Berlin was adroitly playing one German producer off against another in order to obtain generous terms of payment.[227] One of Germany's largest manufacturers of industrial equipment, DEMAG, singed a large contract with the Soviets in early 1926 that required only a 25 percent Soviet deposit in two-and-one-half-year promissory notes and allowed final payment for the order four years after shipment! DEMAG chief executive Wolfgang Reuter moaned that he "had to take the [Soviet] conditions" because he "otherwise had no work for his production facilities." German competitive underbidding in the face of the Soviet state monopoly on trade soured much of German business on the Russian market through 1931. The industrial Reichsverband acknowledged that "what comes out of this German-Russian economic relationship is not particularly much [nicht übermässig viel] for our economy, but it is, after all, something." The Reichsverband doggedly urged its members to "stay in" in Russian market despite the "difficulties, disappointments, and frictions" of trade with the Soviets.[228]

In view of their very modest impact on the value and volume of trade between the two countries, how do we account for the far-reaching political significance of German-Soviet economic agreements in the 1920s? Further, how do we explain Germany's successful use of economic agreements as stepping stones to larger political understandings with the Soviets, the failure of similar German efforts directed toward Poland, and the Reich's inability to sign the desired trade treaty with Czechoslovakia? Ironically, the successful German-Soviet experience in interwar commercial relations was largely the product of the same forces that produced less productive outcomes in German relations with Poland and Czechoslovakia.

The structures of Weimar domestic politics provide the starting point for extracting the common elements from Germany's varied experiences with trade agreements in Eastern Europe from 1920 to 1930. Weimar's corporatist structure and coalition governments granted to each of several major economic groups and their corresponding political parties a veto power over trade policy decisions. For that reason, the system was unable to impose policy solutions that required sacrifices by one or more of these groups. Without some sacrifice on its own part, Germany could not reach meaningful trade agreements with other countries, as Economics Minister Curtius well understood: "… it cannot be the duty of the government to compensate individual industrial sectors within the German economy for all the advantages and disadvantages of a trade treaty, since in following that principle the conclusion of any trade treaties at all must be considered impossible."[229]

These domestic limits prevented the conclusion of serious trade agreements between Germany and its Eastern neighbors regardless of whether German motives for an agreement were political, economic, or a mixture of the two. Weimar Germany did not (and indeed, could not) sign a major trade agreement of genuine substance with Poland, Czechoslovakia, or the Soviet Union. Successive German governments found it impossible to agree to the specific tariff reductions and import allotments required to reach agreements with Poland and Czechoslovakia. Germany could sign only those formal, but essentially empty trade agreements that required no real domestic sacrifices. The general MFN agreements with Czechoslovakia (1920) and the Soviet Russia (Rapallo) contained no specific concessions. The Soviet inability to produce regular exportable surpluses and the state monopoly on foreign trade made the German-Soviet MFN agreement an especially empty formality. The lack of any real opposition to Germany's various trade and financial deals with Soviet Russia is attributable to the fact that each of these deals cost the Reich nothing in terms of measurable domestic economic sacrifice. The 300 million-mark trade credit to the Soviet Union was a logical attempt by the Reich to stimulate exports and to hold onto its share of the Soviet market without making concessions on imports into Germany. In negotiating with Czechoslovakia, the Reich could not progress beyond the early general MFN agreement and a series of ad hoc private industrial agreements. In negotiations with Poland, German domestic opposition eventually forced the government to abandon the idea of a full tariff treaty and to settle instead for a general MFN agreement. In view of low-priced Polish agriculture's potential ability to make real gains in the German market on this basis, even this agreement was eventually abandoned by the Reich.

Because of Germany's position as a quasi-outlaw state in the post-Versailles international order, these largely empty trade agreements could have tremendous political importance. The German side recognized the German-Czechoslovak MFN treaty of 1920 as an important political gain for Germany since the Reich was treated as an equal by one of the Versailles "victors," which still enjoyed many trade privileges unilaterally as part of Versailles treaty. The agreement broke the anti-German front of allied and associated powers and Germany could begin its diplomatic rehabilitation by pointing to the trade agreement with Czechoslovakia. Hitler's use of a full German-Polish trade treaty for political gains with both the Poles and the Western powers in 1934 only underscores what Stresemann lost as a result of Weimar's inability to conclude some type of trade agreement with Poland.

Because of Soviet Russia's position as Europe's other quasi-outlaw state, even economically "worthless" trade agreements could play a particularly important political role in building German relations with the new Bolshevik government. Although the economic results of the agreements struck between the Reich and the Soviets from 1921 to 1926 were almost negligible, these agreements remained invaluable diplomatic tools. Trade agreements preceded and greatly facilitated the conclusion of Germany's two major political understandings with the Soviets – the treaties of Rapallo and Berlin. Despite its weakened condition, Soviet Russia still merited Great Power status; any degree of German-Soviet rapprochement commanded pan-European attention. By anchoring German policy toward the Soviet giant in the East, these agreements provided Germany, and especially Stresemann, with the necessary international and domestic counterweight for a Western Dawes-Locarno strategy of German rehabilitation.

Notes

1. Stresemann to Brentano (Rome), 10 August 1925, cited in Stürmer, *Koalitionen und Opposition,* 104, note 79. As a documentary starting point for an investigation of German relations with Poland, Czechoslovakia, and Soviet Russia in the 1920s consult *ADAP,* Series A, of which twelve volumes have appreared to date, covering the years 1918 to 1925.
2. For general studies of German-Polish relations in this period see Christian Hoeltje, *Die Weimarer Republik und das Ost-Locarno Problem 1919-1934* (Würzburg, 1958); Zygmunt Gasiorowski's two articles on Stresemann's Polish policy, "Stresemann and Poland before Locarno," *Journal of Central European Affairs* 18 (1958), 25-47 and "Stresemann and Poland after Locarno," ibid., 292-317; Jozef Korbel, *Poland between East and West. Soviet and German Diplomacy towards Poland 1919-1933* (Princeton, 1963); Harald von Riekhoff, *German-Polish Relations, 1918-1933* (Baltimore, 1971); Helmut Lippelt, "'Politische Sanierung.' Zur Deutschen Politik gegenüber Polen 1925/26," *VfZ* 19 (1971), 323-73; Martin Brozat, *Zweihundert Jahre Deutsche Polenpolitik,* 2nd ed. (Frankfurt, 1972). Indispensable for the international context are Piotr Wandycz's two volumes, *France and her Eastern Allies 1919-1925* (Minneapolis, 1962) and *The Twilight of France's Eastern Alliances, 1926-1936: French-Czechoslovak-Polish Relations from Locarno to the Remilitarization of the Rhineland* (Princeton, 1988).
3. See, for example the statements presented by Eric Eyck, "Neues Licht auf Stresemann's Politik," *Deutsche Rundschau* 81 (1955), 118; in the memoirs of the former head of the Eastern Department at the German Foreign Office, Herbert von Dirksen, *Moscow-Tokyo-London: Twenty Years of German Foreign Policy* (Norman, OK, 1952), 24; and in the memoirs of the former British ambassador to Berlin, Viscount D'Abernon, *The Diary of an Ambassador* (New York, 1931), vol. 3, 45 all cited in Zygmunt Gasiorowski, "Stresemann and Poland before Locarno," 26, note 8.
4. On Polish diplomacy during the war and in the early years of the Polish republic see Piotr Wandycz, *Polish Diplomacy 1914-1945: Aims and Achievements* (London, 1988) and its bibliographic essay; Anna Cienciala and Titus Komarnicki, *From Versailles to Locarno: Keys to Polish Foreign Policy 1919-1925* (Lawrence, Kan., 1984).
5. Extremely informative in this regard is Peter Nitsche, "Der Reichstag und die Festlegung der Grenze nach dem Ersten Weltkrieg," *HZ* 216 (1973), 335-61.
6. See, e.g, the comments of the head of the Reichswehr, Hans von Seeckt, as cited in Friedrich von Rabenau, *Seeckt: Aus seinem Leben* (Leipzig, 1940), 252.
7. Article 91 contains the following paragraphs: "Within a period of two years after the coming into force of the present Treaty, German nationals over 18 years of age habitually resident in any of the territories recognized as forming part of Poland will be entitled to opt for German nationality .... They will be entitled to retain their immovable property in the territory of the other state where they had their place of residence before exercising the right to opt." Poles living in the reduced Reich also had the right to opt for Polish nationality. Article 297(b): "... Allied and Associated Powers reserve the right to retain and liquidate all property, rights, and interests, belonging at the date of the coming into force of the present Treaty to German nationals, or companies controlled by them within their territories ... including territories ceded to them by the present Treaty." *The Treaty of Peace.*
8. On Reich policy toward the German minority in Poland see Martin Broszat, "Aussen- und Innenpolitische Aspeckte der preussich-deutschen Minderheitenpolitik in der Ära Stresemann," in Wolfgang Mommsen and Kurt Kluxen, eds., *Politische Ideologien und Nationalstaaatliche Ordnung* (Munich, 1968); Norbert Krekeler, *Revisionsanspruch und geheime Ostpolitik der Weimarer Republik: Die Sub-*

ventionierung der deutschen Minderheit in Polen 1919-1933 (Stuttgart, 1973); John W. Hilden, "The Weimar Republic and the Problem of the Auslandsdeutschen," *JCH* 12 (1977), 273-89; Carole Fink, "Stresemann's Minority Policies 1924-1929," *JCH* 14 (1979), 403-22.

9. Older studies concentrating on the economic aspects of the German-Polish relationship include Charles Kruszewski's still useful "The German-Polish Tariff War (1925-1934) and its Aftermath," *Journal of Central European Affairs* 3 (1943), 294-315; for a Soviet-bloc analysis see Berthold Puchert, *Der Wirtschaftskrieg des deutschen Imperialismus gegen Polen 1925-1934* (East Berlin, 1963).

10. BA Potsdam R 3101/2408, Bl. 11-14.

11. BA Potsdam R 3101/2408, 6 March 1919, Bl. 19, 50.

12. German Armistice Commission to the economics and agriculture ministries from 9 May 1919; Agriculture Ministry to various other ministries, 30 July 1919, BA Potsdam R 3101/2408, Bl. 77, 124.

13. BA Potsdam R 3101/2408, Bl. 174, 256. In December 1919, the Germans extended the Polish credit line for coal by another 3 million marks, ibid. Bl.464. As a member of the Commercial Division of the Imperial German Foreign Office, Stockhammern had assisted Körner in the 1903-1904 trade treaty negotiations with the Russians; in March 1920 he became director of the Foreign Office's new Department for Southeastern Europe; in 1922 he became the Foreign Office commissar for trade treaty negotiations.

14. Economics Ministry memorandum on a 9 February interministerial meeting in the Foreign Office, BA Potsdam R 3101/2408, Bl. 516; Riekhoff, *German-Polish Relations 1918-1933*, 25-26 based on evidence in the Paderewski Papers; see also the Economics Ministry's opinion of December 1923 that French policy aimed at "impeding" the trade of East-Central European states with Germany, cited in Schröder, "Zur politischen Bedeutung der deutschen Handelspolitik nach dem Ersten Weltkrieg," 245.

15. On the plebiscites along the German-Polish border, and in Silesia in particular see T. Hunt Tooley, "German Political Violence and the Border Plebiscite in Upper Silesia, 1919-1921," *CEH* 21 (1988), 56 ff. and the literature cited there in note 1.

16. Governor of East Prussia to the Economics Ministry, 16 July 1920; Prussian Ministry for Culture and Education to various Reich ministries, 5 August 1920; Society for the Protection of German Property in Poland to the Economics Ministry, 3 November 1920, BA Potsdam R 3101/2409, Bl. 60, 68, 105.

17. Schmidt to the Foreign Office, 13 February 1920; Economics Ministry minutes of an interministerial meeting at the Foreign Office, 9 February 1920, BA Potsdam R 3101/2408, Bl. 523, 387.

18. Economics Ministry minutes of the 3 July chaired by the Foreign Office's Director for Eastern Europe, Gustav Behrendt; Reich commissar for Import/Export Licenses to all Foreign Trade Offices, 17 August 1920, BA Potsdam R 3101/2409, Bl. 45, 69. The export ban has often been interpreted as a German attempt to undermine Poland at the height of the Polish-Soviet war, see e.g., Riekhoff, *German-Polish Relations*, 30. However, as Edgar Haniel, state secretary in the Foreign Office, explained to export control officers in the Economics Ministry, German policy was designed to "exert pressure on the Polish government by withholding important goods from them so that they might begin the negotiations desired by the German side," BA Potsdam R 3101/2408, Bl.70. See also Gerhard Wagner, *Deutschland und der polnisch-sowjetische Krieg 1920* (Wiesbaden, 1979), 154-55.

19. 13 November 1920 Foreign Office report on negotiations with Poland 3-7 November, BA Potsdam R 3101/2409, Bl. 113.

20. On these developments see Riekhoff, *German-Polish Relations*, 47 ff.; the still authoritative study by Georges Kaeckenbeck, *The International Experiment in Upper*

Silesia – A Study in the Working of the Upper Silesian Settlement 1922-1927 (London, 1942). On the end of the German export ban, a notice in RWW 27-33-4.

21. Wallroth notes, 3 September 1924, BA Potsdam R 901/64561. Wallroth had succeeded Ago von Maltzan as department director in January 1923.

22. The first, rather stiff Polish tariff of November 1919 had been based on the Russian tariff of 1903 with rates increased and expressed in Polish marks. The "new" Polish tariff of June 1924 was generally considered by German manufacturers and exporters to be "prohibitive" in nature; see their complaints in PAAA "Anfrage und Wünsche zum polnischen Zolltarif 1922-1925." On the development of Polish tariff policies see, Harald Braeutigam, *Die Handelspolitik Polens seit Erlangung der Selbständigkeit* (Berlin, 1926), 22 ff., 29 ff.; Drabek, "Foreign Trade," in Kaser and Radice, eds., *Economic History of Eastern Europe*, vol. 1, 408 ff., 476; Ranki and Tomaszewski cite the Polish tariff rates of 1924 as "among the highest in Europe," "Role of the State," in Kaser and Radice, eds., *Economic History of Eastern Europe*, vol. 2, 16.

23. For relations among the key figures on the German side see especially, Lippelt, "Politische Sanierung," which is particularly good on Schacht, Rauscher, Schubert, and Dirksen (although he is erroneously identified as the "director" of the East European department, when in fact he served as deputy director from 1925 through March 1928 and as director only briefly thereafter), but far less satisfying on Wallroth and Zechlin.

24. German Chamber of Commerce confidential report on a 26 November 1924 meeting in the Economics Ministry; Zechlin to the Finance Ministry, 23 December 1924, BA Potsdam R 901/67215, Bl. 150, 80. In October 1924 members of the Economics Ministry sounded the Poles on the possibility of territorial revisions and improving the terms for German transit through the corridor, although Economics Minister Hamm himself favored excluding political questions from the economic negotiations altogether, Hamm to the Foreign Office, 10 October 1924 and 30 July 1924, BA Potsdam R 901/64561, Bl. 176, 31.

25. Consul-General Hentig to the Foreign Office from 4 December 1924, BA Potsdam R 901/67215, Bl. 45-48.

26. Minutes of an interministerial meeting held on 31 October 1924, initialed by Stresemann on 3 November, BA Potsdam R 901/65826, Bl. 66-69. For a detailed examination of Rauscher's career as envoy in Warsaw see Kurt Doss, *Zwischen Weimar und Warschau: Ulrich Rauscher, deutscher Gesandter in Polen, 1922-1930. Eine politische Biographie* (Dusseldorf, 1984).

27. AA, D/2768/5462H/E367 218-219, cited by Riekhoff, *German-Polish Relations*, 165.

28. Minutes of the interministerial meeting, 31 October 1924, BA Potsdam R 901/65826, Bl. 68. Schroeder has pointed out the Foreign Office's earlier "overestimation of German economic-political potential" in 1919, "Deutsche Handelspolitk," 238. In the German-Polish economic confrontation the German advantage appeared overwhelming. In 1925 the German share of Polish foreign trade was ten times larger than the Polish share of German trade. German exports to Poland were 422 million marks, or 4.7 percent of total German exports (8,838 million marks); imports from Poland were 458 million marks, or 3.5 percent of total German imports (13,080 million). On the other side, Polish exports to Germany were 559 million zloty, or 40 percent of total Polish exports (1,397 million zloty); imports from Germany were 511 million zloty, or 31 percent of total Polish imports (1,666 million zloty), *Statistik des deutschen Reichs*, N.F., Bd. 330A, part III, 13, 68-69. Germany was the primary market for each of the major Polish export commodities: coal, agricultural produce, and timber. The German Chamber of Commerce estimated that Polish Upper Silesia mar-

keted 60 percent of its exports in Germany, BA Potsdam R 901/67215, Bl. 150. In the first half of 1925 Polish agriculture had marketed almost 70 percent of its pork and meat exports in Germany; in 1924 Germany had taken 38 percent of Polish lumber exports, Kruszewski, "Tariff War," 305. On the vulnerabilities of the Polish economy at this time see Zbigniew Landau and Jerszy Tomaszewski, *Wirtschaftsgeschichte Polens im 19. und 20 Jahrhundert* (East Berlin, 1986), 144 ff.,168 ff.

29. Stresemann to Count Praschma, 11 October 1924, BA Potsdam R 901/64561, Bl. 182. Minutes of an interministerial meeting held on 31 October 1924, initialed by Stresemann on 3 November, BA Potsdam R 901/65826, Bl. 66-69. Also Lippelt's conclusion that "Stresemann shared the generally widespread anti-Polish prejudice," "'Politische Sanierung'," 367.

30. In addition, in June 1925 Germany still lacked a valid tariff and was fully preoccupied with the complicated French trade negotiations and preparations for the Locarno initiative, all of which inclined the German side to let the negotiations with Poland develop slowly.

31. Henry Bernard, ed., *Gustav Stresemann Vermächtnis*, vol. 2, 15 June 1925, 308. Coal output from the remaining German portion of Upper Silesia had increased from 8,745,000 tons in 1923 to 14,274,000 tons in 1925, an gain of 5.53 million tons, almost completely replacing the 6 million tons the Poles were seeking to place on the German market annually, cited in Kruszewski, "German-Polish Tariff War," 300.

32. For these measures see especially, Kruszewski, "German-Polish Tariff War," 302 ff. and the sources cited there. Lippelt speaks of Germany "stumbling into the trade war" as Stresemann, preoccupied with the initial French response to the German offer of a security pact, turned his attention to the Polish negotiations too late, "'Politische Sanierung'," 332.

33. The existence of an influential, economically motivated anti-treaty coalition belies Lippelt's twice-repeated blanket assertion that in the period "immediately after Locarno, the conclusion of a treaty probably could have been reached quickly" and "easily" if the German Foreign Office had been so inclined, "'Politische Sanierung'," 371, 372.

34. Stähler (Upper Silesian Mining and Metallurgical Association) in a meeting of the German negotiating delegation and its private sector members, 27 October 1926, BA Potsdam R 901/67404, Bl. 188-191. In September 1924 the German representative on the Mixed Commission for Upper Silesia reported to Zechlin that German Upper Silesian heavy industry urged "no concessions" be made to Poland, BA Potsdam R 901/64561, Bl. 69-73. See also the petitions from the following groups to the chancellor and Foreign Office: Oberschlesische Kokswerke und Chemische Fabriken, AG, 12 September 1925; Schlesische Bergwerks und Hüettengesellschaft, 23 September 1925; Rheinish-Westfaëlisch Kohlen-Syndikat, 29 September 1925, BA R 43I/1106.

35. See e.g., the comments of Karszo-Siedlewski (Ostrowiecer Hochofen und Werke) on Polish nonparticipation in the international steel cartel, 25 January 1927, Haniel 4000000/10; on Polish noncooperation with the International Railmakers' Association (IRMA) see Mannesmann-Archiv P7 55 61. A report to the Union of Iron and Steel Industrialists' Governing Committee noted that a trade treaty without some "private understanding" between the two countries would see "Polish iron ... stream into Germany and lead to a serious disturbance of the German market," 22 February 1928, BA R 13I/102. In addition, as the directors at Krupp noted, "the interests of Rhine-Westphalian heavy iron industry (Grosseisenindustrie) in the export of its products to Poland is insignificant," 4 January 1926, RWWA, 20-1128-2.

36. See, e.g. Jakob Reichert's comments that Germany could grant no trade concessions to Poland unless it received Polish guarantees on the treatment of the German minority in Poland, *Stahl und Eisen* 45 (1925), No. 19, 727.

37. "Position of the Governing Committee of the Reich Land Union on the German-Polish Trade Treaty Negotiations," 1 March 1926, BA R 43I/1106. Hog breeding was a mainstay of small- and medium-sized farms across Germany. Pig imports would affect many more farmers (voters) in 1926 than grain imports had before 1914.

38. Joint petition by the Association of East Prussian Timber Industry and the Association of East German Saw Mills from 27 August 1926; unsigned memorandum (Agriculture Ministry?), BA R 43I/1106.

39. Ritter's notes on a meeting with representatives of the miners' union (Verband der Bergbauindustrie Arbeiter Deutschlands), 24 October 1924, BA Potsdam R 901/65826, Bl. 25; Arbeitsgemeinschaft der Bergarbeiter to Luther from 27 August 1925, BA R 43I/1106; W. Eggert (Allgemeine Deutsche Gewerkschaftsbund) in meeting of the German negotiating delegation and its private sector members, 27 October 1926, BA Potsdam R 901/67404, Bl. 188-191; Friedrich Baltrusch (Deutsche Gewerkschaftsbund) at a government – private-sector meeting, 8 October 1925, Mannesmann-Archiv M12 168.

40. See e.g. the Iron and Steel Wares Association to the Economics Ministry from 17 October 1919, BA Potsdam R 3101/2408, Bl. 269; commercial complaints to the Economic Policy Committee of the Reich Economic Council about the ban on exports to Poland, 16 March 1921, BA R 13I/196; German Chamber of Commerce notice advocating the "soonest possible lifting of the so-called Poland-ban," 6 July 1922, RWWA 27-33-4; Breslau Chamber of Commerce to the Foreign Office reminding them of the "great damage" being done to Silesian industry by the lack of a treaty, 17 June 1924, BA Potsdam R 901/64561, Bl. 25.

41. In November 1924 the German Chamber of Commerce reminded its members that Germany must "keep its nerve" in the trade negotiations with Poland, BA Potsdam R 901/67215, Bl. 150. For grumblings about the economic costs of the tariff war see the comments of Bernhard Grund (Breslau Chamber of Commerce), Hans von Raumer (electrical industry) and Engel (Central Assoc. of German Wholesalers) at a government-private sector meeting, 8 October 1925, Mannesmann-Archiv M12 168.

42. Presidium of the Reichsverband to the Foreign Office, 16 June 1926. AA, D/2768/5462H/E367 363-366, cited in Riekhoff, 170

43. Schacht to Economics State Secretary Julius Hirsch, 28 December 1925, Stresemann Nachlass 3144/7323/0610810-11 as cited in Gasiorowski, "After Locarno," 294, note 9. Schacht repeated this demand to both the French in January 1926 and to the British in May, AA, 1426/2945H/571971 and AA, 1426/2945H/572263-66, ibid., 294, 300. On Schacht's role and his connections to Dirksen see Lippelt, "'Politische Sanierung'," 351 ff., 364; *ADAP*, B, vol. 2, 1, No. 200, 203, 213. For other discussions between the German Embassy staff in London and the British government on these issues see *ADAP*, B, vol. 2, 1, No. 72, 97, 116, 148.

44. Stresemann's hint that Germany might "seize the opportunity" [den Zipfel des Gewandes ergreifen] presented by Poland's impending "financial collapse," speech to the Arbeitsgemeinschft deutscher Landmannschaften, 14 December 1925, *ADAP*, B, vol. 1, 1, 745; Stresemann told Ambassador Friedrich Sthamer (London) that "a peaceful solution to the Polish broder questions, one that does real justice to our demands will not be possible until the economic and financial crisis in Poland has reached an extreme degree and has brought the entire Polish entity into a state of impotence [Ohnmacht]." For that reason "it must be our goal" to delay the economic recovery of Poland "until that country has become

ripe for a settlement of the border question that meets our desires," 19 April 1926, *ADAP*, B, vol. 2, 1, No. 150 [also as AA 2339/4569H/E168665-71]; Stresemann's instructions to sixteen German embassies and missions worldwide, 19 July 1925 as cited in Lippelt, "'Politische Sanierung'," 350, note 93.

45. In November 1925 a run on the already shaky zloty produced public unrest that forced the resignation of financial technocrat Wladyslaw Grabski as Polish prime minister. Desperation drove the parties in the Sejm to an improbable and unworkable great coalition under Skrzynski that produced a particularly inept government. When the zloty broke in March-April 1926, Polish unemployment hovered around 30 percent with urban and rural unrest spreading rapidly; for general developments, see Rothschild, *East Central Europe*, 51 ff. On the financial side see Feliks Mlynarski, *The International Significance of the Depreciation of the Zloty in 1925* (Warsaw, 1926); Z. Karpinski, "Poland's Monetary and Financial Policy 1919-1939," in B. Schmitt, ed., *Poland* (Berkeley, 1945); Zbigniew Landau and Jerszy Tomaszewski, "Poland between Inflation and Stabilization," in Gerald Feldman et al., eds., *The Experience of Inflation* (Berlin/New York, 1984), 284 ff.; I Spigler, "Public Finance" in Kaser and Radice, eds., *Economic History of Eastern Europe*, vol. 2, 117-69.

46. The conceptual inadequacies of German preparation and the ultimate failure of the trade war strategy rest primarily with Zechlin at the Polish desk, Wallroth as the director of the East European department, and Dirksen as deputy director. Rauscher, although less enthusiastic about the tariff war strategy, offered no concrete suggestions for improving its viability. Finally, Stresemann himself must take responsibility for leaving Polish policy unattended from 1924 to 1926 and (along with State Secretary Schubert) allowing the anti-Polish element within the Foreign Office to push Germany into an open break with Poland.

47. *Stresemann Vermächtnis*, vol.2, 9 July 1925, 307.

48. See, Lippelt's conclusion that Germany had subordinated other issues in German-Polish relations to the highest goal of border revisions, "'Politische Sanierung'," 334. Hence Schubert's inability to answer British Ambassador D'Abernon's direct question as to what Germany could offer Poland as compensation for intermediate political concessions. D'Abernon concluded that the Germans were putting the cart before the horse if they wanted border revisions as a precondition for improved political and economic relations, Schubert notes, 27 February 1926, *ADAP*, B, vol. 2, 1, No. 71; *DBFP*, series Ia, vol. 1, No. 450. Dirksen's failure was not so much that he "drew economic conclusions from political premises and vice versa" (Lippelt, 345), but rather that he did so with overabundant ambition and insufficient rigor.

49. AA, D/2768/5462H/E367336, cited in Riekhoff, *German-Polish Relations*, 168. Conflicting statements from the Polish side over whether they would accept some connection between political and trade issues added to the confusion. In a 27 December 1924 response to Zechlin, Olszowski had denied any "essential connection" between the upcoming negotiations for an MFN agreement and other outstanding issues, Zechlin to Rauscher, 29 December, BA Potsdam R 901/67215, Bl. 142. See also Stresemann's "unofficial" conversations with Korfanty, *Stresemann Vermächtnis*, vol. 2, 9 July 1925, 543 ff; 7 August, 546 ff.

50. Kackenbeeck, *The International Experiment of Upper Silesia*, 464 ff.; Peter-Heinz Seraphim, "Der polnisch-englisch Kohlenkampf in Nordeuropa und seine wirtschaftliche und politische Bedeutung," *Osteuropa* November 1934, 80-91.

51. Landau and Tomaszewski, "Poland between Inflation and Stabilization," in *The Experience of Inflation*, 286 ff. and the literature cited there.

52. In November 1925 Schubert had warned that extreme demands such as actual territorial revision could never be achieved through economic pressure, AA

2339/4569H/E168402-04, as cited in Gasiorowski, "After Locarno," 294-95, note 11. In July 1926 Dirksen concluded that "it would be futile to expect of a tariff war that it would make Poland pliable to our wishes," AA, D/2768/5462H/E367395, as cited in Riekhoff, *German-Polish Relations*, 171. In a 16 December 1927 speech to the political and economic elites of East Prussia, Stresemann confessed that "the effect of the tariff war, and with it the chances for forcing Poland to economic concessions, have been thwarted by the English coal strike and the economic boom in Poland," a conclusion he appears to have reached about a year earlier, *Stresemann Vermächtnis*, vol. 3, 247.

53. The change in policy was formalized with the Foreign Office memorandum presented to the cabinet on 3 October 1926 in which Stresemann declared that "in view of the general political situation, the speedy conclusion of a [trade] treaty is desirable," BA R 43I/11060, an idea repeated in his notes of 19 December 1927, "the end of the tariff war is also desirable from the foreign policy viewpoint," *Vermächtnis*, vol. 3, 244. On 6 December 1926 the state secretary in the chancellery, Hermann Pünder, told his Under-secretary for trade and tariff affairs, Othmar Fessler, that "In my opinion, a [trade treaty] conclusion is necessary, because as long as we do not have an economic understanding with Poland, the Poles will continually attempt to make our political understanding with the Western powers more difficult." BA R 43I/1106. A similar need for an understanding with the West moved Hitler to an economic and political reconciliation with Poland in 1934 to 1935.

54. Stresemann emphasized that ending French fears of a German attack on Poland was essential to German-French cooperation, AA, 2339/4569H/E169061-69; Nachlass, 3173/7372/166866-73, as cited in Gasiorowski, "After Locarno," 314-15, note 99.

55. Fessler notes of 11 February cabinet meeting; minutes of 31 March 1927 cabinet meeting; Curtius to Pünder, 5 May 1927, BA R 43I/1106. Note: R43I/1106 is the same file as Chancellery, 5748/K2304/K645035-412 in the National Archives T-120 series of microfilms.

56. On these developments see Riekhoff, *German-Polish Relations*, 172, 177, 150 ff.

57. Stresemann admitted as much in December 1927, saying "what impedes the trade treaty negotiations are the conflicts of interest prevailing in Germany itself: agriculture fears the competition of Polish agricultural products, while industry cannot abandon a sales market of 500 million marks," *Stresemann Vermächtnis*, vol. 3, 247.

58. BA Potsdam R 901/67404, Bl. 14 ff.

59. Commercial attache in Warsaw (von Behr) to Lewald, 19 November 1926, minutes of a meeting of the German negotiating delegation and its private-sector members on 27 October 1926, BA Potsdam R 901/67404, Bl. 188-191.

60. Arbeitsgemeinschaft der Bergarbeiter to Luther, 27 August 1925, BA R 43I/1106.

61. Reich representative in Munich to the chancellery, 2 December 1925, BA R43 I/2425.

62. See the very revealing minutes of a meeting of the German negotiating delegation and its private-sector members on 27 October 1926, BA Potsdam R 901/67404, Bl. 188-191.

63. *Stresemann Vermächtnis*, vol. 3, 19 December 1927, 244.

64. Chancellery Under-Secretary Fessler's notes on the interministerial meeting of 11 February 1927; Curtius's memorandum on "The Necessity of a Trade Treaty," 5 May 1927, BA R 43I/1106. Just before the outbreak of the tariff war Stresemann had written sarcastically in his diary about the idea that Germany could afford "to do without" RM 400 million in annual exports to Poland, *Stresemann Vermächtnis*, vol. 2, 15 June 1925, 308.

65. Minutes of an interministerial meting held in the Economics Ministry on 8 October 1926; minutes of the 15 October cabinet meeting, BA R 43I/1106.
66. Schiele to Chancellery State Secretary Pünder from 19 April 1927, BA R 43I/1106.
67. On 19 April 1927 Schiele presented a twenty-seven-page memorandum to the cabinet declaring that any new negotiations "are to be considered as a fully new attempt to regulate bilateral trade relations. Earlier offers and discussion which were made under different conditions, are void," BA R 43I/1106; At a 2 August 1927 meeting with Schubert and Ritter of the Foreign Office, Schiele threatened to resign if the cabinet overrode his position on pig imports, the timber tariff, or the potato tariff, BA Potsdam R 901/67405, Bl.221.
68. In a 21 May 1927 memorandum, Wallroth, Dirksen, and Zechlin warned Stresemann that negotiations with Poland could not move forward as long as there remained "internal uncertainty" about the size and nature of German offers, BA Potsdam R 901/67405, Bl. 144. The 24 October 1927 meeting of the Union of German Iron and Steel Industrialists' Governing Committee noted that "the trade treaty negotiations with Poland have been dead for months," BA R 13I/102.
69. Stresemann met personally with the director of the Political Department in the Polish Foreign Office, who also served as Piłsudski's special envoy, in order to get negotiations going again. The resulting "Stresemann-Jackowski Protokol" of 23 November 1927 renewed the German offer of 200,000 tons of coal, but since the new negotiations were to result first in only a provisional modus vivendi the Germans actually reduced the offer on processed pork imports from an unlimited amount to 600,000 cwt. annually, 400,000 of which the Germans might reexport, PAAA Deutsch-Polnische Wirtschaftsverhandlungen – Verhandlungen allgemeines. Schiele's continued efforts to obstruct even this modus vivendi sparked Stresemann's threat to resign if the government could not pursue negotiations for a treaty in good faith, Stresemann to Marx, 24 November 1927, *Stresemann Vermächtnis*, vol. 3, 235-39.
70. Hermes had been agriculture minister in several "Weimar Coalition" (Center-Democrats-Socialists) cabinets from March 1920 to March 1922. He was chairman of the Center-associated Bauenbund which represented 1.5 million small- and middle-sized farmers in southern and western Germany.
71. The meetings were held on 6-7 December 1927 in Berlin. Unfortunately, representatives of German Upper Silesian mining interests, including Stähler, dominated the German industrial delegation, and the Poles left feeling that "Germany is convinced the Polish side must make wide-ranging concessions without any special compensation." On agricultural issues the German delegation promised to compromise on matters that were not "vital questions." Reichsverband to the Foreign Office, 8 December 1927; confidential report from Warsaw on Polish reactions, 16 December 1927, both in PAAA Deutsch-Polnische Wirtschaftsverhandlungen – Verhandlungen allgemeines. See also Puchert, *Wirtschaftskrieg*, 126 ff.
72. Reich Land Union to Chancellor Marx, 10 March 1927, BA R 43I/2425; Rauscher to the Foreign Office (Köpke), 17 May 1927, BA Potsdam R 901/67405, Bl. 73.
73. Rosenthal, "speaking for export industry" at the presidial meeting of 24 February 1927, Bayer-Archiv 62/10.3, 2. The Reichsverband itself remained divided over Polish issues as heavy industry opposed offering Poland any further increases in the coal quota. See the objections of Peter Klöckner, Ernst Borsig, and Paul Silverberg to a suggestion by Ludwig Kastl, executive secretary of the Reichsverband, that the Poles receive a quota of 200,000 tons monthly, ibid.
74. Curtius's 5 May 1927 memorandum noted that the Reichsverband and the German Chamber of Commerce "emphatically" urged the government to sign a

treaty and that the Reichsverband's Trade Policy Commission had passed a resolution to that effect on 9 February, BA R 43I/1106; Executive Secretary Ludwig Kastl rated a Polish treaty as the second most important outstanding trade issue for the Reichsverband, behind a treaty with France, Main Committee meeting, 19 May 1927, Bayer-Archiv 62/10.5, 1.

75. Ludwig Kastl to Under-Secretary Ritter, 11 August on the Reichsverband meeting with the German Agricultural Council, the Prussian Agricultural Chamber, the Reich Land Union, the Peasants League, and the Reich Forestry Council, BA Potsdam R 901/67405, Bl. 235.

76. On relations between the two groups in toto see the Reichsverband debate at the Main Committee meeting of 27 April 1928, "How Important is German Agriculture to the German Economy?," Bayer-Archiv 62/10.5, 1. See also Panzer, *Ringen um Agrarpolitik*, 111 ff.; Gessner, *Agrarverbände*, 83 ff..

77. Reichsverband notice of 17 November 1928; report of the Präsidial meeting of 23 November 1928, Bayer-Archiv 62/10.3, 2. See also the confidential position statement of the German Chamber of Commerce from 14 November 1928, cited in Dieter Gessner, "Industrie und Landwirtschaft 1928-1930," in Mommsen, ed., *Industrielles System*, 762-78. Panzer identifies the failed agricultural-industrial negotiations of 7-8 November as the final "break" between the two groups, *Ringen um Agrarpolitik*, 139. Vn Hippel's own similar assessment in conversation with Chancellery Under-Secretary Fessler, 15 November 1928, *Akten Müller*, 213, note 3.

78. A plan first presented by Kastl and Simson at the Reichsverband presidial meeting of 23 November 1928 (Bayer-Archiv 62/10.3, 2) and presented to agricultural representatives by Reusch on 20 December 1928, Gessner, "Industrie und Landwirtschaft," 775. On 29 November Reusch told the Lower Rhine Chamber of Commerce he "urgently desired to reach a positive conclusion to the negotiations" with Poland, but that at least the "vital interests" of agriculture should be protected, RWWA 20-1128-2.

79. Kastl to the Foreign Office, 4 November 1929, BA Potsdam R 901/64025, Bl. 115. On 26 April 1929 Hans Kraemer (Reichsverband, Reich Economic Council) told the Main Committee of the Reichsverband that "despite the difficulties, it is necessary to reach a commercial understanding" with Poland and Czechoslovakia and that "the [obviously agricultural] sacrifices required to open these large markets for German exports will have to be made," Bayer-Archiv 62/10.5, 2.

80. See especially Panzer, *Agrarpolitik*, 146 ff.; Gessner, *Agrarverbände*.

81. The Foreign Office had been seeking to force Hermes into resignation since at least May 1929, Ritter to Rauscher, 28 May 1929, PAAA Polen Handel 13A Geheim, Bd. 10. On 29 October 1929 Hippel resigned as agriculture's representative on the German negotiating delegation, BA Potsdam R 901/64025, Bl. 94.

82. *Akten Müller*, 214-215; Trade Policy Committee meeting of 23 November 1928, note of Polish negotiator Twardowski to Hermes from 21 December 1928, PAAA Wirtschaftsverhandlungen mit Polen; Rauscher to Schubert 22 December 1928, AA, StS/2224/4483H/E095, 102-106; cited in Riekhoff, 181.

83. The German-Polish understanding of 21 December was part of the larger negotiations on Polish entry into the international steel cartel and the European Railmakers' Association (ERMA). The bilateral agreement took the form of a "territorial protection agreement" to come into force with the conclusion of a German-Polish trade treaty. At the core of the agreement, the German side agreed to export to Poland only those rolled steel products that the Poles did not produce; German industry also guaranteed scrap iron exports to Poland of 165,000 tons annually. In return, Polish exports of rolled steel to Germany would not exceed 0.5 percent of German domestic sales (c. 48,000-50,000 tons); Polish industry would export no such products to North America; and would offer for

sale first to German industry any unused portion of the Polish quota in the European Railmakers' Association. Jozef Kiedron, President of the Syndicate of Polish Iron Works and director of the Gornoslaskie Zjedoczone Huty Krolewski i Laura (Vereinigte Königs- und Laurahütte) led the negotiations for Poland. Ernst Poensgen (Vereinigte Stahlwerke), Klotzbach (Krupp), Klemme (GHH), and Gerwin (Stahlwerksverband) participated on the German side, Haniel 4000000/10.

84. Chemical industry representative Nikodem Caro (Bayerische Stickstoffwerke A.G.) arrived in Poland on 21 February 1929 to "make clear" to the Poles that their earlier offers to German industry on tariff reductions and import quotas remained "insufficient." PAAA Deutsch-Polnische Wirtschaftsverhandlungen – Verhandlungen allgemeines. At a 9 March meeting, the industrial Reichsverband judged the new Polish offers on German industrial goods made to Caro as "considerable," but "still in need of improvement" for certain industries and products, Ritter's notes on the meeting, BA R 2/10238. On 11 May, Reichsverband members Raumer (electricals), Stähler (coal and steel), Lange (machine-building), Caro (chemicals), Hartmann, and Pietrkowski (chemicals) told Ritter that new Polish offers from 25 April on tariff reductions for German manufactured goods "were sufficient to keep negotiations going," PAAA Poland Handel 13A.

85. BA Potsdam R 901/64025, Bl 101, 142. Even under Hermann Dietrich, the Agriculture Ministry continued to oppose the significant concessions that were needed in order to secure a treaty.

86. Rauscher's negotiations are well recorded in BA Potsdam R 901/67406; for the Reichsverband guarantee (Kastl to Rauscher, 4 March 1930) R 901/67406, Bl. 143; for the official text of the agreement see, *Sten. Ber.* 1928/1930, Anlage Bd. 442, No. 2138.

87. By comparison, a composite index of all German prices stood at 97 in 1931. Jacobs and Richter, "Die Grosshandelspreise," 81. At RM 118/cwt. in 1931, pork prices were more than 20 percent below their 1913 levels (RM 150/cwt.), Gessner, *Agrarverbände*, 86.

88. BA Potsdam R 901/65455, Bl. 257. That file and BA R 2/10238 contain dozens of agricultural petitions against the treaty with Poland.

89. Mining Group of the Reichsverband to Chancellor Brüning, 28 January 1931, BA Potsdam R 901/65455, Bl. 79; petitions from the Rhine-Westphalian Coal Syndicate, the German Brown Coal Industry Assoc., and the Lower Silesian Coal Syndicate in ibid., Bl. 44, 56, 72.

90. Hajo Holborn, *A History of Modern Germany 1840-1945* (Princeton, 1969), 649.

91. Hasslacher (Breslau Chamber of Commerce) 9 May 1931 notes on a conversation with Curtius, BA Potsdam R 901/65455, Bl. 261.

92. *Sten.Ber.*, Bd. 428, 5818-19, 5847, 5905. The Nationals moved for a Reichstag resolution declaring the treaty "completely unacceptable" (völlig indiskutabel), ibid, 5905; see also Puchert's account, *Wirtschaftskrieg*, 166 ff.

93. Including the Nationals and the Bavarians, but not yet the votes of the agrarian factions in the Center and People's Party, the anti-treaty forces had 295 votes in the new Reichstag (577 total deputies).

94. At an 18 February meeting with the Polish envoy in Berlin, Alfred Wysocki, Brüning declared that "he was prepared to bring the Polish trade treaty though [the Reichstag], but had to leave open the timing," Foreign Office State Secretary Bernhard W. von Bülow's notes, BA Potsdam R 901/65455, Bl. 109. The Polish Council of Ministers had approved ratification on 12 December 1930, and the corresponding draft law was published on 31 December 1930. On 12 March 1931 the Sejm and on 17 March the Senate gave their ratifying votes, Puchert, *Wirtschaftskrieg*, 168-69.

95. *Berliner Börsen-Zeitung*, 12 March 1931.

96. Eisenlohr's notes, BA Potsdam R 901/65455, Bl. 230.
97. Foreign Office (Schlesinger) to Count von Holtzendorff at the Saxon Legation in Berlin, BA Potsdam R 901/65455, Bl. 270.
98. The German response to the Versailles terms (Observations on the Conditions of Peace, 29 May 1919) scarcely mentioned the Bohemian boundary and the Germans in the new Czechoslovak state, cited in Wandycz, *France and Her Eastern Allies*, 59. This contrasted sharply with "savage German criticism of the Polish settlement," ibid.
99. The literature on relations between the German Reich and the Czechoslovak republic in the Weimar period is not extensive. F. Gregory Campbell's *Confrontation in Central Europe. Weimar Germany and Czechoslovakia* (Chicago, 1975) treats relations between the two states throughout the period and may be considered the standard work on the subject, but offers only two to three pages (103, 200) on economic issues other than the proposed German-Austrian customs union. Manfred Alexander's *Der deutsch-tschechoslowakische Schiedsvertrag von 1925 im Rahmen der Locarno-Verträge* (Munich, 1970) also covers much of the period. By contrast, the literature on relations between Germans and Czechs within Czechoslovakia is voluminous. The most accessible study is Johann Brügel's *Tschechen und Deutsche 1918-1938* (Munich, 1967) also available in altered form as *Czechoslovakia before Munich* (Cambridge, 1973). Still useful is Elizabeth Wiskemann, *Czechs and Germans: A Study of the Struggle in the Historic Provinces of Bohemia and Moravia* (London, 1938).
100. On relations between the two states in the immediate postwar period see Manfred Alexander, "Die erst Phase der deutsch-tschechoslowakischen diplomatischen Beziehungen, 1918-1919," in Ferdinand Seibt, ed., *Die böhmischen Länder zwischen Ost und West* (Munich, 1983), 228-39; Gerhard Fuchs, "Die politischen Beziehungen der Weimarer Republik zur tschechoslowakischen Republik von Versailler Frieden bis zum Ende der revolutionären Nachkriegskrise," *Jahrbuch für Geschichte* 9 (1973), 281-337; Peter Burian, "Deutsch-Tschechoslowakischen Beziehungen 1918/19," in Kurt Kluxen and Wolfgang Mommsen, eds., *Politische Ideologien und Nationalstaatliche Ordnung* (Munich, 1968), pp. 359-76. Also useful are the several volumes of *Deutsche Gesandtschaftsberichte aus Prag* edited by Manfred Alexander beginning in 1983. For economic histories of the Czechoslovak republic begin with Alice Teichova, *The Czechoslovak Economy 1918-1980* (New York and London, 1988) and the literature cited there. Useful information on Czechoslovak foreign trade in the first years of the republic is contained in Jonathan Bloomfield, "Surviving in a Harsh World: Trade and Inflation in the Czechoslovak and Austrian Republics 1918-1926," in Feldman, et al., eds., *The Experience of Inflation: International and Comparative Studies*, 228-69; Z.P. Pryor and F. L. Pryor, "Foreign Trade and Interwar Czechoslovak Economic Development," *Vierteljahrschrift für Sozial und Wirtschaftsgeschichte* 62 (1975).
101. The German consul-general in Prague (Baron Friedrich von Gebsattel) reported to the Foreign Office that French military and economic experts in General Maurice Pellé's military mission were urging the Czechoslovak government to halt all trade with Germany, 24 February 1919, GStA PK: I.HA/Rep. 120 C, XIII, 2, Nr. 20, Bd. 1, Bl. 87.
102. In response to Entente objections, the Czechoslovak Council of Ministers actually "rejected" the December agreement and one month later approved a "renegotiated" deal with the same substantive terms. Copy of the agreement, Stockhammern and Foreign Office correspondence with Prussian Trade Ministry, 9 January 1919 and 31 January 1919, GStA PK: I.HA/Rep. 120 C, XIII, 2, Nr. 20, Bd. 1, Bl. 2, 18, 33. According to Gebsattel and the German Foreign Office, the "insightful politicians" and "all competent offices" in Prague under-

stood that Czechoslovakia needed economic cooperation with Germany. Gebsattel noted that at the moment the Czechoslovak market was "absorbing every available quantum of German goods," Gebsattel to Foreign Office, 24 February 1919; Foreign Office to Prussian Trade Ministry, 25 February 1919, GStA PK: I.HA/Rep. 120 C, XIII, 2, Nr. 20, Bd. 1, Bl. 87, 58.

103. This characterization is Campbell's from *Confrontation in Central Europe*, 100.

104. Sänger to the Foreign Office from 18 September 1919, GStA PK: I.HA/Rep. 120 C, XIII, 2, Nr. 20, Bd. 1, Bl. 240; Sänger to the Foreign Office from 29 January 1920, GStA PK: I.HA/Rep. 120 C, XIII, 2, Nr. 21, Bd. 1, Bl. 9. In July 1919, Dr. Fafl, head of the Czechoslovak trade-controlling Control and Compensation Office had already indicated that Czechoslovakia would like to "expand" the December 1919 agreement "on a broader basis," GStA PK: I.HA/Rep. 120 C, XIII, 2, Nr. 20, Bd. 1, Bl. 185.

105. All three agreements can be found in *RGBl*. 1920, 2240, 2279, 2284.

106. MFN provisions in *Wirtschaftsabkommen*, Article X, paragraph 1, *RGBl.*, 1920, 2249; appendices B and C and D, ibid., 2260, 2261, 2263.

107. *RGBl* 1920, 2279.

108. Campbell has implied that the liquidation terms were most disturbing element in French eyes, *Confrontation*, 103. Certainly the cluster of German-Czechoslovak agreements contributed to the French fear that the Entente's pro-Polish stance in the Czechoslovak-Polish dispute over Teschen "risked throwing Czecho-Slovakia into the arms of Germany," cited in Wandycz, *France and Her Eastern Allies*, 101.

109. Hans Posse (who was still in the Prussian Trade Ministry at this time prior to his transfer to the Reich Economics Ministry) to the Prussian Trade Ministry from 20 June 1920; Foreign Office memorandum to other ministries, 7 July 1920, GStA PK: I.HA/Rep. 120 C, XIII, 2, Nr. 21, Bd. 1, Bl. 91-96, 107. Hans-Jürgen Schröder has provided additional evidence on this point, citing Foreign Office satisfaction that Germany could once again appear as an "equally entitled" (gleichberechtigt) state, "Deutsche Handelspolitik," 243.

110. For the following see Foreign Office (Marckwald) to the other Reich ministries, 25 February 1921, GStA PK: I.HA/Rep. 120 C, XIII, 2, Nr. 21, Bd. 1, Bl. 357 ff. The two governments chose confidential notes rather than a formal agreement so that other Allied powers could not use their MFN rights to claim identical concessions from Germany.

111. ibid.

112. For the German side, Ernst Stütz (Reichskommissar for coal distribution), headed the talks.

113. Eugen Rümelin, head of Foreign Office Department IIb (Czechoslovakia and Hungary), to the Prussian Trade Ministry, 28 April 1922; Foreign Office to the Prussian Trade Ministry, 25 February 1924, GStA PK: I.HA/Rep. 120 C, XIII, 2, Nr. 21, Bd. 2.

114. Copy of the 31 July protocol and memorandum by Gerhard Köpke (who replaced Rümelin as head of the Foreign Office's department IIb in May 1923) to the other Reich ministries, 31 July 1924, GStA PK: I.HA/Rep. 120 C, XIII, 2, Nr. 21, Bd. 2.

115. This was a recurring theme in Foreign Office instructions to keep the terms of these protocols secret. See, e.g. Köpke to the other Reich ministries, 31 July 1924, GStA PK: I.HA/Rep. 120 C, XIII, 2, Nr. 21, Bd. 2.

116. Minutes of the Chamber's Foreign Trade Committee meeting, RWWA 20-1129-4. In a June 1924 speech to the Central Association of the German Electro-Technical Industry, the executive director of that body and former economics minister, Hans von Raumer, explained that "supranational cartels" as well as tra-

ditional commercial policy tools were needed to control European trade, BA R 131/346. On the government side, Trendelenburg publicly urged the use of private international agreements as a way of "overcoming ... the psychological barriers" limiting European trade in the post-war years. Speech to the Central Association of German Wholesalers carried by the WTB from 4 December 1925, BA R 431/1085.

117. The active role of both governments in supporting these and later private agreements was crucial to the success of the arrangements. These developments in German-Czechoslovak trade relations support Dirk Stegmann's idea that such agreements could "erode" the system of bilateral trade treaties, but do not support his larger implication that state action had possible become dispensable, Stegmann, "Deutsche Zoll- und Handelspolitik 1924/5," in Mommsen et al., eds., *Industrielles System*, 513.

118. For ZEG in the international steel cartel in general see, Alice Teichova, *Kleinstaaten im Spannungsfeld der Grossmächte* (Vienna, 1988), 169 ff.; Ervin Hexner, *International Steel Cartel* (Chapel Hill, NC, 1943), 72 ff., 127 ff., 279 ff.. For ZEG negotiations and agreements with German members of these sales comptoirs 1927-1930 Haniel 40000090/16 and Mannesmann-Archiv Dusseldorf P7 55 61.

119. Hans Posse to the Prussian Trade Ministry, 20 June 1920, GStA PK: I.HA/Rep. 120 C, XIII, 2, Nr. 21, Bd. 1, Bl. 91. On the internal cartelization of Czechoslovakia see several works by Alice Teichova, *Economic Background to Munich*, chapters 2.2, 3.2, 4.2, 5.2; *Kleinstaaten*, 169 ff.; "Industry," in Kaser and Radice, *Economic History of Eastern Europe 1919-1975*, vol. 1, 316 ff.

120. Karl Mobius (executive director of the Iron and Steel Wares Association) to Economics Minister Curtius, 15 December 1926, BA R 431/1085.

121. Foreign Office note to the Czechoslovak legation, 26 June 1924; Prussian Trade Ministry notes on a meeting with State Secretary Trendelenburg in the Economics Ministry, 20 August 1924, GStA PK: I.HA/Rep. 120 C, XIII, 2, Nr. 21, Bd. 3.

122. Exchange of letters between the Foreign Office (Ritter) and the secretary of the Czechoslovak legation in Berlin (Jina), 27 and 29 March 1926, GStA PK: I.HA/Rep. 120 C, XIII, 2, Nr. 21, Bd. 3; exchange of letters between Ritter and Chancellery State Secretary Pünder, 24 April and 4 May 1926, BA R 431/1123. An important consequence of Germany's 1924 tariff failure was now revealed. The Czechoslovak agrarians emerged from the November 1925 elections as the country's largest party (13.7 percent of the popular vote for the Chamber of Deputies). Supported by the German and Magyar farmer's parties, they dominated a bourgeois coalition that was determined to obtain significant agricultural concessions from Germany. Had Germany been ready to negotiate in October 1924, they would have confronted a less unified "red-green" coalition in which the Czechoslovak Social Democrats were the largest party (25.7 percent in the elections of April 1920).

123. Chancellery reports, 14 December 1926 (Pünder), 21 January 1927 (Fessler), BA R 431/1123.

124. Chancellery memorandum, 2 November 1927, BA R 431/1123.

125. Stresemann to Pünder, 6 November 1927, BA R 431/1123 (also reprinted in *ADAP*, B, 7, No. 75); Windel's report with copy of the Czechoslovak declaration, 15 November 1927, GStA PK: I.HA/Rep. 120 C, XIII, 2, Nr. 21, Bd. 5, Bl.180 ff.

126. Schiele's memorandum to the cabinet on German-Czechoslovak trade negotiations, 1 February 1928, BA R 431/1123.

127. See e.g., the government of Württemberg to the Reich government, 9 November 1927, BA R 431/1123. Agriculture Ministry memorandum noting that "large portions of Bavarian agriculture are dependent on barley cultivation," 1 February 1928, BA R 431/1123.

128. Stresemann to Pünder, 6 November 1927, BA R 43I/1123.
129. Cabinet discussion, 9 November 1927; Ministerbesprechung, 11 November 1927; cabinet meetings of 28 January 1928 and 3 February 1928, BA R 43I/1123 (also *Akten Marx III u. IV*, vol. 2, 1051-52). Schiele's unchanged position as outlined in the Agriculture Ministry's eleven-page memorandum "Economic Negotiations with Czechoslovakia," 1 February 1928, BA R 43I/1123.
130. Campbell, *Confrontation*, 200 ff.
131. Zweckverband to its members, 5 October 1928. RWWA 20-1129-4; *Berliner Börsen Zeitung*, 14 September 1928, BA Potsdam R 901/43327 (Windel's file on press reports), Bl. 18.
132. Minutes of Trade Policy Committee meeting, 19 June 1929, GStA PK: I.HA/Rep. 120 C, XIII, 2, Nr. 21, Bd. 6, Bl. 5 ff.
133. Stresemann to the Chancellery, 20 June 1929, Dietrich to the Chancellery, 28 June, Fessler's report, 28 June, minutes of the Ministerbesprechung, 2 July, BA R 43I/1123.
134. In view of Windel's inability to make a German offer on the unsettled issues, the Czechoslovak delegation complained that it "had no idea" what the German position on these issues was, Prussian Trade Ministry notes on the 12 July German-Czechoslovak negotiating session, GStA PK: I.HA/Rep. 120C, XIII, 2, Nr. 21, Bd. 6.
135. WTB report, Prague, 19 July 1929, BA R 43I/1123; meeting of the Reichsverband's Commercial Policy Committee, 12 October 1929, PAAA Sonderreferat W, Zollwesen 4, Nr 1.
136. WTB report from Prague, 19 July 1929, BA R 43I/1123.
137. Trade Policy Committee meeting of 9 December 1929, GStA PK: I.HA/Rep. 120 C, XIII, 2, Nr. 21, Bd. 6; Berliner Börsen Courier, 5 February 1930, BA R 43I/1123.
138. For these reasons, economic relations have generally received some attention in the classic secondary works on Weimar-Soviet relations, E.H. Carr, *German-Soviet Relations between the Two World Wars* (New York, 1951); Gerald Freund, *Unholy Alliance: Russian-German Relations from the Treaty of Brest-Litovsk to the Treaty of Berlin* (New York, 1957); Kurt Rosenbaum's detailed study, *Community of Fate; German-Soviet Diplomatic Relations 1922-1928* (Syracuse, NY, 1965); Klaus Hildebrand, "Das deutsche Reich und die Sowjetunion im internationlen System, 1918-1932," in Stürmer, ed., *Die Weimarer Republik*, 38-61; Karl Dietrich Erdmann and Helmut Grieser, "Die deutsch-sowjetischen Beziehungen in der Zeit der Weimarer Republik als Problem der deutschen Innenpolitik," *Geschichte in Wissenschaft und Unterricht* 26 (1975), 403-26. The standard East German work is Günter Rosenfeld, *Sowjet-Russland und Deutschland 1917-1922* (Berlin, 1960) and its companion volume *Sowjetunion und Deutschland 1923-1933* (Berlin, 1983). Among the memoirs, Gustav Hilger and Alfred Meyer, *The Incompatible Allies. A Memoir-History of German-Soviet Relations 1918-1941* (New York, 1953) is still irreplaceable; Herbert von Dirksen's *Moskau-Tokio-London. Errinerungen und Betrachtungen zu 20 Jahren deutscher Aussenpolitik 1919-1939* (Stuttgart, 1949) is, by contrast, less revealing. For documentation throughout the period see *ADAP*, Series A, twelve volumes to date.
139. The literature on German-Soviet economic relations in this period has grown large; for overviews see Werner Beitel and Jürgen Nötzold, *Deutsch-sowjetische Wirtschaftsbeziehungen in der Zeit der Weimarer Republik* (Baden-Baden, 1979); Robert Himmer, *German-Soviet Economic Relations, 1918-1922* (Ann Arbor, Mich., 1972); Hans Jürgen Perrey, *Der Russlandausschuss der deutschen Wirtschaft: Die deutsch-sowjetischen Wirtschaftsbeziehungen der Zwischenkriegszeit* (Munich, 1985); Berthold Puchert, "Die Entwicklung der deutsch-sowjetischen Handelsbeziehungen von 1918 bis 1939," *Jahrbuch für Wirtschaftsgeschichte* 14 (1973), 11-36.

140. The total turnover of Russian foreign trade (i.e. imports and exports together) was 12,018 million rubles in 1913, with an average value of 11,508 million rubles 1909-1913. For the period 1919 to 1923 total turnover averaged 856 million rubles or 7.4 percent of pre-war values; for the period 1924 to 1928 turnover was 3,556 million or 31 percent of prewar levels, Alexander Baykov, *Soviet Foreign Trade* (Princeton, 1946), Appendix, table I.

141. Between 1909 and 1913, Russia had exported an average of 10.5 million tons of grain annually, large amounts of it going to Germany. Between 1922 and 1927 Soviet grain exports averaged 1.3 million tons or not even one-tenth of earlier levels. In the peak years 1930-31 grain exports averaged 4.9 million tons, still only 47 percent of prewar levels. Roughly similar declines are visible for exports of butter, eggs, and oil-cake, Baykov, *Soviet Trade*, Appendix, table IV.

142. Erdmann and Grieser have pointed out that treaties with the Soviet Union "were passed in the Reichstag with virtually no opposition. All parties from the Communists to the German Nationals voted for them," "Die deutsch-sowjetischen Beziehungen als Problem der deutschen Innenpolitik," 403. See also Jürgen Bellers, *Aussenwirtschaftspolitik und Politisches System der Weimarer Republik und der Bundesrepublik* (Münster, 1988), vol. 2, 399 ff., 412, ff., and the primitive through indicative "cognitive maps," 650, 652.

143. No reliable data are available for the period 1919 to 1922. For the five-year period from 1923 to 1927, the new Soviet state took an average of 5.2 percent of total German exports of chemical and pharmaceutical products, 2.5 percent of ironwares, 6.2 percent of machines, and 3.7 percent of electro-technical products. Only in 1927 and 1928 did exports to the USSR show substantial increases (12.4 percent of all machine exports with higher rates for tool-making machinery), only to slip back again in 1929 (7.8 percent of machine exports), Beitel/Nötzold, *Deutsch-Sowjetische Wirtschaftsbeziehungen*, 217, table 12, as calculated from *Statistisches Jahrbuch für das deutsche Reich*, various vols. Equally disheartening was the decline in the German share of the Soviet import market from 34 percent in 1923 to 21 percent in 1924 and 16 percent in 1925 despite the conclusion of supposedly important economic and political agreements in 1921 and 1922, *Statistik des deutschen Reichs*, N.F., Bd. 339 (1927), part I, 13.

144. A small number of individual firms may have done well. Hilger and Meyer assert without supporting evidence that Otto Wolff, for example, "made a great deal of money on sales to Russia" from 1922 to 1924 through the mixed German-Russian trading company *Rusgertorg*, an assertion not supported by Wolff's pull-out from the arrangement in 1924, *Incompatible Allies*, 172-73. See also Alfred Anderle, "Die deutsch-sowjetischen Verträge von 1925/26," *Zeitschrift für Geschichtswissenschaft* 5 (1957), 487 ff.

145. Peter Alter's statement that "the interest of broad economic circles in an expansion of trade relations with Soviet Russia ... has been convincingly demonstrated" contributes very little to our understanding of the problem, "Rapallo – Gleichgewichtspolitik und Revisionismus," *Neue Politische Literatur* 19 (1974), 514. Of course the private-sector was "interested" in an expansion of trade, but did this vague "interest" endure? Was it real enough to inspire significant, active, or intense private-sector efforts to influence government policy in this direction? If so, did these efforts successful demonstrate a measurable degree of success? For a fine description of the deeply ambivalent attitudes of German business toward trade with the Soviets in the 1920s, see Hans-Jürgen Perrey, *Der Rußlandausschuß der deutschen Wirtschaft*, 49 ff.

146. An interpretation that subordinates the importance of economic motives in German policy toward the Soviets and that sees the primary significance of German-Soviet economic agreements as lubricants for larger political understandings runs

counter to the established West German interpretation of German-Soviet relations in the Weimar period, particularly as reflected in the Rapallo literature: Theodor Schieder, *Die Problem des Rapallo-Vertrages: Eine Studie über deutsch-russischen Beziehungen, 1922-1926* (Cologne, 1956) and "Die Entstehungsgeschichte des Rapallo-Vertrages," *HZ* 204 (1967), 545-609; Herbert Helbig, *Die Träger der Rapallo-Politik* (Göttingen, 1958); Karl Dietrich Erdmann, "Deutschland, Rapallo, und der Westen," *VfZ* 11 (1963), 105-165; Horst-Günther Linke, *Deutsch-sowjetischer Beziehungen bis Rapallo* (Cologne, 1970); Pogge von Strandmann, "Grossindustrie und Rapallopolitik." Not until Hermann Graml reinterpreted Rapallo primarily as an anti-Polish political alliance did the accepted view of powerful German economic motives come into question, "Die Rapallo-Politik im Urteil der Westdeutschen Forschung," *VfZ* 18 (1970), 379. Both Graml and Peter Alter have suggested that an emphasis on practical economic motives served to de-demonize German-Soviet cooperation in the face of Western views that this was an "unholy alliance" directed against the Versailles victors. The rehabilitation of Weimar, as opposed to Nazi, foreign policy served, in turn, to present the second German (Federal) republic as a reliable member of the European community, Alter, "Rapallo – Gleichgewichtspolitik und Revisionismus." The East German literature has also emphasized the role of German economic interests as a way of simultaneously touting the importance of the Soviet economy, exposing the dependence of capitalist economies on foreign markets, and pointing out the mutual benefits of "peaceful coexistence," Rosenfeld, *Sowjet-Russland und Deutschland 1917-1922*, 323 ff.; 346 ff.; Alfred Anderle, *Rapallo und die friedliche Koexistenz* (Berlin, 1963); Berthold Puchert, "Die Entwicklung der deutsch-sowjetischen Handelsbeziehungen von 1918 bis 1939," *Jahrbuch für Wirtschaftsgeschichte* 14 (1973), 11-36.

147. The meeting of 11 April 1919 chaired by Stockhammern, head of the Foreign Office's Commercial Affairs Department, included members of the Foreign Office, Economics Ministry, Office of the Commissar for Import/Export Licenses, and members of private-sector groups such as the German-Russian Association, the Reichsverband (Karl Fehrmann), and the Committee of German Expellees from Russia (Leon Spies), BA R 43I/1172.

148. Summary of Walter Rathenau, Felix Deutsch (both Allgemeine Elektrizitätsgesellschaft), Dr. Alexander (Deutsche Orientbank), and August Müller (former state secretary in the Economics Ministry) to the chancellor, 17 February 1920, BA Potsdam R 901/6231, Bl. 226-228. As in so many policy areas, Rathenau's subsequent views on German-Russian economic cooperation were not typical of any substantial segment of German industry, including the electrical industry. Hans von Raumer (also AEG) favored the Rapallo treaty primarily for political, not economic, reasons, "Dreissig Jahre nach Rapallo," *Deutsche Revue* 78 (1952) 321-30. Raumer's thinking, and possibly that of Hermann Bücher (Reichsverband) as well, is inaccurately cited by Pogge von Strandmann in "Grossindustrie und Rapallo," 298, which, in any event, is too narrowly based on the unrepresentative views of the electrical industry, 275, 276.

149. Meeting at Foreign Office, 3 February 1920 with some thirty commercial and industrial representatives from the German Chamber of Commerce, local chambers (including Hamburg, Bremen, Remscheid, Leipzig, and Breslau), the German-Russian Association, the industrial Reichsverband, and Carl Zeiss (Jena), BA Potsdam R 901/6231, Bl. 59-62.

150. The group endorsed current German policy "in spite of recent attempts by the Entente to enter into trade relations with the Soviets," specifically warning against becoming "nervous" over English efforts in the Russian market.

151. BA Potsdam R 901/6231, Bl. 59-62. See also Stockhammern's notes of 9 March 1920: "In the foreseeable future, German industry will not face a sales crisis

(Absatznot). As a consequence, there is no reason to initiate economic relations with Russia ... not to mention that in the long run Russian foreign trade policy will preclude the free development of capitalist initiative," BA Potsdam R 901/6231, Bl. 220.

152. Foreign Office memorandum initialed by Ago von Maltzan (Foreign Office Russian desk), 20 February 1920, BA Potsdam R 901/6231, Bl. 177. The memorandum again emphasized that arranging talks on economic exchanges "is to be decided primarily in accordance with political considerations" (ist in erster Linie nach politischen Gesichtspunkten zu entscheiden), Bl. 178-79.

153. *Sten. Ber.* (1921) Bd. 346, 21 January, 1993.

154. Maltzan's crucial role in shaping German policy toward Russia from 1920 to 1922 has been universally recognized in the scholarship on German-Soviet relations. Alter calls Maltzan the "key figure in the establishment of relations to Soviet Russia," "Rapallo – Gleichgewichtspolitik und Revisionismus," 517. Graml's work confirms the indispensable role assigned to Maltzan by Schieder (reluctantly), Helbig and Linke. Raumer considered Maltzan "the father of the Rapallo treaty," "Rapallo nach Dreissig Jahren," 326.

155. Hilger claims that Simons gave Schlesinger a "broad ... indefinite mandate" to "see what [he] could do" about finding "a basis for the resumption of German-Soviet diplomatic and economic relations," *The Incompatible Allies*, 65-66. The Foreign Office had earlier pointed out the difficulty that the only Soviet representative in Berlin, Viktor Kopp, "is not recognized as a representative of the Russian government for commercial affairs, but rather only for prisoner-of-war questions," Foreign Office memorandum, 20 February 1920, BA Potsdam R 901/6231, Bl. 178.

156. Hilger and Meyer, *Incompatible Allies*, 66-67; Rosenfeld, *Sowjet-Russland*, 330; also Article I of the agreement, 6 May 1921, *RGBl*, 1921, 929.

157. Interior Minister Erich Koch (Democrats) especially objected to the agreements and doubted their economic value to Germany, Koch to Chancellery State Secretary Heinrich Albert, 25 March 1921; the cabinet refused approval in its meeting of 26 March, both in Karl Dietrich Erdmann and Wolfgang Mommsen, eds., *Akten der Reichskanzlei. Das Kabinett Fehrenbach* (Boppard, 1972), 605-8 (hereafter *Akten Fehrenbach*). Hilger claims that during this time Foreign Minister "Simons instructed Gustav Behrendt [head of the East European Department – RMS] urgently not to let the negotiations with the Russians be disrupted," *Incompatible Allies*, 66-67.

158. Ebert to Fehrenbach, 8 May 1921 in *Akten Fehrenbach*, 669-70. A letter initialled by Maltzan to Schlesinger in Moscow stated plainly that "speedily pushing through the conclusion of these treaties and even the signing of them was possible only because of the London resolutions and the imminent resignation of the cabinet," ibid, 670, note 6.

159. Cabinet approval came on 9 June 1921. In response to a follow-up inquiry from Ebert, Chancellery Assistant Secretary Arnold Brecht noted Maltzan's assertion that Simons had told him "the Cabinet's hesitations have been overcome, the treaties should be concluded now." Brecht noted further that Simons himself "could not explain the error," Karl Dietrich Erdmann and Hans Booms, eds., *Akten der Reichskanzlei. Die Kabinette Wirth I und II* (Boppard, 1973), 57, note 3 [hereafter "*Akten Wirth*"]. For a copy of the delegation expansion agreement see *RGBl*, 1921, 930-932.

160. A year earlier, the Foreign Office had understood that official government-to-government trade talks would be "almost the same as the assumption of diplomatic relations," Foreign Office memorandum initialed by Maltzan, 20 February 1920, BA Potsdam R 901/6231, Bl. 177. See also Hilger's opinion that Article 1

of the 6 May agreement "amounted to a solemn reaffirmation of the de jure recognition which the Imperial German government had already granted the Leninist state in the treaty of Brest-Litovsk," *Incompatible Allies*, 67.

161. It remains for Pogge von Strandmann to substantiate his assertion that unspecified "economic pressure to normalize trade relations must be placed high on the list" of factors leading to the 6 May agreement, "Grossindustrie und Rapallopolitik," 289.

162. As a recurrent member of several cabinets from 1920 to 1923, Raumer relies on his own "daily experience" to remind us "how completely German policy was dominated by the reparation question" during these early years, "Dreissig Jahre nach Rapallo," 322.

163. Carole Fink, *The Genoa Conference* (Chapel Hill, NC, 1984), 21. Fink singularly successful in capturing the pan-European nature of the gathering while so many other studies focus excessively on the German-Soviet agreement at Rapallo. See also Carole Fink, Axel Frohn, et al., eds., *Genoa, Rapallo, and European Reconstruction in 1922* (Cambridge, 1991).

164. With American refusal to attend the conference, Germany's chance of obtaining real reparations relief disappeared. The Allied notes of 21 and 28 March demanding 1.2 billion in gold marks in reparations payments for 1922 only confirmed the unlikelihood of improving the reparations situation in the immediate future.

165. Article 116: "The Allied and Associated Powers formally reserve the rights of Russia to obtain from Germany restitution and reparation based on the principles of the present treaty," *The Treaty of Peace* (London, 1920).

166. The Soviets had acknowledged this possibility as early as July 1920, Linke, *Deutsch-sowjetische Beziehungen*, 107. Since late 1921 the Soviet press had returned to this point frequently, Greiser, *Die Sowjetpresse über Deutschland in Europa 1922-1932, Revision von Versailles und Rapallo-Politik aus sowjetischer Sicht* (Stuttgart, 1970), 18 ff. On Radek's role see M. L. Goldbach, *Karl Radek und die deutsch-sowjetischen Beziehungen 1918-1923* (Bonn, 1973), 107 ff.; Rosenbaum, *Community of Fate*, 26.

167. Wirth at a meeting of the cabinet with the ministers president of the States, 27 March 1922, *Akten Wirth*, 646. Peter Alter suggests that Maltzan considered Soviet recourse to article 116 a bluff (as realism precluded any increase in the German reparations burden), but that Maltzan himself was prepared to accept the Soviet threat as real in order to spur Rathenau and Wirth into active pursuit of an agreement with the Soviets, "Rapallo – Gleichgewichtspolitik und Revisionismus," 515. In any event, Wirth subsequently considered the Rapallo agreement a success primarily because it "prevented an Allied-Russian understanding at the expense of Germany," *Akten Wirth*, 711.

168. Rathenau at a meeting of the ministers with President Ebert on 5 April 1922, *Akten Wirth*, 683-684. In contrast, Lloyd George told the House of Commons on 3 April that even after a British-Soviet economic agreement, diplomatic recognition of the Soviet regime would proceed only in "stages" or "steps," including a "probationary period" during which the Soviets could prove their "bona fides." *Parliamentary Debates*. Fifth Series. Commons, 1922, vol. 152, 1902.

169. Economics Minister Schmidt (SPD) and Rathenau at a meeting of the ministers with President Ebert on 5 April 1922, *Akten Wirth*, 688-89.

170. Rathenau at a meeting of the Ministers with President Ebert on 5 April 1922, *Akten Wirth*, 688. Maltzan and Chicherin had already worked out the basic economic and political contents of what would become the Treaty of Rapallo and the Soviets had presented a draft on 3 April Helbig, *Träger der Rapallo-Politik*, 73 ff; Fink, *The Genoa Conference*, 126-33; Raumer's early (1952) revelation that "Maltzan carried the planned Rapallo treaty finished and ready in his pocket as he left for Genoa," "Dreissig Jahre nach Rapallo," 324.

171. Aside from the daunting political obstacles to this scheme, the plan lacked the support of key players in German big business. Martin Blank (director of the GHH offices in Berlin) cited a recent memorandum from the German Chamber of Commerce in support of his view that the "emphasis" in rebuilding Russia "must come from the private initiative of individual German entrepreneurs." He rejected French plans to have Germany send goods to Russia that would be booked on the German reparations account and characterized as "not promising" plans for "German participation in official reconstruction companies," Blank to Paul Reusch, 8 March 1922, Haniel 30019320/6a.

172. The "Genoa Committee" was established on 11 January 1922 by the RdI Vorstand with the following influential industrial figures as members: Hermann Bücher (VdESI), Carl Duisberg (Bayer), Abraham Frowein (Union of German Employers' Associations), Guggenheimer (MAN), Hans Kraemer (RdI), Paul Reusch (GHH), Behnsen (Krupp). A committee memorandum of 22 February indicated the group would address the issues of raising consumption levels in Central Europe, the "international raw materials situation," and would "take detailed positions on the questions of trade relations – protectionism, free trade, and treaties," Haniel 30019320/6a ("RdI und Genua Konferenz"). Kraemer's notes of 9 March on preparatory discussions reveal hopes for a standard international trade treaty form that could secure long-term trade relations and possibly an end to the unilateral MFN treatment extracted from Germany by the Versailles treaty, ibid. A written report of 20 March 1922 discussed establishing world trade statistics, ending the trade blockade on Germany, and establishing a uniform international tariff scheme, Haniel 300019320/6b.

173. The chamber's governing committee (Vorstand) meeting of 22 February 1922 listed competition, unemployment, international copyright, international trade, and free trade all ahead of Russian reconstruction as issues to be discussed at Genoa, Haniel 30019320/6a. Even after Rapallo, the Economics Ministry considered it "questionable whether in view of the current strain on German export industries, they would take a strong interest in the Russian market as long as the current barriers remain and other foreign countries offer considerably more favorable and more secure markets," Sjöberg at the interministerial meeting of 14 August 1922, GStA PK: I.HA/120c, XIII, 6a, 35, Bd. 1, Bl. 9.

174. The source of German information was the famous "Giannini Conversation" of Wirth, Rathenau, and Maltzan with the secretary of the Italian foreign minister on 14 April. The event is recounted in Foreign Office Press Chief Oskar Mueller's telegram to Berlin (reprinted in *Akten Wirth*, 705, note 2). Fink critically re-examines the conversation in *The Genoa Conference*, 164-66.

175. The characterization of a paralyzed Rathenau is Raumer's, "Rapallo nach Dreissig Jahren," 328. These developments are well recounted by Schieder, "Entstehungsgeschichte," 581 ff. The final notes of Maltzan (who had stepped up from the Russian desk to the directorship of the new Eastern European Department IVa) are available in Ernst Laubach, "Maltzan's Aufzeichnungen über die letzte Vorgänge vor dem Abschluss des Rapallo-Vertrags," *Jahrbücher für die Geschichte Osteuropas* 22, (1975). See also Rathenau's own 16 April telegram to Foreign Office State Secretary Edgar Haniel in *Akten Wirth*, 716, note 1. Schieder also compares the earlier Berlin and final Rapallo versions of the agreement, 602 ff. The latter published in *RGBl*, 1922, vol. 2, 677 ff.

176. Both parties abandoned their claims to any compensation for war damages (article I) and the Germans abandoned any claims on the czarist debt or on compensation for nationalized properties (article II). Diplomatic and consular relations were fully restored with the practical arrangements to be worked out in a subsequent Consular Agreement (article III). Both parties extended MFN sta-

tus to the other in "trade and economic relations" (article IV). Last, the German government promised to "support and facilitate" any contracts signed by private firms in Germany with Soviet agencies (article V).

177. Freund, *Unholy Alliance*, 246, 248 ff. for the malevolent interpretation; Schieder, "Entstehungsgeschichte," 551 for the benevolent view.

178. Freund: "The real significance of the treaty is not to be found in any of its provisions, but rather in the very fact that Russia and Germany, the two outcasts from Western society, dared to defy the Allied powers by signing it," *Unholy Alliance*, 246. Similarly Schieder: "For the Weimar Republic the Rapallo treaty was not only a way out of an acutely dangerous situation at that moment, it was and was supposed to be for the long term an element of 'active foreign policy'," "Entstehungsgeschichte," 600. The fundamental point is recognized by the East German scholarship as well: Fritz Klein, *Die Diplomatischen Beziehungen Deutschlands zur Sowjetunion* (Berlin, 1953), 108; Rosenfeld, *Sowjet-Russland*, 394.

179. For the West German idea that Rapallo helped secure the Dawes Plan agreements, see Schieder, "Entstehungsgeschichte," 601; Erdmann, "Deutschland, Rapallo und der Western," 163 ff.; Helbig, *Träger*, 149 ff.

180. On Soviet thinking on the importance of Rapallo see Rosenfeld, *Sowjet-Russland*, 393 ff.; Soviet press commentaries cited in Himmer, *German-Soviet Economic Relations*, 504 ff.

181. *Sten. Ber.*, Bd. 355, 7704 ff. The Socialists, particularly President Friedrich Ebert, had severe political misgivings about the treaty, but did not oppose it. A few voices of genuine (ideologically motivated) opposition came from the right wing of the German Nationals. The final vote on 4 July 1922 in favor of the treaty was overwhelming, with only a few German Nationals voting against so that the treaty would not receive unanimous approval, *Sten Ber.*, Bd. 356, 8271. On these developments see Erdmann and Grieser, "Deutsch-sowjetischen Beziehungen as Problem der deutschen Innenpolitik;" Bellers, *Aussenwirtschaftspolitik*, 399 ff., 429 ff.

182. The dozens of issues which remained to be cleared up in a "Supplementary Agreement to Fill-Out [ausgestalten] the German-Russian treaty of Rapallo" were outlined in an extensive interministerial meeting held in the Foreign Office on 14 August 1922, GStA PK: I.HA/Rep. 120 C, XIII, 6 a, Nr. 35 A, Bd. 1, Bl. 2 ff.

183. Memorandum by the German Chamber of Commerce on "Complaints of German Firms about the Obstructions of German-Russian Business," 29 September 1922, RWWA 27-33-6. Other economic groups soured on the Soviet trade after Rapallo, as Foreign Minister Frederic von Rosenberg told German Ambassador Brockdorff in Moscow: "The demand for the extension of the Rapallo Treaty's economic provisions did not come from German industrial circles (Wirtschaftskreisen). The great political significance of this treaty was at first not recognized by them. There was disappointment that the treaty brought no progress in the sense of an immediate increase in Russo-German economic dealings ...," cited in R.P. Morgan, "The Political Significance of German-Soviet Trade Negotiations 1922-5," *The Historical Journal* 6 (1963), 257.

184. On Soviet foreign trade organization and the state monopoly see Baykov, *Soviet Foreign Trade*, 7 ff.; Glen Alden Smith, *Soviet Foreign Trade: Organization, Operations, and Policy, 1918-1971* (New York, 1971); Hubert Schneider, *Das sowjetische Aussenhandelsmonolpol 1920-1925* (Cologne, 1973); Franklyn D. Holzman, *Foreign Trade under Central Planning*, (Cambridge, Mass., 1974); also consult the extensive bibliography of Perrey, *Rußlandausschuß* for several pre-1945 German dissertations on this subject.

185. Guggenheimer (MAN) to Paul Reusch (GHH), 15 June 1922, Haniel 300193024/4; Reusch to Guggenheimer, 12 September 1922, Haniel 300193024/4.

186. Report from the Executive Secretariat of the Union of German Iron and Steel Industrialists, 16 December 1925, BA R 13I/246.
187. The German Foreign Office assembled an interministerial delegation composed of five "commissions": State Treaties and Consular Agreement, Private Law, Commercial Shipping, Economic Questions, and Transport. German preparations can be followed in GStA PK: I.HA/Rep. 120 C, XIII, 6 a, Nr. 35 A, Bd. 1, passim.
188. On the course of negotiations from 1923 to 1925 see Morgan, "Political Significance"; Anderle, *Deutsche Rapallo-Politik*, 78 ff., 101 ff., 144 ff.; Rosenfeld, *Sowjetunion und Deutschland, 1922-1933*. Many valuable documents have been reprinted in *Deutsch-sowjetische Beziehungen 1922-1925*.
189. The incident is well recounted in Chapter three of Rosenbaum's *Community of Fate*, 87 ff.
190. Sommer's report to the Prussian Trade Ministry on the German delegation meeting at the Foreign Office, 19 September 1924, GStA PK: I.HA/Rep. 120 C, XIII, 6 a, Nr. 35 A, Bd. 2, Bl. 2. On Stresemann's views toward the Soviet Union at this time see, Martin Walsdorff, *Westorientierung und Ostpolitik: Stresemanns Russlandpolitik in der Locarno Ära* (Bremen, 1971); Gasiaraowski, "Stresemann and Poland Before Locarno." A 30 million-mark German grain purchase from the Soviets in July 1923 (for which the German side provided 15 million in export credits to the Soviets) had been largely politically rather than economically motivated by the German side. Wallroth noted that "the economic and political objections are less important than the political advantages of the agreement," AA, Handakten Wallroth, 5265/317020-2 as cited in Morgan, "German-Soviet Trade Negotiations," 256. See also Stresemann's political arguments for signing an extradition treaty with the Soviets that was clearly unacceptable to most of the German cabinet, *Akten Marx I u. II*, 576 ff.
191. Sommer (Prussian Trade Ministry) and Sjöberg (Economics Ministry) joint report of 29 November 1924, GStA PK: I.HA/Rep. 120 C, XIII, 6 a, Nr. 35 A, Bd. 2, Bl. 49. British-Soviet relations declined precipitously after publication of the "Zinoviev letter" and the subsequent "Red scare" that contributed to Labour's defeat in the 1924 elections and the termination of British-Soviet trade negotiations. Relations remained cold after Prime Minister Stanley Baldwin's Conservative government assumed office in November 1924, culminating in a full diplomatic break in 1927.
192. On the evolution of German demands see GStA PK: I.HA/Rep. 120 C, XIII, 6 a, Nr. 35 A, Bd. 1, especially Wallroth's 17 August 1922 call for "direct business contacts" between German and Russian producers (Bl. 8), Economics Ministry calls for a "penetration of the Russian trade monopoly in personnel and material terms," (Bl. 64), and Körner's statement that "the major goal of the negations from the economic point of view must be to establish the possibility of direct and secure business between Germany and Russia." (Bl. 318). The desire of "German monopolies" to penetrate the Soviet state monopoly in foreign trade is discussed extensively in both volumes of Rosenfeld's *Sowjetunion und Deutschland.*
193. Sommer's 22 and 29 November reports from Moscow, GStA PK: I.HA/Rep. 120 C, XIII, 6 a, Nr. 35 A, Bd. 2, Bl. 35, 45.
194. According to the joint German-Soviet summary of negotiations, the only movement had been Germany's promise to "strive for" private-sector lending to the Soviets "in greater amounts than heretofore." GStA PK: I.HA/Rep. 120 C, XIII, 6 a, Nr. 35 A, Bd. 2, Bl. 68.
195. Within the Foreign Office, Wallroth appeared somewhat out of step with his politically motivated colleagues as he seconded the economically motivated objections of the Chamber of Commerce, Sommer's report, 17 January 1925,

notes on a visit to Bochum on 26 January 1925, GStA PK: I.HA/Rep. 120 C, XIII, 6 a, Nr. 35 A, Bd. 2, Bl. 119, 113; Zweckverband to members, 5 February 1925, RWWA 20-1128-6.

196. See Sommer's report on a first meeting of ministerial representatives and two unnamed private-sector experts held in the Foreign Office, 21 January 1925, his notes on a second meeting of that day at the offices of the Reichsverband, GStA PK: I.HA/Rep. 120 C, XIII, 6 a, Nr. 35 A, Bd. 2, Bl. 106, 103.

197. Zygmunt Gasiorowski, "The Russian Overture to Germany in December 1924," *JMH* 30 (1958), 99-117; Stresemann's "Statement to the Press," 26 April 1926 in *Gustav Stresemann. Diaries, Letters, Papers,* vol. 2, 461; Morgan, "German-Soviet Trade Negotiations," 264.

198. Sommer's report, 6 May 1925, GStA PK: I.HA/Rep. 120 C, XIII, 6 a, Nr. 35 A, Bd. 2, Bl. 270-272.

199. Stresemann to the Chancellery (Kempner), 13 July 1925, GStA PK: I.HA/Rep. 120 C, XIII, 6 a, Nr. 35 A, Bd. 3, Bl. 2-6, reprinted in part in *Akten Luther,* vol. 1, 452.

200. Brockdorff (Moscow) to the Foreign Office, 3 July, GStA PK: I.HA/Rep. 120 C, XIII, 6 a, Nr. 35 A, Bd. 2, Bl. 531.

201. Brockdorff (Moscow) to the Foreign Office, 30 June 1925, GStA PK: I.HA/Rep. 120 C, XIII, 6 a, Nr. 35 A, Bd. 2, Bl. 528.

202. Stresemann to the Kempner, 13 July 1925, GStA PK: I.HA/Rep. 120 C, XIII, 6 a, Nr. 35 A, Bd. 3, Bl. 2-6. The Trade Policy Committee had approved Brock-dorff's plan on 8 July noting both "the danger of a negative political interpreta-tion" of treaty failure by the Soviets and the "not particularly pleasant" consequences for German commercial policy already stuck in negotiations with France, Poland, and Spain, cited in Anderle, *Deutsche Rapallo-Politik,* 144. On 22 July the cabinet authorized Stresemann to continue negotiating with the Soviets along the lines indicated in his cabinet submission of 13 July, *Akten Luther,* 452 ff. Leeser for the Prussian Trade Ministry concluded that "the cabinet had been guided exclusively by political considerations," in reaching that decision, report of interministerial meeting at the Foreign Office, 24 July 1925, GStA PK: I.HA/Rep. 120C, XIII, 6a, 35A, Bd. 3, Bl. 42-45.

203. At the cabinet meeting of 13 May 1925, Under-Secretary Erich Hoffmann had withdrawn Agriculture Ministry objections to the Soviet hog quota when Curtius pointed out that the state of the Soviet economy meant the quota "certainly would not be fully used." In this case, it would be advantageous to Germany to give a larger quota to the Soviets and a smaller quota to the Poles "since Poland will certainly use its quota." Further, the Soviets inexplicably "highly valued this concession … which did not harm Germany" so that in the overall negotiation strategy it made sense to concede this point, *Akten Luther,* 284-85.

204. Rosenfeld, *SowjetUnion und Deutschland 1923-1933,* 154.

205. Foreign Office summary of Brockdorff's 31 August conversation with Chicherin, 2 September 1925, GStA PK: I.HA/Rep. 120 C, XIII, 6 a, Nr. 35 A, Bd. 3, Bl. 93.

206. Hilger and Meyer, *Incompatible Allies,* 184.

207. On 19 September Stresemann had wired to Brockdorff in Moscow that "for prac-tical and political consisderations the earliest possible signing is urgently desired," cited in Schneider, *Das sowjetische Aussenhandelsmonopol,* 132. The Treaty of 12 October 1925 consisted of seven "agreements" covering the following fields: legal protection, economics (trade), railways, navigation, fiscal, commercial arbi-tration courts, legal protection of industrial property. *RGBl,* 1926 (II), 1; Leonard Shapiro, *Soviet Treaty Series 1917-1928* (Washington, D.C., 1950), vol. 1, 288.

208. Stresemann acknowledged that the new agreement had been negotiated "on the basis of" (auf dem Boden) the mutual economic recognition provided for in the

6 May 1921 agreement, "Notes on the German-Soviet Economic Negotiations," 29 September 1925, *Akten Luther*, 588-93.

209. Lesser's report to the Prussian Trade Ministry, 27 July 1925, GStA PK: I.HA/Rep. 120 C, XIII, 6 a, Nr. 35 A, Bd. 3, Bl. 43; Zweckverband to its members, 29 September 1925, RWWA 5-19-12. The Union of Iron and Steel Industrialists also pointed out the "limited value" of many of the agreement's provisions, BA R 131/246. On 23 April 1925 the Westphalian Zweckverband had already posed the question of whether Germany should bother to "work seriously" for a treaty, since "in view of the Russian [government] trade monopoly any trade treaty has only very limited value," RWWA 20-1128-6. See also the evaluation offered by Schneider, *Das sowjetische Aussenhandelsmonopol*, 133 ff.

210. Chamber of Commerce President Edward Hamm to members, 3 October 1925, RWWA 20-1128-6. Hamm's attitude toward an agreement that was considered unsatisfactory but that did not impose any burdens on the private sector was reflected in the Reichstag ratification debate on 12 December 1925. Speaking for the German Nationals, Freytagh-Lovinghoven summarized: "All these [economic] defects do not diminish the political, I would like to say the symbolic importance of these treaties, and because of this importance, we will vote for them." The package of agreements was accepted by overwhelming majority on a show of hands, *Sten Ber.*, Bd. 388, 4826, 4833.

211. East German historians argued extensively that Locarno was in fact an anti-Soviet pact between Germany and the West; see Andreas Dorpalen's review of that East German literature in *German History in Marxist Perspective*, 350 ff.

212. 25 September 1925, *Akten Luther*, 578-79.

213. Stresemann's notes on a conversation with Chicherin, 30 September 1925, *Stresemann. Diaries*, vol. 2, 478-80.

214. Cited in Morgan, "German-Soviet Trade Negotiations, 1922-25," 270. On this see also Anderle, *Deutsche Rapallo-Politik*, 161 ff. Wallroth appears to have been the only one on the German side who thought the October agreement with the Soviets had significantly "strengthened the hand of our negotiators" vis-à-vis the West at Locarno, cited in Morgan, 270-71.

215. Schubert to Ambassador Leopold von Hoesch, 20 January 1926 in Osthoff, *Die Deutsch-Russischen Vertragsbeziehungen*, 92; Stresemann's famous letter to the former crown Prince on "The Tasks of German Foreign Policy," 7 September 1925, *Stresemann. Diaries*, vol. 2, 503-505.

216. The origins of the Soviet request for additional credit are traced in Rosenfeld, *Sowjetunion und Deutschland 1923-1933*, 229 ff.; *ADAP*, B, vol. 2, 1, passim. Under the terms of the credit program, the Reich assumed 35 pecent of the risk, the German states 25 percent, and the seller 40 percent. The bulk of initial financing was supplied by two bank consortia; one under leadership of the Deutsche Bank (RM 120 million) and a second group under leadership of the Darmstaedter bank (RM 110 million). The loans were executed by the new Industrie-Finanzierungs-Aktiengesellschaft Ost (Ifago) with offices in the headquarters of the industrial Reichsverband. On all aspects of the operation see Manfred Pohl, *Die Finanzierung der Russengeschäfte zwischen den beiden Weltkriegen* (Frankfurt, 1975); B. Hahn, "Die deutsche Ausfallbürgschaft für Lieferungen nach Russland (Der 300 Millionen-Kredit)," *Osteuropa* 10 (1925/26), 510 ff.; as well as a number of pre-1945 German dissertations on the subject listed in part B.1 of the bibliography to Perrey, *Russlandausschuss*, 410-11. An interministerial meeting in the Economics Ministry on 11 December 1925 had already "approved in principle" a RM 10 million "export credit insurance" program for German exports worldwide. The "leading economic interest groups" (Spitzenverbände) supported the plan when it was presented to them by the Economics Ministry on 19 December,

some members (Kraemer, Reichsverband) offered "warm support" for the idea. Only the commercial interests from Hamburg opposed it because of potential competition from industrial producers in the export business, Chancellery Assistant Walter Grävell to State Secretary Kempner, 17 December and 22 December 1925, BA R 43I/1174. In his summary for the cabinet discussion on 22 December, Grävell noted that "industry and most of (grosse Teile) the commercial circles liked the idea," BA R 43I/1174.

217. Dirksen to Wallroth and Schubert, *ADAP*, B, vol. 2, .1, No. 49; Schlesinger's comments, 25 February in ibid, 146, note 2.

218. Stresemann and Economics Minister Curtius's joint memorandum on "The Necessity of and the Promotion of German Exports to Russia," 26 January 1926, BA R 43I/1174, reprinted in *ADAP*, B, vol. 2,1, No. 50; Curtius repeated many of the economic arguments in a second memorandum on the subject, 18 February, BA R 43I/1174 which showed the German share of Soviet imports falling from 34.5 percent in 1923 to just 21.1 percent in 1924. Curtius's arguments (pulled together here) captured the reality of German postwar financial weakness and its particularly debilitating effects in competing with the West for Russian orders: "The Russians … can conclude only those deals in which the supplier provides credit. German industrialists are not in a position to assume the full risk for credits of this size and length [two to three years]. Germany's competitor countries offer better payment and credit terms. The danger exists that Germany's share of Russian imports will decline further if special measures are not taken." The cabinet approved the plan "in principle" on 1 February and 9 February 1926, *ADAP*, B, vol. 2, 1, 153, note 6 and Rosenfeld, *Sowjetunion und Deutschland*, 232. The Reichstag Budget Committee gave its approval on 25 February, BA R 43I/1172.

219. Since the Soviets had been prepared for such a political understanding once before in December 1924, it might be more accurate to say that the economic agreement of October 1925 and the new trade credits restored German-Soviet relations to their previous good state by repairing the damage done by Stresemann's understandings with the West (Dawes, Locarno, entry into the League).

220. According to Foreign Office State Secretary Carl Schubert, the Soviets still had a "deep fear" of being "economically isolated and starved-out" by a British-led effort, Schubert to Ambassador Hoesch, 20 January 1926 in Osthoff, *Die Deutsch-Russischen Vertragsbeziehungen*, 91. In that case, nothing could have been more reassuring than an economic agreement, trade credits, and a promise to refrain from any boycott. Rosenfeld, *Sowjetunion und Deutschland*, 224 ff. describes briefly the significance of the loan for the Soviet state; Stresemann's "Statement to the Press," 26 April 1926 in *Stresemann. Diaries*, vol. 2, 461.

221. Shapiro, *Soviet Treaty Series*, vol. 1, 317. On the negotiations for the Berlin Treaty see *ADAP*, Series A, vols. 13 and 14, forthcoming.

222. Stresemann to Curtius, 12 June 1926, cited in Anderle, *Deutsche Rapallo-Politik*, 169. The German banks wanted a 10.75 percent charge (equal to the Reichsbank discount of 7 percent plus 2 percent additional and a Bereitschaftsprovision of 1.75 percent); the Soviets were not prepared to pay more than 10 percent, Reichsverband memorandum, 19 April 1926, RWWA 20-1103-1.

223. Hans Kraemer told the Reichsverband Präsidium that trade developments with the Soviets had discredited the arguments of the "unbridled optimists" such as Felix Deutsch and confirmed the views of the "cautious observers," 29 March 1928, Bayer-Archiv 62/10.3, Bd. 2.

224. *Statistik des deutschen Reiches*, N.F. various vols. especially Bd. 339, 351, 366; *Monatliche Nachweise über den Aussenhandel Deutschlands – Ergänzungsheft: Der deutsche Aussenhandel nach Erdteilen und Ländern, 1929*, 5. Using Soviet data

Baykov shows the German share of Soviet imports declining from 23.3 percent (1925-26) to 22.6 percent (1926-27) and further to 22.1 percent (1929), *Soviet Foreign Trade*, Table VII. Similar data cited in Anderle, *Deutsche Rapallo-Politik,* 170.

225. German Chamber of Commerce to the Duisburg Chamber, 9 November 1927; German Chamber of Commerce Foreign Trade Committee meeting, 9 December 1927, both in RWWA 20-1099-3.

226. Hauptvorstand meeting, 22 February 1928, BA R13I/102, repeated along with the old complaint that "MFN does us no good as long as the Russian government, with the help of the state foreign trade monopoly, is free to bestow contracts on other states for political reasons" in the union's "Tagesfragen der Handelspolitik," 28 February 1928, BA R13I/247. The failure of 300 million marks in credits to spark a sustained increase in trade should not have come as a complete surprise. In December 1925 the German Chamber of Commerce estimated that German exporters had already granted 300 million to 350 million marks in short-term credit to the Soviets through 1925, but the value of German-Soviet trade in the early 1920s remained very small, German Chamber of Commerce memorandum, 30 December 1925, RWWA 20-1099-3.

227. The Reichsverband had warned that the state-sponsored credits would only "make it easier for the Russians to play-off one firm against the other," memorandum of 4 March 1926, Haniel 4001012025/0.

228. Reuter's actions broke the recent "gentlemen's agreement" on terms for Soviet deliveries concluded on 25 February 1926 between DEMAG, AEG, Siemens, Stinnes, Krupp, Borsig, and Gas-Motoren Deutz under the auspices of Karl Lange from the Union of Machine Building Institutes, Martin Blank to Otto Gertung, 26 February 1926; 10 March 1926 meeting of this ad hoc group, both in Haniel 4001012025/0; Reichsverband Main Committee meeting, 19 May 1927, Bayer-Archiv, 62/10.5, Bd. 1. See Also Kraemer's pessimistic forecast for economic relations with the Soviets, Reichsverband Präsidium meeting, 29 March 1928, Bayer-Archiv, 62/10.3, Bd. 2.

229. Curtius to the Foreign Office, 5 June 1929, PAAA Polen, Handel 13 A, Geheim, Bd. 12.

GUARANTEEING THE MARKET 1929-1934

*I*n 1929 Agriculture Minister Hermann Dietrich explained to a Democratic party assembly that in order for the Reich to sign a trade treaty with Poland, Germany must find some way to allow "Polish produce" into Germany without "destroying German price formation."[1] Throughout most of the Weimar period the type of trade arrangement that Dietrich sought was precluded by the international rules of trade (long-term multilateral MFN treaties, few quantitative restrictions), by Germany's own protective mechanisms (moderate tariff protection), and by the domestic system of trade policy formation (corporatist paralysis). The trauma of the Depression catalyzed remarkable developments in each of these three areas: preferences, discriminations, and bilateralization became accepted practices in international trade; high tariffs, foreign exchange controls, and import quotas protected the German economy from world price declines; and the politics of corporatism gave way to a presidential "quasi dictatorship" and then to a one-party state with totalitarian aspirations. Between 1930 and 1934 the new features of these rapidly evolving international and domestic frameworks allowed Germany to conclude the type of trade agreements Dietrich had fruitlessly sought as the basis for an effective German trade policy in Eastern Europe.

Response to World Price Collapse

"The great depression was, in the fields of commercial policies, foreign trade, and capital movements, perhaps more than in other fields,

Notes for this chapter begin on page 237.

the end of an epoch ... in 1933 the European landscape of commercial policies had little in common with that of 1928. The previous multilateral system of trade and payments had been replaced by bilateral agreements, clearings, and quotas."[2] The erosion of the old liberal trade regime and the rise of a new, anarchic international regime was an undirected process in which each of the world's major trading nations played some role. At the very latest the American Smoot-Hawley tariff of the spring of 1930 "made clear that in the world economy no one was in charge."[3] Fear of international competition overwhelmed each of the national actors and produced a snowballing effect of rising tariffs followed by foreign exchange controls and import quotas. As a major trading nation that itself adopted each of these protectionist and trade controlling mechanisms, Germany played a significant role in every phase of the dissolution process. Yet only with Schacht's 1934 New Plan for the complete bilateralization of all German foreign trade, did Germany emerge as a leader in the creation of the chaotic, ad hoc trade regime of the 1930s.[4]

The end of the old international framework for trade began with a worldwide round of tariff increases in 1930 to 1932.[5] In Europe, duty rates and tariff levels soared to heights many times those of the relatively stable years 1925 to 1928. Tariffs on agricultural goods rose first, most quickly, and to the highest levels. These tariff increases disproportionately aggravated the economic strain on the agricultural areas of Europe in the years after 1929. Successive increases beginning in 1929 had pushed German tariff levels for agricultural products to 82.5 percent ad valorem in 1931, or more than three times the 1927 level of 27.4 percent. In Czechoslovakia, agricultural tariffs were similarly high at 84 percent (36.3 percentin 1927), and in Poland agricultural tariff levels reached 110 percent ad valorem (72 percent in 1927). In France and Italy as well, agricultural tariffs in 1931 were more than three times the levels of four years earlier. Even in Sweden, agricultural rates approached 40 percent. Nor were soaring tariffs confined to agriculture. By 1931, tariff levels and duty rates on semifinished and finished articles as well hit unprecedented levels. In Germany, 1931 tariff levels on semifinished goods averaged 23.5 percent (1927 = 14.5 percent), in France 31.8 percent (24.3 percent), in Italy 49.5 percent (28.6 percent). Denmark raised tariffs in October 1931, Sweden in February 1932. Even Belgium and Switzerland increased their tariff levels on semifinished goods by half. Britain abandoned its traditional free-trade policy with the imposition of some duties in autumn 1931 and a general tariff in February 1932.[6]

The upward spiral of tariff increases sent governments scrambling to regain their full tariff autonomy in order to obtain a free hand for tariff increases. This caused cancellation of many treaties that bound European tariff rates. In the summer of 1929 the German cabinet authorized preliminary negotiations with Sweden, France, and Finland for the purpose of unbinding the grain, flour, and dairy tariff rates set in those treaties.[7] On 24 June 1929 the cabinet voted to annul the Swedish treaty effective 15 February 1930. In negotiating a new treaty with Sweden, Germany would refuse to bind its future grain rates and would raise the rates on cattle, sheep, and pigs.[8] These pan-European tariff increases were part of a worldwide trend that contributed to the shrinking volume of European trade.[9] Yet tariffs alone, no matter how severe, could not destroy the multilateral system of trade based on the MFN principle. Import quotas and other "quantitative restrictions" (QRs) were the real causes of death of the old liberal regime.[10]

In early 1931 a number of countries (including France, Czechoslovakia, Spain, Belgium, Sweden, and Hungary) introduced state import monopolies, import licenses, and quotas for some commodities, usually grains. After the financial crisis in Austria and Germany in the summer of 1931, "the system of multilateral trade, already seriously affected, broke down with the collapse of the world monetary system."[11] France pushed ahead in July and August 1931 by imposing quotas on coal, coal products, timber, and wine. A few months later, the "movement towards quantitative restrictions became a landslide and its essential character was changed when sterling, followed by numerous other currencies in every continent, went off gold in September."[12] In the final quarter of 1931, Belgium, Czechoslovakia, Estonia, France, Hungary, Italy, Latvia, Rumania, Spain, Turkey, and Yugoslavia either imposed new licensing/quota systems or expanded previous programs. Some countries responded to the financial crisis with foreign exchange controls that almost inevitably functioned as import controls even when this had not been the primary intent of the imposing governments. By the end of 1931 foreign exchange controls were restricting imports in Austria, Bulgaria, Czechoslovakia, Estonia, Germany, Hungary, Latvia, Portugal, Spain, Turkey, and Yugoslavia. In 1933 the United Kingdom adopted quotas on agricultural imports. That same year France made quotas "an integral part of its bargaining apparatus."[13] Between 1931 and 1934 many governments further expanded and institutionalized their quota systems.

The new quantitative restrictions, especially import quotas, ultimately destroyed multilateral trading arrangements because they lacked an "accepted or plausible principle of quota allocation which could be called non-discriminatory and consistent with the most-favored-nation principle." Any system of allocation preferred some countries and discriminated against others. The need to establish import quotas, unavoidably preferential or discriminatory in nature, pressured European governments into the canceling or unilaterally annulling many trade treaties containing MFN clauses. Even where treaties were not canceled, "the MFN clause lost much of its value in European commercial relationships ... through the use of exchange control and quantitative restrictions."[14]

In the new international environment of preference and discrimination European states began to form regional trading blocs. In May 1931 the Balkan countries of the "Little Entente" concluded a preferential trade pact. In June and July of that year, Germany concluded preferential treaties with Rumania and Hungary in which the Reich granted 25 percent to 50 percent tariff rebates on various grain imports from those countries. However, objections by "discriminated" third parties (Argentina, Czechoslovakia, the USSR, and the U.S.) blocked implementation of the German treaties. Between September 1931 and January 1932, France negotiated and subsequently implemented preferential trade agreements with Hungary, Yugoslavia, and Rumania.[15] The 1932 Ottawa Agreements and the Import Duties Act in Britain established a preferential trading zone within the British Commonwealth and British Empire. In February 1933 Belgium, the Netherlands, and Luxembourg signed the Ouchy Convention for mutual tariff reductions, in violation of their MFN obligations. Protests by nonpreferred trade partners, with the U.S. in the lead, prevented realization of the plan. One year later, many of the "gold bloc" countries (France, Switzerland, Belgium, Luxembourg, and the Netherlands) sought to expand their mutual trade by signing the 1934 Brussels Protocol. A German agreement with Scandinavian dairy producers (Denmark, Finland) in October 1932 allowed Germany to impose preferential and discriminatory quantitative restrictions.[16]

These numerous large and small preferential trading arrangements killed the multilateral trade system which, though shaken by the consequences of World War I, had governed European commercial exchanges since the mid-nineteenth century. When successfully implemented, such treaties clearly meant the end of multilateralism. When such treaties were blocked by third-party objections, that setback inspired many European governments to annul their existing treaties in order to obtain a free hand for negotiating preferential arrangements. By the end of 1932, Germany had made provisions for the termination of the important tariff treaties – those with France, Sweden, the Netherlands, and Yugoslavia – that served as anchors for

Germany's other MFN treaties.[17] With these anchors of the German MFN system removed by early 1933, the new Nazi government set a new course for German trade policy unencumbered by international regime restraints.

These fundamental changes in the international trading system produced a general movement towards bilateralism in Europe and in the world at large. In this new international framework "each bilateral agreement was sui generis, designed to meet the special trade requirements of, and to afford effective reciprocal advantages to, the signatories."[18] The evolution of a new, bilateral trading system was an indispensable prerequisite for a new, more active German trade policy in Eastern Europe. The Foreign Office tested the limits of the evolving system by attempting to bilateralize relations with Hungary and Rumania via the preferential treaties of 1931. As the international rules of trade continued to change from 1932 to 1935, successive German chancellors Heinrich Brüning, Franz von Papen, and Adolf Hitler were able to conclude a number of special deals with Poland, Czechoslovakia, and the Soviet Union. By 1934 the bilateralization of international trade had reached such a degree that Schacht could launch his New Plan, which had as its "cornerstone" in the international sphere the "bilateralization of German foreign trade and external payments ..."[19] Schacht's plan was practical only after the old multilateral system of international trade could no longer prevent its implementation.

With bilateralism came "the endeavor by each country to achieve reciprocity in trade."[20] The move away from MFN-based relations and toward reciprocally based relations allowed Germany to employ individually constructed, reciprocal trade agreements in Eastern Europe. The tendency toward ad hoc reciprocal trade deals was gaining momentum already under the Brüning cabinet in 1932. In a report initialed by Hitler on 29 May 1933, Chancellery officer Franz Willuhn explained how numerous European preferential trade arrangements had already, in effect, undermined the MFN principle to such an extent that with many countries Germany could no longer conduct trade on MFN terms.[21]

In October 1933, Economics Ministry State Secretary Posse presented a plan for Hitler's Germany to launch "an active commercial policy based on the principle of reciprocity."[22] He argued that changes currently underway in the international trade system made it necessary for Germany to commit itself to new trade practices. Papen assured the group that Hitler agreed with Posse's new guidelines for Germany's future trade policy and the cabinet approved the general suggestion that the government "begin with a more active commercial policy."[23] Posse's statements brought home to the cabinet how the evolution of a new order in trade practices not only allowed Germany to embark on a new commercial strategy in Eastern Europe, but in some ways forced the Reich to do so.

The new international framework afforded Germany new opportunities for the use of trade as a foreign policy weapon in the East. Yet by themselves changes in the international trade regime could not ensure that Germany would be in a position to exploit these new international opportunities. The constraints on German trade policy in Eastern Europe from 1920 to 1931 were rooted as much in Weimar's own domestic economic and political structures as in the nature of the international trade regime.[24] Parallel changes in the domestic structures of German trade policy formulation were still required before the Reich could begin to wield the new tools of international trade now available to it.

Authoritarian Politics and the Response to Interests

Successive German cabinets under Müller, Brüning, Papen, and Hitler used newly permissible commercial policies to protect German agriculture from the hideous price declines in the world market. By employing prohibitive tariffs and then state import monopolies and quotas in conjunction with domestic regulations, these governments drove a wedge between German domestic agricultural prices and world prices. By 1931 to 1932 domestic prices for many key German agricultural commodities had become "uncoupled" from world prices, as determined by international market forces. The imposition of agricultural price controls after September 1933 progressively removed even domestic market forces from the German agricultural sector.

In the domestic political sphere, the progressive consolidation of control over tariff and trade policy in the hands of the executive decisively affected the execution of German trade policy from 1930 to 1939. Beginning with Brüning, successive cabinets became increasingly divorced from both parliamentary political support and general social support. Weimar's striving for corporatist consensus gave way to a progressively more authoritarian system with executive powers eventually relying solely on the will of a small clique around the aging president. In divorcing themselves from any social base, these presidential cabinets were able to gain greater degrees of autonomous control over trade and tariff policy than any of their corporatist-based, parliament-bound Weimar predecessors had attained.[25] With the creation of the one-party state in 1933 to 1934,

Hitler assumed control over the strategic course of trade policy, leaving the day-to-day problems to Schacht.

The tariff increases undertaken by the Müller government were an important first step in the long process of divorcing German agricultural prices from world prices. With an eye on the tariff set to expire on 31 December 1929, Agriculture Minister Dietrich (Democrats) warned the cabinet in May that the government should be prepared to offset recent agricultural price declines with tariff increases for cattle, pigs, meat, rye, wheat, spelt, and butter.[26] Although Müller's center-left coalition was not particularly dependent on farmers' support, the plight of German agriculture was so widespread and acute that even opponents of agriculture such as Labor Minister Rudolf Wissel (SPD) and Economics Minister Curtius (DVP) reluctantly agreed to substantial revisions in the Swedish treaty.[27] The industrial Reichsverband as well agreed to "put aside [its] reservations" and to "support the wishes of agriculture" for tariff increases.[28]

Having recovered fully autonomous control over grain duties via a revision of the Swedish treaty, the government considered how to best use the tariff to help German farmers. The agricultural groups were asking for a doubling of the wheat and barley tariffs (from 50 marks/ton to 100 marks/ton) and a near doubling of the rye and oats rates (from 50 marks/ton to 90 marks/ton). The governing parties (People's Party, Center, Democrats, and Socialists) of the Great Coalition all agreed that "something must be done" to support the price of rye which had now fallen to 162 marks/ton.[29] After a series of coalition meetings, Dietrich presented a plan to the cabinet on 19 November that would institute "sliding tariffs" on the major grains.[30] Pressure by President Paul von Hindenburg to get some tariff increases in place before Christmas expedited the final cabinet approval of the plan on 16 December 1929. Rye and wheat tariffs were increased to 95 mark/ton and 100 marks/ton. More important, the government gained the power to adjust individual tariff rates within specified ranges (e.g., between 30 marks/ton and 95 marks/ton for rye), depending on the movement of grain prices.[31]

The long-term economic significance of these new sliding tariffs lay in the establishment of domestic "target prices" for the major grains sold in Germany: 230 marks/ton for rye and 260 marks/ton for wheat. In adopting the concept of target prices, the government implicitly established two important principles. First, that these target prices should obtain in Germany regardless of world market prices; and, second, that tariff rates should be set so as to ensure the attainment of these prices. As early as May 1929, Dietrich argued the need to make German butter producers "independent from the world market."[32] The establishment of these ideas by a Center-Left coalition and the acceptance of them by a majority in the Reichstag provided the starting point for subsequent commercial policies explicitly aimed at making German agricultural prices "independent" of the world market.[33]

The long-term political significance of this tariff legislation lay in its transfer of tariff-setting power from the legislature to the executive. The law of December 1929 allowed the "government" (die Reichsregierung) to set the new sliding tariff rates without the previously required permission of a Reichstag and a Reichsrat committee. The Reichstag party factions felt that this transfer of power would speed up and simplify the process during a time of international crisis, thereby reducing the operating room for grain speculators.[34] Few could have foreseen this as the beginning of a process of "deparliamentization" of tariff and trade policy that would continue and intensify over the next four years.

As prices continued to decline in early 1930, the government responded with more import restrictions. In one of its final acts, the Müller cabinet obtained parliamentary approval for centralization of all corn imports in the new Reich Corn Office. As part of the import restrictive price support strategy, the government was, in effect, imposing a state monopoly on corn imports and sales in the Reich. Discretionary executive power over tariff policy was extended, with a wide range of tariff increases. The upper limit of the sliding scale for wheat was increased to 12 marks, and the government could exceed even this limit with the consent of the appropriate Reichstag committee. Sliding tariffs were introduced for barley and oats.[35]

With the collapse of Müller's Great Coalition in March 1930, the period of genuine parliamentary government in Germany ended. The subsequent governments of Brüning, Papen, Kurt Schleicher, and Hitler rested not on parliamentary majorities, but rather on the executive powers of the president. From March 1930 through the spring of 1933, Germany was governed by an "extraparliamentary" system variously characterized as "authoritarian," "semidictatorial," or a "quasi dictatorship." Whatever label one chooses, the dominant political characteristics of the evolutionary period from 1930 to 1933 are clear: reduction of the Reichstag "to the role of a tolerative body" and a steady "strengthening of the growing executive power over the legislature."[36] On tariff and trade issues, the process of deparliamentizing control over policy accelerated sharply.

At Hindenburg's insistence, Martin Schiele joined the Brüning cabinet (March 1930 to June 1932) as minister of agriculture.[37] Schiele had been among those agricultural leaders who had earlier told Dietrich that tariffs were "more effective" than other means (such as domestic regulations on consumption) in supporting farm prices. Now as a precondition for joining the Brüning cabinet, Schiele presented the chancellor with a list of demands for increased agricultural tariffs as part of a comprehensive plan for enhanced agricultural protection. Schiele demanded that he be empowered to raise and lower the grain tariff without limit in order to maintain the domestic "target" prices for rye and wheat, and that target prices be set for live pigs and pork (750 marks/ton) with the power to adjust the tariff to secure that price. Further, Schiele insisted on new negotiations with Finland ("immediately") for the purpose of unbinding German tariff rates on dairy products.[38] Although Schiele did not get everything he requested from the cabinet, the Law on Tariff Changes from 15 April 1930 did empower the government to adjust the rye, wheat, oats, barley, and pea tariffs without limit and without Reichstag approval. The upper limit on the sliding tariff for feed barley was raised to 100 marks/ton; a target price of 750 marks/ton to 850 marks/ton was established for live pigs; and tariff rates were raised as much as 800 percent on another twenty-five items. Schiele told the cabinet plainly that "the point of these powers" was to establish a "closed system of tariffs ...."[39]

Schiele's tariff policies reflected his general agreement with the position of the radical agricultural groups (now consolidated in the Green Front) that "the price level for all [German] agricultural products be uncoupled from the world market."[40] Over the following six months the Brüning government issued ordinances progressively increasing grain tariffs to levels that exceeded the world market prices for these goods. The wheat tariff went to 185 marks/ton (New York price, 1930 average = 174.2 marks/ton), the rye tariff to 200 marks/ton (price in Polish Posen = 90 marks/ton), and the barley tariff to 150 marks.[41] In May 1930, German farmers paid 180 marks/ton for imported feed barley; 80 to 87 marks covered the price of the goods, and 100 marks paid the duty! Schiele subsequently increased the fodder barley tariff in order to push German farmers over to the use of domestic rye for livestock feeding.[42] Another new Law on Tariff Changes from 28 March 1931 extended the government's powers to adjust tariff rates to all imported commodities. It further instructed the government to eliminate the gap between agricultural and industrial prices.[43] Schiele now turned his attention to other agricultural commodities, especially dairy products and livestock, gradually extending to them the high levels of tariff protection already afforded to wheat, rye, and barley.[44] Only at that point, in the spring of 1932, did Schiele reach the Brüning cabinet's political limits on the further use of tariffs for agricultural protection.

The shift from parliamentary to executive rule was well underway and had been necessary for the rapid increase in domestic economic protection. The sharp swerve toward radical agricultural protection in 1930 indicated that the old corporatist structure of paralytic consensus had been significantly altered by the consolidation of tariff authority in the hands of the cabinet. Although not dependent on a supportive parliamentary majority, Brüning still required Reichstag "toleration" throughout his chancellorship. The composition of his cabinet was broad enough to secure that toleration. That broadness, in turn, continued to impose some limits on Schiele's ability to set trade and tariff policy on an exclusively pro-agrarian course.[45]

The shift from parliamentary to executive rule was also taking place in the control over of foreign trade policy. Step by step, the Reichstag itself and then President Hindenburg transferred primary control over international trade agreements away from the parliament and into the hands of the (nonparliamentary) chancellor. The Law on Tariff Changes from 28 March 1931 empowered the government to "order the temporary application of bilateral economic agreements with foreign countries … in the event of pressing economic need." The law required only that the government present these orders to the Reichstag and that they be rescinded if so demanded.[46] In other words, trade agreements no longer required active Reichstag approval. The new legislation reduced the power of the parliament to a restricted veto right. Problems with this preliminary arrangement arose as a result of the Reichstag's long recess in the autumn of 1931. With the Reichstag out of session, the government could not file its temporary application orders with the parliament, as formally required by the March 1931 law. Signed international agreements entered a state of limbo. In late October 1931, Finance Minister Dietrich suggested that the cabinet obtain a presidential order empowering the government to put signed agreements into force before the Reichstag returned. Because only the 18 July 1931 trade treaty with Hungary was being delayed at this point, the cabinet preferred to wait.[47] By the end of November the Foreign Office felt the situation had become unbearable. Brüning was relying on commercial policies as an important economic and political tool in his international reparations strategy. The Reich had to find some means of proceeding with trade agreements despite the various problems plaguing the Reichstag. In addition to the Hungarian treaty, signed agreements with Czechoslovakia, Austria, Switzerland, France, and Brazil were now on hold. Negotiations with Italy and the Soviet Union were underway. The Foreign Office urged the use of Article 48, Sec. 2 of the Constitution as the basis for issuing a presidential order empowering the government to put bilateral economic agreements in force until the Reichstag returned to session. Ritter explained the Foreign Office position to the cabinet on 30 November, obtaining approval "after a brief discussion."[48] The government received new powers in the Order of the Reichspresident on Tariff Changes and the Temporary Application of Bilateral Economic Agreements from 1 December 1931. Those powers were extended once again in the Order of the Reich President for the Protection of the Economy from 9 March 1932.[49] The transfer of control over international trade agreements from the Reichstag to the nonparliamentary chancellor allowed Brüning and the Foreign Office to pursue their plans for preferential treaties with Hungary and Rumania despite the opposition of the Reichsverband and other important industrial and commercial groups.[50]

Under the Papen government (May to December 1932), Germany approached a qualitatively new level of agricultural protection with the use of restrictive import quotas. Papen had promised farmers that his government would "give more weight to the requirements of agricultural policy in the framework of general economic policy than has been done up to now." Agriculture Minister Magnus Braun told the cabinet "it will now be necessary to detach the processing sector of [German] agriculture from the world market."[51] In July 1932, Braun presented to the cabinet the long-standing agricultural demand for import quotas on key commodities.[52] The government accepted the use of quotas "as far as this is legally permissible according to [our] current trade treaties."[53] The universally hostile international response to these potential import restrictions prevented Papen from implementing most of the planned quotas. Ultimately, an import quota was imposed only on butter (55,000 tons annually).[54]

Export interests and agriculture were deeply split over the continued use of MFN treaties or preferential clauses and the introduction of new mechanisms such as import quotas. Both the Reichsverband and the German Chamber of Commerce clung to the traditional liberal means of managing trade: moderate tariffs, long-term tariff treaties, and MFN clauses.[55] German industrial exporters and commercial groups were apoplectically enraged with Papen for endangering German trade treaties and exports with his plans for quantitative import restrictions.[56] However, Papen's Cabinet of National Forces had cut all ties with the Reichstag, counting on the Nazi-Communist "negative majority" in parliament to prevent any Reichstag challenge to his rule on the basis presidential powers. Armed with extensive new executive powers and dependent only on Hindenburg's support, Papen was able to ignore the conservative opposition of the industrial Reichsverband and the Chamber of Commerce to his plans for severe import quotas. Only the growing gulf between the presidential cabinet on one side and the Reichstag and interest groups as representatives of civil society on the other side prevented the executive government from the type of paralysis that plagued Weimar's parliamentary cabinets.

When Hitler's coalition government came to power in January 1933, Alfred Hugenberg's position as both agriculture and economics minister assured him the ability to implement the radical agricultural program he had advocated since 1930 as head of the German National People's Party.[57] Hugenberg himself readily admitted that "[German] agriculture can be productive only if the price base deviates from the world market." Confronted with the problems of agriculture, Hitler concurred that "in the interest of the national economy," agricultural prices "must be made independent of the world market prices."[58] Using the powers already granted to the government in 1931 and 1932, Hugenberg quickly imposed a series of sharp tariff increases on livestock, meat, fat, eggs, and cheese.[59]

On 4 April Hugenberg established the Reich Office for Oil and Fat, designed to save German dairy farmers from foreign butter and margarine competition by taking control of all imported oil and fat and setting the terms of its sale on the German domestic market.[60] On 5 May Hugenberg reconstructed the Reich Corn Office as the much more extensive Reich Office for Grain, Fodder, and other Agricultural Products with monopoly rights over bread and fodder grains as well as a number of other important commodities.[61] Regulations on fruit and vegetables sales followed in July. With the creation of an import monopoly for dairy products in December 1933, the Oil and Fat Office was expanded as the "Reich Office for Dairy Products, Oil and Fat. At the same time an import monopoly for eggs was established.[62] In describing the functions of the new Reich Office for Eggs, Nazi Agriculture Minister Richard Darré, explained the purpose of these monopolies: "In this way it will be possible to overcome the disruptive effects of an unregulated supply of eggs, and especially as far as foreign eggs are concerned to counter-act the price pressure for imports by levying the difference between the world market price and the domestic price."[63] The proliferation of these all-encompassing marketing monopolies was another important step in the process of shielding German agriculture from international market forces – a process that can be traced in a line from December 1929 through late 1933.

Hitler's government also continued the political process of concentrating control over foreign trade policy and trade agreements in the hands of the executive. The infamous Enabling Act of 24 March 1933 radically expanded the powers of the executive government in all areas, including the conduct of foreign relations and trade treaties. Article 4 removed both the Reichstag and the Reichsrat from the ratification procedure for all international treaties.[64] One month later Konstantin von Neurath (Foreign Office), Hugenberg (economics and agriculture), and Graf Schwerin-Krosigk (finance) presented a draft for a new Law on Temporary Application of Bilateral Economic Agreements with Foreign Countries.[65] The ministers argued that the terms of the Enabling Act still did not make the process "fast enough to put the numerous economic agreements in force as quickly as Germany's economic needs require." For two reasons the terms of the older presidential order of March 1932 also considered inadequate. First, the order required that "in each case the cabinet engage itself with the question of temporary application." Many agreements were too pressing to allow for this procedure. Secondly the presidential order was based on Article 48, Sec. 2 of the Weimar Constitution, "which provides for the participation of the Reichstag." In accordance with the antiparliamentary world view of the Hitler cabinet, the ministers thought it "desirable" to "detach" the application procedure from the old Constitution. The cabinet approved the plan on 4 April and the new law empowering the foreign minister to order the temporary application of economic agreements appeared the same day.[66] The complete concentration of formal control over German trade policy agreements in the hands of Nazi Foreign Minster Neurath marked the end of the process of transferring power from the legislature to the executive that had begun under the Müller government in December 1929.

On the economic side, the Nazi government continued and intensified the existing trend toward isolating the (now recovering) Germany economy from the international market forces that kept the rest of Europe mired in a deep Depression. In the context of protectionist developments after 1929, Nazi economic policy intensified earlier agricultural import controls and then extended them to all sectors of the economy. By April 1933 the Finance Ministry's list of goods requiring import licenses included many non-agricultural items such as coal and coal products, and various chemicals.[67] The number of goods under import controls had grown steadily in 1933 and 1934. A dozen import control offices had already been created to administer the import program.

Schacht completed the process of controlling imports with his comprehensive New Plan of August 1934. In presenting the New Plan, Otto Sarnow at the Economics Ministry explained that "the method employed since March of this year of placing an ever greater range of goods under import controls has reached its conclusion with this arrangement in that now all import goods become controlled."[68] In controlling imports, Schacht relied on bilateral "clearing" agreements with foreign countries and Germany's own foreign exchange controls.[69] The Brüning government had imposed these controls with the Presidential Order on Foreign Exchange Control from August 1931 and the various ordinances issued from 1931 to 1932 to enforce the law. By May 1932, Brüning had limited German importers to 50 percent of their foreign exchange expended in 1930 to 1931. That order stood until February 1934, when Schacht began progressively reducing that limit, so that by July 1934 it was just 5 percent.[70] Beginning in September 1934, Schacht's new system of bilateral clearing agreements provided a systematic, country-by-country import control by controlling payments.[71] In the area of merchandise import controls proper, the New Plan built on the existing arrangements by doubling the number of import control offices. In addition, four of the existing Reich offices for various agricultural products simultaneously acted as control offices.[72]

Schacht's plan has been characterized as an attempt to "steer a national economy against the world economic trend."[73] That attempt completed the process of detaching an increasing number of commodities and then whole economic sectors from the world market, a process hesitantly begun four years earlier. Detachment began with that portion of the German economy most vulnerable to foreign competition – agriculture – but gradually spread to include all economic sectors. The Müller government began the process of extracting some portions of the German economy from the world market by establishing target prices for agricultural goods and the creation of sliding tariffs and a government corn monopoly as means to achieve those prices. Steadily deteriorating economic conditions forced subsequent governments into more radical measures for the preservation of German agriculture – radical tariffs under Brüning-Schiele, import quotas under Papen-Braun, and extensive new government monopolies under Hitler-Hugenberg. All of these measures were designed to uncouple the prices of German products (beginning with rye and wheat) from world market forces.

In the early phases of this process, many contemporary politicians and economists doubted the government's ability to isolate successfully German agricultural prices with the use of tariffs, quotas, and monopolies. In asking for new tariffs in March 1930, Dietrich had told the cabinet that "the whole [protective tariff] system cannot hold out for long." Brüning himself was convinced that "in the long run, [Germany] cannot maintain higher prices than in foreign countries" so that "in the long run, agriculture cannot be helped with high protective tariffs."[74]

Contrary to expectation, Germany was able to show remarkable success in disconnecting many agricultural prices and price developments from those of the world market.[75] The gap between wheat prices in Berlin and New York, which had been only 5.50 marks/ton in early 1929, widened to 82 marks in 1930, to 125 marks in 1931, and to 130 marks in 1932. By that time the gap between Berlin and Polish (Poznan) rye prices was 70 to 75 marks/ton.[76] As early as February 1930, Dietrich reported success in minimizing the price decline for rye. The price of rye in Berlin actually increased from 162 marks/ton in 1930 (monthly average) to 183 marks in 1931. By the end of 1930, Schiele reported that the use of tariffs "had succeeded in making the German grain market largely independent of the catastrophic consequences of world over-production."[77]

Commodities that had received protection somewhat later showed the benefits somewhat later as well. By early 1931 German butter prices exhibited a "certain loosening from the world market" as Fessler noted in his memorandum on The Effects of the Butter Tariff. German butter gained almost 3 percent in price (4 pfennigs) between November 1930 and January 1931, while the world price declined by almost 17 percent (21 pfennigs), pushing the price gap to 220 marks/ton.[78] Even items such as pork, which received protection relatively late and showed serious price declines from 1930 to 1931, remained well above world prices.[79] In 1932 German farmers earned some 2 billion marks of additional revenue from sales on the domestic market due to price increases brought on by import restrictions.[80] By March 1933, Hugenberg noted matter-of-factly that "German agricultural prices are standing on an artificial basis."[81] That artificial basis protected German farmers from the forces of the world market in agricultural products.[82] Artificial prices, marketing monopolies, and eventually full price controls protected Germany's economically most vulnerable sector from the risks of foreign action.

It was only the "tight regulation of its agricultural market" that allowed Germany to take in agricultural imports from those countries that accepted German exports, as the new economics desk officer in the chancellery, Franz Willuhn, noted.[83] Darré advocated the creation of new monopolistic Reich Offices for various agricultural products in December 1933 primarily because these established the preconditions for an effective German commercial policy: "It is not currently possible to conclude trade agreements with foreign countries using the heretofore usual commercial methods ... for that reason monopolies should be created which alone are suitable for the settlement of the import question." Posse vigorously supported these measures as "providing the only possibility for conducting a trade policy. Only via monopolistic regulations is it possible to conclude trade treaties."[84]

As successive German governments put increasing levels of domestic market protection in place, the Reich was able to accept agricultural and other imports without damaging domestic producers. That new ability was the key to a reactivated German trade policy in the Eastern Europe. Germany's ability and willingness to take agricultural and other primary products from the East was the key to various agreements concluded with Poland, Czechoslovakia, and the Soviet Union after 1932.

Notes

1. Dietrich to the DDP Assembly in Württemberg, BA Postdam R 901/63795, Bl. 138.
2. Carlo M. Cipolla, ed., *The Fontana Economic History of Europe* (New York, 1977), vol. 5, 510-11.
3. Charles Kindleberger, *The World in Depression 1929-1939* (Berkeley and Los Angeles, 1973), 134. Three months after Smoot-Hawley, Kraemer remarked to the Reichsverband that "the crisis of trade policy is not only a German crisis, it is a European and beyond that a world crisis," Main Committee meeting, 4 September 1930, Bayer-Archiv 62/10.5, Bd. 2.
4. For historical and theoretical literature on international economic regime change and stability see my earlier essay on the preconditions for applying international trade leverage, *International Organization* 45 (1991), 348 ff., especially note 13.
5. The worldwide economic downturn and resultant international price declines to which these policies were a response have been well described by economic historians. For contemporary documentation see several League of Nations publications: *World Economic Survey* (Geneva, annually); *Review of World Trade* (Geneva, annually); *Statistical Yearbook* (Geneva); *Monthly Bulletin of Statistics*; also Commodity Research Bureau, *Commodity Yearbook* (New York). Also League of Nations special studies: *The Agricultural Crisis*, 2 vols. (Geneva, 1931) and *The Course and Phases of the World Economic Depression* (Geneva, 1931). Detailed secondary studies include Vladimir Timoshenko, *World Agriculture and Depression* (Ann Arbor, Mich., 1953); W.A. Lewis, "World Production, Prices, and Trade 1870-1960," *Manchester School of Economic and Social Studies* 20 (1952), 105-38; J.W.F. Rowe, *Primary Commodities in International Trade* (Cambridge, 1965). Summaries of trade and price trends are available in Kindleberger, *World in Depression*, 97 ff., 143, 172, 188; Z. Drabek, "Foreign Trade Performance and Policy," in Kaser and Radice, eds., *Economic History of Eastern Europe 1919-1975*, vol. 1, 475 ff.
6. On these developments see Heinrich Liepmann, *Tariff Levels and the Economic Unity of Europe* (New York, 1938); League of Nations, *Tariff Level Indices* (Geneva,

1927) and *Commercial Policy in the Interwar Period: International Proposals and National Policies* (Geneva, 1942); H. Raupach, "The Impact of the Great Depression in Eastern Europe," *JCH* 4 (1969), 75-86; Ranki and Tomaszewski, "Role of the State in Industry, Banking, and Trade," in Kaser and Radice, eds., *Economic History of Eastern Europe,* vol. 2, 22 ff.

7. Cabinet meetings from 15 May and 1 June 1929, *Akten der Reichskanzlei, Kabinett Müller II,* [hereafter: *"Akten Müller"*], 656-660; Dietrich cabinet presentation to Chancellery State Secretary Pünder, 30 May 1929, BA R 43I/2425. On the possibility of Germany unilaterally annulling its treaty with Sweden (the "anchor" of agricultural rates for other German MFN treaties) see Fessler's memorandum of 13 June 1929, BA R 43I/2420.

8. *Akten Müller,* 771; Dietrich's 2 October report to Pünder on Trade Policy Committee discussions, BA R 43I/2420; cabinet meeting of 3 October, *Akten Müller,* 996.

9. World trade (as captured in the imports of 75 countries) fell by almost 40 percent in two years; from \$2,998 million in January 1929 to \$1,839 million in January 1931, League of Nations, *Monthly Bulletin of Statistics,* February 1934, 51 as cited in Kindleberger, *World in Depression,* 172.

10. On the other hand, the wisdom and efficacy of these protective tariffs is certainly open to question. The cumulative burden on income and payments caused by a spiral of tariff retaliation weighed down any international economic recovery. See, e.g., the discussion surrounding the Smoot-Hawley tariff in Kindleberger, *The World in Depression 1929-1939,* 133 ff.

11. League of Nations, *Commercial Policy in the Interwar Period,* 70.

12. League of Nations, *Quantitative Trade Controls. Their Causes and Nature* (Geneva, 1943), 16.

13. League of Nations, *Commercial Policy,* 72.

14. League of Nations, *Commercial Policy,* 71.

15. On the German-Balkan treaties see Holm Sundhaussen, "Politisches und Wirtschaftliches Kalkül in den Auseinandersetzungen über die deutsch-rumänischen Präferenzvereinbarungen von 1931," *Revue des Etudes Sud-Est Europeenes* 14 (1976), 405-24; Sundhaussen, "Die Weltwirtschaftskrise in Donau-Balkan-Raum und ihre Bedeutung für den Wandel der deutschen Aussenpolitik unter Brünning," in W. Benz and H. Graml, eds., *Aspekte deutscher Aussenpolitik im 20. Jahrhundert* (Stuttgart, 1976), 121-65; Hans-Jürgen Schröder, "Deutsche Südosteuropa-Politik 1929-1936," *Geschichte und Gesellschaft* 2 (1976), 5-32; William S. Grenzbach, Jr., *Germany's Informal Empire in East-Central Europe. German Economic Policy toward Yugoslavia and Rumania 1933-1939* (Stuttgart, 1988), 14 ff. On the larger question of great power economic rivalry in Balkans see David Kaiser, *Economic Diplomacy and the Origins of the Second World War* (Princeton, 1980); György Ranki, *Economy and Foreign Policy: The Struggle of the Great Powers for Hegemony in the Danube Valley 1919-1939* (Boulder, Co., 1983), 96 ff.

16. Karl Dietrich Erdmann and Hans Booms (hrsgs.), *Akten der Reichskanzlei. Das Kabinett von Papen* (Boppard, 1989), 844, note 2 [hereafter *"Akten Papen"*]. All of these developments should be set in the larger international context provided by the essays in Josef Becker and Klaus Hildebrand, eds., *Internationale Beziehungen in der Weltwirtschaftskrise 1929-1933* (Munich, 1980); Gustav Schmidt, *The Politics and Economics of Appeasement: British Foreign Policy in the 1930s* (New York, 1986); Franz Knipping, *Deutschland, Frankreich und das Ende der Locarno Ära 1928-1931: Studien zur internationalen Politik in der Anfangsphase der Weltwirtschaftskrise* (Munich, 1987); Robert Boyce, "World War, World Depression: Some Economic Origins of the Second World War," in Boyce and Esmonde Robertson, eds., *Paths to War: New Essays on the Origins of the Second World War* (New York, 1989).

17. Report by the Trade Policy Committee on "The Current Situation Regarding Import Quotas on Certain Agricultural Products," 12 December 1932, BA R 43I/1079.
18. League of Nations, *Commercial Policy*, 70-71.
19. Rene Erbe, *Die Nationalsozialistische Wirtschaftspolitik 1933-1939 im Lichte der modernen Theorie* (Zurich, 1958), 71. Petzina calls the "bilateralization of all foreign trade" one of the "most important consequences and characteristics of the 'New Plan'...," *Autarkiepolitik im Dritten Reich* (Stuttgart, 1968), 18.
20. League of Nations, *Commercial Policy*, 70.
21. BA R 43II/329.
22. Cabinet meeting of 4 October 1933, BA R 43II/301a.
23. David Kaiser has suggested that "Posse's proposals cleared the way for a revolution in German trade policy." That conclusion is too sweeping. More accurately, one might say that Posse proposals recognized the fundamentally changed nature of the *international* framework for German trade policy thereby clearing away *one* set of constraints on German trade policy, Kaiser, *Economic Diplomacy and the Origins of the Second World War*, 74.
24. Kaiser himself points out that domestic agricultural objections obstructed German trade policy in the Balkans through 1931 (*Economic Diplomacy*, 20 ff.), yet he does not explain how that opposition was overcome when "under the Nazi government, the Foreign Office and the Economics Ministry ... successfully implemented the policies they had first conceived in 1931 by concluding new, far reaching commercial agreements with the agricultural states of Southeastern Europe" (79-80). Sundhaussen treats German domestic agricultural opposition in 1931 more extensively, but like Kaiser, his closing remarks about Nazi successes being built on "the withdrawal of Germany from world trade" tell us nothing about the fundamental changes in German domestic politics and economics from 1931 to 1933 that underlay the Third Reich's active and successful trade policies in the East, "Weltwirtschaftskrise im Donau-Balkan-Raum," 162.
25. For some early insights into the increasing autonomy of late Weimar presidential cabinets (the gradual "divorce of government from the sphere of political interest-group politics") see T.W. Mason, "The Primacy of Politics – Politics and Economics in National Socialist Germany," reprinted in Henry Turner, ed., *Nazism and the Third Reich* (New York, 1972), 175-200, quotation on 179.
26. Cabinet meetings of 15 May and 1 June 1929, *Akten Müller*, 656-60; Dietrich cabinet presentation to Chancellery State Secretary Pünder, 30 May 1929, BA R 43I/2425. More radical plans for a government grain import monopoly as demanded by some agricultural groups (and some Social Democrats!) were rejected, ibid.; *Vorwärts*, 14 May 1929. According to Dietrich's 30 May presentation, grain prices/ton had fallen sharply: rye to 179 marks (1928 average = 239 marks), wheat to 204 marks (1928 = 234), and oats to 178 marks (1928 = 226).
27. *Akten Müller*, 771; Dietrich's 2 October report to Pünder on Trade Policy Committee discussions, BA R 43I/2420; cabinet meeting of 3 October, *Akten Müller*, 996.
28. The cautiously conservative Reichsverband initially opposed any tariff increases that might "endanger" either German exports or "Germany's painstakingly constructed post-war trade treaty system," industrial Reichsverband executive secretariat to the government from 28 September 1929, Reichsverband Vorstand Position on Commercial Policy, 19 September 1929, but agreed to some increases in Reichsverband (Ramhorst, von Brackel) to Fessler, 26 October, all in BA R 43I/2420.
29. Cabinet meeting of 24 June 1929, *Akten Müller*, 770; Fessler's notes on meeting of party leaders in the Agriculture Ministry, 12 November 1929, *Akten Müller*, 1137.

30. Fessler's notes on meeting of party leaders in the Agriculture Ministry, 12 November 1929; cabinet meetings of 18 and 19 November, *Akten Müller*, 1137, 1151, 1164. Dietrich's presentation of 19 November in BA R 43I/2420.
31. Hindenburg to Müller, 14 December, BA R 43I/2420. Cabinet meeting of 12 December and Dietrich's meeting with party leaders from 16 December, *Akten Müller*, 1250, 1265; *RGBl.* 1929, I, 227 ff.
32. Cabinet meeting of 15 May 1929, *Akten Müller*, 658, note 6.
33. After the final vote on the tariff legislation, Fessler noted how the plight of farmers had brought out "a certain solidarity of the whole people (das ganze Volk) in the interest of agriculture …," 13 January 1930, BA R 43I/2425. That solidarity did not include the leading industrial and commercial groups that opposed any agricultural tariff increases in the form of "sliding rates." At an 11 October 1929 meeting of the Commercial Policy Commission, the industrial Reichsverband urged an "unaltered extension of the [existing] tariff beyond 31 December 1929," PAAA Abt.IV. Zollwesen 4, Nr 1., Bd. 1. In a report to members on the new tariff, the German Chamber of Commerce cited the "objections of all business circles" to the sliding rates, 24 December 1929, RWWA 20-1131-7. The *Berliner Borsen-Courier* of 24 November 1929 called the sliding tariffs "a surprising plan" and lamented the government's "urge to experiment" in commercial policy, BA R 43I/2420.
34. Meeting of Reichstag party leaders, 16 December 1929, *Akten Müller*, 1265-66.
35. These measures were contained in the five laws and one ordinance of 26 March 1930, all in *RGBl.* 1930, I, 87-90. For the origin of these plans see Dietrich's meeting with agricultural interests, 5 March 1930, cabinet meetings of 7 March and 20 March 1930, *Akten Müller*, 1539-1543, 1546-1549, 1588-1589.
36. All three of these characterizations can be found in Karl Dietrich Bracher, *The German Dictatorship* (New York, 1970), 168-78 passim.
37. For literature detailing Hindenburg's role see, Karl Dietrich Erdmann and Hans Booms, hrsgs., *Akten der Reichskanzlei. Die Kabinette Brüning I und II* (Boppard, 1982), 1, note 1 [hereafter: "*Akten Brüning*"].
38. Dietrich's meeting with agricultural leaders, 5 March 1930, *Akten Müller*, 1539; Schiele to Brüning, 29 March 1930, *Akten Brüning*, 1-4.
39. *RGBl.* 1930, I, 131-135; cabinet meetings of 7 and 8 April, meeting of party leaders from 8 April, all in *Akten Brüning*, 23-40.
40. Fessler's 19 January 1931 notes on the demands of the Green Front and Schiele's position on those demands, *Akten Brüning*, 789.
41. Ordinances of 17 April, 22 May, and 26 September in *RGBl.* 1930, I, 1444, 175, 458; ordinance of 5 March 1931, *RGBl.* 1931, I, 62. New York and Posen prices cited in Manfred Nussbaum, *Wirtschaft und Staat in Deutschland während der Weimarer Republik* (Berlin (East), 1978), 343.
42. Fessler's memorandum of 22 May 1930, BA R 43I/2425.
43. *RGBl.* 1931, I, 101.
44. The comprehensive ordinance of 30 April 1931 included, e.g., a 90 percent tariff on pigs, *RGBl.* 1931, I, 139. On 19 January 1932 the butter tariff was increased to 100 marks/cwt., or 1,000 marks/ton, *RGBl.* 1932, I, 30
45. The failed attempt to arrange preference treaties with Hungary and Romania in the summer of 1931 had raised Reichsverband concern over Brüning's commercial policies (despite the earlier 1929 Reichsverband acknowledgement that German agriculture needed increased protection). A notice for the Reichsverband Vorstand meeting of 22 April 1932 warned of the "dangerous development that the conflict with Holland and the Scandinavian countries over the [increased] German butter tariff was taking," Bayer-Archiv 62/10.4. Despite a substantial body of very good work on the politics of economic policy in the Brüning cabi-

net, the role of industrial and commercial dissatisfaction with Brüning's commercial policies in Hindenburg's fateful dismissal of the chancellor has not yet been adequately explored.

46. *RGBl.* 1931, I, 101. Württemberg initially opposed the exclusion of the Reichsrat (upper house) from the modified procedure, but dropped its opposition in exchange for Reich government promises to aid that state's flax and forestry industries. Minister President Otto Braun in Prussia did not oppose Reichsrat exclusion. Pünder to various Reich ministries, 10 March 1931, Württemberg legation to the chancellery, 12 March 1931, both in BA R 43I/2421.

47. Dietrich's presentation to the cabinet, 27 October 1931 and cabinet response as recounted in Foreign Office State Secretary Bülow's memorandum to Chancellery Secretary Pünder, President Hindenburg, and all Reich ministers, 28 November 1931, BA R 43I/1086.

48. Foreign Office State Secretary Bülow's memorandum to Pünder, President Hindenburg, and all Reich ministers, 28 November 1931, BA R 43I/1086. The infamous Article 48, Sec. 2, which underlay all legislation after the collapse of a functioning parliamentary system, allowed the president to take any "necessary measures" to ensure the public order and security. These measures could be vetoed by a Reichstag majority. Cabinet minutes of 30 November 1931, BA R 43I/1086.

49. *RGBl* 1931, I, 689: "On the basis of Article 48, Paragraph 2 of the Reich Constitution it is ordered [that] ... Until the Reichstag returns to session, the Reich government is empowered in the event of pressing economic need, ... to order the temporary application of bilateral economic agreements with foreign countries." Those orders could be annulled by a subsequent Reichstag veto. *RGBl.* 1932, I, 121, 126. "Part Four. Tariff Changes and Temporary Application of Bilateral Economic Agreements." The 1934 Reciprocal Trade Agreements Act in the Unites States marked a similar shift in trade policy authority away from the legislature and toward the executive.

50. As early as 12 November 1930 Carl Duisburg had criticized German "official circles" for "sympathizing" with Balkan countries' proposals for preferential treaties. He noted that these treaties would have the "unavoidable consequence of provoking conflict with those countries that have not joined the [preferential system]." The chemical industry was not willing to risk relations with the rest of the world for the Balkan market that took only 3.4 percent of German chemical exports in 1929, "Die Zukunft der deutschen Handelspolitk," Bayer-Archiv 3/039. See also similar objections by the Reichsverband and German Chamber of Commerce cited in Grenzebach, *Germany's Informal Empire*, 15; Kaiser, *Economic Diplomacy*, 23; Sundhaussen, "Weltwirtschaftskrise in Donau-Balkan-Raum," 139.

51. Papen and Economics Minister Hermann Warmbold addressed the German Agricultural Council on 11 June 1932. German Agricultural Council to Papen, 16 June 1932, BA R 43I/1086. Cabinet meeting of 1 July 1932, BA R 43I/1086.

52. The call for an end to traditional liberal trade practices (MFN, long-term tariff treaties) had been a recurring demand of agricultural groups throughout the Weimar years. In an October 1925 letter to the Foreign Office, the Union of German Farmers' Associations (Vereinigung der deutschen Bauernvereine) warned that if trade treaties could not protect German farm interests, the group would urge that "international trade relations be placed on a completely different basis"; in a 1 March 1927 petition to the Chancellery, the Reichslandbund demanded an end to the practice of using MFN clauses in tariff treaties, PAAA Landwirtschaft 6, Landwirtschaftskammern und -verbände, Bd. 1. At the 61st annual meeting of the traditionally less radical German Agricultural Council a resolution con-

demned "the old methods of trade policy including the system of general MFN" as "no longer adequate for present times and the changed structure of the world economy," PAAA Landwirtschaft 6, Landwirtschaftskammern und -verbände, Bd. 2. On the these developments see Dieter Gessner, *Agrardepression und Präsidialregierungen in Deutschland 1930 bis 1933. Probleme des Agrarprotektionismus am Ende der Weimar Republik* (Dusseldorf, 1977), 31 ff.

53. Minutes of cabinet meetings of 1 July and 21 July 1932, BA R 43I 1086; Braun submitted a detailed plan to the cabinet on 24 August, BA R 43I/1176; minutes of cabinet meeting of 27 August 1932, *Akten Papen*, 457. Justice Minister Franz Guertner pointed out that in view of the existing treaties and other countries' probable reaction, the "legally permissible" qualification "made the [cabinet] resolution practically meaningless," Guertner to Chancellery State Secretary Erwin Planck, 3 September 1932, BA R 43I/1086.

54. Papen had bravely written to steel industrialist Hermann Röchling on 22 October that he "was prepared for defensive measures by the affected [foreign] states," BA R 43I/1176. However after hearing the foreign threats contained in the report of the German Quota Delegation that had sounded the Netherlands, Belgium, Italy, France, and Denmark on the possibility of German import restrictions, the cabinet dropped most of the quota plan and returned to the idea of tariff protection, cabinet meeting of 2 November, Papen's meeting with agricultural representatives, 5 November, *Akten Papen*, 851, 882; cabinet meeting of 3 November, BA R 43I/1177.

55. On these important issues, the leading industrial and commercial interest groups showed no sign of becoming radicalized by the experience of the Depression. On the contrary, they adhered with unimaginative tenacity to classic conservative policies. See Duisburg's defense of MFN in his November 1930 speech "Die Zukunft der deutschen Handelspolitik," Bayer-Archiv 3/039; a similar defense by the German Chamber of Commerce, 23 April 1931, BA R7 VI/350/2, cited in Grenzebach, *Informal Empire*, 15. As late as July 1932 the Reichsverband's Economic Program demanded that "the system of general mutual MFN must be maintained," and that MFN "should be supplemented as far as possible by bound tariff rates," BA Nachlass Kastl 5.

56. As Papen assumed the chancellorship in June 1932, Kraemer expressed the Reichsverband's "growing concern over misdirected tariff actions" by the German government, "Für Unternehmner-Risiko," *Vossische Zeitung*, 25 June 1932, Bayer-Archiv 62.10.5, Bd. 2. See also the Reichsverband's emphatic warning of June 1932 that "German commercial policy may not be used as a means of unilaterally terminating certain uncomfortable [foreign] commitments as the expense of [German] export interests," RdI report of a common position adopted by the Presidium, Vorstand and Main Committee, 25 June 1932, Bayer-Archiv, 62/10.5 By September, as Papen's plans for import controls became clear, the Reichsverband warned that "the decision of the Reich government to place import quotas on certain agricultural articles threatens to provoke a trade policy conflict [with other states] of huge proportions [grössten Ausmasses]." Kraemer outlined Reichsverband "efforts to avert this looming danger" at the Vorstand meeting of 22 September 1932, notice of meeting, 19 September 1932, Bayer-Archiv 62/10.4. Along these lines, the Reichsverband wrote to the chancellery at least six times on this issue between 22 September and 3 November 1932, including two telegrams from Krupp himself to the chancellor, see BA R 43I/1176 and 1177 for these and numerous other industrial and commercial protests against Papen's proposed import control policies.

57. See, e.g. Dieter Petzina's assessment: "In March 1933 the National Socialists still required the German National coalition partners for their own political goals, so

that concessions in agricultural policy were necessary, not least of all because here Hugenberg could count on Hindenburg's full support," "Hauptprobleme der deutschen Wirtschaft 1932-1933," *VfZ*, 15 (1967), 55.

58. Ministerial meeting of 2 March 1933, Konrad Repgen and Hans Booms (hrsgs.), *Akten der Reichskanzlei. Die Regierung Hitler* (Boppard, 1983), 152-155 [hereafter *"Akten Hitler."*]. "Hitler recognized very clearly the domestic political importance of a contented farm sector for the stability of the regime ... later [agricultural policy] took on the autarkization necessary for the war and the function of ideological innovation in the area of economic policy ...," Petzina, "Hauptprobleme," 55. On Nazi agricultural policies see Gustavo Corni, *Hitler and the Peasants. Agrarian Policy of the Third Reich, 1930-1939* (New York, 1990); Horst Gies's contribution on agricultural law in Dieter Rebentisch and Karl Teppe, eds., *Verwaltung contra Menschenführung im Staat Hitlers: Studien zum politisch-administrativen System* (Gottingen, 1986).

59. Hugenberg's ordinances of 8 February and 4 March 1933 increased rates generally by about 100 percent, *RGBl.* 1933, I, 55, 101. For background on these decisions see *Akten Hitler*, 55-56, 119.

60. *RGBl.* 1933, I, 166. On 27 February 1933, Hugenberg presented a memorandum to Chancellery Secretary Hans Lammers asking that the government make a "basic decision" about import quotas at the next cabinet meeting. Claiming that the "catastrophic agricultural conditions threatened the existence of the state and the maintenance of public tranquility, security, and order," Hugenberg urged the use of presidential powers under constitutional Article 48 ("endangerment of public security") to impose import quotas on butter, cheese, and horses, BA R 43II/329.

61. *RGBl.* 1933, I, 313.

62. *RGBl.* 1933, I, 1993-1994, 1104, 1109.

63. Darré's cabinet presentation from 8 December 1933, *Akten Hitler*, 1042, note 26.

64. "Treaties of the Reich with foreign countries, which affect objects of federal law, do not require the consent of those legislative bodies," *RGBl.* 1933, I, 141.

65. Joint presentation by Neurath, Hugenberg, Schwerin-Krosigk to Chancellery Secretary Lammers from 31 March 1933, BA R 43I/1086.

66. *Akten Hitler*, 296; *RGBl* 1933, I, 162-163: "The Reich government has adopted the following law which is hereby announced ... Article 1. The Reich foreign minister is empowered, in the event of pressing economic need, to order the temporary application of bilateral economic agreements with foreign countries."

67. BA R 7/3401.

68. Economics Ministry Assistant Secretary Otto Sarnow to the press, 2 September 1934, BA R 43II/331. Indeed, the domestic "cornerstone" of the plan was the imposition of "quantitative import limits on the total import volume," Rene Erbe, *Nationalsozialistische Wirtschaftspolitik*, 71. Petzina has noted that "the New Plan distinguished itself from the economic policy of the preceding years by moving beyond punctiform intervention toward a larger total concept," *Autarkiepolitik*, 19 In looking at Schacht's plan, Harold James has called attention to the fact that "the decision to ...restrict non-essential imports ... had been made ... already in 1931," James, *The German Slump*, 387.

69. For guides through the labyrinth of German foreign exchange controls as perfected by Schacht and assessments of their workings see United States Tariff Commission, *Foreign Trade and Exchange Controls in Germany*, Report No. 150 (Second Series), 1942; Frank Child, *The Theory and Practice of Exchange Control in Germany: A Study of Monopolistic Exploitation in International Markets* (The Hague, 1958); Larry Neal, "The Economics and Finance of Bilateral Clearing Agreements: Germany, 1934-8," *The Economic History Review*, Second Series, 32 (1979), 391-404;

Jonathan Kirshner, *Currency and Coercion: The Political Economy of International Monetary Power* (Princeton, 1995). On exchange clearing in general see Paul Einzig, *The Exchange Clearing System* (London, 1935); Margaret S. Gordon, *Barriers to World Trade* (New York, 1941); Nyboe Anderson, *Bilateral Exchange Clearing Policy* (London, 1946).

70. As a result of falling prices for imports and a deflation-inspired reduced demand for these goods, the 50 percent foreign exchange limit in 1932 probably did not in fact restrict imports. However, after the economic upturn of 1933, the exchange controls functioned as import controls as well, see Erbe, *Nationalsozialistische Wirtschaftspolitik*, 69 ff. The full merging of both functions is evident in the New Plan's decision to make the import control offices responsible for foreign exchange certificates.

71. According to the rules of the New Plan: "Foreign exchange certificates (Devisenbescheinigungen) are also required when the import will be paid for in Reichsmark via a Payments and Clearing Agreement," Economics Ministry Assistant Secretary Otto Sarnow to the press, 2 September 1934, BA R 43II/331.

72. See Economics Ministry Assistant Secretary Otto Sarnow to the press, 2 September 1934, BA R 43II/331.

73. Petzina, *Autarkiepolitik*, 18.

74. Cabinet meeting of 20 March 1930, *Akten Müller*, 481; Brüning at the ministerial meeting of 9 December 1930, *Akten Brüning*, 711.

75. Numerous and extensive regulations on the domestic economy also helped to support agricultural prices. Successive governments employed a wide variety of measures, including grain purchases by the government-owned Deutsche Getreide-Handelsgesellschaft and the compulsory use of domestic agricultural products, in conjunction with import restrictive policies in an effort to raise agricultural prices.

76. *Statistisches Jahrbuch für das deutsche Reich*, 1933, 115, 143, cited in Nussbaum, *Wirtschaft und Staat*, 343. At 100 marks/ton, the price gap for fodder barley was on the same scale as those for wheat and rye, Fessler memorandum of 22 May 1930, BA R 43I/2425.

77. Dietrich in cabinet meeting of 13 February 1930, *Akten Müller*, 1454; Jacobs und Richter, "Grosshandelspreise;" Schiele to Pünder, 5 December 1930, BA R 43I/2426.

78. Fessler's notes, 28 January 1931, BA R 43I/2426.

79. Nussbaum cites the *Statistisches Jahrbuch* (1931, 117 and 1933, 145) to show a gap between German (Berlin) and world (Copenhagen) pork prices of 535 marks/ton in 1932, *Wirtschaft und Staat*, 344.

80. Kindleberger, *The World in Depression 1929-1939*, 140. Similarly, Harold James estimates that increased wheat, rye, and barley tariff cost German consumers 1.86 billion marks in 1932, *The German Slump*, 282. These estimates vindicate Schiele's 1930 claim that he could recover 1.5 billion marks of the 3 billion loss in German farm incomes by increasing "inadequate tariffs," cabinet meeting of 7 April 1930, *Akten Brüning*, 27. Yet as Tilman Koops has pointed out, "the highly protective tariff policy of the Reich agriculture minister during the world economic crisis remained in the end ineffectual," *Akten Brüning*, XLIV.

81. Ministerial meeting of 2 March 1933, *Akten Hitler*, 152.

82. By the end of 1933 extensive price regulations had removed most of the domestic market mechanisms from German agriculture as well. According to Dieter Petzina, "The organization of the [agricultural] market was perfected through a number of laws and ordinances so that the room for entrepreneurial action by farmers, including the right of disposition over the farm, increasingly diminished" (*Autarkiepolitik*, 17). See, e.g. the Measures for Market and Price Regulation for

Agricultural Products, contained in the comprehensive agricultural law of 13 September 1933, *RGBl.* 1933, I, 626; the 26 September 1933 Law for Securing Grain Prices, *RGBl.* 1933, I, 667; the 29 September Ordinance on Grain Prices, *RGBl.* 1933, I, 707. Petzina argues that for some time Hugenberg's goal had been "the abolition of market economy relations in the agricultural sector," Petzina, "Hauptprobleme der deutschen Wirtschaftspolitik 1932/33," *VfZ* 15 (1967), 52.

83. Willuhn's memorandum, Summary of German Commercial Relations in 1934, 13 January 1935, BA R 43II/323.
84. Cabinet meeting of 15 December 1933, *Akten Hitler*, 1042.

Chapter Six

TRADE IN PREPARATION FOR WAR, 1930-1939

*T*he international economic context of world Depression greatly expanded the opportunities for German use of the Reich's productive powers and consuming capacities as international political levers. After 1930 German leadership redoubled its earlier efforts to use trade policy as the central tool of German foreign policy strategies. Echoing Stresemann, Brüning declared in May 1931 that "the strongest weapon[!] Germany has for its foreign relations is the fact that we are an importer of agricultural goods." For that reason, he argued, Germany would have to orient its tariff and trade policies more closely toward larger foreign policy requirements.[1] Brüning's government did not differ from its predecessors in its plans for a trade-based foreign policy in Eastern Europe. But a marked difference between pre-1930 and post-1930 German governments lay in the ability of these later German governments to achieve progressively larger portions of their ambitious goals for trade policy.

The evolution of new international and domestic frameworks from 1930 to 1934 allowed the German governments from Brüning through Hitler to shape German trade flows effectively and to use these changing shapes to acquire economic and political advantages abroad. Already in 1932 Brüning could show some success in using the new frameworks to obtain a politically motivated trade deal with Poland and to extract significant trade surpluses from Czechoslovakia. Brüning's successes contrasted sharply with Stresemann's repeated failure to secure a trade agreement with Poland as part of his larger strategy for German political rehabilitation.

Notes for this chapter begin on page 279.

As in so many other areas, Hitler adopted existing trade structures and practices, intensified and energized them, and harnessed them to his own monstrous goals. The Nazis greatly accelerated the domestic movements toward economic protection and political authoritarianism that had been underway since 1930. The culmination of these trends in 1934 (New Plan, Gleichschaltung) made it easier for Hitler to direct German trade in the interest of his ultimate goals than it had been for Brüning to control trade in the interests of his governmental program during the early stages of these developments in 1931 and 1932. Yet the "new" instruments used by Hitler and Schacht to control trade – import monopolies, preferential treaties, and foreign exchange controls – were all developed and employed by the Reich before 1933. So, too, the successful use of trade policy for Germany's political advantage under these new frameworks is evident in Brüning's 1932 trade deal with Poland.

In Hitler's world view, Germany's problems could be solved only by the conquest of additional living space. Poland, Czechoslovakia, and the Soviet Union all occupied territory upon which Hitler planned to settle Germanic farmers after destroying the existent state structures and removing the existing populations.[2] No foreign economic policy adopted by the existing Reich -neither autarky or intensified foreign trade – could provide for the "necessary" population increase of the German people. In this view, economic policies were only temporarily more or less useful to the extent they allowed Germany to prepare a war of conquest as a more permanent solution to its fundamental economic limitations.[3]

Hitler generally succeeded in using trade policy for diplomatic, strategic, and even military gains in Eastern Europe because the international and domestic frameworks of the 1930s, which he helped create, were more conducive to this use of trade policy than they had been at any time since the 1880s. Yet within these contexts Hitler succeeded because his worldview determined that trade policy could be only a means toward his ultimate end. Unlike any other previous chancellor, Hitler knew from the time he took office that ultimately he and Germany would stand or fall with the outcome of a major war of conquest. With this knowledge, Hitler could ignore the economic consequences of his trade policy decisions and he understood that only Germany's most immediate and intractable economic problems constrained his use of trade in Eastern Europe.[4]

Hitler's tactical flexibility and willingness to employ any means at his disposal in order to achieve his ends are quite rightly often cited as keys to his success both before and after 1933.[5] One means at his disposal in the conduct of foreign policy was German foreign trade.

Protected from foreign competition, reinvigorated by rearmament, and wielded by an authoritative executive, Germany's productive and consumptive powers were particularly suited to influencing European states ravaged by the Depression. Hitler's own ideas on the use of trade for diplomatic gain were made clear as early as April 1933 when he told the cabinet that "foreign policy interests precede domestic economic interests ... Germany must make economic concessions if political interests determine that."[6] Under these circumstances, one could well expect the successful employment of German trade power in Eastern Europe.

Hitler was willing and able to direct German trade policy in accordance with the diplomatic and strategic needs of enabling Germany to launch a war of conquest. Since that goal had different needs in different countries at different times, Hitler flexibly employed different trade policies for different effects in different countries.[7] Poland received generous trade and payments agreements from Germany as a lubricant for smoother political relations from 1933 to 1936. The same is true for the Soviet Union in 1939. Czechoslovakia was given only what was required to maintain economic peace. Germany's newfound ability to import agricultural and forestry products such as butter, eggs, timber, and hops from Eastern Europe underlay all of these agreements.

Severe trade sacrifices were ordered when Hitler's diplomatic and strategic plans called for them. Germany signed trade and payments agreements with Poland that Schacht resisted and clearly felt Germany could not afford. Similarly, in 1939 Hitler committed Germany to massive exports of sophisticated equipment and weapons to the USSR in order to obtain Soviet "cover" for his invasion of Poland at a time when German industrial capacity was already desperately strained by the rearmament burden. On the other side, in 1935 Schacht lost a chance to secure large-scale, long-term deliveries of badly needed Soviet materials when Hitler, before having heard detailed Soviet requests, refused to allow armaments exports to the USSR.[8]

Poland

At several December 1931 meetings in both Warsaw and Berlin the Brüning government informed the Poles that Germany no longer planned to ratify the trade treaty signed in March 1930.[9] The Poles responded with a series of tariff increases and import bans designed to reduce German exports to Poland to from 315 million zlotys in 1931 to 100 million zl. (45 million to 50 million marks) in 1932. On 19 January Germany imposed a new 70 percent tariff surcharge on butter imports from those countries lacking trade treaties with Germany, including, of course, Poland.[10] When the German envoy in Warsaw, Hans Adolf von Moltke, held a bitter, negative conversation with Foreign Minister August Zaleski in late January 1931, German-Polish relations had sunk to their lowest point since 1925. The situation worsened further on 19 March when Germany ordered the imposition of its new Obertarif (super tariff) on a wide range of Polish goods.[11]

Despite these setbacks in German-Polish relations, Brüning, Moltke, and the Foreign Office felt that Germany had important political reasons for reaching some type of trade accommodation with Poland at this time. Moltke had already pointed out the political advantages that Poland had gained by ratifying the 1930 treaty when Germany had not.[12] Since the summer of 1931 Poland had been working "with all its power for an Eastern Locarno" – something that all members of the German foreign policy establishment were determined to avoid. Zaleski's recent speeches "show how effectively Poland's superior position of having ratified the treaty while we did not can be exploited for these larger political goals." Moltke suspected that at this point, the Poles might even prefer to continue playing the role of "martyr" for their own political gain rather than sign a new treaty. "For this reason alone it appears desirable to remove an effective propaganda tool from Polish hands by ending the tariff war." Chronically poor German-Polish economic relations made it more difficult for Polish leader Josef Piłsudski to fend off the old "right-wing" (Polish National Democrats) proposal that Poland reach an understanding with Russia and then direct its remaining hostility primarily toward Germany. In addition, the economic factor continued to play a role, although now clearly a secondary one. Germany still had to defend its market share in Poland, which was declining once again; in 1931 Germany supplied only 24 percent of Polish imports (1928 = 27 percent).[13] Despite the ravaged state of the Polish economy, a trade agreement would bring some increase in German exports. German Foreign Office Eastern Department Director Richard Meyer advanced Moltke's ideas of a German-Polish trade rapprochement to State Secretary Bülow with the recommendation that "out of general political considerations" Germany open new trade talks. Bülow understood the primarily political character of any negotiations, calling them "a gesture." In a hand-written note, Bülow, citing the "domestic political significance of the question," referred the decision to Brüning.[14]

Since late 1930, Brüning had subordinated all economic policy decisions to his goal of obtaining a radical and permanent reparations revision. In a "go for broke" fulfillment policy far in excess of Wirth's in 1922, Brüning sought to demonstrate through good will that Germany could not pay the amounts demanded from it. One aspect of the government's strategy had been to "force German exports at any price, not only to pay for reparations, but rather to make the effect of these reparation payments clear."[15] The new trade problems with Poland, based on German refusal to ratify the 1930 agreement, left the government vulnerable to charges that it was not doing all that could be done to maintain the Reich's ability to pay. With the major reparations conferences of 1932 on the horizon, Brüning needed the type of "gesture" toward Poland that Bülow was suggesting.[16]

On 2 March 1932 the Trade Policy Committee agreed that Germany should open negotiations with Poland for the purpose of rolling back the tariff increases and import bans introduced since 1 January 1932.[17] Negotiating in Warsaw, Moltke concluded an agreement on 26 March in which Poland promised not to institute any new measures discriminating against German goods. Further, Poland would accept German exports for 80 million zl. in 1932. In view of the ravaged Polish economy's inability to pay for much more than this amount, 80 million had the same practical effect as fully rescinding the import restrictions. In exchange Germany canceled its plans to impose its super tariff on other Polish goods, specifically eggs, and replaced the super tariff rate on Polish butter (170 marks/ton) with the German "autonomous" duty of 100 marks.[18]

At the German Foreign Office, Emil Wiehl's "objective" assessment labeled the economic concessions on each side "roughly equal." He then went on to point out that "the decisive importance of the agreement lies less in the economic than in the political sphere. The conclusion of the agreement was determined primarily by the wish of the chancellor to avoid a worsening of commercial and therewith also political relations with Poland at the moment in view of the upcoming major foreign policy decisions." Moltke noted that the agreement "eased for us the uncomfortable situation that had arisen as a result of not ratifying the [1930] trade treaty."[19]

Brüning's ability to obtain a politically motivated trade agreement with Poland contrasts sharply with Stresemann's frustrated experiences in the 1920s. Germany's new economic and political bases for trade policy allowed Brüning to do what his Weimar predecessors could not. The international wave of protectionism allowed Agriculture Minister Schiele's high tariff walls to create a protected base for German farmers. That level of protection was already sufficiently large to give Brüning room to make tariff concessions on some Polish products – concessions that meant Polish farm exporters would still pay twice the butter duty of 1931 and an egg duty higher than the old rate during the period of no agreement.[20] Politically, the independence of the cabinet from the Reichstag allowed the ministerial majority to override Schiele's objections to butter concessions without fear of coalition breakup and governmental collapse. That immunity from immediate political repercussions also allowed the government to dispense with presenting the deal to the Reichstag at all by framing the agreement as an "exchange of notes" between the two countries.[21]

After January 1933, Hitler also had political motives for concluding some type of trade agreement between the two countries. The tariff issue was only one in a recent series of problems in Danzig's relations with Poland that, in turn, strained German-Polish relations. Combined with Hitler's assumption of the chancellorship and the tumultuous political events in the Reich, tension over Danzig produced a wave of nervous uncertainty about German-Polish relations in 1933.[22] At the same time, Hitler was already preparing his first bold moves in the larger international diplomatic context – withdrawing from the League of Nations and the disarmament conference in October 1933. "Under these circumstances it would make sense to develop better relations, or at least reduce tension, with Poland to offset any possible danger in the West."[23]

On 30 August 1933 Moltke suggested that Germany undertake comprehensive economic discussions with Poland for the purpose of ending the eight-year tariff war between the two countries. Timely negotiations might at least forestall Polish application of its new tariff, scheduled for 11 October, against Germany and prevent a worsening of economic relations. Moltke felt progress could be made if Germany offered to conduct only reciprocally based (i.e., balanced) trade with Poland over the upcoming year.[24] After discussion by the Trade Policy Committee on 21 September, the Foreign Office informed Moltke on 25 September that the committee "shared the opinion that economic negotiations should be rekindled with Poland now as part of a policy designed to decrease tension in German-Polish relations." Despite "serious reservations" about the precedent this might set for German trade relations with other countries, the Reich could even reluctantly agree to the principle of balanced trade "so that the negotiations will not immediately be put onto a dead track again by an argument over the size of the German trade surplus."[25]

By the time German-Polish trade negotiations opened in October 1933, they had become inextricably bound up with foreign policy decisions of the highest level. Most immediately, Hitler would use a new trade agreement with Poland to calm European fears caused by Germany's withdrawal from the League and the European disarmament conference.[26] More significantly, Hitler was already laying the groundwork for the German-Polish nonaggression treaty of January 1934.[27] In October 1933, Hitler had told a closed meeting of NSDAP leaders that he would "sign any treaty of any sort to postpone war until he was ready for it."[28] The nonaggression declaration with Poland would serve as the cornerstone of this strategy. It "broke the ring of French alliances around Germany" while at the same time "at home and abroad the Hitler government could point to this diplomatic triumph as a sign of its peaceful intentions ..."[29] Yet Poland certainly could not be expected to sign the nonaggression agreement Hitler was advancing until and unless the key issues in the long-standing tariff war had been resolved. After an interministerial meeting in Hitler's [chancellor's] office on 16 November, Economics Minister Kurt Schmitt and Bülow prepared to instruct Moltke that "as a parallel to the political negotiations, we are also prepared for cooperation in the economic field, on a more extensive scale than heretofore."[30]

For these reasons Hitler himself ordered major economic concessions by Germany in order to obtain the desired treaty. The talks preceded smoothly until mid-October, when the Poles raised the old issue of sending Polish Silesian coal into Germany as part of the deal. German Foreign Minister Constantin von Neurath felt "that the importation of coal from Upper Silesia could not be permitted" and that "if the Poles took an intransigent attitude, the breaking-off of the negotiations had to be expected." Hitler was similarly disinclined to accept any coal, but did not want the negotiations to fail. He "thought it very important ... that consideration be given as to whether concessions could not be made to the Poles in other fields in the interest of avoiding a breaking-off of negotiations."[31] When the trade negotiations reached a dead end over the coal issue in mid-November 1933, Hitler instructed his ministers "that the negotiations were not to founder on the coal question." Neurath noted that Hitler and the ministers "agreed ... that a way out should be sought."[32] These decisions to adopt a more forthcoming stance in the economic negotiations cleared the way for both the German-Polish nonaggression agreement of January 1934 and the economic agreements signed in Warsaw on 7 March 1934.

The package of economic agreements consisted of a Protocol on Economic Relations, a veterinary agreement with secret appendices, and secret lists of import quotas. In the protocol, both countries terminated all measure of trade warfare still in force, some dating from 1926. Over 100 German export items were freed from anti-German discriminatory measures. The veterinary agreement ended the de facto prohibition against the transport of Polish animals through the

Reich. In the unpublished appendices to the veterinary agreement Germany granted special, preferential terms for Polish livestock entering the Reich. Finally, in the confidential quota schedules each country set out commodity-specific levels of imports that would be permitted. The notes of Franz Willuhn, economics desk officer in the chancellery, make clear that the German government considered this first agreement as the basis for other agreements to follow.[33]

Economic relations between the two countries took another small step forward in October 1934 when the two countries signed an agreement arranging the first government-organized exchanges since the formal end of trade hostilities in March. In the published portion of this 11 October agreement, Poland lifted the export duty on timber destined for Germany and agreed to apply its lowest tariff rates to a wide variety of German manufactured exports with guaranteed import quotas on some items. Germany agreed to employ its lowest rates on a list of Polish products and promised to give "Polish interests proper consideration in the import of butter, eggs, and geese."[34] The unpublished portion of the agreements outlined the import quotas for these items.

These trade concessions were an indispensable part of Hitler's near-term policy of political and economic reconciliation with Poland.[35] The German concessions centered on the very same commodities that had repeatedly obstructed an agreement in the 1920s – Polish butter, eggs, livestock, and coal exports to Germany. Now, however, the protected German economy and the one-party state were quite fully in place. Those new German economic and political frameworks ensured that Hitler would encounter no domestic problems in his use of new international tools such as preferences and quotas to shape German foreign trade for political advantage.

The success of official government negotiations also revived industrial interest in a private-sector agreement that would regulate trade between the two countries in iron and steel products. In October 1933 industrialists from both countries met to update the agreement they had reached in 1928 but had never implemented, owing to Germany's failure to ratify the trade treaty of 1930.[36] A functioning private-sector agreement on trade in iron and steel broadened and deepened the short-term political and economic reconciliation of the two countries after 1933.[37]

Even after both countries had ended hostile trade measures and had concluded the first government-negotiated exchanges, the German government sought to extend further both the economic and political aspects of German-Polish commercial relations. The absence of a comprehensive trade treaty between the two countries remained a central problem. The so-called Barter Agreement of 11 October 1934 had been constructed too narrowly to cover the full volume of bilateral trade. Moltke's lengthy review of the situation in January 1935 prompted a Foreign Office policy statement in the form of a circular composed by Ritter.[38] The Polish government had taken "advantage of the fact that the [trade] balance was momentarily in Germany's favor to suspend most of the autonomous import quotas" in the two 1934 agreements. Further, substantial German imports of Polish timber were taking place outside of the agreement which "render the Agreement meaningless and purposeless because the Poles, in so far as they area still taking any German goods at all, are trying to offset them with Polish products that Germany is not particularly interested in importing." As a result of these problems "the question arises whether the time has not arrived to place German-Polish economic relations on a broader and sounder basis than is provided for by the present agreements. From the point of view of our general policy vis-à-vis Poland, it would in any case be desirable to clarify our economic relations and if possible to extend them." In any comprehensive agreement Poland would insist on either fully balanced trade or a surplus in its favor – an issue that had been avoided in the March 1934 talks. The Foreign Office still opposed the idea of a guaranteed balance, both as a matter of "general policy" and for "commercial reasons."[39]

On the political side, the Foreign Office recognized that it remained "important ... to continue to cultivate and develop general political relations with Poland in accordance with the Führer and Chancellor's instructions ..." Yet Ritter cautioned that "there is, as matters stand, little reason to express this ... political attitude in terms of unilateral economic favors and services unless Poland is also prepared to give us greater opportunities for development in the economic sphere."[40] The economics and agriculture ministries agreed with the Foreign Office assessment that Germany ought not to offer unilateral economic favors to Poland out of political motivations.[41]

In the spring of 1935 the Poles were also seeking a solidification of German-Polish relations.[42] On 11 April Polish Embassy Councillor Lubomirski visited Richard Meyer, director of the German Foreign Office's Eastern Department, explaining that "Warsaw was gripped by anxiety about the pause in economic negotiations between Germany and Poland. This circumstance, which was being exploited by the opposition press, was also politically undesirable and could lead to repercussions on the good relations between Germany and Poland." According to Lubomirski, Foreign Minister Jozef Beck himself "set great store by a very quick resumption of economic negotiations in Warsaw."[43] Lubomirski suggested an agreement for balanced trade that excluded German obligations for the railroad traffic through the corridor, i.e., exactly the Polish offer that Ritter had already internally declared undesirable. On April 26 the Trade Policy Committee agreed that the Polish offer "should not be rejected in principle," but that "every effort should be made during the negotiations" to get German railroad payments included in the 1:1 trade ratio. At the same time, the German reply "should be couched in such terms so as not to exclude the possibility of a comprehensive settlement of future German-Polish relations."[44]

The economic negotiations opened in Warsaw on June 28, with Hans Hemmen of the Foreign Office Economics Department leading the German delegation and Miezyslaw Sokolowski, Director of the Commercial Department in the Polish Ministry for Industry and Commerce, heading the Polish team. Bülow reported to Neurath and Hitler that the opening phases of the talks had gone well. Hemmen convinced the Poles that "the current political and neighborly relations between Germany and Poland" required a "broad" economic agreement, not the limited MFN proposal the Poles had brought with them.[45] After three weeks the talks became stalled over three material issues that were "endangering an agreement, or making one appear impossible." First, the Poles demanded that Germany pay the same high prices (i.e., above world market price) for the most important Polish agricultural products (butter, lard, eggs, cheese) that the Reich had already agreed to pay other countries.[46] In light of Reichsbank's strapped foreign currency position, the Economics Ministry opposed granting these higher prices, which amounted to 6 million marks.[47] Second, in "the coal question," the Poles sought agreement in principle that Germany would accept Polish coal to offset any trade balance that might develop in Germany's favor. After the recent reintegration of the coal-producing Saar area into Germany, the Economics Ministry opposed this concession as well. On the third issue, the transfer of payments for corridor railroad traffic, the German Economics Ministry insisted that the corridor payments problem be solved in this agreement by including those sums in the 1:1 trade ratio. The Foreign Office had suggested compromise solutions for each problem, but Economics Ministry remained firm.[48]

Bülow posed the obvious question: "whether these points are of such importance in relation to the totality of our political and economic relations with Poland as to warrant letting them, should the occasion arise, wreck our economic negotiations with Poland." The answer was reserved for Neurath and Hitler, but Bülow's own "observations" recommended making the necessary economic concessions in order to secure valuable political gain. "Our present political relations with Poland have become an important factor in Germany's foreign policy as a whole. The permanence of these political relations may be endangered or at least impaired if economic relations between the two countries – far from being satisfactory – continue to be strained and even unfriendly."[49] On 25 July Neurath informed Hitler that, in his opinion, the "overall political-economic relations" with Poland required that "a failure of the economic negotiations must be avoided if at all possible." Consequently, he had given orders for Germany to make compromise proposals.[50]

One month later, Bülow was again forced to appeal for a decision from Hitler to resolve an impasse in the Polish negotiations. In further negotiations with the Poles, the German delegation had narrowed the outstanding differences on agricultural prices from the earlier sum of 6 million marks down to only 500,000 marks. Yet Schacht's Economics Ministry still refused to agree to these higher prices; refused to accept any Polish coal imports; and continued to insist on the inclusion of the railroad payments in the trade balance. Schacht's ministry had made the situation more difficult by refusing further cash payments for German orders involving the "finishing of semifinished goods" in Danzig, an issue of 6.25 million marks. Since "no further negotiations with Poland on these four questions will be possible until the Reich Ministry for Economics changes its present negative attitude," Bülow asked for a "discussion with the Führer" at which both Foreign Office representatives and Schacht would be present.[51] At a meeting with Ritter two days later, Schacht gave way on these points, apparently on direct orders from Hitler, as Bülow noted: "The high-level conference under Chairmanship of the Chancellor ... has, at least temporarily, become superfluous. To everyone's surprise, [Reichsbank] President Schacht has given way on the main points outstanding. What may be the cause of this sudden volte face cannot be definitely ascertained. Presumably he received instructions from the Chancellor (who had probably been approached on the matter by a third party) not to let the economic negotiations with Poland fail."[52]

In mid-September 1935 the negotiations stalled again, this time over the technicalities of payment procedures.[53] Hitler again intervened to bring about German financial concessions. Neurath told delegation leader Hemmen that out of "general political considerations" the negotiations could not be broken off; "the Führer himself had declared that the negotiations should not founder on this point." Neurath instructed Hemmen to inform Schacht of Hitler's views on this problem.[54]

Even as Germany's foreign currency situation worsened to a "catastrophic" point in mid-October 1935, the political pressure for a successful agreement mounted.[55] Piłsudski's death in May had created a "psychological void" in Poland and deprived the government of a recognized authority figure who had supported the thaw in relations with Hitler's Germany.[56] The new Polish cabinet was an unpredictable collection of military chauvinists such as Colonel Adam Koc and Marshall Edward Rydz-Smigly surrounded by "numerous opponents of the current policy toward Germany." Moltke pointed out how important it could be "if the new cabinet right at the beginning of its activity could be brought to a positive attitude toward Germany by the conclusion of an [economic] treaty so meaningful for German-Polish relations in their totality."[57] When the Polish government agreed to the German compromise suggestion of conducting reciprocal (balanced) merchandise trade via a clearing agreement, the Economics Ministry and Reichsbank reluctantly agreed to the other concessions necessary for an agreement.[58]

On 4 November in Warsaw, Moltke and Hemmen, Miezyslaw Sokolowski, and Beck's assistant Jan Szembek signed three agreements regulating trade and payments between the two countries: an economic treaty (including a secret protocol and exchange of notes), a payments agreement for merchandise trade (including secret protocol and exchange of notes), and a secret trade agreement (Warenabkommen).[59] Under the terms of the agreements, Germany finally received MFN treatment in the Polish market – something Weimar Germany had never had. In addition, Germany received the guarantee that trade would be balanced 1:1 at the level of 176 million zl. (83 million marks) and paid for in clearing payments only through official government offices: the Deutsche Verrechnungskasse and an agency yet to be named by the Poles. For Germany, balanced trade allowed an effective increase in German exports of 60 million zl., putting an end to recent Polish trade surpluses (53 million zl. in 1934). Bilateral clearing provided a way for the Reich to obtain the raw materials it desired (flax, additional timber, some ironwares, zinc and zincwares, fertilizers) without paying foreign currency for them.[60] In addition, the Poles allowed Germany to pay for 11.5 million zl. worth of "finishing work" in Danzig with merchandise instead of foreign currency.

On the other side, Germany gave quite a lot in these agreements. Not only did the Reich agree to accept agricultural products in which it had little real interest (grain, peas, sugar beets, mustard seed), it also agreed to pay 1.25 millin zl. in higher than world market prices for some items, such as butter and eggs.[61] The Reich had also been unable to incorporate the costs of transit services, transit trade, and the "additional costs" of bilateral trade into the payments agreement as the Economics Ministry had desired; these services still required cash payments. Nor had Germany managed to include the payments for railroad use in the corridor in the balanced trade deal. As a result of these invisible outflows from Germany to Poland, a German payments deficit of 75 million zl. annually was virtually assured – a deficit that Germany was finding difficult to pay already in 1935. Finally, the Reichsbank had been required to supply 10 million zl. for the bridge loan to cover the transition to the new payments system.

If the economic costs to Germany were considerable, so, too, were the political gains. The *Deutsche diplomatische-politische Korrespondenz* praised the creation of MFN status between the two countries after fifteen years as the economic expression of the *Neuordung* of relations between the Germany and Poland. Economic normalization was a "useful, practical result of the desire for political understanding (politischer Verständigungsbereitschaft)." The more sophisticated *Ost Express* understood that the treaty's "importance lies not only in the economic sphere, but much more in the political sphere," because the normalization of trade "supports the general political reconciliation" between the two countries. The Polish *Kurjer Poznanski* reported from Berlin that "the German side evaluates the treaty primarily on the basis of the general international situation and sees it as a political step."[62] Neurath expressed to Hemmen and Moltke his "great satisfaction" at hearing of the successful treaty conclusion. Moltke pointed out how the treaty would fortify the position of Beck as a leader in the new Polish cabinet. The German investment in Beck paid repeated dividends to the Reich over the following years.[63]

Negotiations for a settlement of the still unresolved corridor traffic payments problem dragged on through 1936. Schacht especially resisted the idea of the Germany paying cash (either Reichsmarks or zloty) for Polish rail services. He exasperated the Poles by repeatedly delaying, avoiding, obfuscating, and canceling negotiations on the subject.[64] Hitler had been content to let the issue simmer until the matter took on potentially serious consequences in the wake of the Rhineland crisis. In mid-March Hermann Göring and Hitler both became involved, apparently having decided that the matter must be settled.[65] On Göring's initiative a German delegation traveled to Warsaw on 6 April and the next day signed a generous preliminary agreement for a payments plan with the Poles. The Reich agreed to pay 1.8 million marks (almost 4 million zl.) in cash to the Bank Polski in May 1936 and 1.5 million marks (3.2 million zl.) monthly thereafter.[66] On 9 April Schacht protested vigorously that he was "unable to agree to the preliminary agreement under any circumstances," and that deal had been signed without waiting for his views. The agreement certainly went well beyond anything Schacht or the Foreign Office would have supported.[67] Göring later admitted that "on account of considerations of foreign policy" he had considered it necessary to "met the Polish desires to so great an extent."[68] Once again, for political reasons, Hitler had stretched the Reich finances to breaking point, overriding the protests of his financial "wizard," Schacht.

With these agreements from 1934 to 1936, Hitler, Neurath, and Schacht put in place the structure that would manage German Polish trade until September 1939. In 1936 German-Polish trade balanced almost exactly; Poland imported 143 million zl. in merchandise from Germany and exported 145 million zl. in goods to the Reich. Future trade would be managed by the "government committees" of each country (Regierungsausschusse) established by Article seventeen of the November 1935 trade treaty. The committees met frequently to jointly manage the development of trade and payments under the treaty, setting the terms (prices and amounts) for the commodities to be exchanged under the annual confidential "trade agreements." In July 1936 both parties indicated their willingness to extend the existing arrangement by allowing the terms of delivery or payment for trade deals signed while the treaty was in force to extend beyond the treaty limit if necessary; the same would apply to any deals required to balance accounts at the end of the payments agreement.[69]

In February 1937 the two countries signed a renewal of the November 1935 treaty, extending the terms through February 1939. According to the official German Reporting Service (Deutsche Nachrichtenbüro) the new treaty would "stabilize economic relations for a longer period."[70] The Poles went through the formality of agreeing to bind their tariff rates on some German exports for that period, but with all trade managed by the government committees on the basis of the annual trade agreement, tariff concessions were no longer the point of these negotiations. The new annual trade agreement called for balanced trade of 176 million zl. in 1937. The actual levels of trade (German exports = 173 million zl., imports = 182 million zl.) show how well and comprehensively these agreements controlled trade between the two countries. Both parties also extended the clearing agreement between the two countries administered by the Deutsche Verrechnungskasse and Poland's newly-created clearing agency, the Polski Instytut Rozrachunkowy.[71] The agreement was expanded slightly to include payments for business travel, pate fees, and licenses, and finishing costs. On 2 July 1938 the treaty was reworked to accommodate the incorporation of Austria into the Reich and re-signed by State Secretary Ernst von Weizsäcker and Polish Ambassador Jozef Lipski. The new treaty was scheduled to run through 28 February 1941.[72] In the words of the German reporting Service "an intensified upswing can be expected."[73]

Czechoslovakia

The protectionist policies to which both Germany and Czechoslovakia resorted in 1930 ended whatever slim chance there had been that these two countries might finally sign a tariff treaty that could give some firm substance to the general MFN treaty of 1920. The swing toward protectionism in Czechoslovakia was every bit as sharp and rapid as in Germany. Both countries implemented roughly even, and astronomical, rises in tariff rates from 1930 to 1932. The Germans had imposed a government corn monopoly in early 1930; Czechoslovakia began requiring import licenses for rye and barley that summer. German foreign exchange controls had come earlier (July 1931), but the Czechoslovak foreign exchange controls of September 1931 were both more comprehensive and more restrictive. These policies lead to a dramatic reduction in two-way trade from a level of 1,187 million marks in 1928 to just 350 million in 1932.[74] While trade collapsed, both governments attempted to shift the bulk of the blame for the deteriorating situation onto the other. Each new protectionist measure was perceived by the other party as directed specifically against them and their exports. Both governments accused the other of employing discriminatory policies and adopting measures that violated their MFN guarantees well before either side in fact began to practice such discrimination.[75]

Between 1930 and 1933, the Reich found no special political or economic motives for seeking an improvement in this trade relationship. German political relations with Czechoslovakia had been polite and without any special rancor through 1929 and largely continued in that vein even after the economic downturn. In contrast to German-Polish relations, the German-Czechoslovak relationship was not in need of repair. The Reich could gain little diplomatic capital from any additional warming in relations that might be arranged. At the same time, the existence of the 1920 trade treaty meant that on the formal level at least German-Czechoslovak trade relations were already in order. A dramatic thaw in German-Czechoslovak trade relations was not possible; nor would any improvements in trade relations produce great effects on either the bilateral relationship or the larger European perception of German foreign policy.

In the economic context of Europe from 1929 to 1932, Germany had no reason to be dissatisfied with the development of German-Czechoslovak trade during these years. Although the value and volume of trade had been greatly reduced since the prosperous 1920s, Germany had actually increased its trade surplus with Czechoslovakia in the course of the downturn. In 1928 the German surplus in trade with Czechoslovakia was 111 million marks. For the years 1929 to 1931 the German surplus averaged 175 million marks annually. The Czechoslovak foreign office expressed frustration, concern, and amazement at the ability of certain German industries (resins, cottons, woolens, silks, paper, rubber products, furs) to increase their exports to Czechoslovakia in the Depression year 1931. Despite Czechoslovakia's best efforts, Germany was winning the protectionist battle.[76]

In order to "dissuade the Czechoslovak government from countermeasures against German exports," the Reich was willing to conclude commodity-specific agreements granting preferential access to the German market for some Czechoslovak products.[77] The first of these agreements was the Hops Agreement of 12 November 1931 signed by Bülow and Czechoslovakian Ambassador Frantisek Chvalkovsky in Berlin, and which had begun as negotiations between private-sector groups on both sides. In the secret portions of that agreement Germany promised to issue import certificates for up to 10,000 cwt. of Czechoslovak hops (worth roughly 830,000 marks) and to allow that amount into the Reich at the reduced duty of 60 marks/cwt. instead of 70 marks/cwt. On the basis of the government's authority to order the temporary application of bilateral agreements, this hops concession was extended twice to run through August 1933, despite some resistance by Papen's Agriculture Minister Braun.[78] On 27 November 1931, the Reich also granted preferential tariff treatment for a quota of Czechoslovak timber exports into Germany. Throughout the period, the German side evaded Czechoslovak requests for negotiations on German tariff reductions for a variety of other products, especially barley and malt, something the German government was not prepared to grant.[79] The goal in any German negotiations with Czechoslovakia was simply to "secure the maintenance of German exports at their existing levels" by granting the Czechoslovaks minimal concessions.[80]

German satisfaction with the existing state of affairs diminished over the course of 1932 as the Czechoslovak government imposed ever-stricter foreign exchange controls in their effort to insure sufficient coverage for the koruna.[81] In February 1932 the Czechoslovak government froze German assets on deposit in Czechoslovak banks.

In June the German Minister in Prague, Walter Koch, described the "prohibitive" character of Czechoslovakia's new exchange controls as applied to imported German goods.[82] After lengthy negotiations, a payments arrangement was made in July 1932 that allowed frozen export assets on both sides to be employed preferentially in tourist traffic.[83] Beyond that, the German government hoped to negotiate a foreign exchange agreement that could preserve Germany's trade surplus. In November 1932, the Reich Economics Ministry used I.G. Farben executives to sound out the Czechoslovaks on the possibility of an agreement in which Germany and Czechoslovakia would each make foreign currency available for purchases of the other's products in a ratio of 1:1.5 (i.e., the Czechoslovaks to import from Germany 1.5 times the value of German imports from Czechoslovakia). The Czechoslovaks replied that a fixed ratio of 1:1.5 was "completely out of the question." Repeated attempts to preserve the German trade surplus were rejected by the Czechoslovak government.[84]

In new regulations of April and August 1932, Czechoslovakia expanded the list of goods requiring the approval of the state Foreign Exchange Commission. By September to October 1932 these measures began reducing German exports to Czechoslovakia radically. The German Consulate in Pressburg reported that the new currency and import controls meant "no new sales or business opportunities for German business" in Czechoslovakia. Working from both countries' official statistics, Koch detailed the decline in German exports to Czechoslovakia, which were now falling off faster than exports from many other countries, notably Britain. As of September 1932, German exports of cutlery were down 54 percent from a year before, cottons down 67 percent, machine tools down 54 percent, electrical machines down 54 percent. At 33 million Kcs. (2.6 million marks), the German trade surplus for September was one-quarter of what it had been in September 1931. Koch warned that the statistics for the final quarter of 1932 would look far worse, since the effect of the most recent August restrictions was not yet reflected in the September data.[85]

The period during which Germany had been able to manipulate various protectionist measures in order to hold on to a significant trade surplus was now drawing to a close. The Czechoslovaks were determined to protect the koruna by balancing their trade with Germany, even at the risk of harming Bohemian industry through the disruption of decades-old patterns of exchange. By the time Hitler assumed the chancellorship at the end of January 1933, German exports to Czechoslovakia had practically ceased. German companies with long-standing contacts in Czechoslovakia were being prevented from sending "even the smallest shipments."[86]

Hitler's views on Czechoslovakia and the nature of the relationship between the two states during the Weimar years virtually precluded any dramatic change in relations immediately after 1933. Czechoslovakia's ultimate place in Hitler's world order was already set; defeat, occupation, and population resettlement were the best this "dagger pointed at the heart of Germany" could hope for. Until such time as the necessary force could be applied to achieve his goals in Central Europe, Hitler was content to employ a waiting policy toward Czechoslovakia. That policy in general consisted of clandestinely keeping the German minority issue and Sudeten movement alive while avoiding an open break between the two countries and refusing to become entangled in any project that might bolster Czechoslovakia's position, either a bilateral nonaggression pact on the Polish model or a multilateral Eastern Locarno.[87]

In the German-Czechoslovak trade and payments arrangements of 1933 and 1934 and the subsequent pattern of trade from 1934 to 1938, the Third Reich gave economic expression to its overall "waiting policy" toward Czechoslovakia from 1933 to 1938. In October 1933, Posse had deliberately and explicitly excluded Czechoslovakia from the southeast European countries that Germany was targeting for expanded trade, presumably because Czechoslovakia did not meet his criterion of being a country in which the Reich could "count on a domination of the market by German businessmen."[88]

On the Czechoslovak side, Prime Minister and then President Edvard Benes satisfied himself through 1936 with avoiding conflict with Germany. Having deflected the threatening German proposal for an Austro-German customs union in 1931, the Czechoslovaks sought to maintain their extensive trade and financial relations with Germany, though now on a balanced basis. Shortly after Hitler's takeover in Germany, Benes told the Czechoslovak parliament that he hoped for the same relationship with the new Germany that he had maintained with Weimar. Two years later he told British Foreign Minister Anthony Eden that Czechoslovakia "had no conflicts with Germany and would not have them in the future." Prior to 1938, Benes could not have understood that correct relations with Hitler would not spare the Czechoslovak republic from destruction in accordance with Hitler's long-held goals.[89]

In 1933 Nazi and Czechoslovak policies combined to produce a political relationship in which the two countries stayed "at arm's length."[90] At the same time, both sides continued to spar lightly for the financial advantage in the still-extensive trade relationship between the two. In response to Czechoslovakia's expanded foreign trade controls in 1932, the German Foreign Office acknowledged the "necessity of studying whether our existing waiting policy toward Czechoslovakia must be changed."[91]

Commercial relations took a dramatic turn on 8 March 1933 as Czechoslovakia unilaterally imposed a partial clearing procedure on business with Germany by requiring all Czechoslovak payments to the Reich to be deposited in a "collective German account" at the Czechoslovak national bank (Národní banka Československa). The German Economics Ministry responded on 20 March by suspending trade of the koruna on the Berlin market and imposing a ban on most payments to Czechoslovakia.[92] The Reich really had no choice now but to move toward a clearing agreement with Czechoslovakia. In May, "collective accounts" were established at the Reichsbank and at the Czechoslovak national bank for all payments of merchandise. Yet this measure could not by itself stabilize trade and payment relations. In July 1933 Czechoslovakia unilaterally extended the clearing provisions to include all types of payments to Germany so that the Reich again had no choice but to follow suit.[93]

The economic revival now underway in Germany and the corresponding need for imports soon produced a "clearing surplus" of some 30 million Kcs. in Czechoslovakia's favor.[94] New negotiations were needed to formalize the expanded clearing arrangement and to regulate trade so that the Czechoslovak surplus might be reduced. More comprehensive trade and payments agreements were concluded in November 1934. These 1934 agreements established a framework for German-Czechoslovak trade and payments that typified the frameworks employed by the Reich for regulating trade with countries that employed their own extensive state controls.[95] Under the terms of the new payments agreement, clearing accounts at the German Clearing Agency and the Czechoslovak national bank would receive all payments for merchandise trade (including secondary costs), for finishing processes, and for 8 percent of the value of transit trade purchases. The Protocol on German-Czechoslovak Merchandise Trade established government commissions on each side that met periodically to manage jointly the development of trade. An annual trade agreement negotiated by the two commissions set the structure of two-way trade: import quotas in volume, estimated prices, and import value for each category of commodities. Because of the 30 million kcs. Czechoslovak surplus accumulated under the May 1933 arrangement, it was agreed to allow German exports into Czechoslovakia at the rate of 100 million kcs. monthly and Czechoslovak exports into Germany at the rate of 80 million kcs. monthly. In March 1935, the government commission approved additional compensation deals on the ratio of 1:1.5 to the German export advantage in a further effort to reduce the Czechoslovak surplus, which had grown to 32 million kcs. As an additional incentive, the payments agreement was modified to allow Czechoslovakia to use the remaining portions of its frozen assets to pay for 25 percent of additional purchases. The framework for trade and payments established in November 1934 continued to function as the formal regulator of German-Czechoslovak economic relations through 1938.

In its commercial policies, Germany had responded to Czechoslovak trade and payments initiatives from 1933 to 1934 by doing only what was necessary in order to avoid any formal rupture.[96] Neither the Foreign Office nor the Economics Ministry found political or economic motives for intensifying exchanges between the two countries. Politically, the existing relationship – polite, but cool – satisfied both the traditional diplomats and Hitler's ultimate plans for Czechoslovakia. Economically, the "very similar economic structures of the two countries" precluded the type of "natural complementariness" found in German relations with Rumania and Yugoslavia. Timber was the only raw material from Czechoslovakia in which Germany had a pressing interest. Beyond that, an "intensification of the exchange relationship could take place [only] on a refined basis, for example in the exchange of specific quality products."[97]

The second annual German-Czechoslovak bilateral trade agreement in December 1935 called for holding trade between the two countries to the same level as the previous year. In fact, two-way trade in 1936 declined slightly to 242 million marks (251 million marks in 1935). In July 1936, the Czechoslovak clearing surplus was still 26 million kcs. The new trade agreement for 1937 planned German exports to Czechoslovakia at the same level as 1936, a significant increase in German imports was planned only for the "especially important" Czechoslovak timber exports.[98] Even as the value of trade picked up in 1937 and 1938, Germany's relative position as both a supplier and customer for Czechoslovakia declined slightly after holding steady from 1935 to 1937. By 1937 the German share of Czechoslovak exports had fallen to just 13.7 percent, down from 21.5 percent in 1934; the Reich's 1937 share in Czechoslovak imports was 15.5 percent, down from 19.4 percent in 1934.[99] Trade stagnation (as measured by value) or slight declines (as measured by market shares) were the economic expressions of Hitler's waiting policy toward Czechoslovakia.[100]

Soviet Union

The Soviet decision in the autumn of 1930 to seek credits from Germany for the bulk of the first Five Year Plan's remaining orders for industrial imports decisively shaped economic relations between the two countries for the next half-decade.[101] In 1930 the Soviet need for credit to finance its import purchases was as acute as it had been through the 1920s. Without credit there would be no large-scale sales; and after 1930 the German credits (i.e., the Soviet trade debt) shaped German-Soviet relations more profoundly and for a longer period than did the merchandise transfer of 1931 to 1932 itself.

In November 1930, Soviet president Mikhail I. Kalinin mentioned to German Ambassador Herbert von Dirksen the possibility of the Soviets' placing one billion rubles in new orders to German industry if the German side could provide an unspecified amount of credit to Soviet purchasing agencies. The Soviet offer took more definite shape as it was presented to Peter Klöckner, Wolfgang Reuter, Karl Köttgen and fourteen other leading German industrialists touring the USSR in February and March 1931. They were promised 300 million marks, potentially 500 million marks, in new Soviet orders in 1931 alone if Germany could provide 300 million marks in export credit at better rates than those granted in 1926. Upon their return to Germany, the industrialists brought the matter of new credits, and private-sector hopes for a 70 percent credit guarantee by the Reich, to the cabinet.[102]

After two discussion with the returning industrialists and three cabinet meetings on the subject, the government agreed to provide the necessary guarantees for 300 million in new credits.[103] The proposed project's possible impact on the overall course of German-Soviet political relations emerged as the most important consideration in the cabinet discussions. The credit project was taking shape just as the negotiations for renewal of the 1926 Treaty of Berlin were about to begin in Moscow on 24 March 1931. From Moscow, Ambassador Dirksen had been urging prompt renewal since the subject first arose in February. Ritter thought perhaps the Reich should seek to escape a renewal of the MFN clause as part of Germany new protectionist policies, but evidently no one in the Foreign Office considered letting the treaty lapse. The German decision for a "simple renewal" had been made at the very latest by 16 March, as Curtius's memorandum to Dirksen in Moscow shows.[104] By 16 March, Curtius was just learning the details of the new business proposals. His contributions to the cabinet discussion on the 24th show that he viewed new credits as a continuation of Germany's Russian policy, including the decision for treaty renewal. After all, Germany's strategic position had not changed since the treaty was first concluded 1926 – continued hostility toward Poland required a continued understanding with Soviet Russia. On this central point, Curtius used direct quotes from Stresemann's earlier instructions to Brockdorff about the purpose of a German-Soviet treaty.[105] Germany probably did not need to use economic and financial incentives to insure a treaty renewal. Soviet Foreign Minister Maxim Litvinov had indicated to Dirksen in the first week of February (i.e., three weeks before the German industrial delegation arrived in Moscow) that the USSR was willing to renew the treaty in both form and substance. Yet the emerging overlap of trade and credit negotiations with preparations for the treaty renewal negotiations appeared to establish a link between the economic and political dimensions of German-Soviet relations. Curtius could not allow a Reich rejection of new credit guarantees to endanger the renewal process. Curtius explained that an earlier failure of talks between the Soviets and German industrialists "would not have worsened the political situation." If, however, "the German government refused the guarantee now, the effect would be very significant" since it "would mean a departure from our line of policy towards Russia up to now."[106]

The Reich's own financial position set some limits on the Brüning government's ability to guarantee export credits, even when political considerations favored an expansion of German commercial and financial ties with the USSR.[107] The size and significance of the new credit proposal went well beyond Weimar's previous experiences with Soviet trade. The Foreign Office pointed out that Reich and state governments together had already guaranteed 400 million marks of the 600 million marks in credit extended by German banks and industry to the Soviets from 1926 to 1930.[108] Moreover, 200 million marks in Soviet orders for "regular" new business were expected in 1931. The additional 300 million now hoped for by the industrialists would put total Soviet obligations to Germany at 1,100 million marks and increase the Reich's guarantee obligation from its current 300 million (plus 100 million by the states) to 750 million marks.[109] Both the Prussian government and Foreign Minister Curtius expressed concern about the Soviet ability to repay these debts.[110] Klöckner, speaking for the industrialists, was "convinced that the Russians would pay." He pointed out the necessity of maintaining employment in Germany, and related that the "Berlin banks were of the opinion that the deal must be concluded."[111] The general cabinet uneasiness about the Soviets' ability to repay these vast sums was expressed openly by Labor Minister Adam Stegerwald (Center Party) and State Secretary Schaffer in the Finance Ministry, although both favored the deal. Trendelenburg admitted that from a business point of view, allowing the Soviet debt to rise to over 1,000 million marks was "hardly justifiable" but pointed out that "in comparison to other states" the Soviets' ability to repay was quite good, and finally argued that for "reasons of general policy, it appears correct to stake more on the Russian card than previously." Stegerwald agreed that a "foreign policy orientation toward the East is the right thing."

The cabinet also reviewed the issue with regard to Germany's relations with the Western powers. Stegerwald mentioned how the Swiss newspapers had already pointed out that "Germany does not need foreign loans and a revision of reparations terms if it is rich enough to grant the Russians large sums of credit." Trendelenburg offered an opposite view, declaring that "the Entente states will grant Germany no improvement [in reparations] if Germany does not make this deal." Reichsbank President Luther agreed that "other countries must be shown that in order to pay reparations Germany must make this type of deal."[112] After the failure of the Geneva conference to reduce protectionist measures, Germany was justified in pursuing Soviet contracts. Curtius felt that in view of Germany's continued reparations problems with France "Russia had grown in importance. Continued cooperation with Russia is advantageous [to Germany]. The French want an understanding with Germany in exchange for [German] abandonment of the Russians." "Under these circumstances" Luther favored this new economic deal with the Soviets. Trendelenburg "did not expect any hostility by other countries" if Germany went ahead.[113] Over the financial objections of Interior Minister Wirth and Post Minister Georg Schatzel, the cabinet approved Reich guarantees for 70 percent of an additional 300 million marks in Soviet orders on 24 March.[114]

On 10 April 1131 a Soviet delegation arrived in Berlin to finalize the credit and financial terms of these contracts on the basis of the earlier negotiations with German industrialists in Moscow. The so-called Piatakov Agreement was signed by the Soviets and German industrialists (Kraemer, Köttgen, Reuter) on 14 April 1931.[115] The Soviets received 300 million marks in fourteen-to-twenty-eight-month credits for orders to be placed in Germany by 31 August 1931, i.e., within five months.[116] With this short ordering period and the low levels of current operating capacity in German factories, the Reich funds for providing guarantees in 1931 were exhausted by the end of October 1931. In early 1932, the Reich and the states began to revolve the guarantee funds as they were repaid. In March 1932 the Reichsbank provided another 120 million marks for the redemption of Soviet bills of exchange.[17] New credits totaling at least 185 million were made available in the second half of 1932.[118] The Soviets drew heavily on these credits in placing large orders in Germany in 1931 (920 million marks) and 1932. In 1931 Germany sent 763 million marks in exports to the USSR, or more than twice the 1929 value of 354 million. The carryover of some deliveries into 1932 meant that at 626 million marks exports for that year were also higher than any pre-1931 year.[119]

Although the volume of sales was large; the size of German profits from these Russian orders remains uncertain. German firms competed fiercely for Soviet orders, granting credit and price concessions to the Soviets that deeply eroded profit margins. Limits on this intra-German competition applied only to exports that used government-backed credits.[120] For the majority of Soviet contracts, the desperate business climate of 1931 to 1932 unleashed destructive bidding wars that undermined the value of Soviet orders.[121] Peter Klöckner complained that competition among German producers was driving prices down from 30 percent to 35 percent above production costs to just 1 percent to 2 percent! Applying those figures to the 920 million marks in Soviet orders placed in 1931 means price reductions of over 300 million marks. Klöckner lamented with frustration to a group of fellow industrialists that this intra-German competition was "costing us all a lot of money." In April 1932 he urged the leading Rhine-Westphalian steel producers (including Krupp, Hoesch, GHH, and United Steel) to take a common stand on prices (a minimum of 20 percent above total production costs) and on payments (eighteen months maximum).[122] In fact, intra-German competition in credit concessions to the Soviets diminished after June 1932 as the Comprehensive Delivery Agreement (Rahmen-Lieferungsabkommen) extended the credit terms of April 1931 (in a slightly modified form) to all Soviet orders placed in Germany through May 1933.[123] But just one month later in July 1932 the most important organizations in steel production (including the A-Product Verband, Stabeisen-Verband, and the Grobblechverband) rejected proposals to control competition for Soviet orders.[124]

In the course of their 1931 to 1932 buying spree, the Soviets accumulated a massive debt to Germany of some 1,100 million to 1,200 million marks by the end of 1932. This debt level suddenly acquired special significance in January 1933 with the change of government in Germany. When Hitler assumed the chancellorship, Germany held over one billion marks in Soviet obligations – one of the few significant creditor positions the Reich held. Through 1936, Soviet debt levels played a central role in shaping relations between the two countries. At the same time, huge Soviet repayments between 1933 and 1935 provided a tremendous economic and financial transfusion to a regime spending beyond its means on rearmament.

The territory of the Soviet Union occupied the central place in Hitler's foreign policy program of racial conquest and resettlement.

Hitler's overall strategic goals vis-à-vis the Soviet Union were already irrevocably set. Yet in the half-dozen years before Germany could launch the necessary wars for this program, the Reich had to conduct some type of policy toward the Soviet state. The German-Polish nonaggression declaration of January 1934 ended the Reich's long-standing diplomatic dependence on the Soviets in Eastern Europe. In both deeds and words, Hitler used Germany's new diplomatic freedom in the East to conduct an ambiguous policy toward the USSR that left both the Soviets and the German Foreign Office wondering about his true intentions.[125] Hitler's ultimate plans for the Soviet Union meant that during this 1933 to 1939 period "Germany need have no fixed attitude toward Russia as long as relations were neither too close nor too hostile. For his own domestic political reasons and because of personal preferences, Hitler did not want the relationship to be very close and … was not particularly worried about Soviet hostility."[126]

In this context, it was not necessary for Hitler to employ its trade policy in the service of any larger foreign policy goals. The Foreign Office and Economics Ministry were largely free to manage German trade relations with the Soviets in accordance with the Reich's economic needs and limitations, provided that working relations with the Soviets in the economic sphere did not require significant concessions to them in other areas. Before 1939, Germany would not use trade and financial concessions to create the basis for a new political understanding with the Soviets, as Hitler had done with the Poles in 1933 to 1934. In this way, German-Soviet economic relations 1933 to 1939 more closely resemble German-Czechoslovak economic relations in the same period. The contrast in the Soviet and Czechoslovak experiences lay in the USSR's tremendous natural wealth and its mountain of debt owed to Germany.

In January 1933, Hitler took control of a government that was in a powerful creditor position vis-à-vis the Soviet Union. Largely on the basis of the credit-funded trade deficit of 800 million marks in 1931 and 1932, Soviet obligations to Germany were over 1,110 million marks.[127] In February 1933 Soviet difficulties in maintaining payments on the 650 million marks due to Germany in 1933 forced the Soviets to negotiate a 200 million-mark bridge loan from the Reich.[128] Soviet repayment difficulties coincided with the end of the first Five Year Plan to bring about a dramatic fall-off in new Soviet orders. By 1934 German exports to the Soviet Union were one-tenth of what they had been two years earlier. Yet the existing mountain of Soviet debt provided a cushion that supported massive German imports from the Soviet Union for the next three years in spite of the

Reich's own economic problems (chronic lack of foreign exchange, declining exports, negative trade balance in 1934). From 1933 to the end of 1935, the Soviets used payments of 445 million marks in gold, 356 million in freely convertible currencies, and a 234 million-mark trade surplus during that period to reduce their outstanding debt to the Reich to just 75 million marks.[129]

The dramatic reduction of Soviet debt was a mixed blessing for Germany. On one hand these infusions of gold, foreign currency, and raw materials provided timely relief for Germany's critical financial position and economic problems.[130] The German trade deficit of 373 million marks in 1934 had left the Reichsbank with just 84 million marks in gold and foreign exchange assets at year's end. One must ask how Hitler's government would have met its hard currency obligations for 1934 (424 million marks) without the 227 million in gold and 163 million foreign exchange provided by the Soviet Union in that year alone.[131] At the same time, the 234 million marks worth of unbalanced imports from the USSR from 1933 to 1935 played a crucial role in allowing German rearmament to take off.[132] These imports both supplied the raw materials necessary for expanding armaments production and did not require the use of German factory capacity for the production of compensating industrial exports. On the other hand, the rapid reduction of Soviet debt meant that Germany soon lost the economic and financial upper hand in dealing with the Kremlin. After 1935 the Reich still desired enormous amounts of Soviet materials, but found it increasingly difficult to provided the types of payments that the Soviets began demanding.[133] The shifting balance of power in the economic relationship between the two countries was becoming visible already in early 1935, as the two countries wrangled over the terms of the new German-Soviet trade agreement. By the end of 1934 the Soviets had already reduced their outstanding debt to Germany to a manageable 250 million marks. Further, it was apparent from the successful repayments undertaken in 1933 and 1934 that the Soviets would be able to make the roughly 220 million marks in payments due in 1935, leaving only a small German advantage thereafter.[134]

Negotiations for a new trade and payments arrangement were held in March and April 1935 with the new head of the Soviet Foreign Trade Office in Berlin, David Kandelaki. Schacht attempted to preserve Germany's remaining creditor position by insisting that the proceeds from subsequent Soviet exports "be blocked and are to be released only in proportion to fresh Soviet orders [for German goods] with normal delivery dates." The Soviet side repeatedly and consistently rejected a direct link between the proceeds from Soviet exports and the placement of new Soviet orders. When the Soviets refused to budge on this point Schacht was forced to give in, to the great relief of the German Foreign Office.[135] In the agreements of 9 April 1935 the Soviet Trade Office was explicitly guaranteed "free disposal ... for use inside Germany" of the proceeds from regular Soviet exports under the same terms as an earlier agreement of May 1932. The terms were also set for the remaining Soviet repayments in 1935, totaling 200 million marks. On their side, the Soviets promised to place "regular" orders in Germany for 60 million marks' worth of industrial goods by year's end. As a new means of insuring future German exports to the USSR, and presumably thereby the much-needed continuation of Soviet exports to Germany, Schacht arranged a five-year, 200-million-mark credit at two percent interest for "supplemental" industrial orders to be placed by the Soviets in Germany over the upcoming year.[136] As part of the new credit deal, the Reich insisted that the Soviet Trade Office in Berlin reach agreement with the Russia Committee on general payment and delivery terms (Allgemeine Lieferbedingungen) that would constrain intra-German price and credit competition for Soviet orders.[137] The standardized terms were then enforced by orders of the Reich Economics Ministry to the Export Control Offices.

By the end of 1935 the Soviet debt to the Reich was just 65 million marks, of which some 45 million was due in 1936. Unless Schacht could initiate some new payments provisions, the Reich would be forced to do the very thing Schacht had been successfully postponing for the past three years – pay cash for Russian raw materials. At the end of October 1935 Schacht initiated new talks with the Soviets about trade and payments for the year 1936.[138] In an attempt to fulfill "the most important aim of the negotiations," namely, "to secure the supply of raw materials from the Soviet Union without having to supply foreign exchange," Schacht offered the Soviets a 500-million-mark, ten-year bonded loan. The loan was conditional on Soviet willingness to conduct current trade on a 1:1 balanced ratio at the level of 160 million marks (each way) annually. In essence, Schacht was repeating his 1935 attempt to tie Soviet exports to Germany to new Soviet orders for German products. Kandelaki told the leadership of the Russia Committee that the Soviets would consider the deal only on the condition that they be allowed to order advanced arms and war materials, "warships, aircraft and other things of interest to them ... in particular submarines," as part of the credit. "If this stipulation cannot be fulfilled, then [they] are not interested in the 500 million credit."[139]

In mid-January 1936 Hitler himself forbade "all transactions in war material with Russia."[140] As passed on to the Russia Committee by the War Ministry, Hitler's briefly worded decision had far-reaching consequences, ultimately causing a radical reduction in the volume of Soviet exports to Germany. By banning weapons sales, Hitler scuttled Schacht's plan for securing Soviets exports of 160 million marks annually as part of a 500 million-mark loan offered to the Soviets.[141] Instead of obtaining 480 million marks in Soviet materials for the period 1936 to 1938, as under Schacht's loan plan, Germany in fact received only 200 million in Soviet materials (618 million from 1933 to 1935). The trade and payments agreement of 29 April 1936 initiated a new phase in the economic relationship between the two countries.[142] Schacht was forced to accept a cash basis for all regular (i.e., noncredit) German-Soviet trade. Further, the Soviets continued to have free disposal within Germany of their Reichsmark export proceeds (i.e., they were not committed to future orders outside of the credit agreements).[143] After the Soviets paid off their remaining 1936 obligations to Germany with foreign currency, their only motivation for exporting to the Reich would be to cover Soviet purchases there.

The end of massive Soviet debt to Germany, the continuing German ban on weapons sales to the Soviets, the terms of the 1936 trade and payments agreement, and the economic burden of rearmament in Germany all led to a sharp contraction of Soviet orders placed in Germany and Soviet exports sent to the Reich from 1936 to 1939. In 1936 the Soviets placed new orders totaling just 30 million marks at German factories; in 1937 Soviet new Soviet orders were 25 million to 30 million marks; in 1938 just 30 million. In 1935 German industry had fully expected the Soviets to use all of the 200-million-mark credit granted to them; yet even after the deadline for orders was extended by three months, the Soviets used only 170 million marks of the 200 million credit available to them.[144]

In 1936 Soviet Commissar for Foreign Trade A.P. Rosenholz confused the economic issue by asserting that the Soviet Union's international "peace policy" was playing an increasing role in the USSR's choice of trade partners. The explicit mention of political considerations in trade choices came at a time of declining Soviet trade with Germany and increasing Soviet trade with the United Kingdom.[145] Rosenholz's remarks were obviously intended as yet another expression of Soviet warming toward the West in 1936.[146]

Rosenholz's remarks become even more puzzling in the context of reports from inside Germany indicating that in 1937 and 1938 the Soviets were actively seeking to place new orders with German industrial exporters. Because of German domestic economic developments, these Soviet desires for increased trade could not be realized. After 1936, the greatly intensified pace of rearmament began to strain German industrial capacity.[147] By 1937 German industry was losing one of its traditional commercial strengths – short turnaround time and prompt delivery on export contracts. Because of "long delivery times" most of the goods ordered by the Soviets as part of the 1935 credit were not sent out until 1937; as of May 1938, 22 million marks' worth of those orders still had not been delivered. In its annual report for 1938, the Russia Committee noted that "the high demands on German industry and the long delivery times resulting therefrom have blocked a revival of [Soviet] business. In fact, primarily because of too long delivery times, we have lost many different Soviet contracts that … would have brought us raw materials of equal value."[148] Chairman Reyss of the Russia Committee noted at the annual directors meeting in May 1938 that "in contrast to earlier years when German industry sought as many Russian contracts as possible, in the past year it was the USSR that sought to place contracts in Germany, whereby in many cases Soviet Russian wishes for specialty objects could not be fulfilled."[149] For that reason the Soviets had turned to Britain in 1936 and 1937 and then increasingly to the United States in 1938 and 1939.[150] All of this suggests that the Soviets placed their orders with as least as much practical as political motivation. In that same vein, Rosenholz's comments about the political content of Soviet trade orders can be seen an attempt to gain whatever political advantage was available in the West from trade decisions that the Soviets were forced to make in any event because of economic conditions in Germany.

The inability to place orders with overworked German producers explains why Soviet exports to the Reich fell to such low levels. The Russia Committee of German Industry noted in its 1937 annual report that German currency controls limited the proceeds from Soviet exports to the Reich to use only in Germany and that therefore "the Russians have no incentive to bring raw materials in [to Germany], the proceeds of which in certain circumstances are dead assets. The Soviet foreign trade directors have repeatedly declared that exports to Germany and other countries with foreign exchange controls can take place only in such amounts as the export proceeds are required for payments there."[151] Unable to obtain what they wanted in Germany, the Soviets had to view the sale of raw materials for "dead" Reichsmarks in Germany as less attractive than sales elsewhere in the world for freely convertible dollars or sterling.[152] After 1936 the United Kingdom provided an a sizable alternative market for Soviet commodities.[153]

Ultimately, Hitler's refusal to sell armaments to the Soviets continued to underlay the low level of Soviet orders and contracts placed in Germany after 1935. As the Soviets became more interested in importing weapons in 1937 and 1938, the German armaments ban became a larger impediment to trade. In the course of the preliminary negotiations for the 1938 trade agreement between the two countries, the Soviet Foreign Trade Office in Berlin admitted that "the Russian ordering program is set up primarily according to military-political considerations." The Reich Economics Ministry acknowledged the limitations this put on Soviet orders in Germany and urged the Soviets to order more civilian goods as a way to expand German-Soviet trade.[154]

In early 1939 Hitler again refused to take the necessary steps for an expansion of German-Soviet trade since these actions would have required a deviation from his ideological-strategic goals and from his more immediate rearmament plans. Negotiations between German Ambassador Friedrich-Werner Schulenburg and Soviet Foreign Trade Minister Anastas Mikoyan in February and March 1939 had produced a basic agreement for 145 million marks in Soviet raw materials to be delivered to Germany in 1939 and 1940. These "negotiations with the Soviet Union ... to increase Germany's imports of raw materials" took place "on instructions from Field Marshall Göring and with the agreement of the Foreign Minister." Further, "the Commissioner for the Four Year Plan [Göring], the Minister of Economics [Funk], and the Food Minister [Darré] ... insist on extending this exchange of goods in every possible way in the interests of our raw material supply."[155] However, the German side let these talks go cold when the Economics Ministry informed the interministerial Economic Policy Committee that the "German economy, on account of its preoccupation with certain domestic tasks, is not in a position to make the necessary deliveries [to the Soviets] amounting to 300 million Reichsmarks in the next one to two years."[156] The limits Hitler had set on German-Soviet trade in early 1936, via rearmament at home and ban on armament sales to the Soviets, kept that trade constrained until he was ready to employ trade concessions for a fundamental change in policy 1939.

The strategic considerations and diplomatic events that brought Hitler to a startling about-face in the German-Soviet nonaggression pact of August 1939 have been painstakingly reconstructed in a number of fine studies.[157] German trade and financial concessions played a crucial role in bringing about first a German-Soviet economic agreement and then the infamous political-strategic understanding. The Germans signaled their new cooperative attitude toward the USSR in the spring of 1939 by granting a Soviet request for the fulfillment of Soviet arms contracts held by the Czechoslovak

Skoda works, which had fallen under German control with the occupation of Bohemia-Moravia in March 1939.[158] On 20 May 1939, in response to a Soviet feeler about resuming the economic negotiations that had withered in March, Ambassador Schulenburg met Soviet Foreign Minister Vyacheslav Molotov for discussions on the issue. Schulenburg assured the Soviet foreign minister that the unnamed "difficulties" that had prevented Germany from accepting Mikoyan's trade proposals in the spring had now been removed. The German approach to the Soviets was made much easier when Molotov declared that the Soviets "could only agree to a resumption of the [economic] negotiations if the necessary 'political basis' for them were to be constructed."[159] On 30 May Foreign Office State Secretary von Weizsäcker authorized the German embassy's economics officer in Moscow, Gustav Hilger, to approach Mikoyan about proceeding with economic negotiations. Hilger did so on 2 June, emphasizing to Mikoyan "the sincerity of our intentions about extending economic relations."[160]

The ice had been broken and intentions expressed, yet over the next month little progress in either the economic or political discussions was made as both sides advanced coyly. The Germans moved the negotiations ahead by putting some substance in their economic offers on 10 July by agreeing to grant the Soviets a 200-million-mark credit; to use the items contained in the "lists" of desired goods presented by the Soviets as the basis for discussion of German deliveries; and to "make firm statements on the capacity of German industry to deliver."[161] These substantive pledges had the desired effect on the Soviets. By 16 July Mikoyan responded to Hilger that Soviet Deputy Trade Representative Evgeny Babarin would call on Julius Karl Schnurre in Berlin for "final clarification" before a formal resumption of economic negotiations. The Soviets issued a public statement on the resumption of economic negotiations on 21 July. Thereafter the trade and credit negotiations advanced rather quickly, for after the German promises of 10 July, "the road to a German-Soviet economic agreement was now open."[162]

Only when the economic talks were getting underway was Schulenburg instructed on 22 July to "pick up the threads again" on the "purely political" aspects of the negotiations that had been put on hold by Hitler's earlier order. The Soviets were not unwilling to discuss future political relations, but as Molotov told Schnurre via the Soviet embassy in Berlin on 5 August, the USSR "considered the conclusion of the credit agreement as the first important stage in this direction."[163] On 15 and 16 August, Schulenburg gently indicated the extent of the political cooperation Germany was seeking with the

Soviet Union, suggesting a nonaggression pact and a joint guarantee of Baltic states. Molotov responded on 18 August, undoubtedly on orders from Stalin, that "the first step towards such an improvement in relations ... could be the conclusion of a trade and credit agreement." Later in that meeting he stated plainly and firmly that "the economic agreement must be concluded first."[164]

At the same time the Soviets were insisting the trade agreement be signed as a first step, Hitler's need for "quick results" on a political-strategic understanding was growing more acute.[165] With the German attack on Poland already set for 26 August, the Germans were prepared to grant the Russians the economic terms necessary for the speedy conclusion of the trade agreement. Already in mid-June, Schnurre had understood that Germany's need for a political understanding with the Soviets (which, as Molotov had indicated in statements as early as 20 May, could not be achieved without an economic understanding) meant that "for political and economic reasons we have to reach agreement with the Russians" even if the economic terms (volume of raw material imports) were not entirely satisfactory to the German side. The German statement on economic negotiations from 10 July demonstrated the Reich's willingness to accommodate the major Soviet requests. Similarly, Weizsäcker told Schulenburg on 22 July that in regard to the economic negotiations "we will act in a markedly forthcoming manner, since a conclusion, and this at the earliest possible date, is desired for general reasons."[166]

Under these circumstances it did not take long for the two countries to reach an agreement on 19 August along the lines first suggested by Germany on 10 July.[167] In the interest of concluding the deal quickly, all technical questions that could not be clarified on the spot were left for resolution at a latter date. Germany extended a 200-million-mark credit for Soviet orders of industrial equipment and armaments. Germany would also deliver another 120 million marks' worth of similar products as "current business." German deliveries would include the Reich's most advanced industrial equipment, even "machine tools up to the very largest dimensions."

For the purposes of securing a military-strategic pact with the Soviets, Germany would now deliver 320 million marks' worth of advanced equipment to the USSR when, just five months earlier, the Economics Ministry had effectively terminated budding trade negotiations with the Soviets by declaring German counterdeliveries of 300 million marks' worth of industrial goods over two years a "technical impossibility."[168] Now Germany would even supply the Soviets with 58.4 million marks' worth of various armaments (18 percent of the 320 million mark total). Other products, notably much of the optical equipment, were also in fact destined for military use. In exchange for German military technology, the Soviets agreed to provide 180 million marks' worth of raw material deliveries over the following two years, at a rate of 90 million annually. Predictably, Soviet exports were concentrated in those raw material commodities that Germany urgently needed: timber (92 million marks!), grain (22 million marks), cotton, chrome ore, manganese ore, and 900,000 tons of petroleum products.[169]

The full economic significance of this enormous exchange of products, 500 million marks in two-way trade, still is not generally appreciated.[170] Under the terms of the supplemental agreement signed in February 1940, Germany purchased some 450 million marks of Soviet materials between August 1939 and early July 1940. For their enormity and significance at this critical time, these German-Soviet exchanges may well have been the most important trade in the first half of this century. The importance of these Soviet materials for the German war economy and the strain of producing the necessary German counterdeliveries were both revealed in Göring's October 1940 order placing export contracts for the USSR in "priority category Ia," i.e., on the same priority level as contracts for the German armed forces.[171]

Despite the undeniable economic significance of the August trade and credit agreement, its "immediate importance was more in the political field."[172] The Soviets had insisted since the beginning of German approaches in May 1939 that improved economic and political relations must go together and that an economic agreement must precede any political understanding. The tangible German economic offers of 10 July were crucial in motivating Stalin to the decision that "an economic agreement with Germany was possible, that the Germans were really serious this time, that their offers were adequate for Soviet purposes, and that the Soviet Union could and would make the concessions on its part still needed for an agreement."[173] To the materialistic Stalin, these solid German economic offers (including armaments sales) were the necessary proof of Germany's seriousness of purpose in both the economic and the political spheres. In providing that proof for Hitler, German exports performed their most deadly duty ever in Eastern Europe.[174]

Notes

1. Cabinet session, 27 May 1931; Ritter to Posse, 27 May 1931, both cited by Sundhaussen, "Weltwirtschaftskrise im Donau-Balkan-Raum," 136.

2. On the larger goals of Nazi foreign policy see Gerhard Weinberg, *The Foreign Policy of Hitler's Germany*, 2 vols., (Chicago, 1970, 1980); Hans-Adolf Jacobsen, *Nationalsozialistische Aussenpolitik 1933-1939* (Frankfurt, 1968); Klaus Hildebrand, *The Foreign Policy of the Third Reich* (Berkeley, 1973); Andreas Hillgruber, "Grundzüge der nationalsozialistische Aussenpolitik, 1933-1945," *Saeculum* 24 (1973), 328-45; Norman Rich, *Hitler's War Aims* (New York, 1974); Eberhard Jäckel, "The Evolution of Hitler's Foreign Policy Aims," in Henry Turner, ed., *Nazism and the Third Reich* (New York, 1972), 201-18; Jochen Thies, *Architekt der Weltherrschaft: Die "Endziele" Hitlers* (Dusseldorf, 1976); Bernd Jürgen Wendt, *Grossdeutschland: Aussenpolitik und Kriegsvorbereitung des Hitler-Regimes* (Munich, 1987); Marie-Luise Recker, *Die Aussenpolitik des Dritten Reiches* (Munich, 1990).

3. On Nazi foreign economic strategies in the context of managing the German economy see Dörte Doering, *Deutsche Aussenwirtschaftspolitik, 1933-1935: Die Gleichschaltung der Aussenwirtschaft in der Frühphase des nationalsozialistischen Regimes* (Ph.D. diss., Free University of Berlin, 1969); Dieter Petzina, *Autarkiepolitik im Dritten Reich: Der nationalsozialistische Vierjahresplan* (Stuttgart, 1968); Eckart Teichert, *Autarkie und Grossraumwirtschaft in Deutschland 1933-1939: Aussenwirtschaftliche Konzeptionen zwischen Wirtschaftskrise und Weltkrieg* (Munich, 1984).

4. For an introduction to the political content of Nazi trade policies see Joachim Radkau, "Entscheidungsprozesse und Entscheidungsdefizite in der deutschen Aussenwirtschaftspolitik," *Geschichte und Gesellschaft* 2 (1976), 33-65.

5. "The opportunism to which some have pointed as the essence of Hitler's policy was in fact an integral part of his long term theory of political action, and many of the most extravagant and perplexing instances will be seen to fit most precisely into his general view." Gerhard Weinberg, *The Foreign Policy of Hitler's Germany*, vol. 1, 2.

6. Ministerial meeting of 7 April 1933, *Akten Hitler*, 326. Enthusiastic about the economic aspects of the "national revolution," Germany's leading industrialists "wanted to support without reservation the [Führer's] thesis that foreign policy deserves primacy over commercial policy," Kraemer at the first meeting of the Commercial Policy Committee of the new Reichstand deutscher Industrie (the nazified successor to the industrial Reichsverband), 16 November 1933, BA R 43I/1079. Similarly, the German Agricultural Council, now filled with "new trust and fresh hope" at its 1933 annual meeting, "declined to make specific demands" for the protection of agriculture on the new Hitler government, 5 April 1933, PAAA Sonderref. W, Landwirtschaft 6, Landwirtschaftliche Kammern und Verbände, Bd. 3.

7. In order to maintain economic peace in 1933, the Reich concluded extremely generous treaties with the Netherlands and Denmark in which Germany agreed to pay prices well above world market levels for some Dutch and Danish products. Rene Erbe has described how Germany used a hidden "partial" devaluation of ASKI-Marks to offer German exports at lower prices in South America than in Europe, *Die nationalsozialistische Wirtschaftspolitik 1933-1939 im Lichte der modernen Theorie* (Zurich, 1958). Both Erbe and David Kaiser have pointed out the relatively disadvantageous terms offered by Germany to the Balkan countries, *Economic Diplomacy*.

8. For an introduction to Nazi policies of merchandise exchange exploitation under conditions of wartime occupation (i.e., exchanges that can no longer be termed "trade" in any usual sense) see Hans-Erich Volkmann, "Nationalsozialistischer

Aussenhandel im geschloßenen Kriegswirtschaftsraum," in Friedrich Forstmeier and Hans-Erich Volkmann, eds., *Kriegswirtschaft und Rüstung 1939-1945* (Dusseldorf, 1977); Alan Milward, *War, Economy and Society 1939-1945* (Berkeley and Los Angeles, 1979), 132 ff.; E.A. Radice, "The German Economic Programme in Eastern Europe," in Radice and Kaser, eds., *The Economic History of Eastern Europe 1919-1975*, vol. 2, 299-308.

9. The Polish envoy in Berlin, Alfred Wysocki, met with Brüning on 1 December and with Foreign Office members on 14 December. On 22 December the Foreign Office instructed the German envoy in Warsaw, Hans Adolf von Moltke, to explain the nonratification decision to the Polish government, BA Potsdam R 901/67407, Bl. 67, 85, 97.

10. *RGBl.* 1932, I, 30. Australia, Canada, and Poland would pay an increased duty of 170 marks/ton, while all other countries paid 100 marks. Despite the inclusion of two other countries in the German tariff increase, the Poles felt sure the measure was directed against them, Foreign Office note on Polish protests, BA Potsdam R 901/67407, Bl. 136.

11. Moltke to the Foreign Office, 27 January 1932, BA Potsdam R 901/67407, Bl. 119; *RGBl.* 1932, I, 142.

12. For the following see Moltke's memorandum of 6 October 1931, sent to the Foreign Office on 11 November, BA Potsdam R 901/67407, Bl. 43-50.

13. On 26 January the German Consulate in Kattowitz reported that the new Polish ordinances were allowing Czechoslovakia, France, Sweden, and the United Kingdom to replace Germany in the Upper Silesian market, on 4 February the Mannheim Chamber of Commerce reported that it was "useless" for German exporters to apply for import certificates from the Polish government, both in BA R 2/10237.

14. Meyer to Bülow, 6 November 1931, Bülow's note from 7 November, BA Potsdam R 901/67407, Bl. 52.

15. Finance Minister Dietrich to Brüning, 19 January 1931, *Akten Brüning*, 789.

16. Historians of political economy have extensively debated the wisdom and necessity of Brüning's economic strategy, a dialogue often referred to as the "Borchardt debate" after Knut Borchardt's argument first elaborated in "Zwangslagen und Handlungsspielräume in der grossen Weltwirtschaftskrise der frühen dreissiger Jahren: Zur Revision der überlieferten Geschichtsbildes," Bayerische Akademie der Wissenschaften, *Jahrbuch 1979* (Munich). For responses see Carl-Ludwig Holtfrerich, "Zu hohe Löhne in der Weimarer Republik? Bemerkungen zur Borchardt-These," *Geschichte und Gesellschaft* 11 (1985), 122-41; Charles Maier, "Die Nicht-Determinierheit ökonomischer Modelle: Überlegungen zu Knut Borchardts These von der 'kranken Wirtschaft' der Weimarer Republik," *Geschichte und Gesellschaft* 11 (1985), 275-94; Harold James, *The German Slump: Politics and Economics, 1924-1936* (New York, 1986); Dieter Petzina, "The Extent and Causes of Unemployment in the Weimar Republic," in Peter Stachura, ed., *Unemployment and the Great Depression in Weimar Germany* (New York, 1986). Much of the debate has been summarized in English in the collection of Jürgen Baron von Kruedener, ed., *Economic Crisis and Political Collapse. The Weimar Republic, 1924-1933* (New York, 1990). Useful international comparison is provided by Ekkart Zimmermann, "The Collapse of the Weimar Republic in Comparative Analysis: Putting Borchardt into Perspective," (mimeo, 1990). For all of these developments, Wolfgang Helbich's earlier study, *Die Reperationen in der Ära Brüning* (Berlin, 1962) remains valuable.

17. Emil Wiehl (Foreign Office, Special Economics Department) notes of the committee meeting, BA Potsdam R 901/66000, Bl. 53. Wiehl later directed the Foreign Office's revived Trade Policy Department from 1937 to 1944. On 23

February 1932 the Polish vice-minister for Foreign Affairs, Jozef Beck, told Moltke that Poland was prepared to negotiate some way out of the recent impasse, ibid, Bl. 20.

18. Moltke to the Foreign Office, 23 March 1932, Trade Policy Committee meeting of 23 March; Wiehl notes, 16 April, BA Potsdam R 901/66000, Bl. 129, 165, 199.

19. Wiehl to the President's Office, 16 April 1932, Moltke to the Foreign Office, 23 March, BA Potsdam R 901/66000, Bl. 199-201, 129.

20. By October 1932, new German protectionist measures allowed the Reich to offer a portion of its import quota for butter to Poland in exchange for other concessions, Ritter to Moltke, 29 October 1932, BA Potsdam R 901/66000, Bl. 286.

21. Both the Polish Trade Ministry and Moltke favored negotiating similar, limited agreements for other commodities. The chances for further understandings were cut short by the sudden extension of Poland's new "maximum tariff" to goods entering Danzig, a violation of the spirit, through not the letter, of Article 212 of the 1920 German-Polish Warsaw Agreement, Moltke's summary of a conversation with Assistant Trade Secretary Miezyslaw Sokolowski on 9 April 1932, BA Potsdam R 901/66000, Bl. 217. Article 212 had granted Danzig exemption from Polish import bans on German products. The creation of prohibitive tariffs instead of outright bans and their application to German exports headed for Danzig burdened German-Polish relations from April to December 1932, BA Potsdam R 901/66000, passim.

22. Other incidents included Pilsudski's 6 March 1933 strengthening of the Polish garrison on Westerplatte in Danzig. On the Danzig issues see Ludwig Denne, *Das Danzig Problem in der deutschen Aussenpolitik, 1934-1939* (Bonn, 1959); Herbert S. Levine, *Hitler's Free City: A History of the Nazi Party in Danzig, 1925-1939* (Chicago, 1971). In April, Polish envoy Anatol Mühlstein reported that "rumors about Polish plans of a preventive military action [against Germany] were circulating among 'very serious political circles' in Paris," cited in Wandycz, *The Twilight of French Eastern Alliances, 1926-1936*, 271-72. On this extensively debated question see the opposing views of Hans Roos, "Die Präventivkriegspläne Pilsudskis von 1933," *VfZ* 3 (1955), 344-63 and Zygmunt Gasiorowski "Did Pilsudski Attempt to Initiate a Preventive War in 1933?," *JMH* 27 (1955), 135-53; also Jedrzejewicz, "The Polish Plan for 'a Preventive War' against Germany in 1933," *Polish Review* 11 (1966), 62-91. On the German side, Hitler warned the military that "if France has capable statesmen, it will attack us during the period of [our preparations], not itself, but probably through its vassals in the East," Weinberg, *Foreign Policy*, vol. 1, 27.

23. Weinberg, *Foreign Policy*, vol. 1, 69; see also Christoph Kimmich, *Germany and the League of Nations*, (Chicago, 1976). For the general development of German-Polish relations in 1933 see Weinberg, *Foreign Policy*, vol. 1, 57-74; Wandycz, *The Twilight of French Eastern Alliances, 1926-1936*, 259 ff.; W. Jedrzejewicz, ed., *Diplomat in Berlin 1933-1939: Papers and Memoirs of Jozef Lipski, Ambassador of Poland* (New York, 1968), 46 ff.; Marian Wojciechowski, *Die polnisch-deutschen Beziehungen, 1933-1938* (Leiden, 1971); Günter Wollstein, "Die Politik des nationalsozialistischen Deutschland gegenüber Polen, 1933-1939/45," in Manfred Funcke, ed., *Hitler, Deutschland, und die Mächte: Materialien zur Aussenpolitik des Dritten Reiches* (Dusseldorf, 1976), 795-810.

24. Bülow (drafted by the deputy director in the Foreign Office Economics Department, Ulrich) to Moltke, 25 September 1933, BA Potsdam R 901/67407, Bl. 158, also cited by Weinberg, *Foreign Policy*, vol. 1, 68 from *German White Book*; Moltke to the Foreign Office, 30 September 1933, BA Potsdam R 901/66000, Bl. 328.

25. Bülow to Moltke, 25 September 1933, BA Potsdam R 901/67407, Bl. 158, also cited by Weinberg, *Foreign Policy*, vol. 1, 68 from *German White Book*.

26. Foreign Minister Beck told Moltke on 11 November that Germany's withdrawal from the League made it "hard, without the argument of great economic advantages, such as the possibility of an exportation of Polish coal to Germany would have offered, to overcome present [political] objections" to an economic agreement, *DGFP*, C, vol. 2, No. 58. Neurath had assured the Polish envoy, Lipski, that improvements in political and economic relations would go together, Neurath memorandum from 9 November 1933, ibid, No. 52. Pilsudski reaffirmed the economic-political connection in Polish thinking as he told French military attaché, Colonel Charles d'Arbonneau, on 24 November that he expected a détente with Germany to facilitate settlement of the economic issues between the two countries, Wandycz, *Twilight of the French Eastern Alliances*, 312.

27. Germany's written offer for a nonaggression pact came on 27 November 1933. It had been preceded by an unconventional nonaggression communique signed by both Hitler and Lipski on 15 November. Pilsudski appears to have decided as early as 5 November that Poland could accept a German offer of nonaggression; on these developments see Wandycz, *Twilight of the French Eastern Alliances*, 308 ff.

28. Weinberg, *Foreign Policy*, 70.

29. Weinberg, *Foreign Policy*, 73. In contrast, see Wandycz's view that "it was not so much that the [nonaggression] declaration destroyed an anti-Nazi front, for none in effect existed, but it affected future efforts to construct one. Concentrating on developing thier own system, based on bilateral relations with their big neighbors, the Poles began to distance themselves from the French system," *Twilight of the French Eastern Alliances*, 335. See also Anna M. Cienciala, "The Significance of the Declaration of Non-Aggression of January 26, 1934 in Polish-German and International Affairs," *East European Quarterly* 1 (1967), 1-30.

30. Bülow memorandum with Neurath's additions on a ministers' conference in the chancellor's office on 16 November 1933, *DGFP*, C, vol. 2, No. 73.

31. Memorandum by the Director of Foreign Office's Eastern Department, Meyer, on a Neurath-Hitler conversation from 1 November 1933, *DGFP*, C, vol. 2, No. 38.

32. On 20 November Ritter outlined to Moltke the extent of the coal concession he might offer, *DGFP*, C, vol. 2, No. 70 and 73, note 2.

33. *RGBl.* 1934, II, 99-101 for the published portions; Moltke to the Foreign Office, 28 February, 1934, *DGFP*, C, vol. 2, No. 287; and, 9 March 1934, BA Potsdam R 901/66000, Bl. 339; Willuhn memorandum, 8 March 1934, BA R 43II/323.

34. *RGBl*, 1934, II, 830-833. On 2 October, Willuhn described the trade that would result as "a compensation deal, initiated by both governments, facilitated by tariff reductions, and executed by private business people," BA R 43II/323.

35. On Hitler's early tactical flexibility toward Poland see Weinberg, *Foreign Policy*, 14; Martin Brozat, *Nationalsozialistische Polenpolitik, 1939-1945* (Stuttgart, 1961), 9 ff.

36. The new agreement of 18 October 1933 granted Poland a 0.7 percent annual share of the German domestic market for steel (c. 42,000 tons) through 15 May 1937 and a 0.5 percent share thereafter. German industry would supply Poland with 21 percent of its annual scrap iron needs (c. 150,000 tons) and would refrain from additional exports to Poland except of items not produced by Polish industry. The deal, signed by Poensgen, Reichert, Brennecke and eleven others for Germany and by Surzycki (Friedenshütte, Kattowitz), Rohde and eight others for Poland, ran through June 1937, Haniel 4000000/10.

37. For this reason the private agreement was supported, perhaps even pushed, by both governments. On 19 October 1933 Surzycki told his German counterparts that Polish steel industrialists were in touch were their government and had "complete freedom" in negotiating terms. At a 1 March 1934 meeting of German producers to discuss the costs of scrap iron deliveries to Poland (c. 1.65 million marks) "the Middle German and East German producers argued that the agree-

ment had been forced on the iron industry as a matter of high politics," both in Haniel 4000000/10.

38. The following discussion is based on Ritter's Circular of the Foreign Ministry, 11 February 1935, *DGFP*, C, vol. 3, No. 487.

39. "Germany ... already has a heavily adverse balance of payments vis-à-vis Poland and must therefore endeavor to offset this deficit by a sufficiently large surplus of exports." The payment deficit was caused primarily by German use of Polish railroad facilities through the corridor (governed by Article 218 of the 1920 German-Polish agreement on corridor traffic signed in Paris) in value of some 30 million to 40 million marks annually. "In view of the Reichsbank's precarious foreign currency position, the obligation under article 218 could in practice only be fulfilled if they were offset by the export of German goods to Poland," Ritter, ibid.

40. The paragraph concludes: "Nor are other Great Powers in the habit of signaling by unilateral economic concessions their friendly relations with countries to which they are bound by political ties. In this connection I need only refer to the economic relations between France and its allies."

41. Ministry of Economics from 20 February, Agriculture Ministry from 21 February, *DGFP*, C, vol. 3, No. 487, note 6.

42. The Polish government had progressively abandoned hope for genuine collective security through the League of Nations and, to a lesser extent, through the French alliance system. Collective arrangements had been superseded by bilateral nonaggression declarations with both Germany (January 1934) and the Soviet Union (January 1932 and May 1934), both of which were affected by developments in the spring of 1935. Franco-Soviet negotiations for a Pact of Mutual Assistance (signed 2 May 1935) raised concerns in Warsaw over the USSR's future role in Eastern Europe. Hitler's 16 March 1935 announcement of military conscription in Germany and the goal of a 600,000 man army appeared more ominous. The Poles sought reassurance that German-Polish relations were still amicable. On these developments see Wandycz, *Twilight of the French Eastern Alliances*, 395 ff., 400 ff.

43. Meyer memorandum, 11 April 1935, BA Potsdam R 901/66000, Bl. 363. On 12 April Lipski dined with Neurath and Moltke to discuss the economic negotiations, *Diplomat in Berlin*, #40, 182. In early 1935, Moltke received numerous informal indications from "authoritative representatives" of the Polish government that Poland wanted to enter into negotiations for a broadly based trade treaty. The German Trade Policy Committee considered any negotiations opened on the basis of these approaches to be "not suitable" (nicht angezeigt) and decided to wait for the Polish government to approach the Reich more formally, Trade Policy Committee meeting of 23 March 1935, BA Potsdam R 901/66000, Bl. 360.

44. Ulrich notes on Trade Policy Committee meeting, 27 April, *DGFP*, C, vol. 4, No. 53. On 4 May appropriate instructions were sent to Moltke, who informed Beck on May 7 of German willingness to negotiate all issues, ibid, note 6. At 30 million marks annually the value of German railroad transportation service payments was not much less than the value of German merchandise exports to Poland, c. 40 million marks in 1935.

45. Bülow (drafted by Ritter) to Neurath and Hitler, 23 July 1935, BA Potsdam R 901/66000, Bl. 476, also reprinted as *DGFP*, C, vol. 4, No. 217.

46. Bülow recounted how "on the one hand, the market and price regulations of agricultural produce in Germany, and, on the other, currency devaluations abroad have resulted in world market prices for a number of agricultural products being below the German domestic price levels. The differential between the internal and the world market prices enabled us in previous negotiations with Holland

and Denmark among others, to agree to prices in excess of their world market prices for, e.g., Dutch and Danish butter, without thereby affecting the internal prices charged to the consumer." There is no more succinct explication of how domestic controls in Germany created the basis for singularly effective trade policies after 1933.

47. At the end of 1934 Reichsbank reserves of gold and foreign exchange had fallen to just 83.7 million marks (1928 = 2884.6 million), cited in Rene Erbe, *Nationalsozialistische Wirtschaftspolitik*, 61. On the economic limits imposed by Germany's low foreign exchange reserves see also Dietmar Petzina, *Autarkiepolitik*, 40 ff.; Teichert, *Autarkie und Grossraum Wirtschaft in Deutschland 1930-39*, chapter 2; for the later period see Albrecht Ritschl, "Die Deutsche Zahlungsbilanz 1936-1941 und das Problem des Devisenmangels vor Kriegsbeginn," *VfZ* 39 (1991), 103-23.

48. For Economic Ministry objections see Schacht to Neurath, 11 July 1935, *DGFP*, C, vol. 4, No. 204. The Foreign Office compromise involved (1) granting Poland the higher prices for agricultural goods until the German agreements with Holland and Denmark expired on 1 January 1936, at which point Germany would attempt to stop this practice altogether; (2) allowing Polish coal exports to offset a significant German trade surplus; (3) postponing the corridor payments question until later, Bülow (drafted by Ritter) to Neurath and Hitler, 23 July 1935, BA Potsdam R 901/66000, Bl. 476.

49. Despite recent improvements, Bülow argued that trade relations between the two neighbors "cannot be termed other than unfriendly as long as Germany is the only country (bar Russia) to be subjected to differential treatment on the Polish market. The constant friction and complaints in economic affairs may all too easily have undesirable consequences for general political affairs. We cannot in the long run expect positive and fruitful cooperation between Germany and Poland in the sphere of foreign policy whilst both countries are engaged in differentiating and warring against each other in the sphere of economics, Bülow (drafted by Ritter) to Neurath and Hitler, 23 July 1935, BA Potsdam R 901/66000, Bl. 476, also reprinted as *DGFP*, C, vol. 4, No. 217.

50. Neurath to Bülow with a copy of Neurath's memorandum to Hitler from the same day, BA Potsdam R 901/66000, Bl. 484.

51. Bülow to Neurath, 26 August 1935, BA Potsdam R 901/66000, Bl. 503. Schacht's position on the corridor payments had, if anything, grown more adamant. The representative of the Economics Ministry in the German delegation, Forkel, explained to his Foreign Office counterparts that Schacht responded to Neurath's views by declaring that "he had no more foreign currency at his disposal for the corridor payments," Foreign Office memorandum on an 8 August conversation with Forkel, BA Potsdam R 901/66000, Bl. 493.

52. *DGFP*, C, vol. 4, No. 271, note 4; Schefold (Agriculture Ministry) to the Foreign Office on Schacht's statements to the German delegation on 29 August, BA Potsdam R 901/66000, Bl. 511. Schacht makes no mention of the incident in his memoirs.

53. Schacht insisted that Germany could issue foreign currency certificates to pay for German imports from Poland only in the amount equal to the foreign currency Germany had actually received for its own exports to Poland in the previous month. Schacht also claimed that Germany could advance only 7 million of the 20 million zl. bridge loan required to get the new payment agreement underway. The Poles insisted that Germany supply foreign currency each month equal to one-twelfth of the annual total trade agreement, regardless of Germany's actual monthly income from Polish trade, Hemmen's second memorandum from 13 September 1935, BA Potsdam R 901/66000 Bl. 515; Hemmen memorandum, 19 September, *DGFP*, C, vol. 4, No. 301.

54. Hemmen memorandum on a phone conversation with Neurath (in Nuremberg), 13 September 1935, BA Potsdam R 901/660000, Bl. 513.

55. Economics Ministry (Otto Sarnow) to the Foreign Office, 12 October 1935 and Benzler's notes on a conversation with Sarnow from 24 October in which Sarnow said the Reichsbank could no longer afford even 7 million zl. for the bridge loan to Poland, BA Potsdam R 901/66779 Bl. 18, 26. At the end of 1935 the Reichsbank reserves of gold and foreign currency were still just 87 million marks, Erbe, *Nationalsozialistische Wirtschaftspolitik,* 61.

56. On his deathbed, Pilsudski told Beck to maintain the present reconciliation with Germany as long as possible while preserving the alliance with France, Wandycz, *Twilight,* 403.

57. Moltke explicitly referred to the "political considerations that would give the treaty conclusion special significance precisely at this time," Moltke to the Foreign Office, 23 October 1935, BA Potsdam R 901/66779, Bl. 32.

58. Benzler notes on a conversation with Sarnow, 24 October 1935, BA Potsdam R 901/66779, Bl. 26.

59. Published portions of the treaty and payments agreement are a available in *RGBl.* 1935, II, 768, 810. For the secret provisions see *DGFP,* C, vol. 4, No. 301, note 5, No. 390, note 3, and chancellery memorandum initialed by State Secretary Lammers on 19 November 1935, BA R 43II/323.

60. Some supplies of timber, one of the commodities Germany desired most, had already been assured by a special timber deal signed in August.

61. On 11 October, Moltke told the Foreign Office that in economic terms the "only beneficiary" of the new treaty would be Polish agriculture, BA Potsdam R 901/66779.

62. *Deutsche diplomatische-politische Korrespondenz* from 5 November, *Ost Express,* No. 84, Consulate in Posen to the Foreign Office, 11 November, all in BA Potsdam R 901/66779, Bl. 55, 50, 119.

63. Neurath to Hemmen, 4 November 1935, Moltke to the Foreign Office, 5 November, both in BA Potsdam R 901/66779, Bl. 71, 80. Weinberg points out that at the time of the Rhineland crisis the following spring "[T]here were strong internal pressures [in Poland] for a policy closer to France and less cooperative toward Germany than the one followed by the Polish foreign minister, Josef Beck." Beck's policies played into German hands already at that time as he "gambled on a double-track policy ... both to reassure the advocates of a firm common policy with France in resistance to Germany and to follow in practice a continued policy of aloof but effective cooperation with Germany," Weinberg, *Foreign Policy,* 249. Similarly, Wandycz's disapproving review of Beck's ambiguous "free-hand policy," *Twilight,* 435 ff. On Beck overall see Henry L. Roberts, "The Diplomacy of Colonel Beck," in Craig and Gilbert, eds., *The Diplomats 1919-1939* (Princeton, 1953), 579-614.

64. *DGFP,* C, vol. 4, No. 392, 409, 436, 455, 470, 474, 521, 528, 537, 551, 567; vol. 5, No. 22, 61, 62, 82, 107, 151, 261, 264, 276!

65. On 12 March Moltke reported from Warsaw that the deadlock in negotiations "has caused very great agitation here," DGFP, C, vol. 5, No. 82. On Göring's involvement, ibid. and No. 107. As early as April 1935 Göring had told Lipski that "he [Göring] had a conversation with Hitler, who suggested that, independently of official Polish-German relations, he [Göring] should take the relations between the two countries under his special protection," Lipski, *Diplomat in Berlin,* 41, 189.

66. *DGFP,* C, vol. 5, No. 261, 264

67. Schacht's objections in *DGFP,* C, vol. 5, No. 276. Just three weeks earlier, Conrad Roediger (deputy director in the Foreign Office's newly reorganized Department II) had told Polish ambassador Lipski that "the Polish government were

indulging in illusions if they expected some million of zloty to be transferred monthly in cash in the future. This the foreign exchange situation would by no means permit"[!], ibid., No. 151. Schacht has recorded some aspects of his 1936-37 rivalry with Göring for control of German economic policies in his memoirs, *Confessions of "The Old Wizard"* (Boston, 1956), 335 ff.

68. Explanation to the Economics Ministry, 28 May 1936, *DGFP*, C, vol. 5, No. 356.
69. Agreement signed by Szembek and Moltke in Warsaw on 18 July 1936, *RGBl.* 1936, II, 293. The government committees were empowered to set the final dates of effective terms.
70. *RGBl.* 1937, II, 91; Deutsche Nachrichtenburo from 22 February 1937, BA R 43II/306. Parallel to this, the German-Polish private sector-agreement on iron and steel trade was renewed in Berlin on 20 February 1937 with Polish producers receiving a quota for 0.45 percent of the German domestic steel market and a lump quota of 2,400 tons of refined steel. German scrap iron sales to Poland were reduced to 68.5 percent of the amount of Polish finished steel sold in Germany. In view of the industrial strain already evident in Germany, even these reduced terms were generous, Haniel 4000000/26.
71. *RGBl.* 1937, II, 99.
72. Similarly, the German-Polish private agreement on iron and steel exchanges was rewritten on 15 June 1938 with a Polish quota reduced in percentage terms (now 0.438 percent of German domestic sales) to offset the expanded German(-Austrian) market, Haniel 4000000/26.
73. Deutsche Nachrichtenbuero from 2 July 1938, BA R 43II/306. On material extractions from Poland after September 1939 begin with Martin Broszat, *Nationalsozialistische Polenpolitik*; Jan Tomasz Gross, *Polish Society under German Occupation: The Generalgouvernement, 1939-1944* (Princeton, 1979).
74. The basic data for this discussion of German-Czechoslovak trade 1930-1939 is taken from *Statistisches Jahrbuch für das deutsche Reich*, various volumes 1929-1937. Additional information was taken from the appendix tables in Kaiser, *Economic Diplomacy*; Kaser and Radice, eds., *Economic History of Eastern Europe*, vol. 1, Tables 7.XXIV and 7.XXXI, 511, 518; Doering, *Deutsche Aussenwirtschaftspolitik 1933-1935*, passim; Foreign Office memorandum accompanying the Hops Agreement of 1931, BA R 43I/1123; and from an August 1936 report by the Reichskreditgesellschaft, BA R 2/16470.
75. See, e.g. Foreign Office memorandum on a meeting of the Czechoslovak Envoy Frantisek Chvalkovsky and the director of the Southeastern European department (II), Gerhard Köpke, from 19 September 1931, PAAA Czechoslovakia, Handel 13, Bd. 3.
76. Copy of a Czechoslovak foreign office memorandum Analysis of our Trade with Germany in 1932 sent by the German envoy in Prague, Walter Koch, to the German Foreign Office on 20 February 1933, PAAA Czechoslovakia, Handel 13, Bd. 3. The 1931 German surplus of 180 million marks in trade with Czechoslovakia accounted for 6.3 percent of Germany total trade surplus (2,870 million marks), the 1932 surplus with Czechoslovakia (110.2 million marks) accounted for 10.2 percent of Germany total trade surplus (1,070 millon) that year.
77. Bülow to Chancellery State Secretary Pünder, 18 August 1932, BA R 43I/1123.
78. For the published portions see *RGBl.* 1931, II, 558; for the secret clauses BA R 43I/1123 and Trade Policy Committee meeting of 4 November 1931, GStA PK: I.HA/Rep. 120 C, XIII, 2, No. 21, Bd. 7, Bl. 70. For the renewals *RGBl.* 1932, II, 191, 199. Braun's opposition in ministerial meeting of 19 August 1932, BA R 43I/1123.
79. See GStA PK: I.HA/Rep. 120 C, XIII, 2, No. 21, Bd. 7, passim, e.g. the Czechoslovak note of 11 November 1931 as summarized by Wiehl and the Trade Policy Committee meeting of 30 October 1931, Bl. 68.

80. Trade Policy Committee meeting of 23 June, GStA PK: I.HA/Rep. 120 C, XIII, 2, No. 21, Bl. 144.

81. According to a 17 September 1932 report by the German Chamber of Commerce the Czechoslovaks had only reluctantly abandoned the MFN principle, but were determined "under any circumstances" to support their currency, RWWA 20-1129-4. Only after Czechoslovakia began to benefit economically from the early phases of European rearmament in 1936 were exchange controls on some transactions loosened again.

82. Koch pointed out the already noticeable effects on German porcelain, leather, paper products, electro-technical items, sewing machines, photographic film, and pharmaceuticals, Koch to the Foreign Office, 1 June 1932, GStA PK: I.HA/Rep. 120 C, XIII, 2, No. 20, Bd. 9, Bl. 257.

83. Köpke to the Chancellery and other ministries, 22 December 1931, BA R 43I/1123; GStA PK: I.HA/Rep. 120 C, XIII, 2, No. 21, Bd. 7, Bl. 148.

84. Benzler memorandum for Wiehl and Ritter, 6 December 1932, PAAA Czechoslovakia, Handel 11, Bd. 3. The Germans were offering Czechoslovakia an improvement over the actual ratio of 1931 (1:1.73) and 1932 (1:1.78) in exchange for certainty that the surplus would continue at lower levels.

85. German Consulate in Pressburg (Druffel) to the Foreign Office, 26 October 1932, Koch to the Foreign Office, 29 November 1932, both in PAAA Czechoslovakia, Handel 11, Bd. 3. The German trade surplus in 1932 was just 110 million marks (180 million marks in 1931) of which only 35 million was accumulated after July.

86. Union of Lower Silesian Chambers of Commerce to the Prussian Economics Ministry, 3 February 1933, GStA PK: I.HA/Rep. 120 C, XIII, 2, No. 20, Bd. 10, Bl. 23. Christoph Boyer describes the "significant risks" for both sides in disrupting the "tightly woven net of economic interdependencies" between areas on both sides of the border, "Das deutsche Reich und die Tschechoslovakei im Zeichen der Weltwirtschaftskrise," *VfZ* 39 (1991), 552.

87. On Nazi policy toward Czechoslovakia see Weinberg, "Czechoslovakia and Germany 1933-1945," in Miloslav Rechcigl, ed., *Czechoslovakia Past and Present* (The Hague, 1968), 760-69; Weinberg, "Secret Hitler-Benes Negotiations in 1936-37," *Journal of Central European Affairs* 19 (1960), 366-74; Detlef Brandes, "Die Politik des Dritten Reiches gegenüber der Tschechoslowakei," in Manfred Funcke, ed., *Hitler, Deutschland, und die Mächte: Materialien zur Aussenpolitik des Dritten Reiches*, 508-23.

88. Posse's presentation at the cabinet meeting of 4 October 1933, R 43II/301a. See also Boyer's citation of an August 1933 assessment from Prague that Czechoslovakia stood as a "center of economic resistance to Germany," "Das Reich und die Tschechoslovakei im Zeichen der Weltwirtschaftskrise," 586.

89. Benes's statements cited in Wandycz, *Twilight*, 261, 393. On the Czechoslovak position vis-à-vis Germany see Benes, *The Problems of Czechoslovakia* (Prague, 1936); Gajan Kolomann, "Die Rolle der Tschechoslovakei in Mitteleuropa 1918-1945," *Oesterreichische Osthefte* 8 (1966), 183-91.

90. Weinberg, *Foreign Policy*, vol. 1, 110.

91. Benzler memorandum for Wiehl and Ritter, 6 December 1932, PAAA Czechoslovakia, Handel 11, Bd. 3.

92. Kurt Schneider, *Der Welthandel im Clearingverkehr. 170 Clearing-Abkommen* (Zurich, 1937), 98; Economics Ministry to the Foreign Exchange Control Offices, 25 March 1933, BA R 7/4702.

93. Schneider, *Welthandel im Clearingverkehr*, 98; Economics Ministry to the Foreign Exchange Control Offices, 15 December 1933, BA R 7/4702.

94. The tendency for Germany to run negative clearing balances with a number of countries in 1934 is discussed in Doering, *Deutsche Aussenwirtschaftspolitik 1933-*

1935, 112-13; more recently by Ritschl, "Deutsche Zahlungsbilanz 1936-1941," 110, based on material in Deutsche Bundesbank, *Deutsches Geld und Bankwesen in Zahlen 1876-1975* (Frankfurt/M, 1976), 41.

95. For the following see Schneider, *Welthandel*, 99-101; report by the Reichskreditgesellschaft from August 1936, BA R 2/16470.

96. Dr. Kislinger, Executive Secretary of the German Union of Industry (Prague) reported that after Hitler's assumption of power in January 1933 "large segments" of the Czechoslovak population believed that Germany had "political reasons" for pursuing a hostile trade policy toward Czechoslovakia. That information was passed by Siegert (German Chamber of Commerce) to Ritter at the Foreign Office, where it could only have confirmed the German desire to avoid any break in trade relations, despite Czechoslovakia's unilateral actions on payments, Siegert to Ritter, 8 March 1933, PAAA Czechoslovakia, Handel 11, Bd. 3.

97. "Possibilities for Developing German-Czechoslovak Trade," section 5 (p. 19-20) of the report on Czechoslovakia by the Reichskreditgesellschaft from August 1936, BA R 2/16470. As noted above in chapter four, Posse had remarked on the "similar economic structures" of the two countries already in June 1920.

98. Memorandum by chancellery economics desk officer Franz Willuhn, 6 November 1937, BA R 43II/323.

99. Report on Czechoslovakia by the Reichskreditgesellschaft from August 1936, BA R 2/16470; Kaiser, Table A.7, 325.

100. On the economic and other aspects of the German occupation of Bohemia 1939-1945 see Detlef Brandes, *Die Tschechen unter dem deutschen Protektorat*, 2 vols. (Munich, 1969); J. Krejči, "The Bohemian-Moravian War Economy," in Radice and Kaser, eds., *The Economic History of Eastern Europe 1919-1975*, vol. 2, 452-94.

101. Harvey Dyck dates the Soviet decision to "late October or early November" 1930. He further argues that it was a Soviet attempt to split Germany off from a potential common Western response to Soviet timber and grain "dumping" 1929-1930, *Weimar Germany and Soviet Russia 1926-1933* (New York, 1966), 220 ff. Dyck's dating of the decision is almost certainly correct, but the mixture of political and economic motives in Soviet trade decisions remains (without adequate archival support) impossible to untwine. Dyck discounts any other economic factors and overlooks some obvious political ones, such as the upcoming renewal of the Berlin treaty in 1931, making his explanation for this weighty decision too monocausal. For developments in this period begin with Hartmut Pogge von Strandmann, "Industrial Primacy in German Foreign Policy?," in Richard Bessel and E.J. Feuchtwanger, eds., *Social Change and Political Development in Weimar Germany* (London, 1981), 241-67.

102. The Russia Committee and other organs of German industry had been fishing for an invitation to visit the Soviet Union on a "study trip" since June 1930, Perrey *Rußlandausschuß*, 144 ff. On the "princely treatment" received by the German industrialists, Reuter's report, Mannesmann-Archiv D 1 980/1; Kastl's cautious presentation of trip (before the results were known) to the Reichsverband Vorstand, 20 February 1931, Bayer-Archiv 62/10.4; "Discussion with Representatives of Industry about Business with Russia," 11 March 1931, *Akten Brüning*, 935. The travelers made a second report to economics and finance ministry representatives on 13 March, Zweckverband, 21 March 1931, RWWA 20-1100-1.

103. Meetings with industrialists, 11 March and 16 March 1931, *Akten Brüning*, 935, 948; cabinet meetings of 20 and 24 March, *Akten Brüning*, 971-980.

104. Dyck, *Weimar Germany and Soviet Russia*, 229-36, 231.

105. This point was repeated in Hans Kraemer's (albeit self-serving) declaration to the directors of the industrial Reichsverband: "For political and economic reasons

we must hold absolutely tightly to the Russian card ... there is not the slightest reason for us to let this [card] out of our hand prematurely," 23 April 1931, Bayer-Archiv 62/10.4

106. Cabinet discussions of 20 and 24 March 1931, *Akten Brüning*, 971-80. It is certainly possible that the Soviets timed their offer of additional orders in exchange for credits precisely to create the kind of linkage explained by Curtius, in effect manipulating the German practice of using commercial contacts in support of larger foreign policy moves.

107. In December 1930 the Reich government had refused to assume guarantees for new credits for the Soviets, Perrey, *Rußlandausschuß*, 140-41.

108. The following is based on "Discussion of Business with Russia," 16 March 1931, *Akten Brüning*, 948.

109. According to Kraemer, the Russia Committee and the government had "agreed in past years that the [Soviet] debt should not exceed 500 million." He confirmed that this new program would bring Soviet debts to Germany to "at least one billion ... we must understand this perfectly clearly," 23 April 1931, Bayer-Archiv 62/10.4.

110. In the summer of 1930 the Soviets had fallen behind on payments in numerous contracts with German exporters, some of whom began refusing new Soviet orders, Perrey, *Rußlandausschuß*, 140.

111. Discussion of 16 March 1931, *Akten Brüning*, 948. Klöckner expected 300 million in additional Soviet orders to create 100,000 new jobs in German industry, the Association of German Machine Tool Manufacturers subsequently estimated that 150 million marks in Soviet orders would provide employment for 70,000 workers for six months, both estimates cited in Perrey, *Rußlandausschuß*, 137, 180; Manfred Pohl cites a figure of 150,000 new jobs from the 300 million marks in Soviet contracts, but the source for that estimate is unclear, *Geschäft und Politik. Deutsch-russisch/sowjetische Wirtschaftsbeziehungen 1850-1988* (Mainz, 1988), 91.

112. Here Luther echoed Economic Minister Dietrich's argument of January 1931 on the necessity of an economic agreement with Poland in the helping Germany secure reparations relief from the West.

113. Kraemer told the Reichsverband that "America observes the closer interdependence (Verflechtung) of the German and Russian economies with growing mistrust" and that the Americans had followed recent German industrial overtures to Russia with "the greatest suspicion," 23 April 1931, Bayer-Archiv 62/10.4.

114. On all these developments see as well Perrey, *Rußlandausschuß*, 165 ff.; Pohl, *Geschäft und Politik*, 90-91.

115. The agreement took its name from senior Soviet negotiator Yuri Piatakov, deputy commissar for Heavy Industry and vice-chairman of the Gosplan for the Presidium of the Soviet Supreme Economic Council. A copy of the agreement as circulated confidentially by the "Russia Committee of German Industry" can be found in RWWA 20-1100-1.

116. According to Kraemer, Piatakov told the German industrialists during these negotiations that "we [the Soviets] are forced to place these orders as quickly as possible; we have completed the factories, the buildings are empty, we have to fill them with machines, there are [equipment] shortages of every kind, the people are becoming restless, we absolutely must produce now and we must produce more," Reichsverband Vorstand, 23 April 1931, Bayer-Archiv 62/20.4. The agreement standardized payment terms for these Soviet orders (with a 20 percent deposit) to avoid competition in credit terms among German suppliers, Pohl, *Geschäft und Politik*, 91; Perrey, *Rußlandausschuß*, 168 ff.

117. "Langnamverein" notice of 3 November 1931; notices by the Russia Committee from 12 April and 16 March 1932, all in RWWA 20-1103-1.

118. "Ifago" (bank consortium) action #9 for 15 million, Pohl, *Geschäft und Politik*, 99; action #10 from September 1932 for 110 million and #10 A from December 1932 for 60 million, RWWA 20-1100-1. On these developments see Pohl, *Geschäft und Politik*, 91 ff. and his earlier *Die Finanzierung der Russengeschäfte zwischen den beiden Weltkriegen* (Frankfurt, 1975).

119. Soviet orders cited in Perrey, *Rußlandausschuß*, 174; German exports in *Statistisches Jahrbuch* 52 (1933). Using Soviet data, Baykov show the same dramatic increases in German exports from 852 million rubles in 1929 to 1,799 million in 1931 and 1, 435 million in 1932, *Soviet Foreign Trade*, Table VII.

120. The Piatakov Agreement had standardized the terms for Soviet payments only on German exports that used guaranteed credits. The Russia Committee obtained a government promise that in administering the export credit program, the interministerial committee would withhold state-backed credits from deals concluded by "gross underbidding" of German competitors, Kraemer at Reichsverband Vorstand, 23 April 1931, Bayer-Archiv 62/10.4. In November 1931 Economics Minister Warmbold transferred this approval/withholding power to the Russia Committee itself, Perrey, *Rußlandausschuß*, 191.

121. At the start of the program, Kraemer argued that the risks involved with allowing the Soviets to run up a 1,000-million-mark debt to Germany "can be taken only if the prices to be negotiated with the Russians bring some macroeconomic benefit [to Germany] and here I have the gravest concerns." He criticized the "shameless mutual underbidding" already underway, Reichsverband Vorstand, 23 April 1931, Bayer-Archiv 62/10.4.

122. Klöckner felt that the standard Depression-era practice of unloading inventory at prices based only on variable costs and not on fixed costs "might be right in view of the international market today, but it is, in my opinion, wrong for Russian orders. Currently we have the Russians in our hands, they are dependent on us, and for that reason I cannot understand that we continue to compete with each other." He urged that Soviet orders "be taken on the books only with a large profit (mit grossem Gewinn) so that at least we can cover the risks involved with a 20 percent profit right at the start." Not surprisingly, Klöckner did not suggest that once the risks were covered by large profit, the Reich be allowed to drop its role as the guarantor of export credits. Klöckner to Poensgen et al., 20 April 1932, Mannesmann-Archiv M50 411. See also minutes of a 3 May 1932 meeting of the Stahlwerks-Verband to discuss Handling Russian Contracts in Non-Cartelized (nichtsyndizierten) Products, especially Klöckner's plan for an "understanding ... to reach a price agreement on Russian orders and get the previously existing unbridled competition of the firms into tolerable form," Mannesmann Archiv M 50 411.

123. The Comprehensive Delivery Agreement of 15 June 1932 established the basic terms of delivery and payment for German exports to the USSR, a copy in RWWA 20-1100-1.

124. Notice of Stahlwerksverband to participating firms on plans for an "Ausgleichsabgabe für Mehr-und Minderlieferungen" to the USSR, 2 August 1932, Mannesmann Archiv P 7 55 71.

125. For these reasons, historians who have closely followed Hitler's utterances and decisions on Soviet matters during this period often pose baffling dichotomous questions about German policy and Nazi-Soviet relations such as "continuation of traditional relations or growing opposition?" and "ideology or reasons of state?" These two examples are taken from the tables of contents in Dean Scott McMurry, *Deutschland und die Sowjetunion 1933-1936* (Cologne and Vienna, 1979) and Philipp Fabry, *Die Sowjetunion und das Dritte Reich* (Stuttgart, 1971). Hitler's actions provide abundant evidence for answering both questions either way. For

an excellent introduction to Nazi-Soveit relations, see Geoffrey Roberts, *The Soviet Union and the Origins of the Second World War. Russo-German Relations and the Road to War, 1933-1941* (New York, 1995) which modifies Roberts's earlier work in light of new evidence from Soviet archives. A noteworthy German study for the themes explored here is Rolf-Dieter Müller, *Das Tor zur Weltmacht: Die Bedeutung der Sowjetunion für die deutsche Wirtschafts- und Rüstungspolitik zwischen den Weltkriegen* (Boppard, 1984).

126. Weinberg, *Foreign Policy*, 75.

127. In 1931 and 1932 the Soviets delivered 451 million marks in gold (and a small amount of silver) to Germany, cutting the trade deficit for those years to 363 million. The 1,110 million figure includes the trade deficit from 1931 to 1932, earlier debt, and Soviet orders placed from 1931 to 1932 for German goods not yet delivered. Data on the level of Soviet debt to Germany in *Akten Hitler*, 319, note 28; Foreign Office memorandum on the German-Soviet trade and payments agreement, 20 March 1934, *DGFP*, C, vol. 2, No. 342. Corrected data on German-Soviet trade, including Soviet gold shipments, 1926-1937 provided by the Russia Committee of German Industry from May 1938, BA R 2/16467.

128. On Soviet repayment difficulties see Perrey, *Rußlandausschuß*, 191 ff., 207 ff.; Beitel and Nötzold, *Deutsch-sowjetische Wirtschaftsbeziehungen*, 74 ff. German willingness to provide 200 million marks for the February 1933 bridge loan confirms Hitler's ambiguous early policy toward the Soviets that allowed (new) Reichsbank President Schacht to handle credits for the Soviets in the same forthcoming manner as his predecessor, Pohl, *Geschäft und Politik*, 103.

129. *Akten Hitler*, 319, note 28; Foreign Office memorandum on the German-Soviet trade and payments agreement, 20 March 1934, *DGFP*, C, vol. 2, No. 342. Russia Committee data on German-Soviet trade 1926-1937, including Soviet gold shipments, May 1938, BA R 2/16467.

130. Perrey, Pohl and others have emphasized the economic importance to German industry of exports to the USSR in the depression years 1931 and 1932. By comparison, very little attention has been given to the importance of Soviet debt repayments to the Nazi regime in the years 1933 to 1935; one exception is McMurray, *Deutschland und die Sowjetunion 1933-1936.*

131. By the terms of the German-Soviet Economic Agreement of 20 March 1934, the Soviets agreed to repay 390 million marks of their outstanding debt to the Reich in "gold and foreign exchange," of which sum 227 million was provided in gold, Meyer's memorandum on the agreement, 20 March 1934, *DGFP*, C, vol. 2, No. 342; corrected data on German-Soviet trade 1926-1937 provided by the Russia Committee of German Industry from May 1938, BA R 2/16467; Albrecht Ritschl, "Die deutsche Zahlungsbilanz 1936-1941," table 1, 106, 109, table 3, 111.

132. In 1935 the Soviet Union provided 58 percent of German manganese ore imports, 54 percent of asbestos, 75 percent of the flax, and over half of the pulp wood and pit wood. The import volumes for the years 1934 and 1935 (combined) are a tribute to both the consumptive-productive powers of the Germany economy and the natural richness of Soviet territory: 221,000 tons of barley, 272,000 tons of oil-cake, 42,000 tons of flax, 2,697,000 tons of pulp wood, 701,000 tons of sawn timber, 577,000 tons of motor fuel, 400,000 tons of manganese ore, 311,000 tons of apatite, "On the Question of Vital Raw Material Imports from the USSR," a report by the Russia Committee from March 1937, BA R 43II/332.

133. McMurry appears to have been the first to suggest a periodization of Nazi-Soviet relations on the basis of the Soviet debt repayment.

134. The 20 March 1934 agreement had rescheduled payment on 100 million marks of a February 1933 140-million-mark bridge loan, moving the due date from 1934 to 1935, *DGFP*, C, vol. 2, No. 342.

135. *DGFP*, C, vol. 3, No. 505, 529. Counselor of Legation Bräutigam, who handled economic questions in the Eastern Department of the Foreign Office, commented in mid-March that "in my opinion the German economic interests at stake are too important to allow German-Russian economic relations to become paralysed simply in order to uphold a principle, *DGFP*, C, vol. 3, No. 529. Bräutigam was wrong in supposing that Schacht wanted only to "uphold a principle," but quite correct in asserting that German-Russian trade relations were too important to become paralyzed over this point.

136. The final protocol signed by Schacht and Kandelaki contained two treaties and four letters, *DGFP*, C, vol. 4, No. 21. Soviet payments in 1935 were to comprise 100 million marks in gold and foreign exchange (of which 16 million in gold was in fact delivered) and 100 million in materials, including: 45 million in timber, 20 million in naphtha products, 8.5 million in natural bristles, 5.5 million in manganese.

137. Perrey, *Rußlandausschuß*, 243; copies of these agreements in *DGFP*, C, vol. 4, No. 21.

138. *DGFP*, C, vol. 4, No. 386, 472, 483.

139. *DGFP*, C, vol. 4, No. 483, 524. Geoffrey Roberts does not go nearly far enough in saying merely that the negotiations "floundered in wrangling" because of "Soviet complaints about German restrictions on the type of exports (e.g. military equipment) allowed to go to the USSR," *Soviet Union and the Origins of the Second World War*, 35-6.

140. *DGFP*, C, vol. 4, No. 518.

141. The Soviets were interested in an expansion of trade with Germany only if this would lead to some larger political understanding between the two countries, Roberts, *Soviet Union and the Origins of the Second World War*, 23 ff. Hitler's refusal to accommodate Soviet desires to buy weapons indicated that neither a Nazi-Soviet détente nor even a normalization of relations would be immediately forthcoming. In response, the Soviets declined Schacht's offer for a large new loan. Both sides reiterated their positions in August 1936; again with no positive conclusion, Roberts, *Soviet Union*, 43. On the practical level, it appears from Kandelaki's comments to the Russia Committee that the Soviets also would have resisted German imposition of a 1:1 trade ratio, *DGFP*, C, vol. 4, No. 524.

142. In a final attempt to force the Soviets to use their export proceeds for new orders in Germany, Schacht unilaterally imposed restrictions on payments for Soviet goods in December 1935. This backfired when the Soviets called the German bluff by stopping all exports to the Reich on the last day of 1935 and then issued a decree banning raw material exports to countries blocking the free use of Soviet export proceeds, McMurry, *Deutschland und die Sowjetunion*, 442 ff., *DGFP*, C, vol. 4, No. 502; memo by the Russia Committee, 23 January 1936, RWWA 20-1100-2.

143. For the agreement, signed by Schacht and Kandelaki, *DGFP*, C, vol. 4, No. 302. Many of these changes in 1935 and 1936 were in line with the strategic and tactical shifts in Soviet trade policy outlined by Soviet Foreign Trade Commissar A.P. Rosenholz in *Pravda*, Nr. 308 (7 November 1935), RWWA 20-1100-2: Soviet disinterest in short-term or medium-term credits, a shift to cash payments for imports, building Soviet gold reserves, maintaining a low level of foreign debt, and the explicit warning that with the end of Soviet debts to Germany, the USSR would "put trade relations with Germany on a new basis."

144. Annual reports of the Russia Committee of German Industry from 1935-1936, RWWA 20-1100-2; from 1937-1940, RWWA 20-1088-2; Russia Committee Summary of Contracts in the 200 Million Credit, 16 May 1938, BA R 2/16467.

145. In 1931 to 1933 Britain supplied an average of 9.5 percent of Soviet annual imports. In 1934-1936 the figure had risen to an average of 17.6 percent. Similarly, exports from France rose from an annual average of 1.16 percent of Soviet total imports in 1931-33 to 3.4 percent in 1934 to 36, Baykov, *Soviet Foreign Trade*, Table VII.

146. A copy of Rosenholz's remarks was sent by the press department of the Soviet Trade Office in Berlin to the *National Zeitung* on 29 July 1936. New evidence also supports McMurry's alterative interpretation, i.e., that since the Soviets were no longer compelled by debt to export to Hitler's Germany, the continuation of any such exports should be interpreted as a Soviet desire to preserve some material exchange between the two countries as the basis for a future political understanding with Germany, McMurry, *Deutschland und die Soujetunion*, 455; Roberts, *Soviet Union and the Origins of the Second World War*, 39 ff.

147. According to Erbe, Germany had spent 9 billion marks on the military in 1936 and increased this to 15.5 billion by 1938, *Nationalsozialistische Wirtschaftspolitik*, 25. For an introduction to the various debates and voluminous literature on the economics of German rearmament see Timothy W. Mason, "Innere Krise und Angriffskrieg," in Friedrich Forstmeier and Hans-Erich Volkmann, eds., *Wirtschaft und Rüstung am Vorabend des Zweiten Weltkrieges*, (Dusseldorf, 1975), 158-88; the three-way debate between Mason, David Kaiser and Richard J. Overy, "Germany, Domestic Crisis and War in 1939," *Past and Present* 122 (1989), 200-40. Recently, Ritschl has argued that Germany's chronic foreign exchange crisis peaked in 1937-1938 and diminished after the annexation of Austria, "Deutsche Zahlungsbilanz."

148. Russia Committee Annual report for 1938, RWWA 20-1088-2; Russia Committee Summary of Contracts in the 200 million Credit, 16 May 1938, BA R 2/16467.

149. BA R 2/16467. In January 1937 the Soviets made their one and only explicit offer to Hitler's Germany in this period to normalize relations between the two states, an offer that Hitler rebuffed, Roberts, *Soviet Union and the Origins of the Second World War*, 39 ff.

150. By 1937 and 1938, as Britain began to accelerate its own rearmament; British exports to the USSR declined from their 1934 to 1936 levels of 17.6 percent to 15.6 percent of Soviet total imports. At the same time, the American share of Soviet imports (11.8 percentfrom 1934 to 1936) rose to 18.2 percent in 1937 and 28.5 percent in 1938, Baykov, *Soviet Foreign Trade*, table VII.

151. RWWA 20-1088-2. These practical considerations are missing from every political analysis of Nazi-Soviet trade in this period.

152. However, the accumulation of some 20 million marks in Soviet accounts in Germany supports McMurry's idea that for political reasons, Stalin was prepared to pay for the maintenance of a certain level of trade.

153. In 1937 The USSR sent 566 million rubles worth of goods to the UK, 32.7 percent of total Soviet exports, Baykov, *Soviet Foreign Trade*, Table VII.

154. Spitta to Julius Karl Schnurre, director of the East European section (IV) in the Foreign Office's Economic Policy Division (May 1936 to December 1941), 29 July 1937, PAAA Pol. IV, Russische Handelsvertretung in Deutschland, Bd. 1.

155. *DGFP*, D, vol. 4, No. 488, for the course of negotiations, Nos. 479-495.

156. Emil Wiehl, director of the Foreign Office's Commercial Department, noted that "It is generally agreed that the rupture of credit negotiations with Russia is extremely regrettable in view of Germany's raw-materials position, but that on the other hand, having regard to the actual technical impossibility of carrying out the German counterdeliveries, the responsibility for the conclusion of the credit negotiations cannot be assumed," *DGFP*, D, vol. 4, No. 495.

157. For specialized treatments see Gerhard Weinberg *Germany and the Soviet Union 1939-1941* (Leiden, 1954); Philipp Fabry, *Der Hitler Stalin Pakt* (Darmstadt, 1962); Geoffrey Roberts, *The Unholy Alliance: Stalin's Pact with Hitler* (Bloomington, Ind., 1989, which uses some of the Soviet material just becoming available at that time; Ingeborg Fleischhauer, *Der Pakt. Hitler, Stalin, und die Initiative der deutschen Diplomatie 1938-1939* (Berlin, 1990). The account by journalists Anthony Read and David Fisher is lively but adds no new material knowledge, *The Deadly Embrace. Hitler, Stalin, and the Nazi-Soviet Pact 1939-41* (New York, 1988). With the German attack on Poland already planned by May 1939, Hitler sought some diplomatic means to dissuade the British from adhering to their commitments to Poland. When the Japanese balked at an alliance directed against the British, Hitler was forced to reach an understanding with the other major power potentially capable of dissuading the British from involvement with Poland.

158. Weinberg, *Germany and the Soviet Union 1939-1941*, 25; *DGFP*, D, vol. 6, No. 332. On this much-analyzed event see Roberts, *Soviet Union and the origins of the Second World War*, 68 ff. and his earlier article "Infamous Encounter? The Merekalov-Weizsäcker Meeting of 17 April 1939" which is cited there.

159. *DGFP*, D, vol. 6, No. 424. Like Hitler, Stalin was interested in expanded economic contacts only if these were a promising lead to a political understanding as well.

160. *DGFP*, D, vol. 6, No. 453, 465.

161. *DGFP*, D, vol. 6, No. 628, 642. The lists of desired goods submitted by the Soviets in July have not been found. Since the final agreement for German deliveries contained provisions for 58.5 million marks of "armaments" (Rüstungsgegenstände), one can assume that at least a general request for arms deliveries was made by the Soviets and approved by the Germans at this time. In order to obtain the necessary political-strategic pact, Hitler was now also willing to make substantial arms deliveries to the Soviets, reversing his 1936 ban on weapons sales to the USSR.

162. *DGFP*, D, vol. 6, No. 677, 685, 699; Weinberg, *Foreign Policy*, vol. 2, 604. Oddly, Roberts fails to mention the important German decision of 10 July to sell advanced weapons to the Soviets and its political consequences, he speaks instead of a "month-long lull in German advances to the Soviets" from late June to late July, *Soviet Union and the Origins of the Second World War*, 79.

163. *DGFP*, D, vol. 6, No. 700, 583, 772.

164. *DGFP*, D, vol. 7, No. 70, 75, 105.

165. *DGFP*, D, vol. 7, No. 113.

166. *DGFP*, D, vol. 6, No. 530, 700. These examples, along with much of the account presented here, contradict Geoffrey Roberts's assertion that "the German documents" and "German accounts" consistently paint a picture of Soviet wooing of Berlin," *Soviet Union and the Origins of World War Two*, 72.

167. A copy of the agreement in *DGFP*, D, vol. 6, No. 131; commentary in ibid., Nos. 135, 147, 346; Ordinance (Erlass) of the Economics Ministry to the Export Control Offices (No. 177/39) and to the Foreign Exchange Offices (No. 147/39), BA R 7/4699.

168. *DGFP*, D, vol. 4, No. 495.

169. Report by the Russia Committee, cited in Fabry, *Sowjetunion und Dritte Reich*, 196-219.

170. The economic significance of Soviet deliveries and the role this trade played in Germany's ability to conduct the campaigns of 1939 and 1940 is discussed in Weinberg, *Germany and the Soviet Union*, 65 ff. and in Fabry, *Sowjetunion und Dritte Reich*, 190-94.

171. Copy of the order from 15 October 1940, BA R 7/4699.
172. Weinberg, *Germany and the Soviet Union 1939-1941*, 44.
173. Weinberg, *Foreign Policy*, vol. 2, 604.
174. On the economic exploitation of the USSR after June 1941 see Alexander Dallin, *German Rule in Russia 1941-1945* (New York, 1957); Timothy Patrick Mulligan, *The Politics of Illusion and Empire. German Occupation Policy in the Soviet Union 1942-1943* (New York, 1988)

SEEKING AUTONOMY
Resumption of Trade Relations in the Occupation

After Europe's horrific experiences of conquest, violent economic exploitation, and mass killing during the war, Germany's unconditional surrender provided a radically new framework for West German trade relations with Poland, Czechoslovakia, and the Soviet Union. Under the Occupation regime, the Western Allies exercised full, complete, and exclusive control over Western Germany's foreign trade and foreign trade policy from 1945 through 1949. Unlike the development of the domestic social market economy in which the Germans themselves played an important role, the direction of West Germany's foreign trade remained firmly in the hands of Occupation authorities. The Allies maintained close, careful, and exclusive control over West German foreign trade through 1949, reserving to themselves the right to sign international trade and payments agreements on behalf of the Bizonia and Trizonia.

Within this framework, the Allies made the fundamental decision to reconstruct an advanced industrial (through demilitarized) economy in West Germany. Economic reconstruction necessitated a reintegration of German industrial areas into the European economy and world division of labor. By actively rebuilding and reintegrating an advanced industrial economy in the western zones, the Allies restored West Germany's traditional foreign trade pattern of manufactured exports and raw material imports. Allied reconstruction reestablished the economic basis of German trade with Eastern Europe by allowing West Germany as early as 1948 to reassume much of its traditional

Notes for this chapter begin on page 335.

pattern of trade with Poland, Czechoslovakia, and the USSR despite the disturbing memories of Nazi policies in the East.

The carefully planned resuscitation of West German trade with the rest of Europe was cut short on the eastern side by the gradual emergence two rival political-economic blocs in Europe. Beginning in late 1947, the crystallizing Cold War order provided the dominating international context for West German trade with the East. By 1948 West German trade with Poland, Czechoslovakia, and the Soviet Union became subsumed in the larger concept of East-West trade. American concerns about the national security aspects of Western trade with the Soviet bloc led to the politicization of all East-West trade across a divided Europe.

The combination of economic reconstruction and East-West trade politicization led first to a revival of German trade contacts and formal trade agreements with the East in 1946 and 1947 and then to a constriction of these contacts in 1948 and 1949. As the international framework of a divided Europe became more clear in 1948, the Occupation powers began to employ their unique position of authority in occupied Germany to manipulate West German trade as part of the larger process of politicizing trade across the East-West divide.

Constraints of the Occupation

On 5 June 1945 the Allied powers assumed "supreme authority with respect to Germany, including all the powers possessed by the German government …"[1] With this comprehensive act, the Allies implicitly assumed authority over German foreign trade and foreign trade policy. Over the next six months the Allies explicitly took command of all aspects of trade and trade policy including import/export controls, foreign exchange, and the most basic movement of goods and people. Control Council Proclamation No. 2 of 20 September 1945 listed in detail some "additional requirements imposed on Germany" by the Allies. Section III, Article 7a declared flatly that as of the date of surrender "the diplomatic, consular, commercial and other relations of the German State with other States have ceased to exist." With that declaration, the Allies removed the existing legal framework for German international trade. Germany's international commercial relations entered a void from which they would emerge at a future date. Article 5 insured that the future legal framework for Germany's international commercial relations would be rebuilt by the Allies themselves since it declared that "Allied Representatives will regulate all matters affecting Germany's relations with other countries." In short, control over both current foreign trade and the future direction of German trade policy lay exclusively in Allied hands.[2]

While the Control Council eradicated Germany's previous legal framework for international trade and abrogated German authority in commercial policy, the military government imposed controls on the flow of goods and services into or out of occupied Germany. Military Law No. 53 (Foreign Exchange Control) listed a number of "prohibited transactions," including any involving "property wherever situated if the transaction is between or involves any person in Germany and any person outside Germany." This prohibition effectively cut off Germany from contact with foreign buyers, sellers, middlemen, and international traders of any kind. A second clause expressly forbade "exporting, remitting, or other removal of any property from Germany." These two provisions were reinforced by the blanket rules of Military Law No. 161 (Frontier Control) of 1 December 1945, which limited the passage of persons and property across the German border and the boundaries of U.S. zone.[3]

In war-ravaged Central and East-Central Europe these controls were largely redundant at the time of their promulgation in 1945. The devastated East-Central European economies were not yet capable of significant foreign trade and would not be for another eighteen to twenty-four months. Yet with their comprehensive controls of German foreign trade, the Allies began immediately to determine the direction and content of West German trade, including West German trade with East European countries. Because of traditional German foreign trade dependency (now intensified in the immediate postwar years), control over imports and exports gave the Allies a powerful lever in controlling the entire economy. By controlling German raw material imports and export sales, the Allies could begin to reshape the German economy as they wished.

Long before Allied troops had entered the Reich, a number of occupation strategies had been presented, discussed, and revised in Washington, in London and among the fragmented authorities of the French provisional government.[4] Agreement came easily on the most obvious points, such as the need to denazify, demilitarize, and "democratize" Germany. On the economic aspects of the problem there was also initial consensus on the obvious points, in particular, demilitarization of German industry and decartelization of heavy industry. On other important economic aspects of the Occupation there was very little consensus among the British, French, Americans, and Soviets, or among the three Western powers, or even among American policymakers themselves. In 1945 there was no common Four Power (or even Three Power) conception for the future world economic order, no policy on how Germany should fit into that order, and, as a result, no practical plan for fitting it in.[5] In the absence of a functioning joint Four Power policy or a central German administration, each Occupation zone developed its own economic administration and economic practices, including its own trade policy. Circumstances initially confined the scope of early trade policy to the most basic tasks: controlling imports and exports, locating existing exportable surpluses, and gradually raising the production levels of promising export facilities.

In the western zones, each zone commander was acutely aware of the need to get some exports out of Germany as a means of reducing occupation costs. Already deprived of its foreign balances, external assets, and gold reserves, Germany could pay for Allied support only through merchandise exports. Reviving German exports was absolutely necessary for Germany even to begin covering the cost of feeding itself.[6] For these reasons, export revival in western Germany was pursued as a goal by each of the military governors well before it became official Allied policy and long before the political future of Germany (both West and East) had been decided.[7]

Even though it had emerged from the war as the world's leading economic power, the U.S. had no desire to continue handing out large sums to support German imports indefinitely. Lucius D. Clay, the Military Governor of the U.S. zone of Occupation, recalled explaining to Gen. William Draper, head of the Economics Division at the Office of the Military Government, U.S. (OMGUS), that "we could and must build up our own capital [through exports] until it sufficed to start a real flow of raw materials."[8] Unlike the British and French (who seemed curiously unwilling to exert themselves to promote the sale of German finished goods abroad), OMGUS very actively sought to increase German finished goods exports. The basic production realities of the U.S. zone pushed OMGUS along the path of giving priority to the export of value-added goods.

OMGUS stated very directly and plainly that the "maximum export possibilities for the U.S. Zone, as well as for Germany as a whole, must be found in finished products rather than in raw materials and semi-fabricates." OMGUS openly set a goal of "about 80 percent" of total exports as finished products for 1947.[9] OMGUS saw Germany's future in "cameras, ... pharmaceuticals, surgical equipment, ... shuttle eyes, automatic packing machines" and other value-added goods. As early as December 1945 OMGUS had organized German Export-Import Bureaus (Aussenhandelskontor) in each of the three Länder (states) of the U.S. zone. In February 1946 the first commercial export and import transactions were concluded under the direct auspices of the U.S. military government, and in May the first export show for the U.S. zone opened in Munich.[10]

The export policies pursued by OMGUS since late 1945 amounted to a planned reconstruction of the West German economy along traditional (though demilitarized) lines. These OMGUS actions were a de facto repudiation of the residual elements of the harsh Morgenthau Plan of 1944 still embodied in portions of occupation directive JCS 1067 of May 1945. This repudiation in fact actually preceded Secretary of State James Byrnes's famous "Stuttgart speech" of 6 September 1946 in which Byrnes gave official notice of U.S. intentions to allow the reconstruction of a demilitarized industrial economy in Germany.[11]

At the end of 1946 the still sharply negative balance of trade remained one of the most a serious problems confronting the West German economy. Exports from the British and U.S. zones together totaled $161 million, but this covered just 25 percent of the $643 million in required imports.[12] Export earnings remained overly dependent on sales of two basic raw materials, coal and timber. Problems loomed ahead for both of these commodities. Western Germany had traditionally been a net importer of timber in huge amounts and could not export wood at the current rate for very much longer without irreparable damage to the economy and environment. Coal sales abroad would also have to be cut back as a rise in domestic manufacturing required diversion of some production to the home market. On the administrative side, foreign trade still remained the exclusive prerogative of the Occupation authorities; nothing had been done yet to reprivatize foreign trade or to return to normal business practices.[13]

Substantial physical and administrative progress was made in 1947 after Secretary Byrnes and Foreign Minister Ernest Bevin signed an agreement creating the Bizonia, an "economic fusion" of the British and American zones, effective January 1, 1947.[14] In the agreement itself, the "economic unity of Germany" was highly touted as the principle aim of the new Bizonia. Less ostentatiously presented, but no less directly stated nor less sincerely meant, was another "aim of the two Governments," namely "the achievement by the end of 1949 of a self-sustaining economy for the area." Indeed, "developing a German economy which could be maintained without further financial assistance from the occupying governments" was one of the primary tasks of the new bizonal Joint Export Import Agency (JEIA) over the next three years.[15]

Under its first two cochairmen, Dr. Roy J. Bullock (U.S.) and J.F. Cahan (U.K.), JEIA became the institutional mechanism that put the

American stamp onto the Bizonia's foreign trade plans.[16] Through JEIA, the American military government's emphasis on finished goods exports now made itself felt in the whole area of the Bizonia. JEIA's special position in the bizonal administration reflected Allied awareness that controlling Germany's foreign trade, especially the structure of imports, was a key in expediting the reemergence of a West German industrial economy.[17] Reflecting the explicit statements that had been contained in the original bizonal fusion agreement about the need to raise exports, JEIA had "responsibility for the supervision and control of foreign trade of the Bizonal Area and for the promotion of exports from that area."[18] The American and British governments provided JEIA with an initial capital of $89 million to be used expressly "as a revolving fund to import raw materials essential for export production."[19] The capital was necessary for JEIA to accomplish its two most prominent formal instructions: first, to regulate "all imports and exports and ... such direct procurement as may be required"; and, second, "to ensure that a maximum export program shall be developed."[20] As a result of this mandate, JEIA played the central role in the two administrative processes required for increasing bizonal exports: first, decontrolling and reprivatizing the bizonal export/import trade, and, second, reestablishing the legal basis for bizonal foreign trade by concluding commercial agreements with neighboring countries.

Production factors dictated that a viable economy in western Germany necessarily meant an industrial manufacturing economy, which, in turn, meant an economy heavily dependent on foreign trade, specifically food and raw material imports and value-added manufactured exports.[21] The same arguments the Americans had been making about the necessary structure of foreign trade in the U.S. zone were now repeated and applied to the Bizonia as a unit. "In order to be self-supporting the Area must capitalize on its principal resource, that is, the technical skill of its workers and managers. It must be able to export the product of these skills in order to pay for the imports of food and raw materials without which it cannot live."[22] In April 1947 Clay told the War Department that "the main effort" of the bizonal economic administration should be "concentrated on the export program."[23] That these pronouncements meant reconstructing the West German economy along its prewar lines could not be denied by the bizonal administration, which now accepted that "in general the character of the bizonal Area's [trade pattern] would be similar to that prevailing before the war ..."[24] Yet at the time the Bizonia was launched in January 1947, the existing military law prohibitions on marketing, international transportation, and international payments continued to preclude any rapid expansion of foreign trade.

Significant growth in bizonal exports required two types of administrative action. First, occupation authorities had to ease some of the multitudinous prohibitions on contacts between Germans and foreigners so that at least some portion of international trade could return to private hands. Thereafter, private trade would have to be deregulated as quickly as possible. Second, new commercial arrangements must be made with neighboring countries to regulate the particulars of payments, import licensing, and transport. Virtually all European governments had foreign trade under strict currency and licensing control in the immediate postwar years. Bizonal exports could not move until new arrangements had been made with other countries, especially in the matter of acceptable payment. Occupation authorities had to begin the complicated task of reestablishing international commercial relations with Germany's Eastern and Western European neighbors.

Fully realizing the need for decontrol and new international agreements, Bullock, Cahan, and the rest of JEIA began to attack the major problems hampering the expansion of West German foreign trade. JEIA began immediately with an American plan for establishing branch offices in major cities in order to decentralize procedures and to break up the bottlenecks that had formed at the central import/export offices in the British and American zones. Beginning in the spring of 1947, JEIA issued a steady stream of instructions for gradually decontrolling foreign trade, beginning with exports. In April 1947 JEIA published its Instruction No. 1, Export Procedures for the US/UK Zones of Germany to Be Observed by German Exporters. These regulations were cumbersome and they led to numerous complaints by German exporters. However, their publication showed that the JEIA was in fact making "every effort to return to normal business practices" by allowing the export trade to return slowly to private hands. The JEIA also established Reichsmark conversion factors to be used for calculating minimum export prices in dollars, authorized approved German banks to make payments for export deliveries, and established an export-incentive plan called the Export Foreign Exchange Currency Bonus. The JEIA permitted export firms to use international telephone and telegraph service and arranged procedures for German businessmen to travel abroad. Subsequent measures to decontrol trade and get exports moving as rapidly as possible reflected the growing predominance of American economic policies within JEIA after the revision of the bizonal Fusion Agreement in December 1947. On the basis of this revised agreement, the JEIA received a new charter on January 19, 1948 that more clearly reflected America's increased role in supporting the Bizonia.[25] The new charter ended the previously existing formal parity between the U.K. and the U.S. in JEIA and guaranteed the predominance of American thinking on trade issues. In view of the important role that JEIA played in shaping West German economic reconstruction, American predominance in the JEIA was a crucial big step toward formal and substantive American predominance in answering the vital questions of West Germany's economic future.

In October 1948 JEIA took a big step in promoting the economic unity of all three western zones when the Allies reached agreement for JEIA absorption of the foreign trade agency of the French zone, the Office du Commerce Extérieur.[26] The restructured JEIA continued to promote German exports vigorously and at the same time to reduce and decentralize Allied regulatory procedures. JEIA branch offices were given the power to license deals up to $250,000. The multiple Reichsmark conversion factors were consolidated into one rate (1 RM = 30 cents) and then abolished altogether after the currency reform in June 1948. Another major achievement was the November 1948 revision of JEIA Instruction No. 1 in the form of a new, more liberal export procedure.[27] Export applications (Ausfuhranträge) were no longer required for most items, except industrial raw material in short supply. The removal of export applications was a big step in returning the export trade to normal business practices, since German exporters were now largely free to negotiate and sign export deals on a private basis without prior approval. The revised Instruction No. 1 relieved JEIA branch offices of licensing duties, which now fell on the German foreign trade banks (Aussenhandelsbanken). Exporters could now file their paperwork at any one of some 175 foreign trade banks instead of one of eleven JEIA branch offices.[28] The foreign trade banks reviewed the Export Control Document (Ausfuhrerklärung) submitted by a German exporter and could then itself issue an export license on behalf of the JEIA. The single Export Control Document (in six copies) replaced a multitude of various forms previously required. That earlier procedure had been the source of German criticisms about JEIA "red tape" and the retardant effect these administrative delays were having on exports. In early 1949 the JEIA began liberalizing import procedures along the same lines by which the export trade had been reprivatized and decontrolled in 1948. JEIA itself gradually withdrew from its role as the central procurement agent for the Trizonia. Private agents could then contract for imports, subject to the prior approval of the Import Advisory Committee. The progressive decontrol of bizonal (then trizonal) foreign trade from 1947 to 1949 played a crucial role in reviving exports, reducing the Bizonia's trade imbalance, and stimulating industrial production. From the very first days of the Occupation, OMGUS had considered it unrealistic to expect the level of economic activity in the Bizonia to rise without the necessary food and raw material imports from "better off" European neighbors such as the Netherlands, Italy, and Czechoslovakia. On the other hand, it would be equally unrealistic to hope for a rapid recovery of neighboring European countries without West German exports. These exports included first and foremost West German coal, but also the products of the reviving iron, steel, scrap, metal products, machinery, and motor vehicle industries.[29] An increase in bizonal exports was possible only if provisions were made for other countries to accept and pay for West German exports. Some type of international understanding was required to complement the increase in production and the deregulation of exports in the Bizonia.[30] In short, the Bizonia needed new links to her old trading partners. Restoring physical contact via telephone, telegraph, mail, and travel was only half the assignment here. The Bizonia also needed a new legal basis for trade in order to replace the German commercial agreements abrogated by the Allies. In 1947 the JEIA began restoring these links by signing payments and trade agreements with Bizonia's neighbors.

The shortage of dollars in both Western and Eastern Europe provided the immediate reason for moving to establish a new legal framework of the Bizonia's commercial relations with its neighbors.[31] Beginning in 1947, the JEIA signed a series of bilateral payments agreements establishing "offset accounts" as a means of easing, but not altogether eliminating, the dollar requirement. Under these agreements, offset accounts were set up in European banks in the local currency. (Earlier offset accounts covering payments between the U.S. zone and other countries had always been in dollars.) Bizonal imports from and exports to that country were credited and debited from this local currency account; the outstanding balance was to be calculated quarterly and paid on demand in dollars or sterling. The first agreement was signed with the Netherlands in January, 1947. Similar arrangements were made in 1947 with Norway, Sweden, Hungary, Czechoslovakia, Bulgaria, Greece, and Poland. By November 1947 JEIA had evolved a "standard payments arrangement" that contained the basic features of the offset account system.[32]

The responsibility for planning and negotiating West Germany's reintegration into the larger European economy rested with one of the two principal divisions of JEIA, the Foreign Trade Office.[33] Dr. Ethel Dietrich joined JEIA in January 1948 in the newly created post of deputy for trade negotiations with the task of supervising bizonal international trade negotiations and sending the resulting agreements on to the Bipartite Board.[34] As a means of maximizing the Bizonia's foreign trade and placing it on a more regular and predictable basis, JEIA signed a number of trade agreements between the Bizonia and other European countries. JCS 1779 of July 1947 addressed the problem of "restoration of normal commercial relations between Germany and the rest of Europe" and specifically instructed OMGUS to "consult other European countries and international organizations representing such countries in matters of German production and trade ...."[35] Ethel Dietrich of JEIA's Foreign Trade Division called "the conclusion of trade agreements with those countries which have been Germany's traditional customers in the purchase of her manufactured goods and as providers of raw materials ... one of the most important instruments" in the revival of German foreign trade.[36] By November 1947 JEIA had participated in twenty-three bilateral Conferences on Trade and Financial Arrangements with seventeen European countries. Each conference produced a bilateral Memorandum on Trade. Although these memoranda could "in no sense be called formal trade agreements between governments," they were used "to inaugurate formally export-import trade with sixteen countries of Europe," including six East European countries.[37] Repeatedly emphasizing that "the motivating factor in all these [bizonal] trade negotiations is general European recovery," Dietrich explained what the JEIA hoped to achieve. For JEIA, the "major objective of these trade negotiations is to maximize the volume of commerce, on a two-way basis, of the Bizone with every European country within the limit of what the combined area can produce for export or can afford to buy as imports." Trade maximization as an objective required that "an overriding consideration in all our trade talks is the normalizing of trade relations."[38]

By the time JEIA began self-liquidation in 1949, it had already negotiated trade and payments agreements on behalf of the Bizonia with thirty foreign countries; including twenty-one in Europe and nine overseas. Because the Federal Republic of Germany (FRG) subsequently took over many of these agreements, JEIA's work was immensely important for the future shape of West German foreign trade. In some cases, agreements negotiated by JEIA from 1947 to 1949 continued to provide the legal basis for the Federal Republic's bilateral trade with foreign countries through the 1950s.

JEIA's cumulative actions in decontrolling trade and reestablishing international commercial contacts bore fruit as traditional West German exports revived strongly under JEIA administration from 1947 to 1949 (Tables 7.1 and 7.2).[39] Ultimately more important was the steady increase in the percentage of manufactured and semimanufactured goods in bizonal exports (Table 7.3).[40] Machine exports, for example, increased sevenfold in eighteen months, approaching $30 million for the second quarter of 1949 and regaining their traditional place in the structure of West German exports (Table 7.4). With the success of export revival in 1948 and 1949, the Trizonia had recovered the material basis for a resumption of its traditional trade position vis-à-vis Eastern Europe. The need for capital goods to rebuild Europe enhanced Germany's trade bargaining strength vis-à-vis all her trade partners, both East and West, but especially in relation to the most devastated countries, such as Poland. Foreign desire for West German goods had helped maintain exports even when OMGUS forced Germany's neighbors to pay in scarce dollars for West German exports. Throughout the Occupation period West Germany benefited from a "sellers market" in the type of investment goods that characterized a large portion of German exports.

The German themselves played a very limited role in decontrolling the West German foreign trade from 1945 to 1949. This contrasts sharply with the active German role in decontrolling the domestic economy in that same period. In lifting controls from the domestic economy, both the West German proto-Economics Ministry, called the Department of Economics (Verwaltung für Wirtschaft) and the new West German political parties (the Christian Democrat-Liberal Frankfurt coalition) in the German Economic Council (Wirtschaftsrat) played decisive roles.[41] In contrast, the Allies granted no real authority to these German agents in the complicated process of decontrolling foreign trade and negotiating international agreements.

JEIA's revised charter of January 1948 had stated plainly that "the responsibilities of the Agency shall be transferred to German administration as soon as practicable, and the Board shall prepare a plan for the progressive fulfillment of this policy."[42] Over the course of 1948, JEIA began to draw West German experts into the Bizonia's international negotiations. Responsibility for foreign and interzonal trade (Aussen- und Inter-zonenhandel) in the bizonal German administration rested with Department V A of the Economics Department under the direction of Dr. Vollrath Freiherr von Maltzan, who himself had over twenty years of experience in foreign trade matters.[43]

By mid-1948 JEIA allowed Maltzan's staff to send representatives to bizonal delegations negotiating international trade and payments agreements with foreign countries. Ethel Dietrich commented that "participation by officials of the bizonal Department of Economics (VfW) in all these [trade] talks is a very important part of the proceedings. This German participation and responsibility takes place at all levels of trade talks, from subcommittee deliberations to the final negotiations. The fullest possible use is made of trade, production, and budgetary experts of the VfW ....We anticipate that the participation by the VfW will increase while the role of the Allied officials will proportionately decrease."[44] Unfortunately for the German Economics Department, this prediction was never fully realized during the period of Occupation.

Although German representatives were included in foreign trade negotiations from 1947 to 1949, they possessed no authority either formal or substantive, and their role was very limited. Instead of acting as decisionmakers, they remained the research experts described by Dietrich and the "German technicians" described by Clay.[45] In international negotiations, the West German Economics Department's role was largely confined to submitting a list of suggested imports and exports to the Allies. JEIA and the joint British-American Bipartite Control Office reviewed these lists with the right of final approval. In this review process both JEIA and the control office vetoed numerous German suggestions and radically restructured the West German Economics Department's bilateral trade plans, particularly with East European states.[46] The strong Allied presence along with the subordinate and the narrowly circumscribed role of German staff members must have done a great deal to calm the emotions and allay the suspicions of Czechoslovak, Polish, and Soviet negotiators as they encountered West German representatives for the first time since the war.

The very limited role of the German Economics Department in these negotiations was paralleled by the inability of the bizonal German Economic Council to exercise any authority over West German foreign trade. Even before the creation of the Bizonia, there had been no shortage of opinion about trade and export policy in West German business and political circles. With the establishment of the Economic Council in the Bizonia in May 1947, the Germans had a forum for the public political discussion of all economic issues, including trade policy. However, in matters of foreign trade policy, the Economic Council remained powerless. German frustration with the Economics Department's inability to direct this critical area of the West German economy spilled over in a number of bitter speeches offered by prominent members of the council. Emerging West German political leaders and important German figures of the Occupation period, such as Johannes Semler, Ludwig Erhard,

Heinrich Köhler and Hermann Pünder, all spoke on the injustice of exclusive Allied over foreign trade.[47]

In the very first full session of the Economic Council on June 26, 1947, Holzapfel (Christian Democrats) attacked JEIA for the slow progress made to date on reviving exports of finished goods. Erwin Schoettle (Socialists) went right to the heart of the foreign trade problem as the Germans saw it – the need for "decision-making power by the Germans in their own matters." Schoettle demanded specifically "at least" the right for the Germans to establish "independent foreign trade representations" abroad.[48] Schoettle's thinking found resonance all across the political spectrum over the next two years. In September 1947, Dr. Johannes Semler (Christian Social Union), Erhard's predecessor as director of the Economics Department, sharply attacked the Allied administration for the "obstacles and limits" still plaguing West German foreign trade. Considering the "overwhelming importance" of foreign trade to the West German economy, Semler argued that the Allies "should give us the freedom to fashion our foreign trade in our own responsibility."[49] To a chorus of supportive cries of "Sehr richtig!" from the right of the council chamber, Erhard complained in April 1948 that real growth in finished goods exports would not be possible until the Allies implemented "German suggestions to liberalize imports and exports." He went on to plead explicitly for "greater influence for German authorities and business people in concluding bilateral trade agreements ...."[50] On September 28, 1948 Herman Pünder, Chairman of the Executive Council (Verwaltungsrat) of the German bizonal administration, spoke to the Economics Council about foreign trade as "a matter of life and death to the German people."[51] After preliminary remarks about the substance of foreign trade, specifically the need to increase industrial exports still further, Pünder turned his attention to the execution of West German trade policy, stating "I can bring our formal concerns together quickly under the title 'JEIA'." Pünder noted the "popular criticism of JEIA, which can be heard on every street corner," and reminded the Allies that the original Byrnes-Bevin agreement had promised to return responsibility for foreign trade back over to the Germans "to the maximum extent permitted by [trade] restrictions existing in foreign countries ...." Implying that the Allies had already failed to live up to that earlier promise, Pünder asserted that "now is in fact the time for JEIA's jurisdiction over foreign trade, both in export regulation and in regards to trade treaties, to be handed over to German agents. The [German] Executive Council must be granted the power to conduct direct treaty negotiations with foreign countries and to conclude trade treaties."

Further, the Germans must receive the right to "erect official trade representations abroad." The German criticism voiced in the Economics Council confirmed how little influence JEIA and the control office granted to the Germans in international negotiations. A number of these German demands were not met by the Allies until the Federal Republic received full and final commercial sovereignty in 1952, indicating how far apart West German and Allied views on the subject of foreign trade control were in from 1947 to 1949.

Just as the Allies did, the Germans realized the importance of foreign trade for the survival of a West German economy. Köhler (Christian Democrats) called foreign trade "the alpha and omega of our economic future."[52] It is not surprising that West German authorities should want formal control over their foreign trade fates. Erhard pointed out that the Germans wanted some type of formal role, but, more important, they wanted "greater influence in concluding bilateral trade agreements." If that influence had been forthcoming even on the informal level between JEIA and the German Economics Department members of bizonal trade delegations, it would have gone a long way toward quieting German criticism of JEIA. The *Economist* did not exaggerate when reporting that "during its lifetime, JEIA was regarded by the Germans as a sinister embodiment of Allied ill-will …."[53]

Under these circumstances, the West German business community remained without influence in the formation of trade policy. Itself powerless, the Economics Department could do virtually nothing to translate business wishes into reality. On the other hand, suggestions made by the business community directly to the military authorities produced no results. British failure to respond to the North German exporting community's Hamburg Plan was typical of Allied disregard for German business suggestions in the export field.[54] The West German business community would not regain a voice in foreign trade policy until the West German bureaucracy, specifically the Economics Department, could obtain a more active and responsible role from the Allies.

Constraints of the Cold War

The Western Allies' resuscitation of West German foreign trade was inextricably bound up with the economic and political developments affecting Germany's principal trading partners. As new bilateral trade agreements began reintegrating the Bizonia into the larger European economy, bizonal foreign trade felt the affects of the political and economic pressures that were dividing Europe into two opposing blocs from 1947 to 1949. The division of Europe into two rival economic and military blocs inspired the Americans in particular and the West in general to begin imposing a variety of political considerations onto trade with Eastern Europe. This politicization of East-West trade over the course of 1948 and 1949 decisively affected the evolution of West German trade relations with Eastern Europe in those years and beyond. American and British Occupation authorities did not hesitate to impose their politically motivated trade policy onto West German foreign trade with the East. Because they occupied a unique position of authority in governing West German foreign trade, the British and the Americans could easily and painlessly (for themselves) curtail West German trade with Eastern Europe in accordance with Anglo-American security considerations and political goals.

Cold War politics cut short the eastern half of the process of reconnecting West Germany to its traditional trade partners. The processes of bloc formation from 1947 to 1949 brought western Germany into the western half of a divided Europe and separated it from the eastern half. Inclusion and separation soon required two trade regimes for West German trade; one for trade with the capitalist West and another for the socialist East. From 1947 to 1949 the Allies carefully constructed two distinct trade regimes for West German foreign trade: a depoliticized trade regime for trade with Western economic partners and a politicized regime for trade with East European rivals. The outlines of this bifurcated trade structure were put in place by the Occupation authorities for western Germany before the establishment of the Federal Republic.

The politicization of West German trade with East European countries grew logically out of the formation of two rival political-military blocs in Europe. The formative process had become unmistakable with the Western and Eastern responses to the Marshall Plan in the summer of 1947. By bringing western Germany into the Marshall Plan, the Allies anchored western Germany in the American-sponsored postwar international economy that was inseparable from the European Recovery Program (ERP).[55] The most important steps in the early years of this process are well known: inclusion of the Bizonia in the Marshall Plan and in the Organization for European Economic Cooperation (OEEC) in 1947 and 1948, Trizonal participation in Western multilateral payments systems, Allied introduction of MFN status for General Agreement on Tariffs and Trade (GATT) members in the Trizone in 1948 and 1949, the 1949 Treaty of Economic Cooperation between the Federal Republic and the United States, and full OEEC and GATT membership for the FRG in 1949 and 1950. These events were reinforced along the way by a series of progressively more liberal bilateral trade treaties concluded between the Trizonia and its West European neighbors, including Greece, Italy, Switzerland, France, and the Benelux in 1948, and Switzerland and Holland in 1949.[56]

On the other side, developments in Eastern Europe in 1947 and 1948 led to the withdrawal and exclusion of Eastern Europe from this liberal Western trade system. The Soviets and their Eastern allies refused to join in the "world economy" as it was reconstructed by the Americans after 1945. Although they fished eagerly for international credits from the International Bank for Reconstruction and Development (IBRD) and World Bank, East European governments stayed out of the liberal-capitalist world market created by the Marshall Plan, OEEC, and GATT. Economic decisions went hand-in-hand with political events to drive an economic wedge between Western and Eastern Europe.[57] By refusing to become a member of this American-sponsored system, East European states deprived themselves of the protective benefits that membership in the system provided. Most important, Eastern Europe surrendered the right to maintain the type of depoliticized trade relations with the West that GATT members maintained among themselves. Having no MFN status with the Trizonia, Soviet bloc states gained nothing from the more generous treaties that West Germany signed with Western trading partners. Lack of GATT membership meant that East European governments had no international body to which they could effectively protest about the politically motivated trade discrimination practiced by the West. As a result, JEIA could operate with no holds barred in restricting trade with Eastern Europe for political reasons. The lack of international trade regime restraints on the use of trade diplomacy by the Allies in West Germany complemented the high degree of autonomy possessed by the Bipartite Control Office in its independence from the German business community, whose trade it was manipulating.

The resulting economic divergence between East and West spawned a difference in how Western countries conducted trade among themselves and how they conducted trade with members of the other economic bloc. The incipient formation of two increasingly impermeable trading blocs was perceptible as early as 1948. At that point, trade among the Eastern European countries had grown to almost three times its prewar size; $483 million in 1948 as compared to $168 million in 1938. On the other side, trade among Western European countries had recovered to almost three-quarters of its prewar level: $3,583 million in 1948 compared to $4,993 million in 1938.

However, East-West trade was far short of even one-half of its earlier level: $731 million in 1948 compared to $1,751 million in 1938.[58]

Over the course of 1947 West German trade with Poland, Czechoslovakia, and the Soviet Union became subsumed in the larger concept of East-West trade. Ironically, this new label initially held the promise of reinforcing the necessity of German trade with the East. Both American and Western European leaders expected East-West trade (especially Central and Eastern European exports) to contribute very directly to the economic success of the Marshall Plan. Reviewing Marshall Plan policy some twenty years later, Congress recalled that "Western policymakers on both sides of the Atlantic Ocean were disposed in the early postwar period to regard East-West trade as an important factor in the economic recovery of Europe."[59] Secretary of State Dean Acheson was not alone at the State Department in recognizing "the necessity of existing trade between Eastern and Western Europe and [the] desirability of its increase."[60] The Commerce Department as well recognized that Eastern European grain, timber, coal, and potash were "essential for Western European recovery."[61] The French agreed. In August 1947, Hervé Alphand, head of the economics sections at the French Ministry for Foreign Affairs, told U.S. Ambassador Jefferson Caffery that he thought one of the "assumptions required" for the "viability" of the Marshall Plan was "that some important trade with eastern Europe be established."[62] The British stated essentially the same point, that the "promotion of East-West trade to 1938 levels was a Marshall Plan objective and most important to ERP and U.K. recovery."[63] Writing in *Foreign Affairs* at the time, economist William Diebold, Jr. went so far as to say that the recovery "program is premised [on] the resumption of large-scale commerce between the eastern and western countries of Europe."[64]

In July 1947, the Committee of European Economic Cooperation (CEEC) spelled out very clearly what it expected European Marshall Plan recipients to receive in trade from Eastern Europe: 16 million tons of Polish coal in 1948 (rising to 30 million tons in 1951), timber exports equal to 75 percent of the prewar level by 1951, and a restoration of the prewar East-West grain trade (4 million to 5 million metric tons annually) by 1951.[65] No one doubted that large quantities of Eastern European coal, timber, and grain would be needed in the West over the next four years and beyond. According to the U.S. Commerce Department, ERP countries needed some $5 billion to $6 billion in imports from Eastern Europe over the four years of the plan.[66]

Eastern Europe's earlier position among Germany's foreign trade between the wars was well understood by both American and European planners. OMGUS published information on Germany's pre-war Eastern trade and cited the report of the CEEC in discussing the role of Eastern European trade in the success of the Marshall Plan in West Germany: "It has been assumed that an increasing proportion of the imports of participating countries will be obtained from eastern Europe and Asia and other non-participating areas in cases where they are traditional and economically efficient sources of supply."[67] There was a general consensus that German-Eastern European trade should, could, and would approach prewar levels again. Even as Marshall Plan supplies began to arrive in Germany, the JEIA was negotiating trade-stimulating agreements with Eastern European countries.

Before the effects of trade politicization made themselves felt in mid-1948, the terms and conditions for bizonal trade and payments with Eastern Europe were identical to those applied to Western Europe. In fact the very first dollar offset account was established with Czechoslovakia in October 1946.[68] Speaking on trade with Eastern Europe, Ethel Dietrich of JEIA's Foreign Trade Division stated that "we will do everything possible to increase this trade, in the realization that general recovery cannot take place without it. It is not unreasonable to hope that in the near future the traditional sources of foodstuffs for the German population will once again be developed, if only because the Western Hemisphere cannot possibly provision Western Europe indefinitely, because – and this is elementary economics – Germany requires the vast markets of the East for her manufactures."[69] That type of optimistic, pragmatic thinking on West German trade typified the basic, dollars-and-cents approach to West German economic recovery of Clay, Draper, and OMGUS in general. The process of restoring the Bizonia's commercial relations with the East was already well under way in late 1947 when the widening division of Europe moved the U.S. State Department to introduce a new set of political considerations into Western thinking about trade with Eastern Europe.

The inclusion of German trade with Poland, Czechoslovakia, and the USSR in the larger phenomenon of East-West trade soon began to put limits on some aspects of West Germany's trade with the East. As early as November 1947, political, military, and ideological differences with the Soviet bloc prompted American officials to begin investigating the national security risks involved in U.S.-Soviet bloc trade. That investigation was soon expanded to cover East-West trade in general, including West German trade with Poland, Czechoslovakia, and the USSR. Beginning in 1948, the political considerations that the U.S. imposed on Western trade with the solidifying Soviet bloc began to constrict West German trade with the East. By late 1948, the U.S. export control policy (or "embargo policy" as it is commonly called) dramatically affecting the volume, structure, and conduct of West German-Eastern European trade, as the records of West German/JEIA trade negotiations with Poland and Czechoslovakia show. Over the final two years of the Occupation, the Western Allies introduced a number of political motivations into East-West trade that directly affected West German trade with Poland and Czechoslovakia.

The delicate American diplomatic posturing with carrot and stick that had been so necessary in negotiating a common export control program with West European countries was completely redundant when it came to controlling West German exports.[70] The military government laws and Allied Control Council proclamations of 1945 and 1946 governing control of German foreign trade allowed JEIA to issue "instructions" that authorized or prohibited the export of any commodity or group of commodities. The U.S. and U.K. had already used JEIA instructions to control exports of critical items considered to be in short supply in Germany. To restrict other exports on the basis of their potential strategic value would be an easy task in view of the political authority and administrative machinery already in place for Allied control of German trade. In fact Anglo-American discussions on restricting strategic exports from West Germany to Eastern Europe actually preceded similar negotiations for restricting exports from any other Western European country. U.S. Secretary of State George Marshall's instructions to Averell Harriman, special representative in Europe for the Marshall Plan, in August 1948 "suggested that very informal discussions be undertaken with British and US/UK officials in bizonal Germany prior to approaching others."[71] Marshall thought the Bizonia would be the best place to test British willingness to go along with an export control program. After receiving the American suggestion, the bizonal administration made rapid progress on restricting strategic exports from the Bizonia.[72]

In the Bizonia, the Bipartite Control Office began controlling strategic exports from West Germany to the East in the spring of 1948, a full year before other Western European countries took similarly effective action. Through JEIA and the control office, the West German economy was the first in Western Europe to feel the impact of America's drive to politicize East-West trade as part of the Cold War. The control office was brought into the Bizonia's foreign trade affairs as a counterweight to the economists at JEIA in order to ensure that military security received proper consideration in trade negotiations with the East. Under the Occupation regime, the Bipartite Control Office had the authority to unilaterally inject Allied political considerations into West German trade agreements with Soviet bloc countries. Further, this political injection required relatively little effort by the Allies since they had already constructed a large administrative apparatus in 1945 to 1946 to control economically scarce West German exports. By August 1948, JEIA regularly "consulted with the Control Office in reviewing the export-import programs submitted by the German bizonal economics department."[73] In November 1948, when other West European countries were hesitatingly expressing "agreement in principle" with U.S. export controls, the State Department reported that "the position of the US as an occupying power in western Germany makes it possible to implement the [export control] policy without any major difficulties."[74] At that same time (November/December 1948), the control office's restriction of West German exports to Poland was already shaping the West German-Polish trade negotiations underway in Frankfurt. By 1949 the Americans had sharpened trizonal controls beyond those of any other Western European country. In June, 1949 the Foreign Assistance Correlation Committee reported that the "Trizone of Germany is at the present time embargoing the full [American] 1-A list under licensing control administered by the Joint Export-Import Agency."[75] Throughout the final year of the Occupation (September 1948 to September 1949), political logic often underlay the control office's and JEIA's repeated refusals to import certain commodities from and export particular types of industrial equipment to Poland and Czechoslovakia.

In 1948 the Americans imposed new politically motivated trade-restricting policies onto economically motivated trade-expanding policies that had been in place since 1946 to 1947. As a result, a sometimes confusing multiplicity of economic and political goals characterized the first years of politicized East-West trade. The initial and often-repeated American goal of "limiting Soviet war potential" was counterbalanced by the economic and political goal of successfully concluding the ERP, which in turn implied a maintenance of critical Eastern exports. The State Department and the Economic Cooperation Administration (ECA), but also the Commerce Department and even the Defense Department were acutely aware that a common Western European export control program (or the West German component thereof) must avoid provoking economic retaliation from the East. Throughout the early years of postwar trade politicization, the need to keep exports from Eastern Europe flowing into the West served as a major brake on the Western plans to restrict trade with the East for political and strategic reasons. Into that balance were added a number of secondary goals that might be effected by using a carefully constructed pattern of East-West trade. The British and Americans manipulated trade with the East in the hope of slowing the pace of Eastern European industrialization, retarding the economic integration of the Soviet bloc, and preventing the collectivization of East European agriculture.

The international politicization of trade with the East rebounded onto the politics of Occupation in West Germany by reinforcing Allied control over West German foreign trade. The inclusion of political and strategic considerations in trade policy dramatically reduced the likelihood of the Allies allowing the Germans to regulate their own foreign trade. The Allies could not charge the West German Economics Department with the overtly military-political task of screening exports for "security" violations. (The Germans were not given exclusive control over screening their own exports until after the General Treaty in 1952.) Neither the emergent West German bureaucracy in the Economics Department nor the West German business community had any effective means for influencing Allied policy in this areas. No forum existed for West German dialogue with the Bipartite Control Office or JEIA on this issue; no mechanism existed for appealing Allied export control decisions. Never again would the framers of West German trade policy be so free to subordinate domestic business interests to the considerations of foreign policy.[76]

New and Old Partners 1947-1949

West German trade flows with the East from 1945 to 1949 reflected the larger, Allied-imposed processes of economic liberalization and Cold War politicization that shaped all aspects of postwar West German economic reconstruction. In its overseer's role for West German relations with Poland, Czechoslovakia, and the USSR, the American-dominated Allied administration actively shaped these relations in accordance with American foreign economic policies toward these Eastern states.

Between 1947 and 1949, JEIA signed five different international commercial agreements with Poland and seven with Czechoslovakia on behalf of the Bizonia and Trizonia. Among these were the important trade and payments agreements negotiated in 1948 and 1949. These trade agreements with Eastern Europe reflected the mixture of economic concerns and security fears that characterized Allied thinking on East-West trade. The interaction of these two conflicting sets of concerns created only a brief "window of opportunity" for Allied representatives in western Germany to establish economic relations between the western zones and Eastern European countries. Only for that period from early 1947 through early 1949, when the Allies sought to expand the trade of their zones for economic reasons and when the international military rivalry with the Eastern countries of the emerging Soviet bloc was not yet too great, could the necessary trade and payments agreements between Western Germany and Eastern Europe be concluded. Presumably, the ability to deal with an Allied Occupation agency, JEIA, rather than with some representatives of the emerging West German state made the conclusion of these commercial agreements somewhat easier for the East Europeans as well.

After 1949, the JEIA-East European agreements continued in force for the Federal Republic of Germany. The formal structure that JEIA had given to West German-Polish and West German-Czechoslovak trade in 1947 to 1949 remained effective for years after the dissolution of JEIA itself. For these reasons, the agreements signed by bizonal representatives with Poland and Czechoslovakia proved far more significant than could have been known at the time. Conversely, the Soviet decision not to seek a trade agreement with the Bizonia in 1947 or 1948 had far more lasting consequences than could have been foreseen.

Poland

Against a background of deteriorating political conditions in Poland in 1946 to 1947, the Western Allies entered eagerly into new economic agreements with Germany's war-ravaged eastern neighbor. Even the very first economic deals with Poland were characterized by a mixture of economic and political motives on the part of the West. The Americans and British first sought to secure some of Poland's badly needed coal for export to Western Europe. Beyond that immediate economic consideration, the Allies hoped that through economic contacts with the West they might yet keep Poland out of total immersion in the Soviet economic system.[77]

Over the objections of American Ambassador Arthur Bliss Lane, the United States signed a new Agreement on Economic and Financial Cooperation with Poland on 24 April 1946.[78] An Anglo-Polish financial agreement was signed in London two months later, on 24 June. When Hilary Minc, Poland's minister of industry and future economics czar, arrived in Washington for talks with the State Department in December 1946, he found that the Americans were well aware of the role Poland might play in helping rebuild the European economy. Dean Acheson "thought that Polish exports would be an important factor in restoring the economy of Europe."[79] Despite the steady deterioration in U.S.-Polish political relations that followed the fraudulent referendum in Poland in 1946 and the equally fraudulent elections in January 1947, the Western allies were still very much interested in maintaining and expanding economic contacts between Poland and Western Europe. On 5 May Bevin told the House of Commons that the British Government planned to proceed with ratification of the Anglo-Polish financial agreement signed the year before. Although the Polish government rejected U.S. aid in the form of the Marshall Plan, the U.S. still hoped to make purchases of the most important Polish commodities, particularly coal.[80]

Since both Western Europe and Poland could benefit from an expansion of two-way trade and the Bizonia continued to need trade of all types, JEIA negotiated a trade arrangement for bizonal trade with Poland by signing a Memorandum on Trade Relations and an offset account payments agreement with the Polish government in Warsaw in November of 1947. Both the trade memorandum and the payments agreement were the typical mechanisms used by JEIA in 1947 to govern the Bizonia's foreign trade relations. In both form and content, the terms and conditions for bizonal trade and payments with Poland were identical to those applied to Western Europe, reflecting the still unpoliticized nature of European trade at that time. Like other memoranda negotiated by JEIA, the Warsaw product simply set in writing the information exchanged by bizonal and Polish authorities. The information centered on the basic mechanics of trade, especially "mutual statements of goods available and goods likely to be required" and "the technical manner in which the trade has to be conducted."[81] Poland also received the "standard payments arrangement" in which trade "is paid for through an offset account carried on the books of the central bank of the other country," i.e., Poland. Settlements of the account were due in dollars or sterling quarterly, but only for the outstanding balance at quarter's end. In other words, "for every item set to the account, the party owing has from two to five months to effect payment by a return shipment of goods; payment becomes due in cash only if such return shipments are not made." Reflecting the continued importance of coal and timber in European reconstruction, the new payments arrangement exempted "coal, timber, and potash as commodities which must be paid for in cash, or can be paid for through the offset account only from credit balances."[82]

The results of this first trade agreement remained disappointingly meager. The continuing low level of trade was caused chiefly by the low level of economic activity in the Bizonia, but even more so in Poland, where wartime devastation was extreme.[83] Shortly after the trade memorandum was signed, Ambassador Stanton Griffis told the State Department that "excepting through the use of coal, there is little possibility of any substantial export from Poland for some years and imports ... without outside credits will be small."[84] Polish foreign trade development was also hampered by political differences between the plan-oriented Ministry of Industry under Minc and the more liberal Ministry of Navigation and Foreign Trade under Adam Grosfeld. Grosfeld favored the type of bilateral payments arrangement that had been set up with the Bizonia and that gave Poland the chance to earn dollars or sterling to be used in buying capital goods and other necessities from the dollar area. Minc, on the other hand, "has always been suspicious of this pattern and has favored strict bilateral clearing arrangements ..." The Minc-Grosfeld debate over trade tactics contributed to the Poles not activating the trade possibilities outlined in the trade memorandum with the Bizonia.[85] By April, 1948 Grosfeld had been eclipsed by Minc (whom Griffis now referred to as the "absolute czar over the Polish economy and has also assumed highly important political functions"), with the result that Griffis thought Poland would activate trade with the Bizonia "only if bilateral clearing arrangement established."[86] By October 1948, Minc's rise to preeminence, Poland's strong desire to sell coal and buy scrap metal in Germany (a traditional exchange between the two areas), and the general late 1948 revival in bizonal-Polish trade combined to inspire the Poles to begin sounding JEIA on the possibility of negotiating a new trade and payments agreement.

Negotiations for a new bizonal-Polish trade and payments arrangement opened in Frankfurt on 29 November 1948 and clearly reflected the sharp politicization of East-West trade that had taken place since the previous round of bizonal-Polish trade talks in October 1947. The commerce and state departments had already taken the lead in restricting America's own trade with Poland beginning in early 1948 by holding up Poland's loan application at the IBRD and by refusing to grant an U.S. export license for a nearly completed blooming and slabbing mill contracted for by the Poles. Clayton had told Minc at the United Nations Economic Commission for Europe meeting in July 1947 in Geneva that "Poland could not expect any assistance from the United States in the way of credits or otherwise."[87] The Poles responded by continuing to delay both the conclusion of an agreement on compensation for nationalized properties and settlement of the lend-lease account. In October 1948, Polish President Bolesław Bierut and Foreign Minister Modzelewski complained to the new U.S.

ambassador, Waldemar Gallman, about American export restrictions on advanced machinery desired by Poland.[88] One month later the Poles appealed to the United Nations General Assembly to condemn "discriminations practiced by certain States in international trade obstructing normal development of trade relations and contrary to the purposes and principles of the United Nations Charter."[89]

When Polish representatives sat down with JEIA negotiators in Frankfurt just three days after this Polish appeal to the UN, they knew full well that the U.S. was already subjecting its own trade with Poland to political restrictions.[90] The Poles would soon learn what they might well have already suspected – that Anglo-American Occupation authorities were subjecting West German exports to similar political restrictions. The bizonal administration, specifically the Bipartite Control Office, was, in fact, already an active agent in the American embargo policy, enforcing American standards in exports controls. These export restrictions greatly exacerbated the difficulties of coming to a balanced trade agreement, and finally scuttled the first major agreement between the Bizonia (JEIA) and Poland. Polish frustration with Anglo-American export control policies eclipsed whatever acrimony Polish negotiators might have felt toward West German economic representatives at this, their most extensive meeting since the war.[91]

JEIA negotiators moved the initial negotiations along constructively, and the outlook for trade appeared positive at the first full session with both sides stating their commitment to increase the level of two-way trade. The Poles cited their own low level of imports from the Bizonia in 1948 ($800,000) and the "negligible" bizonal purchases of Polish exports in 1948. Dietrich stated quickly that in the interest of expanding trade the Trizonia would be willing to buy some "nonessential" foodstuffs if the Poles were willing to buy other nonessentials from Germany. From 3 December to 11 December, both sides negotiated their way through a list of commodities available for export: food, minerals, timber, metal products, chemicals, electrical components, and optical equipment.

Almost immediately, economic and politically motivated restrictions on West German exports contributed to the difficulties in reaching a balanced agreement. All through November and December 1948, working parties of JEIA, the Bipartite Control Office, and the West German Economics Department had been assessing trizonal export capabilities. For economic reasons JEIA and the Economics Department continued to restrict exports of specialty items that remained in short supply so that West Germany would not be "bought out" by its neighbors, all of which were starved for the technical equipment needed in reconstruction. The tremendous "competition between the domestic and the export market" about which Clay had warned the State Department in 1947 had not yet diminished.[92]

On top of these economic restrictions, the control office now imposed politically motivated export controls by vetoing certain JEIA and West German Economics Department sale offers to Poland. On 6 December the Poles expressed disappointment that bizonal negotiators refused to export any scrap iron or any amounts of certain steel rolling mill products. The Bipartite Control Office vetoed JEIA and Economics Department offers to sell iron mill and steel rolling mill equipment to the Poles.[93] Together, JEIA, the control office, and the Economics Department prohibited exports of numerous items desired by the Poles, some for economic reasons (e.g., refined steel, aniline dyes), some for political and security reasons (e.g., metallurgic production equipment), and some for both economic and political reasons (e.g. scrap iron and steel products). JEIA directors even declined Polish offers to sell coal, despite the fact that the Poles had made "extensive concessions" by lowering their price substantially in the course of negotiations.[94]

On 11 December, the preliminary lists were presented for review to the JEIA "steering committee" chaired by Cahan. At this point the lists called for bizonal imports of $14.4 million over the next year and exports to Poland of $9.6 million, thereby producing a $5 million deficit for the Bizonia. Cahan stated that, in principle, JEIA was not opposed to a deficit agreement "provided that the dollars were spent on 'hard' imports," which was not the case in these lists. Of the $13.2 million planned for food imports from Poland, only $4.9 million could be considered essentials. In addition, the Poles had not agreed to buy any nonessentials from West Germany. The resulting imbalance was not acceptable to JEIA. Cahan declared that the list would have to be revised and "balanced out." Polish negotiators protested that the real source of the imbalance was JEIA refusal to allow export of some items that the Poles most eagerly wanted to buy, such as rolling mill equipment, scrap iron, drilling machines, rayon, and high-voltage electrical switches.[95]

In fact, both parties contributed to an imbalance that was obviously unacceptable for West Germany in 1948. The Polish policy of absolutely refusing to buy nonessentials from West Germany was understandable under the circumstances of limited foreign exchange and a reorientation of Polish trade toward the Soviet Union, but would not go far toward increasing the volume of trade or the volume of their own exports to the Bizonia. In negotiating their chemical purchases, the Poles had exhibited a real fear of accidentally purchasing something in Germany that might have been available elsewhere.

Nowicki refused German offers to sell glass, leather, paper, and rubber, all of which could have helped balance the deal. When negotiations resumed on 13 December 1948, the Polish delegation clung determinedly to the trade surplus in their favor as contained in the preliminary lists, declaring that they could purchase some nonessentials if the Germans would buy yet more nonessentials in the same amount. Schiffler commented with frustration that Polish "failure to recognize the problem that this creates for us will make the conclusion of an agreement very much more difficult." No progress was made on the next day and Schiffler noted in a message to Maltzan at the Economics Department that the negotiations appeared "dead."[96]

Both sides genuinely wanted a trade agreement and the Poles especially wanted a new payments agreement of the clearing type favored by Minc. On 17 December the Polish delegation met directly with the JEIA steering committee in a session "to which the [West German] Economics Department was not invited."[97] Cahan and Nowicki showed a new willingness to compromise. The Poles accepted some "soft" goods and JEIA saved face by eliminating some soft imports and reclassifying others as soft but "desirable." The new figures resulting from this meeting reduced the West German deficit to $1.4 million, on $14.6 million in imports from and $13.2 million in exports to Poland. The vast bulk of bizonal food imports ($10 million out of a food total of $11.7 million) were now either "hard" or at least "desirable" goods. The Bizonia would receive the foodstuffs it desperately wanted from nondollar sources: rye ($2.8 million), oats ($3.0 million), sugar ($2.5 million), potato starch ($1.35 million), and various types of timber ($600,000). On the West German export side ($13.2 million total) a number of classic German product categories already led the way: machines ($6.2 million), chemicals ($2.9 million), and electrical equipment ($2.2 million). The Poles would place detailed purchase orders after they inventoried their specific needs in each group. Commenting for the Economics Department, Schiffler noted with evident satisfaction the very next day that the agreement "represented a considerable step forward in the formation of German-Polish economic relations." OMGUS described the new trade agreement with Poland as "designed to stimulate the exchange of goods with Eastern Europe and to revive trade with that area ...."[98]

This new trade agreement had significance well beyond the immediate substantial increase in German-Polish trade that could be expected in 1949. By replacing the memorandum on trade of October 1947, this new agreement became the legal basis for West German-Polish trade for years to come. The agreement gave a lasting structure to West German-Polish trade relations by establishing the administrative machinery and the procedures to govern the annual trade talks and by providing a basis for the reconstruction of West German-Polish relations after the war.[99] If mutually acceptable import/export lists were drawn up for a new period, all other provisions of the agreement were automatically extended for another year, including the obligation of the Mixed Commission to meet again. In this way the agreement could continue indefinitely, as long as some exchange of goods could be arranged through the Mixed Commission. A new payments agreement had also been negotiated and initiated at the same times as the new trade agreement. The Payments Agreement provided a long-term system of accounting commensurate with the more stable framework given to trade. A noninterest-bearing offset account in U.S. dollars was established the Narodowy Bank Polski to handle all payments between the three Western zones of Germany and Poland.[100] By bringing coal, timber, potash, and services into the offset system, the new payments arrangement marked a victory for Minc's plan-oriented faction within the Polish economic management administration.[101] These more-conservative communists saw little need to earn dollars with Polish exports in light of the Eastward turn in Polish trade and the Western restrictions on advanced industrial exports from the dollar area.

In January 1949 the Poles began submitting to JEIA their specific purchase orders for the machinery and equipment categories outlined in the December trade agreement. Under the stiffening embargo procedures in the Bizonia, the new Polish list of purchase orders now required additional clearance by the Bipartite Control Office and the ECA. In the course of reviewing the new specifics of the agreement in the spring of 1949, ECA and the control office vetoed $7 million of the proposed West German exports, or slightly over half the planned amount! The Bipartite Control Office and ECA also chopped $5.1 million from West German imports in order to "more nearly balance" the reduced export figures.[102]

In early May the dramatically reduced Polish list was returned to the office of Polish trade representative in Frankfurt. This radical restructuring of the trade lists by the control board and ECA representatives caused a great deal of confusion since JEIA had been operating with the December 1948 agreement already provisionally in force.[103] General M.E.L. Robinson, director of the Foreign Trade Office, and Biernacki met several times in early May to see what could be done in light of ECA/control office actions. Both men agreed that the confusion was substantial and on May 12, Robinson "finally suggested that the best course of action would be for Mr.

Biernacki to recommend to his government that a Mixed Commission be sent to Frankfurt to attempt to write what will be substantially a new trade agreement."[104] Biernacki agreed and a 20 May 1949 date was set for another round negotiations in Frankfurt. JEIA approached the May negotiations with a new appreciation of how important security considerations had become in U.S. thinking on trade with the East: "It can be presumed that if a Polish delegation comes to Frankfurt at the end of May their desires will be very similar to those they expressed in November-December, 1948. Their need for all types of machinery, machine tools and heavy industrial equipment is surely greater now than it was six months ago. From the Allied point of view, therefore, it is of the greatest importance that we have clear instructions of just how far we are to be permitted by higher authorities to go in the export of 'strategic' material."[105] This statement marks an important point in the history of U.S. embargo policy in West Germany and in the evolution of the bizonal foreign trade administration. JEIA's realization that strategic exports must be controlled marks the final step in the transmission of the embargo policy from the highest levels of the State Department all the way down to JEIA negotiators in the Bizonia – a process of policy formulation and implementation that had taken some seventeen months.[106]

The new Polish trade delegation arrived in May, headed by Broniewicz, a director in the new Ministry of Foreign Trade. Almost immediately, the Poles and JEIA agreed to leave the payments agreement of December 1948 and the basic terms of the earlier trade agreement unchanged. New negotiations were confined to working out new, mutually acceptable import and export lists. W. John Logan, the American director of JEIA, and Broniewicz initialed new import/export lists for the full trade agreement on 30 June 1949. Both the trade and the payments agreements received full signature on 5 July, thereby officially replacing the 1947 memorandum.[107]

Two factors greatly facilitated the rapid and successful conclusion of this round of trade negotiations, despite the confusion that had surrounded the scuttling of the December lists. First, both sides agreed that all proposed imports in this new agreement would be "subject to further specification."[108] By including this euphemistic clause in the new agreement, both sides implicitly acknowledged the existence of politically motivated bizonal export restrictions. More important, both sides expressed their willingness to live with those restrictions and to keep trade moving as far as practicable under the politicized circumstances. The large amount of basic foodstuffs offered by Poland for sale to the Trizonia also facilitated the conclusion of a deal based on a large, balanced volume of two-way trade. The Poles promised to deliver $32.2 million in food to the Trizonia over the next year. Food comprised over 90 percent of planned Polish exports to West Germany. Especially attractive were rye ($17.5 million), sugar ($6.5 million), oats ($2 million), eggs ($1.5 million) and pulses ($1.2 million). JEIA negotiators eagerly committed themselves for the full amounts offered by the Poles and undoubtedly would have bought even more of the basic foods if they had been available. In light of the still considerable need for food imports of all kinds into West Germany, food sources from outside the Marshall Plan were desperately needed.

There is also some reason to think that JEIA had political as well as economic motives in signing on for huge food imports from Poland. In January, 1949 the U.K. had signed a trade agreement with Poland for $1 billion in two-way trade over the next five years. Polish exports would be over 70 percent agricultural, which meant sending about $350 million in food exports to the U.K. over the length of the deal. In April 1949, U.S. Ambassador Gallman reported that "from available evidence it appears that agricultural export commitments undertaken by Poland have placed definite brake on collectivization program and may compel pro-Kremlin Communists to relax class struggle against Kulaks in the interest of meeting export quotas." Gallman continued, saying, "We feel that recent U.K.-Polish [trade] pact is case in point of how economic approach may be utilized to foil and delay Soviet plans re Poland and strengthen pro-Western elements without perhaps subtracting unduly from our strategic objectives ..." Without mentioning West Germany specifically, he went on to say that "Other similar opportunities could no doubt be developed."[109] In reply, Acheson said, "[State] Dept agrees large Pol[ish] agricultural export commitments ... may tend retard Sovietization Pol[and]." He asked Harriman in Paris and all U.S. embassies in Europe for suggestions on how to develop this type of trade.[110] The use of increased Polish agricultural export commitments to retard the Sovietization of Polish agriculture would justify the inclusion of a many nonessential foodstuffs in trizonal imports from Poland. Fresh onions, fresh hams, chicory, and malt were all on JEIA's import list from Poland this time. Some items on the June 1949 list, such as poultry, had been specifically criticized by Cahan as nonessential and removed from the previous agreement in December 1948. Now, after Gallman's report on agricultural exports and collectivization in Poland, JEIA approved millions of dollars in nonessential products for import into the Trizonia. The West German Economics Department certainly remained in the dark about these particular U.S. political motivations in manipulating West German-Polish trade. Ludwig Imhoff, director of the Foreign Trade Policy for the Economics Administration, found it "remarkable" that the Trizonia accepted so many nonessentials, especially fresh ham and poultry.[111]

The trizonal-Polish trade agreements of 1948 and 1949 were shaped by a combination of Allied Occupation policy and practices in West Germany, the politicization of trade in divided Europe, and Poland's new socialist economic regime. These powerful postwar factors eclipsed any negotiating difficulties that were rooted in older German-Polish antipathies. The Occupation regime shaped these trade agreements first by rebuilding an advanced industrial economy in West Germany and by restoring its traditional foreign trade structure. The Allies also set the form of negotiations by reserving for themselves the exclusive right to conclude trade agreements for West Germany. The international framework of trade politicization in a divided Europe reinforced Allied trade control in West Germany and allowed Allied manipulation of trade to suit a variety of political goals. Stalinist control in Poland kept West German-Polish trade and payments on a strictly controlled path. Each of these factors – the restoration of traditional West German foreign trade structure, the unique degree of state (Occupation authorities') control over West German trade, the development of two separate trade regimes for East and West, the existence of a variety of political considerations affecting trade with the East, and the consolidation of a Stalinist economy in Poland – was reflected in the form and content of these trade agreements.

The trizonal-Polish trade agreements were milestones along the path of restoring West Germany's traditional foreign trade position as an importer of foodstuffs and an exporter of value-added goods. The 1949 trade agreement proved that despite the ravages of war, the West German economy had the strength to reassume its former relationship with Poland, and, further, that the Allies themselves were actively reestablishing West Germany in its former role. The predominance of machinery, electrical equipment, chemicals, and optical equipment in its exports to Poland so soon after the war meant that West Germany was already on the way in 1948 to reassuming its traditional pattern of trade with Poland (Table 7.6).[112] As the Allied-fostered economic recovery progressed more quickly in West Germany than in Poland, it skewed German-Polish trade even more toward German manufactured exports and food imports than had been the case in the interwar years.[113] The gap between West German and Polish economic performance continued to widen in the early 1950s, opening up dramatic opportunities for the use of trade as a diplomatic weapon.

Occupation practices shaped the course and conduct of West German-Polish negotiations since the Allies alone made the basic decisions about West German trade with Poland. JEIA and the control office confined the German members of the negotiating team to passive and subordinate roles.[114] The Allies did not inform Schiffler, Imhoff, or Maltzan at the Economics Department about a number of factors influencing the outcome of negotiations.[115] The ability of the Economics Department to influence West German-Polish trade actually declined in 1948 to 1949 as the ECA, the Bipartite Control Office, and JEIA began to include new political factors in trade-policy decisions. In the spring of 1949, the control office brought JEIA into the discussion of these political considerations. The Allies did not give the West German Economics Department similar information until after the establishment of the Federal Republic. In his memoirs, Erhard outlined four stages of West German participation in trade treaty negotiations up to 1949: (1) "The Allies negotiated alone, without any German negotiators being present"; (2) "The Allies negotiated but Germans were admitted as observers"; (3) "The Germans conduct the negotiations and the Allies observe"; and (4) "The Germans negotiate and the Allies are silent observers." Measured on this scale, German participation in the 1948 and 1949 trade negotiations with Poland remained stuck between stages one and two, never even remotely approaching stages three or four.[116]

The relatively weak position of the Economics Department in the international negotiation process largely deprived the German business community of any effective means of influencing the negotiations.[117] German business groups tried in vain to have their wishes considered in trade negotiations by petitioning the Economics Department for action. Through 1949 the Economics Department could do little to accommodate these wishes and certainly could promise nothing. The nature and tone of private-sector petitions show that several important industrial groups grossly overestimated the role that the Economics Department was playing in negotiations with Poland.[118]

The 1949 trade and payments agreements with Poland were important steps in the erection of two distinct trade regimes for West Germany. The earlier trade and payments agreements negotiated by JEIA with Poland in October 1947 had not differed in essence from those between the Bizonia and other European countries, Eastern or Western. In contrast, the June 1949 trade agreement formalized Western embargo provisions as a routine part of West German-Polish foreign trade by including the "subject to further specification" clause. The Allies, the West German Economics Department, and the Polish government all acknowledged that export controls as part of a politicized trade policy would be a regular feature of future West German-Polish trade.

In 1947 to 1949 the Allies used this politicized trade policy toward Poland to pursue political and economic goals simultaneously. Initially the Allies wanted imports of Polish grain, timber, and coal for Western European reconstruction. On the export side, the Americans and British restricted West German exports in order to limit Soviet military potential and to prevent the rise of a "Silesian Ruhr," in Ambassador Gallman's words. Beyond that, the Allies entertained a vague hope of using Western food purchases to retard the collectivization of Polish agriculture and to "add to the difficulties of Polish Government in dispensing with pro-Western officials who form negotiating links with the West."[119]

There is no solid evidence that manipulated Western trade helped achieve any of these political goals. In some areas, Western efforts clearly failed. Efforts to increase Polish-West European trade did not preserve the position of "pro-Western" officials in the Polish bureaucracy. Grosfeld's fall and Minc's rise put an stamp of strict state control on Polish foreign trade practices. The embassy in Warsaw also soon lost faith in the West's ability to use trade effectively in influencing basic economic trends in Poland. Gallman, reversing himself, told Acheson in April 1949 that "we feel it is too late to retard Sovietization of Poland through economic measures." By June the State Department concluded gloomily that "the communization of Poland is proceeding steadily along the Soviet model."[120] At the same time, Gallman remained convinced that the "U.S. export control policy ... has unquestionably served as a brake on economic-military planning in the Soviet bloc and on growth of a 'Silesian Ruhr'." As the West lost faith in its ability to use trade to influence political events inside Poland, the narrower material goal of "preventing the Polish economy from contributing to the Soviet military potential" came to dominate Western economic policy toward Poland.[121]

Both the content and the form of Poland's trade arrangements with the West, and West Germany in particular, reflect the Sovietization of the Polish economy along Stalinist lines under the direction of Minc. Plans for the development of Polish heavy industry required enormous imports of capital equipment from Germany that were paid for in food exports. Heavy purchases of West German metal working equipment in 1948 and 1949 intensified the traditional pattern of German-Polish trade characterized by exchanges of German industrial goods and Polish agricultural produce. The formal conditions of trade also reflect the communization of Poland. At the same time the Trizonia's trade treaties in Western Europe were reducing the role of the government and returning trade to private hands in 1948 to 1949, the very opposite was occurring in trade deals signed with the East. The trizonal-Polish trade agreement of June 1949 established a Mixed Commission to negotiate fixed lists of imports and exports covering all trizonal-Polish trade. Through that commission, Poland's communist government had exercised its monopoly right to conduct Polish foreign trade and the Allies had recognized that right. Even the terms of payment for trade between Poland and West Germany reflected the conservative communist cast of the Polish economy. Against the advice of Grosfeld and others, Minc insisted on moving toward an all-inclusive strict bilateral clearing arrangement. The Poles rejected the idea of exporting for dollars or sterling despite their promising position as an exporter of eagerly sought commodities, such as timber, potash, and coal. These terms of payment corresponded to the Eastern reorientation of Polish foreign trade, with Poland embedded in a Soviet-led economic bloc.[122] In this new context, Poland required only minimal, carefully controlled exchanges with the Western economies. One of the best means of control lay in maintaining a nonconvertible currency and bilateral payments arrangements.

By the time officials from West Germany and Poland met again in the summer of 1950 to exchange new lists for the upcoming year, the negotiating framework had changed substantially. On the German side, representatives from the new Federal Republic's Ministry for Economics assumed primary responsibility – although not yet ultimate authority – for trade negotiations with Poland. The Germans would quite rightly begin emphasizing their own economic interests and introducing their own political concerns into the trade talks. How difficult might it prove for Polish representatives or for Allied supervisors of West German-East European trade to adapt themselves to the inclusion of new West German national interests in future trade agreements?

Czechoslovakia

West German-Czechoslovak trade from 1947 to 1949 was subjected to the same pressures for expansion and then restriction that were shaping West German-Polish trade at this time. In both the period of expansion (beginning in January 1947) and restriction (after December 1948), West German-Czechoslovak relations attracted substantial attention from the higher levels of the American administration in

Germany and in Washington. Initially JEIA administrators hoped that the relatively undamaged Czechoslovak economy would be a valuable trade partner for Western Germany. They concentrated special efforts on reviving this trade as quickly as possible. As the international relations across Europe grew more tense in 1948 to 1949, West German-Czechoslovak relations became a focus of American attention because of the common border between Czechoslovakia and the American Occupation zone of Germany.

In the spring of 1946, the United States was negotiating with Czechoslovakia for American grants of some $120 million in loans and credit.[123] As one of Europe's economically "better off" countries adjacent to the American zone in Germany, Czechoslovakia was a prime candidate for early American aid. American enthusiasm for aiding Czechoslovakia diminished considerably when the May 1946 elections produced a communist plurality. Shortly thereafter, the American chargé d'affaires in Prague, told the State Department that "leaders of the more moderate [Czechoslovak] parties … recognize that the Western Powers may well adopt a cooler attitude toward humanitarian relief and loans to Czechoslovakia as long as present degree of Communist control continues."[124] As Communist party strength continued to grow in 1946 to 1947, Czechoslovak relations with the United States cooled rapidly. Already by September 1946 all American financial aid to Czechoslovakia was on hold. After Czechoslovakia withdrew its initial acceptance of Marshall Plan assistance, U.S. Ambassador Lawrence Steinhardt recommended that the "U.S. should extend no substantial public or private loan or credits to Czechoslovakia." Yet relations had not moved to a hostile level: "no attempt should be made to discourage normal flow of trade between U.S. and Czechoslovakia on a cash basis."[125]

Mirroring these developments in U.S.-Czechoslovak relations from 1946 to 1947, the American occupation authorities in Germany were seeking to revive the traditionally extensive German-Bohemian trade links. Czechoslovakia appeared to be one country with which Germany would be able to resume meaningful trade relatively quickly.[126] OMGUS established its very first offset dollar account agreement with Czechoslovakia in October 1946. JEIA's Memorandum on Trade with Czechoslovakia produced at negotiations held in Berlin from 29 January to 1 February 1947 was one of the very first signed on behalf of the new Bizonia.[127] Unfortunately, Czechoslovakia's dollar shortage threatened to curtail further trade with the Bizonia despite the new agreement. In the spring of 1947 new bizonal-Czechoslovak negotiations were held in Berlin to discuss "revised economic arrangements" for "payment for Czechoslovak freight traffic across the British and American zones of occupation." OMGUS argued that it would must continue to require payment in dollars.[128] Acheson responded that he considered Czechoslovakia's "acute shortage of dollars" to be genuine and that from the political point of view it was "desirable that Czechoslovakia continue to trade with the West and ship goods across bizonal area rather than concentrating on transportation facilities in Soviet zone and Polish ports."[129] A new memorandum for expanded trade was signed by the Czechoslovaks and the bizonal authorities in July 1947. In September, a payments agreement was signed, establishing nondollar offset accounts.

These 1947 agreements facilitated the expanding trade between the Bizonia and Czechoslovakia from 1947 to 1949 (Graph 7.1). At $4.4 million in 1947, imports from Czechoslovakia made up 11 percent of the Bizonia's total commercial imports – a proportion exceeding imports from other lightly damaged or undamaged countries such as the Netherlands and Sweden. Imports from Czechoslovakia rose to $10.3 million in 1948 and reached $12.3 million for just the first half of 1949. Coal lay at the core of Czechoslovak exports to the Bizonia, most of it consumed by Bavarian industry in the American zone: 642,000 tons in 1947; 930,000 tons in 1948; and 1,047,000 tons in 1949.[130] Coal export earnings credited through the payments agreement of September 1947 provided Czechoslovakia with a means of increasing its own imports from the Bizonia. The results were readily apparent in the surge of bizonal exports to Czechoslovakia in the first quarter of 1948.

A new, more comprehensive trade and payments agreement negotiated in September and signed in December 1948 put West German-Czechoslovak relations on a more permanent basis. Like the bizonal agreement signed with Poland that same year, this new agreement established a bilateral Mixed Commission and foresaw annual meetings to set the value and volume of two-way trade. Again as in the Polish case, JEIA's 1948 trade agreement with Czechoslovakia unexpectedly continued to serve as the legal basis for trade between the Federal Republic and the Czechoslovak Socialist Republic through the 1950s.

Almost immediately after the conclusion of the promising 1948 agreement, relations between the U.S. and Czechoslovakia began an accelerating deterioration. Beginning in 1948, the United States chose West German-Czechoslovak relations as the primary medium through which they would express American disapproval of developments in Czechoslovakia. The geography of the American Occupation in Germany made a manipulation of West German-Czechoslovak relations an understandable American response to Czechoslovak provocations, although the West Germans did not understand these actions. The U.S. Occupation zone in Germany bordered directly on Czechoslovakia, and American military authorities had complete authority in policing their zonal borders. In effect, the Americans had a common border with Czechoslovakia. Also, the Czechoslovaks were partially dependent on passage through the American zone to Hamburg for their exports destined for overseas markets. The position of American forces in Germany gave the U.S. the unique opportunity to take action along the Bavarian-Bohemian border as a direct response to events in U.S.- Czechoslovak relations.

In December 1948 Czechoslovak authorities stepped up their harassment of Americans assigned to the embassy in Prague. The U.S. was quick to seek retaliation in the U.S. zone of Germany. The embassy in Prague requested American military authorities to consider cutting off facilities and assistance to Czechoslovak representatives in the U.S. zone of Germany. Clay's political adviser, Robert Murphy, had no objection to the plan. On 4 January 1949, Acheson told Murphy that he agreed "retaliation and counter pressure can best be applied [from the] U.S. zone and have no objection to such action."[131] In response to further political friction between the U.S. and Czechoslovakia, Clay recommended closing the Bavarian-Czechoslovak border to international transit traffic. Newly appointed Ambassador Joseph Jacobs in Prague went even further, urging that "closure of the border should include German-Czechoslovak traffic notwithstanding some possible damage to the German economy." From the American perspective, one advantage to using the U.S. zone in Germany as a means of retaliation lay in its immediate proximity to Czechoslovakia. More significantly, "retaliatory steps" by the American military authorities in Germany "are least likely to involve US and Czechoslovakia in retaliatory action against one another." The economic sacrifice of retaliation would be borne by the Europeans, especially the West Germans, but also "Belgium, Netherlands, Denmark (and to less extent France) ..."[132] This was true of Jacobs's alternative recommendation as well, that the U.S. "tighten still further our control over exports to Czechoslovakia."[133]

In response to Cold War pressures, the Americans focused quickly on restricting East-West trade at the point where they could do so most immediately and effectively – along the Bavarian-Czechoslovak border. The American response via Occupation authorities in Germany was based on both political power and geographic logic. The geographic logic was enduring, but American political power in Germany was blunted and encumbered by the evolution of Allied-West German relations from Occupation to alliance. Would this new context allow Western policymakers to balance continuing American concerns about West German exports of strategic commodities to the East and renewed American efforts to close the Bavarian-Bohemian border to trade in 1950 to 1951 with German interests in maintaining supplies of Bohemian coal and preserving Czechoslovak export links to Hamburg?

Soviet Union

Trade between the Soviet Union and the western zones of Germany from 1945 to 1949 existed on only a very small scale and only for a limited time. bizonal exports to the USSR were just $174,000 in 1947, $83,000 in 1948, and only $41,000 for the first half of 1949. bizonal imports from the USSR, which had been very small in 1948 ($1.8 million), dropped to $35,000 in the first quarter of 1949 and to zero thereafter. The disappearance of this small trade volume at a time when economic recovery in western Germany was gaining strength had no lasting economic importance. Much more significant for the future of West German-Soviet relations after 1949 was the lack of a trade and payments agreement, or indeed any type of formal economic agreement between the western zones of Germany and the Soviet Union.

The reasons why no such agreements were concluded are not difficult to understand. On the most basic economic level, the Soviets were busily digesting the exports and reparations extracted from their own Occupation zone east of the Elbe.[134] For the next few years after 1945 the Soviets would dispense with additional material from the western zones, for which they would have to pay as a result of Clay's May 1946 decision to halt further reparations deliveries. Political considerations almost certainly played a role as well. Having rejected the American offer to merge Occupation zones in July 1946, Stalin did not want to recognize the Bizonia or Trizonia as functioning fusions of the western zones by concluding trade agreements with them.[135]

Neither the Soviets nor JEIA administrators could know that the interplay of Occupation politics and Cold War pressures would rapidly foreclose the possibility of a West German-Soviet trade agreement. Once the brief window of opportunity for such an agreement was closed, it could not be reopened for some time since Cold War tensions precluded any expansion or intensification of economic relations between East and West. For these reasons, the Soviet decision not to seek a trade agreement with the Bizonia in 1947 or 1948 had far more lasting consequences than could have been known at the time. The Soviet decision not to act at a time when such an agreement might have been possible could not be remedied easily. Without a formal agreement from the Occupation period upon which they might subsequently rely, the West Germans and Soviets were left without a mutual point of contact after the establishment of the Federal Republic in 1949. The situation in the 1950s was not unlike that of the 1920s as both sides maneuvered for advantage while pondering the role that trade and a trade agreement might (once again) play in rebuilding economic and political relations between two former adversaries.

Despite the rigidities of the European Cold War order in 1949, the future course of West German-East European trade relations after 1949 was filled with questions. Certainly a number of features of the early postwar period remained almost unchanged into the early 1950s. On the physical level, the reconstruction of an advanced industrial economy in West Germany continued apace in the next decade. The performance gap between American-sponsored recovery in the West and Soviet-dictated recovery in the East persisted and widened. The pan-Western politicization of its trade with Eastern Europe remained the enduring characteristic of the international regime for East-West trade for many more years. In that context, the JEIA-negotiated agreements of 1948 and 1949 continued to serve as the legal basis for West German trade with Poland and Czechoslovakia. The absence of a similar agreement with the Soviet Union hampered the normalization of relations between the FRG and the USSR for the next decade.

On the other hand, the domestic political basis for of West German trade policy was fundamentally altered by the creation of the Federal Republic as a new West German state that would coexist with a modified Occupation administration. As of September 1949, Occupation authorities and ministerial bureaucrats from the FRG would share control over West German trade with the East. How would the inherited structures of 1945 to 1949 be employed as West Germany evolved from an occupied territory to a semisovereign state? Could a new framework be constructed that would allow the Allies to supervise the trade of the Federal Republic with Eastern Europe in such a way as to accommodate the interests of both the Americans and the West Germans? How would the governments of East European states respond to the appearance of German negotiators actively pursuing their own national interests? The answers depended in part on whether the new German republic could avoid or overcome the type of divisive paralysis that had left Weimar's Eastern trade policy foundering.

Notes

1. "Declaration Regarding the Defeat of Germany and the Assumption of Supreme Authority with Respect to Germany by the Governments of the United Kingdom, the United States, the USSR, and the Provisional Government of the French Republic," *Official Gazette of the Control Council for Germany*, Supplement I, 7.
2. "Control Council Proclamation No. 2: Certain Additional Requirements Imposed on Germany," *Official Gazette of the Control Council for Germany*, No. 1, 29 October 1945, 8.
3. Military Law No. 53, Articles 2(a) and 2(d); Military Law No. 161: "Except as it is so authorized, all inward and outward movement of property and goods either across said [German] frontier or zonal boundary is also prohibited."
4. The literature on Western Occupation policies has grown voluminous over the past two decades. For earlier studies consult, Gisela Hirsch, *A Bibliography of German Studies 1945-1971: Germany under Allied Occupation* (Bloomington, Ind., 1972) For a more recent introduction see Claus Scharf and Hans-Jürgen Schröder, eds., *Politische und Ökonomische Stabilisierung Westdeutschlands 1945-1949. Fünf Beiträge zur Deutschlandpolitik der westlichen Alliierten* (Wiesbaden, 1977); Theo Stammen, "Das Alliierte Besatzungsregime in Deutschland," in Josef Becker et al., eds., *Vorgeschichte der Bundesrepublik Deutschland. Zwischen Kapitulation und Grundgesetz* (Munich, 1979), 61-92. On British policies, see Scharf and Schröder, eds., *Die Deutschlandpolitik Grossbritaniens und die britische Zone 1945-1949* (Wiesbaden, 1979); Josef Forschepoth and Rolf Steininger, eds., *Die britische Deutschland- und Besatzungspolitik 1945-1949* (Paderborn, 1984); Alec Cairncross, *The Price of War. British Policy on German Reparations 1941-1949* (Oxford, 1986); Albrecht Tyrell, *Grossbritanien und die Deutschlandplanung der Allierten 1941-1945* (Frankfurt, 1987); Ian Turner, ed., *Reconstruction in Post-War Germany: British Occupation Policy and the Western Zones, 1945-1955* (New York, 1989). On the French zone, Heike Bungert, "A New Perspective on French-American Relations during the Occupation of Germany, 1945-1949, *Diplomatic History* 18 (1994), 333-52; Scharf and Schröder, eds., *Die Deutschlandpolitik Frankreichs und die französische Zone 1945-1949* (Wiesbaden, 1983); Klaus-Dietmar Henke, "Politik der Widersprüche. Zur Charakteristik der französischen Militärregierung in Deutschland nach dem zweiten Weltkrieg," *VfZ* 30 (1982), 500 ff.; Rainer Hudemann, "Fragen zur Wirtschaftsgeschichte der französischen Besatzungszone," *Zeitschrift für wüttembergische Landesgeschichte* 46 (1987), 403 ff.; Mathias Manz, *Stagnation und Aufschwung in der französischen Besatzungszone, 1945-1948* (Ph.D. diss., University of Manheim, 1986). On the American experience, Earl Ziemke, *The U.S. Army in the Occupation of Germany, 1944-1946* (Washington, 1975); Edward Peterson, *The American Occupation of Germany: Retreat to Victory* (Detroit, Mich., 1978); Wolfgang Krieger, *General Lucius D. Clay und die amerikanische Deutschlandpolitik 1945-1949* (Stuttgart, 1987).
5. French policy aimed bluntly at weakening German economic power by ending the unity of the German state. The British hoped to control and direct the German economy without impoverishing themselves or the Germans. Official American policy evolved from the harsh Morgenthau Plan of 1944 to a wait-and-see and hope (in vain) for Four Power agreement posture in 1945 and early 1946.
6. In the U.S. zone, the Americans paid $275 million for 1 million metric tons (MMT) of food imports from May 1945 through the end of 1946, OMGUS, *Monthly Report of the Military Governor*, No. 17, Trade and Commerce (Cumulative Review) 8 May 1945 to 30 November 1946, 12.
7. The British concentrated on raising exports of Ruhr coal, which was available in the U.K. zone and was badly needed by other Western European countries. By employing this strategy, the British managed $139 million in exports in 1946, of

which roughly three-quarters was earned by the sale of Ruhr coal, Lucius D. Clay, *Decision in Germany*, (New York, 1950), 199. More rigorous policies in the French zone produced $64 million in exports from 1945 to 1946, of which 88.9 percent went to France. Coal exports generated over 20 percent of this sum as well, Friedrich Jerchow, *Deutschland in der Weltwirtschaft 1944-1947*, (Dusseldorf, 1978), 431 ff. Unlike the British and French zones, the U.S. zone had no coal for ready export to a waiting Western Europe; the U.S. zone had traditionally imported brown coal from Bohemia.

8. Clay, *Decision in Germany*, 196.
9. OMGUS, *Monthly Report of the Military Governor*, No. 17, 11.
10. The physical and administrative obstacles prevailing in Germany in 1945 and 1946 kept export earnings disappointingly low, especially in the resource-poor U.S. zone. Despite what Clay termed an "unbelievable effort," exports from the U.S. zone earned just $3 million in the second half of 1945 and not quite $25 million in all of 1946, *Decision in Germany*, 224. OMGUS commented with tired resignation that "what happened in 1946 – both as to the volume and composition of exports – reflects the exhaustion of the Germany economy in the wake of defeat," *Monthly Report of the Military Governor*, No. 17, Trade and Commerce (Cumulative Review) 8 May 1945 to 30 November 1946, 9.
11. Drafted to rebut Molotov's accusations following the failure to reach Four-Power agreement on the economic administration of Germany at the Paris meeting of the Council of Foreign Ministers in July 1946, the Byrnes speech was the first official and public confirmation of the constructive Occupation policy that OMGUS had already been practicing in the U.S. zone since 1945. Byrnes emphasized the economic reconstruction of Germany and the necessary role of foreign trade: "Germany must be given a chance to export goods in order to import ..." The reasoning was two-fold: first, to make the German economy "self-sustaining;" and, second, to foster recovery in the neighboring European states. Reviving German exports, including "steel, iron and coal," was openly acknowledged to be an important part of both short-term and long-range American plans for Germany and Europe, reprinted in Royal Institute of International Affairs, Beate Ruhm von Oppen, ed., *Documents on Germany under Occupation 1945-1954* (Oxford, 1955), 152-60.
12. OMGUS, *Monthly Report of the Military Governor*, No. 49, July 1949. Statistical Annex, Issue No. XXIX, Table 601.
13. Through the first half of 1946 export policy was neither orderly nor planned, as OMGUS itself admitted: "Occupation authorities, manufacturers, and German officials formulated policies, and generally built up an organization to export what they could when they could, and to whatever countries could pay in dollars," *Monthly Report of the Military Governor*, No. 17, 9.
14. Convinced that "conditions in Germany ... were leading to economic chaos," Clay and the political adviser in the U.S. zone, Ambassador Robert D. Murphy, approached Secretary Byrnes in April 1946 with the idea of merging the economic affairs of the British and American zones. As Clay made clear, basic economic considerations motivated his proposal: "Separated, neither zone appeared capable of self-sufficiency; combined their chance was greater," *Decision in Germany*, 165, 199. In July 1946 the Americans presented their offer to merge zones both at the Paris Council of Foreign Ministers meeting and in the Allied Control Council. Predictably, the French and Soviets declined the offer; the British accepted. On 9 August 1946 the British and American deputy military governors established a Bipartite Board to hammer out the details of the merger. On these consequential developments begin with John Gimbel, *The American Occupation of Germany: Politics and the Military* (Stanford, Calif., 1968), 56 ff.; Wolfgang Benz,

Von der Besatzungsherrschaft zur Bundesrepublik Deutschland. Stationen einer Staats-gründung, 1946-1949 (Frankfurt, 1985), 35 ff.

15. "Agreement Between the Government of the United Kingdom and the United States on the Economic Fusion of their Respective zones," in Ruhm von Oppen, ed., *Documents on Germany under Occupation 1945-1954*, 195-99.

16. Bullock had just recently headed the Import-Export Section at in the American zone. Before that he had served with the Foreign Economic Administration and before the war had directed the Business School at Johns Hopkins University. Cahan came from service at the British Treasury.

17. JEIA was established at the end of 1946 pursuant to the Bizonal Fusion Agreement of December 2, 1946 (the Byrnes-Bevin agreement) and was rechartered in accordance with the Revised Bizonal Agreement of December 17, 1947 (the Lovett-Strang agreement). JEIA was not subordinated to the Bipartite Control Group for Economics as one would have logically expected. Rather, JEIA was placed on equal footing with the Economics Control Group and brought directly under the control of the higher-ranking Bipartite Panel for Economics, which, in turn, dealt directly with the highest-level Bipartite Board. When bizonal administration was reorganized in early 1948, the JEIA retained its "independence." Unlike other bipartite groups (e.g., finance, commerce and industry, transport), JEIA was not subordinate to the Bipartite Control Office, but retained its direct link to the Bipartite Board, see War Department, Civil Administration Division, *The Evolution of Bizonal Administration*, Charts No. 1 and 3; Walter Vogel, *Westdeutschland 1945-1950. Der Aufbau von der Verfassungs-und Verwaltungseinrichtungen über den Ländern der drei westlichen Besatzungszonen* (Boppard, 1964), 157 ff.

18. War Department, Civil Administration Division, *The Evolution of Bizonal Administration*, Appendix X, "Joint Export-Import Agency Charter," 87. It was legally impossible for a German agency to exercise these functions at this time since German foreign assets were still blocked by U.S. and U.K. wartime law, and German authorities were not permitted to deal in foreign currency.

19. War Department, Civil Administration Division, *The Evolution of Bizonal Administration*, 13. Gen. Clay cites a figure of roughly $90 million for JEIA's initial capital in Clay, *Decision in Germany*, 173. However, John Backer cites the JEIA original balance sheet from the OMGUS records as showing a starting capital of $72.6 million, Backer, *Priming the German Economy*, (Durham, N.C., 1971), 135. Walter Vogel claims a figure of $121 million in his *Westdeutschland 1945-1949*, 163. While Vogel's figure seems to include some monies paid in later, the discrepancies between the other three figures remain.

20. War Department, Civil Administration Division, *The Evolution of Bizonal Administration*, "Joint Export-Import Agency Charter," 89.

21. In April 1947, General Sir Brian Robertson presented a British Memorandum on the Operation of the Fusion Agreement after the Moscow Conference, which declared that "Measures shall be taken to develop greater freedom of trade between Germans in the Combined zones and other countries ...." In response, Draper at OMGUS commented drily that the British statement "added nothing to the current understanding" since this had been U.S. policy for some time already, for Robertson's Memorandum and Draper's comments on it, *FRUS*, 1947, vol. 2, 479 ff.

22. OMGUS, *Report of the Military Governor*, No. 29, Trade and Commerce (Cumulative Review) 1 December 1946 to 30 November 1947, 6.

23. "The Political Advisor in Germany (Murphy) to the Director of the Office of European Affairs (Mathews)," *FRUS*, 1947, vol. 2, 910.

24. OMGUS, *Report of the Military Governor*, No. 29, 7.

25. The offices of co-chairmen were replaced by an American director general and British deputy director general. Cahan stayed on as deputy director for the

British, while W. John Logan took the American post of director. Logan was a New York banker who had served as a director in the Distribution Bureau of the War Productions Board and had followed Bullock as U.S. co-chairman in the old JEIA in October 1947. The new charter established a board of directors composed of both U.S. and U.K. members, each group to vote as a unit on trade policy questions with "voting strength in relation to the other group equal to the proportion which the appropriated funds made available by their respective governments" in supporting the Bizonia, War Department, Civil Administration Division, *The Evolution of Bizonal Administration,* "Joint Export-Import Agency Charter," 88. The revised fusion agreement had already reduced British contributions to bizonal imports for the upcoming year to £17.5 million, largely in goods and services. The Americans agreed to pay in dollars for all remaining "category A" imports (food, fertilizers, and petroleum) to the Bizonia through the end of 1948.

26. The French Director became a JEIA deputy director, French representatives were added to the JEIA board of directors, and the French foreign trade agency's headquarters in Baden-Baden became a JEIA branch office, see Buchheim, *Wiedereingliederung,* 41 ff. Along with French participation in the currency reform, the extension of the old bizonal import/export regime to the French zone was a key step in unifying all three zones.

27. JEIA Instruction No. 1, Revision 1, in *JEIA Monthly Report,* Dec. 1948. The official German text of the revised Instruction No. 1 can be found in BA B 102/2000 H.1.

28. Backer, *Priming the German Economy,* 185.

29. Byrnes had connected German and European economic recoveries in his Stuttgart speech of September, 1946. By 1947 the Allies understood the inseparability of a German economic recovery and a general European economic recovery. Economic experts at OMGUS reported that "[T]he Bizonal Area can and must play an important role in general European recovery. Germany, and especially western Germany, has always been an integral and vital part of the Western European economy; and it is difficult to envisage a healthy economic system in Western Europe without a very substantial German contribution," OMGUS, *Report of the Military Governor,* No. 29, 7.

30. The U.S. had been calling for a "resumption of normal business practices" since mid-1946, Department of State, *United States Economic Policy toward Germany* (Washington, D.C., 1946), 48. Official instructions to "take measures which will bring about the establishment of stable political and economic conditions in Germany" and "to return foreign trade … to normal trade channels" were given to OMGUS in July 1947 as part of JCS 1779, Press Release accompanying publication of JCS 1779, 15 July 1947, in U.S. Department of State, *Germany 1947-1949. The Story in Documents* (Washington, D.C., 1950), 34; JCS 1779 (paragraph 18d), U.S. Department of State, *Germany 1947-1949. The Story in Documents,* 38.

31. At its creation, the JEIA had inherited the long-standing OMGUS practice of accepting only dollars for West German exports. That policy had been heavily criticized by German exporters in the U.S. zone, who quite rightly perceived its limiting affect on sales abroad. The dollar policy was even more harshly criticized by other countries, especially the Netherlands and Belgium, where dollar shortages prevented them from ordering eagerly desired capital goods from Germany. In early 1946 a meeting of economic advisers of American embassies in Europe discussed the problem in Paris. As Frederick Winant (Trade and Commerce Branch, OMGUS) told Draper, the Paris group urged that "the dollar requirements be eased as soon as possible and plans be developed for the acceptance of other currencies in payment for European exports," OMGUS records, 123-2/3 as cited in Backer, *Priming the German Economy,* 149; Buchheim, *Wiedereingliederung,*

42 ff.; memorandum of Wesley Haraldson to Robert Murphy on Clay's views, 5 March 1948, National Archives, Department of State, Central European Division, 1944-1953, Box 1, Folder [no heading]. Clay himself only very reluctantly compromised on the dollar policy, as his letter to Secretary Marshall in May 1947 shows, *Decision in Germany*, 225; *FRUS*, 1947, vol. 2, 915.

32. By August 1, 1948, JEIA's Foreign Exchange Agency had accounts in thirty-five foreign banks with assets totaling $158 million and outstanding letters of credit totaling another $106 million, Clay, *Decision in Germany*, 205.

33. As part of its 1948 reorganization, JEIA was divided into two principal divisions, the Foreign Trade Office and the Comptroller's Office. George J. Santry, a New York business executive who had joined OMGUS at the beginning of the Occupation, served as director of the Foreign Trade Office, with General M.E.L. Robinson serving as the deputy director and British representative. The Foreign Trade Office was itself further subdivided into four branches: policy and planning, imports, exports, and trade negotiations.

34. Dietrich had been professor of economics at Mount Holyoke College and then deputy chief of the Trade and Commerce Branch in the Economics Division at OMGUS before assuming her new duties with JEIA.

35. JCS 1779 (paragraph 18c) in U.S. Department of State, *Germany 1947-1949. The Story in Documents* (Washington, D.C., 1950), 38.

36. Ethel Dietrich, "The Bizonia's Trade Agreement Program," *OMGUS Information Bulletin*, No. 142, August 24, 1948, 3.

37. OMGUS, *Monthly Report of the Military Governor*, No. 29, Nov. 1947, 23. The extensive control of European trade in the immediate postwar years accounts for the unusual contents of the early trade memoranda negotiated by JEIA. These agreements were not contracts to exchange merchandise, but rather were simply government agreements to issue import/export licenses for specified volumes of itemized commodities. "None of the trade pacts is on a compensation basis, guaranteeing the exchange of specific quantities of items agreed upon. They represent guarantees on the part of each government to grant authority, in the form of licenses, if and when private contracts can be satisfactorily arranged," Dietrich, "The Bizonia's Trade Agreement Program," *OMGUS Information Bulletin*, No. 142, 24 August 1948, 5.

38. Dietrich, "The Bizonia's Trade Agreement Program," *OMGUS Information Bulletin*, No. 142, 24 August 1948, 3.

39. In 1946 exports from the British and American zones were just $161 million. In 1947 the Bizonia exported $225 million worth of goods, and in 1948 exports were almost $600 million. For the first seven months of 1949 bizonal exports average $96.7 million per month, a rate that projected a 1949 yearly total of $1.1 billion in exports and exceeded targets for 1949 that had been set in 1947. By 1949 these export earnings paid for more than 50 percent of the Bizonia's rapidly growing imports, with the remainder financed by GARIOA and U.K. contributions (28 percent) and ECA funds (21.7 percent), OMGUS, *Report of the Military Governor*, No. 50, 132.

40. In the first eleven months of 1947 coal (56 percent) and timber (18 percent) had together accounted for almost 75 percent of bizonal exports, OMGUS, *Report of the Military Governor*, No. 29, Trade and Commerce (Cumulative Review) 1 December 1946 to 30 November 1947, 2. By June 1949 coal exports were just 32 percent of total exports and timber exports just over 1 percent of the total. In that same period exports of finished and semifinished goods rose from 12 percent of total exports to 56 percent. By 1949 five traditional German industrial categories (metalware, machinery and vehicles, chemicals, scientific equipment, and pharmaceuticals) accounted for one-quarter of West German exports.

41. On the creation of a domestic "social market economy" in West Germany and the Federal Republic, see Gerold Ambrosius's excellent study, *Die Durchsetzung der Sozialmarktwirtschaft in Westdeutschland 1945-1949* (Stuttgart, 1977); Alan Peacock and Hans Willgerodt, eds., *Germany's Social Market Economy: Origins and Evolution* (New York, 1989).

42. War Department, Civil Administration Division, *Evolution of Bizonal Administration in Germany*, Appendix X, 91. As early as April 1947 JEIA had created a "policy & planning section" headed by G.N. McClusky and A.W. Moran to serve as "the point of contact between JEIA and the Main Department of Foreign Trade" of the West German Economics Administration, JEIA memorandum signed by Bullock and Cahan, 2 April 1947, BA B 102/1770.

43. As the German administration expanded, the original Main Department (Hauptabteilung) D was renamed Main Department V (Foreign Trade) and its subordinate Department V A was assigned responsibility for foreign trade policy, Walter Vogel, *Westdeutschland 1945-1950*, 134-135. Maltzan had served before the war as a trade expert in the German Foreign Office. He began his postwar career in the State Ministry for Economics and Transportation in Hesse, first as a consultant for foreign trade matters, and then as department head. In June 1946 he was nominated by the Council of States (Länderrat) in the U.S. zone as special representative for interzonal and foreign trade. In November 1946 he moved to Main Department D (Foreign and Interzonal Trade) of the newly established Economics Administration in the West German bizonal administration at Minden. Maltzan remained department head for Foreign Economic Relations in the New West German Federal Ministry for Economics from 1950 to 1953, and in 1953 moved to the newly revived Foreign Office as head of the Trade Policy Division.

44. Ethel Dietrich, "The Bizonia's Trade Agreement Program," *OMGUS Information Bulletin*, No. 142, August 24, 1948, 5.

45. Clay, *Decision in Germany*, 205.

46. A 1953 memorandum on East-West trade by the Trade Policy Department of the West German Foreign Office recalled how "German administrators were initially practically excluded from the resumption of trade relations" with East European countries, PAAA 311.22.

47. Manfred Knapp, "Die Anfänge westdeutscher Aussenwirtschafts- und Aussenpolitik im bizonalen Vereinigten Wirtschaftsgebiet (1947-1949)," in Manfred Knapp, ed., *Von der Bizonengründung zur ökonomisch-politischen Westintegration* (Frankfurt, 1984); and Institut für Zeitgeschichte und Der Deutsche Bundestag (hrsg.), *Wörtliche Berichte und Drucksachen des Wirtschaftsrates des Vereinigten Wirtschaftsgebietes 1947-1949*.

48. *Wörtliche Berichte und Drucksachen des Wirtschaftsrates*, Bd. 2, 9-10.

49. *Wörtliche Berichte und Drucksachen des Wirtschaftsrates*, Bd. 2, 96.

50. *Wörtliche Berichte und Drucksachen des Wirtschaftsrates*, Bd. 2, 444.

51. For the following, *Wörtliche Berichte und Drucksachen des Wirtschaftsrates*, Bd. 2, 954 ff.

52. *Wörtliche Berichte und Drucksachen des Wirtschaftsrates*, Bd. 2, 960.

53. "The Passing of the JEIA," *The Economist*, 29 October 1949.

54. Friedrich Jerchow, *Deutschland in der Weltwirtschaft 1944-1947*, 289 ff.

55. Leaving aside the extensive debate on the role of the Marshall Plan in promoting West German domestic economic recovery, the role of the plan in reintegrating western Germany into the larger European economy and the importance of this for the overall success of American policies in Europe has been explored by Alan Milward, *The Reconstruction of Western Europe 1945-1951* (London, 1984), 320 ff.; Christoph Buchheim, *Wiedereingliederung*, 171 ff. Both the war and state departments agreed that the Bizonia must be included in the European Recovery Pro-

gram, as Marshall indicated in September 1947, "Secretary of State to the Embassy in the United Kingdom," *FRUS*, 1947, vol. 3, 409. The British concurred. In Paris, the Benelux countries told the Committee of European Economic Cooperation (CEEC) that "there can be no Western European economic recovery in the true sense unless there is a rapid utilization of the resources of western Germany," "The Ambassador in France (Caffery) to the Secretary of State," *FRUS*, 1947, vol. 3, 333.

56. Several recent studies have brought out the role played by foreign trade in anchoring the future Federal Republic in the liberal Western economic order. See Friedrich Jerchow, "Aussenhandel im Widerstreit. Die Bundesrepublik auf dem Weg in das GATT 1949-1952," in Heinrich Winkler, ed., *Politische Weichenstellungen im Nachkriegsdeutschland 1945-1953* (Gottingen, 1979), 254-89; the contributions by Manfred Knapp and Bernhard Welschke in Knapp, ed., *Von der Bizonengründung zur ökonomisch-politischen Westintegration. Studien zum Verhältnis zwischen Aussenpolitik und Aussenwirtschaftsbeziehungen in der Entstehungsphase der Bundesrepublik Deutschland 1947-1952* (Frankfurt, 1984), 14-93 and 187-286; Harald Guldin, "Aussenwirtschaftspolitische und aussenpolitische Einflussfaktoren im Prozess der Staatswerdung der Bundesrepublik Deutschland (1947-1952)," in *Aus Politik und Zeitgeschichte*, B32/87, 8 August 1987, 3-20; Werner Bührer, "Erzwungene oder freiwillige Liberalisierung? Die USA, OEEC und die Westdeutsche Aussenhandelspolitik 1949-1952," in Ludolf Herbst et al., eds., *Vom Marshallplan zur EWG. Die Eingliederung der Bundesrepublik in die westliche Welt* (Munich, 1990), 139-62.

57. Nationalization and collectivization in the people's democracies, the fraudulent Polish elections, refusal to participate in the Marshall Plan, exclusion from the OEEC, and the Czech coup are the best-known events in this process, see Laszlo Lang, *International Regimes and the Political Economy of East-West Relations* (New York, 1989), 18 ff., 26 ff.; Gier Lundestad, "Der Marshall-Plan und Osteuropa," in O. Haberl and L. Nietzhammer, eds., *Der Marshall-Plan und die europäische Linke* (Frankfurt, 1986), 59-74.

58. All figures in 1938 f.o.b. prices. United Nations Economic Commission for Europe, *Economic Survey of Europe in 1948* (Geneva, 1949), table 82.

59. Committee on Foreign Relations, United States Senate, *A Background Study on East-West Trade*, 89th Congress, 1st Session, Washington, 1965, 2.

60. "Acting Secretary of State to the Embassy in France," *FRUS*, 1947, vol. 3, 387.

61. "Report by the Ad Hoc Subcommittee of the Advisory Committee of the Secretary of Commerce," *FRUS*, 1948, vol. 4, 536.

62. "Ambassador in France (Caffery) to the Secretary of State," *FRUS*, 1947, vol. 3, 394.

63. "The Ambassador in the United Kingdom (Douglas) to the Secretary of State," *FRUS*, 1948, vol. 4, 562.

64. William Diebold, Jr., "East-West Trade and the Marshall Plan," in *Foreign Affairs* 26, no. 4, 709-22.

65. See *Committee of European Economic Cooperation, Technical Reports*, vol. 2, July-Sept 1947 (Department of State Publication 2952)

66. "Report by the Ad Hoc Subcommittee ...," *FRUS*, 1948, vol. 4, 536.

67. OMGUS, *Monthly Report of the Military Governor*, No. 29, 7.

68. OMGUS, *Monthly Report of the Military Governor*, No. 17, 17.

69. Ethel Dietrich, "The Bizonia's Trade Agreement Program," *OMGUS Information Bulletin*, No. 142, 24 August 1948, 5.

70. On American initiatives for the construction of common Western export control program see Michael Mastanduno, "Trade as a Strategic Weapon: American and Alliance Export Control Policy in the Early Postwar Period, *International Organi-*

zation 42 (Winter 1988), 121-50; Robert Mark Spaulding, "'A Gradual and Moderate Relaxation.' Eisenhower and the Revision of American Export Control Policy 1953-1955," *Diplomatic History* 17 (1993), 223-49. Less useful now is Gunner Adler-Karlsson's classic study, *Western Economic Warfare 1947-1967. A Study in Foreign Economic Policy* (Stockholm, 1968).

71. "The Secretary of State to the Embassy in France," 27 August 1948, *FRUS*, 1948, vol. 4, 564.

72. British compliance with American wishes to restrict West German exports to the East is hardly surprising in light of the dominant American position in determining bizonal policy (especially the American majority voting position in JEIA itself), Britain's overall financial dependence on the U.S., and genuine British agreement with the need to control some strategic exports.

73. War Department, Civil Administration Division, *The Evolution of Bizonal Organization*, 13. Since JEIA was technically independent of the control office, that office had previously played no part in regulating West German foreign trade.

74. "Current Economic Developments," *FRUS*, 1948, vol. 4, 587.

75. "Policy Paper Approved by the Foreign Assistance Correlation Committee," *FRUS*, 1949, vol. 5, 131. The Foreign Assistance Correlation Committee contained representatives from State, the National Military Establishment, and ECA. In contrast, the British were controlling only 128 out 163 items on the U.S. 1-A list at that time, and other European countries remained even further behind in implementing controls.

76. Executives at Bayer heard with frustration that "the German administration could make no concrete suggestions" about how Bayer might appeal an Allied refusal to allow exports of rubber-treating chemicals to the East, Bayer-Archiv 67/2, vol. 1 (trade policy reports of Bayer's Verbindungsstelle in Frankfurt, headed by the usually well-informed Jost Terharr. Bayer later moved this office to Leverkusen and renamed it the Handelspoltisches Büro), 16 June 1949.

77. On the consolidation of communist power in Poland from 1944 to 1948 see Norman Davies, "Poland," in Martin McCauley, ed., *Communist Power in Europe 1944-1949* (New York, 1977), 39-57; Teresa Toranska, *"Them"; Stalin's Polish Puppets* (New York, 1987); Krystyna Kersten, *The Establishment of Communist Rule in Poland, 1943-1948* (Berkeley, Calif., 1991). Among the memoirs, Stanisław Mikołajczyk, *The Pattern of Soviet Domination* (London, 1948); the service memoirs of American Ambassador Arthur Bliss Lane, *I Saw Poland Betrayed: An American Ambassador Reports to the American People* (New York, 1948).

78. The agreement is reprinted in *United States Statutes at Large*, vol. 60, 1946, part 2, (Washington, D.C., 1947), 1609. The Americans agreed to provide Poland with an initial $90 million in credit, $50 million to purchase surplus American war supplies and equipment in Europe, and a $40 million credit line at the U.S. Export-Import Bank. For Lane's position see *I Saw Poland Betrayed*; *FRUS*, 1946, vol. 6, 374-554.

79. "Memorandum of a Conversation, by the Acting Secretary of State," in *FRUS*, 1946, vol. 6, 540. Acheson, Clayton (Under-Secretary for Economic Affairs), Llewelleyn Thompson (chief of the Division of Eastern European Affairs), and even Ambassador Lane agreed on the importance of Polish coal for Western European recovery.

80. In late July 1947, Clayton told Under-Secretary Lovett that "since increased production of coal in Europe in the quickest possible time is the most important problem in European reconstruction, I recommend that the [State] department raise no objection to consideration by the International Bank [for Reconstruction and Development] of the extension of credit to Poland for reequipping her coal mines and such reconstruction of her ports as may be necessary to move the coal

export," *FRUS*, 1947, vol. 6, 436. Secretary of State George Marshall himself acknowledged that Poland "had coal which was badly needed [in Europe] and she had needs herself which could only be supplied from outside Poland," "Memorandum of Conversation, by the Secretary of State," *FRUS*, 1947, vol. 6, 439. For this reason R.L. Garner, vice-president of the International Bank for Reconstruction and Development, supported a loan "of about $47 million [in order to] support a substantial increase in Polish coal production," saying that the bank was "of the opinion that the value of this coal to other members of the bank is sufficient to justify the risk," "Memorandum by the Vice President of the International Bank for Reconstruction and Development (Garner)," *FRUS*, 1947, vol. 6, 454. The new U.S. ambassador in Poland, Stanton Griffis, supported the bank's conclusion, having himself decided that the "tremendous need of western Europe for Polish coal and the probability of receiving it overwhelm the political dangers," "The Ambassador in Poland (Griffis) to the Secretary of State," in *FRUS*, 1947, vol. 6, 456.

81. OMGUS, *Monthly Report of the Military Governor*, No. 29, 22; a German-language copy of the agreement, which was negotiated without West German participation, found in Bayer-Archiv 700/608. Each side offered a "list of those goods that are available for export." The Anglo-American delegation also accepted a Polish list of industrial contracts "that they wished to place in the British-American Occupation zones," but the Allies refused to extend a "promise" that these contracts would be filled.

82. Ibid., 22.

83. On this begin with E.A. Radice, "The Collapse of German Hegemony and its Economic Consequences," in Kaser and Radice, eds., *The Economic History of Eastern Europe 1919-1975*, vol. 2, 497 ff.

84. "The Ambassador in Poland (Griffis) to the Secretary of State," in *FRUS*, 1947, vol. 6, 456. The October 1947 Polish list of goods available for export from Poland had been heavily skewed toward agricultural exports to Germany: fruits, vegetables, potatoes, eggs, poultry. Yet in contrast to Polish industry, which by 1948 had surpassed the production levels of 1938, the 1948 output of Polish agriculture had risen to only 75-82 percent of prewar levels. Even for the period from 1948 to 1952 the Polish potato harvest was only 85 percent of prewar levels, W. Brus, "Postwar Reconstruction and Socio-Economic Transformation," in Kaser and Radice, eds., *Economic History of Eastern Europe*, vol. 2, 624 ff., tables 22.17, 22.19. In the first quarter of 1948, the Poles bought just $23,800 worth of bizonal exports! (See Table 7.6). Not until the final quarter of 1948 did bizonal exports to Poland begin to pick up.

85. "The Ambassador in Poland (Griffis) to the Secretary of State," *FRUS*, 1948, vol. 4, 529.

86. "The Ambassador in Poland (Griffis) to the Secretary of State," *FRUS*, 1948, vol. 4, 529

87. "The Under-Secretary for Economic Affairs (Clayton) to the Under-Secretary of State (Lovett)," *FRUS*, 1947, vol. 6, 436.

88. "The Ambassador in Poland (Gallman) to the Secretary of State," *FRUS*, 1948, vol. 4, 572.

89. The Polish resolution was defeated in the General Assembly on November 26, 1948, with only the Soviet bloc states voting for it. See United Nations Department of Public Information, *Yearbook of the United Nations 1948-49* (New York, 1950), 482-85.

90. The trizonal JEIA delegation for the Frankfurt negotiations was chaired by Schlepegrell, who was assisted by Ethel Dietrich. The West German Department of Economics was represented by Schiffler from Main Department V (Foreign

Trade), Section A (Trade Policy), Referat 7 (Eastern Europe). Neumann from the West German Agricultural Department was present as the German agricultural expert for food imports. The Polish delegation was chaired by Nowicki and Muszquinski (Navigation and Foreign Trade Ministry) and backed up by the Biernacki, the foreign trade representative at the Polish general consulate in Frankfurt, Schiffler's notes, 29 November 1948, BA B 102/2312.H1

91. The worsening atmosphere surrounding East-West trade had made itself felt even before substantive negotiations began as the Poles arrived complaining "with a certain undertone of bitterness" that JEIA had waited two months to respond to Polish efforts to arrange this new trade meeting, Schiffler's notes, 7 December 1948, BA B 102/2312.H1

92. "The United States Military Governor for Germany (Clay) to the Secretary of State," *FRUS*, 1947, vol. 2, 917. JEIA's revised Instruction No. 1, which went into effect during these negotiations with Poland, listed items in thirty key West German industrial categories as still in short supply and requiring special JEIA and/or Economics Department approval for export, a copy in BA B 102/2000.H1.

93. BA B 102/2312.H1. This production equipment was essentially the same type of metallurgical industrial equipment for which the U.S. itself had refused export licenses to Poland in April 1948.

94. The Poles lowered their price from $11.75 c.i.f. (cost, insurance, and freight) for delivery at Hamburg on 9 December to $7.60 c.i.f. on 11 December. Schiffler noted that at $7.60 Polish coal was now $1.10 under the English c.i.f. price, and that the West German Economics Administration "strongly supported" buying coal at the lower price. He himself was clearly puzzled as to why JEIA was not buying. On 27 December, Maltzan commented vaguely that "fundamental considerations" (grundsätzliche Erwagungen) prevented West Germany from buying Polish coal, Schiffler's notes, 9, 11, 18 December; Maltzan's commentary on the final agreement, 27 December 1948, all in BA B 102/2312.H1. I suspect that U.S. representatives declined to make coal purchases that would only emphasize the importance and desirability of Polish coal for the Bizonia at the very same time the U.S. was blocking a modernization loan for Poland at the International Bank for Reconstuction and Development.

95. Schiffler's notes, 11 December 1948, BA B 102/2312.H1

96. Schiffler's notes 8, 13, 14 December 1948, BA B 102/2312.H1

97. Schiffler's notes, 14 December 1948, BA B 102/2312.H1

98. Unsigned English language summary, 17 December 1948; Schiffler's notes, 18 December 1948; copy of the agreement with Economics Administration commentary, all in BA B 102/2312.H1; OMGUS, *Monthly Report of the Military Governor*, No. 43, 89. JEIA General Director Logan initialed the deal for the Trizonia on 20 December 1948 with the commodity lists valid through December 31, 1949. The agreement still required an official signing by the military governors in order to take effect.

99. Article 2 established a Mixed Commission of German and Polish representatives to "supervise and facilitate commerce and payments." Article 5 prescribed that the Mixed Commission should meet again not later than November 15, 1949 to "suggest and recommend" lists for the following period.

100. All credits and debits were to be booked in this account, including the value of imports and exports, the costs of transit trade (harbor, canal fees, etc.), and the periodic settlement of accounts between railroad and postal administrations. The balance of the account was to be calculated quarterly and the creditor could demand payment of the outstanding quarterly debt in dollars or alteratively at any time the account balance showed more than $500,000 in their favor. The new payments agreement was valid for one year, with an automatic annual

extension if neither side chose to terminate. Like the trade agreement, the payments agreement required an official signing by the military governors to become effective, but Logan took the liberty of setting it provisionally in force for sixty days.

101. Minc's victory was completed by the 1949 creation of a new Polish Ministry of Foreign Trade to replace the old Ministry of Navigation and Foreign Trade. That ministerial reorganization served as a cover for easing the too pro-Western Grosfeld and Horowitz out of their jobs at the old ministry. Tadeuz Gede, "a comparative nonentity," according to U.S. Ambassador Gallman, became the new minister for foreign trade. "The Ambassador in Poland (Gallman) to the Secretary of State," *FRUS*, 1949, vol. 5, 98, note 3.

102. Memorandum from George Wyeth (JEIA) to Logan, Robinson, Dietrich, and Schlepegrell, 13 May 1949, in BA B 102/2312.H1. Schiffler later confirmed that "because of political considerations" (wegen politischer Bedenken) the December 1948 agreement had never received final approval, 23 May 1949, BA B 102/2312.H1.

103. JEIA had already allowed West German authorities to sign import contracts for $6.8 million worth of goods listed in the 20 December agreement while West German exporters had delivered only $1.4 million in goods to Poland. This imbalance might cause "considerable difficulty" if not corrected, since the West German Bank deutscher Länder was already operating under the terms of the new payments agreement (also provisionally in force) that would allow the Poles to demand a quarterly payment of some $5 million to balance the account, Wyeth memorandum, 13 May 1949, BA B 102/2312.H1.

104. Wyeth memorandum, BA B 102/2312.H1.

105. Wyeth memorandum, BA B 102/2312.H1.

106. In Washington, the State Department's Policy Planning Staff under George Kennan first considered the subject in December 1947; in Europe, Harriman's ECA headquarters in Paris received instructions on this issue in August 1948; in West Germany, the Bipartite Control Office was actively involved by November 1948, and by May 1949 JEIA was asking for instructions so that security considerations could be factored into trade agreements at the start of international negotiations.

107. A summary of the trade agreement was published in OMGUS, *Monthly Report of the Military Governor*, No. 49, 116 ff.

108. That clause was written into the agreement at several points so that it covered all bizonal exports, even relatively benign items such as "machinery for the shoe and leather industry." See agreement annexes A and B, the English language "lists of commodities to be imported," BA B 102/2312.H1.

109. "The Ambassador in Poland (Gallman) to the Secretary of State," *FRUS*, 1949, vol. 5, 98.

110. "The Secretary of State to the Embassy in Poland," *FRUS*, 1949, vol. 5, 103.

111. Imhoff's notes, 12 July 1949, BA B 102/2312.H2

112. OMGUS commented proudly on the December 1948 agreement that "traditional exports of chemicals, metal manufactures, precision instruments, optics, machinery, and electrical equipment will be sent to Poland," OMGUS, *Monthly Report of the Military Governor*, No. 43, 86. In both West German-Polish agreements, over 50 percent of German exports to Poland were machines of various types; over 90 percent of Polish exports to the Bizonia were food.

113. Machinery had comprised 34 percent of German exports to Poland in 1938; food had been only 38 percent of Polish exports to Germany.

114. Manfred Knapp has asserted as a general rule that the "German economic administration was able to receive generous opportunities ... from the occupy-

ing powers ... to participate in the reestablishment of normal foreign trade relations." In the case of negotiations with Eastern Europe at least, his assertion is
certainly an overstatement of the German role. Manfred Knapp, "Die Anfänge
westdeutscher Aussenwirtschafts- und Aussenpolitik im bizonalen Vereinigten
Wirtschaftsgebiet (1947-1949)," in Knapp, ed., *Von der Bizonengründung zur
ökonomisch-politischen Westintegration,* 58.

115. The list of examples in this area (for only the Polish negotiations of 1948 to
1949!) is long: the Economics Department as a passive recipient of Bipartite
Control Office decisions on restricted exports; the Economics Department uninformed about U.S. reasons for not buying Polish coal; the Economics Department not included in the key 17 December 1948 meeting between JEIA and the
Polish delegation that broke the negotiating deadlock; the Economics Department's originally proposed import/export schedule more than doubled by JEIA
in the June 1949 trade agreement; the Economics Department's unawareness of
American thoughts on using food purchases to retard the pace of collectivization
in Polish agriculture.

116. Ludwig Erhard, with the assistance of Maltzan, *Germany's Comeback in the World
Market,* (London, 1954), 88. The Trade Policy Department of the West German
Foreign Office recalled that "the first trade and payments agreements with East
bloc states were concluded by the Western Occupation powers with delegates of
the Eastern bloc states without German participation," memorandum on East-
West trade, 9 March 1953, PAAA, 311.22, vol. 1. In the case of Poland, Imhoff's
recollection about the general role German participants in trade negotiations
played during the Occupation, i.e. that "JEIA conducted the trade treaty negotiations, we Germans sat alongside and could make suggestions," is far more
accurate than Erhard's version, *Weite Welt und Breites Leben* (Frankfurt, 1955),
396. Although in the Polish negotiations of 1948, German representatives did
not even "sit alongside" at some key meetings!

117. On the other hand, JEIA's occasional use of West German technical advisers
brought some advantages. Presumably the technical advice given by Dr. Lahr
(from the private-sector Arbeitsgemeinschaft Chemie) during the Polish negotiations of December 1948 allowed Bayer executives to know some weeks in
advance that the negotiations would not produce a big deal (grosser Abschluss)
for chemical sales to Poland, Terhaar report from Frankfurt, 4 December 1948,
Bayer-Archiv 67/2, vol. 1.

118. As early as October 1948, the South Hanover Chamber of Commerce had
presented its "export goods requests for the trade treaty negotiations with
Poland" to the Economics Department, 1 October 1948, BA B 102/2312.H1. In
1949, the traditionally influential interest group of the metal products industry (Wirtschaftsverband Eisen-, Blech-, und Metalwaren Industrie) demanded
that the Economics Department secure for them metal exports to Poland worth
at least $3 million in the June 1949 agreement, BA B 102/2312.H2. The
Economics Department was, of course, in no position to deliver these $3 mil-
lion; the June trade agreement in fact called for metal goods exports of just
$1.3 million.

119. "The Ambassador in Poland (Gallman) to the Secretary of State," 27 April 1949,
FRUS, 1949, vol. 5, 108.

120. "The Ambassador in Poland (Gallman) to the Secretary of State," 27 April 1949,
FRUS, 1949, vol. 5, 107-8; "Department of State Policy Statement," 25 June
1949, ibid., 502. The tentative nature of Polish agricultural collectivization that
Gallman had attributed to Western food purchases in 1948 was in fact a result of
the ideological struggle underway between the factions of Party Secretary
Władysław Gomułka and President Bierut, with Gomułka's "homeland" faction

opposing any Soviet-style collectivization attempt. Western trade policies could neither win the argument for Gomułka nor prevent his demotion in September 1948. On agricultural developments see Andrzej Korbonski, *The Politics of Socialist Agriculture in Poland, 1945-1960* (New York, 1965); Ernst Koening, "Collectivization in Czechoslovakia and Poland," in Irwin T. Sanders, ed., *Collectivization of Agriculture in Eastern Europe* (Lexington, KY, 1958), 103-139. On the broad range of issues, Adam Ulam, *Titoism and the Comintern* (Cambridge, Mass., 1953), "Crisis in the Polish Communist Party," 146-88.

121. "Department of State Policy Statement," *FRUS,* 1949, vol. 5, 502. In the absence of hard evidence on this point, the "success" of the embargo policy in this area remained an article of faith, one in which the Truman administration believed more strongly than its Western European allies, see e.g. "Report to the President of the United States on Policies and Programs in the Economic Field which may Affect the War Potential of the Soviet Bloc," *FRUS,* 1951, vol. 1, 1026-44; NSC Planning Board Report, *FRUS,* 1952-1954, vol. 1, 969; the discussion in Robert Mark Spaulding, "Eisenhower and the Revision of American Export Control Policy," *Diplomatic History* 17 (1993).

122. The Polish-Soviet trade agreement of January 1948 called for two-way trade of 2 billion rubles over the next four years. In 1948, Poland's trade with other Soviet bloc countries was $176 million; that trade had been just $18 million with these same East European countries in 1938, *Economic Survey of Europe 1948,* table 84, 146.

123. *FRUS,* 1946, vol. 6, 197, 200, 203, 224.

124. "The Chargé in Czechoslovakia (Bruins) to the Secretary of State," *FRUS,* 1946, vol. 6, 204.

125. "The Ambassador in Czechoslovakia (Steinhardt) to the Secretary of State," *FRUS,* 1947, vol. 4, 224. On political developments in Czechoslovakia 1945-1949 see Vladimir V. Kusin, "Czechoslovakia" in McCauley, ed., *Communist Power* (New York, 1977), 73-94; Karel Kaplan, *The Short March: The Communist Takeover in Czechoslovakia, 1945-1948* (London, 1987); John F.N. Bradley, *Politics in Czechoslovakia, 1945-1990* (Boulder, Colo., 1991), 9-39.

126. As early as October/November 1945 executives at Bayer in the British zone had been contacted by Czechoslovak agencies about compensation trade deals, Bayer-Archiv 700/678.

127. On 21 January 1947, Bayer again received an inquiry from Prague about the availability of chemicals for export to Czechoslovakia, Bayer-Archiv 700/678.

128. OMGUS to the State Department, 10 March 1947, *FRUS,* 1947, vol. 4, 198 footnote 1.

129. "The Acting Secretary of State to the United States Political Advisor for Germany (Murphy), at Berlin," 25 March 1947 *FRUS,* 1947, vol. 4, 198. On 8 April Acheson again urged that "renewed efforts be made to reach agreement with Czechoslovak authorities on the payment of transit charges for Czechoslovak freight crossing the United States zone of Occupation in Germany," *FRUS,* 1947, vol. 4, 204 footnote 3.

130. Data on West German imports from Czechoslovakia in OMGUS, *Report of the Military Governor,* No. 31, Statistical Annex, Figures 4, 8; *Report of the Military Governor,* No. 42, Statistical Annex No. XXII, Table 91; *Report of the Military Governor,* No. 43, Statistical Annex No. XXIII, Table 609; *Report of the Military Governor,* No. 49, Statistical Annex, No. XXIX, Table 603, 604. Coal data cited in a report by the Upper Franconian Chamber of Commerce, 13 December 1950, BA B 102/18446.H2.

131. "The Acting Secretary of State to the United States Political Advisor for Germany (Murphy), at Berlin," *FRUS,* 1949, vol. 5, 381.

132. Jacobs was prepared to have Clay "order cessation of all passenger and freight traffic across Bavarian Czechoslovakian border. This order would include trains, truck and barge traffic (if any). There should be no exceptions." To make these measures "watertight" the U.S. could "seal US-Soviet [zonal] border to Czechoslovak-bound or Czechoslovak-origin traffic and seek British assistance in similarly sealing British-Soviet [zonal] border," Jacobs to Acheson, *FRUS*, 1949, vol. 5, 394-95, 396. The border had already been "semi-closed" to passenger traffic for some weeks already as a response to the "arbitrary arrest and expulsion" of British Cap. Philip Waldish of the Combined Military Permit Office in Prague, on this affair and the "Hill-Jones" espionage case see ibid., 391-92, 397, note 8.

133. At Bayer's Trade Policy Office in Leverkusen, Jost Terhaar noted two weeks later that Allied "refusal to grant export licenses" (die Nichterteilung von Exportgenehmigungen) for numerous commodities destined for Czechoslovakia had "increased unexpectedly" recently, 23 April 1949, Bayer Archiv 67/2.H1.

134. On Soviet Occupation policies in Germany begin with the encyclopedic work of Martin Broszat and Hermann Weber, eds., *SBZ-Handbuch: Staatliche Verwaltungen, Parteien, gesellschaftliche Organisationen und ihre Führungskräfte in der Sowjetischen Besatzungszone Deutschlands 1945-1949* (Munich, 1990) and the literature cited there.

135. For Soviet (and French) protests that the Anglo-American Bizonia violated the Potsdam Agreement see, Christoph Klessmann, *Die doppelte Staatsgründung. Deutsche Geschichte 1945-1955* (Gottingen, 1982), 99 ff.; John Gimble, *The American Occupation of Germany: Politics and the Military, 1945-1949* (Stanford, Calif., 1968), 114, 116.

Chapter Eight

POLITICAL ECONOMY RESUMED
Recreating the Networks 1949 to 1955

Enforcing Embargo

*I*n the years of the Federal Republic of Germany's semisovereignty after 1949, the Allies employed an elaborate structure of overlapping rights, powers, and institutions to monitor West German foreign trade, and in particular, trade with the East. That structure reached its peak of complexity in 1951 and was then gradually dissolved from 1952 to 1954 as the Allies returned full trade policy sovereignty to the West Germans themselves.

In June 1948, the three Western allies agreed that any new West German state could not immediately wield full sovereignty over all of its own affairs.[1] A July 1948 draft of the Occupation Statute that would regulate future relations between the occupying powers and the West Germans stated plainly that the Allies intended to "reserve to themselves such rights as are necessary to ensure the fulfillment of the basic purpose of the Occupation." In foreign trade, the Allies planned to exercise a "minimum control over German foreign trade, and over internal policies and measures which could adversely affect foreign trade ..."[2] Clearly the foreign trade sovereignty so eagerly sought by the German Economics Department and Economic Council (Wirtschaftsrat) would not be immediately forthcoming. The prominent listing of foreign trade among the areas remaining under Allied control (just behind "foreign affairs" and well ahead of "observing the new Constitution") indicated that the Allies planned to take this control function very seriously.

Notes for this chapter begin on page 400.

The finalized Occupation Statute enumerated the fields in which "powers ... are specifically reserved" to the Allies; "control over foreign trade and exchange" (Article 2g) was naturally among them. Significantly, the Allies this time used a short, simple, and comprehensive phrase with no restrictions or elaborations attached to those controls; earlier draft statements about "minimum control" were gone. These broad powers were given to a new trilateral Allied High Commission that would "exercise control over the Federal Government and the Governments of its constituent Länder."[3]

The Agreement on Basic Principles for Trizonal Fusion (published along with the Occupation Statute) continued the practice of "weighted voting" among the three powers in matters of West German foreign trade and exchange.[4] Weighted voting insured that the existing American dominance of West German trade policies (heretofore through JEIA) would continue under the new High Commission. On the basis of its financial position, the U.S. could outvote both France and the U.K. combined, so that, in effect, the Americans alone could determine West German trade policy. Because of the weighted voting system in matters of foreign trade and exchange, the East-West trade policies developed by the Office of U.S. High Commissioner for Germany became definitive for all three zones of the Federal Republic of Germany. U.S. High Commissioner for Germany John J. McCloy arrived at his post with a good understanding of America's evolving economic policy toward the Soviet bloc. As president of the International Bank for Reconstruction and Development from 1947 to 1949, McCloy had already seen Western credits to Eastern Europe dry up; indeed he had been an active participant in that process.[5] Within the High Commission, the Council of the three commissioners themselves oversaw the work of tripartite committees, subcommittees, and ad hoc working parties. The commission charter prescribed five principal committees: political affairs, foreign trade and exchange, finance, economics, and law. [6]

The High Commission charter charged the Foreign Trade and Exchange Committee with the "orderly liquidation of JEIA at the earliest possible date." The new committee would "assume any control functions presently exercised by JEIA as may warrant retention when the liquidation of JEIA is completed."[7] With this mandate, the Foreign Trade Committee assumed control over the Federal Republic's strategic exports to the East, a task that had been one of JEIA's function since May/June 1949. In establishing a subcommittee for East-West trade and a working group for export controls, the High Commission paid its respects to the rapidly intensifying American commitment to control trade with the Soviet bloc.[8]

In addition to the export controls based on the Occupation Statute and enforced by the High Commission and by the U.S. High Commissioner's Office, the Allies also brought the Federal Republic into the informal pan-Western system of export controls that had grown out of Harriman's export control negotiations with the Western Europeans in 1948 and 1949 and that were administered by the Coordinating Committee (COCOM) in Paris. After several preliminary discussions among the Allies themselves and then with the Germans in the autumn of 1949, the High Commission invited representatives from the new federal government to participate in the January 1950 COCOM discussions. Thereafter, the Federal Republic participated regularly in both COCOM and in its superior body, the Consultative Group (CG) which determined embargo policy.

The Americans largely ignored the organizational distinction between the trade restrictions administered variously by the Allied High Commission, the U.S. High Commissioner's Office, and COCOM. A number of personal and organizational overlaps often hid the exact source of authority for each step in the construction of an export control system for Germany. For example, the invitation to join COCOM came from the high commissioners whose East-West Trade Subcommittee (and its Export Control Working Party) gradually assumed the function of monitoring Federal Republic compliance with COCOM rules, although it was never clear how the formal powers of the High Commission under Article 2(g) of the Occupation Statute related to the informal COCOM agreements. Similarly, it remained unclear whether American suggestions to the Germans about their export control program were made on the basis of McCloy's authority as high commissioner or on the basis of his position as representative of the ECA in Germany.[9] What emerged from this situation of overlapping authorities was a very comprehensive set of controls on West German trade with the East forged by steady pressure applied by the Americans from several sources.[10]

This combination of formal and informal powers provided the Americans with three means of shaping the flow of West German trade with the East. First, the Allies very actively oversaw the conclusion of trade and payments agreements between the Federal Republic and foreign countries, all of which required the expressed approval of the High Commission. Second, the Allies ensured Federal Republic compliance with the evolving COCOM program for the control of strategic exports. Units from both the High Commission and the U.S. High Commissioner's Office closely supervised the construction of an elaborate German bureaucracy for the control of exports. In the period before the German administration was prepared for its new duties, the Allies themselves approved export licenses for West German exports. Finally, in some instances, the Allies themselves took direct action at the borders in controlling German trade. Each high commissioner held the final responsibility for allowing passage of goods across his zonal border to the East. Occupation troops could, and did, physically detain questionable shipments at the border.

On September 21, 1949 the new federal government presented its credentials to the High Commission at the Petersburg just across the Rhine River from Bonn. Five days later Vollrath von Maltzan as Director of the Economics Ministry's Department for Foreign Economic Affairs, sent an "urgent" memo to Economics Minister Ludwig Erhard noting that "following the establishment of the Federal Republic and the simultaneous dissolution of JEIA, the question arises as to who shall conduct foreign economic negotiations and especially who shall sign the resulting agreements."[11] The Occupation Statute had not expressly addressed this issue and the uncertainty of the new situation was already causing a hiatus in the negotiations with Austria. For that reason, Maltzan requested that "the Chancellor immediately consult with the High Commissioners concerning the authority to conduct negotiations and to sign trade and economic agreements."[12] On 12 November 1949 the Allied General Secretariat sent to Chancellor Konrad Adenauer a directive containing "the principles and procedure to be followed in foreign trade as well as in the negotiation of trade and payments agreements."[13] The Allies directed that "as a matter of principle the Federal government conduct the negotiation of trade and payments agreements with other states" while the High Commission retained the right to send its own representatives to negotiations as "observers." Further, the federal government was empowered only to initial international agreements, but not to sign them formally until after they had been presented to the High Commission and "the High Commission had informed the Federal government whether it objected to the signing of this document or not."

The November 1949 Petersburg Protocol granted the Federal Republic permission to "initiate the gradual reestablishment of consular and commercial relations with those countries where such relations appear advantageous" but did not relax Allied supervision of the trade agreements.[14] The Revised Occupation Statute of March 1951 softened these procedures substantially except as they applied to countries of the Soviet bloc, where the only change was the imposition of a twenty-one-day limit for the High Commission to respond to the agreements submitted to it.[15] By signing the General Agreement on Tariffs and Trade (GATT) in October 1951, the Federal Republic received full commercial sovereignty from the Allies, with East European relations again excepted; trade and payments agreements with those countries still required Allied approval.

During this period of closely supervised trade from 1949 to 1951, Allied observers frequently complained that German negotiators from the Economics Ministry were too soft in their dealings with the East. In April 1951 Deputy ECA Administrator Karl Bode presented American concerns on this issue to the Economics Ministry. Claiming that Economics Ministry negotiators had not used "sufficient hardness," on a number of occasions involving Poland, Hungary, and Bulgaria, Bode asked Erhard to see to it that negotiations would be conducted "somewhat harder" in the future.[16] The same points were raised by the Chairman of the High Commission's Economics Committee, MacReady, in a letter addressed to the Erhard. He specifically cited the "tendency on the part of Federal negotiators to accept imports of secondary economic importance in exchange for the export of industrial equipment and other goods of high economic value." He understood that although the Germans had a "natural desire to maintain contacts in traditional markets, ... security must take precedence over trade."[17]

In the course of negotiating the general treaty and the contractual agreements with the Occupying powers in the spring of 1952, the federal authorities successfully pressed the Allies to give up their remaining rights to approve or reject Federal Republic trade agreements with Eastern Europe. That information was particularly well received in the Economics Ministry, where it was noted that "with the signing of the General Treaty the Federal Republic will be made fully equal with the other States of the international community in the areas of embargo policy, general East-West trade, and especially in interzonal trade."[18] Unfortunately, these self-congratulatory tones proved premature. When the complexities of French politics delayed passage of the European Defense Community (EDC) plan, the general treaty and the contractual agreement entered a state of limbo from which they did not soon emerge. In the meanwhile, procedures remained as they had been since the first revision of the Occupation Statute in March 1951 – with the federal government obligated to present its economic agreements with Soviet bloc states to the High Commission for approval.

Direct supervision of West German export control procedures provided the Allies with a second means of injecting themselves into West German trade with the East. From the very earliest days of the Federal Republic, the Allies had explained to federal authorities the need for the Federal Republic to construct an export control program. Over the next four years the Americans applied direct and effective pressures on the Germans for construction of an adequate export control system. By 1953 the federal authorities had put in place inside the Economics Ministry a large and effective bureaucracy for control exports to the East in accordance with American wishes as expressed through the High Commission, the U.S. High Commissioner's Office, and COCOM.

On October 17, 1949 McCloy informed the State Department, the ECA, and the Commerce Department that the High Commission was prepared to approach the new German government on the issue of controlling exports to the Soviet bloc. The State Department, the ECA, and McCloy all agreed that "an oral understanding with the West German Government regarding export controls would be unsatisfactory and that written instructions from the Allied High Commission would be necessary."[19] On 25 November the Allied council instructed JEIA to send a letter of instructions "regarding the establishment of a program of export security controls" to the Economics Ministry. When Erhard responded vaguely about the need for instructions from Adenauer, the Allies lost no time in applying convincing pressure to the chancellor. In a December 8 meeting between the Allied council and Adenauer, McCloy bluntly presented the American position; he "stressed to Adenauer the necessity of implementing strict export controls to ensure that certain commodities did not move to the East, and he pointed out the relationship of the control program to the entire United States aid program."[20]

McCloy's implied threat to cut off further Marshall Plan aid to the Federal Republic unless the Germans moved to put a satisfactory export control program in place brought immediate results. Two weeks later Erhard informed Robert Hanes, chief of the ECA Mission in Germany and head of Economics Division in the U.S. High Commissioner's Office, that he would "cooperate fully with the export control plan outlined in the November 25 letter."[21] Years later, when the Economics Ministry and the Foreign Office independently reviewed the origins of West German embargo policy, both agencies stressed how the Americans had explicitly connected compliance with American export control wishes to continued participation in the Marshall Plan.[22] Through 1951 the threat of severance from Marshall Plan funds hung like a sword of Damocles over the West German economy. In May 1951, Hanes's successor, Jean Cattier, threatened to withhold Marshall Plan counterpart funds from any firm engaged in illegal trade with the East. In June McCloy made that same threat in a public speech.[23]

German officials took these threats seriously. Heinrich Brentano, Chairman of the Christian Democratic Union/Christian Social Union parliamentary group and future Foreign Minister, warned Erhard that American dissatisfaction with West German export controls could lead to the U.S. Congress making "exceptionally dangerous decisions" about the upcoming ECA budget.[24] In light of the overwhelming pressure America could exert as sole underwriter of the Marshall Plan and as the dominant member of the High Commission, the German government saw little alternative but to comply with American suggestions. As Erhard understated to Brentano: "Considering the important political and economic factors involved, we thought it right to accommodate ourselves to the policy line followed by the American government."[25]

Accommodation to American policy meant constructing an elaborate bureaucratic apparatus for export controls. After the Erhard-Hanes conversation of 22 December 1949, an Allied-German working group met on 23 and 28 December to discuss German plans for an export control administration. Federal authorities planned to establish a Federal Agency for Merchandise Trade (Bundesstelle für den Warenverkehr) within the Economics Ministry to deal with import/export questions at the national level.[26] Within that agency, the Central Export Control Group (Zentralausfuhrkontrolle), with its nine departments, assumed the important task of setting guidelines to cover exports to the Soviet bloc.[27] Problems soon arose with the lack of coordination between export control policy as determined by the Central Export Control Group and normal commercial policy toward the East as conducted by other elements of the Economics Ministry.[28]

Not until the Economics Ministry reorganized itself in early 1951 was the situation resolved by creating a new Group on East-West Trade within the Foreign Trade Department specifically for the purpose of coordinating commercial policy in Eastern Europe and the "pure control side" of the issue.[29] As head of that group, Hans Kroll himself took over Federal Republic representation at the Paris COCOM meetings and established a direct line of communication with Josef Seiberlich, who assumed responsibility for routine commercial negotiations with Eastern and Southern Europe. By the end of 1951, American pressure to improve control procedures had stimulated the growth of Kroll's group to the point where it had generated three desks within the Economics Ministry to cover all aspects of embargo policy.

The growth of embargo thinking led the Americans to abandon their earlier preference for a decentralized export licensing procedure. Reversing their actions of 1948, the High Commission now demanded that licensing authority be withdrawn from the foreign trade banks (Aussenhandelsbanken, some 450 in number) and concentrated in a single, central agency. Beginning in June 1950 applications for restricted goods would be centralized in the Frankfurt-based Central Licensing Office (Zentrale Genehmigungsstelle) under control of the Central Export Control Group. In questionable cases the Central Permission Office would pass these applications to the U.S. High Commissioner's Office for final approval. But the Licensing Office staff of twenty persons (who had planned to handle 1,000 applications per day) was soon overwhelmed by the scope of the export control task. In November 1950 McCloy took back export licensing control from the Germans.[30]

Throughout the summer of 1951 American officials met repeatedly and personally with federal authorities, including Chancellor Adenauer, Economics Minister Erhard, and Economics State Secretary Ludgar Westrick, to exchange views on improving German export controls.[31] In July 1951, the High Commission informed the German government that unless German export controls could "satisfactorily ensure the security of the Allies," the commission would retain its export control powers even after the contractual agreements" were signed.[32] When, in the summer of 1951, German authorities removed licensing permission even for nonstrategic exports to the East from the foreign trade banks and transferred it to the internal customs units of the new Federal Customs Office, the High Commission indicated that it was prepared to approve German proposals for the commission's Export Control Working Party to transfer the "responsibility for the final approval of applications for the export of certain commodities" to German authorities.[33]

Yet even in the long period between the signing of the contractuals in May 1952 and their eventual implementation, the U.S. High Commissioner's Office continued to monitor German export controls to the East, offering unasked-for advice and commenting on every minor change in the German organization.[34] Meanwhile, the emotion surrounding the embargo issue in the U.S. made congressional "inspection" trips to Germany a favorite activity as the 1952 elections approached. The new German administration had its hands more than full trying to keep pace with a continuous stream of Allied requests for improvement in export control procedures.

A third way in which the Allies continued to play a role in shaping West German-Eastern European trade was through direct intervention on the West German borders. The High Commission Charter (Article V, Sec. 2b) guaranteed to each commissioner the powers necessary to ensure the security of the Allied Occupation forces. Under these provisions, a commissioner could order exports to be halted on the grounds that they adversely affected the security of the Allies. The U.S. High Commissioner's Office repeatedly used this authority to prevent the transport of various West German exports into Eastern Europe. The Americans imposed a much stricter standard of controls on exports moving from the U.S. zone into Eastern Europe than the British applied on exports from their zone.[35]

In late 1950 the U.S. Military Police Customs Unit on the Bavarian border began halting "illegal" export shipments headed East, stopping sixty-nine shipments with a value of DM 1.49 million in October 1951 and fifty-three shipments with a value of DM 1.37 million in November.[36] Aside from keeping the legal department at Gustav Schmoller's Institute for Occupation Issues (Institut für Besatzungsfragen) absorbed with the question of who should pay the damages for unjustified stops, these actions provoked a real crisis in West German-Czechoslovak trade relations, with very serious consequences for the Bavarian economy. Despite promises by U.S. High Commissioner's Office that these military police would be withdrawn by December 1952, they remained troublesomely active until September 1953.

When the American military police were withdrawn, it marked the beginning of a twenty-month period during which the Federal Republic gradually gained complete and genuine sovereignty in its trade relations with Eastern Europe. Two overlapping developments made that gain possible. First was the "gradual and moderate relaxation" of embargo policy initiated by the Eisenhower administration in March 1953. This modified American policy allowed COCOM to adopt radically reduced "international lists" of restricted goods in August 1954.[37] With the hysterical phase of the embargo over at home, the American element in the High Commission and even the U.S. High Commissioner's Office itself adopted less-intrusive postures in regard to German export controls. In the Federal Republic, these changes were manifested institutionally by the reduction of the Economics Ministry's special group on East-West Trade from three sections down to one by the end of 1953.

A second, more momentous, development, was the West German acquisition of nearly total political sovereignty as a byproduct of French rejection of the proposed European Defense Community. With new arrangements made for the military defense of Western Europe, including an almost fully equal West German ally, the Western powers declared their intent "to end the Occupation regime in the Federal Republic as soon as possible, to revoke the Occupation Statute and to abolish the Allied High Commission ... In the meantime, the Three Governments are instructing their High Commissioners to act forthwith in accordance with the spirit of the above policy. In particular, the High Commissioners will not use the powers which are to be relinquished unless in agreement with the Federal government."[38] On 12 November 1954 the High Commission informed the Commercial Affairs Department of the West German Foreign Office that the commission no longer intended to review copies of export licenses for strategic goods, nor did it desire to have trade agreements with the Soviet bloc countries presented to it for approval. The long process of returning trade policy sovereignty to the Federal Republic had been completed.[39]

Despite the frustrations that West Germans naturally felt as Allied export control policies were imposed on the semisovereign Federal Republic, the continued politicization of East-West trade across a divided Europe in the 1950s offered the new West German state certain international advantages. Dramatically weakened militarily, diplomatically, and politically as the successor to the defeated, divided, and occupied German Reich, the Federal Republic was fortunate to operate in the peculiar European international order of the 1950s. The Cold War framework sanctioned and encouraged the use of the one form of statecraft still available to the FRG: economic diplomacy.[40] Not only did the international trade regime allowed the use of politicized trade pressure toward the Soviet bloc, but the lack of other contacts across politically divided Europe actively encouraged the use of this economic diplomacy. In the absence of other forms of contact, trade assumed a central place in German-Eastern European relations. The lack of diplomatic, cultural, and other relations with Eastern Europe helped the Federal Republic turn its trade advantage to political advantage.

Further, the American sponsors of the Federal Republic supported the use of economic diplomacy. Within the framework of a common Western export control program, the Allies allowed the West Germans a wide degree of latitude in pursuing their own trade strategies in the East.[41] That latitude allowed the Federal Republic to pursue its own national interests in the East, even when these had clear potential for friction within the Alliance. As long as the Federal Republic's occasional pursuit of its own national interests did not lead to identifiable violations of the international embargo lists, it generated surprisingly little German-American tension.[42] The United States repeatedly supported the FRG's efforts to reestablish a vigorous West German commercial and political presence in Eastern Europe.[43] In return, the West German federal government made a good-faith attempt to enforce the embargo rules and informed the

Allies openly and honestly about West German thinking on trade with the East.[44]

In sum, the Federal Republic of the 1950s was fortunate that the postwar structures of East-West interaction established a framework that facilitated the employment of West Germany's reemerging economic power toward the East. For the West Germans, fortune was indeed a factor, since the FRG did not play a decisive role in developing the structures of the postwar international economic regime. The FRG remained largely a "market taker" in terms of this international framework.

A Revived Corporatism?

Nominally, the Allies turned the control of trade policy over to the West German "federal government." Yet this general formulation left the real questions of power open. How would the authority over trade policy be distributed between the two poles of the new governmental system – the executive ministerial bureaucracy on one side and the Parliament (Bundestag) on the other side? Within the bureaucracy, which ministry or coalition of ministries – economics, finance, agriculture, Marshall Plan, and (after 1951) the Foreign Office – could best produce a functioning trade policy? The still-desperate economic situation demanded a more smoothly functioning arrangement than the policy deadlock that Weimar had produced.[45]

A second set of questions revolved around the relations between the authority of new state and the power of private economic groups, specifically, the ability of the bureaucracy to maintain its integrity vis-à-vis the reemerging industrial and commercial interest groups. For some thirty years before 1945, the interest groups had been closely intertwined with state agencies in determining the course of German foreign trade, with disastrous results during the Weimar years. Might the interest groups similarly erode state authority in the second republic, despite the fresh political start provided by the Allied Occupation? With the crucial importance of foreign trade for West Germany's continued economic recovery apparent to all, it would be no easy task to find a properly balanced partnership between government and private groups in defining Eastern trade policy objectives.[46]

Based on its organizational development under the Allies from 1945 to 1949, the Economics Ministry clearly had the strongest claim among the existing ministries to assume control of foreign trade policy in 1949. A Department for Foreign Economic Policy (Main

Department V) had been established under Maltzan's direction in the old Economics Department in 1946. Normal commercial relations with those East European countries that had signed trade agreements with JEIA were handled by the foreign economic policy department's geographically organized country desks (Länderreferate).[47] The Economics Ministry also assumed major responsibility for the country's new embargo duties; Kroll's special group on East-West trade had been established in the Economics Ministry for this purpose.

The peculiarities and complexities of West Germany's Eastern trade required input from other ministries as well. The predominantly agricultural character of Eastern Europe made trade negotiations there a subject of special interest for the Agriculture Ministry, just as it had been for the old Reich Agriculture Ministry. The Finance Ministry administered the Customs Service, whose internal customs offices now played a major role in controlling exports to the East. Traditionally the Transportation Ministry had been accorded a secondary a voice in trade policy. Finally, American threats to withhold Marshall Plan moneys in the case of embargo violations brought the Ministry for the Marshall Plan into East-West trade.In order to fortify the position of the Economics Ministry among these potential competitors, Maltzan himself shaped the charter of a new interministerial Trade Policy Committee.[48]

After the formal establishment of a new West German Foreign Office in the spring of 1951, primary authority over trade policy was gradually divided between the Foreign Office and the Economics Ministry. Initially, the Foreign Office kept itself out of trade policy questions concerning Eastern Europe, noting that in view of the "unclear political conditions" in Eastern Europe (i.e., lack of diplomatic recognition between the Federal Republic and the "people's democracies") a high-profile involvement by Foreign Office "would only cause additional problems."[49] At the same time, the Foreign Office was planning to "guarantee decisive participation by the Foreign Office in the basic questions [of East-West trade] and in the composition and dispatch of trade delegations or permanent trade representatives" to Eastern Europe.[50] In preparation for raising its voice in interministerial meetings on these matters, the Foreign Office established its own East-West Trade desk inside its Commercial Affairs Department.

Between 1951 and 1953 the Foreign Office grew tremendously with the lateral transfer of Economics Ministry employees. Maltzan himself moved over to the Foreign Office as head of the Commercial Affairs Department in 1952. Zahn-Stranik, who had worked on embargo policy under Kroll in the Economics Ministry, now went over to the East-West trade desk in the Foreign Office.[51] By November 1953, Foreign Office representatives had been added to the Federal Republic delegation at the Paris COCOM meetings.[52] In January 1954 Dr. Scholz of the Economics Ministry explained that responsibility for East-West trade was now "divided" between the Foreign Office (responsible for the "foreign policy direction of the embargo policy") and the Economics Ministry (responsible for "all trade policy, economic, and technical questions" as well as for control of the Central Export Control Group).[53] Particularly in the area of embargo policy and export controls, the Foreign Office gained ground steadily, emerging as an equal to the Economics Ministry by 1954.[54]

At the same time the Federal Republic's refusal to recognize formally the governments of the Soviet satellite states constrained Foreign Office participation in negotiations with East European states. While interministerial West German trade delegations negotiated deals with Poland and Czechoslovakia, members of the Foreign Office stayed away, fearing that their presence might imply a softening of the Federal Republic position on diplomatic recognition of the Eastern countries. This de facto ban on Foreign Office involvement in the negotiations bolstered the relative position of all other participating ministries.

By 1954 the Foreign Office, Economics Ministry, and Agriculture Ministry had come to broad agreement on the basic goal of expanding West German trade with the East while continuing to observe the restrictions of the Western export control program.[55] That ministerial agreement reflected broad private-sector consensus on this point and was based ultimately on the divergent economic fortunes of the Federal Republic on one side and the Soviet bloc on the other. The successful restoration of a profitable, sophisticated, export-oriented industrial economy gave West Germany a decided advantage in economic relations with the problem-riddled economies of Eastern Europe.[56] As the relative performance of the Soviet bloc economies deteriorated in the early 1950s, imports from Eastern Europe no longer threatened any important part of the West German economy, even agriculture.[57] Economic developments in the East spurred the evolution of a nearly universal West German private-sector consensus on the desirability of expanding trade with Eastern Europe.[58]

As the executors of trade policy in the East, members of ministerial bureaucracy were most immediately in touch with current trade developments. Within the state structure, the federal ministries passed information "down" to the state (Länder) governments and "over" to the Parliament. The Economics Ministry kept the governments and economics ministries of the Länder informed on East-

West trade issues via the Länder Committee on Foreign Trade.[59] Ministerial officials also met with parliamentarians in the Parliamentary Council on Trade Agreements, a small group chosen by members of the Bundestag's Trade Policy Committee. Here the government offered previews of proposed trade treaties, made preliminary arguments for their approval, and prepared the parliamentary discussion of them.[60]

Oddly, the peculiarities of Germany's trade agreements with the East exempted them from Bundestag approval, thereby fatally weakening the ability of the legislature to influence trade policy in the East.[61] Trade treaties required parliamentary approval only in cases where they involved federal legislative action (e.g., changing the tariff, granting MFN status, altering copyright law). The annual trade agreements negotiated by the Federal Republic with various Eastern European countries contained no such provisions, and, as a result, did not require parliamentary approval.[62] The annually negotiated lists were the exclusive trade regulating instruments in trade between the Federal Republic and Eastern Europe. Since the Bundestag could not determine the shape of these agreements, it played a secondary role to the ministerial bureaucracy in determining Eastern trade policy.[63] On the positive side, the exclusion of the Bundestag from an active role in shaping or ratifying the annual trade agreements allowed the Federal Republic to respond quickly and quietly to changing circumstances in Eastern Europe.

Discussions on the general direction of trade policy and on the larger developments in East-West trade did surface on the floor of the Bundestag. In February 1950, Communist party representatives asked some embarrassing questions about Western embargo policy at a time when even the existence of COCOM was still a secret matter. A Social Democratic (SPD) inquiry into embargo policy in the context of the upcoming contractual agreements led to a lengthier debate on Germany's Eastern trade in May 1952. After hearing from Johannes Semler (CDU), Helmut Kalbitzer (SPD), and Erhard, the Bundestag resolved unanimously on May 6 that "the remaining limits on German freedom of action in the control of merchandise trade and – so far as is legally possible – in the conclusion of trade treaties with East bloc countries must be eliminated as soon as possible."[64] The Bundestag's involvement in East-West trade policy remained largely on this general level.

The inability of the Bundestag to influence directly the flow of West German trade with the East affected both the distribution of power within the government and the relations between the state and the business community. Parliamentary weakness in this area tilted the balance of power within the state apparatus decisively in favor of the ministerial bureaucracy. Bundestag exclusion from the process also meant that, on this issue, Bundestag representatives could not fulfill the traditional parliamentary function of linking civil society to the state. The system lacked a parliamentary link capable of effectively representing the views of concerned private groups to the government bureaucracy. In the absence of such a link, interest groups had little choice but to appeal directly to the ministries themselves. In this way, parliamentary weakness catalyzed the regeneration of a network of organizational ties linking the bureaucracy and interest groups for the purpose of formulating trade policy toward the East.

Bundestag weakness was not the only reason for the rise of a number of formal and informal institutions that served as intimate channels of communication between the ministerial bureaucracy and the private-sector on matters of Eastern trade policy. Certainly the corporatist tradition of close bureaucratic-business collaboration on trade policy as it had evolved since 1914 played a strong role. In the "hierarchically organized chancellor democracy" of the new Federal Republic the "modes of conduct within the ministerial bureaucracy … complimented the leadership style of the peak associations" and vice-versa, so that both bureaucrats and businessmen were more comfortable dealing with each other than with the democratic Parliament.[65] The international Cold War context also contributed to the growth of direct bureaucratic-industrial links since the federal government needed some type of intimate government/private-sector forum to communicate confidentially the content of embargo policy and COCOM decisions to export industries. Finally, Eastern trade and trade policy in general were certainly not the only issues on which the interest groups sought to exert their influence on the bureaucracy. The revival of the interest groups and the rapid increase of their real (and imagined) influence in all areas, even cultural, was noted by critical observers at the time and has been studied extensively since.[66]

Like the Occupation authorities and the new federal government, the West German business community also realized the crucial importance of foreign trade for the economic future of the FRG. As soon as reconstituted economic interest groups began to emerge in 1945 and 1946, the business community began to stake out positions on trade issues.[67] In 1948 a large number of iron, steel, and metalworking groups in the British zone came together in a single industrial interest group with a foreign trade committee of its own. In 1949 thirty-five industrial interest groups joined together in the new suprasectoral industrial interest group that eventually adopted the name Bundesverband deutscher Industrie in obvious reference to the old industrial Reichsverband deutscher Industrie. In May 1950 this powerful group established a foreign trade committee chaired by Wilhelm Mann (I.G. Farben).[68] In June 1948 Germany's most powerful industrial and commercial associations combined their resources on the study of foreign trade problems in the new Working Group on Foreign Trade (Arbeitsgemeinschaft Aussenhandel). This tremendously influential group sought the "common ground" in the private-sector on the "fundamental questions" of trade policy that "interested all economic sectors"[69]

The Economics Ministry fostered a number of "neocorporatist" links with the reemergent private groups for the management of trade policy.[70] Most generally, the Economics Ministry's Academic Council (Wissenschaftliche Beirat) allowed professional economists to offer advice on a wide range of policy issues. Another body, dealing specifically with foreign trade issues, was the Advisory Board on Foreign Trade (Aussenhandelsbeirat). Numbering about thirty, this group contained members of the economics and agriculture ministries, the Foreign Office, the federal bank, the trade unions, and various industrial groups.[71] The advisory board met regularly as a forum in which all interests could express their opinions about the Federal Republic's position in the world economy, the development of trade, and the direction of trade policies. The advisory board, however, was not an association concerned primarily with trade with Eastern Europe; its attention was naturally focused on those areas where the Federal Republic traded most intensively: Western Europe and (increasingly) North America.

Since 1948 the private-sector Working Group on Foreign Trade had maintained a private reporting service (the Trade Treaty Bureau) that transmitted information from the Economics Ministry to the interest groups in the working group, which, in turn, passed that information down to their individual members. The Economics Ministry had actively encouraged the establishment of this bureau and considered the reporting service "in effect the execution of a public commission" which "relieved" Economics Ministry of itself having to supply such information.[72] The ministry even directed all members of Main Department V to provide the working group with copies of new international trade agreements.[73]

For the specific purpose of discussing and executing trade policy toward the East, two other crucially important bodies existed; the Working Committee on Central Export Control (Arbeitsausschuss Zentrale Ausfuhrkontrolle) and the Eastern Committee of German Business (Ostausschuss der deutschen Wirtschaft). Both of these groups displayed neocorporatist characters in their fusion of government and private-sector functions.[74] The first of these two, the Committee on Central Export Control, arose from the government's need to communicate directly and confidentially with German exporters on matters of embargo policy. Its origins lay in a 23 July 1951 meeting between officials of the Economics Ministry (State Secretary Westrick and export control specialist Hans Kroll) on the one side and "leading members of interested German economic circles" on the other side.[75] For ninety minutes Kroll "laid out in confidential terms the political reasons for the Western embargo policy toward Soviet bloc countries." The private-sector members accepted the situation as outlined by Kroll and expressed their "gratification" at receiving this information. On 23 January 1952, another, similar meeting was held between the Economics Ministry and the "top-ranking organizations of the private-sector" to discuss "the development of East-West trade and the trade policy of the Federal Government." Shortly thereafter Wilhelm Beutler and Edgar Meyer of the industrial Bundesverband asked Erhard to formalize this group and hold additional meetings on a regular basis. In response, the Economics Ministry formally established the Committee on Central Export Control, which then met bimonthly beginning in February 1952.[76]

Over the next three years, the Committee on Central Export Control served as an important forum for intimate communication in both directions between industry and government. The ministerial members used the Committee on Central Export Control to explain the limits imposed on them by Allied embargo decisions and to inform industry of the most likely future direction of Western embargo policy, based on COCOM discussions and other international signals. The government also used the Committee on Central Export Control to collect information from German industry. Information on export capabilities and desires was especially important in regard to COCOM's annual quota allocations for "quantitatively restricted" exports to the Soviet bloc. The Committee on Central Export Control became the primary forum for the transmission of this information from industry to the ministries, where it was reviewed and used as the basis for the Federal Republic's position in COCOM negotiations. The private-sector used the Committee on Central Export Control to communicate to the government how the required embargo rules could be administered in a way that met international obligations, yet made compliance by West German industry as convenient as possible. For all these reasons, the Committee on Central Export Control served as an important forum for working out a government-industry consensus on how to respond to the international problems and obligations arising from the Western embargo.[77]

In both the range of its functions and the scope of its authority, another group, the Eastern Committee, went far beyond the Committee on Central Export Control in giving a direct role in Eastern trade policy formation and execution to the private West German business community. The private-sector Eastern Committee was called into being by the federal government as a neocorporatist solution to "two difficult problems in trade between the Federal Republic and the Eastern bloc countries."[78] The first of these was a problem familiar to German exporters from the interwar period of German-Soviet trade: preventing the centrally directed foreign trading companies of a planned economy from gaining excessive concessions on prices, credits, and delivery terms by exploiting the competition between private German firms. Drawing on private-sector experience with Soviet buyers in the interwar period and the efforts of the Russia Committee to counter the Soviet state trade monopoly in the 1920s and 1930s, the new Eastern Committee hoped to set uniform "terms of delivery, acceptance, and payments" for trade with all East European countries."[79] When the federal government subsequently made adherence to the Eastern Committee's standard terms a prerequisite for participation in the government-backed export insurance program, those privately established practices took on an official character.

A second, immediate concern was to devise a means by which the West Germans could negotiate with the foreign trade organizations of those Soviet bloc countries that did not yet officially recognize the Federal Republic. With the signing of the general treaty between the FRG and the Allies and the scheduled abolition of the High Commission, the lack of international recognition between the Federal Republic and the Soviet satellite countries threatened to become a real obstacle in the negotiation of new trade treaties in the East. With the Allied authorities gone, the question arose as to how the Federal Republic planned to negotiate at all with states with which it had no diplomatic ties. In response to a question from the chairman of the Bundestag's Economic Policy Committee on this point, Erhard admitted that "the establishment of diplomatic relations and international recognition is not to be expected in the foreseeable future" and therefore "a way must be found that makes possible the conclusion of trade agreements after the General Treaty is in force, yet that does not prejudice our negative position on international recognition of these countries."[80] With countries where old JEIA treaties were in place (Poland, Czechoslovakia, Hungary, and Bulgaria) a simple solution was found in the extension of these treaties without any mention of their previous legal basis. However, relations with the Soviet Union, Rumania, and China required some other solution. The Economics Ministry found that solution in the Eastern Committee, a private group that would assume the task of "making trade policy contact with those East bloc countries with which JEIA agreements do not exist."[81] The Eastern Committee would act as an agent of the West German state by conducting international trade negotiations in the name of the Federal Republic. Conversely, the state would act as an agent of the committee by enforcing the committee's standards for business practices with the East onto the entire German economy.

By October 1952 the membership and organization of the Eastern Committee had been formalized.[82] Immediately thereafter the Eastern Committee became a central actor in the formation and execution of German trade policy in Eastern Europe. In March 1953 Eastern Committee members appeared as special advisers to the ministerial members of the Federal Republic's delegation at the UN Economic Commission for Europe Conference on East-West trade, with the Foreign Office praising the "adaptability and initiative" of the Eastern Committee in its international activities.[83]

By May 1953 the Eastern Committee was challenging the ministries for control of West German trade policy in the East. The Eastern Committee informed the Foreign Office that negotiations on establishing permanent trade missions in Eastern Europe would be best handled by the committee itself, not by the ministries.[84] By May 1954, Seiberlich was complaining to his department head, Assistant Under-Secretary for Foreign Trade Hermann Reinhardt at the Economics Ministry, that the Eastern Committee was overstepping its bounds by extending its negotiating activities to all Eastern European countries, even those that had JEIA trade treaties with the Federal Republic.[85]

Although created primarily for the purpose of overcoming a specific set of political and commercial obstacles, both the government and the private-sector used the Eastern Committee to tackle other problems as well. The Eastern Committee's other generally defined duties ("advising the Federal government and the private-sector on basic questions of Eastern trade" and "compiling [German] desires for trade treaty negotiations") meant that virtually no area of trade policy toward the East was outside this committee's competence. The Eastern Committee and the Federal Office for Foreign Trade Information even jointly published the Eastern Economic Newsletter *(Ostwirtschafts-Mitteilungen)*.[86]

The Eastern Committee concentrated a tremendous amount of across-the-board private-sector influence into a single organization concentrating on East-West trade. This influence was magnified by the committee's position as a recognized agent of the federal government in international negotiations and by the support that the federal government had given to the committee's decisions on how to conduct business in the East. The Eastern Committee's uniquely influential position lent credence to Seiberlich's fears that it might eventually usurp the government's ability to determine the course of trade policy toward Eastern Europe. A dominion of the interest groups seemed a very real possibility in the area of Eastern trade policy.

Yet throughout the 1950s, the interest groups remained subordinated to the government's direction of Eastern trade policy. When government/private-sector differences arose over the management of Eastern trade, government officials invariably prevailed over commercial and industrial groups in determining policy. The strength of the federal government in these policy disputes was rooted in the legacy of Allied Occupation. As part of U.S. and British Occupation policy against an overconcentration of private economic power in Germany, the Allies sought to maintain the integrity of the fledgling West German administration in relation to the dormant, but by no means dead, interest groups. This meant both protecting the administration from interest-group pressure and forbidding the administration to transfer administrative authority to the interest groups.[87] The Bipartite Control Office had expressly forbidden the private interest groups from exercising any administrative authority in matters of trade.[88] The Anglo-American vision of distinctly separate public and private duties left no room for the German concept of private-sector "self administration" (Selbstverwaltung) that had been an essential element of German trade regulation since 1914.

After 1949 the Allied High Commission allowed many of these restrictions to fall away. The interest groups were no longer forbidden from exercising any regulatory authority. In many areas, West German society returned to the practices of economic self-administration, generating numerous neocorporatist bodies to take on these tasks.[89] Yet in the management of foreign trade, the High Commission continued to limit the role of private interest groups, instructing Adenauer to have the West German government "obtain special permission from the High Commission before delegating any authority in matters of foreign trade to the economic interest groups."[90]

The West German administration, particularly the Economics Ministry, used these Allied restrictions to fend off interest-group pressure for more influence in trade policy. By using the threat of Allied disapproval, the Economics Ministry could hide behind American and British authorities, thereby protecting itself from the interest groups.[91] Using these vague concerns, Maltzan responded in a cool and uncommitted manner to the German Chamber of Commerce's request that private-sector representatives (Vertreter der Wirtschaft) be included in Federal Republic's international trade negotiating delegations. The contrast with the intrusion of private interest groups into Weimar's porous ministerial structure is striking.[92]

Because the West German administration's autonomy derived in part from Allied authority, the government bureaucracy sought to preserve its monopoly on contacts with Occupation authorities.[93] Federal officials repeatedly denied interest-group requests for members of the German business community to meet directly with Allied authorities on Eastern trade issues. As early as June 1949 the Association of the German Precision Mechanics and Optical Industry tried in vain to gain access to Allied authorities through Maltzan. Throughout 1951 Kroll turned a polite but deaf ear to repeated request from the Export Committee Iron and Steel to "participate in discussions with the U.S. High Commissioner's Office." As late as December 1954, the Economics Ministry rejected a private-sector call for a full Embargo Committee that would have given German exporters more direct information about common Western embargo decisions.[94] The German government's monopoly on receiving information from the Occupation administration gave the Federal bureaucracy a strong position in dealing with the interest groups.

The state's strong position in embargo matters lent the authority to the Economics Ministry and Foreign Office in other Eastern trade policy issues as well. In an action reminiscent of imperial government authority, the Economics Ministry intervened to settle an organizational dispute in 1951 between the industrial Bundesverband and the German Chamber of Commerce within the Working Group on Foreign Trade. Maltzan actually compelled the industrial Bundesverband to scrap its plans to erect a separate Trade Treaty Bureau.[95]

In the area of trade policy toward the East, the federal bureaucracy managed to establish a measure of authority over the interest groups that had always eluded the Weimar state. That authority was based initially on a skillful exploitation of the remaining Allied restrictions on government-business association. After 1949 the hierarchical structure of Adenauer's authoritative Chancellor democracy, which appealed to the industrialists, also lent authority to the new government in the crucial early years of an emerging political culture. The broad ministerial consensus on the basic lines of trade policy toward the East (a consensus that soon included even the Agriculture Ministry) prevented cracks in the government's external facade that might serve as opening to excessive private-sector influence. Erhard's successful economic policies and his poorly hidden dislike of a number of the industrial Bundesverband's leading personalities (particularly Fritz Berg) also helped keep the industrialists at bay. Ultimately, the interest groups had no statutory right to the large role the government had granted them in the determination of Eastern trade policy. If and when the government could summon the political will to overrule the interest groups, the interest groups had no assured path of recourse.[96] Finally, the changes that had taken place in Eastern Europe itself since the war also contributed to a decline in the ability of the German interest groups to control the Eastern trade. With the Sovietization of the Eastern economies, the ability to control the production and movement flow of commodities through international cartels and other private agreements had vanished.

The Allies returned control over West German trade relations with Eastern Europe to a neocorporatist coalition between the Federal Republic's ministerial bureaucracy and the business community that relegated both the Bundestag and organized labor to distant secondary roles. Government and business acknowledged their mutual coalition by constructing a number of public and private working groups, councils, and committees that embodied the Federal Republic's corporatist approach to managing its Eastern trade. Some of these bodies, such as the Advisory Board on Foreign Trade, were the indirect successors to similar institutions dating back to Caprivi's Tariff Council or Bülow's Economic Committee. Others, such as the Eastern Committee, were the direct successors to Weimar institutions like the Russia Committee. Unlike the corporatism of the Weimar years, the neocorporatism of the Federal Republic's domestic framework for trade policy gave the government the upper hand in dealing with the interest groups by preserving for the German ministries a good portion of the bureaucratic autonomy inherited from the Occupation regime.

The Federal Republic's neocorporatist institutions faced a succession of thorny problems in the decade ahead. Most fundamentally, the West German trade policy bureaucracy had to advance vigorously the national interest of the Bonn republic against the still recent background of trade problems in the interwar period and the atrocious German policies implemented between 1939 and 1945. With Allied intermediaries now completely absent from West German negotiations with the new people's democracies, the emotions and suspicions of earlier periods would unavoidably be closer to the surface, making the contentious issues of the 1950s that much more difficult to resolve. Between 1949 and 1960 West German trade with the East brought a number of economic issues to the surface for debate, such as protection for West German agriculture in the course of negotiations with Poland; the economic burdens of the Western embargo program in the course of trade problems with Czechoslovakia; and developing appropriate strategies for reestablishing a West German presence in the Soviet market. In addition, trade relations with each of these countries were complicated by the Federal Republic's increasingly reliance on trade leverage of various types in pursuit other foreign policy goals, such as securing the return of ethnic Germans; forging an new West German political identity in relations with the USSR; and supporting Polish efforts at political and economic reform in the crisis of 1956. At the same time, the Federal Republic had to balance pursuit of its own goals in the East with continued West German participation in a larger, pan-Western approach toward the Soviet bloc. Confronted with an equally difficult cluster of political and economic issues in its Eastern relations after 1920, Weimar Germany had produced trade policies of paralysis punctuated by aggressive convulsions. Would the new West German neocorporatism be able to overcome unhappy earlier legacies in responding to the complicated issues of political economy across a divided Europe?

Impoverished Partners

Between 1949 and 1960, the much-vaunted West German Wirtschaftswunder (economic miracle) provided the solution for many of the Federal Republic's major domestic problems: unemployment, integration of the Eastern expellees, balance of payments, and currency stability. The West German economic miracle – in particular, the impressive adaptation to the forced loss of the Eastern market – also underlay the Federal Republic's early successes in Eastern Europe. Particularly after 1950, as the economic fortunes of the Federal Republic and the people's democracies moved sharply in opposite directions, West Germany gained an unprecedented advantage in its economic relations with the declining economies of Eastern Europe. By 1955 the Federal Republic could deliver both the food supplies and the industrial goods that Eastern Europe badly needed, along with short-term financing for West German export sales and long-term loans for capital equipment and consumer items. Superior economic performance was the sine qua non for a policy of using trade as the narrow end of a wedge for opening Eastern Europe to West German influence.

Superior economic performance was further magnified by successful reorientation of the West German economy away from the

East European market and toward Western Europe and North America. Since the Eastern trade did not reassume its traditionally important role for the West German economy, the FRG emerged less vulnerable to economic disturbances from the East than any German regime of the previous sixty years. By 1954, portions of the West German business community that were well-informed about the Soviet bloc economies had come to the realistic assessment that Eastern trade could play only a very limited role in the Federal Republic's foreseeable economic future.

The Federal Republic's greatly reduced economic stake in the Eastern trade allowed the Federal Government more easily to incorporate political considerations into trade policy calculations; the economic losses that might result from pursuing political demands in the East via trade policies could be absorbed by the German economy. That ability was embodied in the Foreign Office's position that West German trade policies should go beyond strictly commercial considerations and should instead be used to raise the overall political standing of the Federal Republic in Eastern Europe. By 1954, government and business in the FRG had come to agree that West German trade policies in the East would prioritize political interests over economic interests.[97]

On this basis, the Federal Republic employed trade policies to reestablish itself as a political and commercial force in Eastern Europe. Trade and trade policy played a role in each of the Federal Republic's early achievements in Eastern Europe: wringing Polish concessions on repatriation of the German minority, establishing a West German commercial presence in the Soviet market, and opening diplomatic relations with the Soviet Union. In these ventures, the burden of subordinating potential West German business profits to the achievement of certain political goals was easily borne by the otherwise prosperous West German economy.

The explicit prioritization of politics over economics was reflected in the federal government's unambiguous ability to assert itself vis-à-vis the private sector as it did when insisting on compensation deals in the Soviet trade from 1952 to 1954 and when canceling the Eastern Committee's planned trip to Moscow in June 1954. The Foreign Office and Economics Ministry both were jointly determined that the search for profits should not imperil either long-term economic strategy or other, noneconomic goals. Supported by Erhard and Adenauer, ministerial policymakers had the strength to impose long-run commercial strategies and political considerations, decisively shaping the emerging government/business consensus on West German priorities. Within the boundaries set by a primacy of politics, a second point of government/private-sector consensus emerged supporting increased trade with the East. Weimar's divisive private-sector battles and interministerial feuds over the economic content of Eastern trade policies disappeared in the economically reinvigorated Federal Republic.

Against the (comfortable) background of their continuing economic recovery after 1949, the West Germans managed to use both the international framework imposed on them by the Allies and the domestic framework that they themselves had fashioned to formulate and execute a very successful Eastern trade policy between 1949 and 1955. Ultimately, it was West German economic power – revived by the international and domestic frameworks of postwar Europe and the new Federal Republic – that made successful trade policies possible. The forceful hands of the ministerial bureaucracy in turn insured that West German economic power was thoughtfully applied in the pursuit of both political and economic goals in Eastern Europe. If, as the West German Foreign Office insisted, the goal was to raise the Federal Republic's overall political stature in the East, then the years 1949 to 1955 comprise one of the most successful periods in the history of German relations with Eastern Europe.

Poland

Between 1949 and 1955 familiar political problems pushed West German trade with Poland through several ups and downs. Initially, politics in the Federal republic revisited the issue of agricultural protectionism, and specifically the proper role of Polish agricultural imports in the new West German economy. On this point the Economics Ministry and the Agriculture Ministry clashed violently in 1949 to 1950. In postures reminiscent of the protectionist debates that had paralyzed Weimar trade policy, the Agriculture Ministry hoped to limit agricultural imports into the Federal Republic through obstructionist tactics, while the Economics Ministry sought to open the German market to these imports as a means of securing reciprocal export opportunities. A familiar tone was also heard in the political sparring that surrounded trade negotiations between the two countries, as the two sides wrestled again with the status of a German minority unwillingly residing within the new borders of Poland. Yet unlike the Weimar era, when these problems dragged on unresolved for the life of the regime, these clear parallels with trade policy debates of the interwar period soon ended with both issues essentially resolved within five years of the creation of the Federal Republic.

Sadly, the steady and rapid decline of the Polish economy after 1949 provided the solution to the early problems between the FRG and the new Polish republic. As Polish agriculture sank into the abyss of declining productivity, it lost the ability to generate regular exportable surpluses on a scale that could genuinely threaten German farm incomes. As Polish agricultural surpluses disappeared, so, too, did the problem of protecting German farmers from the impact of trade with Poland. The Poles continued to export some agricultural goods to the Federal Republic, but by 1954 the Polish communist government (and other Soviet satellites) was buying heavily on the West German market to cover domestic shortages in the East. A program for protecting German farmers from Polish competition would have been laughable in 1954 and 1955. The across-the-board economic decline in Poland was so severe that the Poles could not resist German economic pressure to begin transferring part of the remaining German minority from Poland to the Federal Republic. Defiant in 1952, the Poles softened under German trade pressure in 1954, and formally agreed to begin repatriation of some Germans in 1955.

As early as December 1949, the West German Economics Ministry and the Agriculture Ministry recorded their first disagreements over the future course of West German trade policy. Agriculture Minister Wilhelm Niklas (CSU) resented the sacrifices imposed on his ministry by Erhard's emphasis on increasing German exports. Niklas complained about expensive food purchases forced on him by Economics Ministry negotiators who "allowed price considerations to play no role in import purchases if an intransigent [German] position would endanger exports." Erhard simply denied Niklas's criticism, although it is clear that the Economics Ministry frequently bought high-priced foodstuffs and raw materials that the Federal Republic did not need urgently in order to secure reciprocal export sales – a practice that the Western Allies had already criticized as a feature of Erhard's economic strategy.[98] Erhard's policy might function smoothly when importing industrial raw materials, but it evoked bitter hostility when applied to East European agricultural products that threatened German farm prices and incomes.

The issue resurfaced in concrete terms in the 1950 trade negotiations with Poland. On 12 June German delegation leader Josef Seiberlich of the Economics Ministry complained to Erhard that the Agriculture Ministry's refusal to accept a number of Polish agricultural products (especially live pigs and pork) was blocking finalization of a deal in which the Poles had already agreed to buy $35 million in German manufactured exports. Seiberlich suggested that the German accept $5 million in live pig/pork imports in order to secure the deal. Erhard took the issue to the cabinet for resolution.[99]

The 20 June cabinet meeting produced a "lengthy discussion on the condition of German agriculture and on the factors to be considered when negotiating trade treaties," but neither Erhard nor Niklas would concede their positions. Erhard agreed to try to keep the pigs out of the new agreement in the next round of negotiations, but warned that "he could not let the negotiations fail over this point" because of the "unfavorable repercussions" that failure might have on the FRG's Marshall Plan aid.[100]

By this point, the industrial Bundesverband had become concerned over the Agriculture Ministry's protectionist position and the resulting impasse with the Poles. On 24 June it telegraphed Adenauer – having already written twice to Erhard – asking for a cabinet decision that would "make possible the conclusion of a treaty beneficial to the growth of industrial exports." Further, the industrial Bundesverband feared that a breakdown in negotiations "would have prejudicial effects on future negotiations with Eastern and Southeastern European countries," as well as "very disadvantageous political consequences."[101] Erhard asked for another cabinet discussion on 30 June so that something might be done to appease the Polish delegation, which had threatened to depart Frankfurt if the Germans had not made a "fundamental decision" by the end of the month.[102]

In the cabinet, Erhard attacked Niklas for obstructing trade agreements with several European countries, currently Poland and Italy. This left the Federal Republic open to charges that it had not done every thing possible to close the "dollar gap." He went on to point out that the government's economic strategy had been to lower industrial prices "as a precondition for our export ability." Now the cabinet had to take responsibility for that strategy by signing a trade agreement with Poland. Franz Blücher, minister for the Marshall Plan, said that only an "active and successful trade policy" could reduce unemployment and raise purchasing power. Niklas held firm; the meeting ended in disagreement.[103] Again the issue went unresolved after Adenauer, Erhard, and Niklas met on the evening of 30 June.

Then on 3 July, State Secretary Schalfejew of the Economics Ministry informed his counterpart, Theodor Sonnemann at the Agriculture Ministry, that Adenauer had given his approval to $5 million in pork imports. On that basis, the German delegation agreed to accept $4.8 million in pork imports from Poland. The negotiations went ahead and the full lists were initialed in Frankfurt by Seiberlich and Polish trade delegation leader Wiktor Muszynski on July 7. The Federal Republic agreed to accept $32.6 million in imports, of which $26.3 million were agricultural goods (rye for $13 million, sugar and eggs for $3 million each.) The Germans also took $3 million in Polish coal exports. Among West German export industries, machine building ($10 million), chemicals ($4 million), iron and steel products ($3 million), motor vehicles ($2 million), and the electrical industry ($1.5 million) were the major beneficiaries of the new agreement.[104]

The similarity between these most recent negotiations and German-Polish trade talks in the Weimar era was frightfully apparent: a conflict of interest between protectionist farmers and export-oriented industries over the terms of a trade treaty with Poland manifested itself in ministerial deadlock in a coalition government. The deadlock, in turn, elevated a negotiating position involving less than $5 million to a cabinet-level decision and brought on direct pressure from Germany's most powerful industrial interest group in order to avoid a break in the negotiations. Finally, the affair ended acrimoniously in a disputed decision by the chancellor.

The prospect of this drama replaying itself annually (probably in increasingly intensified terms as both agriculture and industry in West Germany became more productive) did not bode well for the future of West German-Polish trade. Despite the wide-ranging consensus on West Germany's need to export its manufactures, these negotiations had demonstrated that it would not be easy to fulfill that need and satisfy German farmers simultaneously. The Economics Ministry's Foreign Trade Department (V) expressed concern about the "dangers posed to Germany's entire foreign trade by a short-sighted and radical agricultural protectionism."[105]

The Agriculture Ministry was capable of blocking trade deals in Eastern Europe; it scuttled the 1953 trade agreement negotiated between the Eastern Committee and Rumania (the first ever between the Federal Republic and Rumania) by rejecting German plans to buy 50,000 tons of wheat as part of the deal.[106] Adenauer's Bundestag majority had been just one vote in September 1949. CSU votes and farm votes were crucial ingredients in that majority, so therefore their ability to obstruct trade deals with Poland was very real.

In subsequent years, Adenauer's cabinet was spared additional anguish over the agricultural side of Polish trade issue. The rapid decline in Polish agriculture after 1950 transformed Poland from an agricultural exporter to an agricultural importer, from a competitor to a customer. With that transformation, the domestic political issue of protecting German farmers from Polish exports evaporated.[107]

Following the October 1950 finalization of the trade agreement, the Poles did well in delivering pork supplies, but as of March 1951 they had failed to deliver any of the promised rye. By that time, the FRG had already accumulated a surplus of $5.1 million in their clearing account at the Narodowy Bank Polski.[108] The High Commission pressured the Germans to slow the pace of their own exports until the Poles came through with counter-deliveries.[109] In the trade agreements for 1951 to 1952 and for 1952 to 1953 the Poles also failed to deliver their rye and timber exports.[110] By December 1952 the Poles were asking to buy grain (20,000 tons of wheat) from the Federal Republic. In 1954 Poland had trouble making its promised deliveries of pork and live pigs, traditionally a strong point of its agricultural exports.[111] In December 1954 the Poles admitted the obvious – that grain, except for specialized brewers' barley, would no longer be available for export from Poland.[112] In March 1955, the Foreign Office noted the "strained state of the food supplies in Poland"; the Poles were making hurried purchases of West German wheat flour, a sure sign of an emergency at home.[113] Six months later the Poles approached the Germans for 200,000 tons of wheat and 100,000 tons of rye (c.$18 million total). In order to complete that deal in December 1955, the Germans had to provide $18 million in credit, since the Poles could not deliver the reciprocal amounts of coal and wood for at least another 18 months.[114]

Under these tragic circumstances, the issue of protection from Polish agriculture would have been a cruel joke. In sporadic fits, Poland could still occasionally export some goods, usually sugar, occasionally pigs, but the balance of trade in agricultural goods was turning sharply in West Germany's favor. Since late 1952 the Agriculture Ministry had been transformed into an agency for promoting West German agricultural exports to Poland.

Polish economic problems were not limited to the agricultural sector, but were gradually engulfing the entire economy. Because of the predominantly rural character of the Polish economy, low agricultural productivity acted as a massive deadweight on general economic development. Progress in Stalinist-style heavy industry was impressive, but housing, consumer goods, and food supplies were all just barely sufficient to prevent civil disturbances. Years later the party leadership admitted that Polish standards of living actually declined between 1949 and 1954. Under the direction of the powerful Central Planning Commission, the Polish economy was heading rapidly down the path of failure, leading to the Poznan workers uprising in June 1956.[115]

By the spring of 1951 it was clear that Poland could not deliver many of the export goods it had promised in July 1950 for the 1950 to 1951 year. As of March 1951 Poland had delivered none of the promised $3 million in coal.[116] Instead of the $32.6 million in exports they had promised for 1950 to 1951, the Poles in fact managed to deliver only $17.5 million. The next year exports to the Federal Republic fell off to $15.6 million when "planned" exports to the FRG ought to have totaled $62 million for the period January 1952 to June 1953.[117] The Polish trade delegation leader, Wiktor Muszynski, repeatedly emphasized to Seiberlich that Poland needed additional credits from the Federal Republic, claiming that "Poland can import German goods only if it finds some concessions in the payments area."[118]

The faltering Polish economy desperately needed trade concessions to maintain food supplies and some hard currency credits for industrial and consumer imports. Against this background, the Federal Republic used its superior economic and financial position to extract concessions from the Poles on the matter of the German minority remaining in Poland.

Minister for All-German Questions Jakob Kaiser (CDU) was besieged throughout 1950 with requests to help German family members who had been left behind in Eastern Europe, especially in Poland, where a substantial German minority remained.[119] West German concern focused initially on the 20,000 to 50,000 Germans living in Poland who had immediate family in the Federal Republic. Protest notes by the High Commission on behalf of the Federal Republic had no effect. Since trade talks were the only official meetings between West German and Polish representatives at any level, Kaiser asked Erhard "whether the possibility exists of bringing up political issues in the negotiations for the commodity lists." A month later he sounded out Erhard on the idea of paying a "ransom" as part of the trade agreements.[120] The Polish trade representative in Frankfurt rebuffed Seiberlich's attempts to discuss the issue and the matter slumbered until the summer of 1951.

With implementation of their new Law on Citizenship in 1951, the Poles cut off the existing trickle of emigration to the West and launched a new campaign to force the remaining Germans to "opt" for Polish citizenship. Heinz Trützschler at the Foreign Office's legal department called for an interministerial meeting to consider whether "some German action" could be taken to influence Polish authorities.[121] At that meeting, Seiberlich discouraged the thought of using economic pressure, saying it was "doubtful whether an economic dispute with Poland would not bring very considerable economic disadvantages to the Federal Republic, especially as such disputes could spread to the whole of the Eastern trade."[122]

The Foreign Office pressed on, asking the Economics Ministry for a written opinion on "which, if any, economic measures the Federal Republic can use to counter the actions of the Polish authorities." In the Economics Ministry, Assistant Under-Secretary for Foreign

Trade Hermann Reinhardt overruled Seiberlich's objections that mixing politics and economics needlessly complicated trade negotiations. Reinhardt instead suggested raising the issue in the 1951 round of trade talks with Poland and basing further German actions on the Polish response. Foreign Trade Director Maltzan and State Secretary Ludgar Westrick supported Reinhardt's cautious plan.[123] When the Poles rebuffed German attempts to discuss the matter, the Economics Ministry was content to let it drop, and Erhard himself worried about the "delicate character of this question."[124] As of March 1952, when the trade agreement for 1952 to 1953 was signed, nothing had been achieved concerning the return of separated German family members living in Poland.

Frustrated by this lack of progress, the Foreign Office now pressed for a cabinet resolution instructing German negotiators to raise the matter in the very next meeting of the Mixed Commission. Meanwhile the Economics Ministry was to prepare a carrot for Poland by "checking" the possibility of offering increased exports of those hard goods in short supply in Poland and making West German deliveries "dependent on concessions in the question of exit permission" for Germans living in Eastern Europe. Finally, the stick was readied in the form of an Economics Ministry report on "whether, and to what extent, reprisals in the area of trade must be taken" in the event that no satisfaction was obtained.[125] When Muszynski again declared that he could not possibly discuss this issue, the Germans began immediately to apply trade pressure.[126] The German delegation under Seiberlich and Otto Stalmann, desk officer for Eastern Trade in the Agriculture Ministry, revoked earlier German offers to buy $8 million of Polish pork and 30,000 tons of Polish sugar, a revocation that severely limited Poland's ability to reduce its debt to the Federal Republic.[127] At a West German interministerial meeting on January 8, both Seiberlich and Koch, of the Agriculture Ministry, argued against a further coupling of the "political complex of reuniting families" with economic questions. Seiberlich claimed that Germany's interest in getting a trade agreement was "at least as strong" as the Polish interest. Trützschler argued instead that "the political, human and social importance of family reunification can by no means be subordinated to our interest in reaching a trade agreement."[128] The divided opinions of the West German foreign trade bureaucracy were reflected in the German-Polish negotiations of early 1953 as steady economic progress was made while the Poles refused to discuss family reunification.

In June 1953, the Germans faced the decision of whether or not to sign the next annual bilateral trade agreement with Poland in view of continued Polish intransigence on the family reunification issue. Chancellor Adenauer declared in cabinet discussion on 30 June that he was disinclined to sign a new trade agreement with Poland at that time.[129] At the interministerial meeting on the following day Seiberlich declared flatly that Germany must stop "burdening" its commercial interest with "political demands which obviously cannot be met" by Poland. Albert Hilger van Scherpenberg, chief of the Foreign Office's Trade Policy Division and future state secretary in the Foreign Office, countered that in the larger context, the issue went beyond "commercial interests" and "concerned the overall political standing of the Federal Republic in the East." Trützschler flatly opposed signing. Otto Stalmann proposed the compromise of not signing the agreement but allowing its terms to come into force for a limited period of three months in order to give the Poles a final chance to make some concessions. Full, formal signing of the deal would remain dependent on these concessions.[130]

This uneasy stalemate of limited trade without a formal agreement dragged on through most of 1954.[131] In July 1954 the Germans refused to participate in the annual discussions for a new trade agreement. Stalmann told the Poles that any expansion of trade depended on Polish compliance with "certain German political demands."[132] In August the West German federal bank (Bank of the German Länder) canceled previous plans to increase the Polish credit limit (the "swing") in German-Polish trade. The Poles vaguely expressed a willingness to negotiate on the issue if they could entice an official German delegation to Warsaw -something that could not be arranged until the end of the year.[133]

At the October 1954 sessions of the UN Economic Commission for Europe's Trade Committee in Geneva, Zahn-Stranik (Foreign Office desk officer for Eastern trade) managed to speak twice to the Polish delegate, Wolynski, about the current West German-Polish trade impasse. Zahn-Stranik stated bluntly that "the return of the Germans is a precondition by the German side for a better negotiating climate." After some renewed sparring about the possibility of a German delegation traveling to Warsaw for negotiations, Wolynski came to the substantive issues. Any negotiations on returning Germans must also include discussion of the following economic issues: "a long-term investment loan; a $10 million loan for consumer goods; and a favorable recasting of the German-Polish Payments Agreement, including the swing credit."[134]

Wolynski's comments made it clear that at least some portion of the German minority was now for sale. In the absence of other exportable commodities, the Poles would now start exporting their

Germans; after all, Poland had no other goods guaranteed to bring in at least $10 million in hard currency.[135] In mid-November the Trade Policy Committee and Adenauer agreed to comprehensive negotiations in Warsaw; the German delegation, chaired by Foreign Office East-West Trade Officer von Lupin arrived on 29 November.[136] Two months later the Germans arranged a trade, credit, and financial deal with Poland that included an eighteen-month trade agreement, a revised payments agreement reducing Poland's interest-free swing credit line from $7.5 million to $6 million, and the promise of $10 million in government-guaranteed private loans over four years ($4 million for consumer goods and $6 million for investment goods).[137] In exchange the Germans received oral assurances that the Poles would begin providing exit visas for 20,000 Germans already identified with immediate family in the Federal Republic.[138]

Between January and September 1955, a mere 428 Germans arrived in the Federal Republic from Poland. The federal authorities were furious at this low number.[139] When a Polish delegation came to West Germany in September 1955 looking to buy grain, the Germans were determined to use their commercial advantage to gain the repatriation of immediate family members. On 2 September the Poles outlined to the Germans a plan to purchase 300,000 tons of German grain in exchange for Polish deliveries of coal and wood. Since the Poles wanted the grain as soon as possible, but could not deliver their own exports for another twelve to eighteen months, the deal required German financing. At the end of the month, Stalmann told the Polish negotiators, Jazdon and Stanislaw Strus, that the financing would require a government guarantee of the loans, something the federal government was not prepared to give as long as "the problem of repatriation remained unsolved."[140] Four days later Strus and Wachowiak, a director in the state import and export firm, POLIMPEX, told Stalmann that "in the matter of food supplies, Poland had been left in the lurch this year by the Soviet Union and could expect no supplementary deliveries from there. For that reason the supply situation in Poland was catastrophic and necessitated quick deals with the West."[141]

On 19 October Stalmann repeated the West German conditions while Strus complained of "extortion."[142] On 28 October the West Germans presented a memorandum of demands on family reunification to the Poles; at the same time the Germans threatened to suspend further negotiations on grain purchases. The consequences were not long in coming; on 9 November the first group of Germans in over two months left Poland for the West; on 18 November Stalmann arrived in Warsaw at Polish invitation to negotiate the modalities of a larger repatriation. In early December negotiations, the Polish Red Cross agreed to return from Poland to the Federal Republic 800 to 1,000 persons per month throughout 1956.[143] The Federal Republic responded immediately by fulfilling a Polish request for an additional $2 million timber-for-machinery deal, a deal the Germans had rejected seven months earlier. On December 19 in Warsaw, Stalmann finalized the grain deal (including government-guaranteed financing of $18 million). Ten months later, he reported that the return action was progressing "without a hitch" and that the goal of 10,000 returnees for 1956 would be met.[144]

Czechoslovakia

In the early 1950s, the pan-Western embargo policy and the manner of its execution in the Federal Republic affected West German trade with Czechoslovakia more immediately than West German trade with either Poland or the Soviet Union. Repeated interruptions of trade and unpredictable border stoppages by units of the American forces stationed in Bavaria brought legal and illegal West German-Czechoslovak trade to an almost complete standstill in the first half of 1951. The decline in trade severely strained the Bavarian economy, which depended on Czechoslovakian coal and other raw materials for its native glass and ceramic industries.

American actions succeeded in elevating the otherwise routine trade relations between the Federal Republic and Czechoslovakia to a matter of West German national attention between 1950 and 1953. The situation on the Bavarian border focused public attention on the Western embargo policy and engendered a good deal of debate on what role Eastern Europe might play in West Germany's economic future. Only after the American-inspired embargo policy declined in scope and intensity from late 1953 through 1955 did the West Germans gradually come to a more realistic assessment of the limited role that Eastern Europe was capable of playing in their economic future.

In mid-September 1950, shortly before the beginning of German-Czechoslovak negotiations for the next annual trade agreement covering 1951, U.S. Military Police Customs Units stopped and held at the Bavarian border twenty-one duly licensed railroad cars containing pipes and fittings (by Mannesmann and Stahlunion) on their way to Czechoslovakia.[145] In the course of following German-Czechoslovakian trade negotiations, the American representatives from the Allied High Commission vetoed several German offers to export iron and steel scrap to Czechoslovakia, and then finally allowed the small amount of 10,000 tons. The Americans almost certainly did not plan to initiate a tit-for-tat sequence with Czechoslovakia that would reduce German-Czechoslovakian trade to very nearly nothing within six months (see Tables 8.2a/b). Nor did they realize at the time that their actions along the border had just begun such a sequence. However, the subsequent actions of the High Commission indicate that it was unlikely the British or the Americans would have modified their actions in order to help preserve the reemerging pattern of German-Czechoslovak trade.

On 1 December 1950 the Czechs began reducing their coal and kaolin exports to West Germany in the hope of freeing the pipes and fittings that were still held at the Bavarian border. By the end of December Czechoslovakian exports had "almost fully ceased." The *Wiener Wirtschaftskorrespondenz* quickly pointed out that American interference had brought even "the legal Eastern trade practically to a standstill."[146] As a prerequisite for renewed coal deliveries, the Czechs demanded the 15,000 tons of scrap promised them (but never delivered) under the 1950 trade agreement and a "guarantee of regular deliveries of hard goods on the basis of the new [21 December 1950] commodity lists."[147] Together this meant 25,000 tons of scrap exports at a time when the Allies were not inclined to allow any.[148]

Intensifying embargo restrictions culminated in Allied refusal to grant entry visas to the Czechoslovakian trade delegation in November 1951. In April 1952, the U.S. High Commissioner's Office expelled one member of the new Czechoslovakian trade delegation and transferred the cite of future negotiations from the Czechoslovak consulate in Düsseldorf to Bonn. Parallel to those negotiations, Seiberlich tried in vain to reach a "comprehensive agreement with the Allies" that would prevent the type of last-minute problems on the Bavarian border that plagued trade with Czechoslovakia.[149]

As a Bavarian himself, Erhard was particularly sensitive to the economic damage being caused there by the lack of Czechoslovak industrial raw materials. The West German porcelain industry specialized in the manufacture of hard porcelains composed of 50 percent kaolin. Since medieval times the Bavarian ceramic industry had used Bohemian kaolin from the exceptionally pure deposits at Karlsbad and Zeltlitz. In order to maintain its export reputation and market share, the Bavarian porcelain industry required 10,000 to 15,000 tons of Bohemian kaolin annually. More serious disruptions were caused by the loss of Czechoslovak coal supplies. As early as February 1951 Erhard received reports of an "industrial flight" by fuel-dependent industries (glass, iron, porcelain, ceramics) from northern Bavaria.[150] Meanwhile, the need to supply Bavaria with Ruhr coal strained German supplies, in part because of the International Ruhr Authority's program for exporting German coal.[151] The Bavarian

Economic Ministry warned that any reduction in supplies from the Ruhr would force the Bavarian ceramic industry onto a two-day work week.[152] When Erhard met with members of the High Commission's Economics Committee in August 1951, he "very urgently pointed out the necessity of supplying the Federal Republic with coal, especially Bavaria and Northern Franconia, in order to avoid not only an economic, but also a social and political crisis." In response the Americans would say only that the commission "agreed in principle" with the points made about trade with Czechoslovakia, but could make no specific promises to remedy the situation.[153]

Discussion of the economic situation in Bavaria (which could hardly remain a secret) propelled the Western embargo policy into the center of German national attention in the spring of 1951. On 28 April Adenauer issued a Public Declaration on the Question of East-West Trade that explained the need to prevent the export of militarily usable goods to the East; in this statement the chancellor spoke plainly about the "unavoidable sacrifices for the German economy" that this policy entailed.[154] In the spring of 1951, Hans Kroll initiated a dialogue with the business community, explaining to several interest groups the reasons for the Western embargo policy and the Federal Republic's need to comply with international agreements in this area. The private-sector Working Committee on Central Export Control was established as a confidential forum for discussion of embargo enforcement. On the whole, both the business community and the public at large accepted the reasoning behind the embargo policy.[155] A realistic perception that the semisovereign Federal Republic had little choice but to go along with Allied policy, combined with a feeling that the Soviet bloc was a genuine threat to Western security, produced a West German consensus that the Federal Republic ought to participate in the common Western export control program.

Yet the Germans could not overcome the gnawing fear that the Federal Republic was participating more fully in the program than were other Western states. The idea that supposedly "common" Western export restrictions were being unfairly manipulated to restrict West German exports more severely than exports from other countries was the great recurring nightmare of West German exporters. The British in particular were suspected of plotting to thwart West Germany's natural recovery of East European markets. Kroll acknowledged that "the prevailing opinion in German economic circles is that only the Federal Republic" (among European countries) adhered strictly to the embargo rules, and that most West German exporters were convinced that other Western European countries are "quite generous" with their export licenses.[156] In virtually every discussion of West Germany and the embargo policy the word Diskriminierung very quickly appeared.

The intrusive activities of the U.S. Military Police Customs Unit confirmed West German fears of discrimination against their exports. This was especially true in the years 1952 to 1953 when the general treaty and the contractual agreements had raised German expectations that this sort of activity would cease. Those expectations had been reinforced by a period of relative American restraint for most of 1952 and the first half of 1953, despite Economics Ministry failure to obtain any comprehensive guarantee from the Americans about the passage of exports over the border.

In the summer of 1953, a new flurry of U.S. Military Police activity on the border caused the Czechoslovaks to postpone signing the trade agreement for 1954.[157] The Czechoslovak trade representative in Frankfurt pleaded with Seiberlich not to let the "well-known difficulties of the past" reach destructive proportions again.[158] In the West German business community, grumbling about the "unfair" aspects of the embargo policy grew louder. The frustration of West German export industries was typified in the comments of the machine-building interest group to the Economics Ministry: "In our opinion it is intolerable that even now exports of goods that according to the international guidelines are not restricted items should be subjected to this unjustified chicanery, despite German officials having already testified as to the legality of the export." Even the normally subdued *Deutsche Finanz- und Wirtschaftszeitung* demanded that the matter finally be resolved. In 1953 the *Handelsblatt* regularly published articles pointing out the injustices of U.S. interference in West German trade.[159]

Fortunately, the new Eisenhower administration had already initiated a policy of "relaxing" the Western embargo program. The U.S. Military Police soon abandoned their reactivity and were withdrawn at the end of 1953, so that the border actions of September 1953 remained an isolated incident. By that time, the U.S. delegates to COCOM had already adopted a more tolerant attitude toward Western European requests for specific embargo exemptions. At the same time, the negotiations had already begun in Washington and London that would culminate in the mid-1954 reductions of banned and restricted commodities on the International Lists.[160]

As these external political obstacles to trade were removed, the Federal Republic had its first opportunity to evaluate German-Czechoslovak trade purely on the basis of economic capabilities, free from major political restrictions.[161] Any such evaluation could not lead to very optimistic conclusions in 1954 as even the relatively advanced Czechoslovak economy ran short of hard currency for trade with the West. By 1954 it was clear that Czechoslovakia's own limited economic performance lay at the source of a disappointingly slow growth rate for German-Czechoslovakian trade.

The embargo-related disruptions in East-West trade had only partially masked Czechoslovakian debt and export problems in the years 1950 to 1953. The embargo could not be blamed for early Czechoslovak failures to deliver scheduled agricultural exports, through which the Czechoslovakia fell $5 million behind in payments to the Federal Republic by June 1950.[162] By November 1951 the Czechoslovak debt (expressed in terms of the German account surplus at the Statni Banka Československa) had risen to $8.2 million, exceeding its $7.5 million credit line by over half a million dollars; by July 1952 the debt was $11 million. Over the next five years the Germans progressively lowered the swing credit limit to $4.1 million and introduced interest charges on the outstanding balance as a way of forcing Czechoslovakia to reduce its debt.[163]

This debt reduction was possible only by severely limiting exports from the Federal Republic, which, at $15.1 million for 1955, barely exceeded the 1949 level of $14.5 million, despite the fact that by 1955 the Federal Republic had become Czechoslovakia's premier Western trading partner (Tables 8.2a/b and 8.3). Throughout the 1950 to 1955 period, Czechoslovakia was consistently unable to fulfill its scheduled trade volumes with the Federal Republic (Table 8.4). For example, the 1953 agreement called for German exports to Czechoslovakia of $16.2 million, but the Czechs actually bought only $7.7 million worth of goods. In May 1954, the Czechoslovakian trade representative in Germany had to admit that a shortage of hard currency continued to prevent Czechoslovakia from making its scheduled purchases.[164]

Consistently short of agricultural deliveries, Czechoslovakia had only a limited range of manufactured goods with which to supplement its only exports truly desired by the Federal Republic – coal and kaolin. In November 1949 the Czechs had admitted that they really did not want to export agricultural goods to Germany at all, but did so only to "bridge the gap between planned volume of German exports and the limited Czechoslovakian export possibilities from the manufactured sector."[165] The Federal Republic was prepared to accept only a limited amount of "soft" manufactured goods such as glass, ceramics, textiles, wood products, or beer. Other, more desirable Czechoslovakian manufactured exports were sent East under the terms of the 5 April 1952 Czechoslovak-Soviet trade treaty.[166] (Table 8.2b shows the steady decline in Czechoslovakian exports to West Germany for the two years following the treaty with the Soviets.) Czechoslovakian exports to Germany were actually larger at the height of the embargo in 1951 than they were thereafter.[167] Czechoslovak economic performance was further damaged by "the most extensive" purge in Eastern Europe, which swept through the Czechoslovakian administration in 1951 and 1952.[168]

Confronted with the economic limits of the Polish and Czechoslovakian economies, the Germans now began toning down their expectations about East-West trade in a post-embargo Europe. Between 1950 and 1953 the West Germans, like the Allies before them, had assumed that Germany's Eastern trade would and could be revived. In June 1950 Erhard himself thought the Eastern trade might reasonably soon increase to 10 percent of the Federal Republic's total foreign trade.[169] As late as 1952 Erhard declared that the "structural preconditions" still existed for a significant expansion of trade with the East.[170] The view of the *Frankfurter Allgemeine Zeitung* that Eastern trade should be used to reduce Germany's "dollar gap" was widely shared in government and industry.[171] An official government statement from July 1952, titled *On Germany's Eastern Trade* emphasized its "great importance" for the future of the German economy.

Yet the 1954 rounds of trade negotiations with the East failed to produce the dramatic increases in exchange generally hoped for in the West now that the embargo program had been greatly pared down. In September 1953 the Foreign Office reminded its officers that well before the embargo had begun to affect trade, Eastern Europe had not been able to deliver even half of the $3 billion in exports to the Western countries called for by the Marshall Plan. The "decline in agricultural production and the falling-off of earlier export possibilities," the "reckless industrialization and one-sided preference for heavy industry" and the "integration of the Eastern bloc countries" combined to drastically reduce Eastern European ability to trade with the West.[172] Gradually the Germans and other West Europeans came to realize that the "major difficulties" in East-West trade were not caused by the embargo rules, but rather by the "insufficient export abilities or export willingness" of Soviet bloc countries. Even "complete freedom of trade" after the embargo could not restore the old trade volume.[173] In January 1955 Scholz of the Economics Ministry told the representatives of the state governments (Länder) that the Soviet bloc appeared to be in an autarky drive and that exports in 1954 had dwindled to a very low level. Consequently "no unusual increases [in East-West trade] could be expected in the near future." He warned specifically against the "exaggerated expectations of the private-sector" in East-West trade.[174]

Throughout 1954 and 1955 the Economics Ministry spent a good deal of time and effort dampening the "unrealistic" hopes of West German industry about the future course of Eastern trade. By 1954, earlier government and private-sector visions of a substantial revival of East-West trade had faded. Speaking for a number of leading West German industrialists in the Eastern Committee, Otto Wolff von Amerongen and Hans Reuter (DEMAG) told Adenauer they approached East-West trade issues "without any great illusions about the scale or success of trade with the Eastern bloc."[175]

For the Federal Republic, trade with the East in 1955 was roughly half as important as it had been six years earlier. In 1949 the Federal Republic had used the Soviet bloc for 4.2 percent of total imports and 3.6 percent of total exports; for 1955 the numbers were 2.1 percent and 1.9 percent. Only the growth of trade with the Soviet Union prevented an even larger decline.[176] Those numbers reflect how successfully the West Germans had reoriented their export economy toward Western Europe and North America. In the spring of 1956 Erhard remarked to a group of leading German industrialists that sales to the East were "interesting, but not necessary in order to achieve a healthy economic foundation."[177]

Soviet Union

West German exporters still found the Eastern trade "interesting" (to use Erhard's own characterization) and after 1953 they found trade with the Soviet Union particularly interesting. As German-Soviet business picked up in the second half of 1952 the Federal Republic faced a thicket of commercial and political problems that had to be cleared away if West German-Soviet trade were to regain a portion of its earlier scope and significance. Most fundamentally, commercial success in the Soviet market required a significant expansion of exports to the USSR, so that West German industry could "reconquer" its traditional position as the Soviets' leading Western trade partner. For West German exporters, genuine commercial success also required some means of limiting intra-German price and credit competition for Soviet orders, either through a new West German private-sector organization or through a renewed understanding with the Soviets on credit and delivery terms, or both. In this regard, the lessons of the interwar period appeared clear, i.e., without some organizational defense against the trade practices of the Soviet state monopoly, German producers would be played off against one another in an expensive bidding war for Soviet orders that would reduce German profits to the very thinnest margins. Only by bringing German exporters together in a single organization, the Russia

Committee, and having that organization work closely with the German government, had it been possible in the early 1930s to negotiate standard payment and delivery terms with the Soviets and to enforce these terms on German exporters, thereby reducing intra-German competition and preserving profits. In view of this interwar legacy, it could come as no surprise that the West German private-sector sought to restrain West German competition by negotiating some new form of agreement with the Soviets.[178]

As various commercial strategies began to increase the volume of West German-Soviet trade in late 1952, the Federal Republic faced a second, and a diplomatic problem. That was how to regulate the trade and payments relations between the FRG and the USSR. Most fundamentally, the negotiating task was complicated by the absence of West German-Soviet diplomatic relations 1949 to 1955. Further, any trade agreement must not compromise the Federal Republic's stated positions on the questions of German reunification and Germany's eastern border.

In this context, the new private-sector Eastern Committee came into being as a neocorporatist mechanism for the pursuit of West German trade strategies vis-à-vis the Soviet Union. Most fundamentally, the Eastern Committee could serve as a way of conducting trade negotiations with the Soviets in the immediate postwar framework of international relations that prevented any official contacts between the two countries. The West Germans were also hopeful that the Eastern Committee would serve as a means of preventing the centrally directed foreign trading companies of the Soviet economy from exploiting the competition between private German firms to gain excessive concessions on prices, credits, and delivery terms.[179]

As a corporatist body, the Eastern Committee reflected a cross-current of economic and political motives that came from the business community and the ministerial bureaucracy (chiefly the Economics Ministry and Foreign Office). Significant for the 1950s and beyond was the unambiguous primacy of political considerations over economic calculations in the formation of West German trade policies toward the Soviet Union. The primacy of politics in West German-Soviet relations was a view shared by the business community, which provided the material wherewithal for any economic interaction with the Soviets, and by the governmental bureaucracy, which determined trade policy. Ironically, the West German prioritization of political over commercial concerns allowed significant commercial success in the early 1950s, but prevented the political successes that might have come with a trade agreement or normalized trade relations. The shifting currents of international politics prevented the Federal Republic (or the Eastern Committee) from signing a formal trade treaty with the Soviets until early 1958.

From 1949 to mid-1952 West German-Soviet exchanges amounted to less than $4 million in two-way trade; for eleven consecutive quarters from late 1949 to mid-1952, West German imports from the Soviet Union amounted to a meager $0.5 million; imports were nonexistent (Table 8.5).[180] In the increasingly acrimonious Cold War atmosphere of 1946 to 1949, Soviet officials preferred to sell their goods elsewhere in Western Europe. Even during the years 1948 to 1952, when the Soviets were buying from and selling to other Western Europeans in substantial amounts, Soviet foreign trade companies avoided West German contacts.[181] At the same time, the Federal Republic concentrated its Eastern efforts on the politically less complicated task of building trade and trade contacts in those countries with which old JEIA agreements existed.

After the Soviet-sponsored Moscow World Economic Conference of April 1952 failed to produce significant European defections from the Western embargo program, Soviet export agencies began offering supplies of wood, grain, and oil to West German import firms.[182] Against the background of the Bundestag resolution on East-West trade from 6 May 1952 and the cabinet's resolution and public statement on 24 June endorsing an expansion of the "legal trade" with the East, the Economics Ministry welcomed Soviet offers of raw materials and encouraged such imports.[183] These earliest exchanges were constructed as "compensation deals" – essentially barter transactions in which the West German import/export firm arranged for both the import of Soviet products and the export of an offsetting amount of German goods (leather, textiles, machines, chemicals, and some consumer goods). Since the High Commission had earlier forbidden the Federal Republic from establishing a clearing system for payments with the Soviets, an internal Economics Ministry meeting had agreed that compensation deals were the best way to proceed.[184]

As West German purchases from the USSR began to pick up in 1953, pressure increased on the Economics Ministry to facilitate increased West German imports by authorizing direct payments to the Soviets in TAA-pounds. (TAA refers to Transferable Accounts Area, an international payments system to which both the FRG and the USSR belonged and in which accounts were carried in sterling.) Within the Economics Ministry, the Department for Industrial Policy (Main Department IV) urged the approval of direct payments with transferable pounds to take advantage of Soviet export offers on timber and especially oil (20,000 tons/month).[185] Seiberlich responded that "imports from the Soviet Union on the basis of compensation deals are in every case to receive preference, since export opportunities for the German economy must be created, and Germany gains importance as a direct trade partner."[186]

The conscious and explicitly articulated strategy of insisting on bilaterally balanced compensation deals as the basis for trade with the USSR forced the Soviets to accept West German products as payment for Soviet raw materials marketed in the FRG. The West German policy countered lingering Soviet reluctance to take West German exports as long as the FRG refused to recognize the postwar settlement in Central and Eastern Europe.[187] On 20 October 1953, the interministerial Trade Policy Committee reaffirmed the policy of "preference" for compensation deals, although it did allow Seiberlich to permit transferable pound payments in exceptional cases.[188]

Over the next eighteen months the Economics Ministry steadily pursued its goal of expanding West Germany's position in the Soviet market by linking German exports to German imports via compensation trade. Economics Ministry "preference" for compensation deals led to the cancellation of dozens of proposed West German cash purchases from the Soviets; only in exceptional cases would the ministry authorize pound or dollar payments. The Economics Ministry held firmly to its policy, claiming to take the "long-term view" of German-Soviet trade and stating plainly that "the point of all our efforts is the development of the German export trade through expansion of the market space available to it."[189] The Economics Ministry chose to interpret the trade statistics for 1952 to 1954 as supporting its claims that it was possible for the Federal Republic to force-feed exports to the Soviets (Table 8.6). From 1952 to 1955, the FRG rose steadily from last among the West Europeans to become the Soviets' third most important Western European trade partner, behind only the U.K. and France. The very substantial Soviet orders to West German shipyards (DM 100 million by December 1953, DM 500 million by March 1954) might also be credited to the Economics Ministry export policy.

Yet the compensation system had a number of disadvantages, notably the high degree of dissatisfaction it engendered in the West German business community. The Economics Ministry was showered with applications by German firms for exemptions to the compensation rules. Industrial and commercial firms (Klöckner, Kupferberg & Co., Gratenau, Ohlert) complained bitterly to the Economics Ministry that negotiating a purchase from the cumbersome Soviet bureaucracy was trying enough even in the best of times; negotiating a purchase and a sale simultaneously with two different Soviet foreign trade companies was frequently impossible. Each had numerous examples of import deals that had died while waiting for the Soviets to sign a deal for the corresponding counter-purchase. Therefore, the Soviet trade would not expand significantly until or unless the Economics Ministry authorized payment for German imports in TAA-pounds. At the very least, the Economics Ministry must allow a West German bank to issue the backup letters of credit, since this would help speed up the payments process and eliminate fees to the foreign banks.[190]

Steel export firms Stahlunion-Export and Otto Wolff told Boris Meissner at the Foreign Office's Soviet desk that a clearing agreement was the "absolute precondition" for a real expansion of trade with the Soviets.[191] Other industrialists explained that without a full-scale West German-Soviet trade agreement, the Soviets could not plan their exports to the Federal Republic. As a result, West German importers generally could obtain only insufficient quantities or poor quality "leftovers" from planned Soviet trade with other countries. A similar situation prevailed for West German exports. Maltzan noted that a chief drawback of the current compensation system was the Soviet use of West Germany primarily as a "stop-gap ... while regular business, especially in the consumer goods sector, which is important for us, goes to those countries which, like England and France, have concluded merchandise trade agreements with the Soviet Union."[192] Insisting on compensation deals also meant foregoing advantageous import purchases worth millions of deutsche marks when offsetting exports could not be arranged. These major problems in the West German-Soviet economic relationship could be resolved by devising some form of trade and payments agreement with the Soviets. In addition, an understanding on delivery terms had to be arranged before the West German shipyards completed work on Soviet ship orders.

Some political motives also spoke in favor of a properly regulated trade relationship with the Soviets. Kroll had foreseen as early as the spring of 1952 that the SPD's parliamentary inquiry into embargo policies and increasing interest in Soviet contracts among the business community would require improved trade relations with the Soviets.[193] The West German Foreign Office subsequently saw advantage in a trade agreement since it would place the Western embargo restrictions in economic perspective by "making clear the limited volume of exchange which trade with the Soviet Union by its very nature must have." This, in turn, would "reduce to a proper scale criticisms of the Federal government, that are based on overly high expectations in the private-sector."[194] This combination of macroeconomic, microeconomic, and political considerations brought the

Economics Ministry, the business community, and the Foreign Office together in the conviction that some type of general trade agreement with the Soviets should be pursued.

In May 1952, the federal government began to consider in earnest the problem of reaching a comprehensive commercial agreement with the Soviets. Despite the creation of the Eastern Committee, pursuit of a trade agreement was complicated by the larger political issues surrounding the unresolved German question, including diplomatic and public relations posturing on a possible reunification of the two Germanies, the uncertainty of the Oder-Neisse line, West German refusal to recognize the Soviet bloc people's democracies, and lack of diplomatic relations between the FRG and the USSR. Along with the "general consensus" in the Economics Ministry that the Federal Republic must somehow get a regular trade relationship with the Soviets, there was a corresponding realization that the political "preconditions" would require "substantial time" to iron out.[195] The Foreign Office well understood that finding "the most suitable form for [German-Soviet] economic agreements in accordance with the political situation and trade interests" would be no easy task.[196]

The first West German attempts to arrange some more general trade agreement with the Soviets came via the West German private-sector and were supported by the Americans. In response to a Soviet inquiry, members of the West German steel industry met with Soviet foreign trade officials in Copenhagen in August 1952.[197] Erhard favored renewed contacts with the Soviets, but refused to let the meeting take place until he had "informed the Allies and obtained their permission." At a meeting with Herbert Blankenhorn, head of the Political Department of the Foreign Office, and State Secretary Otto Lenz of the Chancellor's Office, Allied representatives Kiefer (U.S. high commissioner's East-West Trade Group) and Colonel Griffin (British High Commissioner's Office) "explicitly denied" having any hesitations about the proposed discussions with the Soviets. Griffin "explicitly emphasized" his hope that the meeting contribute positively to the "reconstruction of economic relations between the Federal Republic and the Soviet Union."[198] In Copenhagen the Germans suggested a "broadly based trade agreement," citing the existing West German trade treaties with Poland, Czechoslovakia, and Hungary. Soviet Vice-Minister for Foreign Trade Borisov acknowledged the German offer as "serious and interesting" but as something that would require "detailed consideration" by the Soviet government, adding his "personal opinion" that the treaty suggestion would not meet "fundamental opposition" in Moscow.[199] The Soviets then inexplicably failed to pick up on the trade treaty suggestion or on the German suggestion for another round of more detailed talks on a list of commodities for exchange.[200]

After key personnel decisions were finalized in October 1952, the private-sector Eastern Committee was ready to assume its prescribed function as the contact point between the Federal Republic and the Soviet Union. A first round of very preliminary discussions between the Eastern Committee and Soviet trade representatives took place in the background of the April 1953 United Nations trade development meeting in Geneva. Wolff, Edwin von Carnap, and Ziegesar (machine-building interest group) met with members of the Soviet Ministry for Internal and Foreign Trade and established a working relationship with the Soviet trade attaché stationed in Bern, Kurepov.[201] At their next meeting with Kurepov at his offices in Bern, the Eastern Committee members presented their idea for the conclusion of a "framework agreement" (Rahmenabkommen) that would set the basic terms for all West German industrial sales to the Soviets.[202]

Over the following two years political uncertainties first inside the Soviet Union (the first phase of the Stalin succession struggle) and then within the Western alliance (the EDC debacle) prevented sustained negotiations between the Soviets and the Eastern Committee, so that no real progress was achieved between July 1953 and August 1954. After the Central Committee's expulsion of Politburo member Lavrenty Beria from the party in July 1953 opened the political struggle in the USSR, the Soviets failed to respond to Eastern Committee letters of 16 September and 19 October 1953.[203] Only "loose discussions" were held at the Leipzig Trade Fair in October, although the Soviets did extend an invitation for German industrialists to visit Moscow. Reporting to Economics Ministry's Advisory Board on Foreign Trade, the Eastern Committee declared that its talks with the Soviets so far "had come to nothing" and that the invitation to Moscow did not, in itself, promise any progress.[204] The Germans let their Soviet contacts lapse over the winter of 1953 to 1954.

After Molotov used the Berlin Conference in early 1954 to hint at an expansion of East-West trade, the Soviets took the initiative. On 9 February Kurepov asked the Eastern Committee for a preliminary meeting in Bern to arrange a second, larger meeting in April at the Soviet Embassy in East Berlin. In Berlin, the Soviets asked for a "larger economic delegation" of about eighteen members from "the most important firms" to travel to Moscow to discuss deals "in concrete terms." At the United Nations conference on European trade in May 1954, representatives from the West German Foreign Office took an active part for the first time in the negotiations. Zahn-Stranik told the Soviets that only a small Eastern Committee delegation could travel to Moscow. The Soviets accepted and a West German delegation of six prepared to depart for Moscow in late May to discuss the "volume and composition of a German-Soviet commodity exchange as well as the arrangement of a clearing system" of payments.[205]

At the last minute Adenauer delayed and then forbade the Eastern Committee's planned trip to Moscow. Since that time, it has been widely assumed that the Americans pressured the chancellor not to allow the overly eager pursuit of the Soviet market indicated by this highly publicized trip. In fact, the Americans had no objections to the proposed Moscow visit. In response to Eastern Committee inquires on this very point, the office of the U.S. high commissioner had already assured Carnap that members of the Eastern Committee would experience no subsequent "difficulties" in visiting the United States as a result of traveling to Moscow as part of a quasi-official delegation from the Federal Republic.[206] This is not surprising in light of new information about American support for the 1952 Copenhagen meeting at a time of generally much higher East-West tension. Wolff has asserted that Foreign Office State Secretary Otto Hallstein (the hardest of the anti-Soviet hardliners) "lied" to Adenauer about the American attitude toward the planned trip in order to bring Adenauer out against the Moscow visit.[207] Wolff's account is supported by Adenauer's confidential statements that "not all officials of the Foreign Office had acted intelligently (klug gehandelt) in relations with the Eastern Committee," regarding the proposed trip and that he himself "had not been informed or only inadequately informed by the gentlemen of the Foreign Office."[208]

In the end, the mutual accusations surrounding American approval of the trip were only an informative sideshow; Foreign Office notes indicate that Adenauer stopped the planned visit in order to spare French sensibilities rather than American ones. French perceptions of West German foreign policy were especially critical in the summer of 1954 as France finally prepared itself to vote on the EDC initiative.[209] Any perception of an emerging West German-Soviet rapproachment beginning with a trade agreement (and the cries of "Rapallo!" that would certainly follow) would only complicate Adenauer's drive to recover German sovereignty as it approached a critical juncture.[210]

Furious over the abrupt public cancellation of the trip and the consequent implication, widely circulated in the West German press, that the Eastern Committee's business activities were not in the best interests of the FRG, Wolff arranged a meeting with Adenauer to clear the air.[211] That meeting on 22 June explicitly confirmed a broad consensus between Adenauer and the members of the Eastern Committee about the priorities and goals of West German policy toward the Soviet Union. Adenauer posited the "primacy of politics over economics, especially in relations with East." Reuter and Wolff confirmed the "subordination of economic interests to the political" in dealing with the Soviets, noting that they "had no great illusions about the scale and success of trade with the Eastern bloc."[212] With these fundamental priorities established, Adenauer listened to the business view that "trade with the USSR must be normalized … brought into a treaty-like state."[213]

On 30 June 1954, the presidium of the Eastern Committee wrote to the Soviet Trade Office in East Berlin explaining that "timing of the trip had been unfortunate" since "in view of the situation at the moment such a trip could lead to misinterpretations." It suggested that "in the interest of future trade relations, a postponement [of the trip] might be the proper thing."[214] Having cleared the air with Adenauer, the Eastern Committee itself accepted the postponement as a temporary setback; the rest of the German business community took its cue from the Eastern Committee and found little cause for concern.[215]

While anxious to avoid the possible negative diplomatic repercussions that might have resulted from a public German-Soviet trade agreement in the summer of 1954, federal authorities were nonetheless eager to do everything possible to expand German-Soviet trade. The Trade Policy Committee fulfilled one of the main purposes of the scuttled trip (a payments arrangement with the Soviets) by authorizing the Rhein-Ruhr Bank (Dusseldorf) to establish a pound-sterling account for the Soviet State Bank.[216] With this low-visibility move, the Trade Policy Committee authorized a de facto, though unofficial, clearing system for German-Soviet trade payments. The Economics Ministry thereafter loosened its compensation requirements.[217] During the annual Soviet "buying season" in the autumn, Soviet foreign trade companies placed sharply increased orders in West Germany. The small surge in West German exports the following year, 1955, was helped along by the new payment modalities.

Despite the May 1954 setback, the Eastern Committee resumed contact with the Soviets at the next opportunity, the October 1954 meeting of the United Nations European Trade Committee in Geneva.[218] On October 16 and 18, Zahn-Stranik and members of the Eastern Committee (including, again, Wolff and Carnap) had substantial discussions with the head of the Soviet delegation, Cheklin. At these meetings both sides agreed that the Eastern Committee should submit a draft agreement on terms of delivery, payment, and "other general rules" governing German-Soviet trade. To this agreement would be appended the annual commodity lists specifying the volume and composition of trade for the upcoming year. (This was the form of the trade mechanism negotiated by the Eastern Committee with Rumania in 1953.) Cheklin cited the availability of manganese, chromium, soft timber, pit-props, cellulose, asbestos, and oil for delivery against German ships and machinery. Both sides agreed to continue the negotiations "at a quicker pace than had previously been the case" and to use Kurepov at the Soviet trade office in Bern as the intermediary.[219] At this point, continuing uncertainty in the Soviet leadership and the abandonment of Politburo member Georgi Malenkov's New Course in the spring of 1955 caused considerable delay in the following negotiations. A January 1955 meeting in Bern had to be canceled because Kurepov was recalled to Moscow for consultations in conjunction with Malenkov's impending demotion.[220]

On 26 April 1955, Reuter asked Hallstein for permission to approach the Soviets again about resuming negotiations at a neutral site or, if necessary, in Moscow. Noting that "the previous foreign policy considerations against the departure of the Eastern Committee delegation for Moscow have since ceased to exist as a consequence of the ratification of the Paris Treaties," the Foreign Office's Commercial Affairs Department recommended that the Eastern Committee be given permission both to open negotiations at a neutral site and to accept the expected invitation to Moscow.[221] At this point the efforts of the Eastern Committee to negotiate quietly with Soviet trade officials were once again overtaken by larger political considerations.

On 7 June 1955 a Soviet note inviting Adenauer to Moscow for high-level talks on the possibility of establishing formal diplomatic relations between the Federal Republic and the USSR was handed to Maltzan at the West German embassy in Paris. The Soviet note of 7 June and the follow-up note of 3 August expressly mentioned the "establishment of diplomatic, trade and cultural relations." The Federal Republic's answering notes of 30 June and 19 August accepted trade talks as part of the overall negotiations.[222]

Across the board, the West Germans believed that Soviet economic difficulties played a major role in the desire to normalize relations with the FRG.[223] Adenauer himself was convinced that "the Soviet government endeavored to establish diplomatic relations with us in the special hope of thereby being able to expand their trade relations with us."[224] Because the Eastern Committee had been conducting informal trade negotiations with the Soviets for almost three years, it was widely assumed on the West German side that those economic negotiations would now fall together with political discussions in Moscow. The Foreign Office saw the overlapping of commercial and political discussion as an opening for the use of economic diplomacy: "Within the framework of the other questions to be discussed [in Moscow], the conclusion of an [economic] agreement suitable to the Soviets is an important negotiating tool held by the Federal Republic."[225] Yet in the absence of any detailed instructions from the chancellor on how he planned to proceed in the Moscow negotiations, no operational plan could be drafted that tied West German economic favors to Soviet political concessions.[226]

Detailed suggestions for the use of West German economic and financial strength to bring forth Soviet political concessions came from Economics Minister Erhard. He was convinced that "economic concessions ... carry substantial weight" in Soviet calculations, and he understood that "our present state of economic development puts us in the position to offer significant economic compensation for important political concessions." Erhard suggested that Adenauer could offer "generous export credits, perhaps even in the form of transferable DM." In exchange, the FRG would demand the "fulfillment of genuine political demands in the direction of reunification," specifically, free access to West Berlin in the form of international road and rail connections, creation of an all-German court for human rights; free circulation of books and newspapers, the right to travel between East and West Germany, and full freedom for the churches.[227]

One theme that connected all West German thinking on these issues was the view that, from the economic perspective, the FRG did not need an economic agreement with the Soviets.[228] With West German industry operating at near capacity and at full employment, it was actually questionable whether significant Soviet orders for industrial equipment could be accommodated![229] Members of the Eastern Committee admitted that a significant increase in total exports from the FRG was not possible and that "a shift in trade relations to the detriment of new markets won since the war was not economically justified." A month later, Carnap and Reuter acknowledged that the West German machine-building industry had additional industrial capacity for Soviet orders but that obtaining and holding the corresponding number of additional workers would be "exceedingly difficult."[230] On the import side, West German industry had interest in Soviet raw iron, nickel and manganese ores, timber, anthracite coal, and oil.[231] Here, the FRG faced the question of how it might import substantially increased quantities of these goods from the East without reducing the imports from the West that ultimately secured foreign markets for West German exports.[232]

Any plans to sign an economic agreement in exchange for Soviet political concessions went too far, too fast for Adenauer. His economic goals for the Moscow visit went no further than establishing a Mixed Commission that would begin substantive economic negotiations at a later date.[233] Adenauer's strategy reflected Erhard's sound advice not to allow the Soviets to cover up a political deadlock between the two states with a "superficial partial success" in the form of an economic agreement."[234]

Much to the surprise of the Germans, substantive trade talks with the Soviets never emerged in the course of the five-day Moscow visit. The Soviets offered the usual platitudes about the mutual gains of closer economic relations, but consistently refused to get involved in concrete discussions. On September 10, Hallstein waved some economic bait in a short speech devoted to the advantages to be had from a "revival of the traditional trade between the Federal Republic and the Soviet Union" and the need for discussions about the volume and composition of an exchange of goods. Nikita Khrushchev, emerging as the preeminent figure in the Soviet Politburo, noted that the day's sessions had been "interesting," but he never responded directly to Hallstein's offer. The Soviets also ignored Adenauer's idea for the immediate establishment of a Mixed Commission.[235] Albert Hilger van Scherpenberg, head of the Trade Policy Department in the Foreign Office, concluded from his unofficial talks with Soviet trade representatives, including Deputy Foreign Trade Minister Kumykin, that the Soviets had made a "political decision at the highest level" not to engage in "concrete" economic negotiations at this time.[236] When the German delegation departed Moscow on September 14, nothing specific had been done about a trade agreement, a payments agreement, or about a list of commodities for immediate exchange; nor had a Mixed Commission been established.

On the positive side, both parties had agreed in the final sentence of the 13 September joint communique that "consultations on the question of trade development will be held between the Soviet Union and the Federal Republic in the near future."[237] With the establishment of full diplomatic relations, trade talks could resume, now on the official level. After the on-again-off-again, semiclandestine negotiations of 1952 to 1954, the prospect of regular, official contact was clearly encouraging.

On the other hand, it was unclear how the addition of official German representatives to the negotiations would affect the existing relations between the Soviets and the Eastern Committee (which, despite the fits and starts of the past three years, had already reached the point of submitting a draft agreement for Soviet review). Nor was it clear how the direct inclusion of the federal ministerial bureaucracy would alter the mixture of political and economic motives in West German trade policy toward the Soviet Union. These questions could be answered only after trade negotiations resumed in 1956.

Notes

1. The London Conference of Deputy Foreign Ministers communique stated that the Germans would be allowed "to assume those governmental responsibilities which are compatible with the minimum requirements of occupation and control and which ultimately will enable them to assume full governmental responsibility," London Six-Power Conference, Text of Communique, with Annex on International Control of the Ruhr," 2 June 1948 in United States Department of State, *Germany 1947-1949: The Story in Documents,* European and British Commonwealth Series 9, Publication 3556 (Washington, D.C., 1950). On political developments in the period 1949-1952/54 see Elmer Plischke, *The Allied High Commission for Germany* (Bonn, 1953); Plischke, *History of the Allied High Commission for Germany. Its Establishment, Structure, and Procedures* (Bonn, 1951); Manfred Funcke, ed., *Entscheidung für den Westen: vom Besatzungsstatut zur Souveränität der Bundesrepublik Deutschland* (Bonn, 1987); Ludolf Herbst et al., eds., *Vom Marshallplan zur EWG. Die Eingliederung der Bundesrepublik Deutschland in der westlichen Welt* (Munich, 1990); Thomas A. Schwartz, *America's Germany. John J. McCloy and the Federal Republic of Germany* (Cambridge, Mass., 1991); Hermann-Josef Rupieper, *Der besetzte Verbündete: die amerikanische Deutschlandpolitik 1949-1955* (Opladen, 1991).
2. "Instructions from Military Governors of U.S., U.K., and French Zones to German Ministers President," in State Department, *Germany 1947-1949*, 275-76.
3. The Occupation Statute was published at the conclusion of the Washington Foreign Ministers Conference 8 April 1949; "Text of Occupation Statute," State Department, *Germany 1947-1949*, 89-91; "Charter of the Allied High Commission for Germany, art. II.1," State Department, *Germany 1947-1949*, 92-97.
4. Paragraph five of the Trizonal Fusion Agreement stipulated: "In cases in which the exercise of, or failure to exercise, the powers reserved under paragraph 2(g) of the Occupation Statute would increase the need for assistance from United States Government appropriated funds, there shall be a system of weighted voting. Under such a system the representatives of the occupation authorities will have a voting strength proportionate to the funds made available to Germany by their respective governments. This provision shall not, however, reduce the present United States predominant voice in Joint Export-Import Agency and Joint Foreign Exchange Agency while these organizations, or any successor organization to them, continue in existence and are charged with the performance of any of their present functions," Trizonal Fusion Agreement, State Department, *Germany 1947-1949*, 91-92. This was one of two exceptions to the usual practice of majority voting, the other – amendments to the West German Basic Law – required unanimous approval from the High Commission.
5. On McCloy as president of the IBRD see Schwartz, *America's Germany*, 26 ff. For a perspective on McCloy throughout a lengthy career see Alan Brinkley, "The Most Influential Private Citizen in America," *Harpers*, February 1983, 31-46. Within McCloy's office, the Office for Economic Affairs was headed first by Robert Hanes, an industrialist from North Carolina and then by Jean Cattier, a Belgian by birth who made his career with the White, Weld & Co. investment house in New York. Finally, M.S. Harris came over from the ECA to assume the post until it expired. Within the Office for Economic Affairs John C. Renner headed the Eastern Economic Relations Division, with primary responsibility for implementing U.S. policy on East-West trade within the U.S. zone. Whyner, who had worked with JEIA on trade negotiations with Eastern Europe just at the time that JEIA began imposing security controls on Eastern trade, was also brought into the Eastern Economics Relations Division.

6. Plischke, *History of the Allied High Commission for Germany*, 107; Charter of the High Commission, Article III.1(b).
7. Charter of the High Commission, art. III.3(b).
8. The Foreign Trade Committee established five subcommittees: JEIA liquidation, customs, current affairs, interzonal trade, and export control. Both the export control and the customs subcommittees took part in reviewing and restricting West German exports to the Soviet bloc. When the Foreign Trade Committee was dissolved as part of the commission's reorganization in the spring of 1951, the customs subcommittee was reformed as working party and transferred to the Economics Committee. A second reorganization in December 1951 brought about the merger of the previously independent economics and finance committees. A new East-West Trade Subcommittee was formed to review West German trade with the Soviet bloc. Shortly thereafter an Export Control Working Party was established specifically to contain the flow of strategic exports to the East. On these developments see Plischke, *History of the Allied High Commission*, 107-135, passim.
9. Thomas Schwartz has noted that "McCloy directed almost all his appeals [for stricter export controls] to the Adenauer government from his position as American High Commissioner and Chief of the ECA in Germany," see "European Integration and the 'Special Relationship': Implementing the Marshall Plan in the Federal Republic, in Charles Maier and Günter Bischof, eds., *The Marshall Plan and Germany* (Providence, 1991), 203.
10. Specifically by Kiefer in the East-West Trade Subcommittee of the Allied High Commission; by Renner in the Eastern Economic Relations Division of the U.S. High Commissioner's Office; by Cattier as Head of ECA Special Mission and of the Economic Affairs Office of the U.S. High Commissioner's Office; and by Harriman in the Coordinating Committee negotiations in Paris.
11. Maltzan to Erhard, 26 September 1949, BA B 102/1986.
12. BA B 102/1986.
13. AGSEC (49) 160 in BA B 102/1986.
14. Article IV of the Petersburg Protocol. November 22, 1949.
15. AGSEC (51) 413, March 7, 1951; AGSEC (51) 550, March 30, 1951; and AGSEC (51) 1121, July 3, 1951 in Plischke, *History of the Allied High Commission*, 164. The generally well-informed foreign trade adviser to the Bayer chemical firm, Jost Terhaar, considered it "questionable" whether the West German "foreign trade bureaucracy" was capable of properly executing the new responsibilites handed to it, 2 September and 25 November 1949, Bayer-Archiv 67/2, vol. 1.
16. Internal Economics Ministry memo to Erhard in BA B 102/7196 H.1; Kroll's notes in BA B 102/2366 H.1
17. MacReady's letter, 14 July 1951, BA B 102/7196 H.1. Maltzan responded bravely that "when negotiating the trade volume of strategically important goods, German negotiators are instructed to adhere to the internationally agreed upon practices [i.e. COCOM] and to stubbornly and toughly present German positions," Maltzan to MacReady, 8 August 1951, BA B 102/7196 H.1
18. Hans Kroll, director of the Economics Ministry's special East-West trade group, to Economics Minister Erhard and State Secretary Ludger Westrick, 21 April 1952, BA B 102/7196 H.1
19. The French and British unenthusiastically supported the American decision, "The United States High Commissioner for Germany (McCloy) to the Secretary of State," *FRUS*, 1949, vol. 5, 154, notes 5 and 6.
20. *FRUS*, 1949, vol. 5, 172-73.
21. Ibid.
22. Classified report on the "Development and Construction of COCOM" by the Economics Ministry's desk for International Questions on East-West Trade (V A

6), April 1953, BA B 102/7196 H.2; "Report on East-West Trade," March 1953 by Trade Policy Department of the Foreign Office, PAAA 311.22/1.

23. BA B 102/3266 H.1; BA B 102/55998; McCloy's speech, 26 June 1951, *Department of State Bulletin*, 9 July 1951, 66

24. Brentano to Erhard, Jakob Kaiser, minister for Intra-German Affairs, and Robert Lehr, interior minister, 1 June, 1951, BA B 102/2366 H.1

25. Erhard to Brentano, 19 June 1951, BA B 102/2366 H.1

26. The agency was classified as an Oberbehörde by the German authorities, McCloy to the secretary of state, 30 December 1949, *FRUS*, 1949, vol. 5, 182-83. Since the creation of a separate Ministry for Foreign Trade had already been rejected, the Economics Ministry was the logical choice for the location of this new unit, Edgar Randall, *Das Bundesministerium für Wirtschaft*, 24-25.

27. BA B 102/7228 H.1

28. The Central Export Control Group received its information on export policy directly from the Federal Republic's COCOM representative, Witzel, at the Economics Ministry's desk for Import and Export Policy Questions (V D 2). Routine commercial policy toward the East, including the negotiation of the annual import/export lists, was the job of the Economics Ministry's subdepartment for Foreign Trade with Eastern Europe (V A 7). The lack of a direct line of communication either from Witzel or from the Central Export Control Group to the East European foreign trade desk meant that relevant export control information often did not reach the officials responsible for normal commercial negotiations with Eastern Europe. As a result of this confusion, Economics Ministry negotiators promised exports of goods that the Germans themselves and the High Commission's Export Control Working Party later vetoed. The situation was similar to that prevailing in the Bizonia in 1948 and early 1949 when JEIA remained uninformed about the Bipartite Control Office's export restrictions, and promised goods that were later vetoed.

29. Memorandum of conversation between Witzel and members of the High Commission's East-West Trade Subcommittee, 2 February 1951, BA B 102/7233. The West German business community also urged some organizational clarification so that "one office of the federal government could take full responsibility" for East-West trade, the influential private-sector Working Group on Foreign Trade to Adenauer, 15 March 1952, BA B 136/7807.

30. On the development of the Central Licensing Office see BA B 102/7228 H.1; Terhaar's well-informed reports (2 March, 28 April, 23 June), Bayer-Archiv 67/2, vol. 2; for McCloy's action, McCloy to Adenauer, 24 November 1950, cited in Schwartz, "The 'Special Relationship'," 204 note 63. In his report of 21 April 1950 Terhaar remarked that the U.S. High Commissioner's Office had "noticeably sharpened" its licensing procedures.

31. John Renner, head of the Eastern Economic Relations Dvision in the U.S. High Commissioner's Office, explained to Westrick how the "mood" of the American public had made Congressional action (the Kem amendment and the Battle Act) unavoidable. Zahn-Stranik's notes, 25 March 1952, BA B 102/7201 H.1.

32. "Confidential Allied Statement on Foreign Trade and Exchange and Strategic Commodities Export Controls," 18 July 1951, BA B 102/2366 H.1.

33. BA B 102/2366 H.1.

34. HICOG's statement that "this mission has long been intimately acquainted with the development and functioning of the Central Export Control Agency" was no exaggeration. As late as February 1953 the Americans intervened to express disapproval of a planned reduction in the Central Export Control Agency's staff from the current level of 140 persons, HICOG Aide-Memoire to the Cancellor's Office, 13 February 1953, BA B 136/7807.

35. As early as June 1950 Erhard had told Adenauer that "the English are most deci-sively" in favor of rebuilding economic relations with Eastern Europe, while the Americans tend to view East-West trade "more from the political angle," Erhard to the Chancellor's Office, 23 June 1950, BA B 102/55998. These conflicting views on East-West trade reflect basic economic realities. The U.K. held the largest share of Western Europe's trade with the East; 25 percent of Western Europe's imports from the East went to the U.K. and 18 percent of Western Europe's exports to Eastern Europe came from the U.K. Although imports from Eastern Europe made up only 2.5 percent of the U.K.'s total imports, they accounted for roughly one-third of its total grain imports and one-fourth of its soft timber imports. U.S. trade with the East was negligible at this time.

36. Central Licensing Office report for November 1951, BA B 102/7233.

37. For explanations of the shift in Western export control policy see Robert Mark Spaulding, "'A Gradual and Moderate Relaxation': Eisenhower and the Revision of American Export Control Policy," *Diplomatic History* 17 (Spring 1993), 223-49 and the literature cited there.

38. "Final Act of the Nine-Power Conference Held in London 28 September to 3 October 1954," Ruhm von Oppen, *Documents on Germany Under Occupation*, 600-09.

39. PAAA 311.22/3. A few institutional changes dragged on through 1955, e.g. not until the summer of 1955 did the High Commission's Military Security Board (MSB) pass out of existence in accordance with Article 2(2) of the Protocol on the Termination of the Occupation Regime in the Federal Republic. Its duty to mon-itor the import and export of directly applicable military goods was assumed by the Economics Ministry.

40. An explicit elaboration of the obvious parallels with Weimar Germany's position in the international order of the 1920s has been reserved for the Conclusion.

41. Thomas Schwartz has even suggested that American officials in Germany did not consider strict West German compliance with the embargo program to be an important issue and that the High Commissioner's office pressured the Germans only to appease congressional and American public opinion, "The Special Rela-tionship," in Maier and Bischof, eds., *The Marshall Plan and Germany*, 205.

42. Erhard noted that these issues had been discussed with the High Commission's "economic advisers" at a meeting in the Petersberg on 7 June 1950 in which the Occupation authorities "expressly declared that the Federal Republic is allowed to trade with the East-bloc countries within the limits set by the embargo lists." Further, the Allies had "no qualms" about the conclusion of trade treaties between the FRG and Soviet bloc countries, and were prepared to place their own diplomatic missions in Soviet bloc countries at the disposal of the FRG in order to facilitate the conclusion of trade treaties, Erhard to Adenauer, 13 June 1950, BA B 136/7807.

43. See below for a number of these cases treated in some detail. Studies that focus on German-American trade and economic issues in the 1950s have tended to empha-size the embargo issue and the publicly-aired differences of opinion between the less informed elements of public and parliamentary/congressional opinion in both countries. See Hanns-Dieter Jacobsen, *Ost-West Wirtschaftsbeziehungen als deutsch-amerikanisches Problem* (Baden Baden, 1986), 54-69; Angela Stent, *From Embargo to Ostpolitik* (Cambridge, 1981), 31 ff.; Gunther Mai, "Osthandel und Westintegration 1947-1957," in Ludolf Herbst et al., eds., *Die Eingliederung der Bun-desrepublik Deutschland in die westliche Welt* (München, 1990), 203-26.

44. Although made in reference to a single specific meeting in 1952, Kroll's comment that he "thought it correct to infrom [the Americans] about the real attitude (tat-sächlice Haltung) of the Federal Government regarding East-West trade" was

characteristic of West German governmental views in the early 1950s, Kroll memorandum, 5 December 1952, BA B 136/7807.

45. Institutional surveys of the West German political system are available in Thomas Ellwein, *Das Regierungssystem der Bundesrepublik Deutschland* (Opladen, 1973) and Hans Pohl et. al., eds., *Deutsche Verwaltungsgeschichte*, vol. 5. (Stuttgart, 1987).

46. Substantial factual information on the organization of the Federal Republic's Eastern trade structures, including those participating directly in the COCOM program, is available in the contemporary West Germany accounts by W. Trautmann, *Osthandel – Ja oder Nein* (1954); Hans-Jürgen Lambers, *Das Ostembargo* (Frankfurt, 1956); R. Haase, *Theorie und Politik des Embargos* (Cologne, 1973). Using these sources summaries early developments in *Osthandel und Ostpolitik* (Baden-Baden, 1978), 37-51.

47. From 1950 through 1954 Josef Seiberlich manned the foreign trade desk for Eastern and Southeastern Europe, supervised by assistant undersecretary Hermann Reinhardt until Reinhardt succeeded Maltzan as head of Foreign Economic Policy Department in late 1952.

48. The Economics Ministry would provide both the chairmanship and the secretariat for the new Trade Policy Committee. Since the Trade Policy Committee was to "establish a unified line for German trade policy and coordinate the activity of the participating ministries in this sphere," holding the chairmanship could be used as a powerful weapon by the Economics Ministry in the event of intramural trade policy disputes. For the origins and organizational history of the Trade Policy Committee see BA B 102/1986. Both the idea for and name of the committee were borrowed from the important interministerial Trade Policy Committee of Weimar period.

49. Memorandum by Dr. Schwarz of the Foreign Office's organizational desk to Herbert Blankenhorn (head of the important Political Division) and State Secretary Otto Hallstein, 4 August 1952, PAAA 413.22, vol.1. Schwarz's notes were a response to Chancellery State Secretary Otto Lenz's comment of May 1952 that the Economics Ministry remained the "preferred ministry for the conceptualization and conduct of East-West trade."

50. Ibid.

51. In May 1951 the Foreign Office employed 307 upper-level civil servants; less than one year later this number had grown to 469, Wilhelm Haas, *Beitrag zur Geschichte der Entstehung des Auswaertigen Dienstes der Bundesrepublik Deutschland* (Bonn, 1969), 58. A number of Foreign Office officials who would play important roles in the Federal Republic's Eastern trade policies had been working in the Economics Ministry: for example, Rolf Lahr, Albert Hilger van Scherpenberg, and Lupin.

52. Dr. Scholz, responsible for East-West Trade in the Economics Ministry (V A 7) to the sixteenth meeting of the Committee on Central Export Control, 19 November 1953, BA B 102/7203.

53. Scholz speech on East-West trade to the forty-fourth meeting of the Länder Committee on Foreign Trade, 28 January 1954, BA B 102/7198 H.2.

54. Through 1952, Allied representatives had dealt exclusively with the Economics Ministry when discussing matters of East-West trade. However, by 1954 Scholz was complaining that membes of the U.S. High Commissioner's Office now went to the Foreign Office instead of the Economics Ministry to discuss trade problems, Scholz's notes, 15 November 1954, BA B 102/55998.

55. In an article "On the Question of East-West Trade" to appear the *Braunschweigerischen Industrie- und Handelsblatt* in August 1954, Maltzan summarized West Germany policy by saying that "within the limits set by political necessity, the federal government seeks to increase the Eastern trade beyond its present low level," BA B 136/7807.

56. In 1951 the five traditional leading German export industries (machinery, motor vehicles, electricals, metal products, and opticals) produced a combined trade surplus of DM 5,552 million and finished goods accounted for three-quarters of West German exports. By 1952 the FRG as a whole had achieved a positive trade balance and had the largest accounts surplus in the European Payments Union, Economics Ministry, *Deutschland im Wiederaufbau* (Bonn, 1952), 114. For studies of the West German economic revival in the 1950s see Henry Wallich, *Mainsprings of German Revival* (New Haven, 1955); Erhard, *Germany's Comeback in the World Market* (London, 1954); Simon Reich, *The Fruits of Fascism. Postwar Prosperity in Historical Perspective* (Ithaca, 1990). More generally, Werner Abelshauser, *Wirtschaftsgeschichte der Bundesrepublik Deutschland 1945-1980* (Frankfurt, 1983); Eric Owen Smith, *The West German Economy*, (London, 1983); Hans-Joachim Braun, *The German Economy in the Twentieth Century* (New York, 1990), 165 ff.

57. In the most dramatic case, Poland was transformed from an exporter of substantial agricultural surpluses in the interwar period to an importer of foodstuffs from the Federal Republic beginning in 1953! On these postwar transactions and their political consequences, see below.

58. Only producers on the very low end of the manufacturing spectrum (makers of basic glassware, ceramics, and textiles for consumers) were vulnerable to competition from Soviet bloc exports.

59. In this group Economics Ministry staff met regularly with Länder representatives to discuss trade issues; East-West trade was a regular item on the agenda. Members of the Economics Ministry were especially attentive to the commercial concerns of Hamburg and Bremen, often visiting there and addressing the governments of these still important city-states, BA B 102/54281, 54285-86, 56567.

60. BA B 102/5932 H.1 and B 102/5933 H. 1 & 2. Reactions by the Trade Policy Office at Bayer show that the private-sector rejected the Parliamentary Council as part of the "feared democratization" of West German trade policy and as an "unnecessary impediment" to trade policies already "burdened" by the involvement of the High Commission, Terhaar report, 4 August 1950, Bayer-Archiv 67/2, vol. 2.

61. According to article 59, paragraph 2 of the Basic Law of the Federal Republic, "treaties that regulate the political relations of the Federal Government, or that affect areas of Federal authority require the approval or the participation of the appropriate bodies in the form of a Federal Law," Schuster, ed., *Deutsche Verfassungen*, 153.

62. In response to an inquiry from Parliamentary Council member Hellmut Kalbitzer (SPD) to Reinhardt in July 1951 as to why so few of the Federal Republic's "trade treaties" required ratification, the Economics Ministry explained that the annual exchange of lists negotiated between the Federal Republic and Poland or Czechoslovakia on the basis of the JEIA agreements required only administrative action, and no new laws, in order to be effective. These lists guaranteed only that the administrative prerequisites (e.g., import licenses, foreign currency availability) would be arranged for the exchange of the agreed-upon amounts of specific goods. The Economics Ministry and the Finance Ministry themselves initiated or authorized these arrangements; no parliamentary action was necessary, internal memorandum of the Economics Ministry's Trade policy desk, 19 July 1951, BA B 102/2272 H.1.

63. The Economics Ministry reassured Kalbitzer and other SPD politicians that they were being kept fully informed of East-West trade developments through the Parliamentary Council. By and large this was true, but "being kept informed" was no substitute for a direct role in shaping the content of the all-important trade agreements.

64. *Verhandlungen des deutschen Bundestages*, I. Wahlperiode 1949, Stenographische Berichte, vol. 11, (Bonn, 1952), Drucksache Nr. 3282, 9012; for the debate, 8961-8967. SPD inquiry, 17 January 1952, Drucksache Nr. 2935, ibid., vol. 10, 7933. On 12 November 1952 Kroll's two-hour report to the Parliamentary Council on Foreign Trade on implementation of the May resolution met with "unanimous approval," Kroll memorandum, 14 November 1952, BA B 136/7807.

65. Volker Berghahn, *The Americanization of West German Industry 1945-1973* (New York, 1986), 187-88.

66. As early as the mid-1950s Theodor Eschenberg pointed out the dangers of a "dominion of the interest groups" (Herrschaft der Verbände) in a speech to the German Chamber of Commerce in Dusseldorf; his book of the same title [2nd ed., (Stuttgart, 1963)] remains a classic on the role of the interest groups in the FRG. Less pessimistic views of interest group activity have been taken by Wilhelm Hennis, "Verfassungsordnung und Verbandseinfluss," *Politische Vierteljahresschrift* 2 (1961), 23-34; Klaus von Beyme, *Interessengruppen in der Demokratie* (Munich, 1970) and by Wolfgang Budzio in *Die organisierte Demokratie. Parteien und Verbände in der Bundesrepublik*, 2nd ed. (Stuttgart, 1982). Introductions to the topic of interest groups in the FRG are provided by *Die Bundesrepublik Deutschland Staatshandbuch.* Teilausgabe. *Verbände, Vereinigungen, wissenschaftliche Einrichtungen* (Cologne, 1979); Jürgen Weber, *Die Interessengruppen im politischen System der Bundesrepublik Deutschland* (Stuttgart, 1977), and by Hartmut Krueger, *Interessenpolitik und Gemeinwohlfindung in der Demokratie* (Munich, 1976). Volker Berghahn's *Unternehmer und Politik in der Bundesrepublik* (Frankfurt, 1985) is the most recent study of note.

67. By April 1946, twenty-four "economic associations" (Wirtschaftsvereinigungen) and twenty-six industry specific interest groups (Fachverbände) had been founded in the three Western zones, Roland Raithel, *Wirtschaft und Außenpolitik. Der Bundesverband deutscher Industrie e.V. als Faktor im außenpolitischen Entscheidungsprozeß der Bundesrepublik Deutschland*, (Ph.D. diss., University of Erlangen-Nürnberg, 1984), 77. Among the most important of the new groups, the chemical industry interest group in the British zone (Wirtschaftsverband chemische Industrie, Britisches Kontrollgebiet) had established a special committee for foreign trade in 1946; in October 1947 the new iron and steel industry interest group established its foreign trade committee, Bayer-Archiv, 62/22, vol. 1; Werner Bührer, *Ruhrstahl und Europa. Die Wirtschaftsvereinigung Eisen- und Stahl Industrie und die Anfänge der europäische Integration 1945-1952* (Munich, 1986), 52. As early as November 1946 the Union of German Machine Building Establishments (Württemberg-Baden) had written to the Economics Department reminding it bluntly that "machine-building is one of the most important export industries," 30 November 1946, BA B 102/62. In September 1949 the machine-building interest group sent a Resolution on Foreign Trade Policy to Erhard and Maltzan, Karl Lange to Erhard, 10 September 1949, BA B 102/1986.

68. On the origins of the industrial Bundesverband see Gerard Braunthal, *The Federation of German Industry in Politics* (Ithaca, 1965); Georg Brodach, *Der Bundesverband deutscher Industrie* (Dusseldorf, 1987); Raithel, *Wirtschaft und Außenpolitik*, 77 ff. and the literature cited there.

69. Maltzan memorandum on a conversation with Beyer and Peterson (German Chamber of Commerce), 24 February 1951, BA B 102/2262 H.1 Among the founding eight organizations were three of West Germany's most influential: the industrial Bundesverband, the German Chamber of Commerce, and the Combination of German Export Groups (Arbeitsgemeinschaft der Exporteurevereine).

70. On "neocorporatism" as it applies to the FRG, see Rolf Heinze, *Verbändepolitik und "Neokorporatismus". Zur politischen Soziologie organisierter Interessen* (Opladen,

1981); G. Lehmbruch and Ph. Schmitter, *Patterns of Corporatist Policy-Making* (London, 1982); Ulrich von Alemann, *Neokorporatismus* (Frankfurt, 1981).

71. A variety of commercial groups had regular representation: the German Chamber of Commerce, the Rhein-Ruhr Bank, the Combination of German Export Groups, and the new industrial Bundesverband represented by Fritz Könecke (Daimler-Benz). Specific industrial sectors also received representation on the Advisory Board; for example, industrialist Ludwig von Heyl appeared for the leather industry, Walter Schwede (Handelsunion, AG, Dusseldorf) for steel, and Rudolf Sies for ceramics. Hirche from the Federation of German Trade Union's Parliamentary Liaison Office represented the trade unions.

72. Maltzan memorandum on a conversation with Beyer and Peterson (German Chamber of Commerce), 24 February 1951, BA B 102/2262 H.1.

73. Memorandum from Seeliger (Economics Ministry V D, 4) to all members of Main Department V, 17 March 1951, BA B 102/2272.

74. At the forty-fourth meeting of the Länder Committee on Foreign Trade, Scholz (Economics Ministry) declared that in matters of trade with the East "discussions between the authorities and the private-sector take place essentially only in the conversations with the Eastern Committee and the Committee on Central Export Control," 28 January 1954 in BA B 102/7198 H.2

75. For the following on that meeting see Kroll's notes of 31 July 1951 in BA B 102/2366 H.2; Carnap's notes, 24 July 1951, BdI, OA/4. Kroll had spoken alone to a "small group" of steel and machine industrialists in Cologne on 4 April 1951, Carnap's notes, BdI, OA/4.

76. Wilhelm Beutler (executive secretary of the Bundesverband) and Meyer (executive secretary of the Bundesverband's foreign trade committee) to Erhard, 29 January 1952, BA B 102/7203. The government sent members of Economics Ministry, Foreign Office, and Finance Ministry to these meetings with agents of the German Chamber of Commerce, the industrial Bundesverband, the Combination of German Export Groups, the Union of German Machine Building Establishments (VDMA), the electronics industry, non-ferrous metals, the chemical industry, and representatives from the Chambers of Commerce of Cologne, Dusseldorf, and Wiesbaden.

77. On all these activities see the Economics Ministry's records of the committee, BA B 102/7203.

78. Zahn-Stranik notes, 22 March 1954, PAAA 311.22, vol. 3. On the origins of the Eastern Committee see Robert Mark Spaulding, "'Reconquering Our Old Position': West German Osthandel Strategeies of the 1950s," in Volker Berghahn, ed., *Quest for Economic Empire. European Strategies of German Big Business in the Twentieth Century* (Providence, 1995), 123-43.

79. Reinhardt to Westrick and Erhard on "Organization and Function of the Eastern Committee," from 23 March, 1956. BA B 102/58158. The need for such an agreement on East bloc deliveries had been discussed confidentially in the West German private-sector since early 1950 [!], beginning with Gerhard Schauke (Mannesmann) to Meyer, 8 February 1950, BdI, OA/4. For similar reasons the federal government assisted in the creation of two corporations in Bavaria with monopoly purchasing rights for Czechoslovakian coal and kaolin.

80. Draft response of Erhard to Wilhelm Naegel (Christian Democrats), November 1952, PAAA 411.22, vol. 1.

81. Reinhardt to Westrick and Erhard on "Organization and Function of the Eastern Committee," from 23 March, 1956. BA B 102/58158. On 24 June 1952 the cabinet approved Erhard's plan to set up the Eastern Committee, Bundesarchiv, *Die Kabinettsprotokolle der Bundesregierung*, 1952, vol. 5, 403.

82. After a good deal of wrangling between July and October 1952, the private-sector Working Group on Foreign Trade selected the following men to lead the East-

ern Committee: Senator Wenhold (C.F. Corssen, Bremen) of the German Chamber of Commerce for the trading community, W. Alexander Menne (Hoechst) and Hans Reuter (Demag) of the industrial Bundesverband for manufacturers, and Hermann Abs (Deutsche Bank) for the banking community. With these members, the most powerful organizations of commerce, industry, and finance were all present at the highest levels. Wolf von Amerongen chaired the "committee on the USSR" and even the nonpresidium members were powerful men: Richard Carstenjan (MAN), H. Köhler (Bayer), Alfred Toepfer, Carl Haiblen (Felten & Guilleaume), Fritz Berg (president of the industrial Bundesverband), Wilhelm Beutler (Bundesverband), Karl Lange (VDMA) and Erwin von Carnap (Bundesverband). The selection process is documented in BdI, OA/4. At the same time, the government managed to deflect SPD calls for some trade union representation on the Eastern Committee. Kalbitzer raised the issue at the 12 July 1952 meeting of the Parliamentary Trade Council. The chairman of the Bundestag's Foreign Trade Committee, Kuhlemann (CDU), promised to look into the matter; labor members subsequently did not join the Eastern Committee, BA B 102/5932 H.1. Just as in Weimar, the ministerial bureaucracy acquiesced in private-sector efforts to keep corporatist bodies on trade policy as exclusive preserves of owners and managers.

83. Outline on East-West Trade by the Foreign Office's Commercial Affairs Department, March 1953, PAAA 311.22, Bd.1.

84. Lupin's 20 May 1953 memorandum to the files of the Foreign Office's Trade Policy Department with a copy to Maltzan at the Economics Ministry, BA B 102/7196 H.2.

85. Seiberlich to Reinhardt, 19 May 1954, BA B 102/7196 H.1 citing Diehlmann, Wolff von Amerongen, and Reuter as being especially aggressive. In December 1953 both the *Handelsblatt* and the *New York Herald Tribune* (Paris) ran stories on the increasing activity of the Eastern Committee.

86. Reinhardt to Westrick and Erhard on "Organization and Function of the Eastern Committee," 23 March, 1956, BA B 102/58158.

87. U.S. Military Law No. 56 and British Military Ordinance No. 78 had forbidden the creation of interest groups, syndicates, or cartels that exercised regulatory authority.

88. Appendix A, paragraph 1(c) of Control Office memorandum (48)13 from 12 February 1948 as cited by Control Office Chairmen Adcock and MacReady to the Chairman of the Administrative Council (Pünder), 12 July 1948: "Economic organs (Verbände) have only advisory functions. They are forbidden from exercising administrative authority (behördliche Befugnisse) in whole or in part, from limiting or controlling trade, or from assuming direction of distributions, sales, prices, rates and charges, the allocation of material and fuel, the issuance of licenses to firms or persons, or instructions for production or deliveries," BA B 102/62. In their sharply worded instructions, the Control Office chairmen ordered a revocation of the arrangement by which the Economics Department had granted the private Scrap Metal Association (Schrottgemeinschaft) the right to approve scrap iron export contracts. This "flagrant violation" of Allied policies would "not be tolerated"; in subsequent cases the Control Office would ask the Bipartite Control Board to "dismiss and remove" West German economic officials who participated in such arrangements.

89. Perhaps the most important of these bodies were the industry-specific private-sector Fachtellen that oversaw the use of scarce economic resources, *WiGBl*, 1949, 73; *BGBl*, 1950, 5. In 1951 their duties were transferred to the private-sector "groups" attached to the new Federal Agency for Merchandise Trade in Industrial Commodities (Bundestelle für den Warenverkehr im Bereich der gewerblichen

Wirtschaft). The Export Committee for Iron and Steel (Exportausschuss Eisen und Stahl) in Dusseldorf was another private group that assumed a corporatist character in trade policy by issuing the government-required allotment certificates for exports of iron and steel products in short supply. For other examples of West German corporatist solutions to economic problems in the 1950s see Werner Abelshauser, "Ansätze 'Korporativer Marktwirtschaft' in der Korea Krise der früheren Fünfziger Jahre," *VfZ* 30 (1982), 715-56; W. Herrmann, "Der Wiederaufbau der Selbstverwaltung der deutschen Wirtschaft nach 1945," *Zeitschrift für Unternehmensgeschichte* 23 (1978), 81-97.

90. The High Commission to Adenauer, 12 November 1949, AGSEC (49)160, BA B 102/1986

91. Terhaar reported that West German officials had received "strict instructions" not to discuss export control issues with the business community and were exercising "strict discretion" on the subject so that it was "still impossible" to have a "thorough conversation" with the authorities on this issue, 24 March 1950, 12 May 1950, Bayer-Archiv 67/2, vol. 2.

92. Maltzan's notes, 24 February 1951, BA B 102/2262 H.1.

93. After July 1949 JEIA agreed to meet "unofficially" with members of the West German Economics Department to review rejected export applications for shipments headed to the Soviet bloc, creating in effect an informal appeals process on Allied embargo decisions, Terhaar report, 1 July 1949, Bayer-Archiv 67/2, vol. 1.

94. BA B 102/2262; Wallenhorst (Export Committee Iron and Steel) to Kroll, 28 June 1951, BA B 102/2366 H.2; 1 December 1954 meeting of the Economics Ministry export control officials, BA B 102/7203.

95. Chamber of Commerce (Fermerling) complaint to the Economics Ministry, 19 February 1951, BA B 102/2272; BA B 102/2272 and 2262 H.1., passim.

96. Because most West German organizations have no "statutory claim.. to participate in government" Lehmbruch considers corporatism in Germany to be "medium" strength, as opposed to the "strong" corporatism of Austria, Sweden, and the Netherlands, where such statutory guarantees do exist. By this same criterion, Weimar is more strongly corporatist than the Federal Republic because private participation in government was guaranteed through the constitutionally institutionalized Reich Economics Council, Lehmbruch and Schmitter, eds., *Patterns of Corporatist Policy-Making.*

97. Further, Adeanuer unambiguously subordinated his diplomacy in Eastern Europe to the necessity of sound politcial relations with the West. For an introduction to West German foreign policies in the 1950s begin with Waldemar Besson, *Die Aussenpolitik der Bundesrepublik* (Munich, 1970); Christian Hacke, *Weltmacht wider Willen: Die Aussenpolitik der Bundesrepublik Deutschland* (Stuttgart, 1988;) Wolfram Hanreider, *Germany, America, Europe: Forty Years of German Foreign Policy* (New Haven, 1989); Adolf Birke, *Nation ohne Haus: Deutschland 1945-1961* (Berlin, 1989); Frank Pfretsch, *West Germany: Internal Structures and External Relations: Foreign Policy of the Federal Republic of Germany* (New York, 1988). On Adenauer's conceptions in particular consult Hans-Peter Schwarz, *Die Ära Adenauer 1949-1957* (Stuttgart, 1981); and *Adenauer,: Der Aufstieg, 1872-1952* (Stuttgart, 1986); Dieter Blumenwitz et al., eds., *Konrad Adenauer uns seine Zeit,* 2 vols. (Stuttgart, 1976).

98. Exchange of letters between Niklas and Erhard on 12 and 13 December 1949, BA B 102/1986. Erhard himself described West German trade policy from 1949 to 1953 as "deliberate priority is ... given to the German import market as an instrument to create opportunities for German exports. Import quotas are used as instruments of an expansionist trade policy," *Germany's Comeback in the World Market,* 90.

99. Erhard sent Seiberlich's report and a cover letter to the Chancellor's Office on 15 June 1950, BA B 136/1261; Hans Booms (hrsg.), *Die Kabinettsprotokolle der Bundesregierung* Bd. 2, *1950* (Boppard, 1984), 471.

100. *Die Kabinettsprotokolle der Bundesregierung*, Bd. 2, *1950*, 471-72. Erhard's statements, especially that Germany must demonstrate every effort to close the "dollar gap," parallel Brüning's 1932 plan to obtain a trade deal with Poland because of the otherwise unfavorable repercussions on Germany's reparations negotiations with the West.

101. BA B 136/1261. Two days later the industrial Bundesverband repeated its concerns and urged a German concession of $3 million to $5 million in pork imports, Beutler and Stein to Adenauer on 26 June 1950. BA B 102/2312 H.2.

102. Josef Rust (Chancellor's Office) to Vice-Chancellor Blücher, 29 June 1950, BA B 136/1261.

103. *Die Kabinettsprotokolle der Bundesregierung*, Bd. 2, *1950*, 504-05.

104. A copy of the agreement can be found in BA B 102/2312 H.2. The affair took another twist when five days later Niklas told Erhard that he was "astounded" at the final terms of the deal, having been under the impression that on June 30 Adenauer had supported the Agriculture Ministry's position in this matter, Niklas to Erhard on 12 July 1950, BA B 102/2312 H.2. Since the negotiations had already ended (and the Polish delegation departed), the Agriculture Ministry was presented with a fait accompli to which it would have to reconcile itself. The agreement was submitted to the High Commission, which approved it in early October. Formal signing by Seiberlich for the Federal Republic took place on 9 October.

105. A series of internal Economics Ministry memoranda on this point from July 1950, BA B 102/1986; Seiberlich's complaint about agricultural protection and Balkan produce, 7 November 1952, BA B 102/7204.

106. Seiberlich note, 26 May 1953, BA B 102/7196 H.2

107. The Polish land reform of 1944 to 1946, followed by a half-hearted collectivization campaign from 1948 to 1955, had produced an especially inefficient agricultural pattern. Dwarf farms of less than five hectares in size held 61 percent of the land. This uneconomical system "did not provide a surplus of grain or other agricultural food stuffs for the [domestic] non-farm population." By 1952 Poland's agricultural production had barely improved over the 1949 level (1952 = 104 percent of 1949). Under these circumstances, Poland could not regularly generate exportable surpluses, Zbigniew Brzezinski, *The Soviet Bloc. Unity and Conflict* (Cambridge, Mass., 1967), 13, 101; *Report of the F.A.O. Mission to Poland* (Washington, 1948), 39 as cited by Brzezinski; N. Spulber, *The Economics of Communist Eastern Europe* (Cambridge, Mass., 1957), 245 ff.

108. Economics Ministry (V A, 7) Report on Trade with Eastern Europe, 29 March 1951, BA B 102/7210 H.1.

109. Kaiser (Economics Ministry) 16 April 1951 notes on a meeting of Bode with several members of the Economics Ministry, BA B 102/7196 H.1.

110. Seiberlich's notes on a meeting of the German-Polish Mixed Commission 22 November 1952, BA B 102/7208 H.2.

111. For the period July 1952 to December 1954, Polish live pig exports were only $1.7 million ($5 million planned); none of the planned Polish wheat exports (60,000 tons!) were realized, Weekly report of the East-West Trade desk (413A), 27 March 1954, PAAA 311.22/4; report on German-Polish negotiations in Warsaw, 20 December 1954, PAAA 413.85.00/114.

112. Zahn-Stranik memorandum from Warsaw, 4 December 1954, PAAA 413.85.00/114.

113. Weekly report of the East-West Trade desk (413A), 21 March 1955, PAAA 311.22/4.

114. For the evolution of the December 1955 grain deal see: PAAA 311.22/4; BA B 102/56565.
115. On the economic origins of the 1956 Polish crisis, see chapter nine.
116. Economics Ministry (V A, 7) Report on Trade with Eastern Europe, 29 March 1951, BA B 102/7210 H.1.
117. Statistical Office of the United Nations, *United Nations Statistical Papers Series T. Direction of International Trade*, Vols. I-VII, (1949-1955); Economics Ministry circular on foreign economic policy Nr. 31/52, PAAA 413.85.00/114. Because of its continued export shortfalls, Poland was overdrawn on its $7.5 million "swing" line of credit with the Federal Republic by some $300,000 at the end of 1952, memorandum from the Economics Ministry's Foreign Exchange desk to Reinhardt, 23 February 1953, BA B 102/55998. Fearful that the Germans would invoke the dollar payment clause of the 1949 payments agreement, the Narodowy Bank Polski limited the foreign exchange available to Polish importing agencies until the outstanding balance was back under the $7.5 million limit, Seiberlich memorandum on trade with Poland, 6 January 1953, BA B 102/7208 H.2.
118. Seiberlich memorandum from 22 November 1952, BA B 102/7208 H.2.
119. Some 40,000 Germans had been brought to West Germany in 1949 to 1950 as part of the Operation Link program negotiated by the Allies with the Polish government. At least 20,000 persons remained in Poland separated from their immediate families in the West; the number of persons separated from more distant relatives must have been very much greater.
120. Kaiser to Erhard on 17 October and 20 November 1950, BA B 102/7197.
121. Trützschler to the other involved ministries, 2 May 1951, BA B 102/7197.
122. Trützschler's report on the 8 May 1951 meeting, BA B 102/7197. Seiberlich retained this (overly pessimistic) opinion of the prospects of success through economic pressure while the issue was played out from 1952 through 1955. Over in the Agriculture Ministry, desk officer Otto Stalmann was similarly pessimistic of the chances for political success through trade pressure, Stalmann to Maltzan, 17 June 1953, PAAA 413.80.07/116.
123. Seiberlich's 9 May 1951 draft and Reinhardt's 16 May final memorandum, BA B 102/7197.
124. Erhard to Blücher, 8 November 1951, BA B 102/7196.
125. Foreign Office cabinet submission of 11 November, 1952, BA B 102/1261. In the Trade Policy Committee meeting on October 2, Reinhardt and Kroll gave the Economics Ministry's approval to the Foreign Office's plans, Reinhardt to the Foreign Office, 18 October 1952. Maltzan approved the Foreign Office's draft of the instructions on November 17, BA B 102/7197. The cabinet approved these instructions in its November 21st meeting, BA B 136/1261.
126. West German delegation leader Otto Stalmann noted that Muszynski claimed to have been "expressly forbidden by his government from discussing this political issue" and that the Poles were not willing to link (verkoppeln) political and economic questions, Stalmann notes, 29 November 1952, PAAA 413.80.07/116.
127. Muszynski well understood what was happening; on 25 November both sides agreed to break off negotiations until January 1953, Stalmann's report, 29 November 1952, BA B 102/7197.
128. From 13 January 1953 Foreign Office report of the 8 January meeting, BA B 102/7197. Trützschler was now serving as personal representative of Herbert Blankenhorn, head of the influential Political Department in the Foreign Office.
129. Trützschler summary for the Chancellor's Office, 5 December 1953, BA B 136/1261; *Die Kabinettsprotokolle der Bundesregierung*, Bd. 6, *1953*, 371-72.
130. Foreign Office report, 1 July 1953, BA B 102/7197. In a 6 July memorandum to the cabinet, Scherpenberg argued that, "Success in the question of repatriating

Germans from Poland would justify a [West German] claim for the same resolution of this question with other satellite countries. Therefore, we must attempt at one point to break the existing closed front of the satellites in the question of repatriation," PAAA 413.80.07/116. Stalmann's temporary solution was approved by the cabinet in discussion on 7 July.

131. Between 1 July 1953 and 1 October 1954 the FRG had imported $18.6 million worth of merchandise from Poland or just 50 percent of the amount called for in the July 1953 trade agreement. German exports in the same period were $20.2 million, or just 60.3 percent of the planned level of $33.5 million. These low levels were caused by Poland's own economic problems coupled with German unwillingness to offer any trade-boosting aid until the family reunification issue was settled.

132. Weekly report of Foreign Office's East-West Trade desk, 19 July 1954, PAAA 311.22/3. Seiberlich and Lupin communicated that same message to Polish trade negotiators at various times in June and July 1954, Lupin memorandum, 30 June 1954, PAAA 413.85.00/144; unsigned East-West Trade desk memorandum, 9 July 1954, ibid.

133. Negotiations in Warsaw would allow the Poles to "save face" while making concessions, Schmoller (at the Foreign Office's desk for refugees) notes, PAAA 413.80.07/116. Agriculture Minister Heinrich Lübke considered the question of repatriation "so important politically" that the West Germans should go to Warsaw. Reinhardt pointed out that trade relations would enter a state of limbo should the Poles take the bold step of canceling the 1949 JEIA-Polish trade agreement, Seiberlich's undated memorandum on Trade with Poland, PAAA 413.85.00/114. Despite these pressures, Adenauer himself decided against negotiations in Warsaw until after the French parliamentary vote on the EDC initiative had been held, memorandum by Zahn-Stranik (East-West trade desk at the Foreign Office), 11 May 1954, PAAA 413.85.00/114; memorandum by Lupin (East-West trade desk at the Foreign Office), 13 October 1954, PAAA 4113.85.00/114.

134. Zahn-Stranik report, 20 October 1954, PAAA 311.22/3.

135. In November, Wolynski specified Polish demands as $6 million in credits for consumer goods and $10 million in six-year credits for investment goods, Zahn-Stranik memorandum, 15 November 1954, PAAA 413.85.00/114. Prior to the opening of negotiations, the West Germans assumed that it would be possible to reduce Polish credit demands to $4 million for consumer goods and $6 million for investment equipment, East-West Trade desk memorandum, 23 November 1954, ibid. At $16 million for the 20,000 Germans separated from their immediate families, the Poles were asking $800 per person; at $10 million, the Germans were offering $500 per person.

136. On 24 November Lupin had informed Kiefer at HICOG of West German plans to visit Warsaw. On 29 November, Whyner replied that Washington had "strong sympathy for the humanitarian goals of the trip" and that HICOG supported West German efforts to achieve repatriation via trade talks. On the other hand, Washington remained unenthusiastic about West German credits for Poland, despite $10 million in recent Belgian credits to Poland and the projected positive outcome of ongoing Franco-Polish credit discussions, Lupin memorandum on conversation with Whyner, 29 November 1954, PAAA 413.85.00/114.

137. The new terms of the swing credit still must be considered a concession by the FRG in light of original German plans to reduce the swing to between $3.5 million and $4 million and to introduce an interest charge on the outstanding balance, Walter Steidle (Economics Ministry) report on an "Interministerial Meeting on the Upcoming Economic Negotiations with Poland," BA B

102/58124. Polish imports of West German rolled steel products ($5.4 million) and chemicals ($7.3 million) made up just over half of the $23.5 million to be imported from the FRG in regular trade over the next eighteen months, Lupin memorandum, 5 January 1955, PAAA 413.85.00/114.

138. Both parties understood the exceptional nature of the deal. For the FRG, government guarantees of credits to Poland violated West German principles on loans to Soviet bloc countries. The Poles repeatedly emphasized that the linkage of trade and other issues was a "one-time exception." Zahn-Stranik noted that "in view of Polish dependence on trade with the FRG, they fear that the FRG could employ its economic superiority (wirtschaftliches Übergewicht) in the solution of political problems," memorandum, 16 December 1954, PAAA 413.85.00/114.

139. The reasons for this low number remain unclear. In the West German Foreign Office, Schmoller (desk officer for refugees) claimed from unnamed "reliable sources" that the Foreign Ministry of the German Democratic Republic had intervened with the Soviets to block repatriation, memorandum, 17 March 1955, PAAA 413.80.07/116. Other information obtained from Karol Szymanowski, chief desk officer for West Germany and West Berlin in the Polish Foreign Ministry, indicated that general East-West tensions of early 1955 (Paris treaty, West German entry into NATO) made it difficult for Poland to repatriate at that time, report to the Political Division of the Foreign Office, 15 July 1955, ibid. On West German dissatisfaction, Zahn-Stranik memorandum of conversation with Walter Steidle (Economics Ministry) and Jazdon, the Polish trade representative in Frankfurt, 11 May 1955, PAAA 311.22/4.

140. Lupin memorandum of conversation, 29 September 1955, PAAA 311.22/4.

141. Lupin memorandum of conversation, 3 October 1955, PAAA 311.22/4. The Foreign Office estimated the Polish grain shortfall for 1956 at about 1 million tons, which meant that even with purchases from other Western countries as well, the Poles could hardly avoid buying some grain from West Germany, especially since the Germans could provide the necessary short-term financing.

142. Lupin's memorandum, 20 October, PAAA 413.80.07/116. Inside the West German Foreign Office, the Political Division and the area studies group for Eastern Europe agreed that economic relations with Poland "must be viewed exclusively from the foreign policy angle," memorandum from the refugee desk, 20 October 1955, ibid.

143. Steidle memorandum, 9 December 1955, BA B 102/56565. The West Germans contented themselves with a clause inserted into the Red Cross agreement that the repatriation would be "facilitated by the Polish authorities," Lupin memorandum, 9 December 1955, PAAA 413.80.07/116.

144. Weekly report of the East-West Trade desk, 12 December 1955, PAAA 311.22/4; Stalmann at the thirty-fourth meeting of the Parliamentary Council for Foreign Trade Agreements, 4 October 1956, BA B 102/5933 H.1. In fact, as Zahn-Stranik noted on 7 December, c. 12,500 Germans arrived from Poland in 1956, PAAA 413.85.00/111.

145. The inclination to use American powers along the border as a means of influencing Czechoslovakia had been evident since Clay suggested closing the border in the spring of 1949. After the outbreak of hostilities in Korea, U.S. forces sought to punish the monolithic communists wherever they could. The Bavarian-Czechoslovakian border being one of the few points of direct contact, these American actions were almost foreseeable.

146. Seiberlich's memorandum on trade with Eastern Europe, 29 March 1951, BA B 102/7210 H.1.; Wiener Wirtschaftskorrespondenz, 7 June 1951.

147. Seiberlich memorandum, 29 May 1951, BA B 102/7211 H.1

148. The chairman of the High Commission's Economics Committee, MacReady (U.K.), told Erhard plainly that "the Allied High Commission would not approve any such proposal" for even 15,000 tons of scrap exports to Czechoslovakia, MacReady to Erhard, 14 July 1951, AGSEC(51)1199 ECON, BA B 102/7196 H.1.

149. Seiberlich to the fifteenth meeting of the Parliamentary Council on Foreign Trade Agreements, 5 April 1951, BA B 102/5932 H.2.

150. Otto Seeling to Erhard, 3 February 1951, BA B 102/7210 H.1.

151. Expected coal imports from Czechoslovakia were 1.4 million tons for 1951; without them Bavaria faced an average monthly shortfall of 116,000 tons.

152. Memorandum, 26 February 1951, BA B 102/7211 H.1.

153. Seiberlich memorandum from 24 August 1951, BA B 102/7211 H.1.

154. Press release Declaration of the Chancellor on the Question of East-West Trade, 28 April 1951, PAAA 304.11. The theme of conscious economic sacrifice was repeated by members of the government throughout the early embargo years. See e.g., Maltzan's public statement that "to the extent that foreign policy factors require us to forego a possible expansion of trade with the East, we are prepared for that," Maltzan, mauscript "On the Question of East-West Trade," August 1954, BA B 136/7808.

155. See above, the business response to Kroll's explanations; Schaefer of the German Chamber of Commerce to Erhard, 11 June 1951, BA B 102/2366 H.2.

156. "Klarheit im Osthandel," *Bulletin der Presse- und Informationsamt der Bundesregierung*, Nr. 146, 1329. The German Chamber of Commerce also reported that "in the opinion of the German business community the current [export] restrictions are not administered fairly," chamber memorandum to all members, 30 June 1952, BA B 102/7230.

157. Seiberlich cursed "this new border chicanery" in a note to Lupin, 10 July 1953, BA B 102/7233. The agreement covering trade for 1954 had been concluded on 23 June 1953.

158. Urban to Seiberlich, 29 July 1953, BA B 102/7211 H.2.

159. "Verschärfte Embargopolitik," *Deutsche Finanz- und Wirtschaftszeitung*, 11 March 1953; *Handelsblatt* examples include "Neuer US-Angriff auf den Osthandel," and "Embargo – so und so," 4 February 1953 and 18 November 1953.

160. Notice from the Foreign Office's Commercial Affairs Department to all diplomatic representatives, 9 March 1953, BA B 102/7196 H.2.

161. The problem of the residual German minority in Czechoslovakia had been largely solved from 1945 to 1949 by the forced expulsion of some 3 million ethnic Germans. For an introduction to this problem see the rather one-sided work of Alfred de Zayes, *Nemesis at Potsdam. The Anglo-Americans and the Expulsion of the Germans* (London, 1977). Documentary material has been collected in Bundesministerium für Vertriebene, *Dokumentation der Vertreibung der deutschen aus Ostmitteleuropa* (Bonn, 1953-1961). On the basis of the 31 January 1950 agreement between the American permit officer of the High Commission in Prague (Martin Bowe, Jr.) and the division chief of the Interior Ministry of the CSSR (Miroslav Sapara), another 15,000 Germans were allowed to move from Czechoslovakia to the FRG in 1951 to 1952.

162. Memorandum of Seiberlich conversation with Czechoslovakian trade attaché Junek on 23 June 1950 BA B102/7210 H.1.

163. The 1955 trade and payments agreement instituted interest charges of 1.5 percent on that portion of the outstanding swing between $1.5 million and $2.7 million and 3 percent on that portion between $2.7 million and $4.1 million.

164. Urban to Seiberlich, 10 May 1954, BA B 102/7211 H.2.

165. Memorandum of conversation between Schiffler and Czechoslovakian trade attaché Junek, 25 November 1949, BA B 102/7210 H.1.

166. In 1948 Czechoslovakia sent 16 percent of its total exports to the USSR, of which 36 percent were industrial machinery and industrial consumer goods. By 1953, 33 percent of total exports went to the Soviets, of which 37 percent were industrial. See Paul Marer, *Soviet and East European Foreign Trade, 1946-1969. Statistical Compendium and Guide* (Bloomington, Ind., 1972) 36, 81. Both Seiberlich and Kroll were convinced that the new Czechoslovak economic obligations toward the USSR had caused the Czechs to suddenly and dramatically scale back their trade offers to the FRG during the April 1952 German-Czechoslovak negotiations for a new agreement, Seiberlich to Reinhardt, 26 April 1952, BA B 102/7211 H.1.

167. The chronic shortage of foreign currency brought into question Czechoslovakia's ability to pay off the substantial bills it ran up by using the West German transportation system, especially the port services and facilities at Hamburg. Shipping almost 750,000 tons of freight through Hamburg annually was costing Czechoslovakia about $8 million per year, with estimates of $10 million for 1956. Average Czechoslovak tonnage passing through Hamburg for the years 1951 to 1953 was 705,000 (1,204,000 in 1936). The estimate for 1956 was discussed at the twenty-fifth meeting of the Parliamentary Council on Trade Agreements on 9 December 1955, BA B 102/5933 H.2. Czechoslovakia repeatedly threatened to reroute its export traffic through Szczecin (Stettin) unless the Federal Republic accepted increased imports of Czechoslovakian manufactures to help with payment, e.g., Czechoslovak trade delegation leader Matousek to Seiberlich, 30 January 1954, BA B 102/7211 H.2. The West Germans certainly bought more glass and textiles than they otherwise would have, using the increased purchases as an indirect subsidy to Hamburg while the port city adjusted to the loss of eastern and middle Germany, BA B 102/7211 H.1 & 2, passim.

168. Brzezinski, *The Soviet Bloc*, 94-95. The Economics Ministry noted in October 1951 that the "changing of the guard," underway since April was now affecting the Czechoslovakian Foreign Trade Ministry. The pragmatic Czechoslovakian trade representative in the FRG, Dr. Fisl, was replaced by Urban at this time, Seiberlich memo from 18 October 1951, BA B 102/7210 H.1.

169. Erhard to Adenauer, 13 June 1950, BA B 136/7807; similarly in Erhard's presentation to the cabinet, 23 June 1950, BA B 102/55998 and *Die Kabinettsprotokolle der Bundesregierung*, Bd. 2, *1950*, 519.

170. Economics Ministry, *Deutschland im Wiederaufbau* (Bonn, 1952), 113.

171. Der Ost-West Handel, 16 May 1952. The Foreign Office estimated that Western Europe could close the dollar gap by $300 million annually if Eastern supplies of grain, coal, and wood could be fully reactivated to prewar levels, Commercial Affairs Department memorandum to all diplomatic officers, 9 March 1953, PAAA 311.22/1.

172. Foreign Office Commercial Affairs Department to all diplomatic officers, 9 March 1953, PAAA 311.22/1.

173. Maltzan to the Parliamentary Council for Trade Agreements, 19 January 1954, BA B 102/5933; similarly and at greater length in his article "On the Question of East-West Trade," August 1954, BA B 136/7808.

174. BA B 102/7198.

175. Wolff to Director Carl Haiblen (Felten & Guilleaume) et al., 24 June 1954. BdI, OA/1. The similarity of Wolff's statement to Maltzan's formulation from August 1954 (that the federal government "has no illusions about the possibilities of a rapid increase" in East-West trade) shows the high degree of genuine consensus between the government and the private sector in evaluating the potential of the Eastern trade, Maltzan, "On the Question of East-West Trade," August 1954, BA B 136/7807.

176. West European trade with the East grew at depressingly slow rates in the years immediately following the list reductions. For eight major Western European economies in the period 1947 to 1949, trade with Eastern Europe accounted for an average of 3 percent of total exports at this time and 4.4 percent of total imports. In 1956 trade with Eastern Europe made up only 2.8 percent of Western Europe's total exports and the same for imports. This meant a meager increase of 0.3 percent for exports and 0.8 percent for imports since the peak of embargo in 1952, an average of the figures for Belgium-Luxembourg, France, West Germany, Italy, Netherlands, Denmark, Norway, and United Kingdom as given in Gunnar Adler-Karlsson, *Western Economic Warfare 1947-1967*, (Stockholm, 1968), 48-49, and United States Senate Committee on Foreign Relations, *A Background Study on East-West Trade*, 89th Congress, 1st Session, April 1965, 2-5. Both of these publications base their figures on United Nations data, primarily the annual *Economic Survey for Europe* and the *Yearbook of National Account Statistics*.

177. Erhard's assessment conforms almost identically with that of the German Chamber of Commerce regarding the "Russian business," namely that it remains "interesting" even if "one has no illusions regarding it," German Chamber of Commerce (Altenburg) to the industrial Bundesverband (Carnap), 8 June 1954, BdI, OA/1.

178. Kroll used the phrase "reconquering our old position" in the East in an 18 January 1952 meeting with West German industrialists at the Economics Ministry, memorandum to the files, BdI OA/4.

179. Drawing on experience with Soviet buyers in the interwar period, the Eastern Committee hoped to establish a set of uniform "terms of delivery, acceptance, and payments" for trade with all East European countries – a project insistently advanced by the business community and supported by the government, Reinhardt to Westrick and Erhard on "Organization and Function of the Eastern Committee," 23 March 1956, BA B 102/58158.

180. Statistical Office of the United Nations, *United Nations Statistical Papers*, Series T. *Direction of International Trade*, Vols. I-IV, (Geneva 1950-). Some small portion of Soviet exports to other Western European countries may have been reexported to the FRG, although no mention of that trade is found in the Economics Ministry or Foreign Office files, which indicates that this amount must have been very small indeed.

181. In 1948 the Soviets signed trade treaties with Belgium, the Netherlands, Italy, and Norway. Two-way trade between the USSR and twelve Western European countries reached $354 million in 1948, $470 million in 1952.

182. In June 1952 the Soviet wood exporting agency, EXPORTLES, offered pitprops and plywood to a West German import firm. At the same time E. van Hazebrouck, one of the oldest German trading firms, negotiated to buy DM 15 million in grain and seed-cake from the Soviets.

183. Seiberlich to the firm E. van Hazebrouck from 8 July 1952, BA B 102/7214b.

184. Ahlbrecht, the Economics Ministry's desk officer for Compensation Trade, memorandum of conversation with Kroll, Seiberlich, Achener at the Economics Ministry's Far East desk, and Schmitt in Economics Ministry's Department of Economic Policy, 29 May 1952, BA B 102/7196 H.2. As early as June 1950 Erhard declared he had "no objections" to "private compensation deals" between West German firms and Soviet agencies, Erhard to Adenauer, 13 June 1950, BA B 136/7807. Erhard's cabinet submission on the creation of the Eastern Committee (approved 24 June 1952) had explicitly mentioned compensation deals as the best method for reviving trade with the East, BA B 102/7204. Compensation deals were "insured" by letters of credit drawn on London banks in TAA-pounds sterling.

185. Görs in the Economics Ministry's Department of Industrial Policy to Seiberlich, 13 August 1953, BA B 102/7196 H.2.; Boecker, also in Industrial Policy, to Seiberlich, 5 September 1953, BA B 102/7214b.

186. Seiberlich to Boecker, 10 September 1953, BA B 102/7214b.

187. In a global context, the use of compensation deals with the Soviets was only a regional variant of Erhard's general trade strategy of using the West German import market to create opportunities for German exports. Balanced compensation deals cannot fail to bring to mind German mechanisms for increased trade with Southeastern Europe after 1930, when preferences for Hungarian and Romanian produce in the German domestic market stimulated German imports, which then had to be bilaterally balanced by increased East European purchases of German exports. Although the specific mechanisms differed, in both cases the German government used German imports to wedge open East European markets for increased German exports.

188. Seiberlich memorandum, Trade with the USSR, 20 October 1953, BA B 102/18446.H.2.

189. Ahlbrecht to the firm Kupferberg & Co., 26 March 1954 and to Seiberlich, 19 February 1954, BA B 102/7214b. The policy itself and Seiberlich's "inflexible execution of the Trade Policy Committee's resolution" continued to draw sharp criticism from the Department of Industrial Policy on the grounds that unwieldy compensation deals did not always allow the FRG to take advantage of Soviet export offers and that payment in transferable pounds would relieve the West German position in the European Payments Union. Both objections were valid but failed to acknowledge the long-term perspective of West German trade strategy, Görs to Assistant Under-Secretary for Industrial Policy, Hoffmann-Bagienski, 8 January 1954, BA B 102/18446.H.2.

190. See BA B 102/7214b, passim for the correspondence from these firms to the Economics Ministry in October-November 1953. Maltzan admitted that under the current compensation system "settlements are usually made via [banks in] third countries that earn a substantial middleman's profit," Maltzan to Blankenhorn and Hallstein, 29 May 1954, PAAA 311.22/2.

191. Meissner memorandum of conversation with Kraus (Otto Wolf) and Bergmann (Stahlunion-Export G.m.b.H.), 10 June 1954, PAAA 311.22/2.

192. Maltzan to Blankenhorn and Hallstein, 29 May 1954, PAAA 311.22/2.

193. Kroll's Memorandum on the Results of the Moscow [Economic] Conference, 19 April 1952 and Memorandum on the SPD Inquiry Regarding Eastern Trade, 2 May 1952, both in BA B 136/7807.

194. Memorandum by the Foreign Office's East-West Trade desk from 6 May 1955, PAAA 311.22/4.

195. Ahlbrecht memorandum, 29 May 1952, BA B 102/7196 H.2; Seiberlich to the firm A.W. Faber-Castell, 6 May 1952, BA B 102/7214b.

196. Foreign Office Commercial Affairs Department to all diplomatic offices from 9 March 1953, PAAA 413.22/1.

197. Gerhard Bruns, head of the Rolled Steel Group within the industry chaired the German delegation, which included Wolff von Amerongen, von Carnap (industrial Bundesverband), Ernst Wolf Mommsen (Phoenix-Rheinrohr AG and Iron and Steel Association), Blankenagel (Refined Steel Group), and H. Polenz (Rheinische Röhrenwerke).

198. Kroll memorandum, 31 July 1952, BA B 136/7807; Kroll relayed the same information to the newly-formalized Eastern Committee on 2 August, Stein memorandum, BdI, OA/1. On 1 August State Secretary Westrick (Economics Ministry) reported to the cabinet that the Americans "have nothing against this contact" with the Soviets, *Kabinetsprotokolle der Bundesregierung*, Bd. 4, 1952, 500.

199. Memorandum of Results, signed by members of the German delegation, BA B 136/7807.

200. Maltzan to Hallstein and Blankenhorn, 29 May 1954, PAAA 311.22/2. Possibly the Soviets were disappointed with a statement drafted by Kroll and read by Bruns that the federal government would allow an expansion of trade only "within the framework of its international obligations," i.e., the COCOM/embargo program, Memorandum of Results, including prepared German statement, Bruns to Westrick, 7 August 1952, BdI, OA/1.

201. Memoranda by Wolff, 20 April 1953 and Zahn-Stranik (desk officer for East-West trade in the *Handelspolitische Abteilung* of the West German Foreign Office), 21 April, 1952 both in BdI, OA/1.

202. Memorandum of Results, signed by Wolff and other Eastern Committee members, 3 July 1952, BdI, OA/1.

203. BdI, OA/1.

204. Fifty-seventh meeting of the Foreign Trade Council, 9 October 1953, BA B 102/7196 H.2.

205. The planned delegation consisted of Wolf von Amerongen (now chairman of the Eastern Committee's Working Group on the USSR), Carl Haiblen (Felten and Guilleaume), and Konrad Wernecke (Zellstoff Fabrik Waldhof) for industry; Helmut Pollems (Rhein.-Westfälische Bank) for the banks; Karl Senff (timber importing firm Gratenau, Bremen) and Wilhelm Hansen (grain import/export firm Mackprang, Hamburg) for the trading community, Maltzan to Hallstein and Blankenhorn, 29 May 1954, PAAA 311.22/2. Boris Meissner (Soviet desk, Foreign Office) considered the signing of some type of payments agreement to be "the main purpose" of the trip, Meissner memorandum, 10 June 1954, PAAA 311.22/2.

206. Carnap to Hans Reuter et al., 1 June 1954, BdI, OA/1. Otto Wolff has subsequently stated that he held written assurances of American support for the trip from the office of the U.S. high commissioner, Otto Wolff von Amerongen, personal interview with the author, Cologne, 3 July 1991.

207. Wolff interview, Cologne, 3 July 1991. Maltzan had summarized the circumstances surrounding the proposed visit in favorable terms in a memorandum to Blankenhorn and Hallstein, 29 May 1954, PAAA 413.85.00/96.

208. Adenauer to Fritz Berg (BdI), 15 June 1954, BdI, OA/1; Wolff to Carl Haiblen et al. on the 22 June meeting with Adenauer, 24 June 1954, BdI, OA/1. Wolff has since recounted that at the 22 June meeting, Adenauer "exploded" at Hallstein and gave him an astonishing dressing down in front of the small group that included Maltzan, Hans Reuter, W. A. Menne (BdI, Hoechst), and Robert Pferdmenges (Cologne banker and mutual friend of Adenauer and Wolff), Wolff interview, Cologne, 3 July 1991.

209. Weekly report of the Foreign Office's East-West Trade desk, 8 June 1954; Zahn-Stranik memorandum, 4 May 1955, both in PAAA 311.22/4; Wolff's notes on a 16 September converstaion with Scherpenberg, BdI, OA/1. Adenauer's secondary concerns were the open attack on East-West trade restrictions and the suggestion for diplomatic negotiations with Moscow being carried on by Bundestag member Pfliederer (FDP) and the recent speeches of former Chancellors Heinrich Brüning and Hans Luther at the Rhein-Club in Dusseldorf, both of which attacked Adenauer for his pro-Western policies that allegedly forfeited German independence and the possibility of reunification, Wolff to Haiblen et al., 24 June 1954, BdI, OA/1.

210. This interpretation is further supported by evidence of similar motives cited in Adenauer's decision not to allow a German trade delegation travel to Warsaw in June 1954.

211. Wolff used Pferdmenges to obtain a meeting with Adenauer in which he could express the Eastern Committee's "complaints about the manner of cancellation" including "false information" from the Foreign Office that resulted in "skewed" (verzerrt) press reports, Carnap memorandum of a 12 June 1954 telephone conversation with Pferdmenges, BdI, OA/1; Wolff interview, Cologne, 3 July 1991; Wolff to Haiblen, et al., 24 June 1954, BdI, OA/1. A sampling of the press coverage from 9-10 June on the subject is available in the Otto Wolff Nachlass, RWWA 72-189-16.

212. Berg had already confirmed in his 12 June letter to Adenauer that "the industrial Bundesverband has consistently emphasized that … political demands must have primacy over economic demands," BdI, OA/1.

213. Wolff's summation for Haiblen et al., 24 June 1954, BdI, OA/1. On 16 September 1954 the Economics Ministry's Assistant Under-Secretary for trade with the East, Daniel, noted that "at the economic level, the opinions of the Foreign office, the Economics Ministry and the Eastern Committee are in absolute conformity. We are convinced of the necessity of normalizing the Eastern trade with those countries with which we have no trade treaties; however, we must acknowledge the primacy of politics in these questions," Wolff's notes BdI, OA/1. More than any other factor, this broad "conformity" of opinion separates the Bonn Republic's Eastern trade experiences from those of its Weimar predecessor.

214. Eastern Committee (Working Group on the USSR) to the Trade Office of the USSR in East Berlin, PAAA 311.22/3.

215. Wolff to Haiblen, et al., 24 June 1954, BdI, OA/1; Reuter to Hallstein, 26 April 1955, PAAA 311.22/4. In one of the few sharp criticisms, one of Bremen's representatives to the Bundesrat told Maltzan plainly that he did not agree with the decision and that the government ought to get on with the "expansion of East-West trade without considering possible questions of prestige," [Reinhardt's hand-written commentary on a memorandum regarding] Special Meeting on East-West Trade of the Bundesrat's Committee on Foreign Affairs, 14 October 1954, PAAA 311.22/3.

216. Weekly report of the Foreign Office's East-West trade desk, 8 June 1954, PAAA 311.22/2. Shortly thereafter the Rhein-Main Bank also established similar accounts.

217. Seiberlich to the Hamburg import/export firm of Maltzan & Timm, 28 July 1954, BA B 102/7214b.

218. After the collapse of the EDC project in August 1954, the Foreign Office's East-West trade specialist, Scherpenberg, told Wolff on 16 September 1954 that "in view of the now completely unclear political situation of the Federal Republic, any step toward a new Moscow trip by a German delegation would not be expedient. The situation, especially in view of world public opinion, is more explosive now than at the originally scheduled time of the trip," Wolff's notes, BdI, OA/1.

219. Zahn-Stranik memorandum, 20 October 1954, PAAA 413.22/3. In the 1953 Geneva discussions, the Soviets had proposed two-way trade of 500 million rubles, a figure that apparently continued to serve as the basis for discussions in 1954, PAAA 413.85.00/96.

220. At the direction of the Foreign Office, West German economic policy toward the Soviets remained on hold in the spring of 1955. In January, Maltzan told Carnap to "maintain the existing line" which meant "continued negotiations for the purpose of preparing an [economic] agreement, without concluding any binding agreement at the moment and without travelling to Moscow," Carnap memorandum, 4 January 1955, RWWA 72-189-14. These same instructions were repeated by the Foreign Office to the Eastern Committee in March, Carnap memorandum, 9 March 1955, RWWA 72-189-14.

221. Zahn-Stranik memorandum, 4 May 1955, PAAA 311.22/4; Scherpenberg to Hallstein, 6 May 1955, PAAA 311.22/4.

222. Bundesministerium für Gesamtdeutsche Fragen (hrsg.), *Dokumente zur Deutschlandpolitik*, III Reihe, Bd. 1, (Frankfurt, 1961) 76, 251. The diplomacy of Adenauer's September 1955 trip to Moscow has been explored by Josef Foschepoth, "Adenauers Moskaureise 1955," *Aus Politk und Zeitgeschichte*, B 22/86 (31 May 1986), 30-46. Whatever the Soviet motives for the June note, it coincided with Adenauer's plans; Bräutigam at the Foreign Office told Wolff that "the view of the Chancellor appears to be heading toward establishing diplomatic relations with the counties of the Eastern bloc as soon as possible," Wolff's notes on a 4 March 1955 conversation, RWWA 72-189-14.

223. The Foreign Office briefing paper on German/Russian Economic Negotiations in Moscow opened with a pessimistic assessment of the "economic situation in the Soviet Union" and went on to discuss at several points how the Soviets might use increased trade with FRG to improve the economic situation at home, PAAA 413.85.00/96. Erhard mentioned the "difficult [economic] situation in the East" in his 25 August letter to Adenauer offering thoughts on the interplay of "economic policy" and "political goals" in the upcoming negotiations, BA B 136/655. See also Khrushchev's own statements that in the mid-1950s Soviet machine tools were not of sufficient quality to develope the Soviet oil and gas industries, and that imports were needed, Jerrold Schecter, ed. and trans., *Khrushchev Remembers. The Glasnost Tapes* (Boston, 1990), 110-11.

224. Adenauer, *Erinneruungen 1953-1955* (Stuttgart, 1966), 553.

225. Foreign Office report, 10 August 1955, 14, PAAA 413.85.00/96.

226. Scherpenberg admitted vaguely that "it can not yet be determined at which level economic negotiations in Moscow will be conducted, rather this will be one point of the Chancellor's conversations in Moscow," memorandum Economic Negotiations with the Soviets, 8 August 1955, PAAA 413.85.00/96.

227. Erhard to Adenauer, 25 August 1955, BA B 136/655. See also Hans-Peter Schwarz's earlier, undocumented report that Erhard and Mueller-Armack, Under-Secretary for Economic Policy in the Economics Ministry, advocated using economic incentives such as long-term loans as a means of gaining concessions from the Soviets, Hans-Peter Schwarz, *Die Ära Adenauer 1949-1957*, (Stuttgart, 1981), 274.

228. Erhard concluded that "the current economic situation [in the FRG] is characterized by full employment. With that, there is no economic motive for making concessions," Erhard to Adenauer, 25 August 1955, BA B 136/655. Similarly, the Foreign Office assessment: "In the short run, there is from the purely economic perspective no special interest in intensifying trade relations with the Soviet Union. In the long run, the Soviet Union could gain some importance as an 'evening-out' [of cyclic fluctuations] market," report of 10 August 1955, PAAA 413.85.00/96

229. Erhard noted that the "labor force and capacity limit our room for additional foreign economic activity. Trade agreements, except in special cases, must be seen as sacrifices or at least as concessions," Erhard to Adenauer, 25 August 1955, BA B 136/655. Similarly, Scherpenberg on 8 August: "In the current economic circumstance of the Federal Republic, a large-scale economic agreement with the Soviets would require extraordinary exertions on the German side and would be by no means purely benficial for us," PAAA 413.85/96.

230. Scherpenberg, Reinhardt, et al. meeting with the Eastern Committee on Problems of Future Economic Relations with the Soviet Union, 18 July 1955, BdI, OA/1; Lupin memorandum, 19 August 1955, PAAA 413.85.00/110.

231. Carnap notes on a meeting of Wolff, et al. with members of the Foreign Office, 29 June 1955, BdI, OA/1.

232. Maltzan manuscript on The Question of East-West Trade, BA B 136/7808. An additional concern was avoiding any significant degree of West German "dependence" on Soviet materials, see e.g., Hallstein's questions at the interministerial meeting of 2 August 1955, PAAA 413.85.00/110.

233. Lupin told members of the Eastern Committee that "the Chancellor's negotiations will emphasize political questions" and that on economic issues the Germans would "receive Russian suggestions" but that real economic negotiations would be carried on at a later date by a German "commission" and its Russian counterpart, Wolff memorandum on a 29 June 1955 meeting at the Foreign Office, RWWA 72-189-14. Similarly, Reinhardt on 31 August: "On the basis of a conversation between the Chancellor and Prof. Erhard, there is no thought of reaching an economic agreement [in Moscow]." At that same meeting Foreign Office representative Bräutigam emphasized that "the Chancellor does not intend to sign any agreements, also no political agreements ... a trade treaty will certainly not be concluded during the visit to Moscow," Carnap memorandum, BdI, OA/1; Wilhelm Grewe, *Rückblenden 1976-1951* (Frankfurt, 1979), 248.

234. Erhard to Adenauer, 25 August 1955, BA B 136/655. For this reason, high-visibility personalities such as Erhard and Wolff were dropped from the delegation, Fritz Berg to Wolff on recent conversations with Pferdmenges, Erhard, and Finance Minister Fritz Schäffer, 16 August 1955, RWWA 72-189-14. Yet with the inclusion of Eastern trade experts Reinhardt and Scherpenberg in his delegation, Adenauer was prepared for serious economic talks if the need arose. Scherpenberg later told the Parliamentary Council that the German side had made "exhaustive" preparations for economic negotiations, Reinhardt to the twenty-second meeting of the Parliamentary Council of 28 September 1955, BA B 102/5933 H.2.

235. *Dokumente zur Deutschlandpolitik*, III, vol. 1, 326; Adenauer *Errinerungen*, 518.

236. Scherpenberg to the Parliamentary Council, 28 September 1955, BA B 102/5933 H.2.

237. *Dokumente zur Deutschlandpolitik*, III, vol. 1, 332-34.

Chapter Nine

FAMILIAR CLIENTS
West German Trade Policy in Eastern Europe 1956-1960

Politicized Trade in the Polish Crisis of 1956

*I*n the second half of the 1950s, West German trade toward Poland displayed essential continuity with the period of limited German sovereignty from 1949 to 1955. Most fundamentally, West German trade with Poland remained a very small portion of the enormous economic activities of the Federal Republic. Two-way trade with Poland lingered at less than 1 percent of West German total trade. In this economic context, political considerations rather than economic calculations continued to dominate West German trade policies toward Poland. Merchandise flows between the FRG and Poland remained sensitive to these political influences because West German policies largely determined the size and scope of trade. Although the primacy of political considerations over economic remained a central point of continuity in German trade policy toward Poland, German political goals toward Poland from 1956 to 1960 differed markedly from political motivations in the first half of the decade.

The dominating event of the period was the Polish October of 1956, which brought Wladyslaw Gomułka to power. The "right-wing nationalist deviation" that had cost Gomułka his party and government positions in 1949 was well known in the West. Coming on the heels of the Poznan workers' riot, Gomułka's appointment as first secretary appeared to Western leaders as a real chance for Poland to establish some degree of independence from the USSR.

Notes for this chapter begin on page 459.

Western governments, including the American, Canadian, and West German, sought to strengthen Gomułka's position, both within his own party and in his relations with the Soviets, by offering trade concessions and financial aid to the Polish regime. Between October 1956 and December 1958, the Federal Republic granted some DM 200 million in economic and financial aid to Poland. Although the West German federal bank, the Finance Ministry, and the private sector all advised against loans to Poland on economic grounds, the Foreign Office convinced the Economics Ministry that the change of leadership in Poland offered a unique political opportunity that justified Western economic assistance despite the accelerating deterioration of the Polish economy. By the spring of 1958 the Foreign Office had become disillusioned with Gomułka's policies and began urging a more cautious approach toward economic concessions for Poland. That caution translated into the end of West German financial charity toward Poland and a new slump in the importance of Polish trade for the FRG.

Events in Poland once again demonstrated the utility of trade-based economic diplomacy as the only tool of statecraft that the FRG could employ in the East. The international framework of the Cold War division of Europe continued to deprive the FRG of other forms of influence in Eastern Europe. In the end, the attempt to influence Gomułka away from Leninism failed, but the conscious West German decision to apply trade policies as a form of support for reform-minded regimes in the Soviet bloc emerged as an enduring West German political strategy for Eastern Europe over the following thirty years, and one that would help to shape events in the political tumult of 1989 and 1990.

In the six months prior to Gomułka's dramatic rehabilitation as first secretary in October 1956, West German-Polish trade relations had settled into what might be called a normal commercial relationship for countries operating across Europe's East-West divide. Resolution of the first round of the repatriation issue in 1955 had allowed both countries to shift the focus to the economic aspects of trade. The results were mixed; West German imports from Poland were up sharply in early 1956, but exports had grown only with the Federal Republic's extension of substantial loans in 1954 and early 1955 ($30 million) connected to Polish concessions on repatriation[1] (Graphs 9.1 and 9.2).

Between January 1955 and June 1956, the Poles had delivered 90 percent (c. $50 million) of their scheduled exports under the terms of the eighteen-month trade agreement signed in February 1955. The Germans were "especially satisfied" with $18.6 million in Polish coal that they received. West German exports reached 100 percent of the scheduled amount ($47 million) for the same period.[2] German exports were stimulated by the $10 million in loans granted by the Federal Republic to Poland as part of the 1955 repatriation agreement. Of the $6 million slated for purchases of West German investment goods, $5.4 million had been spent by July 1956.[3]

When preliminary negotiations began in May 1956 for a new agreement, the Polish trade representative, Jazdon, suggested that the existing 1955 agreement be extended for one year. The West German federal bank (Bank of the German Länder) was concerned about the amount of credit already extended to the Poles and sought to lower at least the short-term "swing" credit from $6 million to $5 million (already down from the original 1949 limit of $7.5 million).[4] The bank also wanted to transform the West German-Polish clearing accounts from dollars to limited convertibility deutsche marks. The Germans offered a four-month extension of existing arrangements (to 31 October), with the lower swing effective immediately. The Poles accepted the trade extension, rejected the swing reduction, and hinted at the need to increase the 1955 capital goods loan from $6 million to $10 million in order to finance the construction of the Pommerenzdorf power plant outside Szczecin.

When formal negotiations opened on 1 October 1956, both sides remained far apart on the financial arrangements for future trade. The Germans pressed for the elimination of the swing credit over the following two years, with a 3 percent interest charge on the outstanding balance. The Poles argued for the swing reduction over a period "longer than two years" with no interest charged on the balance. The Poles also wanted an bridge loan of $4 million to help with the swing reduction, while the Bank of the German Länder felt it could offer just $1.5 million.[5]

Beyond the swing credit, the Polish delegation made two additional and surprisingly large requests. First, the Poles asked for a $20 million "investment loan" for the completion of the Pommerenzdorf power plant, with the bulk of the money to be used for purchases from the gigantic West German elctrical firm AEG (Allgemeine Elekticitäts-Gesellschaft). The German delegation had reckoned with a request for some financing for the Pommerenzdorf project, but had expected the Poles to ask for about $4 million. Secondly, the Poles wished to buy 300,000 tons ($20 million) of grain from West Germany to help cover Poland's 1956 shortfall, now estimated at between 1 million and 1.2 million tons. Due to the magnitude of the new loan request and the potential grain sale (which might also require financing), the German delegation referred both questions to the interministerial Trade Policy Committee for evaluation.[6] How-

ever, before the Trade Policy Committee met to discuss these commercial ventures, the pent-up frustration in Poland came to a head in
the events of the "Polish October."

The trends that combined to produce a crisis atmosphere in
Poland during the summer and autumn of 1956 were long-term,
numerous, and complex.[7] Widespread dissatisfaction with the Stalinist system had been a constant feature of Polish society since the
fraudulent referendum and dishonest elections of 1946 and 1947.
Stalin's death, the initiation of Malenkov's New Course, and the
"Swiatlo Affair" combined to crystalize discontent within the party.
In December 1954, the Central Committee subjected the Politburo to
scathing criticism over its management of affairs during the past five
years. With nothing positive to offer in response to these criticisms,
the Stalinist leadership triumvirate (Boleslaw Bierut, Jakob Berman,
Hilary Minc) sought to reduce the accumulated tension by gradually
relaxing cultural and political censorship. At this point, the Politburo
made no personnel changes, although Gomułka was released from
house arrest. Meanwhile, the Central Committee waffled on economic policy, incomprehensibly endorsing both Malenkov's New
Course in the Soviet Union and chief Soviet ideologist Dimitri Shepilov's subsequent rejection of it.

This stagnation was broken by the twentieth party conference of
the Communist Party of the Soviet Union (CPSU) and the death of
Polish President Bierut, both in February 1956. Bierut's replacement
by Edward Ochab opened the door to a more general shake-up in
leadership. In May, Berman was ousted as part of the reform of the
security apparatus. In June, Minc's vulnerability as economic czar
was revealed when the Congress of Polish Economists openly repudiated Shepilov's reaffirmation of Stalinist economic policy. After
the Poznan riots in June, the party polarized into the Natolin (Stalinist) faction, and the "evolutionist" faction. The Seventh Plenum in
July 1956 laid out the issues facing the country: degree of external
identification with the USSR, press censorship, agrarian policy,
release of Cardinal Stefan Wyszynski, wage increases, rehabilitation
of Gomułka. The differences between the two factions were clear
and the Seventh Plenum failed to make any policy decisions.

Both factions sought to co-opt Gomułka for their side, but his
views on collectivization, on the party history from 1949 to 1954,
and on relations with the USSR prevented an agreement with the
Natolin group. In October, Ochab joined the evolutionists who then
came to an arrangement with Gomułka that sparked Minc's resignation on 9 October. Over the weekend of 13-15 October Gomułka
was brought into a reconstituted Politburo and the way seemed clear

for an across-the-board reform policy. During the next week, the new Politburo managed to survive an attempted coup by the Natolin faction and a visit by a powerful and nervous Soviet delegation. On 21 October, Politburo elections were repeated as part of the Eighth Plenum and Gomułka was elected first secretary.

Since his release from confinement in December 1954, Gomułka had grown into a universally recognized symbol of the deStalinization drive in Poland: "His 'right-wing' deviation appealed to nationalists outraged at Soviet domination. To the anti-communists, he was the leader of a movement toward independence; to the revisionists, toward democratic socialism. To the concerned Communists, he was the savior of crumbling Communist rule."[8] Although his election ended the immediate crisis in the upper levels of the party, it remained unclear how he planned to balance the wide variety of political hopes that had been pinned to him and at the same time solve the economic problems facing the country.

On 20 October 1956 Gomułka addressed the Central Committee in a lengthy speech that unmercifully attacked the general economic mismanagement and the agrarian policies of the previous Six Year Plan. He ridiculed the "clumsy attempt to present the painful Poznan tragedy as the work of imperialist agents and provocateurs" and attributed the riots instead to the "profound discontent of the entire working class" with the meager results of the highly touted Six Year Plan. The following day, the Eighth Plenum closed with a resolution that broke free from the most objectionable Stalinist goals and methods of economic planning.[9] Thanks to the unprecedented and prompt publication of numerous government documents in the Polish press, Western observers had been able to closely follow the events in Poland since the Seventh Plenum at the end of July 1956.

Like most other observers outside and inside Poland, the West German federal government had no clear picture of Gomułka's future plans. It was clear to all that Gomułka sought more independence from Moscow than his predecessors had done. How much more independence Gomułka sought, how much he could obtain, or what forms this independence might take was clear to none. Still, any degree of additional independence that Poland might be able to obtain from the USSR was welcomed by the West.[10]

On 29 June 1956 SPD Chairman Erich Ollenhauer commented in the Bundestag on the "loosening of the situation" in Eastern Europe and urged the federal government to work for "better" or even "normal" relations with the Eastern countries.[11] On the evening of 21 October, Adenauer declared that "in my ... opinion an understanding between ourselves and a free Poland, i.e., a Poland that is no longer a slave to Moscow, is absolutely possible, even probable."[12]

By the time the West German Trade Policy Committee met on October 23 to discuss Polish trade and financial questions, the economic aspects of the earlier Polish requests had been almost fully eclipsed by the political events of the preceding weeks. The technical details surrounding the reduction of the swing credit fell into the background as the Trade Policy Committee declared that a "fundamental political decision is required" as part of the West German response to Polish grain and financial requests.[13] The Foreign Office's Commercial Affairs Department presented the political case for an economic accommodation of Poland. The committee was reminded of Adenauer's public statements about cultivating Poland's "efforts toward independence." The Foreign Office considered it "desirable that the results of the economic negotiations should be in keeping with those [Polish] efforts, i.e., that as far as possible the grain deliveries should carried out and the Pommerenzdorf power plant project realized."[14] Representatives from the Agriculture Ministry reminded the group in an understated way that "grain sales to Poland were not commercially disadvantageous" for the FRG and that financing the sale "should be possible."

Yet the economic arguments spoke loudly against further financial favors for Poland. The Finance Ministry pointed out that the federal government had already guaranteed a number of private purchasing credits to Poland as part of its export development program ("Hermes" obligations) and the funds for the program were limited. In addition, members of the Finance Ministry reported that private exporters had voiced objections to granting extended payment conditions to Poland out of fear that other Soviet bloc countries might demand the same benefits.[15]

After "exhaustive discussions," the committee agreed that the "technical preparations" for both of the special deals should begin, including the question of including the Pommerenzdorf project in the government-guaranteed export credit program. The final decision on both issues would be made by the cabinet. In addition, the Trade Policy Committee authorized a renewal of the existing eighteen-month trade agreement for the period June 1956 to December 1957 and the extension of an "appropriate loan" to Poland to smooth over the progressive reduction of the swing credit and the transformation of the clearing accounts from dollars to marks.

The very next day, Adenauer told a press conference that it remained too early to say anything definitive about the final outcome of events in Poland, but that it was "probable" that relations between the Federal Republic and Poland would change for the better. Adenauer again reassured Poland that the Federal Republic sought to resolve its differences with Poland only through "peaceful negotiations."[16] Over the following weeks Adenauer repeatedly expressed his "sympathy" for both Poland and Hungary and praised Poland's "desire for freedom."[17]

Despite the fact that Gomułka had yet to generate a concrete program for Poland, the Foreign Office was determined to do what it could to support the new Polish Politburo. That thinking had already been apparent at the Trade Policy Committee meeting on 23 October, and it decisively influenced the renewed trade agreement with Poland, which, together with a letter on payments, was signed in Bonn on 16 November. The agreement called for $140 million in two-way trade over the eighteen-month period from July 1956 to December 1958, a 20 percent increase over the amount set out in the previous agreement of February 1955. West German imports totaled $68 million, including $24 million in agricultural goods, $40 million in nonagricultural goods, and $4 million in transportation services. Almost two-thirds of West German imports were spread across just four commodities: coal ($20 million), timber ($6 million), eggs ($9 million), and poultry ($6 million). Among West German exports the leading categories were large iron and steel products ($22 million), machinery ($10 million), chemicals ($9 million), electrical products ($2.1 million), and small iron and steel products ($1.9 million). In addition to this expansion of normal trade, the Germans agreed in a separate letter "to carry out a delivery of grain from the Federal Republic of Germany to the People's Republic of Poland" and that both sides "will return to this question in two to four weeks, as soon as the Polish side has given exact information about the amounts and types" of grain desired. More significantly, the German allowed the Poles to take both investment goods and grain deliveries on credit. On the payments issue, both sides agreed to convert their accounts from dollars to marks beginning the first of the year, but the "technical details" of the conversion were left to further negotiation between the Bank of the German Länder and the Narodowy Bank Polski.[18] In total the Germans offered Poland quite a lot in this economic package: a substantial expansion of two-way trade, supplementary grain deliveries, credit for industrial equipment and food, and further negotiation on the terms of payment. The West German press reported very favorably on the new agreements, on the general increase in trade, and especially on increased deliveries of Polish coal.[19]

West German generosity reflected both the Foreign Office's conviction that the FRG must support the new Polish government and the existing diplomatic situation, which continued to limit the ways in which the Federal Republic could show goodwill toward any Polish regime. The determination not to prejudice the West German stand on the Oder-Neisse border question meant that the Federal Republic could not offer formal recognition to Gomułka's government by establishing diplomatic relations, as Brentano repeatedly made clear. Adenauer and Brentano both warned that overly friendly, public statements of Western support might do more harm than good to Gomułka's position.[20] The international framework of Cold War Europe compelled the Federal Republic to use trade and trade financing when seeking some means of affecting politics in Poland.[21]

Trade and trade financing were particularly suitable tools for demonstrating support for Gomułka's new course. No one inside or outside Poland doubted that economic failure had played a major part in sparking the Poznan riots and bringing down the Stalinist Politburo. Gomułka himself had admitted as much in his 20 October speech. The Soviets realized this as well. Immediately following the Poznan riots Soviet Politburo members Nikolai Bulganin and Georgi Zhukov arrived in Warsaw offering $25 million in consumer goods to alleviate immediate shortages and to shore up the regime. This was followed in November by a Polish-Soviet joint Communique on Military and Economic Co-operation, in which the USSR canceled Polish debts, extended credits for Polish purchases of grain and other commodities, and raised the price offered for Polish coal.[22] The West, with the Federal Republic in the lead, was also eager to expand its economic aid to Poland in 1957. In December 1956 Brentano told the *Politisch-Soziale Korrespondenz* that the Federal Republic hoped to intensify its cultural and economic relations with Eastern Europe.[23]

As the Polish economy stumbled through 1957, it became clear that intensified economic contact between the two nations would require the FRG to underwrite any increase in trade. In 1957 the Federal Republic granted two massive financial relief packages to Poland, one in July and another in December. As early as January 1957, the Economics Ministry had received parliamentary inquiries as to whether the "political changes" in Poland might impair Polish ability to repay the credits granted in 1955 and 1956. Walter Steidle, the Economics Ministry's desk officer for East and Southeast Europe, replied that the Poles had adhered to all repayment terms so far, and that the Economics Ministry expected this to continue.[24] By mid-year this optimism had faded; it was clear that the Polish economy was in very deep trouble.

From 17 to 19 June, Stalmann met with Polish trade officials in Warsaw for a briefing on economic relations between the two states.[25]

The news was all bad. Poland was far behind in its coal deliveries. Further, the Polish Foreign Trading Companies had used their new decentralized freedoms to go overboard in ordering goods from Germany. As a result, the Poles had recentralized the import licensing procedure to confront an immediate foreign currency crisis. Polish Vice-Minister for Foreign Trade Bajer predicted a Polish debt to the Federal Republic of $30 million to $35 million by year's end. He explained that the "Polish government was extremely anxious to expand trade [with the FRG] partially for non-economic reasons," but that even maintaining the existing trade volume would not be possible "if special measures are not taken." The Poles could, with "the greatest difficulties," finish repaying the 1955 grain loan, but without some relief action, would be unable to make any additional purchases of investment goods. Officials of the Polish Foreign Trade Ministry spoke of avoiding an "abrupt interruption of the otherwise very positive development of German exports to Poland."

The Poles offered two solutions for their financial difficulties. First, a "long-term" coal contract through 1958 that would increase the Polish coal quota in the West German market to 2 million tons, with the possibility of renewal for 1959. Coal was the decisive commodity since "an expansion of Polish exports to the Federal Republic in either the agricultural or the industrial sector is not to be expected."[26] Second, Bajer asked "whether a private bank consortium, with a guarantee from the federal government, would be prepared to take over [Poland's] existing obligations and possibly also offer an advance on the long-term coal contract."

Within and among the West German ministries there was considerable divergence of opinion about the best response to Poland's economic problems. The Economics Ministry acknowledged the political argument for aiding Poland, maintaining that "in view of the current political conditions in Poland, which must be considered, everything should be tried in order to at least partially satisfy Polish wishes."[27] At the same time, these experts thought it "extremely doubtful" that Poland could deliver 1.5 million to 2 million tons of coal by the end of 1958, claiming Polish export capabilities were "at most" 1 million to 1.5 million tons. In any event, the German market could not absorb more than 350,000 additional tons of Polish coal.[28] On the financial side, Steidle considered it "hardly possible" that the banks would agree to cover a Polish payments moratorium. In the course of several interministerial meetings in early July, the Finance Ministry repeatedly rejected advance West German payments on a Polish coal contract, citing both financial and legal problems. The federal bank also saw little chance for additional long-term credit for Poland.[29] Under these circumstances, the meeting of the German-Polish Mixed Commission in July could make little progress toward covering Polish obligations of DM 190 million due by the end of 1957[30] (Graph 9.3 and Table 9.1).

In the face of these formidable problems the Foreign Office presented to the cabinet a large-scale financial aid relief plan for Poland.[31] After summarizing the constraints on West German-Polish trade caused by Polish export deficiencies, the Foreign Office focused on the political aspects of the problem, reminding the cabinet that "heretofore the Federal government has consistently been of the opinion that an intensification of [West] German-Polish trade is politically expedient. This opinion has been strengthened by Polish developments of the past autumn. At the moment, the greatest possible trade with the West provides one of the few counterweights to Poland's extraordinary dependence on the Soviet Union." Any decline in trade between the two countries at this time was "politically undesirable" because it would "create the impression in the West and in Poland that the Federal Republic is showing no understanding for the difficult economic and political situation of Poland."[32] A "partial moratorium" of DM 30 million was established for Polish debts due in the remainder of 1957.[33]

With this DM 30 million short-term prop for German-Polish trade in place, economic talks resumed in Berlin at the end of October 1957 in the hope of finding a sounder, long-term basis for an expansion of trade. Both parties agreed that "Polish coal exports to the Federal Republic have become the central problem of German-Polish trade." For this reason the negotiating delegations included Director Wilhelm Pape from the private West German coal importing consortium, Polimport, and Director Wolski from the state-run Polish coal exporting company, Wenglokoks, as well as the resident coal expert at the Polish Ministry for Foreign Trade, Horowitz.[34] As a prerequisite for any price concessions, the Poles insisted on a long-term contract that assured future West German purchases. Pape insisted on Polish guarantees on delivery and quality as well as substantial price reductions before he would make any West German commitment. Otherwise, he insisted, Poland could never regain its declining share of the German market. The Poles countered with requests for changes in railroad freight rates and taxes in order to help Polish coal compete with U.S. imports. When the official talks ended on 30 October, Polimport and Wenglokoks were instructed to continue negotiations on a private level until an agreement could be reached.[35] In the absence of a coal agreement that would necessarily set the parameters for a new trade agreement, both sides considered extending the existing trade agreement until 31 March 1958. But the

Poles needed more than an extension; they asked for increased exports allowances for hogs, pork, brewer's barley, sugar, and spirits. In addition, the Poles were interested in more loans – a long-term investment goods credit and a short-term credit – provided that the Federal Republic promised to facilitate repayment by accepting more Polish exports.[36]

With West German-Polish negotiations stuck on a range of issues and the Polish economy still in deep trouble, only additional trade concessions by the FRG could prevent a downturn in trade between the two countries. By November 1957 Brentano felt compelled to present a second financial relief package to the cabinet, reminding his colleagues that the July relief had been granted with the "assumption that political considerations would make further repayment concessions necessary in the coming months."[37] The Foreign Office plan suggested two important financial concessions: first, a one-year moratorium on payments due from Poland in the first half of 1958 for goods covered by the federal export credit guarantee program (c. DM 20 million); second, a one-year moratorium on DM 6.3 million due on 31 December 1957 as part of the five-year swing reduction negotiated in 1956. Except for the federal bank (since renamed as the Bundesbank), which opposed a moratorium on swing reduction payments, other portions of the ministerial bureaucracy backed the Foreign Office plan.

The Economics Ministry recognized that Poland would be unable to pay its 1958 debts to the Federal Republic (DM 61 million) out of earnings from exports to the Federal Republic. Poland was already 95,000 tons behind in coal deliveries for the first nine months of 1957, which meant that the target of 1.5 million tons over eighteen months would never be reached.[38] Since the Foreign Office considered some type of relief necessary "for political reasons," Reinhardt could certify for the Economics Ministry that "from the economic standpoint there are no objections to that sort of help."[39] On 21 November the cabinet approved only the first portion of the plan; on the advice of Bundesbank President Wilhelm Vocke the moratorium on swing repayments was rejected "unless negotiations would collapse over this point."[40] As in the earlier July economic concessions to Poland, political considerations dominated West German thinking in supplying further debt relief to the Poles. Brentano reiterated "the political importance of economic relations with Poland" and pointed out again that the FRG had only trade and trade financing to use as a "counterweight" to Soviet influence.

The FRG was not alone in the use of trade to influence the direction of Polish politics. In 1957 virtually all of the leading Western powers were offering generous trade and financial choices to Poland, including a loosening of the remaining embargo restrictions.[41] After economic negotiations in April and May, the U.S. agreed to provide $90 million in credit to Poland. On 24 September COCOM approved a U.S. motion for a "temporary" rule allowing unlimited exports of quantitatively restricted items to Poland and applications to COCOM for some exports of previously banned goods to Poland.[42] The United States also encouraged the Federal Republic toward a "positive development of relations with Poland."[43]

Armed with new relief proposals for Poland and confirmed in their judgments on the approach to Gomułka's Poland by a Western consensus, the German delegation began a new round of economic negotiations in Warsaw on 25 November. By 3 December a bundle of agreements had been reached that extended the trade agreement of 16 November 1956 to 31 March 1958, that put in place a one-year moratorium on DM 16.5 million due from Poland in the first half of 1958, and that increased German imports of five Polish agricultural commodities.[44]

Although the December 1957 agreements represented substantial economic relief to Poland on the part of the Federal Republic, they offered far less than the Poles were requesting. The Poles sought financial relief in the form of a DM 40 million bank loan [!] and a moratorium on the swing repayment (DM 6.3 million) that was now due at the end of 1958. In other words, Poland sought financial aid totalling almost three times the DM 16.5 millions that the Federal Republic granted. In trade, the Poles asked for Germany to accept 5,000 live pigs/week and doggedly stuck to this number. Only after lengthy personal negotiations between Stalmann and Bajer would the Poles agree to 1,100 animals/week and the right to lodge a written protest asking that the question be reconsidered.

The West German refusal to grant even greater trade concessions was based on a mixture of economic calculation and political considerations. There were genuine economic obstacles. A bank loan for DM 40 million was out of the question; the banks would insist on a federal government guarantee of the loan, whereas the current government guarantee program covered only commodity exports and could not be used for capital transactions. Similarly, the growth of West Germany's own hog livestock (20 million head in 1957, up from 15 million head just a few years previously) dissuaded the Agriculture Ministry from accepting 250,000 Polish hogs in the next year.[45] These economic obstacles were real, but hardly insurmountable.

More important in dampening German support for Poland was the changing political assessment of the Gomułka regime that had been underway in the Foreign Office since late summer. Based on Gomułka's first year in power, the Foreign Office doubted whether he was really the independent-minded national communist they had assumed him to be. In both his economic and political policies, Gomułka was proving a disappointment to Western hopes. Through May 1957 Gomułka still had to accommodate himself to the remaining Stalinists in the party. Hence he delivered his early "hard-line" speeches, even those extolling the security organs.[46] After the complete defeat of Stalinist remnants in May 1957, Gomułka was no longer in any danger; by October 1957 his control was "well consolidated." Yet thereafter Gomułka intensified the repression against his former "revisionist" allies.[47] The remaining dogmatists in the Economic Committee of the Council of Ministers, led by Eugeniusz Szyr, who became a deputy premier in 1959, blocked implementation of the decentralization plans submitted in May 1957 by Oskar Lange and others at the reform-minded Economic Council. In early 1958 the reform proposals were rejected outright. Shortly thereafter, Gomułka limited the right to strike, and the Workers' Councils were brought under control by the imposition of a Workers' Self-Government Conference.

In foreign relations as well, Gomułka disappointed the West. The "Polish path" to socialism did not require any serious break with the USSR. The November 1956 Polish-Soviet Communique on Military and Economic Cooperation had initiated a steady improvement in official Polish-Soviet relations. At the same time, the similarities in background and training between Gomułka and Khrushchev led to good personal relations between the two leaders, culminating in Gomułka's successful trip to the USSR in 1958.

By late 1957 the Foreign Office had become suspicious of Gomułka's political, economic, and foreign policies. Even at the time that Brentano submitted his second financial aid proposal to the cabinet in November 1957, the Foreign Office was sounding a cautious note in its approach to Gomułka. In preparing that aid proposal, Zahn-Stranik explained that trade and credit concessions would remain "small" for the present; "truly meaningful" decisions would be made in the spring "if we succeed in establishing a clear political line regarding Poland." At an interministerial meeting on the issue, the assistant under-secretary for commercial policy, Harkort, summarized "the Foreign Office's current political line toward Poland" by "emphasizing that in view of the current political state of the Gomułka system, one should help Poland somewhat, but not too much."[48]

By the spring of 1958, Adenauer was publicly writing off the Gomułka experiment as a failure.[49] With this, the West Germans began slowly to move away from major new trade concessions and debt relief for Poland. When German-Polish economic negotiations resumed early 1958, the Germans were offering only a straight, three-month extension of the November 1956 agreement, but no new loans and no concessions designed to increase the volume of trade. Over the next two years the existing agreement was extended repeatedly at three- or six-month intervals, each time without significant new financial aid or trade concessions for Poland. In October 1958 the West Germans rejected a Polish suggestion for a major new trade agreement between the FRG and Poland to replace the old JEIA agreement of 1949 – something the Poles hoped might be a first step toward normalized diplomatic relations.[50] At the same time, the Foreign Office dropped plans to ask the cabinet for yet another major debt restructuring for Poland, settling instead for a smaller "consolidation" of DM 42 million in Polish debt. The political situation in Poland remained the chief determinant of West German commercial policy. As Ambassador Georg Duckwitz, head of the new Eastern Department in the Foreign Office explained, "In view of the pro-Soviet, anti-Federal Republic position of the Warsaw government, there is no reason to accommodate Polish financial desires with the public funds of the Federal Republic."[51]

Without the type of politically motivated external stimulation that had brought on a surge in West German exports to Poland in 1958 (up $13.3 million), German exports to Poland stagnated again after 1959, which meant that they declined in significance for the West German economy (Graphs 9.4 and 9.5). In its relationship to the total exports of the West German economy, the Polish market was less significant in 1961 than it had been in 1951. The supplemental agreement of April 1960 called for an increase of DM 230 million ($55 million) in two-way trade for each of the next two years. Without special financing, however, West German exports to Poland could not increase. In fact, they declined by 3 percent ($2.1 million) from 1960 to 1961. The slightly better performance of Polish exports (although these, too, declined in significance for the Federal Republic) went toward paying off the Polish debt accumulated from 1956 to 1958.

The Federal Republic's experiences with trade diplomacy and the Gomułka regime forced the ministerial bureaucracy to confront the effectiveness and utility of trade-based economic diplomacy in shaping the course of events in Poland. The limits of West German economic diplomacy vis-à-vis Poland in the 1950s lay in its obvious inability to counteract Soviet "military diplomacy." Even on the assumption that Gomułka sought genuine independence from the Soviets, radically increased Western economic aid could not provide a counterweight to the presence of the Red Army. Reporting from Warsaw, the Economics Minstry's expert on East and Southeast Europe, Schauenburg, explained to Under-Secretary Reinhardt that "the *political power relations* are what remain decisive. The Russian Occupation force and Russian tanks stand in bases in Poland not far from Warsaw and would be prepared, in the event of a genuine deviation from Moscow's line, to march at any time in order to prevent Poland from deviating toward the West. Even greatly increased economic help for Poland would not change this."[52] While in Warsaw, Schauenburg had conferred with the Austrian ambassador to Poland about the question of using Western trade to influence Polish policies. The Austrian trade representative in Poland told the Germans bluntly that the Polish regime would not respond to that kind of action: "If you wish to practice charity toward Poland, you are free to do so. But a political change by Gomułka for that reason – not to be expected."[53] Somewhat later, the Foreign Office acknowledged that economic leverage was not moving Gomułka. Duckwitz admitted in December 1958 that "even a mild influence on Warsaw's aggressive German policies is hardly to be expected from financial favors."[54]

Ironically, in view of these disappointing results, events in Poland once again demonstrated the utility of trade-based economic diplomacy as the only form of leverage that the FRG could employ in the East. Throughout the 1950s, the Cold War division of Europe continued to deprive the FRG of virtually all other mechanisms for exerting influence in Eastern Europe. For this reason, trade contact was never broken off, even in the bitter disappointment over Gomułka in 1958 and 1959. The Trade Policy Committee explicitly instructed that trade contact with Poland "not be broken" even though the immediate economic and political grounds for economic diplomacy toward Poland had disappeared. The motives for this instruction lay in the long-term constraints of the international order. The West Germans well understood that the FRG had to "stay in touch [with the Poles] through trade discussions in order to use this path perhaps again later to broach political themes."[55] Indeed, the West Germans would frequently return to the "path" of trade diplomacy over the next thirty years as they struggled toward a more normal relationship with their Polish neighbors.

Business as Usual with Czechoslovakia

Between 1955 and 1960 the Federal Republic developed a trade relationship with the Czechoslovakia that differed fundamentally from the German-Polish and German-Soviet trade relationships. The absence of any looming, unresolved political differences between West Germany and Czechoslovakia provided the key to this development. Other than the general security considerations associated with the Western embargo policy, the Federal Republic had no overriding political motives affecting its trade with Czechoslovakia.[56] This meant that when revisions in the pan-Western embargo policy slowly reduced the political considerations affecting Western trade with Czechoslovakia over the course of the 1950s, West German-Czechoslovak trade become largely depoliticized. Thereafter, Czechoslovak abilities to export successfully to the West largely shaped the flow of trade. As a result of Czechoslovak economic limitations, trade stagnated in the later half of the 1950s.

As it had with other East European countries, West German trade with the Czechoslovakia had been politicized in 1948 to 1949 as part of the American-initiated trade embargo policy reflecting the division of Europe. As the Western countries gradually relaxed the Western embargo policy toward the East, they removed the most obviously politicized aspect of West German-Czechoslovakian trade. The Western countries had implemented a first major relaxation of export control policy toward the Soviet bloc in August 1954. In 1958 the Western allies announced another major revision of the Western embargo lists (International Lists I and II). Together, these actions removed the most overt political obstacles limiting East-West trade, except for those restrictions still affecting a very small percentage of genuinely strategic items. In the absence of first-rate bilateral political conflicts, West German-Czechoslovakian trade stood to benefit substantially from this gradual reduction of the Cold War embargo.

That contrasts sharply with the conditions surrounding German-Polish and German-Soviet trade. In each of those situations, the Federal Republic had its own political considerations, which it imposed on trade relations even as the Western embargo policy was waning. West German relations with Czechoslovakia lacked the raw material for the type of high-level political and emotional exchanges that characterized German-Polish and German Soviet relations. Unlike their Silesian, Pomeranian, and Prussian compatriots in Poland, the German minority had largely disappeared from Czechoslovakia by 1950. There were no emotionally charged territorial issues. Unlike the superpower USSR, Czechoslovakia had no real or imagined international responsibility for German reunification. Finally, the dreary stability of the Czechoslovakian communist regime in the 1950s ruled out a dramatic opening such as the "Polish October."

For each of these reasons the Federal Republic had little political motive either to restrict or to expand trade with Czechoslovakia. Similarly, the world wide success of the West German economy meant that the Federal Republic had no economic motive to initiate any dramatic changes in its trade relationship with Czechoslovakia. Political considerations had artificially catalyzed German trade with Poland from 1956 to 1959 with trade concessions, export credits, and debt relief. At the same time, another round of political sniping with the USSR over German reunification in 1955 limited the growth of German-Soviet trade. In the Czechoslovak case, once the embargo restrictions were toned down, "business as usual" characterized trade with the FRG. Unfortunately, business with this centrally directed economy was, as usual, not booming.

Between 1955 and 1957 German-Czechoslovakian trade began to recover from the slump it had experienced in 1952 to 1954. In 1955 and 1956 West German exports to and imports from Czechoslovakia grew strongly, as measured both in dollar value and as a percentage of Federal Republic total trade (Graphs 9.6-9.9). After 1957, however, growth slowed markedly. Although in most years from 1957 to 1961 trade showed small increases in its dollar value (current prices), this growth did not keep pace with the expansion in the Federal Republic's trade with other partners. Consequently, Czechoslovakia's share of West German trade began to decline again. By 1961 the Czechoslovak market absorbed just about the same percentage of Federal Republic exports as it had taken at the height of the Western embargo a decade earlier in 1951 – just 0.6 percent!

More than any other single factor, Czechoslovakia's own export abilities continued to determine the volume of German-Czechoslovakian trade. By 1956 the Soviet Union and the rest of the Soviet bloc had greatly reduced their demands on Czechoslovak exports from the earlier high levels of 1952 to 1954. In 1956 the Czechoslovaks sent "only" 30.8 percent of their total exports to the USSR (1954 = 34.6 percent). In 1956 Czechoslovakia could send 35.1 percent of its exports out to market economies (1953 = 21.8 percent). More important, Czechoslovakia now had more of the "desired" goods, especially coal and machinery, to send to the West.[57]

The reduction in demands from the East left Czechoslovakia free to increase exports to the West. Czechoslovak commitments on coal exports to the Federal Republic increased steadily throughout these years: 650,000 tons ($4.5 million) in 1955; 950,000 tons ($6.8 million) in 1956; 1,000,000 tons ($10.5 million) in 1957; and 1,100,000 tons ($12.3 million) in 1958.[58] Coal provided between 20 percent and 25 percent of Czechoslovakia's exports to the Federal Republic, and increased fuel exports provided the core of increased West German imports from Czechoslovakia during these years. Czechoslovak earnings from coal exports helped finance the growth in West German exports to Czechoslovakia from 1955 to 1959.

This period of increased trade was short-lived. By 1957-1958 Czechoslovakia was again facing the economic and political limits of its ability to export to the West. In 1956 the Soviets once again began stepping up their imports of Czechoslovak industrial machinery. In 1957 the Soviets and Czechoslovaks concluded a number of "far-ranging agreements" for the integration of Soviet and Czechoslovakian economic plans as part of Khruschchev's new strategy for Soviet economic growth. Accordingly, by 1965 Czechoslovakia was slated to conduct 42 percent of its foreign trade with the USSR, 32 percent with other centrally planned economies and only 26 percent with market economy countries. Soviet expert Zbigniew Brzezinski noted as early as 1960 that "Soviet economic ties with Czechoslovakia, combining the desirable characteristics of an advanced, highly skilled industrial base and a hyper-loyal regime, went beyond any arrangement concluded with other states."[59]

These Soviet-Czechoslovak agreements immediately affected Czechoslovak manufacturing industries, which had been reemerging gradually as successful exporters to the West, including to the FRG. In 1956 machine exports to the USSR had been just $113.8 million, or 31.7 percent of Czechoslovak exports to the Soviets. After five years of steady increase they were $293.2 million or 48.1 percent of Czechoslovak exports to the Soviets.[60] On the other side, the 1958 trade agreement with the Federal Republic showed no increase for Czechoslovakian exports of iron and steel products ($4 million). The 1959 agreement showed no increases for either iron and steel or machinery exports to the Federal Republic.

The dollar value of West German exports to Czechoslovakia stagnated from 1958 to 1960; the same happened to German imports from Czechoslovakia in 1960 to 1961. As the decade drew to a close, the Czechoslovakian share of West German trade – not large to begin with – began to slip again. After the downs and ups of the 1950s, the Czechoslovakian share of West German trade (both imports and exports) at the end of the decade was close to what it had been in 1951. Together, the West German share of Czechoslovak total trade showed only small improvement. In 1961 West Germany took only 3 percent of Czechoslovakia's total exports (1951 = 2 percent) and supplied 3.7 percent of total imports (1951 = 2.3 percent).

This overall stagnation should not conceal significant changes occurring within the distribution of Czechoslovak trade with the

West. The Federal Republic had strengthened its position, regaining a traditional German role as Czechoslovakia's premier Western trade partner. By 1961 the Federal Republic's share of Czechoslovak market economy trade had increased to 10.2 percent of Czechoslovak exports (1951 = 5.2 percent) and 12.1 percent of Czechoslovak imports (1951 = 6 percent).

The uniqueness of the German-Czechoslovak trade relationship after 1954 lies in the absence of substantive political conflict between the two countries. The lack of basic raw material for conflict had its origins in a variety of political and historical factors: the role of Czechoslovakia in the war and its settlement, the quick resolution of the German minority issue from 1945 to 1950, and the stable loyalty of Czechoslovakia's communist regime to the Soviet Union. Under these circumstances, the performance of the Czechoslovak economy, specifically its ability to export to the West, determined the volume of German-Czechoslovak trade. For Czechoslovakia, this was not good news. By the late 1950s Czechoslovak agricultural and industrial productivity had fallen far behind that of West Germany. After 1957 a new series of economic agreements with the USSR and other Soviet bloc countries further constricted Czechoslovak exports to the West. As a result, West German trade with Czechoslovakia struggled to keep pace with the Federal Republic's rapidly expanding worldwide trade.

Trade Treaty Politics with the Soviet Union

After the establishment of diplomatic relations between the Federal Republic and the USSR in September 1955, another two-and-a-half years elapsed before the two countries normalized trade relations with a treaty. The central importance of the USSR for any solution to the "German question," however defined, meant that West German-Soviet trade relations – as the primary point of contact between the two countries – carried momentous political overtones. Adenauer, Brentano, and Erhard continued to link progress toward a Soviet trade treaty with the FRG's international goals in Eastern and Western Europe, so political issues largely determined the schedule for reaching a West German-Soviet trade agreement.

By connecting political issues to economic issues, the West Germans slowed progress toward a trade treaty in two ways. First, they delayed the start of treaty negotiations for almost two years. West German dissatisfaction with the outcome of the two Geneva conferences in 1955 prevented the Federal Republic from entering into trade negotiations with the Soviets for almost two full years after Adenauer's return from Moscow. During that time, the Eastern Committee tried in vain to reach a private agreement with the Soviets, while the Soviets sought a formal agreement with the Federal Republic. During this time, 1955 to 1956, trade itself showed a quickening pace of growth over the previous years but remained modest in comparison to the post-treaty period of 1958 to 1960.

A second reason for the lengthy lag in reaching a treaty lay in the complicated nature of the negotiations that finally began in July 1957. A variety of political considerations underlay Adenauer's decision to open trade talks at that time, and the negotiations touched on a range of mixed political and economic issues. The two countries had to resolve two economic issues (trade, payments); a mixed economic-political issue (consular relations); and a political issue (repatriation) in order to fully normalize trade relations.

The results were clearly worth the effort. The treaty's three-year commodity agreement gave structure and stability to the exchange of goods, and German-Soviet trade took off immediately thereafter. In that way, the 1958 agreements encouraged the Soviets to experiment with a policy of import-led growth in the 1960s and 1970s, which opened up the period of rapid trade growth from 1960 to 1975. More significantly, the 1958 treaty confirmed West German assumptions that trade concessions could be used to lubricate the sticking points in relations with the Soviets. The 1958 treaty closed the first postwar period by restoring fully normal trade relations between the FRG and the USSR. At the same time, it opened a new era of West German-Soviet economic agreements upon which improved political relations were built.

Contrary to the general West German expectation, Adenauer's September visit to Moscow visit produced nothing definite on future trade talks. Both sides agreed only that "consultations on the question of trade development will be held between the Soviet Union and the Federal Republic in the near future."[61] This vague formulation left the FRG free to manipulate the start of negotiations as part of its well-established strategy of subordinating any economic agreements with the Soviets to larger West German political strategies in Western and Eastern Europe.

Political relations between the Federal Republic and the USSR in late 1955 and early 1956 were soured by the outcome of the Geneva Foreign Ministers' Conference (27 October to 16 November 1955).[62] West German hopes for some progress on the division of Germany had been raised by the 23 July 1955 directive to the foreign ministers, which had put "European Security and Germany," including "the settlement of the German question and the reunification of Germany by means of free elections" at the top of the agenda for the Foreign Ministers' Meeting.[63] Soviet acquiescence in this formulation raised hopes in the West that something might be accomplished. Nonetheless, three weeks of negotiation proved once again that the Four Powers could not resolve fundamental elements of the German question and that reunification was not in the foreseeable future. The Western foreign ministers declared jointly on November 16 that the conference's "result must bring a sense of cruel disappointment to the German people, East and West of the zonal border …"[64] The next day in Vienna, Brentano declared the conference a "deep disappointment" for the German people. That disappointment was readily apparent in the federal government's review of West German foreign policy given by Brentano in the Bundestag on 1 December.[65]

The Federal Republic expressed its disappointment to the Soviets by delaying the start of trade treaty negotiations. The very limited variety of West German-Soviet contacts steered the Germans once again toward an economic response to Soviet intransigence. In addition, Molotov had repeated in Geneva that the Soviets desired to increase their trade with the West, so a delay in trade treaty negotiations could serve as a particularly clear expression of West German dissatisfaction with the outcome of the conference.[66]

In the months following the Geneva conference, the Soviets continued to express their interest in opening trade treaty negotiations with the Federal Republic. Those Soviet expressions were closely followed in the upper levels of the West German Economics Ministry.[67] One could not deny the sharp increase in German-Soviet trade in 1955 over 1954. West German exports to the Soviet Union for 1955 had grown by over 50 percent, and imports were up 40 percent from a year earlier. More than any public statements, these increases indicated genuine Soviet interest in expanding trade in a variety of legal goods. In the spring of 1956 Soviet requests to buy West German patents and licenses were increasing daily; so, too, was pressure from the Soviet embassy in Bonn for permission for Soviet foreign trade representatives to visit West German production facilities before placing any orders there. Economic developments and commercial contacts all pointed to the need for a trade treaty to regulate the growing volume of business between the two countries.[68]

Despite the pleasantly surprising growth of trade, Adenauer, Brentano, and Erhard continued to base West German trade policy toward the Soviet Union primarily on political considerations; they would not automatically follow commercial trends. As early as January 1956 Matthias Schmitt, who handled general questions of trade policy in the Economics Ministry, warned members of the industrial Bundesverband that "Minister Erhard is against the conclusion of a trade treaty with Russia [*sic*]." Otto Wolff, who chaired the Eastern Committee's Working Goup on the USSR, heard from Bundesverband members that "indications are that conclusion of a German-Russian [*sic*] trade agreement is not being considered."[69] In early March Brentano cautioned the Eastern Committee about a trade treaty with the Soviets, asking for continued support of the established West German position that "economic considerations be subordinated to considerations of political principle."[70] The Economics Ministry then arranged a "strictly confidential" meeting with Foreign Office members and the Eastern Committee to discuss the recent upsurge in German-Soviet business activity. In preparation for that meeting, where discussion would forseeably center on the issue of opening treaty negotiations with the USSR, Reinhardt and Erhard reaffirmed their view that political considerations required a postponement of trade negotiations with the Soviets: "After the results of the Second Geneva Conference in October 1955, for political reasons, the beginning of trade treaty negotiations are not foreseen at this time."[71]

At the government/private-sector meeting on 26 March, Erhard turned to the larger political context, reminding the group that "an economic agreement between the Federal Republic and Russia is something different from a similar agreement between France or England and Russia."[72] He then declared flatly that "in politics, we must constantly consider the division of Germany and reunification, for that reason no formal trade treaty will be concluded until further notice." Having reaffirmed the primacy of politics over economics, with disappointing consequences for the Eastern Committee, Erhard went on to console the business representatives by explaining that "there was no reason not to maintain a normal exchange of goods in the framework of existing trade with Russia." He also reassured the group that the Federal Republic would not "conduct an ambiguous policy at the expense of industry." Scherpenberg (soon to succeed Hallstein as state secretary in the Foreign Office) expressed concurrence with this position, saying "the Foreign Office also views positively the maintenance of normal trade, but the question of concluding a trade treaty must be judged politically." The government's point had been made emphatically. When the Eastern Committee met with State Secretary Hallstein one month later on 28 April, Wolff opened the discussions by declaring that "the Eastern Committee is aware of the Federal Government's position on the question of a trade treaty with the Soviet Union: there will be no trade treaty with Soviet Union."[73]

The Eastern Committee saw little no choice but to accommodate itself to this vigorously stated government policy on a trade treaty with the Soviets.[74] At the 26 March meeting with Erhard, Wolff rather timidly declared that the Eastern Committee and the industrial Bundesverband "could make no recommendation on this point [a trade treaty with the Soviets] since numerous important arguments could be presented both for and against a treaty." Nor was accommodation to government policy particularly uncomfortable for the Eastern Committee. The business community could easily forego the formality of a trade treaty if some of the substance of a treaty could be arranged with the Soviets on a less formal basis. In effect, this would be a return to the situation of 1953 to 1955, when the Eastern Committee had come close to concluding a private understanding with the Soviets on general terms of sale and delivery.

After hearing the government's rejection of treaty negotiations on 26 March, Wolff immediately assured Erhard that the business community did not insist on a treaty, but would find it "useful" if some general rules could be obtained on the "basic questions" of trading with the Soviets, especially terms for delivery, acceptance, payment, and arbitration. Rules were necessary, according to Wolff, in order to counter the "well-known" Soviet tactic – and oft-repeated German complaint – of "playing off both the Western countries and individual firms against each other." The Eastern Committee suggested that it begin negotiating these general rules with the Soviets; appropriate industrial associations could then arrange industry-specific rules. According to Wolff, "it would be more appropriate if the first discussions [with the Soviets] were not about a trade treaty, but rather about these problems."

Reinhardt stated immediately that he favored the establishment of some general rules for German-Soviet trade. Wolff went on to point out the advantages of this procedure "especially emphasizing that negotiations between the Eastern Committee and Soviet authorities about general terms would give the Federal Government the opportunity *not* to negotiate about a trade treaty for the time being." Scherpenberg reserved judgment for the Foreign Office, but personally agreed with Wolff's assessment that private-sector talks might relieve Soviet "pressure to begin trade treaty negotiations." At the 28 April meeting with Hallstein, Wolff again explained the need for "general, binding trade rules" for business with the Soviets. Hallstein confirmed the private-sector approach Wolff had suggested at the 26 March meeting in the Economics Ministry.

These West German plans to use a private level understanding with the USSR in place of a trade treaty were thwarted by the Soviets, who wanted an official treaty and were not willing to accept a private understanding in its place. As a result of these conflicting aims, both sides spent the next twelve months in an unproductive circle of negotiations. The Eastern Committee sought in vain to reach a private agreement with Soviet representatives, while the Soviets saw private negotiations primarily as a forum for mobilizing the West German business community to exert pressure on the federal government for a full treaty. At the same time, West German government officials continued to deflect Soviet requests for official negations by referring them to the Eastern Committee.

These circular negotiations began when, at the following meeting of the Eastern Committee on 23 May 1956, Scherpenberg gave the "green light" to open private negotiations with members of the Soviet embassy.[75] On 31 May Wolff met with members of the the Soviet embassy, including Medvedkov, the head of the embassy's trade department. Wolff asked "whether one could come to an agreement between the Eastern Committee and an agent of the Soviet government to be named later about certain general rules such as arbitration and payment terms." Wolff explained that these rules would be negotiated by both sides, not imposed by the Germans, and that the Eastern Committee could sign an agreement with either the Soviet Foreign Trade Ministry, the Soviet Embassy in Bonn, or the All-Union Chamber of Commerce. After some three hours of discussion, the Soviets agreed to further negotiations on a private basis.[76]

On June 13 Reinhardt gave Economics Ministry approval to the Eastern Committee's plans to hammer out specific terms for "routine payments" and for arbitration procedures with the Soviets. In addition, the Economics Ministry agreed that two important West German industrial delegations (iron/steel and machine-building) could begin negotiating "acceptance terms" for the delivery of German exports to the Soviets.[77] On July 7, the Eastern Committee sent detailed proposals covering an arbitration board and payment conditions to Medvedkov at the Soviet embassy. The Eastern Committee promised that if the Soviets approved the terms, "we will see to it that they are declared obligatory for Soviet-German trade." The Eastern Committee also indicated that West German industrial representatives would soon be approaching their Soviet counterpart foreign trade companies with the intention of arranging industry-specific delivery and acceptance terms.[78]

On July 17 Medvedkov acknowledged Wolff's letter. In mid-September Medvedkov and Wolff met again at the industrial Bundesverband's offices in Cologne to discuss the Soviet response to the Eastern Committee's draft proposals. After inviting Wolff to the All-

Union Industrial Exhibition in Moscow, Medvedkov came to the point. The Soviets had studied the offer and were convinced that "a general agreement on arbitration questions and payment conditions could not hurt, but would not be particularly useful, and that they therefore preferred to dispense with any such general agreement." Wolff countered smoothly that he could "understand" the Soviet point, and that the Germans had thought of the arbitration clause only as a means of "simplifying" things; "it is certainly not a pressing interest for German business."[!][79]

Yet at the same time they were rebuffing the Eastern Committee's attempts to forge some kind of private agreement, Soviet representatives continued to use public and private pressure in an effort to stampede the Federal Government into treaty negotiations. The Soviets targeted the West German business community with repeated assertions that the federal government's refusal to sign a treaty was hampering the growth of German-Soviet trade. In May 1956, Ambassador Valerian Sorin told a group of West German businessmen at the Hannover Trade Fair that as part of Adenauer's 1955 visit to Moscow, the federal government had agreed to sign a trade treaty. This fully erroneous statement brought a sharp protest from Scherpenberg when he met with Sorin on May 28. Sorin privately retracted his statement, but used the occasion to explain that "the Soviet foreign trade monopoly requires a legal basis in the form of a trade treaty for relations with foreign countries, especially when accepting large amounts. If the Federal Government now declares that it does not need a trade treaty, this obviously means that it has no interest in expanding [German-Soviet] trade."[80] Sorin's Hannover statement was followed by a 1 June German-language Radio Moscow broadcast arguing that an "expansion of trade between the Federal Republic of Germany and the USSR would contribute to a normalization of economic relations and thereby be beneficial to both countries." The problem, in the Soviet view, lay in the "behavior of the ruling circles in Bonn, which stubbornly adhere to the American embargo policy."[81] Meeting with Steidle on 7 June Medvedkov extended Sorin's line of argument by "repeatedly pointing out that a trade agreement was the necessary pre-condition for a substantial increase in German-Soviet trade," because "budget resources are generally available only in the context of the Plan, which, in turn, is based on treaties with foreign countries." The lack of a "legal basis" for trade meant that "at the present, the Federal Republic can only fill-in the gaps which appear in the Plan."[82] The Soviets renewed their public appeal for a treaty in September when Foreign Trade Minister Kubanov gave a lengthy interview in the West German conservative daily, *Die Welt*. Kubanov blamed the federal government for the lack of negotiations and stated that trade could not increase "because West German firms and the Soviet foreign trade organizations do not have sufficient perspective on the stability of the trade."[83]

These Soviet arguments found some resonance among the German industrial and trading communities.[84] After all, many of the points raised by Sorin, Medvedkov, and Kubanov had been mentioned in 1954 and 1955 by West German businessmen and had been recognized by the Economics Ministry and Foreign Office. This was particularly true of the idea that the Federal Republic needed a treaty so that German imports and exports could be included in Soviet economic plans. German traders knew better than anyone that the inflexible Soviet economy could not respond to changing market conditions and instead needed an agreement that would establish target amounts for trade in specific commodities.

Despite the mixture of public and private pressure from the Soviets and appeals from West German business, the federal government remained firm in its conviction not to sign a trade treaty with the Soviets at this time. Responding to the arguments put forward by the import/export firm Anton Olhert AG (Hamburg) in favor of a treaty, Steidle commented that "from an economic perspective these observations may be correct, however, from the political point of view, negotiations with the Soviets must be shelved for the time being."[85] In his 28 May 1956 meeting with Ambassador Sorin, Scherpenberg explained that a treaty was impossible since "the conclusion of a trade treaty requires an atmosphere of mutual trust, which, in view of the current political differences, does not yet exist. As is well known, one of the decisive pre-conditions is the satisfactory resolution of the reunification question."[86]

The Eastern Committee repeatedly warned the Soviets that a trade treaty would not be forthcoming. In his very first approaches to the Soviets in May 1956, Wolff made clear to Medvedkov and Krestov that the recent inauguration of German-Soviet diplomatic relations meant that the Eastern Committee was "no longer in the position to discuss anything like a trade treaty."[87] When Medvedkov rejected Wolff's offer of a private understanding, Wolff felt compelled to warn the Soviets sharply that "if you think your rejection of our suggestions brings you closer to a trade treaty, I am of quite a different opinion." As late as March 1957 Wolff again told Medvedkov that "the conclusion of a classic trade treaty is out of the question as the political situation is not ripe [for that]."[88]

The economic data from 1955 and 1956 did not support Soviet arguments on the necessity of a treaty. In fact, the rapid and continuing growth of German-Soviet trade since 1954 eroded the credibility of Soviet claims that a treaty was indispensable for trade expansion, as both Scherpenberg, Steidle, and even Adenauer pointed out on numerous public occasions.

Although political considerations prevented the Federal Republic from signing a trade treaty at this time, the federal government remained committed to facilitating trade expansion. In May 1956 Scherpenberg suggested, and the Soviets accepted, a meeting between German Foreign Office, Economics Ministry, and Soviet embassy officials to "exchange information" on the current level of trade.[89] A follow-up meeting was delayed until after the Soviets had received and studied the Eastern Committee's July 1956 offers on private negotiations. Only then did Medvedkov ask Steidle if the Economics Ministry was prepared to discuss "the areas in which Germany has import desires," mentioning barley and other grains as an initial Soviet offering.[90] Steidle's willingness to pursue this exchange and the prospect that at least some type of talks could take place on the official level probably confirmed the Soviet decision to reject an agreement with the Eastern Committee. After the Soviets rejected Wolff's offer on 14 September, Steidle wondered whether the Federal Republic should continue these discussions on the official level. However, on September 27, Zahn-Stranik gave the Foreign Office's approval for the Economics Ministry and the Agriculture Ministry to hold an "unofficial" meeting with the Soviets, which should be kept "as confidential as possible."[91]

With approval from Reinhardt and the Foreign Office, Steidle met Medvedkov again on 12 October. The Agriculture Ministry agreed to accept a "small" amount of barley, pending further information on the Federal Republic's own harvest, and some rye. The West Germans then presented their own list of "delivery possibilities" for Russian exporters, heavily weighted toward coal, iron ore, manganese, and chromium. The Economics Ministry informed the Eastern Committee of the results of the meeting and Steidle planned to include Eastern Committee members in future discussions with the Soviets.[92]

By the end of 1956 the two countries no longer seemed very far apart on how to proceed on trade relations. The West Germans still maintained that they wanted an increase in trade, but insisted that they would not sign a trade treaty at this time. On the other side, the Soviets had not given up on a treaty, but had apparently subordinated that quest to the task of increasing the volume of trade. Steidle emphasized to the Foreign Office that Medvedkov had "mentioned neither a trade treaty ... nor any other type of trade agreement." Steidle's own opinion was that the "Russians are interested in a quiet expansion of

Soviet-German trade and perhaps wish to incorporate information on German import needs into the planning for 1957."[93] The huge surge in West German exports to the USSR in 1956 indicated that trade, rather than a trade treaty, was the top priority for the Soviets.

Soviet Premier Nikolai Bulganin's February 1957 letter to Adenauer provided the impetus to move beyond the curious state of trade relations that had developed between the two countries in 1956 and to begin formal treaty negotiations.[94] In a rambling epistle, Bulganin touched on all aspects of German-Soviet relations, blowing alternately hot and cold. On the problem of reunification he had nothing new to offer, repeating well known Soviet claims about "two German states." On trade, Bulganin hung out the lure of the Soviet market, describing the possibilities for developing economic relations as "colossal." Most significantly for the development of future relations between the two countries, Bulganin declared that the "Soviet Union considers the development of such [trade] relations as a secure basis for the improvement of the political relations between the countries." In other words, the Soviets were receptive to West German economic diplomacy, would welcome it, and were prepared to "sell" some improvement in political relations if the West German were willing to "buy" it with an expansion of trade. Detailing the offer, Bulganin suggested negotiations on a number of "pressing questions" such as "an increase in trade between the two countries and a trade treaty, a Convention on cultural and academic-technological cooperation, and a Consular Convention that would assure the rights of both sides in protecting its citizens and would ease the solution of questions involving the repatriation of citizens."

On 22 February Adenauer answered Bulganin with a declaration that the federal government was prepared to negotiate on "trade relations," academic-technological cooperation, and consular rights.[95] This inspired another exchange of brief letters from Bulganin (18 March) and Adenauer (16 April) in which the federal government confirmed its willingness to "enter into negotiations with the Government of the Union of Soviet Socialist Republics about the resolution of questions in German-Soviet relations," specifically on trade, consular authority, and repatriation.[96] The resulting long-term trade agreement with the Soviets had profound political and economic consequences for West German-Soviet relations.

What had changed so profoundly in West German thinking that Adenauer should now reverse established policy and begin trade treaty negotiations with Soviets? In his memoirs, Adenauer characterized Bulganin's initial offer as something "about which fruitful negotiations were possible." He felt the Kremlin's overture "confirmed his suspicions" that the Soviets were hard-pressed; that "economic difficulties inside the Soviet bloc" had cast doubts on the strength of the USSR; and that the Soviets now wished to improve their relations with a several other countries.

In addition, 1956 had been a year of extreme instability and there is no doubt that the chancellor was deeply worried about the international situation.[97] The problems within both the Eastern and Western blocs (Poland and Hungary on one side, and the Suez crisis on the other) seemed to indicate a wave of uncertainty about the stability of the postwar order. Even more worrisome for the Federal Republic in particular were the numerous East-West arms control plans floated between 1955 and 1957: the Eden Plan, Rapacki Plan, Gaitskill Plan, Radford Plan, and "Disengagement." Adenauer rightfully saw each of these plans as a threat to German reunification since they implied *peaceful East-West coexistence on the basis of a divided Germany.* In Britain and France the priority of arms control over some improvement in the German question was no longer disguised.[98] Under these circumstances, Adenauer sought to establish direct talks with the Soviets as a way to counter German fears of an East-West agreement concluded over the head of the Federal Republic.[99] The spring of 1957 provided a desirable starting point for negotiations with the Soviets. Renewed strength and unity in the West (Treaty of Rome, post-Suez American reconciliation with the U.K.) was paired with Soviet realization that the USSR could not achieve its domestic goals while at the same time maintaining an aggressive foreign policy.[100]

More significantly, the decision to begin substantive trade negotiations with the Soviets provided the first definite indication of the fundamental revision in Adenauer's foreign strategy taking place in 1957 to 1958. Adenauer frankly admitted that in Bulganin's letter "the Soviet standpoint on the German question was unchanged." At the same time, he justified a positive response by saying that "some progress could be recognized … in the friendly tone of the letter" in contrast to earlier notes. This second point reveals an essential modification of Adenauer's judgements since 1955.[101] Faced with the dead end in the German question that his "policy of strength" had produced between 1949 and 1956, and recognizing that the Western powers were no longer prepared to actively pursue the question of German reunification, Adenauer now began to alter his approach to the Soviet Union. Beginning in 1957, Adenauer committed the FRG to a policy of improving relations *(Entspannungspolitik)* with the Soviets as part of the general East-West thaw then underway and beyond his control. In addition to preventing an East-West understanding that excluded the Germans, an improved West German-Soviet relationship set in the context of generally improved East-West relations now appeared to be the only possible way of creating a climate for a renewed discussion of the German question.[102]

West German-Soviet trade negotiations and the resulting treaty served as *de facto* announcements of an evolving demarche in the Federal Republic's Soviet policy. The Soviets had desired a trade treaty for some time and Bulganin has explicitly mentioned the role that trade could play in improving political relations between the two states. Under these circumstances, Adenauer's decision to reverse his position on a trade treaty with the Soviets must be regarded as a critical step in reversing the general policy of deliberately emphasizing West German dissatisfaction with Soviet policies.[103]

Finally, a trade treaty could be used as leverage for the repatriation of German civilians still detained in the USSR – a highly sensitive political issue in the FRG and one that Adenauer had specifically addressed in his 17 February letter as a "main obstacles to ... good and friendly relations between our two countries."[104] A trade agreement that secured the release of ethnic Germans and paved the way for other, more significant political talks with the Soviets would quiet the restive voices both outside and inside Adenauer's coalition, perhaps in time for the September 1957 elections. For all of these reasons Adenauer took the step of opening trade talks.

One common theme connects each of these explanatory factors – the dominance of political considerations over economic considerations. Economic motivations played a distant secondary role in the decision to open trade negotiations with the USSR. The economic situation of the FRG had improved further since 1955; there was no pressing need to increase economic interaction with the East. The industrial Bundesverband told Scherpenberg that they "did not expect any spectacular increases from a trade agreement that, meanwhile, has become primarily a political matter."[105] Commerce and industry in the Federal Republic remained interested in raising the volume of trade with the Soviets, but only within the limits imposed by successful existing commercial arrangements in the West.[106]

None of the principal decisionmakers on the West German side weighed the economic factor as a motivation for improving trade relations. Both in public and in private, they denied any pressing economic need for a trade treaty. In his 22 February reply to Bulganin, Adenauer repeated the Federal Republic's long-standing and well-founded contention that trade had developed nicely from 1954 to 1956 despite the absence of a treaty. On 25 July just two days after the German-Soviet negotiations opened in Moscow, Adenauer told the press that "in itself, trade [with the USSR] means nothing to me

...″[107] Zahn-Stranik opened internal Foreign Office preparations for the negotiations with the matter-of-fact statement that "commercially, the German side has no special interest in a trade agreement with the Soviets."[108] The chairman of the German negotiating delegation, Special Ambassador Rolf Lahr, explained to his mother in a letter from Moscow that "the trade agreement is my battle horse: the Soviets are obviously very interested in this, especially as far as it concerns acquiring investment goods for their multi-year plans, while we, in view of the full employment in our economy and a world-wide demand for our investment goods that already can hardly be met, can be coy without any risk." To his sister, Lahr wrote that West Germany's "important industrialists (die Grossen von Rhein und Ruhr)... have such strong positions in world trade that they never pressured us in the Moscow negotiations."[109]

The composition of the German delegation, the course and conduct of the negotiations, and the cluster of agreements that were produced all confirm the priority of politics over economics in the federal government's thinking. Within the German delegation, Foreign Office members held the key positions, while representatives from the ministries concerned with the economic substance of trade negotiations (Economics Ministry, Agriculture Ministry, Bundesbank) occupied positions of secondary importance. Lahr was a good and logical choice as chairman of the German delegation.[110] The Soviets also used a career diplomat, Deputy Foreign Minister Vladimir Semenov, as chairman of their delegation. Revealingly, the Soviets used Deputy Minister for Foreign Trade P. N. Kumykin to head the subcommittee on trade questions, while the Federal Republic again used a Foreign Office man, Zahn-Stranik, to lead their trade negotiating team. This despite the fact that both Steidle (Economics Ministry) and Stalmann (Agriculture Ministry) had extensive experience in hammering out trade deals with other Eastern European countries.[111]

Schellpeper, who represented the Economics Ministry in the trade subcommittee, soon realized that political considerations rather than economic calculation would determine the outcome of the trade negotiations. He reported to his ministry in Bonn that "... the economic negotiations cannot be conducted according to the principle of *do ut des,* but rather are fully overshadowed by the political attempt to come to an agreement with the Soviets in the repatriation question, thereby improving the climate of political relations"; for this, the West Germans would have to make "economic sacrifices."[112] Schellpeper repeatedly expressed his concern that the Foreign Office's desire for a treaty was eroding the ability of the German delegation to dig in its heels in the tough economic negotiations.[113]

Throughout the nine-month course of the negotiations, the political desire to get an agreement with the Soviets determined the actions of the German delegation.[114] Before he left for Moscow in July, Lahr had spent an hour with Adenauer, who "underlined how important it was for the Federal Government that these first negotiations with the Soviet Union be concluded successfully ..."[115] Even when the Soviets deliberately provoked a crisis in the negotiations by unilaterally declaring that the repatriation question "had been removed from the agenda," the Foreign Office refused to let the negotiations collapse. After consulting with Brentano, Hallstein, and Adenauer, and after reporting to the cabinet, Lahr returned to Moscow with instructions to proceed with the economic side of the negotiations despite the dead end reached on repatriation.[116] At each subsequent impasse, this pattern repeated itself; Lahr received instructions to move around the point of impasse and keep the negotiations going.

The final products of these negotiations – the Long-Term Agreement on Trade and Payments, the Agreement on General Questions of Trade and Navigation, the Protocol on Commodity Trade for 1958, and the Consular Treaty – show in concrete and specific terms the numerous economic and political concessions made by the West Germans. The overwhelming political desire for a trade treaty accounts for significant economic and financial concessions that the Federal Republic granted to the USSR, concessions that the Bundesbank often opposed and the Economics Ministry agreed to only because of the political need for a treaty.

The trade and payments agreement contained several formalities that were notable concessions on the part of the West Germans. By signing a multiyear agreement for the period 1958 to 1960, the Germans gave in to a key Soviet demand, although the Federal Republic had refused this type of multiyear deal with any other trade partner. The same applies to the multiyear import/export lists. Lahr and Zahn-Stranik agreed to three-year lists despite initial Foreign Office promises to the economics and agriculture ministries that the Federal Republic would not make import commitments more than one year in advance. Equally significantly, the FRG signed a long-term agreement that did nothing to address the chief concern of the West German private-sector, establishing some general contract and delivery terms for exports to the Soviet Union.[117] Rather than insisting on some uniform terms as part of the trade agreement, the FRG accepted an exchange of letters between Lahr and Kumykin in which both states agreed to "recommend" that the West German "private-sector" and the "foreign trade organizations" of the USSR enter into negotiations on "general delivery terms and questions of arbitration."[118] Kumykin's letter committed the Soviets to nothing beyond some additional discussions and the Soviets ultimately refused to sign any binding rules for business with West German exporters.[119]

The FRG also made numerous concessions in the composition of trade, most importantly in the composition of West German imports from the USSR.[120] On a wide variety of items, from asbestos to zinc, the Federal Republic agreed to allow imports in excess of what was required or desired.[121] On the export side, the Federal Republic abandoned its position that 10 percent of Federal Republic exports in this period must be consumer goods, settling in the end for about 4 percent (DM 50 million to 70 million). After lengthy negotiations the Federal Republic also dropped its demand that the Soviets buy some German agricultural goods. The final agreement had no provision for German agricultural exports.

The payments agreement between the two states was another area of significant West German concessions. Despite opposition from the Bundesbank, the Federal Republic granted the Soviets a DM 15 million interest-free swing credit. This was a major breach of prevailing West German practice since the Federal Republic had spent the past three years reducing the swing credits of other East bloc countries. The Germans also met a Soviet request to include nontrade payments in this agreement, which, again, had not been granted to other centrally planned economies.

On noneconomic issues as well, the Federal Republic reworked its demands and concessions, even on the emotional questions of repatriation, in order to reach agreements. Despite Adenauer's public statements that repatriation was the issue that concerned him most, the Germans dropped their demand for a written guarantee of future Soviet action on the repatriation question. Instead, the FRG obtained only an oral "promise" from the Soviets; real progress on repatriation remained hostage to the future development of relations between the two countries, as Deputy Chairman of the Council of Ministers Anastas Mikoyan made clear.[122] In the Consular Agreement, the Federal Republic agreed to the long-standing Soviet request for an extraterritorial trade mission in Cologne.

These numerous and diverse West German concessions were not made in vain. They enabled the FRG to sign a cluster of economic and political agreements with the Soviets that marked an important turning point in the development of West German relations with the Soviet bloc. The agreements were used immediately in West German domestic politics to help quiet the rising chorus of domestic criticism directed at Adenauer's foreign policy. Widespread frustration with a situation that had stagnated since the Second Geneva Conference in 1955 erupted in the Bundestag *Redeschlacht* on 23 January 1958. On that day, the SPD attacked Adenauer's government as never before for its "immobility" in the face of the Rapacki Plan (and Kennan's "Disengagement" idea), for the obvious limitations of the Hallstein Doctrine, and for the general dead end reached in the German question.[123] Now, with the new Soviet agreements in hand and Mikoyan arriving in Bonn for the formal signing ceremonies, Adenauer could point to some real accomplishments in improving relations with the East.[124]

The economic agreements also allowed Adenauer to speak extensively with Mikoyan during the latter's visit to Bonn for the signing ceremonies on 25 April 1958. These discussions capped a year-long effort by Adenauer to open direct substantive communication with the Soviet leadership. Unfortunately, the renewed turbulence in the Soviet politics brought on by the fall of Bulganin in March 1958 precluded any immediate concrete results emerging from these talks with Mikoyan.

The importance of the trade, navigation, and consular agreements in Adenauer's goal of securing a more normal relationship with the Soviets was evident in the government arguments put forward for their parliamentary ratification.[125] Khrushchev's Berlin Ultimatum of November 1958 disrupted what had been expected to be a smooth process of ratification.[126] Adenauer remained committed to the necessity of the FRG "improving relations with the Soviet Union" despite the current Soviet "policy of pinpricks" toward the FRG. In pursuit of this goal, Adenauer was prepared to use "all available opportunities," including ratification of navigation and consular agreements concluded in Moscow as part of the trade negotiations.[127] In a statement to the Foreign Affairs Committee of upper house of Parliament (Bundesrat), Brentano acknowledged the role of economic diplomacy in improving relations with the Soviets. He explained that "despite deep disappointment with the Soviet attitude in the fate of the German people," the federal government still favored ratification "in the hope that in this way it will be possible to create the base for a solution of the important political questions" and that "on this foundation it should be possible to solve the political questions that remain between Germany and the Soviet Union and to come to good and lasting relations."[128]

The 1958 trade, payments, and navigation agreements with the USSR mark an important development in the evolution of Adenauer's *Ostpolitk*. Viewed together with Adenauer's proposal for an "Austrian solution" for the German Democratic Republic and his agreement to put disarmament before more general political questions in the London disarmament conference, the economic agreements with the Soviets marked a shift in Adenauer's priorities. With each of these three plans, Adenauer had in fact shifted his emphasis away from territorial revision in East-Central Europe (i.e., formal reunification). Instead, Adenauer was now working toward an improvement in political relations on the basis of the existing territorial settlement in Eastern Europe.[129]

In signing a cluster of economic agreements with the USSR, Adenauer unambiguously entered a period of improved relations with the USSR in spite of the unacceptable situation in East Germany and new Soviet provocations over Berlin. Two years earlier the Foreign Office had insisted on progress in the German question as a "precondition" for trade negotiations. Now Adenauer had signed the Long-Term Agreement and the Consular Treaty, thereby entering into fully normal commercial relations with the Soviet Union, although the Soviets had refused meaningful discussion on the German question since 1955.[130]

Although German motives for the Long-Term Agreement were primarily political, the economic results were substantial. The 1958 agreements ushered in a quantitatively and qualitatively new era in German-Soviet trade. Most immediately, the Long-Term Agreement and the Protocol for 1958 brought about a dramatic rise in two-way trade between these countries.[131] The agreement called for DM 3.3 billion ($785 million) in balanced two-way trade over the three years 1958 to 1960. On the import side the Germans concentrated heavily on a half-dozen raw materials: oil (unrefined, diesel, and heating), timber, grain (wheat and barley), coal, and iron and manganese ores (Graph 9.13). This list had not changed substantially since Steidle's October 1956 preliminary conversations with Medvedkov on possible West German imports. The volume of West German was now so large that the Soviets were ordering complete factory infrastructures, rather than categories of machines.[132] That type of ordering, which required deliveries over two or more years, was possible only with a comprehensive, long-term agreement.

The multiyear agreement also allowed the Soviets to incorporate German-Soviet trade in their economic plan. With lengthy advance notice, the Soviets were able to meet West German import desires. This, in turn, meant that the scheduled trade volume of $785 million was 90 percent fulfilled ($706 million) by the end of 1960.[133] German-Soviet trade under the 1958 agreements was more than twice what it had been for the three previous years, 1955 to 1957. By 1960 to 1961 the Russian market was approaching 2 percent for both West German imports and exports (see Graphs 9.14 and 9.15). There is no doubt that the 1958 agreements enabled the Federal Republic to recapture Germany's traditional role as Russia's premier Western trade partner, surpassing Finland in 1959. In 1960 the Federal Republic supplied over 42 percent of the Common Market's exports to the Soviets.

The long-term significance of the 1958 agreements can hardly be overestimated. Despite the federal government's reluctance to admit so, the Long-Term Agreement on Trade and Payments, the Agreement on General Questions of Trade and Navigation, and the Protocol on Commodity Trade for 1958, established fully normal commercial relations between the two states. The Soviets had failed to act during the brief "window of opportunity" in 1947 to 1948 when, like other Eastern countries, they might have been able to sign a trade agreement with the western zones of Germany. Six years had passed since the first informal German-Soviet contacts on the subject of regulating trade relations had taken place in Copenhagen in 1952. Throughout that period, political considerations had overshadowed and repeatedly interrupted efforts to regulate the merchandise trade between the two countries. The new agreements finally provided the stable basis for German-Soviet trade that had been missing for the past decade. The Berlin crisis of 1958 demonstrated clearly that short-term political problems would no longer disrupt on West German-Soviet trade. The new stability was enhanced by another three-year Long-Term Agreement signed on 31 December 1960, which governed trade for the period 1961 to 1963. That stability must have played a role in Soviet thinking when they opted for a strategy of "import-led growth" in the 1960s. In this way the Federal Republic's 1958 agreements opened the door on the era of rapid German-East European trade growth that began in the early 1960s and ran through the late 1970s. Expanding trade, in turn, brought new possibilities for the use of economic diplomacy in a changing international environment 1960 to 1990.

The years 1956 to 1960 comprise a critical transition period in the postwar history of West German trade relations with Poland, Czechoslovakia, and the USSR. West German trade policy preserved the essential features of the earlier postwar periods, especially the highly politicized nature of trade with the East. Trade-based economic diplomacy remained the FRG's only tool for crafting relations with the Soviet bloc, and the West Germans had adapted themselves fully to this international constraint by deciding on an unequivocal "primacy of politics" when planning Eastern trade strategies.

Yet trade politicization after 1955 differed from politicization in the earlier postwar years as the Federal Republic increasingly pursued its own national political interests. In some cases, West German goals overlapped with those of the larger Western alliance, for example, the attempt to lure Gomułka onto a "liberal" course. In other cases, the West Germans pursued their own interests even at the expense of other Western countries, for example, by using a trade treaty to open a direct political line to the Soviets, thereby enhancing the political status of the Federal Republic within the Western alliance and regaining the traditional German role as Russia's premier Western economic partner.

Beyond this foreseeable shift in the political motivations of managed trade, a more important change in the very nature of trade politicization was occurring. Between 1956 and 1960, the Federal Republic gradually abandoned the type of overt, short-term, tit-for-tat trade politicization that had been practiced since 1948 and had marked West German trade strategy during the embargo, the repatriation issue, early talks with the Soviets, and the attempt to influence Gomułka. By the end of the decade, Adenauer had made a calculated political decision to change the nature of trade politicization by moving away from the short-term use of sticks and carrots. This shift created a more stable economic relationship with the Soviets that might be used for a general improvement in political relations, thus preparing the ground for some future movement on the German question. This directly lead to the Federal Republic's willingness to sign a multiyear trade agreement with the USSR. Of course, the Federal Republic could not genuinely depoliticize its trade with the East to the same extent that it had done with Western partners; the abandonment of one type of politicized trade policy in the East was in itself a political decision. Nor did a lessening of immediate politically motivated trade manipulation automatically lead to increased trade. For Poland, it meant the end of politically inspired West German trade concessions and a consequent decline in trade. Yet the years 1958 to 1960 are a watershed; they mark the end of the first overtly politicized postwar phase of West German-East European trade and the beginning of a more positive and more subtle West German trade strategy toward Eastern Europe, which itself continued to change.

Notes

1. Data on merchandise trade in United Nations, *Statistical Papers, Series T. Direction of International Trade* (Geneva, 1949-) vols. I-XI (1949-1961), all values in current prices.

2. Memorandum by East and Southeast Europe desk in the Economics Ministry, 28 May 1956 and Walter Steidle (chief desk officer for East and Southeast Europe) memorandum, 14 September 1956, BA B 102/58124.

3. The chief West German beneficiaries of these purchases were MAN ($3 million), AEG ($900,000), and Siemens ($900,000), memorandum of the East and Southeast Europe desk, 25 July 1956, BA B 102/58124. This $47 million in West German exports did not include the $18 million in special grain deliveries from the FRG in the first months of 1956; these were booked on a separate account at the Narodowy Bank Polski. As of July 1956 the Poles had repaid $2 million on that interest-bearing debt, with $1.3 million due monthly over the next fourteen months.

4. The Finance Ministry and the Bank of the German Länder earlier expressed "reservations" about the 1955 grain deal since it would raise West German credits to Poland to a total of $30 million on a volume of less than $60 million in two-way trade, Lupin memorandum of an interministerial meeting on 12 September 1955, PAAA 311.22/4.

5. Within the West German delegation, Otto Stalmann cautioned the bank representatives that their offers were "insufficient" and that in order to "make progress" toward a new agreement the bank would have to do more for the Poles, memorandum, 17 October 1956, BA B 102/58124.

6. Minutes of Trade Policy Committee meeting #27/56, 23 October 1956, BA B 102/58124.

7. For an introduction to these problems see Paul E. Zinner, ed., *National Communism and Popular Revolt in Eastern Europe* (New York, 1956); Zbigniew Brzezinski, *The Soviet Bloc,* rev. ed., (Cambridge, Mass., 1967), 230 ff.; Joseph Rothschild, *Return to Diversity. A Political History of East Central Europe since World War II* (New York, 1989) 150 ff. For greater detail on the economic issues begin with Wlodzimierz Brus, "1950 to 1953: The Peak of Stalinism" and "1953 to 1956: The 'Thaw' and the 'New Course'," in Kaser and Radice, eds., *Economic History of Eastern Europe 1919-1975,* vol. 3, 3-39, 40-70.

8. Brzezinski, *The Soviet Bloc,* 339.

9. For Gomułka's speech see *Trybuna Ludu,* 21 October 1956; *Nowe Drogi,* No. 10, 1956, 21-46; reprinted in translation in Zinner, ed., *National Communism,* 197-239. For the Resolution Adopted by the Central Committee of the Polish United Workers Party at its Eighth Plenary Session, October 19-21, see *Trybuna Ludu,* 25 October 1956; *Nowe Drogi,* No. 10, 1956; Zinner, *National Communism,* 239-62.

10. In his memoirs, Adenauer claims the Foreign Office told him that Gomułka's "political goal is an independent, national-communist Poland in friendly association with the Soviet Union," Adenauer, *Erinnerungen 1955-1959,* (Stuttgart, 1967), 299.

11. *Verhandlungen des deutschen Bundestages,* II Wahlperiode 1953, Stenographische Berichte, Bd. 31, 8508 B ff.

12. Rudolf Morsey and Hans-Peter Schwarz, eds., *Adenauer. Teegespräche 1955-1958,* (1986), 420-21. Longer sections of this speech to the Landesverband Westfalen der Jungen Union in Dortmund are available in *Dokumente zur Deutschlandpolitik,* Series III, vol. 2, part 2, 813-24.

13. The following is based on minutes of Trade Policy Committee meeting #27/56, 23 October 1956, BA B 102/58124.

14. As early as 1954 the West German Foreign Office had considered "whether the economic self-interest of the satellite countries could mobilize centrifugal ten-

dencies and whether these, once existent, could be activated by Western trade policy actions," 3 November 1954 meeting of experts on East Bloc and Eastern Questions with members of the East-West Trade desk, PAAA 311.22/3.

15. The Eastern Committee (Otto Wolff) repeated that objection to Reinhardt, 11 July 1957, BA B 102/18434.H.1.

16. Adenauer went on to explain that this reassurance was designed to counter Soviet claims that the Federal Republic had rearmed in order to attack Poland, *Adenauer. Teegespräche 1955-1958*, 153-54. In a 3 July 1956 interview with *Die Welt* McCloy urged the West Germans to do everything possible to reduce Polish and Czech "fear" of Germany since this caused the satellite countries to seek Soviet "protection." This same view is expressed at length in McCloy's "Forward" to H. L. Roberts, *Russia and America. Danger and Prospects* (New York, 1956).

17. See, e.g., Adenauer's 26 October 1956 campaign speech in Hannover in *Dokumente zur Deutschland Politik*, III, vol. 2, part 2, 832; Declaration of 8th November in *Verhandlungen des deutschen Bundestages*, II Wahlperiode 1953, Stenographische Berichte, Bd. 32, 9259 D ff.

18. A copy of the 16 November 1956 agreement, the protocol on payments, and the letter on future grain deliveries can be found in BA B 102/58124. The unresolved "details" concerned the rate of interest on the Polish swing credit. The Bank of the German Länder insisted on 2.8 percent while the Narodowy Bank offered just 1.05 percent, unsigned Economics Ministry memorandum from 9 November 1956, BA B 102/58124.

19. See e.g., "Handel mit Polen erweitert," *Hamburger Anzeiger*, 17 November 1956; "Polen stellt auf Beko-Mark um," *Handelsblatt*, 19 November 1956.

20. See e.g., Brentano's press conference in Berlin on 30 November 1956, *Dokumente zur Deutschlandpolitik*, III, vol. 2, part 2, 933-39; Brentano also warned that "we must avoid the impression that we are attempting to influence the internal political development of Eastern Europe," ibid., 978-79; Adenauer's statement of 24 October 1956, *Adenauer. Teegespräche 1955-1958*, 154; similarly in *Erinnerungen 1955-1959*, 367. As a political concession to the Poles, Stalmann urged a new trade treaty between the FRG and Poland to replace the 1949 JEIA agreement, but was overruled by the Foreign Office, Sartorius (East-West Trade desk) memorandum, 10 November 1956, PAAA 413.85.00/111.

21. Wilhelm Grewe, the head of the Foreign Office's Political Department, understood that the FRG must use of trade missions and trade policy as "substitute arrangements for the lack of diplomatic relations" and as a "platform for political activity" in Eastern Europe. Grewe, *Rückblenden*, 263.

22. Brzezinski, *The Soviet Bloc*, 249; Vacslav Benes and Norman Pounds, *Poland* (London, 1970), 309. Brzezinski estimates Soviet credits to Poland in 1956 at 1.1 billion gold rubles, 285.

23. Brentano interview, 14 December, *Dokumente zur Deutschlandpolitik*, III, vol. 2, part 2, 978-79.

24. Minutes of the thirty-seventh meeting of the Parliamentary Council for Trade Agreements, 30 January 1957, BA B 102/58124.

25. For the following see Stalmann's memorandum, Conversations in Warsaw on Questions of German-Polish Economic Relations, 24 June 1956, BA B 102/58124. Stalmann's partners included Vice-Minister for Foreign Trade Bajer; the Foreign trade Ministry's coal expert Horowitz; and the regular chairman of the Polish delegation in Polish-German trade talks, Stanislaw Strus.

26. An Economics Ministry memorandum of 18 March 1957 had already confirmed that West German importers had "little interest" in other commodities offered by the Poles for payment of the grain deal, BA B 102/18434.H.1.

27. Steidle to Reinhardt from 17 July 1957, BA B 102/58124.

28. Schauenburg (East and Southeast Europe) to Roegner (coal), 27 June 1957, BA B 102/58124.

29. Schauenburg memorandum on the 1 July 1957 interministerial meeting on Upcoming Polish Negotiations, BA B 102/58124; Steidle to Reinhardt, 17 July 1957, BA B 102/58124.

30. A balance sheet showing the net Polish debt to the FRG for 1957 at DM 110 million (DM 190 million in Polish obligations and DM 80 million in projected receipts for Polish coal and agricultural exports) in BA B 102/58124. That balance sheet (with rounded totals) corresponds to the data given by Strus on 10 July showing Polish obligations of DM 186 million due by year's end, BA B102/18434.H.1.

31. Wilhelm Grewe, head of the Political Department, drafted the Foreign Office cabinet submission Economic Aid for Poland, 22 July 1957; it was approved by the cabinet on 24 July, BA B 136/1260.

32. Similarly, the political emphasis in Stalmann's 22 July summation for Agriculture Minister Heinrich Lübke: "In view of the courageous steps underway in Poland toward independence from the Soviet Union, the Federal Republic would create the impression that it was exerting anti-Polish pressure if it [the Federal Republic] were to bring about a decline in trade with Poland at this time," BA B 102/58124.

33. The Finance Ministry would deposit DM 30 million at the Kreditanstalt for Wiederaufbau to cover both existing and new bills presented by German exporters. The Poles would pay 5.5 percent interest on the DM 30 million, (4.5 percent rediscount rate and 1 percent bank margin). In addition, the Hermes export credit guarantee would be extended for one year and increased to cover 100 percent of the outstanding bills. Stalmann also warned his minister that "more comprehensive" help for Poland would be needed later, Stalmann to Lübke, 22 July 1957, BA B 102/58124.

34. For the following see German delegation member Schellpeper's Report on German-Polish negotiations in Berlin from 28 to 30 October 1957 as well as three individual memoranda, one on each day of negotiations, BA B 102/58124. On the problems of Polish coal exports to the FRG one should consult Walter Pape's manuscript "Die polnische Kohle in der BRD und West Berlin," available in the BdI library.

35. In fact, cheaper American coal had already driven Polish coal out of the northern German market and the southern German industrial market; by 1956 Polish coal was used only by domestic consumers in Bavaria. For these reasons Polimport had bought only 250,000 tons of Polish coal so far in 1957, and the firm faced great difficulty placing even this amount in the German market, ibid.

36. Despite the failure to reach agreement on these issues, Schellpeper was impressed by the "friendly and understanding atmosphere" of the negotiations, BA B 102/58124.

37. Foreign Office cabinet submission Economic Aid for Poland, 15 November 1957, BA B 102/58124. Brentano had ordered preparation of this document on 24 October, Assistant Under-Secretary for General Commercial Policy Harkort to Zahn-Stranik, 14 November, PAAA 413.85.00/111. On 8 November Brentano prepared Adenauer for further aid by reminding him that the cabinet had recognized in July that "additional concessions on credits would be unavoidable in the next economic negotiations" with the Poles, BA B 136/1260.

38. The decline in Polish coal exports to the Federal Republic between 1956 (845,000 tons) and 1957 (450,000 tons), accounts for roughly 40 percent of the $10 million decline in West German imports from Poland from 1956 to 1957.

39. Reinhardt to Erhard on Economic Aid for Poland, cabinet submission by the Foreign Office from 15 November 1957, BA B 102/58124. Already on 18 November, the plan had been recommended for approval in the Chancellor's Office, BA B

136/1260. The interministerial economic Committee of Five gave approval on 21 November, Schauenburg (Economics Ministry) memorandum on that meeting, 21 November 1957, BA B 102/58124.

40. Hallstein to Commercial Affairs Department from 21 November 1957, BA B 102/58124.

41. In making the political argument for an expansion of trade in his submission to the cabinet, Brentano had noted that "this is also the opinion of the major powers in NATO."

42. Schellpeper memorandum of a conversation with Campbell, 10 October 1957, BA B 102/58124. In November, the French proposed reducing the number of fully embargoed goods on the international list as it applied to Poland. The West German Economics Ministry favored a reduction of the embargo lists in order to make available "exports that are calculated to reinforce the influence of the West on Poland or to link the Polish economy with the Western world, or which to raise the living standards and serve to improve the economic situation in Poland," Assistant Under-Secretary for Foreign Economic Policy Stedtfeld to the COCOM delegation head, Kruse, via Zahn-Stranik, 29 November 1957, BA B 102/58124.

43. Grewe, *Rückblenden 1976-1951*, 292.

44. Economics Ministry Foreign Trade Circular Nr. 74/57, 18 December 1957; Schauenburg memorandum, both in BA B 102/58124; Zahn-Stranik's Memorandum of Results, 8 December 1957, PAAA 413.85.00/111. On the coal issue nothing was resolved since the private negotiations between Polimport and Wenglokoks had produced no agreement. For its part, the federal government agreed to allow as much coal as Poland could deliver, with a "goal" of 2 million tons annually, and it promised that Polish coal would have resale tax parity with U.S. coal imports.

45. In the late October round of talks, the Agriculture Ministry told the Poles that the FRG could not agree to any additional imports of live pigs, memorandum on negotiations on 29 October 1957, BA B 102/58124.

46. Prior to the Ninth Plenum in May 1957, the Stalinist "Natolin" faction could still control twenty to twenty-five out of seventy-seven votes in the Central Committee. E.g., Gomułka's speech to a national conference of party activists in Warsaw on November 4, 1956, *Trybuna Ludu*, 5 November 1956 and Zinner, *National Communism*, 284-306.

47. Brzezinski, *The Soviet Bloc*, 353. In October 1957 "the mainstay of the liberalization and democratization movement," the weekly *Po prostu*, was banned because of its alleged "nihilistic and deviationist tendencies." The editorial board was expelled from the party, Benes and Pounds, *Poland*, 312.

48. Zahn-Stranik memorandum approved by Assistant Under-Secretary for Commercial Relations with Foreign States von Bargen, PAAA 413.85.00/111; Schauenburg memorandum on the Committee of Five meeting, 21 November 1957, BA B 102/58124. In late December 1957 Schauenburg characterized the Foreign Office's position as "recommending, in view of the political situation in Poland, restraint in granting large-scale economic aid until further notice." The Americans, too, he noted, had granted only one-third of aid Poland requested; $90 million instead of $300 million, Schauenburg to Daniel, assistant under-secretary for economic relations with countries outside the EPU, and Reinhardt, on the "controversial political question of whether the Federal Republic should grant greater economic aid in order to win Poland for the West" as part of his report on the November-December economic negotiations, 20 December 1957, BA B 102/58124.

49. On 20 May 1958 Adenauer told John Midgley and a small group of reporters that "there is no freedom in Poland, there is perhaps a certain freedom to curse, but

nothing more, and Gomułka has moved further and further from freedom," *Adenauer. Teegespräche 1955-1958*, 282.

50. On this West German decision, Stalmann's report on negotiations with Strus in Berlin, 9 October 1958 and Foreign Office East-West Trade desk summary of the Trade Policy Committee meeting of 28 October 1958, both in PAAA 413.85.00/111. In December, the Foreign Office rejected the establishment of a trade mission in Warsaw "as a pre-step or in-between-step to diplomatic contact," memorandum by Dr. Lane, desk officer for Poland in the new Eastern Department of the Foreign Office, and Ambassador Georg Duckwitz, assistant under-secretary for Eastern Europe, 22 December 1958. To soften the rejection, the Germans offered a one-year moratorium on DM 16 million still owed (and due in 1959) from past grain deals.

51. Memorandum by Lane and Duckwitz, 22 December 1958, PAAA 413.85.00/111. On 7 January 1959 Harkort ,now the under-secretary for commercial affairs, acknowledged that "suggestions for economic aid are politically and economically less justified since the Gomułka has turned onto a course of aggressive policies toward the Federal Republic," ibid.

52. Schauenburg to Daniel and Reinhardt, 20 December 1957, BA B 102/58124.

53. Schauenburg to Daniel and Reinhardt, 20 December 1957, BA B 102/58124.

54. Memorandum, 22 December 1958, PAAA 413.85.00/111. The Trade Policy Committee had already concluded that "no change in the [Polish] political situation could be expected in the immediate future," Foreign Office East-West Trade desk summary of the meeting of 28 October 1958, PAAA 413.85.00/111.

55. Minutes of Trade Policy Committee meeting Nr. 3/59, 27 January 1959, PAAA 413.85.00/111.

56. The parallel with German-Czechoslovak relations during Weimar is obvious. In this way, West German relations with Czechoslovakia allow us to control for economic problems and highlight the political considerations that so strongly affected West German trade with Poland and the USSR.

57. Czechoslovak fuel (i.e. coal) deliveries to the USSR fell from $149 million in 1953 to $120 million in 1956. Exports of machinery to the Soviets also fell; from $145 million in 1954 to $113 million in 1956. In 1953 these two items made up 83.7 percent of Czechoslovakian exports to the USSR, in 1956 only 60 percent, Paul Marer, *Soviet and East European Foreign Trade, 1946-1969. Statistical Guide and Compendium*, 24, 26, 36, 81.

58. The annual protocols on West German-Czechoslovakian trade are published in the *Ministerialblatt des Bundesministers für Wirtschaft*, various vols.

59. Brzezinski, *The Soviet Bloc*, 288.

60. Marer, *Soviet and East European Foreign Trade, 1946-1969. Statistical Guide and Compendium*, 24, 26, 36, and 81.

61. *Dokumente zur Deutschlandpolitik*, III, vol. 1, 332-334. *Der Volkswirt* (Frankfurt) had assumed that "at least an agreement for the date of future talks about a trade treaty" would be set in Moscow, "Der Handelspartner im Osten," 27 August 1955.

62. Documentation of the second Geneva Conference is available in Department of State, *The Geneva Meeting of Foreign Ministers, October 27-November 16, 1957* (Washington, 1955); La Documentation Francaise, *La Conference de Geneve (Octobre-Novembre 1955)* (Paris, 1956); *Documents relating to the Meeting of the Foreign Ministers of France, the United Kingdom, the Soviet Union and the United States of America. Geneva October 27-November 16, 1955*, (London, 1955 (Cmd. 9633); *Dokumente zur Deutschlandpolitik*, Series III, vol. 1.

63. *Dokumente zur Deutschlandpolitik*, III, vol. 1, 214-15.

64. *Dokumente zur Deutschlandpolitik*, III, vol. 1, 719.

65. "Statement on Foreign Policy," *Dokumente zur Deutschlandpolitik*, III, vol. 1, 741 ff.

66. Molotov had explained the Soviet view that "the main question in the problem of developing contact between East and West is the development of economic relations and international trade," *Dokumente zur Deutschlandpolitik*, III, vol. 1, 693. Some West Germans saw this as nothing more than an a Soviet maneuver to accelerate Western thinking toward another major reduction of the embargo lists, see e.g., Brentano's declaration to the Bundestag in *Dokumente zur Deutschlandpolitik*, III, vol. 1, 750: "The course of negotiations revealed that the Soviets were interested only in the end of the embargo for strategic goods, and not in peaceful trade ... ."

67. Reinhardt reported to Erhard that the "activity of [Soviet] Ambassador Sorin in economic areas" as well as the presence of "several official and semi-official visitors groups in the Federal Republic" supported Soviet claims about their desire for a treaty, Reinhardt to Erhard, 23 March 1956, BA B 102/58158.

68. In late October 1955, Wolff told a group from the Federation of British Industries that the Federal Republic would "probably" begin trade talks with the Soviets in the upcoming year, 1956, Hipp (industrial Bundesverband) to Reinhardt on a meeting with the Federation of British Industries to discuss East-West Trade, BA B 102/58158. In January 1956, one of the junior clerks at the Economics Ministry's East-West Trade desk assumed that treaty negotiations with the Soviets would begin "shortly," Fischer report to desk officer Scholz, 30 January 1956, PAAA 413.85.00/101.

69. Hipp (Bundesverband) memorandum, 20 January 1956, RWWA 72-189-14.2; Hipp to Wolff, 27 January 1956, ibid. Bundesverband President Berg had heard a few days earlier from Lupin in the Foreign Office that "the federal government does not intend to conclude a trade treaty with the USSR," Wolff to Brentano, 13 January 1956, RWWA 72-189-14.

70. Reinhardt to Erhard, 23 March 1956, including summary of Brentano's 7 March letter, BA B 102/58158.

71. Reinhardt summation for Erhard, 23 March 1956, BA B 102/58158.

72. At that meeting for the Economics Ministry: Erhard, Reinhardt, Steidle, Scholz; for the Foreign Office: Scherpenberg, Lupin, Zahn-Stranik; for the Eastern Committee: Wolff, Berg, Menne, Wenhold, Koehler, Beutler, Hipp, Carnap. The following account is reconstructed from Carnap's undated report on the meeting and Steidle's report from 28 March, both in BA B 102/58158.

73. Sartorius (Foreign Office desk for East Bloc Trade) memorandum of 2 May on the meeting of 28 April 1956, BA B 102/55998. Wolff's notes on that meeting and Reinhardt's report to Erhard in BA B 102/57785.

74. On a "purely private" basis Wolff had urged Brentano and Erhard to consider instead signing "a trade treaty with a very small volume" with the Soviets since even this would reveal Soviet export difficulties and relieve the pressure on the Eastern Committee coming from "small and medium" firms where the "romance of the Russian business in the 1920s and 1930s remains stuck in many heads," Wolff draft to Brentano, 13 January 1956, RWWA 72-189-14. Wolff had at least one meeting with Brentano on the subject and one with Erhard on 27 January 1956, Wolff memorandum, 27 January 1956, RWWA 72-189-14. Wolff tried to win over the influential Cologne banker Robert Pferdmenges, a mutual friend of his and Adenauer's, for the project in a 4 February 1956 letter on the "pros and contras of a possible trade agreement with the USSR," RWWA 72-189-14.

75. Wolff to Reinhardt, 5 June 1956, BA B 102/58158 and RWWA 72-189-14.2. For accounts of the 23 May meeting of the Eastern Committee, Scholz's report, BA B012/57785 and a copy of the minutes, BdI OA/3.2. Scherpenberg's 9 May memorandum on Economic Relations with the Soviet Union reveals that he was searching for some form of "talks with the Soviet side that offer us the possibility of fulfilling our Moscow obligations" [i.e., to hold "consultations on the question of trade development"], PAAA 413.85.00/96.

76. Wolff to Reinhardt, 5 June 1956, BA B 102/58158. Medvedkov headed the embassy's trade division, having previously performed the same function for the Soviet embassy in East Berlin.
77. Scholz memorandum on meeting of Wolff with Reinhardt, Steidle, Schmitt, and Scholz in the Economics Ministry on 13 June 1956, BA B 102/58158.
78. The Eastern Committee (Wolff) to Medvedkov, copy to Reinhardt, 7 July 1956, BA B 102/58158.
79. Wolff memorandum, 14 September 1956, BA B 102/58158.
80. For an account of this meeting, Lupin's notes, 1 June 1956, BA B 102/58158. At an 8 December 1955 meeting of West German mission chiefs, Brentano felt the need to "correct emphatically" the "widespread contradictory reports" that during Adenauer's visit to Moscow the FRG had undertaken an obligation to conclude a trade treaty with the Soviets, Lupin memorandum, 23 January 1956, PAAA 413.85.00/96.
81. Transcript in BA B 102/58158. See also Brentano's complaint to Erhard about Soviet radio broadcasts and the Soviets' "long term effort to exploit the interests of the German business community for the benefit of the Soviet negotiating position," 23 May 1957, BA B 136/1260 and PAAA 413.85.00/101. In March 1957 Medvedkov asked Wolff whether the West Germans would consider "raising the question" in COCOM of "easing" Western export control policies, Wolff memorandum, 28 March 1957, PAAA 413.85.00/101.
82. Lupin memorandum, 7 June 1956, BA B 102/58158.
83. Kubanov directly goaded West German exporters by saying that "of course it will be possible in the future for Soviet foreign trade organizations and West German firms to sign deals for the purchase or sale of particular commodities, however, because of the conditions mentioned above, one cannot expect any substantial increase in trade …. we can wait, because the USSR has the option of developing mutually beneficial trade with those countries that wish to," see "Handelsvertrag verbessert die Beziehungen," *Die Welt*, 10 September 1956.
84. See e.g., the nineteen-page outline in favor of a treaty sent by Erich Berndt of the Hamburg trading firm of Anton Ohlert AG to Erhard in January 1956, BA B 102/58158. In a report of 18 August 1955 the Press and Information Office of the federal government had warned the Foreign Office that most of the print and broadcast media in West Germany favored an expansion of trade with the Soviet bloc and did not accept political arguments for restricting trade with the East, PAAA 413.85.00/110.
85. Steidle to Erhard's personal assistant, Seibt, 9 April 1956, BA B 102/58158.
86. For an account of this meeting, Lupin's memorandum, 1 June 1956, BA B 102/58158.
87. Wolff to Reinhardt from 5 June 1956, BA B 102/58158.
88. Wolff memorandum, 14 September 1956, BA B 102/58158; Wolff memorandum, 28 March 1957, PAAA 413.85.00/101.
89. For an account of this meeting, Lupin's memorandum, 1 June 1956, BA B 102/58158.
90. Steidle memoranda on his 10 and 11 September 1956 discussions with Medvedkov, BA B 102/58158.
91. Steidle notes, 17 and 28 September 1956, BA B 102/58158.
92. Steidle's report, 23 October 1956, BA B 102/58158. Wolff had been invited to this first meeting, but was unable to attend.
93. Steidle notes, from 17 September and 28 September 1956, BA B 102/58158.
94. Bulganin's 5 February 1957 letter in *Dokumente zur Deutschlandpolitik*, III, vol. 3, part 1, 299-315.
95. *Dokumente zur Deutschlandpolitik*, III, vol. 3, part 1, 421-23.

96. Adenauer's response in *Dokumente zur Deutschlandpolitik*, III, vol. 3, part 1, 615. The West Germans suggested that negotiations take place in Moscow and declared themselves prepared to send a delegation with a Chairman in the rank of Ambassador at any time.
97. See, e.g. Adenauer, *Erinnerungen 1955-1959*, 113-20; Felix von Eckardt, *Ein unordentliches Leben*, 474-75.
98. The British and French had already stated plainly that the German question would not be allowed to "block" progress in future negotiating rounds in the subcommittee of the United Nations Disarmament Commission, cited in Gregor Schöllgen, "Kontrollierte Abrüstung" Konrad Adenauer, der Kalte Krieg, und die Entspannungspolitik," in Schöllgen, *Die Macht in der Mitte Europas* (Munich, 1992), 132.
99. Hans Peter Schwarz has interpreted the positive response to Bulganin "as part of a predominantly intra-Western balancing policy designed to fortify the rank of the Federal Republic in negotiations with the Soviet Union and to counter-balance Western detente maneuvers," *Die Ära Adenauer*, 355. Peter Siebenmorgen has also explored Adenauer's growing recognition that the FRG needed a direct line to the Soviets, *Gezeitenwechsel. Aufbruch zur Entspannungspolitik* (Bonn, 1990), 141, 144.
100. Klaus Gotto, "Adenauer's Deutschland- und Ostpolitik 1954-1963,"in Gotto, *Konrad Adenauer. Seine Deutschland- und Aussenpolitik 1945-1963* (Munich, 1975), 197-98. In contrast to Adenauer's view that economic problems motivated Soviet desires for a trade treaty, Scherpenberg felt that the Soviet negotiating offer was "purely political," a way of placing the GDR on "equal footing" with the FRG by concluding trade treaties with both German states, Scherpenberg's draft memorandum for Adenauer, 8 January 1957, PAAA 413.85.00/96.
101. Adenauer, *Erinnerungen 1955-1959*, 353-360, passim.
102. Recent scholarship has made great progress in illuminating this important transition in Adenauer's foreign policy thinking. Identifying and explaining this change in Adenauer's thinking is a major theme in Siebenmorgen's, *Gezeitenwechsel*. Schöllgen has used Adenauer's views on disarmament to reach a similar conclusion about the evolution of Adenauer's foreign policy conceptions between 1955 and 1960, "Kontrollierte Abrüstung."
103. Press Secretary Felix von Eckardt had hinted at a softening West German position in a press conference on 4 January 1957 by stating that "we have returned to the idea of conducting fruitful talks" on "German-Soviet trade;" by announcing that the chancellor "is prepared to take-up this subject;" and by denying that a trade treaty could be signed only by a reunified Germany, transcript in PAAA 413.85.00/96. In a parallel statement to the Bundestag on 28 June 1956, Adenauer denied that a disarmament agreement would have to wait until after reunification, cited in Schöllgen, "Kontrollierte Abrüstung," 133.
104. The complicated repatriation issue involved not only *Altreichsdeutschen* (i.e., East Prussians), "a clear case" according to the German delegation, but also Memel Germans, the settlers from the Baltic countries, Bessarabia, and Vohlynia, ethnic Germans from Poland, Germans from the areas transferred to Poland in 1918, and ethnic Germans from the Soviet Union; "all of these ethnic Germans are either 'booty Germans' i.e., became German citizens during the war, or if not are still burningly interested in emigrating to the Federal Republic." In 1955 Adenauer claimed 130,000 persons fell into these categories, by July 1957 the Foreign Office had revised its estimate to 80,000 (still "more a guess than a certainty"), the final agreement accommodated 25,000. Rolf Lahr, *Zeuge von Fall und Aufstieg. Private Briefe 1934-1974*, (Hamburg, 1981) 262, 267.
105. Beutler to Scherpenberg, 23 May 1957, PAAA 413.85.00/97. An internal memorandum from the Bundesverband's Foreign Trade Committee to Berg reaffirmed

the general "primacy of politics in the Eastern trade," and specifically acknowledged the "priority of foreign policy considerations" in these negotiations, 16 January 1958, RWWA 72-189-15. The parallel with business assessments of Stresemann's 1925 trade treaty with the Soviets is evident.

106. The Hamburg Chamber of Commerce told Wolff plainly that "Hamburg importers ... have no intention of injuring relations with existing suppliers for the benefit of increased imports from the Soviet Union," 13 May 1957, RWWA 72-189-14.2 Similarly, the iron and steel interest group told the Economics Ministry that they did not intend to include Russian iron ore in their principal sources of supply, 7 May 1957, ibid. Most of the private-sector suggestions reaching the Foreign Office in June 1957 focused on smoothing out and speeding up procedural aspects of business deals with the Soviets rather than on increasing the volume of trade, PAAA 413.85.00/101.

107. *Adenauer Teegespräche 1955-1958*, 206

108. Memorandum, 19 March 1957, PAAA 413.85.00/96.

109. Lahr, *Zeuge*, 262, 295. At the final interministerial preparation for the Moscow negotiations on 17 July 1957, Lahr "emphasized that the impetus for trade negotiations had come from the Soviet side. In the FRG, neither the government nor the private sector has considered a treaty urgent." Scherpenberg considered the business community's "current cautious judgment of the commercial opportunities in the USSR" to be a significant advantage for the German delegation, Zahn-Stranik memorandum, 22 July 1957, PAAA 413.85.00/97.

110. Lahr had received his early training in the Reich Economics Ministry (1934 to 1935 and 1939 to 1945). After the war he joined the Economics Ministry. Since 1953 he had been with the Western European Section of the Foreign Office's Commercial Affairs Department, where he led the German delegation in the extraordinarily difficult Saar negotiations with France. He rose to state secretary in the Foreign Office (1961 to 1969) and thereafter served as ambassador to Italy.

111. Zahn noted that the Economics Ministry was "relatively weakly" represented in the German delegation, memorandum, 1 June 1957, PAAA 413.85.00/108.

112. Schellpeper to Steidle, 21 December 1957. BA B 102/18489 H.2. As early as 1 April 1957 Zahn-Stranik had cautioned Steidle that "in the opinion of the Foreign Office, the upcoming negotiations cannot be conducted purely from the economic perspective," Steidle memorandum, PAAA 413.85.00/97.

113. On 17 March 1958 he reported from Moscow that "I am concerned about the outcome of the negotiations because I fear that at the most the Foreign Office would let the negotiations fail because of the repatriation question, but on no account because of economic questions," BA B 102/18489 H.1

114. A detailed, day-by-day account of the course of negotiation can be reconstructed from the documents in BA B 102/18489 H.1 & 2 and PAAA 413.85.00/96-105.

115. Lahr to his mother on 18 July 1957 in Lahr, *Zeuge*, 261. In his memoirs, Adenauer states plainly that he told Lahr to "hold out in Moscow until a positive result has been achieved", *Erinnerungen*, 370.

116. Lahr, *Zeuge*, 269-75; Toepfer (Economics Ministry) report, 24 September 1957, BA B 102/18489 H.2. On 25 June 1957 *Pravda* had run three columns denying the existence of any repatriation issue involving ethnic Germans in Soviet territory, Ambassador Haas to the Foreign Office, 25 June 1957, PAAA 413.85.00/97. On 6 July the Soviets presented that position in an official note to the West German embassy in Moscow, ibid.

117. On 29 May 1957 Carnap had again reminded the Foreign Office that the Eastern Committee considered it "necessary" to have these points "fixed" in the agreement or in an exchange of letters, PAAA 413.85.00/107.

118. PAAA 413.85.00/106.

119. On the failure of these negotiations from 1958 to 1960 see Robert Mark Spaulding, "Reconquering Our Old Position," in Berghahn, ed., *Quest for Economic Empire*, 135 ff.

120. Finding some way to balance West German exports to the USSR with Soviet exports to the FRG was a recurring problem of the negotiations, becoming the major issue in the final phase, February 1958 to March 1958. On 14 and 15 February Lahr and Kumykin held a special two-day meeting to try to close this gap, PAAA 413.85.00/99. As Lahr explained to an interministerial meeting back in Bonn on 24 January 1958, the "difficulties on the [West German] import side" were caused by the very limited interest that Soviet export offers aroused in the Federal Republic, PAAA 413.85.00/103.

121. Typical in this regard was the 11 December 1957 telegram from the German delegation in Moscow (Zahn-Stranik?) to the Economics Ministry in Bonn: "Regarding oil, please consider that economic negotiations must be conducted under strong political considerations, that oil belongs to the classic export commodities of the Soviet Union, and that for these reasons the greatest possible concessions should be made. Similar arguments apply for non-ferrous metals, especially zinc," BA B 102/18489 H.2. On 12 March the West Germans agreed to "additional concessions" of 700,000 tons of oil, 15,000 tons of gasoline, and 150,000 tons of pyrite, PAAA 413.85.00/97.

122. According to Lahr, Mikoyan told him at the initialing ceremony in Moscow on 8 April 1958 that "if relations with the Federal Republic develop positively then there will be many German repatriates; if [relations] develop poorly, there will be fewer," *Zeuge*, 293.

123. *Verhandlungen des deutschen Bundestages*, III Wahlperiode, Stenographische Berichte, Band 39, 297-419. For background and a summary of the debate, including the government's lackluster performance, see Gordon D. Drummond, *The German Social Democrats in Opposition, 1949-1960. The Case Against Rearmament* (Norman, Okla., 1982), 217 ff.

124. From Moscow, Lahr urged that the "political value and consequences" of the agreements be emphasized at the signing ceremonies, and for this reason he favored having Soviet Foreign Minister Gromyko come to Bonn, Lahr to the Foreign Office, 9 March 1958; Welck (Soviet desk) to Hallstein, 6 March 1958, PAAA 413.85.00/106. When reports from the West German embassy in Paris indicated that Gromyko's appearance in Bonn at a time when negotiations over East-West disarmament talks were just beginning would lead to "wild combinations" in the Western press, the Germans switched to Mikoyan, Knocke (Soviet desk) memorandum, 27 February 1958, ibid. Wolff advocated Mikoyan over Gromyko because the former's generally more pleasant, less confrontational nature increased the likelihood of a politically successful visit, Wolff interview, 3 July 1991.

125. Only the Consular Treaty and the Navigation Agreement required parliamentary approval, but the role of the merchandise agreements in anchoring the entire bundle of accords was generally recognized and the government's appeals for public and parliamentary support most usually referred to "the treaties" or "the agreements."

126. In December 1958, the CDU Bundestag faction put the treaty on hold, telling Adenauer and Brentano that they would continue the ratification process in mid-January, Duckwitz summation for Adenauer and Brentano, 9 January 1959, PAAA 413.85.00/106.

127. Duckwitz summation, 9 January 1959, PAAA 413.85.00/106; Adenauer interview with the *Politisch-Soziale Korrespondenz*, 30 December 1958.

128. Further, the agreements would be a "contribution to peace and to the solution of the larger political issues," Brentano's declaration to the Bundesrat's Foreign

Affairs Committee, 26 February 1959, PAAA 413.85.00/106. Similarly, Adenauer in his memoirs offered the justification that the trade agreements "might create a better climate between Moscow and Bonn which could possibly be useful in the reunification question," *Erinnerungen 1955-1959*, 359.

129. Adenauer realized this constituted a radical departure from previous policy. He warned Soviet Ambassador Vladimir Smirnov that if the Austrian proposal "should become known to the German public, I risk being stoned by my own people." *Erinnerungen 1955-1959*, 378. On the evolution of Adenauer's own Ostpolitik see Siebenmorgen, *Gezeitenwechsel*; Horst Osterfeld, *"Ich gehe nicht leichten Herzens ... ": Adenauers letzte Kanzlerjahre; Ein dokumentarischer Bericht* (Mainz, 1986).

130. At a press conference on 8 April 1958, Eckardt sought to cover over this change in priorities by denying that the agreement with the Soviet was equivalent to a "classic" trade treaty which, as he explained vaguely, would have covered a "broader range of issues."

131. These two documents are available in the *Ministerialblatt des Bundesministers für Wirtschaft*, 1958, Nr. 9, 273-278. Commodity exchanges for 1959 and 1960 were finalized in an additional protocol, also available in the *Ministerialblatt* 1959, Nr. 5, 125 ff. and 1960, Nr. 6, 171 ff.

132. For example, the first item on the 1958 protocol's German export list read: "Seven complete infrastructures for factories producing plywood, each with an annual capacity of 15,000 tons." In addition, the Federal Republic was to deliver complete freezing and cooling infrastructures for fishing trawlers, assembly line technology for bottling plants, extractive technology for whale-oil processing plants, and more.

133. Yet Soviet inability to expand its hard currency exports beyond coal, timber, and oil remained the greatest barrier to further increases in trade. Reinhardt warned that the West German market "has not proven very receptive to Soviet goods" and that the FRG would have to "go to the extreme limit of the economically responsible" in accepting unwanted amounts of Soviet exports in order to balance the scheduled volume of West German exports for 1960, Trade Policy Committee meeting 18/59, 22 December 1959, PAAA 413.85.00/109.

THE STRUCTURES AND PATTERNS OF GERMAN TRADE POLICY

The Structural Framework

*D*espite the position of trade as one of the most important international activities of any sovereign state, the formation of national trade polices remains an understudied and poorly understood process. Trade itself has been the subject of increasingly sophisticated analytic modeling since Ricardo's work nearly two hundred years ago, yet trade policies have come under ambitious academic inquiry only in the past twenty years. As a result, the economics of most trade phenomena are now understood with mathematical precision, while the political economy of trade policy remains a subject with few analytic tools and no generally accepted models. As I have suggested elsewhere, most studies of trade policy formation have had difficulty moving beyond the debate over an appropriate conceptual framework.

Of necessity then, one goal of this book has been to construct an interpretive framework for understanding German trade policy decisions vis-à-vis Eastern Europe. That goal grew naturally and logically out of a desire to compare in some systematic manner German trade policies over an extended period from the late nineteenth century through the first decades of the post-1945 order. At the time I undertook this study, the relevant historical, political, and economic literature provided few clues for analyzing German trade policy decisions in any one of the four periods I sought to compare. By extension, there had been no articulation of a set of concepts around which I could fashion a comparative analysis of trade policies over several periods. In response, I sought to identify recurring considerations in trade policy formulations that might serve as the starting points for a methodical comparison of these policies.

Working through the historical record that comprises the empirical foundation of this study, I began to generate a set of analytic factors that have served as the vehicles for my explanations of German trade policy decisions. Eagerly receptive to theoretical insights offered by social science colleagues working in international political economy, I nonetheless extracted my conceptual tools for an analysis of trade policy from the historical record of German experiences in Eastern Europe. There, I was able to identify recurring concerns, considerations, and constraints of German policymakers across several regimes as they grappled with some of their nation's most difficult economic and political problems. Although the components of my investigative framework have been drawn from German experiences in Eastern Europe, I suspect that the recurring factors, issues, structures, and questions around which I have centered my inquiry might be relevant to issues of trade relations and foreign economic policy in other contexts.

The first part of this conclusion lays out the conceptual tools employed in dissecting German trade policy. Those readers who are not reading these conclusions first will already have seen these categories of trade policy comparison employed over the preceding pages. Nonetheless, it is worthwhile to extract these concepts and present them here explicitly before reviewing the German experiences in the Eastern trade from the 1890s through the 1950s.

1. The foundation for any international trade policy must be sought in the role of each country in the international division of labor. National economic performance provides objective measures of each country's relative strength in a given trade relationship – the starting point for any trade policy. Germany held the upper hand economically in its relations with Eastern Europe throughout the period under consideration by virtue of exchanging its more sophisticated consumer and capital goods for Eastern Europe's primary products.

   Yet the strength of the German economy in the international framework provided only the starting point for trade policy formulation. A methodical analysis of trade policy across several regimes must take into account other, political factors that played determinant roles in shaping German policies. Because German industrial superiority vis-à-vis Eastern Europe was continual throughout this period, I have used economic performance as a constant. As such, the role of German economic strength in the fashioning of trade policies has receded somewhat into the background and the influences of these other, more political and more variable factors occupies the foreground.

2. An unavoidable consideration in shaping German trade policies throughout the entire period was the prevailing international trade regime. The record of German activities shows the international trade regime played an important role in shaping both the form and content of German trade policies in the Eastern Europe. A powerful economic actor such as Germany is not merely a passive recipient of changing regimes, but neither did it fly in the face of prevailing trends. Germany worked within the Western trading system, but was always a leader in protectionist departures from existing norms.

   Four distinct trade regimes have emerged since the late nineteenth century. The pre-1914 liberal trade regime was secured by most-favored-nation (MFN) clauses and limited state powers of regulation. The transitional regime of 1920 to 1929 sought in vain to restore the full liberty of prewar trade. The fractured regime of the Depression years, 1930 to 1939, was characterized by bilateralism and trading blocs. The post-1945 order produced a bifurcated European trade regime with neoliberalism in the West and state control in the East. These successive regimes prevented, impeded, allowed, and then encouraged the execution of trade leverage policies. German policymakers had to choose their tools for shaping trade flows with Eastern Europe (tariffs and treaties, administrative action, cartels) from the set of trade policy tools deemed permissible by the prevailing trade regime.

3. Recognizing the potential of trade leverage and accepting the use of that leverage as a foreign policy tool was a recurring deliberation in the various Eastern trade policies examined by this study. A growing awareness after 1890 of the potential of trade policy as a foreign policy tool was not unique to Germany. After 1918, European policymakers recognized the new opportunities offered by the crumbling liberal trade regime. Particularly in Germany, however, the reduction and (by 1950) the elimination of other means of influence in Eastern Europe hastened the acceptance of trade leverage as a foreign policy tool. Increasing reliance on trade agreements as foreign policy tools further increased the difficulties of reaching satisfactory trade agreements. In those circumstances, trade agreements had to perform double duty, producing political as well as economic concessions abroad.

4. Trade policy requires a special understanding between the state as the director of foreign policy on one side and the private sector as the owner of economic resources on the other side. That understanding may rest on a private-sector consensus – in the form of a coalition of interests – that accepts the distribution of sacrifices and rewards generated by government policy. In the absence of such a consensus between commercial, agricultural, and industrial private-sector groups, coordination between the state and private sector must come from the regime's own autonomy – its ability to impose the necessary sacrifices on society. In order to generate a functioning trade policy, successive German governments had either to build a consensus with the private sector on the costs and benefits of the government's trade policies or, alternatively, the government had to impose those policies on a fractious private sector through tariff and other trade regulations. The choice for consensus, imposition, or some combination of the two and the ability to execute these choices has been as important as any other factor in determining Germany's ability to frame viable trade policies for Eastern Europe. Success in these endeavors has varied greatly across the four German regimes reviewed here. A fundamental supposition of this work has been that an investigation into these choices and the causes for success of failure in their execution provides new and valuable insights into the distribution of economic and political power within the authoritarian, corporatist, dictatorial, and neocorporatist regimes of modern Germany.

5. The ability to control imports and exports effectively on a selective basis directly determined the ability of German governments to apply any trade policies on a differential basis in Eastern Europe. In cases involving major trade partners or large volumes of trade, selective trade control policies required a virtual army of personnel possessing the technical expertise to determine the origin of every imported commodity and the ability to police the destination of every exported item (because foreign buyers and sellers naturally sought to circumvent any prohibitions).

The Patterns of German Trade Policy

An effort at systematic comparison of trade policies must not lead to a "leveling" of the vastly different experiences among the four German regimes examined here. As a combination of varied responses to the recurring challenges of trade policy formation, each regime brought forth its own policies on the Eastern trade – policies that varied tremendously over the extended period under consideration here. In this, exceptional policies and recurring policies illuminate patterns of German policy equally well. Further, in producing or failing to produce its own characteristic responses to recurring pressures on policy, each regime revealed essential elements of its political and economic systems. As channels of insight into the international and domestic arrangements that characterized each of the regimes we have examined, German experiences in the Eastern trade merit summary review. For the historian, a variety of experiences precludes a schematic presentation of the results, despite the methodical nature of the inquiry. The unique character of each period as captured in the historical findings, rather than the systematic nature of the social scientific inquiry, determines the form of what follows.

After 1890 the conflicting material and organizational interests of the leading sectors of the German economy precluded a functional private-sector consensus on the fundamental questions of Germany's future trade policies in the East. At the core of this conflict stood a German agrarian response to Eastern trade policies that might be characterized as obstructionism. Because any expansion of trade with Eastern Europe required Germany to import East European agricultural products, German agriculture actively sought to block the conclusion of trade agreements between Germany and its Eastern neighbors. Hereafter, German agriculture's input on trade policy grew increasingly one-dimensional and negative. Private-sector consensus on any policy that might increase trade was possible only if and when Eastern imports did not threaten domestic German agricultural price levels.

Wilhelmine governments overcame these bitter private-sector divisions with a quasi-democratic state structure in which a largely autonomous authoritarian administration was repeatedly capable of imposing trade policy settlements on fractious private groups. Maintaining most of the autocratic autonomy they had inherited from the preconstitutional era, the Imperial Reich and royal Prussian administrations successfully insulated themselves from the demands and pressures of competing interest groups. The authoritarian monarchical structure of the regime lent the bureaucratic apparatus more than enough prestige, authority, and discipline to fend off intrusive inquiries from a badly fragmented private-sector. Caprivi's Tariff Council proved to be no more than a brief flirtation with private-sector partners. The Bülow government simply ignored private-sector demands that representatives of commerce and industry be allowed to participate in preparing and negotiating the new round of trade treaties in 1904 and 1905, even when these demands came from the Reich's most powerful private interest groups. In Germany, Bülow's fortuitous success in negotiating the 1904 German-Russian trade treaty against the backdrop of the Russo-Japanese war vindicated the closed-door manner in which the government had prepared for and negotiated the treaty. In Russia, on the other hand, his calculated exploitation of Russian weakness helped poison political relations with Germany in the final decade before the Great War. Imperial Germany's ratification procedures for trade treaties also contributed to a high degree of executive autonomy. Trade agreements were presented to the Reichstag as inviolable whole packages subject only to a single yes-or-no vote, thereby precluding legislative refashioning of parts of the deal.

Prior to 1914 control over trade policy remained exclusively in the hands of the state bureaucracy, concentrated chiefly in the persons of the chancellor and the interior state secretary and executed by the Foreign Office bureaucracy. This concentrated authority allowed the wide fluctuations that characterized Imperial German trade policy: from protectionism under Bismarck in the 1880s to dramatic tariff reductions under Caprivi in the 1890s and back to highly protectionist policies under Bülow. However, political culture and state structure could not fully insulate the chancellor from the political realities of German society. Caprivi was capable of reversing Bismarck's protectionists policies but paid the price in unrelenting agrarian hatred and intrigue, which helped secure his dismissal after ratification of the Russian trade treaty in 1894. The quasi-democratic structures of the Imperial Reich allowed the chancellor to dominate trade policy formation, but could not always afford absolute or permanent protection against the reactions of powerful political opponents.

Executive autonomy also played a crucial role in German governments overcoming the emerging domestic debate on the use of trade policy as a tool of foreign policy. Bismarck had always maintained a strict separation of foreign economic policies from the political and military elements of *grosse Politik*. In this, the still-dominant European liberal trade doctrines, which had been strong in Prussia through the 1870s, and Germany's position as a net grain exporter until 1876 reinforced Bismarck's natural inclination to avoid entanglements that might limit his diplomatic room to maneuver. In addition, before 1914 Germany had available to it other forms of leverage, especially military and diplomatic tools, that might influence Russian policy. For these reasons, Bismarck felt no need to support his allies with trade or financial considerations. The German-Austrian Dual Alliance covered over a de facto trade war that had originated with new increases in the German tariff of 1881. Similarly, in 1887 Bismarck raised the (primarily anti-Russian) grain tariff for the third time in ten years, while at the same time he proposed, negotiated, and signed the Reinsurance Treaty with the Russians and arranged for the czar's visit to Germany in 1887.

Bismarck's successor, Caprivi, on the other hand, publicly embraced the idea of using trade in support of larger foreign policy goals. He argued in 1894 that economic sacrifices were required in order to secure a Russian trade treaty that Germany needed, in part, to reestablish a line to St. Petersburg after the lapse of the Reinsurance Treaty in 1890. Caprivi's logic may have been sound, but his argument caused a small sensation since it so obviously departed from Bismarck's practice of refusing to commit the Reich to the economic support of its allies. Notwithstanding the self-serving nature of their arguments, the agrarian conservatives, who instinctively clung to Bismarckian practices, feared the loss of German diplomatic freedom that the political overtones of Caprivi's long-term trade agreements implied. The Junkers' preindustrial worldview could not easily accommodate Caprivi's policy of strengthening Germany's allies through trade and economic cooperation. At the same time, Junker belief in German military superiority meant that most conservatives would not accept the idea that Germany "had to pay for peace" by maintaining harmonious trade relations with its neighbors.

In sum, a high degree of state autonomy was crucial for the state's resolution of conflicting economic claims and emerging foreign policy debates. That executive autonomy was indispensable for the conclusion of the 1894 and 1904 Russian treaties. Those agreements allowed the highly productive German economy to assume a controlling position in Russian foreign trade, capturing 45 percent of the Russian import market and 30 percent of the Russian export market in 1913. Yet these figures represented "only" 9 percent of German total exports and 13 percent of total imports. Although a number of other countries could serve Germany well as alternative sources of Russian agricultural exports, the German market, with its densely packed mass of consumers, was irreplaceable for Russian grain exporters. Further, Russia needed German exports; few other, or, in some cases, no other countries could deliver the advanced chemical, electrical, and machine exports that the Reich sent to Russia.

For Imperial German governments secondary difficulties in framing trade policy toward Russia lay in the international trade regime where an extensive network of MFN treaties and the lack of a rigorous trade control mechanism left Germany unprepared to handle Russian agricultural exports in a discriminating manner. Prior to

1914, the liberal European trade regime worked to prevent Germany from isolating its trade relations with Russia. Beginning with the Anglo-French Cobden-Chevalier Treaty of 1860, European commercial relations had been regulated by an expanding web of trade treaties containing the most-favored-nation clause. This treaty practice made it difficult and unusual to discriminate against or grant preference to any subset of trading partners in an enduring manner since any bilateral tariff reduction became a multilateral reduction.

Under these circumstances, Germany did not develop a rigorous German import/export control bureaucracy. Prior to 1914 Germany did not possess the effective administrative control mechanism required to manipulate the flow of trade as either a reward or a punishment for Russia. The Prussian Finance Ministry (responsible for customs administration) explained this defect to Caprivi in 1894 and the Reich Treasury Office returned to this shortcoming in response to Bülow's questions in 1903. The German customs service could not even administer a discriminatory tariff against Russian grain! When negotiating with Russia in 1894 and 1904, the absence of a sufficiently sophisticated customs service virtually compelled the Reich to sign MFN treaties with Russia. This, in turn, further hindered German ability to apply tariff and other discriminations or preferences. Both directly and indirectly, the pre-1914 trade regime of MFN treaties handicapped the Reich's attempts to bring the full German economic advantage to bear during German-Russian treaty negotiations. This combination of negative factors compelled Caprivi to place Russia on equal footing with Germany's other trade partners in 1894 and explains why his use of trade as a means of influencing relations with Russia could consist only of granting this unavoidable concession.

The shattering of the Russian and Habsburg Empires into a number of smaller successor states in Eastern Europe only increased the previously existing German trade advantages during the interwar years. In 1929 the German share of Polish foreign trade was more than ten times larger than the Polish share of the German trade (29 percent and 2.5 percent respectively)! Czechoslovakia's position was only a little better. The Reich absorbed one-quarter of Czechoslovak exports and supplied more than one-third of imports, while Czechoslovakia was a market for just 5 percent of German exports and supplied only 3.5 percent of German imports. Although the Soviets remained largely withdrawn from the European economy in the 1920s, the trade they did conduct with the Reich was skewed to the German advantage. The Germans held 22 percent of the Soviet import market in 1929, yet this represented just 2.6 percent of German foreign sales. Germany bought 23 percent of Soviet exports, yet these were only 3.1 percent of German total imports.

At these levels, the Eastern trade continued to spark domestic debates over the content of the Reich's Eastern trade policies. By the 1920s this policy conflict had widened precisely at a time when the economic burdens of the Versailles settlement made a German trade surplus imperative. Domestically oriented producers (agriculture, textiles, and heavy industry) argued for an emphasis on home protection and reduced imports. In opposition, those industrial sectors that could compete successfully in the world market (machine tools and electro-technicals) urged a priority of export growth, which required a reduction of home protection in order to lower the costs of industrial production and to secure export-facilitating trade agreements.

Unlike the imperial regime, Weimar lacked the strong state capable of imposing a settlement on the splintered agricultural and industrial interests. The heavy-handed Imperial regime was followed by a porous republic that proved incapable of standing above the intensifying private-sector disputes or imposing a solution on them. Weimar's corporatist structure and coalition governments allowed the private interest groups to carry their differences over trade policy directly into the Reichstag, and, more significantly, into the cabinet, the ministerial bureaucracy, and on occasion even inside German trade delegations as they negotiated with foreign counterparts. In this way, Weimar granted to each of several major economic groups and their corresponding political parties a veto power over trade policy decisions on each of several different levels. For that reason, the system was unable to impose trade policies on the private-sector that would have required sacrifices by one or more of these groups. These domestic limits, expressed in the form of an agricultural veto on trade policy, prevented the conclusion of serious trade agreements between Germany and its Eastern neighbors regardless of whether German motives for an agreement were political, economic, or a mixture of the two. Weimar trade policy remained paralyzed. Seven years of laborious negotiations failed to produce a trade treaty with Poland during the life of the German republic. Similarly, the agricultural veto allowed only a preliminary general treaty with Czechoslovakia which was signed in 1920; subsequent substantive agreements remained elusive. Only because of the pariah status of both great powers did the economically insignificant German-Soviet trade agreements of the 1920s acquire political significance. As a result of these domestic shortcomings, Weimar governments could not even begin to realize Foreign Minister Gustav Stresemann's desire to exploit Germany's superior trade position vis-à-vis the East.

Domestic restraints caused particular frustration in the 1920s because changes in the international trade regime and in Germany's ability to control imports and exports more effectively appeared to open new possibilities for the use of trade as an instrument of foreign policy. After 1920 the liberal trade regime reemerged, badly damaged by the bitter experience of 1914 to 1918. The war unleashed a wave of economic nationalism heralded by the six-power Allied Economic Conference in June 1916 and confirmed by the Versailles settlement. The economic and reparations clauses of Versailles (Part X, Economic Clauses, Articles 264 to 270) legitimized the continued use of commercial and financial weapons in the pursuit of foreign policy goals during peacetime. Even in the relatively normal years between 1925 and 1929, many European countries strictly controlled trade in many important commodities (e.g., coal in Germany). In East-Central Europe more so than in the West, economic nationalism shaped tariffs, state budgets, and private investments. At the same time, the goal of essentially free, multilateral trade was still acknowledged in Western and Central Europe, and the MFN principle (though often without the necessary tariff substance) was included in most German trade treaties in the 1920s.

By relying heavily on the private interest groups as control administrators Germany created a corporatist system of extensive and effective trade controls from 1914 to 1924. In 1920 Weimar's mixed private-public system of economic self-administration was processing 20,000 to 30,000 import and export applications per day. This extensive trade control regime gave early Weimar governments something their imperial forerunners never had – a means of controlling foreign trade so effectively that German policies could now differentiate among East European partners.

The new circumstances of politicized trade in the interwar period were well suited to Stresemann as foreign minister. He had long argued for an active integration of international economic and political concerns. As a product of the Saxon industrial environment, Stresemann understood that for the near term, Germany's remaining strengths in the new European order were limited to the areas of economic power. He was not alone in seeking to employ Germany's economic resources in the service of its foreign policy. As a net capital importer, Weimar Germany did not have the financial resources to counter British and French financial diplomacy in Eastern and Southeastern Europe. Weimar's status as an economic great power was restricted to trade, relying on the Reich's export capabilities and appetite for imports. In light of this, Weimar's general inability to produce working trade policies in Eastern Europe deprived Stresemann of what ought to have been Germany's most useful foreign policy tool for compelling a peaceful revision of the terms of Versailles.

Only as the political structures of corporatism gave way to an increasingly authoritarian presidential quasi-dictatorship from 1930 to 1933 and then to a one-party state with totalitarian aspirations after 1933 could Germany employ economic diplomacy in the East. By 1932 these transitions had progressed far enough that Chancellor Brüning offered concessions and obtained a small trade agreement with Poland. That agreement served Brüning's "go for broke" policy, which was designed to obtain a radical reduction in reparations by demonstrating to the West that despite German goodwill the Reich could not pay the amounts demanded from it.

The fraying system of multilateral trade did not survive the currency turmoil of 1931. State import monopolies, quantitative restrictions, foreign exchange controls, and preferential treaties killed the multilateral trade system, which, though shaken by the consequences of World War I, had governed European commercial exchanges since the mid-nineteenth century. These fundamental changes in the international trading system produced an international trade regime based on bilateral trade relations fashioned sui generis with the new tools of import quotas and exchange controls. Whereas the pre-1914 multilateral trade regime had restricted the options in German trade policy, the bilateral regime of the 1930s did just the opposite – it dramatically widened the range of policy choices available to the German government in crafting trade policies with individual East European states. The collapse of the multilateral trade regime deprived East European countries of any possible communal international protection. In 1933 and especially in 1934 as part of Reichsbank President Hjalmar Schacht's New Plan, the Nazis greatly accelerated the wave of trade controls that had been surging since the final years of the Weimar Republic. In administering its system of import controls and export promotion, the Third Reich, too, relied on the mixture of government and private bureaucratic administration. The resurgent Reich then isolated its smaller neighbors in bilateral deals shaped by radical new measures such as state-run import monopolies for key commodities.

Ominously, the new foreign policy opportunities afforded by changes in the international trade regime arrived coincidentally with Hitler's assumption of power in Germany. After 1933, Hitler's worldview determined that trade policy could be only a means toward his ultimate ends. Unlike any other chancellor, Hitler knew from the time he took office that ultimately he and Germany would stand or fall with the outcome of a major war of conquest. With this knowledge, he ignored the short-term economic consequences of his trade policy decisions and he allowed only Germany's most immediate economic problems to constrain his use of trade in Eastern Europe.

Hitler's use of trade policy in the East aroused little opposition at home. Unprecedented economic protection for agriculture, rearmament, and political suppression provided the Nazi regime with a mixture of consensus and control more than sufficient to pursue its politically motivated Eastern trade polices. For the first time since the 1880s, genuine, across-the-board private-sector consensus on expanding German trade in the East emerged under the Nazis in 1933 and 1934. Hitler allowed Agriculture Minister Alfred Hugenburg to build on protectionist measures initiated in 1930 in order to nullify the East European agricultural threat with radical tariff, quota, and price control protection for German farmers. By 1934 radical agricultural protection, culminating in guaranteed prices, gave farmers the income stability they had so desperately sought in the 1920s. This put an end to agrarian obstructionism. At the same time, a state-sponsored export drive, public works, and rearmament prevented the downturn in industrial production that labor, industry, and commerce had long feared as the ultimate result of increased domestic agricultural protection. Full employment and healthy industrial profits provided the Nazis with an economically pacified private-sector. By 1934 all independent political parties and trade unions had been dissolved; other independent associations such as the German Chamber of Commerce were reconstituted as part of political synchronization *(Gleichschaltung)*. In this way, economic and political developments combined to give the government a passive consensus on managing Germany's Eastern trade however it chose in accordance with the bases of Nazi agricultural and industrial programs.

In sum, Hitler's Nazi government enjoyed an anarchic international trade regime and an autonomous domestic regime from 1933 to 1939. The combination worked synergetically to produce both the opportunity and the ability for German policies of economic diplomacy in Eastern Europe. Beginning in 1934, the Reich applied trade leverage in Eastern Europe, hoping to open the area to German influence in the period before Germany could impose military control. Nazi economic penetration into the Southeastern Europe and the Balkans is generally well known. Less well known is the Nazi use of economic diplomacy in German-Polish relations at this time. Hitler ended a decade of German-Polish tariff conflict by accepting imports of Polish coal and voluntarily reducing the size of the German trade surplus. As part of Hitler's near-term policy for Poland, those concession paved the way for the 1934 German-Polish nonaggression pact of March 1934, which effectively ended the prospect of containing Germany by French-East European alliances. The critical role played by German trade incentives in the July to August 1939 negotiations with the Soviets is still not sufficiently well appreciated. The Soviets demanded material proof about the sincerity of German feelers for a nonaggression pact. In order to obtain the political-strategic cover for his invasion of Poland, Hitler offered the Soviets 320 million marks in advanced industrial equipment and armaments, 200 million of this on credit. In terms of both its enormity and its ultimate political significance it may well be the most important single trade deal of this century.

After 1945 West German trade with Poland, Czechoslovakia, and the Soviet Union became subsumed in the larger concept of East-West trade. Like other Western countries, the new Federal Republic participated in two distinct trade regimes: a depoliticized trade regime for Western partners (embodied in GATT) and a politicized regime for East European rivals (COCOM). The nonparticipation of the Soviet bloc in the world economy excluded Eastern Europe from the depoliticizing protections of the postwar neoliberal trade regime. In contrast, the new American-sponsored regime for East-West trade not only allowed the use of trade leverage, it demanded that use of trade as part of the American embargo policy on trade with the Soviet bloc. By both allowing and demanding carefully managed trade with the East, the politicized regime of East-West Trade worked at different times either to widen or narrow the range of West German trade policy choices in Eastern Europe. Because allowances for politicized trade in pursuit of West German national interests far exceeded demands for politicized trade in pursuit of common Western interests, the net effect of the post-1945 trade regime for trade with Eastern Europe was to dramatically increase the set of West German trade policy choices with Soviet bloc countries.

In conjunction with the politicization of East-West trade, the Allies insisted that the Bonn republic construct an adequate export control program as part of the pan-Western embargo policy. When the West German Economics Ministry reorganized itself in 1951, a comprehensive Group on East-West Trade was created within the Foreign Trade Department specifically for the purpose of coordinating commercial policy in Eastern Europe and the pure control side of the issue. By 1953 the federal authorities had put in place a large and effective bureaucracy within the Economics Ministry, whose primary purpose was to control exports – initially in accordance with American wishes, but increasingly in accordance with the FRG's own foreign policy initiatives in the East.

After 1949, the lack of diplomatic, cultural, and all other forms of normal relations with Eastern Europe virtually compelled the Federal Republic to recognize the use of its economic advantage for political advantage. In the absence of other forms of contact, the annual trade negotiations assumed central places in West German relations with several East European countries. By the early 1950s, political questions were often discussed at the annual trade negotiating sessions. This formal linkage naturally invited the Federal Republic to use trade leverage for the resolution of political issues. In 1953 the new West German Foreign Office advanced the idea of using trade policy to secure other advantages in the East. In interministerial debates, West German Foreign Office officials declared flatly that the purely commercial considerations of trade agreements should be subordinated to raising the overall standing of the Federal Republic in the East. Members of the agriculture and economics ministries, eager to establish and reestablish a German economic presence in the East, balked at the proposed connection. Adenauer's decision to back the Foreign Office recognized that trade had, of necessity, become the FRG's foreign policy tool of greatest utility in Eastern Europe.

As the Allies returned control over West German trade relations with Eastern Europe to the Federal Republic, that control became imbedded in a neocorporatist coalition between the ministerial bureaucracy and the business community. However, unlike the corporatism of the Weimar years, the neocorporatism of the Federal Republic's domestic framework for trade policy was based on an economic consensus vis-à-vis Eastern Europe. Consensus and a measure of bureaucratic autonomy inherited from the Occupation regime gave the ministries the upper hand in dealing with the interest groups.

After 1950, the Federal Republic saw a reemergence of German private-sector consensus on expanding trade with the East. This consensus did not rest on protectionism and state controls as in Germany of the 1930s, but on the political and economic consequences of Stalinism (i.e., on the poor economic performance of the new people's democracies, specifically their inability to produce exportable agricultural surpluses or competitive manufactures). As Czechoslovakia and Poland sank into the abyss of declining productivity after 1950, they lost the ability to genuinely threaten German agriculture or industry. By 1954 a large program for protecting German farmers from East European or Soviet competition would have been laughable.

The economic success of the Federal Republic from 1949 to 1960 gave the West Germans a strong position from which to plan trade strategy toward Eastern Europe. By 1955 the previously existing disparity between living standards in Eastern and Western Europe had widened into an unbridgeable gulf, affecting even the most advanced industrial areas of Czechoslovakia. The divergence in economic performance between Germany and its Eastern neighbors had never been greater. The Federal Republic could deliver both the food and the investment goods Eastern Europe needed. West Germany could also supply short-term financing for its export sales and long-term loans for both investment and consumer purchases. The Federal Republic's successful reorientation away from the Eastern market and toward Western Europe and North America meant that West Germany could easily afford to politicize its Eastern trade. Foreign Office and Economics Ministry policymakers had the latitude to balance both short- and long-run commercial goals with political considerations.

One narrow yet consistent aim of post-1945 West German foreign economic policy was the expansion of the West German commercial presence in the East. This began in 1953 as a conscious plan by the West German Economics Ministry to (re)gain an "appropriate" share of the Soviet market. The Economics Ministry countered a Soviet policy of not buying in West Germany by insisting that German-Soviet trade be balanced bilaterally on a deal-by-deal basis. This forced the Soviets to accept German exports or else risk losing the German market – a policy reminiscent of German actions in Southeastern Europe in the 1930s (which does not imply any further similarity between that German regime and the Federal Republic). By 1959, aggressive and innovative commercial policies had propelled the FRG into the position of the premier Western economic partner for the Soviet Union.

The federal government also used commercial policy as a link to a number of foreign policy agreements between the FRG and East European countries. One recurrent theme here has been coupling economic incentives to the status and treatment of German minorities in the East. As early as 1954 the FRG used 300,000 tons of German grain, provided on credit, to force open the minority issue and to obtain the first Polish concessions on repatriation.

Trade treaties and economic agreements have also been invaluable in helping the FRG establish diplomatic relations in the East. Trade played a role in opening diplomatic relations with the Soviet Union in 1955; three years later a DM 3.3 billion multi year trade treaty opened a direct political line to the Soviets with Vice Premier Anastas Mikoyan's February 1958 visit to Bonn. The trade treaty and state visit enhanced the political status of the Federal Republic within the Western alliance and crowned the Federal Republic's position as the Soviets' premier Western economic partner.

The third, most interesting, and ultimately most significant use of West German economic diplomacy in Eastern Europe was as an incentive to and a form of support for reform-minded regimes in the East. With the first post-Stalinist reform attempts of the mid-1950s, the West German Foreign Office argued consistently (if somewhat vaguely) that Western economic assistance could increase the likelihood of reform success by granting reform regimes some measure of maneuvering room *(Spielraum)* for their policies. From October 1956 to 1958 the FRG granted DM 200 million in debt relief, trade concessions, and financial aid to Gomulka's "reform" regime in Poland. At that time the West German Foreign Office insisted that the change in leadership in Poland offered a unique opportunity, which justified Western economic assistance despite the accelerating deterioration of the Polish economy.

It is of course ironic that the Federal Republic as Germany's most humane regime and the Third Reich as its most inhumane have both experienced a similarly favorable combination of international and domestic factors for the formation of very successful trade policies in the East (i.e., a highly politicized international trade regime and a domestic consensus providing the regime with autonomy in setting trade policy).

CONTINUITIES 1960-1990

At the end of the 1960s and into the early 1970s a new West German federal government led by the Social Democrats moved to fully normalize the Federal Republic's political and economic relations with the East in accordance with an extended division of Europe. This policy of normalization, most frequently referred with the general-sounding name of Ostpolitik, and the debate surrounding it dominated German politics for the better part of a decade. Normalized trade relationships with Soviet bloc states were both a means and an end of the new Eastern policy. A steady expansion of trade was closely bound up with the step-by-step normalization of political relations, and trade policy decisions played a crucial role in the slow process of building trust between the two sides. For these reasons, the nature and role of West German economic cooperation with Soviet bloc governments also became a subject of intense debate in the Federal Republic, in Western Europe, and in the United States. At the center of that debate, as the primary form of potentially increased cooperation, stood West German-East European trade.

Despite a fundamental redefinition of the West German political relationship with the East as a result of normalization, the West German trade policies since then have demonstrated some very noticeable parallels to policies in earlier periods. The means and ends of West German trade with and trade policy toward the East displayed some direct continuities with trade as it had evolved in the first postwar period, 1945-1960. They also bore resemblances to strategies and goals that stretched back in time over several decades.

Notes for this section begin on page 500.

This epilogue cannot undertake an encyclopedic account of developments in trade and trade relations between the Federal Republic and the Soviet bloc states in the years since 1960. Instead, the following pages offer an episodic review of developments between 1960 and 1990, highlighting continuities by situating more recent decisions in the larger context of enduring German foreign trade designs.[1]

Structural Continuities

Most fundamentally, the essential character of the merchandise exchanges between the Federal Republic and the Soviet bloc states changed little between 1960 and the end of the 1980s. Although the value of two-way trade between the Federal Republic and its Eastern neighbors increased more than fifteen-fold between 1960 and 1990, the composition of the Eastern trade and its significance for the Federal Republic varied little or only temporarily from the patterns that had been (re)established in the 1950s.[2] First, throughout the long period from 1960 to 1990, trade with the East remained only a small component of the Federal Republic's growing commercial activities worldwide. Despite the steady and more secure growth in trade with the USSR that began with the 1958 trade treaty and continued through the 1960s and 1970s, both the Soviet market proper and the Soviet bloc as a whole gained only marginally in importance for West German exports during this period. Some deviation from these generally low levels occurred for a brief period in the mid-1970s. In 1975 West German exports to the Soviet bloc peaked at 7.2 percent of total West German exports for that year. Soviet bloc imports rose above 4 percent in 1973 and reached 5.1 percent in 1979. The West German domestic debate and the trans-Atlantic debate with the Americans over whether the FRG was developing too large an economic stake in trade with East quickly became moot as trade trailed off again at the end of the 1970s. By the late 1980s, trade with East was no more important than it had been twenty-five years earlier, at the start of the 1960s! The West German export boom that produced large trade surpluses between 1986 and 1989 was achieved with only a minuscule contribution from the sputtering East European market.

For the FRG, the limited economic stakes of the Eastern trade allowed successive governments of both major parties to continue Adenauer's strategy of prioritizing politics over economics in framing trade policy toward the East. At the same time, a growing convergence of West German political and economic interests in an expansion of trade with the East muted the choice between political and economic priorities. Nonetheless, the obvious disparity between the enormous political consequences and the minor economic gains of the Federal Republic's relations with the USSR meant that for most West Germans involved in these decisions the Eastern trade served primarily larger political goals.[3] The historic inability of the Soviet bloc economies to break out of the very limited economic roles that they played in the FRG's foreign economic activities was not lost on the West German private sector. Experienced traders continued the cautious practices established in the mid-1950s of not risking any damage to trade in well-established Western markets in order to accommodate possible trade increases in East.[4]

The economic continuities of West German-East European trade in the Cold War era went hand-in-hand with a continuity in the international political structures that shaped trade policies. European international relations in general and West German foreign policy in particular remained dominated by the division of the continent and the political, military, and economic integration of the two German states into rival blocs. East-West détente in 1970s may have smoothed the very roughest edges of this divide, but the fundamental gulf in political and economic organization that separated the two halves of Europe remained the defining characteristic of the postwar period. For these reasons, security considerations continued occasionally to interfere with West German exports to Eastern Europe. In the best-publicized cases of the period, large diameter seamless steel pipes and other types of equipment for the Soviet oil and gas industries were embargoed in 1962 and 1982 on U.S. initiative.[5]

More important, the enduring division of Europe meant a lack of formal diplomatic contact with Poland and Czechoslovakia through the 1960s. The limits placed on cultural relations and other forms of international contact meant that trade continued as the most extensive and intensive form of contact between the FRG and Soviet bloc governments. All types of nontrade issues continued to find an airing in the only truly substantive talks occurring between the two sides – the annual trade negotiations. The opening of West German trade missions as substitutes for embassies in Warsaw (1963), Prague (1967), and other East European countries further highlighted the continued centrality of trade in West German-East European relations. Even after diplomatic relations were opened with Poland (1970) and Czechoslovakia (1973), trade continued to occupy the central place in these relationships.

The endurance of economic patterns and political structures formed in the 1950s helped preserve an international environment in which the Federal Republic could successfully employ its strategies of economic diplomacy. Cold War limitations continued to emphasize the importance of trade and trade credits as the primary channel of interaction between the FRG and Soviet bloc states, and it was precisely in these areas – export capabilities and financing – that the West Germans held the greatest advantage over their Eastern neighbors.[6] Although trade policies have not always been effective in influencing Polish, Czechoslovak, and Soviet policies, they remained the Federal Republic's most useful tool in advancing West German interests in the East.

Significant changes in the larger international structures governing West German trade with the East came about with the continuing integration of the European Community (EC). In 1973 the EC began to apply a common commercial policy toward state-trade countries. Thereafter, the ability of the FRG to pursue its own independent trade policies toward the East was constrained. For the EC, one important result of the common commercial policy has been the multilateralization of many aspects of West German policy toward the East as West German desires were implemented by the community.[7]

Continuities in German Policy

In view of the long-term continuities in the larger economic and political structures in which the Federal Republic operated during the Cold War era, we should not be surprised to find some recognizable continuities in West German trade policies toward the East as well. Most fundamentally, the primacy of politics continued to dominate the shaping of Eastern trade policy well beyond the Adenauer years. Adenauer's successor in the chancellor's office, Ludwig Erhard, had supported and even advocated the use of economic diplomacy vis-à-vis Eastern Europe and the Soviet Union as Economics Minister in the 1950s. As chancellor from 1963 to 1966, Erhard maintained the politicized nature of trade with the East generally within the bounds inherited from Adenauer.[8]

Politicized trade played a central role in the new Ostpolitik of Chancellor Willy Brandt and the Social Democrats. Steadily improving trade relations played a important part in the "policy of small steps" that aimed ultimately at "change through rapprochement" with the East.[9] Social Democratic Ostpolitik emerged slowly in the Great Coalition with the Christian Democrats from 1966 to 1969 and then moved forward much more rapidly in the Social-Liberal coalition under Chancellors Brandt and Helmut Schmidt, with Liberal leader Hans-Dietrich Genscher as Foreign Minister from 1969 to

1982.[10] The series of agreements on trade and economic cooperation concluded by Brandt and Schmidt with the Soviets in the 1970s were political as well as economic acts.

When Helmut Kohl brought the Christian Democrats back into power with Liberal support in 1982, Genscher helped provide continuity for what had become by that time a traditional West German policy of politicized trade with the East. The two bundles of economic agreements concluded with the Soviets in 1988 and 1989 were heavily laden with political motivations in the context of Gorbachev's reform program. Shortly thereafter, Chancellor Kohl did not hesitate to employ heavy-handed economic leverage in relations with the Soviets and the Poles during the tumultuous political developments of 1989 to 1990.

Throughout the period, leading West German industrial groups continued to support the Federal Republic's strategy of viewing the Eastern trade first as a political matter and second as an economic issue. The government private-sector corporatist consensus that had been forged on this point in the mid-1950s remained in place. Speaking for the Eastern Committee in 1971, for example, Wolff reaffirmed business community support for the Brandt government's position that Soviet participation in a new international agreement on the status of Berlin must precede a new long-term West German-Soviet trade agreement of the type sought by the Soviets since Premier Alexi Kosygin's visit to Bonn in August 1970.[11]

Guided by the primacy of politics, the Federal Republic continued to seek both commercial and political advantages from its Eastern neighbors. The pattern of West German economic diplomacy in the East from 1960 to 1990 reveals three overlapping yet distinct policy thrusts, whose general outlines are recognizable from their roots in the 1950s.

One narrow yet consistent aim of German foreign economic policy was the continued expansion of the West German commercial presence in the East. We have seen that this began in 1953 as a conscious plan by the West German Economics Ministry to (re)gain an "appropriate" share of the Soviet market. By 1959, aggressive and innovative commercial policies had propelled the FRG into the position of the premier Western economic partner for the Soviet Union.

In the détente period of 1960s and 1970s, successive German governments from Erhard to Schmidt liberalized export and credit policies to allow the negotiation of huge, multi year deals for Soviet infrastructure construction, thereby securing West German industry's premier position.[12] Larger political considerations may have periodically constrained the development of West German-East

European economic relations in this period, but within the limits of those constraints no opportunity for the expansion of economic interaction was left unused. These efforts culminated in the unprecedented twenty-five year agreement on trade and economic collaboration signed by the two governments in May 1978. As a result of these achievements in the 1970s, the Christian Democrats, returning to power in 1982, did not need to modify the existing framework for exchange until after Soviet leader Mikhail Gorbachev had radically altered Soviet trade and investment practices beginning in 1987.

In addition to these important and highly visible actions, the federal government facilitated an expansion of trade through far less obvious daily practices. One important practice has been to allow into the West German domestic market substantial imports of low-end East European manufactures, such as ceramics and glassware, along with some agricultural produce. Allowing these essentially unwanted Soviet bloc products into the Federal Republic has played a key role in the expansion of trade with Poland and Czechoslovakia in particular. This practice, too, had its origins in the early 1950s, when Erhard viewed the West German domestic market primarily as vehicle for securing reciprocal export opportunities, and the Allied authorities demonstrated flexibility on financing imports of "soft" goods from the East.

Encouraged and aided by these government actions, the West German business community has been eager to expand its presence in the Soviet bloc markets, although it has never pursued that goal recklessly. Soviet orders for large-scale infrastructure projects in the 1958 treaty had already revealed significant export opportunities for some West German industrial sectors. The size of Soviet orders increased steadily throughout the 1960s and 1970s, culminating in 1981 with the gigantic $15 billion Trans-Siberian Gas Pipeline project concluded by the Soviets and a consortium of Western European countries. West German business was quick to take advantage of the new commercial opportunities made available by Gorbachev's perestroika. For example, beginning in 1987 West German industry jumped on the new joint venture investment vehicle, pouring over DM 600 million into the USSR in joint venture investment over the following two years.

A second familiar and easily recognizable role of West German commercial policy has been as a link to a number of important political agreements between the FRG and East European countries. This critically important use of trade policy also had its origins under Adenauer in the 1950s. By the end of that decade, Adenauer had agreed to a trade treaty and a substantial expansion of trade with the

Soviets as a means of improving the general climate of political relations between the two countries in the hope that this might eventually induce some movement on the German question.

The policy of improving political relations by improving trade relations was enthusiastically adopted and pushed forward after 1966 by the Social Democrats under Brandt. At the core of the seminal Moscow, Warsaw, and Prague treaties that normalized relations with the USSR, Poland, and Czechoslovakia was the Federal Republic's acceptance of the post-1945 territorial settlement in Eastern Europe. Brandt's willingness to recognize this reality was the sine qua non for a better political relationship with the East Europeans. Despite the political nature of the treaties themselves, trade and trade policy actions played a crucial role in preparing the ground and smoothing the path for their successful conclusion. Since the FRG had no other lubricants to apply to these contentious treaty negotiations, it is difficult to image that normalization of relations could have been achieved at this time if the FRG had not used improving trade relations to help the process along. As so often in the past, German economic concessions played a crucial role in reassuring the suspicious Soviets that a German demarche toward improved political relations reflected a genuine desire for a change in relations between the two countries.

In October 1968 Soviet Foreign Minister Andrei Gromyko questioned the sincerity of Brandt's announcement that the Federal Republic sought a renunciation of force agreement with the USSR. This Soviet maneuver was essentially a repetition of the tactics of 1925 and 1939, i.e., insisting on material progress in the form of trade and economic cooperation before agreeing to any major new political agreement between the two states. Brandt had no trouble providing the required material assurances. By the time the two men met again in September 1969 the West German foreign minister could point to a number of "practical measures" in trade and trade negotiations that served as "tokens of goodwill."[13] Three months later, in December, the two governments opened negotiations for an agreement on the renunciation of force and the improvement of political relations. Conclusion of the milestone Moscow Treaty in August 1970 was followed immediately by the relaxation of extensive West German import restrictions previously imposed on Soviet bloc goods. The political agreement of August 1970 was framed between two sets of trade concessions that provided the Soviets with the direct material signals that they understood best.

In the Polish case, improvement in political relations began with a new long-term trade and economic cooperation agreement initialed in June 1970 – an important step toward de facto diplomatic recognition of the postwar Polish state and its communist regime. With the new trade treaty having prepared the way, Brandt made his dramatic visit to Warsaw in December 1970 and concluded the Warsaw treaty normalizing relations between the two states. After that contentious treaty was ratified by the Bundestag in May 1972, a new agreement on economic cooperation with Poland was concluded in November 1974.

Similarly, the improvement of relations with Czechoslovakia moved forward in an alternating progression of economic and political agreements that normalized relations between the two neighboring states. When that process was successfully concluded in December 1973, the existing West German trade mission in Prague was upgraded to an embassy – an appropriate and revealing decision on the centrality of trade in the evolution of West German-Czechoslovak relations in the postwar period. Just one year later, in January 1975, the two governments confirmed their new relationship with another long-term agreement on economic cooperation.

The West Germans also turned to economic leverage in linking the political status of Berlin to any further substantial improvement in trade relations or economic cooperation. Economic pressures were applied directly in an attempt to influence the Soviets during the negotiations leading up to the Four Power Berlin Accord of 1971. Having used trade to oil the wheels of the political negotiation with the Soviets during the bilateral normalization process in 1969-1970, the Federal Republic then halted further progress in trade development as a means of moving the Soviets to accept a new multilateral Berlin agreement, which emerged in September 1971.

For the Federal Republic, the political utility of trade relations and trade agreements with Soviet bloc states was by no means exhausted with the dramatic improvements made between 1970 and 1973 by the Moscow, Warsaw, and Prague treaties and by securing the status of West Berlin. Subsequent agreements on trade and economic cooperation from the mid-1970s to the end of the decade also served larger political ends. In a political strategy already discernible at the end of Adenauer's chancellorship and clearly evident in SPD policies since 1966, the federal government engaged in a long-term, open-ended pursuit of improved political relations with the Soviets. The political goal of this strategy was a steadily improving political atmosphere that might reduce international and bilateral political tensions and culminate in some softening of the German division, hence the SPD slogan "change through rapproachment."

In this strategy, commercial exchanges and economic relations continued to play important roles in West German-Soviet relations.

Constructive, cooperative bilateral economic activity would provide a steady reassurance to the Soviets that improved political relations could benefit both parties. West German commentary on the May 1978 Agreement on Developing and Deepening Long-Term Cooperation between the Federal Republic and the Union of Soviet Socialist Republics repeatedly emphasized the importance of the agreement to the continued development of positive political relations between the two states. Chancellor Schmidt told the Bundestag that for "political reasons" he had been glad to sign the agreement. He emphasized that the "economic agreement extends far beyond the range of economic affairs. It provides orientation for the development of political relations in general, for long-term peaceful development..."[14] This was the same argument Brentano had made in the Bundestag nearly twenty years earlier in defense of the 1958 trade treaty.

When a Christian Democratic-Liberal coalition assumed power from the previous Social Democratic-Liberal coalition in 1982, Chancellor Kohl and continuing Foreign Minister Genscher committed the government to maintaining the best possible relations with the Soviets, despite the troublesome Soviet foreign policy decisions of the early 1980s and the instability at the top of the Soviet leadership. When Mikhail Gorbachev's policies provided a new opportunity for improved relations between the two countries, Kohl used economic cooperation to warm up political relations. In October 1988 Kohl traveled to Moscow accompanied by a West German industrial delegation that signed numerous business deals with Soviet foreign trade officials who were enthusiastic over perestroika. That scene was repeated in Bonn during Gorbachev's visit to the FRG in June 1989.

Beyond the issues of high politics surrounding the German question and the Federal Republic's political relations with the Soviet Union, trade remained the FRG's general utility tool for influencing all manner of political developments in Eastern Europe. For example, in September 1989 the Hungarian government allowed thousands of East German refugees to pass over its border into Austria. In return for this decisive act, the FRG promised and, two weeks later, the EC delivered some $300 million in trade-related material aid to Hungary. During his December 1989 visit to Budapest, Kohl repeated his promise of additional economic aid for Hungary, explicitly connecting this to Hungary's role in "knocking the first brick out of the [Berlin] wall."[15]

One recurrent theme that stands out in the formation of West German trade policies and practices toward East European states has been the coupling of economic incentives to the status and treatment of ethnic German minorities in the East, mainly in Poland. We have seen that as early as 1954 the FRG used grain exports and credits to

force open the minority issue and to obtain the first Polish concessions on repatriation. Since that time, the German minority issue has
never been far from the center of West German-Polish negotiations.
The partial resolution of the issue between 1970 and 1975 closely mir-
rors the story we have told for the earlier period, 1951 to 1955.

After the economic agreement of June 1970 cleared the path for
more comprehensive negotiations on normalization, the status of the
German minority in Poland emerged as a major issue between the
two countries. In the course of those negotiations, the Polish government agreed to a plan that copied the earlier 1954 Red Cross repatriation arrangement, this time allowing 60,000 to 100,000 persons to be
repatriated.[16] In January 1971 the first group of new returnees arrived
in the Federal Republic, but the West Germans remained dissatisfied
with the small number of new arrivals, which amounted to only
10,000 to 15,000 over the following two years. Not until the West Germans offered additional financial incentives did the Poles move more
seriously on this question. In 1974 the federal government offered the
Poles a twenty-year low interest credit of DM 1 billion, apparently in
exchange for prompt delivery of the 50,000 Germans still waiting to
leave Poland under the terms of the 1970 agreement. The Poles, who
had initially sought a DM 3 billion credit, accepted the terms, and by
the end of 1975 another 50,000 returnees had been transferred to the
FRG.[17] Subsequent negotiations between the two governments on the
issue were generally not matters of high politics, in part because the
humanitarian provision of the 1975 Helsinki Accords had, in theory,
provided a forum for the resolution of the remaining cases.[18]

After the elections of June 1989 brought a noncommunist government to power in Poland, the West Germans reopened the issue
by applying financial pressure. The new Solidarity government desperately needed debt relief from major creditors, including the FRG,
in order to restructure some $40 billion in debts acquired by the
communist regime in its failed strategy of import-led growth in the
1970s and 1980s. Yet the FRG refused to enter into financial negotiations until the new Solidarity government had "met part way" the
FRG's "wishes" on the minority issue.[19] German economic pressure
catalyzed production of a West German-Polish joint declaration in
November 1989 that guaranteed the German minority the right to
maintain and develop its German identity.[20] In exchange for this
declaration, the new Polish government received a high-profile visit
from the West German chancellor, new terms for the repayment of
existing West German credits, and promises of DM 3 billion in economic aid over the next three years. German minority rights were
explicitly guaranteed with more precision in Articles 20 to 22 of the

German-Polish Friendship and Cooperation Treaty signed in June 1991. Germany's DM 1 billion debt relief action of November 1990 may have helped secure those terms.

West German federal governments have also continued to use trade as an incentive to and a form of support for reform-minded regimes in the East – a practice that began with DM 200 million in debt relief, trade concessions, and financial aid to Gomulka's "reform" regime in Poland. Thirty years later, the FRG jumped eagerly at the opportunity to help Gorbachev's reform program of political glasnost and economic perestroika. Early on, Genscher correctly character-ized Gorbachev's accession to power as an "historic opportunity" that "should not be passed up."[21] Practical support began when Kohl lead a delegation of some fifty West German industrialists on a trip to the Soviet capital in October 1988. The two governments signed a gen-eral agreement on scientific and technological cooperation and a spe-cific agreement promoting cooperation in the food-processing sector. The West German private representative signed numerous deals with Soviet state agencies and shortly thereafter a West German bank con-sortium concluded a loan deal to the Soviet Union for £ 1 billion. When Gorbachev paid a visit to Bonn in June 1989, he signed a clus-ter of economic agreements designed to encourage more West Ger-man participation in the Soviet economy, including liberalized rules on the protection of German investments in the Soviet Union. Yet the new West German-Soviet agreements of 1988 to 1989, quite substan-tial in themselves, were eclipsed that summer and autumn by the dramatic political events in Eastern Europe.

The West German response to the evolution of Polish politics in 1989 shows clear parallels with West German policies from 1956 to 1957. Upon conclusion of the Polish round table agreement in April 1989, the FRG again took the lead in promising increased Western support. A unanimous Bundestag resolution of 19 April 1988 urged West German "economic and financial support" for the new Solidar-ity-led Polish government. In familiar tones, West German Foreign Minister Genscher repeatedly mentioned the need for Western aid to provide reform governments with "room to maneuver" while Liberal Party Chairman Otto Graf Lambsdorff implied that West Germany must grant Poland some debt relief or else risk a revocation of Polish reforms.[22] Both Chancellor Kohl and Finance Minister Theo Waigel insisted on outside support to provide "a chance" for the reform process in Poland.[23] Joint statements to this effect with France and Italy preceded Genscher's appeal to the EC in July. Massive EC trade concessions contained in the EC-Polish agreement of 19 Sept 1989 gave Poland greatly expanded export chances to the West. But Western aid was conditional on Poland's continued transition to political pluralism and a market economy, as Solidarity leader Bronislav Geremek was informed during his July 1989 trip to Bonn.[24]

The German commitment to supporting genuine political and economic reform has acquired immense proportions. The new Germany has shouldered the bulk of the international financial burden in subsidizing economic reform in the former Soviet bloc, with concessions in various forms of almost DM 80 billion to the former Soviet republics between 1990 and 1993 and another DM 87 billion granted to the new regimes in Eastern Europe. At the close of 1996, Germany held almost half of Russia's $125b foreign debt.[25]

Prospects

The profound changes in Europe since 1989 have begun to alter the domestic determinants of German trade policy. Increased East European productivity resulting from the postcommunist processes of economic and political reform may upset the private-sector consensus that has underlaid the federal government's ability to employ a broad range of trade policies in the East. Eastern economic impotence has been the ultimate source of the West German consensus that Eastern trade policy was not an economic issue of the highest order for the FRG. If, as is hoped, economic reform reinvigorates the historically productive agricultural and manufacturing sectors in Poland, the Czech Republic, and the Soviet Union, some Western producers will begin to feel the pinch of Eastern competition. That sort of economic pressure will reactivate domestic debates in the Federal Republic and Western Europe over Eastern trade policies. European Union (EU) [formerly the EC] farmers will feel the pressures of increased agricultural output in the historically productive areas of eastern Europe. Other, less sophisticated industries have already begun to react as textiles, shoes, furniture, and household items move from East to West. The new availability of legal and illegal East European workers has already disrupted relatively tranquil labor markets in Western Europe. Even if new institutional arrangements soften the impact of East European developments on West European farmers, manufacturers, and workers, many economic sectors in EU countries will unavoidably feel some effects of the economic transformation underway in the East. For the Federal Republic and other western governments, finding suitable trade policies toward Eastern Europe will have greater economic consequences in the 1990s than at any time since the 1930s. Regardless of how EU members respond to these new pressures, western governments' wide latitude in setting Eastern trade policies is disappearing with a raising of the economic stakes, as the broad and lengthy debate on extending EU membership to Poland, Hungary, and the Czech Republic shows.[26]

Ultimately, the new international institutions that govern relations between the economies of Eastern and Western Europe will play a crucial role in determining how the changes in the East effect the West. The breakdown of the Cold War order in 1989 to 1990 affected the international determinants of German trade policy in the East almost immediately. The dismantling of the international structures that held together the old Soviet bloc has transformed Eastern Europe into an institutional no-man's land. Poland, Czechoslovakia, and other former members of the bloc no longer have the economic insulation against Western pressures that was provided by a planned economy locked into Soviet-imposed organizations such as the Council for Mutual Economic Assistance (CMEA or COMECON). In the years immediately following, no new international organizations were fashioned that might give some institutional cohesion and international strength to the states of the region and no existing international organizations such as the EU or the European Free Trade Association (EFTA) were extended to the area. In a situation not unlike that of the 1930s, individual East European countries currently lack any larger international protections as they face a new round of German economic persuasion. In a parallel development, democratic reforms ended the domestic political immunity that communist East European regimes had used to insulate themselves from domestic and foreign economic pressures. The more or less desperate economic circumstances of all former Soviet bloc countries made them particularly sensitive to Western economic policies.

When the Soviet hold on Eastern Europe crumbled in 1989, the FRG immediately sought to adjust the framework of economic interaction with the East to help create new opportunities there. After the elections of June 1989 brought a Solidarity government to power in Poland, the FRG advanced a battery of self-serving arguments about the transition to a market economy to insist that the Poles open their economy to greater German participation. Neither Chancellor Kohl nor President Richard von Weizsäcker would accept Polish invitations to visit Warsaw until the Poles had signed an agreement for the Protection of German Investment in Poland, a joint set of Guidelines for Future Economic Cooperation, and new terms for the repayment of earlier West German loans.

At the same time, the steady reduction of common Western restrictions on exports to Eastern Europe since 1989 has increased the national discretion of the Federal Republic and other Western governments in sales of advanced technology and equipment to East European states. This may result in increased influence for countries such as Germany that can deliver the latest production technologies demanded by the East, for example in computer-controlled machine tools.

In sum, the 1990s probably offer fewer international restraints on German trade policies in Eastern Europe than we have seen at any time in the past century. The near-term international economic order invites an active German trade policy in the East. The economic base for those active policies develops daily. In a pattern reminiscent of the interwar period, Germany has become the dominant trade partner of several East European countries while other Western countries (this time the United States rather than Britain and France) have become the leading investors in Eastern Europe.

On the other hand, long-term developmental trends in the international trade regime may work to constrain future German trade policies in the East. The continued supranational integration of Western Europe and the transformation of the European Community to the European Union means any German trade policy toward the East must be multilateralized through the EU. This was readily apparent in 1989 to 1990, when trade concessions for Poland and economic aid for Hungary were delivered via the EC at the urging of West German Foreign Minister Genscher. In theory, multilateralization might serve to restrict German options in the East, although it is true that the EU, as with the EC before it, has been content so far to follow the German lead in relations with Germany's neighbors. That, too, may change with the arrival of Sweden and Finland into the Union as additional experts on Eastern Europe. One result might be an increased importance for trade financing as one component of trade policy that remains under national discretion. In the near-term, the huge financial burdens of reconstructing the former German Democratic Republic might limit the German government's willingness to increase government spending on guarantees for export credits.

In the more distant future the wide latitude hitherto enjoyed by German trade policies in the East will be narrowed as the Eastern economies are brought back into the institutions of the world economy. As that process proceeds, Polish, Czech, Slovak, and Soviet membership in GATT and, in some cases, eventually in the EU will essentially eliminate the Federal Republic's ability to apply discriminatory or preferential trade policies to these countries. In trade policy, as in many other areas, the inclusion of East European nations in a common supranational institution with the Germans would be an historic event and would mark the end of an era.

Notes

1. All studies of Germany's Eastern trade policies in the more recent past, this one included, must rely almost exclusively on information available from published sources rather than on the government and private-sector documentation comparable to that available for earlier periods. Still important is Angela Stent's *From Embargo to Ostpolitik. The Political Economy of West German-Soviet Relations, 1955-1980* (Cambridge, 1981); Rajendra K. Jain's *Germany, the Soviet Union and Eastern Europe, 1949-1991* (New York, 1991) is a detailed narrative account. Michael J. Sodaro's *Moscow, Germany, and the West from Khrushchev to Gorbachev* (Ithaca, 1990) is survey and analysis based on international relations theory. The most recent study of note is Timothy Garton Ash, *In Europe's Name. Germany and the Divided Continent* (New York, 1993).

2. Data on West German trade is taken from United Nations Department of Economic and Social Affairs Statistical Office, *Yearbook of International Trade Statistics* (New York: various years).

3. Although the tradition of Ostpolitik in the FRG as a primacy of politics over economics and the economic situation of the Soviet bloc as well understood by West German big business both speak loudly against a primarily economic interpretation of Ostpolitik, some have advanced that economic argument. See, e.g. Claudia von Braunmühl's essay that sets Ostpolitik in a context of economic imperialism, "Ist die `Ostpolitik' Ostpolitik?," in Egbert Jahn and Volker Rittberger, eds., *Die Ostpolitik der BRD* (Opladen, 1974), 13-28.

4. Volker Berghahn has made this point in "Lowering Soviet Expectations. West German Industry and Osthandel during the Brandt Era," in Berghahn, ed., *Quest for Economic Empire* (Providence, 1996), 145-57.

5. On these controversies see especially, Hans-Dieter Jacobsen, *Ost-West-Wirtschaftsbeziehungen als deutsch-amerikanisches Problem* (Baden-Baden, 1986).

6. Since 1960 the financial instruments of trade (trade credits) and debt relief have gradually assumed equal weight with import allowances and price concessions on merchandise trade.

7. Michael Kreile was among the very first to point out the larger international consequences of this development, "Ostpolitik Reconsidered," in Ekkehart Krippendorff, ed., *The Foreign Policy of West Germany* (Beverley Hills, 1980), 124.

8. Stent cites a number of quotes by Erhard as chancellor that demonstrate an essential continuity with the policies of politicized trade leverage that he elaborated as Economics Minister, *From Embargo*, 149.

9. These two oft-quoted and revealing phrases come from Egon Bahr's July 1963 speech at the Evangelische Akademie in Tutzing. Bahr was Brandt's press secretary, confidante, and special envoy; his speech is generally viewed as the formal starting point of the SPD's new Ostpolitik.

10. On the dramatic achievements of Brandt's Ostpolitik in Eastern Europe in the early 1970s begin with Arnulf Baring, *Machtwechsel* (Stuttgart, 1982); Benno Zündorf, *Die Ostverträge* (Munich, 1979); Günther Schmid, *Entscheidung in Bonn* (Cologne, 1979); Michael Kreile, "Ostpolitik Reconsidered;" Peter Bender, *Neue Ostpolitik,* (Munich, 1986).

11. Wolff's statement that "a Berlin solution comes first" cited in Rajendra K. Jain, *Germany, the Soviet Union and Eastern Europe, 1949-1991* (New York, 1993), 153, note 28.

12. Willy Brandt, for example, never denied that his government was eager to "open up new fields of economic opportunity" in the East, Brandt, *People and Politics. The Years 1960-1975* (Boston, 1978), 169.

13. According to Brandt, "trade was shaping up well, talks were in progress on the purchase of natural gas, a Soviet proposal to exchange technological know-how had aroused our interest, and fresh negotiations on air traffic would be held before too long," Willy Brandt, *People and Politics. The Years 1960-1975* (Boston, 1978), 194-95. Brandt could point to the government's role in providing some DM 600 million in state-backed guarantees for West German credits that were essential to moving the gas deal forward.

14. *Verhandlungen des deutschen Bundestages,* 8 Wahlperiode, 90 Sitzung, 11 May 1978, 7066 cited in Stent, *Embargo to Ostpolitik,* 206.

15. Cited in Gebhard Diemer, ed., *Kurze Chronik der deutschen Frage* (Munich, 1990), 132.

16. Brandt, *People and Politics,* 404 ff.

17. Jain, *Germany, the Soviet Union, and Eastern Europe,* 79.

18. Brandt notes that in 1970 the German Red Cross estimated 280,000 ethnic Germans would like to leave Poland, *People and Politics,* 405. A Polish estimate from 1991 cites 300,000 to 400,000 ethnic Germans in post-communist Poland; German estimates run between 600,000 and 800,000, Joachim Rogall, "Die deutschen Minderheiten in Polen Heute," *Aus Politik und Zeitgeschichte,* B 48/93, 35.

19. "Genscher: Rasche Hilfe fuer Polen," *Deutschland Nachrichten,* 10 May 1989, 2.

20. In January 1990 a local German group in Kattowice established the first officially recognized German minority organization in postwar Poland. Since that time, numerous local and national organizations of ethnic Germans have appeared, Rogall, "Die deutschen Minderheiten," 34-35.

21. Genscher's statement of 1 February 1987, cited in Jain, *Germany, The Soviet Union, and Eastern Europe,* 199, note 15.

22. "Genscher: Rasche Hilfe für Polen," *Deutschland Nachrichten,* 10 May 1989, 2.

23. "Deutsche un EG-Hilfsmassnahmen für Polen und Ungarn," *Deutschland Nachrichten,* 28 September, 1989, 2.

24. As in 1956, the West Germans were not alone in these efforts. U.S. President Bush offered the same deal to the new Polish government (more aid for more reforms) during his 1989 trip to Poland. During his February 1990 visit to Europe, Secretary of State James Baker plainly told both the Romanian and Bulgarian governments that Western aid would be tied directly to the time and manner of future elections.

25. "Deutschland finanziert GUS," *Deutschland Nachrichten,* 30 October 1992; "Bisher 167 Milliarden Mark für die Reformstaaten," ibid., 12 November 1993; "Deutschland gewährt Russland Zahlungsaufschub," ibid., 7 February 1997.

26. I am less pessimistic now than when I first suggested this possibility in "German Trade Policy in Eastern Europe, 1890-1990: preconditions for applying international trade leverage," *International Organization* 45, no. 3 (1991), a portion of which has been reproduced here.

GRAPHS AND TABLES

Graphs

Graph 1.1 Index of Wholesale Prices in Germany 1868-1890 (1800 = 100)

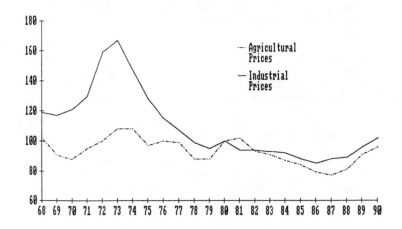

Source: A. Jacobs and H. Richter, "Die Grosshandelspreise in Deutschland von 1792 bis 1934," Sonderhefte des Institute für Konjunkturforschung, Nr. 37 (1935)

Graph 1.2 German Exports to Russia 1880-1893 (excluding precious metals)

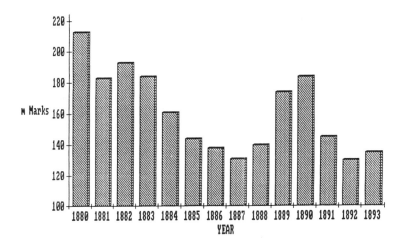

Source: Schriften des Vereins fuer Socialpolitik, 1900, IV, P. 282; Sdr, NF, Bd. 47, 4B, 51

Graph 1.3 German Imports from Russia 1880-1893 (excluding precious metals)

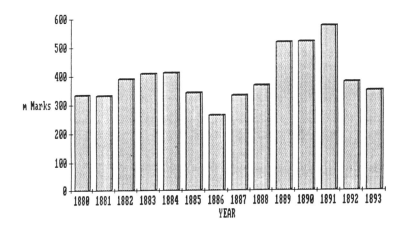

Graph 1.4   German Balance of Trade with Russia 1880-1893 (excluding precious metals)

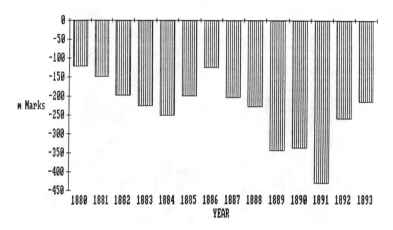

Graph 1.5   Index of Wholesale Prices in Germany 1880-1890 (1880 =100)

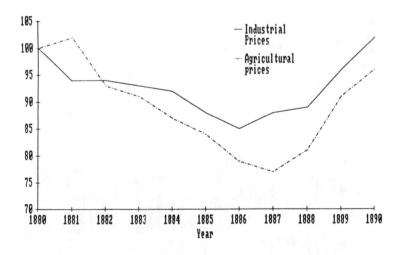

Source: A. Jacobs and H. Richter, "Die Grosshandelspreise in Deutschland von 1792 bis 1934," Sonderfefte des Instituts fuer Konjunkturforschung, Nr. 37, 1935

Graph 2.1 German Two-Way Trade with Russia 1892-1904 (mil. Marks)

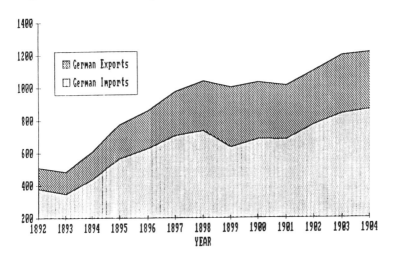

Graph 2.2 German Two-Way Trade with Russia 1880-1904 (mil. Marks)

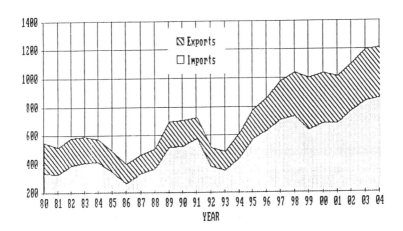

Graph 2.3 German Exports to Russia 1892-1904 (mil. Marks)

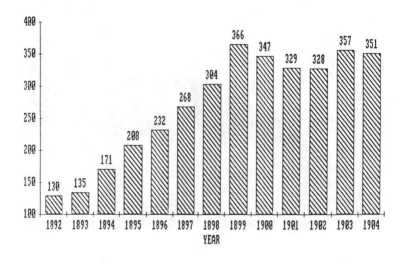

Graph 2.4 German Exports to Russia 1880-1904 (mil Marks)

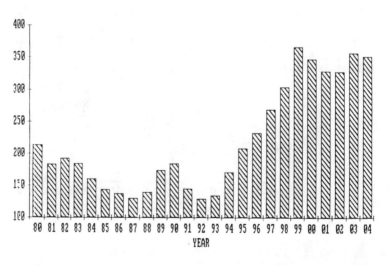

Graph 2.5   German Exports to Russia as a % of Total German Exports

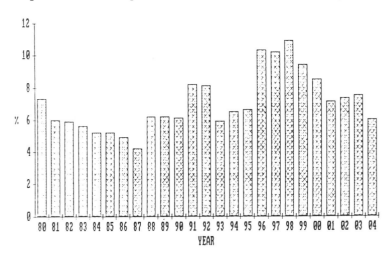

Graph 2.6   Structure of German Exports to Russia in 1903
(357 mil. Marks)

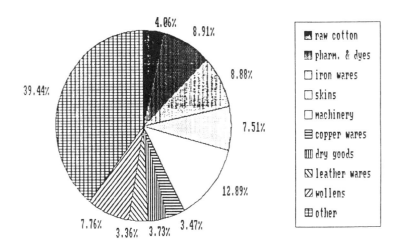

Graph 2.7   German Imports from Russia 1892-1904 (mil. Marks)

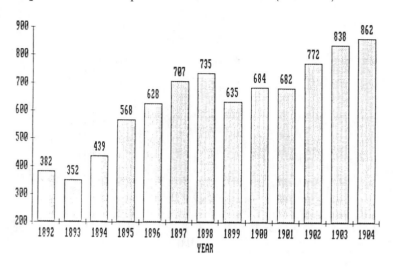

Graph 2.8   German Imports from Russia 1880-1904 (mil Marks)

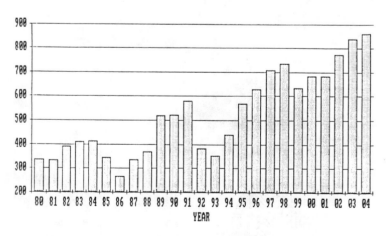

Graph 2.9 Structure of German Imports from Russia in 1903 (838 mil. Marks)

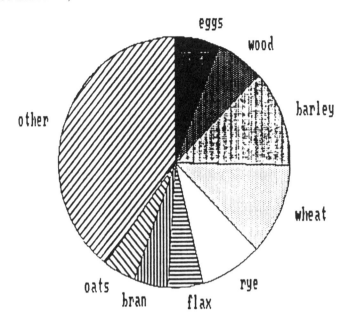

Graph 2.10 Index of Wholesale Prices in Germany (1913 = 100)

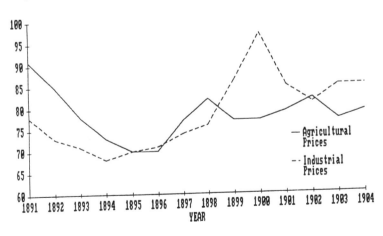

Source: A. Jacobs and H. Richter, "Die Grosshandelspreise in Deutschland von 1792 bis 1934," Sonderfefte des Instituts fuer Konjunkturforschung, Nr. 37, 1935

Graph 2.11   German Total Trade with Russia 1894-1913 (mil. Marks)

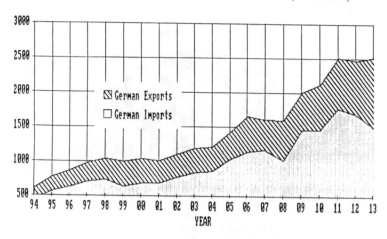

Graph 2.12   German Total Trade with Russia 1880-1913 (mil Marks)

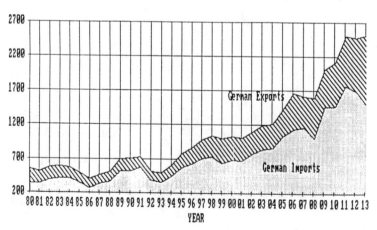

Graph 2.13   German Exports to Russia 1880-1913 (mil. Marks)

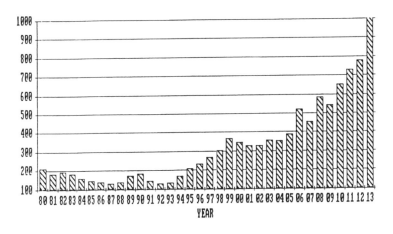

Graph 2.14   German Trade Deficit with Russia 1894-1913 (mil. Marks)

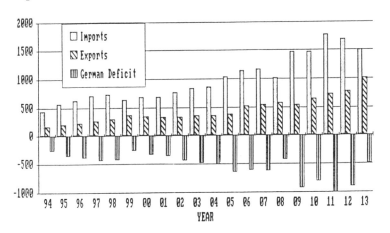

Graph 2.15 Composition of German Exports to Russia in 1913
(1011 mil. Marks)

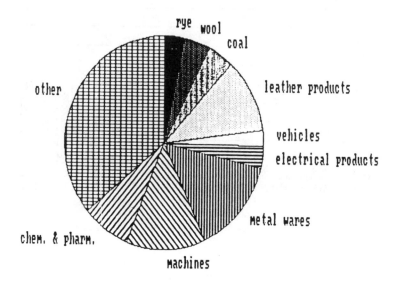

Graph 7.1 West German Trade with Czechoslovakia 1947-1949
(thousand $ US)

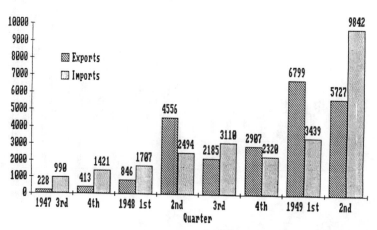

Graph 9.1 Federal Republic Imports from Poland 1948-1961

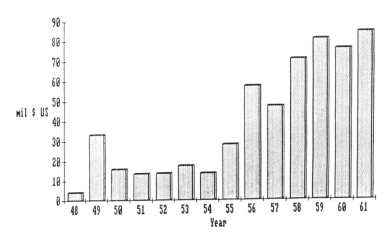

Graph 9.2 Federal Republic Exports to Poland 1948-1961

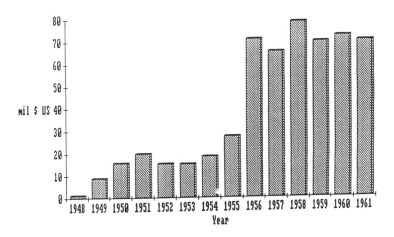

Graph 9.3 The Composition of Polish Debt to the FRG in 1957
(total = DM 190m)

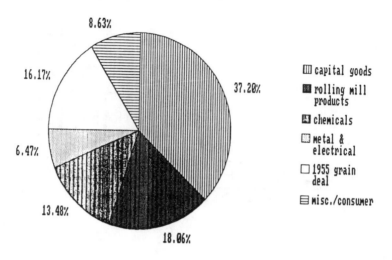

Graph 9.4 FRG Imports from Poland as a % of FRG Total Imports
1948-1961
Source: Calculated from United Nations Stastical Papers. Series T. Direction

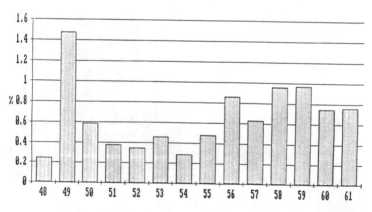

of Internaitonal Trade, vols. i-xi.

Graph 9.5 FRG Exports to Poland as a Percentage of FRG Total Exports

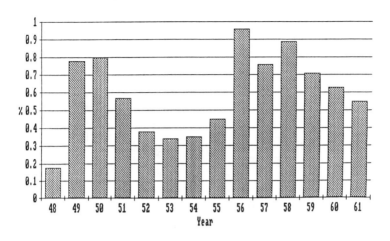

Graph 9.6 FRG Exports to Czechoslovakia 1948-1961

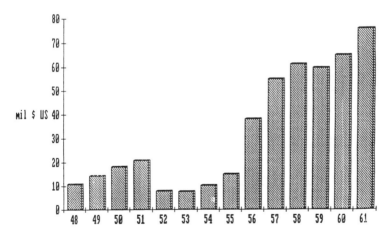

Source: United Nations Stastistical Papers. Series T. Direction of International Trade, vols. i-xi

Graph 9.7   FRG Imports from Czechoslovakia 1948-1961

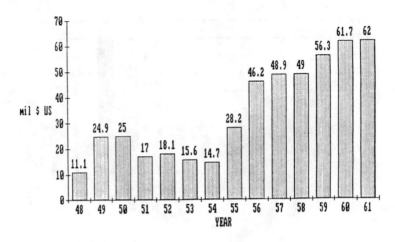

Source: United Nations Statistical Papers. Series T. Direction of International Trade, vols. i-xi

Graph 9.8   FRG Imports from Czechoslovakia as a % of FRG Total Imports 1948-1961

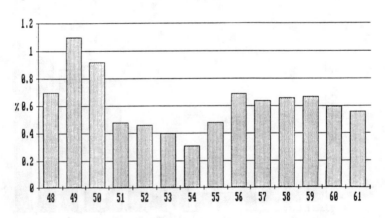

Source: United Nations Statistical Papers. Series T. Direction of International Trade, vols. i-xi

Graph 9.9 FRG Exports to Czechoslovakia as a % of FRG Total Exports
1948-1961

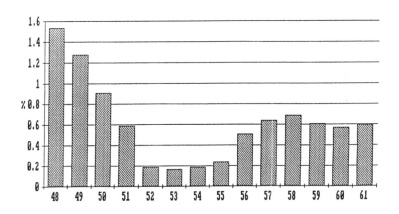

Source: Calculated from United Nations Statistical Papers. Series T.
Direction of International Trade, vols. i-xi

Graph 9.10 FRG Two-Way Trade with the USSR 1948-1961

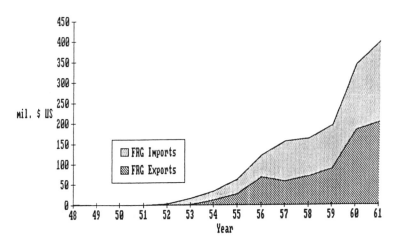

Source: United Nations Statistical Papers. Series T. Direction of
International Trade, vols. i-xi

Graph 9.11   FRG Imports from the USSR 1948-1961

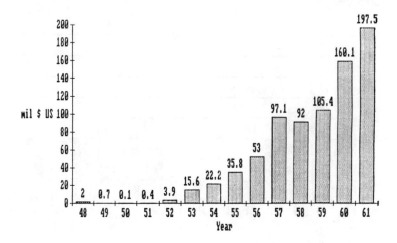

Source: United Nations Statistical Papers. Series T. Direction of
International Trade

Graph 9.12   FRG Exports to the USSR 1948-1961

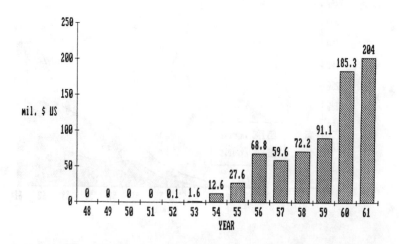

Source: See Graph 9.11

Graph 9.13 Scheduled Commodity Composition of FRG Imports from the USSR in 1958 (total = DM 550m)

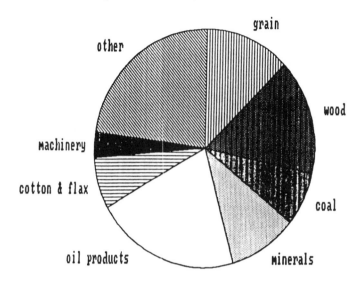

Source: Ministerialblatt des Bundesministers fuer Wirtschaft, 1958, Nr. 9

Graph 9.14 FRG Imports from the USSR as a % of FRG Total Imports 1948-1961

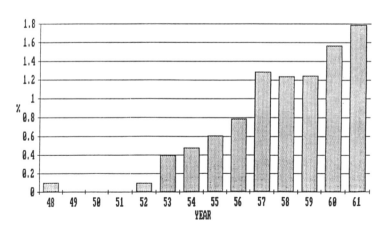

Source: Calculated from UN Statistical Paper, Series T. Direction of International Trade, vols. i-xi

Graph 9.15 FRG Exports to the USSR as a % of FFRG Total Exports 1948-1961 (0 = values less than 0.1%)

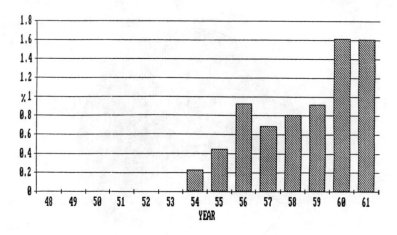

Tables

Table 7.1: The Growth of Bizonal Foreign Trade 1945-1949

	(million $ US in current prices)		Exports as a % of Imports
	Export Deliveries	Import Arrivals	
1945 (Aug-Dec)	40	96	41.6
1946	161	643	25.0
1947	225	734	30.6
1948	599	1,400	42.7
1949 (Jan-June)	564	852	66.2
Total (Aug 1945-June 1949)	1,489	3,725	39.9

(*Source:* OMGUS, *Report of the Military Governor*, No. 49, July 1949, Statistical Annex, No. XXIX, table 601.)

Table 7.2: The Growth of Bizonal Exports 1948-1949.

Qtr	(million $ US in current prices)	Index (1st Qtr 1948 = 100)
1948 1st Qtr	91	100
2nd Qtr	139	152
3rd Qtr	167	183
4th Qtr	202	221
1949 1st Qtr	265	291
2nd Qtr	299	328

(*Source:* OMGUS, *Report of the Military Governor*, No. 49, July 1949, Statistical Annex, No. XXIX, table 601.)

Table 7.3: Bizonal Exports of Five Groups of Finished Products: metal products, machinery and vehicles, chemicals, scientific equipment, pharmaceuticals.

Qtr	thousand $ US in current prices	Index (1st Qtr 1948 = 100)	As a % of total Bizonal exports
1948			
1st Qtr	11,705	100	12.9%
2nd Qtr	20,729	176	14.8%
3rd Qtr	24,549	209	14.6%
4th Qtr	42,543	363	21.0%
1949			
1st Qtr	60,253	514	22.7%
2nd Qtr	72,530	619	24.2%

(*Source:* Calculated from OMGUS, *Report of the Military Governor*, No. 49, July 1949, Statistical Annex, No. XXIX, table 602.)

Table 7.4: Bizonal Exports of Machinery and Vehicles 1948-1949.

Qtr	thousand $ US in current prices	Index (1st Qtr 1948 = 100)	as a % of total Bizonal exports
1948			
1st Qtr	4,195	100	4.5%
2nd Qtr	12,999	314	9.2%
3rd Qtr	11,925	290	7.1%
4th Qtr	21,926	534	10.8%
1949			
1st Qtr	22,551	546	8.4%
2nd Qtr	29,215	709	9.7%

(*Source:* Calculated from OMGUS, *Report of the Military Governor*, No. 49, July 1949, Statistical Annex, No. XXIX, table 602.)

Table 7.5: The Value of Bizonal Exports to Poland 1947-1949. (thousand $ US in current prices)

1947	3rd Qtr	152.0
	4th Qtr	71.0
1948	1st Qtr	23.8
	2nd Qtr	168.5
	3rd Qtr	113.0
	4th Qtr	977.5
1949	1st Qtr	1361.3
	2nd Qtr	2286.0

(*Source:* OMGUS, *Report of the Military Governor*, No. 49, Statistical Annex No. XXIX, table 603; *Report of the Military Governor*, No. 42, Statistical Annex No. XXII, table 91; *Report of the Military Governor*, No. 31, Statistical Annex, figure 8.)

Table 7.6: The Structure of West German Exports to Poland as Planned by the Trade Agreements of 1948 and 1949.

	December 1948 Agreement		June 1949 Agreement	
	million $ US	as % of total exports to Poland	million $ US	as % of total exports to Poland
Machinery	$6.2	46.9%	15.2	42.9%
Electrical Machinery	2.3	17.4	3.2	9.0
Chemicals	2.9	21.9	4.6	12.9
Metal Products	0.3	2.4	1.3	3.8
Fine Mechanics	0.4	2.8	0.5	1.2
Textiles	--	--	1.5	4.4
Total	$12.1	91.4%	$26.3	72.4%

(*Source:* BA, B 102/2312 H.1 and H.2)

Table 8.1: Trade between the Federal Republic and Poland 1949-1955, million $ U.S. and as a percentage of FRG total trade.

	FRG Imports		FRG Exports	
	million $ US	% of total M	million $ US	% of total X
1949	33.4	1.4%	8.9	0.7%
1950	16.1	0.5	15.9	0.8
1951	13.6	0.3	19.9	0.5
1952	13.8	0.3	15.4	0.3
1953	17.6	0.4	15.3	0.3
1954	13.8	0.2	18.6	0.3
1955	28.0	0.4	27.6	0.4

Source: Statistical Office of the United Nations, *United Nations Statistical Papers Series T. Direction of International Trade,* VOLS. I-VII, (1949-1955).

Table 8.2a.: Quarterly FRG Exports to Czechoslovakia 1950-1955. (million $ US)

1949	Q2	4.5	
1950	Q1	3.7	
	Q2	3.9	
	Q3	5.8	
	Q4	4.8	
1951	Q1	6.0	
	Q2	5.4	
	Q3	4.9	
	Q4	4.5	--- FRG account surplus reaches $8.2 million
1952	Q1	3.5	
	Q2	1.8	--- Cz - Soviet Trade Treaty; FRG account surplus reaches $11 million
	Q3	1.3	
	Q4	1.4	--- FRG ranks 4th among West European exporters to Cz. for 1952
1953	Q1	1.6	
	Q2	1.2	
	Q3	1.6	
	Q4	3.3	--- FRG ranks 3rd among West European exporters to Cz. for 1953
1954	Q1	1.9	
	Q2	1.8	--- Urban admits hard currency shortage as limiting factor
	Q3	2.4	
	Q4	4.1	--- FRG ranks 2nd among West European exporters to Cz. for 1954
1955	Q1	3.3	
	Q2	3.1	--- FRG ranks 1st among West European exporters to Cz. for 1955

Source: Statistical Papers Series T. Direction of International Trade, VOLS. I-VII, (1949-1955).

Table 8.2b: Quarterly FRG Imports from Czechoslovakia 1950-1955. (million $ US)

```
1949 Q4    3.9

1950 Q1    6.1
     Q2    4.7
     Q3    7.9
     Q4    6.9

1951 Q1    1.2    --- Cz. response to HICOG border stoppages
     Q2    1.8
     Q3    6.8
     Q4    7.2

1952 Q1    4.1
     Q2    5.1    --- Cz. - Soviet Trade Treaty
     Q3    4.7
     Q4    4.2    ---  FRG  ranks  2nd  among  West  European
                  importers from Cz. for 1952

1953 Q1    3.5
     Q2    3.0
     Q3    4.0    --- "isolated" HICOG border stoppages; US MPs
                  withdrawn
     Q4    5.1

1954 Q1    2.7
     Q2    3.1
     Q3    3.9
     Q4    5.0

1955 Q1    5.8
     Q2    6.3    ---  FRG  ranks  1st  among  West  European
                  importers from Cz. for 1955
```

Source: Statistical Office of the United Nations, *United Nations Statistical Papers Series T. Direction of International Trade,* VOLS. I-VII, (1949-1955).

Table 8.3: Trade between the Federal Republic and Czechoslovakia 1949-1955, million $ U.S. and as a percentage of FRG total trade.

	FRG Imports		FRG Exports	
	million $ US	% of total M	million $ US	% of total X
1949	24.9	1.1%	14.5	1.2%
1950	25.0	0.9	18.2	0.9
1951	17.0	0.4	20.8	0.5
1952	18.1	0.4	8.0	0.2
1953	15.6	0.4	7.7	0.1
1954	14.7	0.3	10.2	0.2
1955	28.2	0.4	15.1	0.2

Source: Statistical Office of the United Nations, *United Nations Statistical Papers Series T. Direction of International Trade,* VOLS. I-VII, (1949-1955).

Table 8.4: Trade betweeen the Federal Republic and the CSSR 1949-1955, amounts actually traded as compared to amounts scheduled by the annual Trade Agreements. (million $ US).

	FRG Exports		FRG Imports	
	actual	scheduled agreement	actual	scheduled agreement
1948	10.9	n.a.	11.1	n.a.
1949	14.5	n.a.	24.9	n.a.
1950	18.2	29.0	25.0	29.0
1951	20.8	13.9	17.0	16.1
1952	8.0	14.0	18.1	22.9
1953	7.7	16.3	15.6	17.8
1954	10.2	17.5	14.7	19.5
1955	15.1	22.0	28.2	24.0

Source: Statistical Office of the United Nations, *United Nations Statistical Papers Series T. Direction of International Trade,* VOLS. I-VII, (1949-1955).

Table 8.5a: Quarterly FRG Imports from the Soviet Union 1950-1955. (million $ US)

1949	Q4	0.0	
1950	Q1	0.0	
	Q2	0.0	
	Q3	0.1	
	Q4	0.0	
1951	Q1	0.2	
	Q2	0.0	
	Q3	0.2	
	Q4	0.0	
1952	Q1	0.0	
	Q2	0.0	--- Moscow "World Economic Conference"
	Q3	0.6	
	Q4	3.3	--- FRG ranks 9th among 12 West European importers from the USSR for 1952
1953	Q1	3.8	
	Q2	1.3	
	Q3	4.7	
	Q4	5.8	--- FRG ranks 5th among 12 West European importers from the USSR for 1953
1954	Q1	5.0	
	Q2	2.2	--- Rhein-Ruhr and Rhein-Main banks establish accounts for Russian State Bank
	Q3	4.0	
	Q4	10.5	--- FRG ranks 5th among 12 West European importers from the USSR for 1954
1955	Q1	5.2	
	Q2	4.9	--- FRG ranks 3rd among 12 West European importers from the USSR for 1955

Source: Statistical Office of the United Nations, *United Nations Statistical Papers Series T. Direction of International Trade,* VOLS. I-VII, (1949-1955).

Table 8.5b: Quarterly FRG Exports from the Soviet Union 1950-1954. (million $ US)

1949	Q4	0.0	
1950	Q1	0.0	
	Q2	0.0	
	Q3	0.0	
	Q4	0.0	
1951	Q1	0.0	
	Q2	0.0	
	Q3	0.0	
	Q4	0.0	
1952	Q1	0.0	
	Q2	0.0	---- First meeting of FRG industrialists with Soviet trade officials; Eastern Committeee formed.
	Q3	0.1	
	Q4	0.0	
1953	Q1	0.0	
	Q2	0.0	
	Q3	0.1	--- HPA gives formal approval to BMfW policy of "prefernce"for compensation deals.
	Q4	1.5	--- FRG ranks 11th among 12 West European exporters to the USSR for 1953
1954	Q1	2.5	
	Q2	2.3	--- Cancellation of Eastern Committee trip to Moscow.
	Q3	3.4	
	Q4	4.4	--- FRG ranks 8th among 12 West European exporters to the USSR for 1954
1955	Q1	1.8	
	Q2	2.3	--- Soviet invitation for talks on establishing diplomatic relations; FRG ranks 3rd among 12 West European exporters to the USSR for 1955

Source: Statistical Office of the United Nations, *United Nations Statistical Papers Series T. Direction of International Trade,* VOLS. I-VII, (1949-1955).

Table 8.6: Trade between the Federal Republic and the Soveit Union 1949-1955, million $ U.S. and as a percentage of FRG total trade. ("–" = less than 0.1%).

	FRG Imports		FRG Exports	
	million $ US	% of total M	million $ US	% of total X
1949	0.7	--	0.0	--
1950	0.1	--	0.0	--
1951	0.4	--	0.0	--
1952	3.9	0.1	0.1	--
1953	15.6	0.4	1.6	--
1954	22.2	0.4	12.6	0.2
1955	35.8	0.6	27.6	0.4

Source: Statistical Office of the United Nations, *United Nations Statistical Papers Series T. Direction of International Trade,* VOLS. I-VII, (1949-1955).

Table 9.1: The Polish Balance Sheet with the FRG in 1957

I. Polish Obligations:

Capital Goods	c. 69	m DM
Rolling Mill Products	c. 33.5	m DM
Chemicals	c. 25	m DM
Metals and Electrical	c. 12	m DM
Payment for old grain deal	c. 30	m DM
Misc. (including consumer goods)	c. 16	m DM
Total	185.5 m DM = c.190 m DM	190 m DM

II. Polish Receipts from Polish Exports: 80 m DM

(Mainly coal deliveries of 250,000 tons and agricultural deliveries of 30.5 m DM)

Polish Deficit on 31 December 1957   c. 110 m DM

(*Source:* BA, B 102/58124)

SOURCES

I. Archival Materials

A. Public Archives

1. Bundesarchiv, Koblenz and St. Augustin, abbreviated "BA".

pre-1945
The Reich Chancellery (R 43 I and R 43 II)
The Reich Economics Ministry and precursors (R 7)
The Reich Finance Ministry and precursors (R 2)
The Union of German Iron and Steel Industrialists (R 13 I)
The Chemical Industry Interest Groups (R 13 XII)
Nachlass Hermann Pünder
Nachlass Ludwig Kastl
Nachlass Hans Posse
Nachlass Paul Silverberg

post-1945
The Chancellor's Office (B 136)
Federal Ministry of Economics (B 102)
Nachlass Vollrath von Maltzan (B 62)

2. Politisches Archiv des Auswärtigen Amtes, Bonn, abbreviated "PAAA".

pre-1945
Special Economics Department (Sonderreferat W)
Department II and IIb for Czechoslovakia
Department IV and IVa for Poland, USSR
Microfilms of the German Foreign Office 1920-1945 (T-120 Series):
Office of the Foreign Minister
Office of the State Secretary
Handakten Karl Ritter

post-1945, (Neues Amt)
Area Studies Department (Länderabteilung)
Commercial Department (Handelspolitische Abteilung)
Eastern Department (Ostabteilung)

3. Bundesarchiv, Abteilungen Potsdam, abbreviated "BA Potsdam" (formerly "Zentrales Staatsarchiv Potdam" of the GDR).

Foreign Office (R 901):
Poland (1920-1935)
Russia/Soviet Union (1893-1925)
Czechoslovakia (Handakten Windel)

Reich Economics Ministry (R 3101):
Poland (1918-1920)

4. Geheimes Staatsarchiv Preussischer Kulturbesitz, Berlin-Dahlem, abbreviated "GStA PK" (formerly "Zentrales Staatsarchiv Merseburg" of the GDR).

Prussian Trade Ministry (Rep. 120C):
Russia (1890-1895)
Czechoslovakia (1918-1935)

B. Private Archives

1. Rheinisch-Westfälisches Wirtschaftsarchiv, Cologne, abbreviated "RWWA".

Münster Chamber of Commerce (Abt.5)
Cologne Chamber of Commerce (Abt. 1)
Duisburg-Wesel Chamber of Commerce (Abt. 20)
Neuss Chamber of Commerce (Abt. 27)
Nachlass Otto Wolff (Abt.72)

2. Bayer-Archiv, Leverkusen.

Reich Association of German Industry (Reichsverband deutscher Industrie), 62/10.3-62/10.5.
Berichte Dr. Jost Terhaar, Handelspolitisches Büro, 67/2.
Russia 1946-1957, 700/353.4.
Poland, 700/608.
Bayer Revue

3. Mannesmann Archiv, Dusseldorf.

Demag AG (Bestand D)
Mannesmann (Bestand M)
Phoenix AG (Bestand P)
Phoenix-Rheinrohr AG (Bestand PR)
Deutsche Röhrenwerke AG (Bestand R)

4. Haniel Archiv, Duisburg.

Nachlass Paul Reusch

5. Bundesverband deutscher Industrie, Cologne, abbreviated "BdI".

The Eastern Committee (Ostausschuss)

6. Ludwig Erhard Archiv, Bonn

Tages-Nachrichten (Economics Ministry).

II. Other Nonpublished Sources

Interview with Otto Wolf von Amerongen, Cologne, 3 July 1991
"Der wirtschaftliche Aufstieg des Hauses H. Lanz," manuscript provided
    by John Deere Werke, Mannheim.
"100 Jahre im Dienst der Gesundheit 1886-1986," manuscript provided by
    Knoll AG.

SELECT BIBLIOGRAPHY OF
PUBLISHED SOURCES*

Documents, Documentary Collections, Statistical Material

Adenauer, K. *Teegespräche,* vol. 2, 1955-1958. Berlin, 1986.

Akten zur Deutschen Auswärtigen Politik 1918-1945. Boden-Boden, 1950-1995. Series B: 1925-1933. 1960-1967; Series A: 1918-1925. -1995.

Allied General Secretariat of the Allied High Commission for Germany. *Laws, Regulations, Directives, and Decisions of the Allied High Commission for Germany.*

Allied High Commission for Germany. *Official Gazette.* 1949-1954.

Booms, H., ed. *Die Kabinettesprotokolle der Bundesregierung.* Boppard, 1982-.

Booms, H. and Erdmann, K.D., eds. *Akten der Reichskanzlei.* Boppard, 1970-1989.

Booms, H. and Wernicke, K.D., eds. *Der Parlementarischer Rat. Akten und Protokolle.* Boppard, 1975.

Bundesgesetzblatt. Bonn, 1950-

Bundesministerium fur Gesamtdeutsche Fragen. *Dokumente zur Deutschlandpolitik.* Series III: 1955-1957. Frankfurt and Berlin, 1963.

Control Council. *Official Gazette of the Control Council for Germany 1945-1948.*

Der Deutsche Bundestag. *Verhandlungen des deutschen Bundestages.* Bonn, 1949.

Der Deutsche Reichstag. *Stenographische Berichte über die Verhandlungen des deutschen Reichstages.* Berlin, 1867-1938.

Documents on British Foreign Policy. 1st Series. London, 1946-.

Documents on German Foreign Policy 1918-1945. Series D: 1937-1945. Washington, D.C., 1950-1957; Series C: 1933-1937. Washington, D.C., 1957-1966.

Goetz, W., ed. *Briefe Wilhems II an den Zaren 1894-1914.* Berlin, 1920.

Great Britain, Parliamentary Papers. *Reports on Tariff Wars between Certain European States.* London, 1904.

Handelskammer zu Bremen. *Statistische Mitteilungen betreffend Bremens Handel und Schifffahrt.* Bremen, various years.

Handelskammer zu Hamburg. *Jahresbericht.* Hamburg, various years.

---

* This is a select bibliography. For additional information on specific points, consult the notes attached to the discussion in the text.

Institut für Zeitgeschichte and Der Deutsche Bundestag, eds. *Wörtliche Berichte und Drucksachen des Wirtschaftsrat des Vereinigten Wirtschaftsgebietes 1947-1949.* Munich, 1977.

Kaiserliches Statistisches Amt. *Statistisches Jahrbuch des deutschen Reiches.* Berlin, 1880-1918.

Kaiserliches Statistisches Amt and (after 1918) Statistisches Reichsamt. *Statistik des deutschen Reiches*, 1873-1881 [Alte Folge]; 1881-1944 [Neue Folge]. Berlin, 1873-1944.

___, *Monatliche Nachweise über den auswärtigen Handels des deutschen Zollgebiets.* Berlin, 1892-1939.

Lepsius, J. et al., eds. *Die grosse Politik der europäische Kabinette, 1871-1914.* Berlin, 1922-1927.

Ministerium für Auswärtige Angelegenheiten der DDR. *Von Brest-Litovsk bis Rapallo. Deutsch-sowjetische Beziehungen von den Verhandlungen in Brest-Litovsk bis zum Abschluss des Rapallovertrages. Dokumentensammlung.* Berlin (East), 1971.

Office of the Military Government for Germany (U.S.). *Monthly Report of the Military Governor.* 1945-1949.

___, *OMGUS Information Bulletin.* 1945-1949.

___, *Miltary Government Gazette.* 1945-1949.

___, *Central German Agencies. Special Report of the Military Governor.* 1946.

Reichsanzeiger. Berlin, 1871-1944.

Reichsgesetzblatt. Berlin, 1880-1944.

Ruhm von Oppen, B., ed. *Documents on Germany under the Occupation 1945-1954.* Oxford, 1955.

Statistical Office of the United Nations. *United Nations Statistical Papers Series T. Direction of International Trade.* Geneva, 1950-.

Sutton, E., ed. Gustav Stressemann. *His Diaries, Letters, and Papers.* New York, 1937.

The Treaty of Peace between the Allied and Associated Powers and Germany, and other Treaty Engagements signed at Versailles, June 28, 1919; together with The Reply of the Allied and Associated Powers to the Observations of the German Delegation on the Conditions of Peace. London, 1920.

United Nations Economic Commission for Europe. *Economic Survey of Europe.* Geneva, 1948-.

United States Department of State. *Germany 1947-1949: The Story in Documents.* Washington, D.C., 1950.

___, *Papers Relating to the Foreign Relations of the United States.* Washington, D.C., various years.

___, *United States Economic Policy Toward Germany.* Washington, D.C., 1946.

United States War Department, Civil Administration Division. *The Evolution of Bizonal Administration.* 1948.

Zinner, P., ed. *National Communism and Popular Revolt in Eastern Europe. A Selection of Documents on Events in Poland and Hungary February-November 1956.* New York, 1956.

Zwoch, G., ed. *Gustav Stresemann, Reichstagsreden.* Bonn, 1972.

Memoirs

Adenauer, K. *Erinnerungen.* 4 vols. Stuttgart, 1965-1967.

Berlepsch, H. von. *Sozialpolitischeerfahrungen und Erinnerungen.* M. Gladbach, 1925.

Blankenhorn, H. *Verständnis und Verständigung. Blätter eines politischen Tagebuchs 1949 bis 1979.* Frankfurt, 1980.

Brandt, W. *People and Politics. The Years 1960-1975.* Boston, 1978.

Bueck, H.A. *Der Centralverband deutscher Industrieller 1876-1901.* 3 vols. Berlin, 1903-1905.

Bülow, B. von. *The Memoirs of Prince von Bülow*. 4 vols. Boston, 1931-1932.

Clay, L.D. *Decision in Germany*. Garden City, NY, 1950.

Curtius, J. *Sechs Jahre Minister der deutschen Republik*. Heidelberg, 1948.

Dirksen, H. von. *Moskau-Tokio-London. Erinnerungen und Betrachtungen zu 20 Jahren deutscher Aussenpolitik 1919-1939*. Stuttgart, 1949.

Eckardt, F. von. *Ein unordentliches Leben. Lebenserinnerungen*. Dusseldorf, 1967.

Erhard, L. *Deutschlands Rückkehr zum Weltmarkt*. London, 1953.

____, *Germany's Comback in the World Market*. London, 1954.

Grewe, W. G. *Rückblenden 1976-1951*. Frankfurt, 1979.

Haas, W. *Beitrag zur Geschichte der Entstehung des Auswärtigen Dienstes der Bundesrepublik Deutschland*. Manuscript, 1969.

Hilger, G. and Meyer, A. *The Incompatible Allies. A Memoir-History of German-Soviet Relations 1918-1941*. New York, 1953.

Imhoff, L.P. *Weite Welt und breites Leben. Meine Erlebnisse in fünf Erdteilen*. Frankfurt.

Lahr, R. *Zeuge von Fall und Aufstieg. Private Briefe 1934-1974*. Hamburg, 1981.

Lipski, J. *Diplomat in Berlin: 1933-1939*. New York, 1968.

Luther, H. *Politiker ohne Partei. Erinnerungen*. Stuttgart, 1960.

Posse, H. *Aus der Werkstaat der Handelspolitik*. Cologne, 1949.

Raumer, H. von. "Dreissig Jahre nach Rapallo." *Deutsche Revue* 78 (1952).

Schacht, H. *Confessions of the "Old Wizard"*. Boston, 1956.

Wermuth, A. *Ein Beamtemleben*. Belin, 1923.

Witte, S. *Memoirs of Count Witte*. Garden City, NY, 1921.

Secondary Works

Abelshauser, W. *Wirtschaft in Westdeutschland*. Stuttgart, 1975.

____, *Wirtschaftsgeschichte der Bundesrepublik Deutschland 1949-1980*. Frankfurt, 1983.

Albrecht-Carrié, R. *The Meaning of the First World War*. Englewood Cliffs, NJ, 1965.

Aldcroft, D. *From Versailles to Wall Street*. Berkeley and Los Angeles, 1977.

Alemann, U. von., ed. *Neokorporatismus*. Frankfurt, 1981.

Amberger, E. *Geschichte der Behördenorganisation Russlands*.

Arndt, P. "Zum Abschluss eines neuen deutsch-russischen Handelsvertrages." *Schriften des Vereins für Socialpolitik* 92 (1901).

Aubin, H. and Zorn, W. *Handbuch der deutschen Wirtschafts- und Sozialgeschichte*. 2 vols. Stuttgart, 1976.

Backer, J. *Priming the German Economy. U.S. Policies 1945-1948*. Durham, NC, 1971.

Ballod, C. "Die deutsch-russischen Handelsbeziehungen." *Schriften des Vereins für Socialpolitik* 90 (1900).

Barkin, K. *The Controversy over German Industrialization 1890-1902*. Chicago, 1970.

Baykov, A. *Soviet Foreign Trade*. Princeton, 1946.

Beckmann. F. "Die Entwicklung des deutsch-russischen Getreideverkehrs unter den Handels-Vertägen von 1894 und 1904." *Jahrbücher für Nationalökonomie und Statistik* 101 (1913).

Beitel, W. and Nötold, J. *Deutsch-sowjetische Wirtschaftsbeziehungen in der Zeit der Weimarer Republik*. Baden-Baden, 1979.

Benes, V.L. and Pounds, N.J.G. *Poland*. London, 1970.

Berghahn, V., ed. *Quest for Economic Empire. European Strategies of German Big Business in the Twentieth Century*. Providence, 1996.

Bischof, G. and Maier, C., eds. *The Marshall Plan and Germany*. New York, 1991.

Boyer, C. "Das deutsche Reich und die Tschechoslowakei im Zeichen der Weltwirtschaftkrise." *Vierteljahrshefte für Zeitgeschichte* 39 (1991).

Brzezinski, Z. K. *The Soviet Bloc. Unity and Conflcit*. Cambridge, MA, 1960.

Caves, R.E. and Jones, R.W. *World Trade and Payments*, 3d ed. Boston, 1981.

Cecil, L. *The German Diplomatic Service, 1871-1914*. Princeton, 1976.

Cecil, L. *Wilhelm II.* Chapel Hill, NC, 1989.

Cippola, C., ed. *The Fontana Economic History of Europe.* 5 vols. New York, 1977.

Committee on Foreign Relations, United States Senate. *A Background Study on East-West Trade.* 89th Congress, 1st Session. Washington, D.C., 1965.

Conrad, J. "Die Stellung der landwirtschaftlichen Zölle in den 1903 zu schliessenden Handelsverträgen Deutschlands," *Schriften des Vereins für Socialpolitik* 90 (1900).

Crisp, O. *Studies in the Russian Economy before 1914.* London, 1976.

Dade, H. "Die Agrarzölle." *Schriften des Vereins für Socialpolitik* 91 (1900).

Das Bundesministerium für Wirtschaft. *Deutschland im Wiederaufbau.* Bonn, 1952.

____, *Gutachten des wissenschaftlichen Beirat bei der Verwaltung für Wirtschaft in dem Vereinigten Wirtschaftsgebiet.* Frankfurt, 1947-1949.

Diebold, W. "East-West Trade and the Marshall Plan." *Foreign Affairs* 26 (July 1948).

Dix, A. *Wirtschaftskrieg und Kriegswirtschaft. Zur Geschichte des deutschen Zusammenbruchs.* Berlin, 1920.

Döring, D. "Deutsche Aussenwirtschaftspolitik 1933-1935. Die Gleichschaltung der Aussenwirtschaft in der Frühphase des nationalsozialistischen Regimes." Ph.D. dissertataion, Free University of Berlin, 1969.

Doss, K. *Das deutsche Auswärtige Amt im Übergang vom Kaiserreich zur Weimar Republik. Die Schuler'sche Reform.* Dusseldorf, 1977.

Dyck, H. *Weimar Germany and Soviet Russia. A Study in Diplomatic Instability.* New York, 1966.

Ehlert, H.G. *Die wirtschaftliche Zentralbehörde des deutschen Reiches 1914-1919.* Wiesbaden, 1982.

Ellwein, T. *Das Regierungssystem der Bundesrepublik Deutschland.* Opladen, 1973.

Erbe, R. *Die nationalsozialistische Wirtschaftspolitik 1933-1939 im Lichte der modernen Theorie.* Zurich, 1958.

Eschenberg, T. *Jahre der Besatzung 1945-1948.* Stuttgart, 1958.

Fabry, P. *Der Hitler-Stalin Pakt 1939-1941. Ein Beitrag zur Methoder sowjetischer Aussenpolitik.* Darmstatdt, 1962.

Facius, F. *Wirtschaft und Staat. Die Entwicklung der staatlichen Wirtschaftsverwaltung in Deutschaland vom 17.Jh. bis 1945.* Boppard, 1959.

Fink, C. *The Genoa Conference.* Chapel Hill, NC, 1984.

Fischer, F. *Griff nach der Weltmacht. Die Kriegziele des kaiserlichen Deutschlands 1914/18.* 2nd ed. Bonn, 1979.

____, F. *War of Illusions.* New York, 1975.

Fischer, W. *Wirtschaft und Gesellschaft im Zeitalter der Industrializierung.* Göttingen, 1972.

Freund, G. *Unholy Alliance: Russian-German Relations from the Treaty of Brest-Litovsk to the Treaty of Berlin.* New York, 1957.

Gasiorowski, Z. "Stresemann and Poland before Locarno." *Journal of Central European Affairs* 18 (1958).

____, "Stresemann and Poland after Locarno." *Journal of Central European Affairs* 18 (1958).

Gessner, D. *Agrarverbände in der Weimarer Republik,* Dusseldorf, 1976.

Geyer, D. *Wirtschaft und Gesellschaft im vorrevolutionaeren Russland.* Cologne, 1975.

Gotto, K. *Konrad Adenauer. Seine Deutschland- und Aussenpolitik 1945-1963.* Munich, 1975.

Gregory, P. and Stuart, R. *Soviet Economic Structure and Performance,* 4th ed. New York, 1990.

Graml, H. "Die Rapallo-Politik im Urteil der Westdeutschen Forschung." *Vierteljahrshefte für Zeitgeschichte* 18 (1970).

Garml, H. and Benz, W. *Aspekte deutscher Aussenpolitik im 20. Jahrhundert.*

Grupp. P. *Deutsche Aussenpolitik im Schatten von Versailles 1918-1920: Zur Politik des Auswärtigen Amts vom Ende des Ersten Weltkriegs und der November Revolution bis um Inkrafttreten des Versailler Vertrags.* Paderborn, 1988.

Gulden, H. "Aussenwirtschaftspolitische und aussenpolitische Einflussfaktoren im Prozess der Staatswerdung der BRD 1947-1952." *Aus Politik und Zeitgeschichte* B32/87 (1987).

Haberland, G. *Elf Jahre staaatlicher Regelung der Ein- und Ausfuhr. Eine Systematische Darstellung der deutschen Aussenhandelsregelung in den Jahren 1914-1925.* Leipzig, 1926.

Hardach, G. *The First World War.* Berkeley and Los Angeles, 1977.

Hardach, K.W. "Die Haltung der deutschen Landwirtschaft in der Getreidezoll-Diskussion 1878/79." *Zeitschrift für Agrargeschichte und Agrarsozologie* 15 (1967).

Hayes, P. "Industrial Factionalism in Modern German History." *Central European History* 24 (1991).

Helbig, H. *Die Träger der Rapallo-Politik.* Gottingen, 1958.

Henning, F.-W. *Das Industrialisierte Deutschland 1914-1972.* Paderborn, 1972.

Hentschel, V. *Wirtschaft und Wirtschaftspolitik im wilhelmischen Deutschland. Organisierter Kapitalismus und Interventionsstaat.* Stuttgart, 1978.

Hertz, F. *The Economic Problem of the Danubian Countries.* New York, 1970.

Hirschmann, A. O. *National Power and the Structure of Foreign Trade.* Berkeley and Los Angeles, 1980.

Hoffmann, W. G. *Das Wachstum der deutschen Wirtschaft seit Mitte des 19 Jahrhunderts.* Berlin, 1965.

Holborn, H. *A History of Modern Germany 1840-1945.* Princeton, 1969.

Hubatsch, W. *Entstehung und Entwicklung des Reichswirtschaftsministerium, 1880-1933.* Berlin, 1978.

Jacobs, A. and Richter, H. "Die Grosshandelspreise in Deutschland von 1792 bis 1934." *Sonderhefte des Instituts für Konjunkturforschung* 37 (1935).

Jain, R. *Germany, the Soviet Union and Eastern Europe.* New York, 1993.

James, H. *The German Slump. Politics and Economics 1924-1936.* New York, 1986.

Jerchow, F. *Deutschland in der Weltwirtschaft 1944-1947. Anfänge der Westdeutsche Aussenwirtschaft.* Dusseldorf, 1978.

Jeserich, K. et al., eds. *Deutsche Verwlatungsgeschichte,* 5 vols. Stuttgart, 1983-1987.

Kaeble, H. *Industrielle Interessenpolitik in der wilhelmischen Gesellschaft. Centralverband deutscher Industrieller 1895-1914.* Berlin, 1967.

Kaiser, D. *Economic Diplomacy and the Origins of the Second World War. Germany, Great Britain, France and Eastern Europe, 1930-1939.* Princeton, 1980.

Kaser, M.C. and Radice, E.A., eds. *The Economic History of Eastern Europe 1919-1975,* 2 vols. New York, 1986.

Kehr, E. *Primat der Innenpolitik.* Berlin, 1965.

Kellenbenz, H. *Deutsche Wirtschaftsgeschichte,* 2 vols. Munich, 1977-1981.

Khromov, P.A. *Ekonomicheskoe razvitie Rossii v XIX-XX vekakh, 1800-1917.* Moscow, 1950.

Kindleberger, C. *The World in Depression.* Los Angeles, 1973.

Klein, A. "Der Einfluss des Grafen Witte auf die deutsch-russischen Beziehungen." Ph.D. dissertataion, Univeristy of Bielefeld, 1932.

Knapp, M, ed. *Von der Bizonenegründung zur ökonomische-politischen Westintegration. Studien zum Verhältnis zwischen Aussenpolitik und Aussenwirtschaftsbeziehungen in der Entstehungsphase der Bundesrepublik Deutschland 1947-1952.* Frankfurt, 1984.

Krohn, C. D. *Stabilisierung und Ökonomische Interesssen. Die Finanzpolitik des deutschen Reiches 1923-1927.* Dusseldorf, 1974.

Kruszewski, C. "The German-Polish Tariff War (1925-1934) and its Aftermath." *Journal of Central European Affairs* 3 (1943).

League of Nations. *Commercial Policies in the Interwar Period: International Proposals and National Policies.* Geneva, 1942.

____, *Quantitative Trade Controls. Their Causes and Nature.* Geneva, 1943.

Lerman, K. A. *Chancellor as Courtier. Bernhard von Bülow and the Governance of Germany 1900-1909.* Cambridge, 1990.

Liepmann, H. *Tariff Levels and the Economic Unity of Europe.* New York, 1938.

Lieven, D. *Russia's Rulers under the Old Regime.* New Haven, 1989.

Link, H.-G. *Deutsch-sowjetischer Beziehungen bis Rapallo.* Cologne, 1970.

Lippelt, H. "'Politische Sanierung.' zur deutschen Politik gegenüber Polen 1925/26." *Vierteljahrshefte für Zeitgeschichte* 19 (1971).

Lohmann, A. *Das Auswärtige Amt.* Frankfurt, 1966.

Lohr, B. *Die "Zukunft Russlands": Perspektiven russischer Wirtschaftsentwicklung und deutsch-russische Wirtschaftsbeziehungen vor dem Ersten Weltkrieg.* Wiesbaden, 1985.

Lotz, W. "Die Ideen der deutschen Handelspoltik von 1860-1891." *Schriften des Vereins für Socialpolitik* 50 (1892).

____, "Die Handelspolitik des deutschen Reiches unter Graf Caprivi und Fürst Hohenlohe." *Schriften des Vereins für Socialpolitik* 92 (1901).

Lyashchenko, P.I. *A History of the National Economy of Russia to the 1917 Revolution.* New York, 1949.

Maier, C. *Recasting Bourgeois Europe. Stabilization in France, Germany, and Italy in the Decade after World War I.* Princeton, 1975.

Marer, P. *Soviet and East European Foreign Trade 1949-1969. Statistical Compendium and Guide.* Bloomington, Ind., 1972.

McKay, J. *Pioneers for Profit. Foreign Entrepreneurship and Russian Industrialization 1885-1913.* Chicago, 1970.

McMurry, D.S. *Deutschland und die Sowjetunion 1933-1936.* Cologne, 1979.

Mielke, S. *Der Hansa-Bund für Gewerbe, Handel, und Industrie 1909-1914.* Gottingen, 1976.

Mitchell, B. *European Historical Statistics 1750-1970.* New York, 1975.

Mommsen, H. et al., eds. *Industrielles System und politische Entwicklung in der Weimarer Republik.* Dusseldorf, 1974.

Morgan, R.P. "The Political Significance of German-Soviet Trade Negotiations 1922-5." *The Historical Journal* 6 (1963).

Motz, W. "Die Regelung des Aussenhandels in Deutschland von 1945-1949." Ph.D. dissertataion, University of Basel, 1954.

Mueller-Link, H. *Industrializierung und Aussenpolitik. Preussen-Deutschland und das Zarenreich von 1860 bis 1890.* Göttingen, 1977.

Nichols, J.A. *Germany After Bismarck.* Cambridge MA, 1958

Nussbaum, H., ed. *Die bürgerlichen Parteien in Deutschland. Handbuch der Geschichte der bürgerlicher Parteien und anderer bürgerlicher Interessenorganisationen vom Vormärz bis zum Jahre 1945.* Leipzig, 1970.

Nussbaum, M. *Wirtschaft und Staat in Deutschlaand während der Weimarer Republik.* Berlin (East), 1978.

Ol', P.V. *Inostrannye Kapitaly v Rossii.* Petrograd, 1922.

Olshausen, H.-P. *Friedrich List und der deutsche Handels- und Gewerbeverein.* Jena, 1935.

Panzer, A. *Das Ringen um die deutsche Agrarpolitik von der Währungsstabilisierung bis zur Agrardebatte im Reichstag im Dezember 1928.* Kiel, 1970.

Pasvolsky, L. and Moulton, H. *Russian Debts and Russian Reconstuction.* New York, 1924.

Perrey, H.-J. *Der Russlandausschuss der deutschen Wirtschaft: Die deutsch-sowjetischen Wirtschaftsbeziehungen der Zwischenkriegszeit.* Munich, 1985.

Petzina, D. "Hauptprobleme der deutschen Wirtschaftspolitik 1932/33." *Vierteljahrsheft für Zeitgeschichte* 15 (1967).

———, *Autarkiepolitik im Dritten Reich. Der nationalsozialistische Vierjahresplan.* Stuttgart, 1968.

———, *Die deutsche Wirtschaft in der Zwischekriegszeit.* Wiesbaden, 1978.

Plischke, E. *History of the Allied High Commission for Germany. Its Establishment, Structure and Procedures.* Bonn, 1951.

———, *The Allied High Commission for Germany.* Bonn, 1953.

Pogge von Strandmann, H. "Grossindustrie und Rapallopolitik." *Historische Zeitschrift* 222 (1976).

Pohl, H. *Weimars Wirtschaft und die Aussenpolitik der Republik 1924-1926.* Dusseldorf, 1979.

Pohl, M. *Geschäft und Politik. Deutsch-russische/sowjetische Wirtschaftsbeziehungen 1850-1988.* Mainz, 1988.

———, *Geschäft und Politik. Deutsch-russisch/sowjetische Wirtschaftsbeziehungen 1850-1988* (Mainz, 1988).

———, *Die Finanzierung der Russengeschäfte zwischen den beiden Weltkriegen* (Frankfurt, 1975).

Posse, H. *Grundlagen der künftigen deutschen Handelspolitik.* Berlin 1924.

Puchert, B. *Der Wirtschaftskrieg des Deutschen Imperialismus gegen Polen 1925-1934.* Berlin (East), 1963.

Pühle, H.J. *Agrarische Interssenpolitik und preussischer Konservatisumus im wilhelmischen Reich 1893-1914.* Hannover, 1966.

Randel, E. *Das Bundesministerium für Wirtschaft.* Bonn, 1966.

Riekhoff, H. von. *German-Polish Relations, 1918-1933.* Baltimore, 1971.

Ritschl, A. "Die Deutsche Zahlungsbilanz 1936-1941 und das Problem des Devisenmangels vor Kriegsbeginn," *VZG* 39 (1991), 103-23.

Röhl, J.C.G. *Germany With out Bismarck. The Crisis of Government in the Second Reich.* Los Angeles, 1967.

Rosenbaum, K. *Community of Fate. German-Soviet Diplomatic Relations 1922-1928.* Syracuse, NY, 1965.

Rosenfeld, G. *Sowjet-Russland und Deutschland 1917-1922.* 2nd ed. Berlin (East), 1983.

———, *Sowjetunion und Deutschland 1922-1933.* Berlin (East), 1983.

Rothschild, J. *East-Central Europe between the Two World Wars.* Seattle, 1974.

Samuelson, P.A. *Principles of Economics,* 9th ed. New York, 1973.

Scheel, "Der auswärtige Handel des deutschen Zollgebiets im letzten Jahrzehnt." *Schriften des Vereins für Socialpolitik* 49 (1892).

Scheider, T. "Die Entstehungsgeschichte des Rapallo-Vertrages." *Historische Zeitschrift* 204 (1967).

Schmidt, M. *Graf Posadowsky. Staatssekretär des Reichschatzamtes und des Reichsmates des Innern.* Halle, 1935.

Schmidt, C. *Russische Presse und deutsches Reich 1905-1914.* Cologne, 1988.

Schmoller, G. "Die Befügnisse der Besatzungsmachte in der Bundesrepublik Deutschaland." *Dokumente und Berichte des Europa-Archivs* 8 (1950).

Schneider, H. *Das sowjetische Aussenhandelsmonopol 1920-1925.* Cologne, 1973.

Schneider, K. *Der Welthandel im Clearingvekehr. 170 Clearing Abkommen.* Zurich, 1937.

Schöllgen, G. *Die Macht in der Mitte Europas.* Munich, 1992.

Schulthess, H. *Schulthess' europäischer Geschichtskalender,* Reprint. Nendeln, 1976-77.

Schulze-Gävernitz, G. von. *Volkswirtschaftlichen Studien aus Russland.* Leipzig, 1899.

Schuster, R., ed. *Deutsche Verfassungen.* Munich, 1979.

Schwarz, H.-P. *Die Ära Adenauer 1949-1957.* Stuttgart, 1981.

Sheehan, J., ed. *Imperial Germany.* New York, 1976.

Slover, R. "The Bizonal Economic Administration of West Germany." Ph.D. dissertataion, Harvard Universuty, 1950.

Smith, G. A. *Soviet Foreign Trade. Organization, Operations, and Policy, 1918-1971.* New York, 1973.

Sonnemann, R. "Der Verin zur Wahrung der Interssen der chemischen Industrie Deutschlands." *Wisenschaftliche Zeitschrift der Friedrich Schiller Iniversität Jena* 14 (1965).

Stegmann, D. *Die Erben Bismarcks. Parteien und Verbände in der Spätphase des Wilhelmischen Deutschlands.* Cologne, 1970.

Stegmann, D. et al., eds. *Industrielle Gesellschaft und Politisches System. Beiträge zur politischen Sozialgeschichte.* Bonn, 1978.

Stent, A. *From Embargo to Ostpolitik. The Political Economy of West German-Soviet Relations 1955-1980.* Cambridge, 1980.

Stürmer, M. *Koalition und Opposition in der Weimarer Republik, 1924-1928.* Dusseldorf, 1967.

Teichova, A. *An Economic Background to Munich.* London, 1974.

Tirrell, S. *German Agrarian Politics after Bismarck's Fall. The Formation of the Farmers' League.* New York, 1951.

Turner Jr., H. A. *Stresemann and the Politics of the Weimar Republic.* Princeton, 1963.

Ullmann, H-P. *Der Bund der Industriellen. Organisation, Einfluss, und Politik klein- und mittelbetrieblicher Industrieller im deutschen Kaiserreich 1895-1905.* Gottingen, 1976.

Vogel, W. *Westdeutschland 1945-1950. Der Aufbau von der Verfassungs- und Verwaltungseinrichtungen über den Ländern der drei westlichen Besatzungzonen.* Boppard, 1964.

Wagner, G. *Deutschland und der polnisch-sowjetischer Krieg 1920.* Wiesbaden, 1979.

Wehler, H.-U. *Krisenherde des Kaiserreichs 1871-1918.* Göttingen, 1970.

_____, ed. *Moderne deutsche Sozialgeschichte.* Berlin, 1966.

Weinberg, G. *Germany and the Soviet Union 1939-1941.* Leiden, 1954.

_____, *The Foreign Policy of Hitler's Germany. Diplomatic Revolution in Europe 1933-1936.* Chicago, 1970.

_____, *The Foreign Policy of Hitler's Germany. Starting World War II 1937-1939.* Chicago, 1980.

Wernecke, K. *Der Wille zur Weltgeltung. Aussenpolitik und Öffentlichkeit im Kaiserreich am Vorabend des Ersten Weltkrieges.* Dusseldorf, 1970.

Witt, P. C. *Die Finanzpolitik des deutschen Reiches von 1903 bis 1913. Eine Studie zur Innenpolitik des Wilhelmischen Deutschlands.* Hamburg, 1970.

Wittschewsky. "Die Zoll- und Handelspoltik Russlands während der letzten Jahrzehnte." *Schriften des Vereins für Socialpolitik* 49 (1892).

Zink, H. *The United States in Germany 1945-1955.* Princeton, 1957.

INDEX